Shaping the Law of Obligations

Professor Ewan McKendrick KC OUImages/Rob Judges.

Shaping the Law of Obligations

Essays in Honour of Professor Ewan McKendrick KC

Edited by
EDWIN PEEL
REBECCA PROBERT

Great Clarendon Street, Oxford, OX2 6DP,
United Kingdom

Oxford University Press is a department of the University of Oxford.
It furthers the University's objective of excellence in research, scholarship,
and education by publishing worldwide. Oxford is a registered trade mark of
Oxford University Press in the UK and in certain other countries

© The multiple contributors 2023

The moral rights of the authors have been asserted

First Edition published in 2023

All rights reserved. No part of this publication may be reproduced, stored in
a retrieval system, or transmitted, in any form or by any means, without the
prior permission in writing of Oxford University Press, or as expressly permitted
by law, by licence or under terms agreed with the appropriate reprographics
rights organization. Enquiries concerning reproduction outside the scope of the
above should be sent to the Rights Department, Oxford University Press, at the
address above

You must not circulate this work in any other form
and you must impose this same condition on any acquirer

Public sector information reproduced under Open Government Licence v3.0
(http://www.nationalarchives.gov.uk/doc/open-government-licence/open-government-licence.htm)

Published in the United States of America by Oxford University Press
198 Madison Avenue, New York, NY 10016, United States of America

British Library Cataloguing in Publication Data

Data available

Library of Congress Control Number: 2023944934

ISBN 978–0–19–888976–2

DOI: 10.1093/oso/9780198889762.001.0001

Printed and bound by
CPI Group (UK) Ltd, Croydon, CR0 4YY

Links to third party websites are provided by Oxford in good faith and
for information only. Oxford disclaims any responsibility for the materials
contained in any third party website referenced in this work.

Foreword

This collection celebrating the work of Professor Ewan McKendrick is a notable new addition to what has become a popular academic literary genre, in law as in other fields of study. It is worth pausing to reflect on what a reader may expect or hope to find in a volume of this kind. What are the qualities of a good festschrift?

To answer that question it is necessary to consider the book's purpose. The purpose of a festschrift is to celebrate and honour the work of the eminent scholar to whom it is dedicated (the honoree). But how can a volume of chapters on topical legal issues honour an individual? It can do so, I apprehend, by showing the honoree's impact on their chosen field of learning—in this case the law of obligations—and on other scholars in this field.

That impact may be measured in two dimensions: first, the identity and range of the contributors; second, the quality and range of their contributions to the book. If many distinguished scholars who are themselves foremost in the field so admire the honoree that they wish tangibly to acknowledge their debt and show their respect by contributing a piece of writing to the collection, that is itself a mark of influence and achievement. Ideally, the range of contributors will also illustrate the full trajectory—temporally, geographically, and thematically—of the honoree's career. The ideal contribution, I would suggest, is a piece of original work, valuable in its own right but written specially for the occasion, which reflects—either directly, or indirectly by pursuing ideas which the honoree has helped to inspire—the influence of the honoree on the topic discussed in the chapter and on its author. Again, the range of contributions will ideally reflect the range of the honoree's own work.

If these are suitable criteria, how does this book measure up? Readers will make their own judgments, but I submit: outstandingly well.

Look first at the list of contributors. Not only do their associations with Ewan reflect every stage of his career, but anyone interested in the law of obligations will see here a roll call of the leading names of jurists in this field. One might almost say, to paraphrase John F Kennedy, that they represent the most extraordinary collection of talent, of legal knowledge, that has ever been gathered together in one book on this subject—with the possible exception of when Ewan last wrote one of his own.

As for the contributions, it is enough to say that they surely meet Ewan's exacting standards and that a remarkably high number of the twenty-three chapters in this volume written by twenty-five authors display the ideal qualities that I have proposed.

As this foreword is itself a small part of the book's homage to Ewan, it is fitting that I should include a short tribute of my own. It reflects the strength of the impression that he made on me, personally and intellectually, and the sense of connection that I felt, that I can remember clearly our first meeting—at a conference in honour of another great legal scholar, Gareth Jones, in Cambridge in 1997 (at which Ewan spoke). Not long afterwards Ewan decided to qualify as a barrister and was required to complete a programme of professional education for new practitioners. This allows me to claim with at least some verisimilitude that I share with *Hector L MacQueen* the accolade of having had Ewan as my student, since he dutifully attended lectures that I organized on behalf of the Commercial Bar

Association, including my own tutorial on professional ethics. He was courteous enough never to complain at having to play this role and generous enough to contribute a lecture of his own in the following year. It was a lecture on the then recent case of *Alfred McAlpine Construction Ltd v Panatown Ltd*, which was as fine a demonstration as I have ever heard of the ideal that has guided Ewan throughout his career: that legal education should develop the ability both to focus intensely on the facts of a particular case and to identify the point of legal principle raised by the facts, and not one of these skills at the expense of the other.[1]

Skipping forward to the present, I was recently contemplating trying to write an essay or lecture on the subject of certainty in commercial law—an attribute often advertised but seldom analysed. Then Ewan sent me a copy of a lecture he had recently given on the subject at the University of Leiden. I read it and breathed a sigh of relief. There was no need for me to try to write the essay, as Ewan had said everything worth saying.

George Leggatt
London, 5 June 2023

---

[1] See Ewan McKendrick, 'The Common Law at Work: The Saga of *Alfred McAlpine Construction Ltd v Panatown Ltd*' (2003) 3 OUCLJ 145, 146./

Ewan McKendrick and the Administration of Oxford University

I am delighted to contribute to this Festschrift celebrating the contributions of Professor Ewan McKendrick to legal education and contract law. The chapters that follow detail his productive and influential career latterly at University College London and Oxford University and his scholarly publications on the law of contract. However, in this contribution, I want to focus on another side of Ewan's professional life, his role and impact as an academic administrator and leader at the highest levels of one of the world's top universities. His legacy in this area is immense and can be seen by the remarkable success of Oxford during his time in leadership there from 2006 to 2017, during which the University was the UK's pre-eminent in the 2007 and 2014 Research Excellent Framework (REF) exercises and rose to the top of the Times Higher Education Global Rankings.

Ewan was first lured into senior leadership in 2006 at a time of considerable turbulence for Oxford University. These were the latter years of John Hood's Vice-Chancellorship when the University engaged in a prolonged and contentious debate around proposed, but ultimately thwarted, governance changes. During this time, Ewan served in the roles of Pro-Vice-Chancellor (PVC) for Research and PVC for Education. In the former, he oversaw the 2007 REF submission which is no mean feat for such a large and decentralized University as Oxford. His success in corralling both the breadth and the varied impact of scholarship from the University and its Colleges was seen in the top ranking and sizeable funding increases that were received. Ewan's dedication to teaching came through during his time as PVC for Education and he steered the University through ever-increasing bureaucracy from the then regulators, HEFCE. Both PVC roles spanned the time of the global financial crisis and its, somewhat delayed, impact on the funding structures for higher education in the UK.

My first interaction with Ewan came when I arrived as Vice-Chancellor of Oxford University in September 2009. I immediately detected a kindred spirit with whom I would enjoy working and someone who could help me navigate the sometimes choppy waters of Oxford's governance landscape. At that time, he was already PVC for Education, having stepped unexpectedly into the role a few months earlier, in typically selfless fashion, upon the untimely death of his predecessor. A few months later, the role of Registrar at Oxford opened up and, to my pleasant surprise, Ewan decided to apply. The role of Registrar in UK universities is a hybrid one with elements of a chief operating officer's responsibilities (with many of the operational directors—IT, finance, capital projects, HR, etc—reporting in) as well as some of the academic oversight functions (quality assurance, student, and faculty discipline) normally associated with an American-style provost. In most UK universities, the Registrar's role is occupied by a staff member and is often viewed as the pinnacle of career achievement within the non-academic track, not unlike the Ministry Permanent Secretary role within the civil service. But to have a renowned scholar with legal training as Registrar, particularly in a university like Oxford which values above all scholarly prowess, was very appealing. So, I was delighted when the search committee chose Ewan McKendrick to be the next Registrar.

The challenges we faced together at that time (2009–2016) of turmoil in UK higher education were significant. But our first goal was to settle down the political turbulence within Oxford that had been created by the fight over governance reforms and to push for a more coordinated and aligned approach between the University and its autonomous colleges to the financial and academic challenges faced by the institution. As a former head of the Law Faculty and a long-standing member of Lady Margaret Hall, Ewan was well positioned to work with colleagues throughout the collegiate University to develop productive new ways of collaboration. A formal process of joint working between the University and its thirty-eight Colleges was established and in time approved by all of their governing bodies. This led to several years of relative calm both at Council (essentially the Board) and Congregation (equivalent to a faculty/senior employee Senate) levels and allowed a renewed focus on the core financial, teaching, and research dimensions of the institution during a period of national economic turmoil. A measure of this was seen by the passing in Congregation in 2011 of almost (but not quite) all of the governance reforms that had been the cause of so much strife in the earlier years.

Those years of Ewan's Registrarship also coincided with a period of radical reform to the funding structure of UK higher education. A series of draconian (and much feared) Comprehensive Spending Reviews took place in Whitehall which resulted in a steady reduction in government support for undergraduate teaching. This eventually led in 2010 to the proposal to replace those lost funds by the tripling of tuition fees to £9,000 for the individual student. Unsurprisingly, the reaction from students and many faculty was loud and vituperative. Violent demonstrations took place in London and in Oxford the iconic Radcliffe Camera was occupied. In many universities, including Oxford, faculty resolutions were proposed to resist the government reforms. All of this needed careful handling not just in the acceptance of different fee structures but also in considering the potential, reputational, and financial damage caused by getting it wrong. Ewan played a key role at every level in charting our response to the reforms and their unhappy reactions. Fortunately, the judicious and relatively gentle use of police in entering the barricaded Radcliffe Camera through an underground tunnel meant that its occupation only lasted two days, unlike the several weeks suffered by the comparable occupation of Senate House in Cambridge. And in the end, by 2012, a new tuition fee structure was approved by Congregation and smoothly introduced in Oxford after almost complete removal of public funding for undergraduate teaching. A key part of its acceptance was our ensuring the provision of the most generous financial aid package in the UK to students from low-income backgrounds. This generosity was possible, in large measure, due to a series of remarkable gifts (including £75 million from the Silicon Valley venture capitalist Michael Moritz) from philanthropists aimed at reducing the impediment to study that high cost might have for disadvantaged students; all of which Ewan played a role in stewarding. Other progress was made in the securing of gifts for the support of graduate students (more than £150 million) with particular focus on those studying the humanities and as Rhodes scholars and, from the corporate world, Eni graduate scholarships for African students.

The sign of a thriving university is not just demonstrable academic excellence but also a sustainable financial model with sufficient annual budget surpluses to allow continual reinvestment in the physical and intellectual capital of the institution. Ewan's period of responsibility for the financial health of Oxford resulted in seven years of a balanced and growing budget (average income growth of 5 per cent per annum to £2 billion in 2015) with the generation of sizeable annual surpluses (average £120 million) for strategic investment; all of which was achieved despite major reductions in government support. In the realm of competitively won research income from government, foundations, or corporations, academic excellence collides with the bottom line. For Oxford, research funding increased on average 9 per cent per annum during Ewan's time as Registrar to more than half a billion pounds making the university the most funded in the UK and 30 per cent higher than those of its larger rivals (Cambridge and UCL).

Creating new academic programs in a nine-hundred-year-old institution is notoriously difficult; however, with Ewan's stewardship, a new School of Government was established in Oxford thanks to a gift of $120 million from the American industrialist, Leonard Blavatnik—the largest single gift at that point in the recent history of Oxford University. A few years after its founding, a dramatic new Herzog-De Meuron designed building for the school was constructed on the Radcliffe Observatory Quarter. Even more than that gleaming building in the centre of historic Oxford, perhaps our most noteworthy architectural achievement was the building of a new wing of the Said Business School dedicated to executive education. Not only did this building provide a luxurious learning environment for visiting executives but, thanks to careful stewardship by Ewan and Dean Peter Tufano, it was also named at the request of the donor for that most unpopular of Oxford personages, Margaret Thatcher. (Those of you with long, or perhaps scarred, memories will remember that the University with much fanfare denied an honorary degree to the former Prime Minister in the early 1980s).

In every large, modern university, the medical enterprise, in the form of both the medical school and its affiliated hospitals, is playing an ever more important role. Research in biomedicine and clinical innovation attracts large amounts of government and corporate funding and the translation of discoveries to the bedside leads both to improved patient care and sizeable patent royalties. For several years, there had been strained relations between Oxford University's world-renowned Medical Sciences Division and the legally separate Oxford John Radcliffe Hospital, limiting their ability to grow together as a modern Academic Health Science Center. Using his considerable legal skills, Ewan stewarded a series of joint working committees and a strategic partnership committee that led to the hitherto unthinkable transfer of the University's name and with it the creation of a symbolic and functional partnership in the form of the Oxford University Hospitals NHS Trust. This now provides a firm foundation for the mutual growth and support of the clinical enterprise and biomedical research within Oxford.

An almost immediate benefit of the improvements in Oxford's clinical infrastructure was the establishment of a formal partnership between the University and the major national research complex at Harwell (located 15 miles from Oxford). The enhanced strategic collaboration led to the renaming of the facility as Harwell-Oxford and not long after the location there of a new government funded biomedical research facility, the Rosalind Franklin Institute.

Sometimes our greatest successes come from the most unexpected sources. The city of Oxford has one of the worst housing shortages in the UK. Like the rest of the country, the Oxford City Council was constantly being exhorted to protect green space by building on unwanted brownfield sites. So, it was not a surprise that when a truly unsavoury plot of land—an oil-polluted former railway siding right next to Oxford Station and the main line, no less—became available, the University acquired it and submitted plans for desperately needed graduate student housing. The City Council conducted its normal review and public consultation, deemed the project suitable for approval, and construction on the now named Castle Mill began. A few months later as the project neared completion, outrage and consternation from some quarters erupted! The series of residential buildings were visible from the ancient open land known as Port Meadow. And although this was true for many other modern Oxford buildings (in addition, of course, to the dreaming spires), a group of activists called for the buildings to be demolished or reduced in size. Demonstrations were held in the city, fulminating columns and letters were written in *The Times*, and numerous angry emails were sent to the University leadership. In the way of Oxford, this all led to a resolution laid down by members of the University to demolish the top floors of Castle Mill and a 'Congregation Debate' ensued of the kind that had defeated the governance reforms seven years earlier and is often seen as a vote of confidence in the leadership.

In this maelstrom of intense Oxford politics, Ewan McKendrick was masterful. His endless patience, supreme ability to marshal argument, strategic brain, and attention to detail came into their own. He meticulously planned the administration's response to the resolution, he identified and persuaded speakers from across the University to argue for the importance of graduate accommodation, and, in a masterstroke, he, as Registrar, spoke to the assembled academics in a packed Sheldonian Theatre emphasizing the rigour of the consultation process and promising to learn lessons in the future. He was, in short, the quintessential academic leader, strategic behind the scenes but willing to step into the fray. The resolution was roundly defeated on the day and a subsequent postal vote of the several thousand members of congregation gave a five to one majority against the resolution and in favour of the actions of Oxford's leadership.

In this Festschrift, we celebrate Ewan McKendrick, the King's Counsel and legal scholar. But I am happy to have a chance to highlight his other contributions to the academic enterprise through his many accomplishments as a university administrator of the highest level and wise academic leader.

Andrew Hamilton

Ewan McKendrick at the Bar

Apart from Ewan McKendrick's standing as a leading jurist, he is also a barrister who frequently appears in litigation and international arbitrations. He is regularly asked to give expert opinions on English law. This is not surprising. It is hard to find anyone who has better credentials to explain principles of English law in an authoritative manner.

Ewan also practises as an advocate in high-profile commercial disputes. He is a member of 3 Verulam Buildings. As a practising barrister, the challenges are different from those of an academic. He is no longer giving his opinion on issues of English law. When appearing as a barrister, his personal opinions do not matter as far as the decision-maker is concerned. He presents the arguments that assist the client on the theory that the judge or arbitrator will come to the truth by testing the rival arguments of the parties. An important skill of an advocate is to simplify arguments based on the facts of the case and Ewan knows how to do this. He was made a King's Counsel (Hon) in 2015 as recognition of his skills.

In crafting his submissions for a judge or a tribunal, Ewan brings to bear all the clarity, eloquence, and voluminous knowledge of English commercial law that distinguish his academic writings, enabling him to advance persuasive arguments firmly grounded in authority and to detect and exploit the flaws in his opponent's case.

Moreover, those who have worked with Ewan as counsel can testify to the intellectual generosity and curiosity so familiar to his students and colleagues. He is always keen to consider and debate a point with any member of the legal team, no matter how junior, in the search for the winning answer and in showing empathy and kindness.

Ewan enjoys working this way and in particular the collegiality that comes in working with other barristers and advocates in a team. Clients also want to know about his views on the likely outcome of cases. This is not just about legal rules and theory but about prediction based on the facts of the case. It is also about experience and knowledge of how the decisions are made. Procedural law affects the outcome of cases and Ewan understands this as a practitioner. I suspect his work as a skilled practitioner makes him a better academic.

Whether appearing as an independent expert on English law or as an advocate, Ewan has the skill of mastering the facts that matter. This includes cases involving oil and gas, minerals, cryptocurrency, Covid business interruption claims, joint ventures, and sanctions.

Finally, it is worth concluding these brief remarks with a mention to Ewan's work in teaching practitioners and young barristers. He has authored numerous textbooks on Contract Law which are a go-to resource for law students. Law firms regularly ask him to give lectures on recent developments in commercial law. He covers a large number of recent cases in a short time and identifies their importance and what they establish. He is also a Bencher of the Gray's Inn and this puts him in touch with those aspiring to become barristers as well as practitioners and the judiciary. It is hard to think of anyone who has given such an important contribution to the development of commercial law and also its practical application.

Ali Malek

Preface—Shaping a Career in the Law of Obligations

It has been both a pleasure and a privilege to put together this collection in honour of Professor Ewan McKendrick. Our task was greatly facilitated by the speed and enthusiasm with which our contributors responded to our initial invitation, and by the erudition and insights that they have brought to their contributions.

The collection includes reflections on contract law, tort law, commercial law, and restitution, reflecting the key areas that Ewan has shaped over the course of his career. Many contributors also have included their own recollections of Ewan at different stages in his long and successful career, or commented on particular aspects of his work. This preface draws together these recollections and comments, to recount what we might term Ewan's life story in the law, or the shaping of a career in the law of obligations.

We begin with Ewan's undergraduate studies in Edinburgh in the early 1980s, where he was taught by *Hector L MacQueen*, who (unsurprisingly) notes that he was one of the leading lights of the contract law class. As Hector also notes, Ewan's earliest publications appeared in Scottish journals, the *Scottish Law Gazette* and the *Scots Law Times*. While Hector expresses his regret that Ewan went on to focus on English law rather than Scots law—after leaving Edinburgh for Oxford to study for the BCL—John Cartwright sees that initial training in a different legal system as being key in shaping Ewan's appreciation of the role of comparative law, to which he and others pay tribute in their chapters.

Richard Taylor picks up the story of Ewan's academic career in his recollections of Ewan's first academic post at what was then Lancashire Polytechnic, where he spent a year before moving on to a lectureship at Essex. His comments on Ewan's penetrating—but always patient and polite—observations are echoed by many contributors. Andrew Burrows, who first encountered Ewan at an SPTL conference in the mid-1980s, was similarly struck by his 'almost unrivalled ability to cut straight through to the heart of any legal issue'.

That clarity of analysis is most obviously reflected in Ewan's textbook on contract law, the first edition of which appeared in 1990 when Ewan was a lecturer at the LSE. As students, Rebecca Probert recalls reading it in its first edition, Stefan Vogenauer in its second, and Tim Dodsworth in its sixth, and its continuing influence is evident from the many other contributors who cite its latest incarnation (the fifteenth) in their chapters. In 2016 an Australian edition was published, co-authored with Qiao Liu.

In 1991, as Andrew Burrows recalls, Ewan returned to Oxford when he was appointed as Fellow of St Anne's College and Linnells Lecturer in Law. Ewan had married Rosemary in 1983, and their four daughters were born over the next few years. As a devoted family man, he was often seen in college with his young daughters in tow. On occasion they even sat in on his tutorials!

At Oxford, his career entwined with that of a number of contributors, including Mindy Chen-Wishart and Louise Gullifer, with whom he taught commercial law. Both editors of this collection were fortunate enough to be students of Ewan: Edwin Peel in seminars on Restitution on the BCL; and Rebecca Probert as one of Ewan's students at St Anne's, during which time she acquired an insight into the depth of research involved in an academic career when employed as a research assistant on *Cases and Materials on the Law of Restitution*, which Ewan co-authored with Andrew Burrows.

In 1994 Ewan became one of the editors of *Chitty on Contracts* for its twenty-seventh edition, a role he has continued through to its current (thirty-fourth) edition. Hugh Beale, the current general editor, notes that Ewan 'has not only brought enormous learning to the book, but has also carried out substantial restructuring of the material to make it more accessible and has been a wonderful source of advice and support to me as general editor'.

One specific topic on which Ewan wrote extensively in the 1990s was that of frustration, and his edited collection, *Force Majeure and Frustration of Contract*, was published in 1995. William Day and Robert Stevens both focus on this topic in their own contributions. As Donal Nolan notes, Ewan also made a distinctive contribution to the law of tort during this period, with publications addressing issues such as product liability, pure economic loss, and fundamental questions of personal property.

After moving to London to take up a chair at University College London in 1995, Ewan was called to the Bar in 1998 and became a tenant at 3 Verulam Buildings, Gray's Inn. His contribution in that role is reflected in the foreword from Ali Malek. A fellow tenant at 3VB, Louise Gullifer, notes that Ewan's practice at the Bar contributed to the 'commercial astuteness' evident in his 'conception of many parts of contract law, such as interpretation, frustration and remedies'. In a similar vein, another tenant at 3VB, Adam Kramer, reflects on the importance of interpreting contracts 'from a pragmatic and practical standpoint' and describes Ewan as similarly being a 'pragmatic moderate' in his approach. The example he gives—of Ewan's reaction to a controversial case being to survey a huge body of case law to review how it was working in practice—illustrates Ewan's undogmatic approach. The issue of contractual interpretation, and Ewan's detailed analysis of the topic, is also considered by Philip Sales in his contribution.

Ewan returned to Oxford in 2000 as Professor of Private Law and Fellow of Lady Margaret Hall (where James Edelman recalls a stimulating lunchtime discussion that led to a subsequent publication and another debate at the SPTL). Another Fellow at LMH, Helen Scott, describes Ewan as an 'invaluable colleague and mentor' to her 'and to many others'.

During the 2000s Ewan made a significant contribution to the Study Group on a European Civil Code (and later to the Co-ordinating Committee for the European Civil Code project as a whole), as recalled by Hugh Beale in his chapter. Comparative law also continued to be a key theme of Ewan's own work. With Nili Cohen, he co-edited a collection on *Comparative Remedies for Breach of Contract* in 2005.

Roy Goode begins his chapter by thanking Ewan for taking on the editorship of what was then *Goode on Commercial Law* for its fourth edition in 2010. Ewan's contribution to the field of commercial law was cemented with his co-authorship of *Transnational Commercial Law: Texts, Cases and Materials*. As Roger Halson notes, a key characteristic of Ewan's scholarship has been his ability to make technical areas of commercial law more accessible to non-specialists.

In 2011 Ewan took up the role of Registrar of the University of Oxford. Various contributors pay tribute to the superb administrative skills he demonstrated in this role, which is addressed specifically by Andrew Hamilton in his foreword. Despite this heavy administrative burden, he continued to be active as a scholar, with new editions of *Contract Law*; *Contract*

Law, Text, Cases and Materials; *Transnational Commercial Law, Text, Cases and Materials*; and *Goode on Commercial Law* all appearing during this time, as well as numerous contributions to edited collections, including most recently one edited by two contributors to the present collection, William Day and Sarah Worthington.

What shines through the contributions to this volume is the warm regard in which Ewan is held. Mindy Chen-Wishart and Jodi Gardner describe him as 'supremely talented, hardworking, humble, understated (although utterly compelling when lecturing), encouraging, kind and excellent with people'. As his former students and, in Edwin's case, later his colleague, we concur.

Edwin Peel and Rebecca Probert

Contents

Table of Cases	xix
Table of Legislation	xxxv
List of Contributors	xli

PART I: CONTRACT

1. Facility, Circumvention, Economic Duress, and the Corporate Veil *Hector L MacQueen*	3
2. Good Faith in English Contract Law: Lessons from Comparative Law? *John Cartwright*	23
3. Rethinking Reliance Damages for Breach of Contract *Richard Taylor*	39
4. The Illegality Defence in the Courts Today *Andrew Burrows*	59
5. Schrödinger's Lawful Act Duress: Dead or Alive? *Mindy Chen-Wishart and Jodi Gardner*	75
6. Contracts and Relationships of Love and Trust *Rebecca Probert and Tim Dodsworth*	93
7. Shades of Frustration *William Day*	111
8. Repeal the Law Reform (Frustrated Contracts) Act 1943 *Robert Stevens*	125
9. Contractual Interpretation: Meaning, Intention, and Disembodied Spirits *Adam Kramer*	141
10. Contractual Interpretation: Antinomies and Boundaries *Philip Sales*	153
11. The Damage in Negotiating Damages *Sarah Worthington*	171
12. The Critical Reception of *Cavendish Square Holdings v Makdessi* *Roger Halson*	193

PART II: TORT

13. Direct and Vicarious Liability of Corporations *James Edelman*	211

xviii CONTENTS

14. Damage to 'Other Property': Exploring the Boundary Between Property
Damage and Pure Economic Loss 227
Donal Nolan

15. Procuring Wrongs 245
James Goudkamp

PART III: COMMERCIAL

16. Who Can Sue the Obligor When Receivables Are Financed? 265
Louise Gullifer

17. The 'Tripartite Guide' to Uniform Instruments in the Area of International
Commercial Contracts: Background, Content, and Legal Effect 283
Stefan Vogenauer

18. The Sale of Goods Act and the Nature of Sales 301
Hugh Beale

19. Transnational Commercial Law and Impediments to Its Development 319
Roy Goode

PART IV: UNJUST ENRICHMENT

20. Mistakes of Law, Again 339
Helen Scott

21. The External Shield of a Contract—Torts, Equity, and Restitution 351
Nili Cohen

22. Unjustified Enrichment in China: An Uncertain Path 367
Qiao Liu

23. Implied Terms and Restitution 383
Edwin Peel

List of Publications 397
Ewan McKendrick
Index 403

Table of Cases

UNITED KINGDOM

Aberdeen City Council v Stewart Milne Group Ltd [2011] UKSC 56 . . . . 150n.40
Ackworth v Kempe (1778) 1 Dougl 40; 99 ER 30 (KB). 214n.11
AG v Guardian Newspapers (No 2) [1990] 1 AC 109 (HL) 189nn.101–2
Ahuja Investments Ltd v Victorygame Ltd [2021] EWHC 2382 (Ch) 197n.37,
   202n.79, 205, 205n.100
AIB Group (UK) Plc v Mark Redler & Co Solicitors [2014] UKSC 58 (SC) 189n.106
Al Nehayan v Kent [2018] EWHC 333 (Comm); [2018] EWHC 614 (Comm);
   [2018] 1 CLC 216 . . . . 34n.56, 34n.59, 35nn.62–63, 82n.45
Alfred McAlpine Construction Ltd v Panatown Ltd' (2003) 3 OUCLJ 145 . . . . vin.1
Ampurius Nu Homes v Telford Homes [2012] EWHC 1820 (Ch); 144 Con LR 72;
   ([2013] EWCA Civ 577; [2013] 4 All ER 377 . . . . 40n.6
Anderson v Beacon Fellowship 1992 SLT 111. . . . . .8n.26, 13n.53
Anglia TV v Reed [1972] 1 QB 60. . . . . 42n.9, 43, 44–45
Anglo-African Shipping Co of New York Inc v J Mortner Ltd [1962] 1 Lloyd's Rep 81;
   [1962] 1 Lloyd's Rep 910 . . . . 308n.39
Anglo-Russian Merchant Traders and John Batt & Co Ltd, Re [1917] 2 KB 679 (CA). 122n.89
Anns v Merton London Borough Council [1978] AC 728 (HL). 229n.13, 236n.49
Antuzis v DJ Houghton Catching Services Ltd [2019] EWHC 843 (QB),
   [2019] Bus LR 1532 . . . . 254n.63
Appleby v Myers (1867) LR 2 CP 651 . . . . 131n.18, 135n.31
Arcos Ltd v EA Ronaasen & Son [1933] AC 470. . . . . 311n.56
Ardila Investments NV v ENRC NV [2015] EWHC 1667 (Comm); [2015] 2 BCLC 560 . . . . 280n.112
Arnold v Britton [2015] UKSC 36, [2015] AC 1619 . . . . . . 150n.40, 155n.5, 159n.28, 162–63, 162n.41
Arris v Stukely (1677) 2 Mod 260 . . . . 360n.57
Ashley v The Scottish Football Association Ltd [2016] CSOH 78. . . . . 17n.74
Associated Newspapers Group plc v Insert Media Ltd [1988] 1 WLR 509 (Ch D) 514 261
Astor Management AG v Atalaya Mining plc [2018] EWCA Civ 2407, [2019] Bus LR 106 . . . 151n.47
Attorney General of Belize v Belize Telecom Ltd [2009] UKPC 10, [2009] 1 WLR 1988. . . . . . 391n.53
Attorney General v Blake [2001] 1 AC 268 (HL) 172n.12, 179n.44, 184n.72, 184n.74, 186n.89
Attwood v Lamont [1920] 3 KB 571 (CA) 73n.35

Bacardi-Martini Beverages Ltd v Thomas Hardy Packaging Ltd [2002] EWCA Civ 549,
   [2002] 2 Lloyd's Rep 379 . . . . .234–35nn.40–43
Bahamasair Holdings Ltd v Messier Dowty Inc [2018] UKPC 25, [2019] 1 All ER 25 . . . . 228n.7
Bailey v De Crespigny (1869) LR 4 QB 180 . . . . 150n.36
Bain v Fothergill (1874) LR 7 HL 158. . . . . 54, 54n.44, 54n.46
Balfour v Balfour [1919] 2 KB 571 (CA) 106n.98
Bank Line Ltd v Arthur Capel & Co [1919] AC 435 (HL) 120nn.72–73
Bank of Credit and Commerce International v Ali [2001] UKHL 8,
   [2002] AC 251. . . . . 161n.35, 169n.73
Bank of New York Mellon (International) Ltd v Cine-UK Ltd [2022] EWCA Civ 1021 . . . . . . 120n.71
Bank of New York Mellon (International) Ltd v Cine-UK Ltd, London Trocadero
   (2015) LLP v Picturehouse Cinemas Ltd [2022] EWCA Civ 1021, [2023] L&TR 2 . . . . . .385n.16,
      388–89, 388n.36, 388n.38, 388n.40, 389n.43, 390, 391–92, 392n.62, 393, 394
Barclays Bank Ltd v Willowbrook International Ltd [1987] 1 FTLR 386. . . . . 270n.29
Barclays Bank Ltd v WJ Simms, Son & Cooke (Southern) Ltd [1980] QB 677 . . . . 339n.7
Barnes v Eastenders Cash & Carry Plc [2014] UKSC 26, [2015] AC 1 . . . . . . 384n.3, 384n.12, 385n.15,
      386–87, 387n.31, 387n.33, 388–89, 391–92, 393, 394, 395n.81, 395n.85, 395n.88

Barton v Morris [2023] UKSC 3 . . . . 131n.19, 168n.72, 182n.59, 384n.8, 385n.17, 388n.36, 389–92, 390n.51, 391n.54, 391n.58, 392n.65, 393, 393n.69, 393n.72, 394, 395n.84

Bates v Post Office Ltd [2019] EWHC 606 (QB) 34n.56, 34n.59

Behzadi v Shaftesbury Hotels Ltd [1992] Ch 1 . . . . 312n.75

Bellefield Computer Services Ltd v E Turner & Sons Ltd (2000) 2 TCLR 759 (CA) 238n.63

Benedetti v Sawiris [2013] UKSC 50, [2013] 3 WLR 351. . . . . 395n.83

Berkeley Community Villages Ltd v Pullen [2007] EWHC 1330 (Ch); [2007] 3 EGLR 101 . . . . 87n.82

Bexhill UK Limited v Abdul Razzaq [2012] EWCA Civ 1376. . . . . 273n.56, 278n.95, 279n.99, 279nn.100–1, 280n.110, 281n.115, 281n.121

Blackburn Bobbin Co v Allen & Sons [1918] 2 KB 467 (CA) 119n.65

Blackburn v Smith (1848) 2 Ex 783; 154 ER 707 . . . . 126n.5

Black-Clawson International Ltd v Papierwerke Waldhof-Aschaffenburg AG
 [1975] AC 591 . . . . 153, 154n.1

Blake v Lanyon (1795) 6 TR 221 . . . . 354n.15, 359n.55

Bloomsbury International Ltd v Department for Environment, Food and Rural Affairs
 [2011] UKSC 25; [2011] 1 WLR 1546 . . . . 157n.21

Blu-Sky Solutions v Be Caring Ltd [2021] EWHC 2619 (Comm) 196n.22, 205–6, 205n.102, 206n.104

Blue v Ashley [2017] EWHC 1928 (Comm) 106, 106n.91

Boissevain v Weil [1950] AC 327(HL) 61n.5

Borrelli v Ting [2010] UKPC 21, [2010] Bus LR 1718 . . . . 83, 83n.49, 88

Borrowman, Phillips & Co v Free & Hollis (1878) 4 QBD 500 . . . . 312n.68

Boxfoldia Ltd v National Graphical Association (1982) [1988] ICR 752 (QBD) 255n.73

BP Exploration Co (Libya) Ltd v Hunt (No 2) [1979] 1 WLR 783 . . . . 133n.26

BP v Hunt [1979] 1 WLR 783 . . . . 136, 137n.34

BP v Hunt [1983] 2 AC 352 . . . . 137n.33

Brack v Brack [2018] EWCA Civ 2862. . . . . 102n.65, 102n.67

Bremer Handelsgesellschaft mbH v Vanden Avenne-Izegen PVBA
 [1977] 1 Lloyd's Rep 133 (Com Ct). 112n.9

Brewer Street Investments Ltd v Barclays Woollen Ltd [1954] 1 QB 428 (CA) 135n.29

Brice v Bannister (1878) 3 QBD 569. . . . . 270n.32

British Bank for Foreign Trade v Novinex [1949] 1 KB 623 (CA). 164n.48

British Westinghouse v Underground Electric Railways [1912] AC 673. . . . 46n.23, 47–49, 48n.29, 58

Broad Idea International Ltd v Convoy Collateral Ltd [2021] UKPC 24, [2022] 2 WLR 703 . . . . . . 248n.29

Bromarin AB v IMD Investments Ltd [1999] STC 301, 310 . . . . 149n.32, 150n.39

Broom v Morgan [1953] 1 QB 597 . . . . 215n.21, 216

Broster v Galliard Docklands Ltd [2011] EWHC 1722 (TCC), [2011] PNLR 34 . . . . 238n.67

Brown's Bay Resort Ltd v Pozzoni [2016] UKPC 10 . . . . 198, 198n.49

Bunge Corp v Tradax SA [1981] 1 WLR 711 . . . . 312n.73

Business Computers Ltd v Anglo-African Leasing Ltd [1977] 1 WLR 578 . . . . 271n.39

C & P Haulage v Middleton [1983] 1 WLR 1461 . . . . 41n.8, 42n.11, 43–46, 47

Cadogan Petroleum Holdings Ltd v Global Process Systems [2013] EWHC 214 (Comm);
 [2013] 2 Lloyd's Rep 26 . . . . 200n.62

Callisher v Bischoffsheim (1870) LR 5 QB 449 (QB) 88n.92

Cambridge Water Co v Eastern Counties Leather plc [1994] 2 AC 264 (HL) 304 . . . . 259n.96

Campbell Discount Co Ltd v Bridge [1962] AC 600. 36

Canary Wharf (BP4) T1 Ltd v European Medicines Agency [2019] EWHC 335 (Ch);
 183 Con LR 167. . . . . 115n.29, 117n.48, 119nn.63–64, 121n.81, 123n.92

Cargill International Trading Pte Ltd v Uttam Galva Steels Ltd
 [2019] EWHC 476 (Comm) 205, 205n.98

Carlos Federspiel & Co SA v Charles Twigg & Co Ltd [1957] 1 Lloyd's Rep 240 . . . . 307n.30

Carmichael v National Power Plc [1999] 1 WLR 2042 (HL) 163n.45

Carter v Boehm (1766) 3 Burr 1905, 1910; 97 ER 1162 . . . . 31n.42

Cassidy v Ministry of Health [1951] 2 KB 343 (CA). 218n.37, 218n.40

Cassidy v Ministry of Health [1951] 2 KB 343 . . . . 222n.58

TABLE OF CASES   xxi

Cavendish Square Holding BV v Makdessi; ParkingEye Ltd v Beavis (Consumers'
  Association Intervening) [2015] UKSC 67, [2016] AC 1172 . . . . . . .193, 193n.1, 193n.3, 194–95,
    194n.9, 195n.16, 196n.19, 196n.23, 196n.24, 197n.36, 198n.42, 199–200,
    200n.59, 200n.60, 201, 201n.63, 202n.72, 202n.77, 203, 204, 204n.87, 205n.96,
    206n.103, 206n.105, 206n.107, 206n.110, 207–8, 207n.111, 207n.114
CCC Films v Impact Quadrant Films [1985] 1 QB 16 . . . . 44–45, 44n.19
Cehave NV v Bremer Handelsgesellschaft mbH (The Hansa Nord) [1976] QB 44. . . . . 311n.58
Central Insurance Co Ltd v Seacalf Shipping Corporation (The Aiolos)
  [1983] 2 Lloyd's Rep 25 . . . . 273n.55, 274n.61
Chandler v Webster [1904] 1 KB 493 (CA) 118n.60, 130–31, 130n.15, 132–33, 134, 139
Chapman v Honig [1963] 2 QB 502 (CA) 260n.107
Charnesh Kapoor v National Westminster Bank [2011] EWCA Civ 1083,
  [2012] 1 All ER 201. . . . . 273nn.56–57, 277n.84, 277n.86, 277n.88, 278n.93, 279n.107, 280n.114
Chocosuisse Union des Fabricants Suisse de Chocolat v Cadbury Ltd
  [1998] RPC 117 (Ch D) 127 . . . . 259n.93
Clark v Malpas (1862) 4 De G F & J 401, 45 ER 1238 (Ch). 5n.16
Clarke v Dickson (1858) EB & E 148; 120 ER 463. . . . . 126n.5
Clunie v Stirling (1854) 17 D 15 . . . . .7, 8n.25, 12n.46
CMX v EJX (French Marriage Contract) [2022] EWFC 136. . . . . 102n.66, 103n.70
Co-operative Insurance Society v Argyll Stores [1998] AC 1 (HL) 357n.37
Coco v AN Clark (Engineers) Ltd [1968] FSR 525 (Ch) 189n.102
Cole, Re [1931] 2 Ch 174 . . . . 88n.92
Colonial Bank Ltd v European Grain & Shipping Ltd [1988] 3 WLR 60 (CA) 269n.18
Commissioner of Public Works v Hills [1906] AC 368 . . . . 201n.67
Compania Colombiana de Seguros v Pacific Steam Navigation Co [1965] 1 QB 101 . . . . 272n.49
Compass Group UK and Ireland Ltd v Mid Essex Hospital Services NHS Trust
  [2013] EWCA Civ 200, [2013] BLR 265. . . . . 35n.60
Compound Photonics Group Ltd, Re [2022] EWCA Civ 1371. . . . . 87n.82
Cook v Wright (1861) 1 B & S 559, 121 ER 822 (QB) 88n.92
Cooper v Parker (1855) 15 CB 822, 139 ER 650 . . . . 88n.92
Cotman v Brougham [1918] AC 514 (HL) 224n.70
Council of the City of York v Trinity One (Leeds) Ltd [2018] EWCA Civ 1883 . . . . 149n.30
Courtney & Fairbairn Ltd v Tolaini Brothers (Hotels) Ltd [1975] 1 WLR 297 (CA) . . . 33n.47, 33n.48
Couturier v Hastie (1856) 5 HLC 673. . . . . 117n.41, 118n.52
CPC Group Ltd v Qatari Diar Real Estate Investment Company [2010] EWHC 1535 (Ch),
  [2010] CILL 2908 . . . . 87n.82
Cresswell v Potter [1978] 1 WLR 255 (Ch D) 83n.53
Crossley v Crossley [2007] EWCA Civ 1491 . . . . 99n.36
Crossley v Volkswagen AG [2021] EWHC 3444 (QB). 143n.8, 144n.10, 144n.11
CTN Cash and Carry Ltd v Gallaher Ltd [1994] 4 All ER 714 (CA). 80n.26, 90n.103
Customs & Excise Commissioners v Barclays Bank plc [2006] UKHL 28,
  [2007] 1 AC 181 . . . . 258n.91
Cutter v Powell (1795) 6 Term Rep 320; 101 ER 573 (KB) 131, 131n.18, 135–36, 390n.50

D & F Estates Ltd v Church Commissioners for England [1989] 1 AC 177 (HL) 229n.15, 230n.21
Dalton v Angus (1881) 6 App Cas 740 (HL) 221n.54
Dargamo Holdings Ltd v Avonwick Holdings Ltd [2021] EWCA Civ 1149;
  [2021] 2 CLC 583 . . . . 384n.5, 384n.7, 384n.10, 388–89nn.41–42, 392n.62
Darling Island Stevedoring and Lighterage Co Ltd v Long [1957] HCA 26,
  (1957) 97 CLR 36 . . . . 215–16, 215n.17, 215n.22
Davis Contractors Ltd v Fareham UDC [1956] AC 696 (HL). 120n.77, 149n.35, 151n.44
De Francesco v Barnum (1890) 45 Ch D 430 . . . . 354n.15, 359n.55
Dearle v Hall (1828) 3 Russ 1. . . . . 271n.38
Debenhams Retail plc v Sun Alliance and London Assurance Co Ltd
  [2005] EWCA Civ 868, [2005] 3 EGLR 34. . . . . 149n.33, 150n.38
Deposit Protection Board v Dalia [1994] 2 AC 367 . . . . .270–71nn.34–35, 273n.53, 273n.56

xxii TABLE OF CASES

Deutsche Morgan Grenfell Group plc v Inland Revenue Commissioners
  [2006] UKHL 49, [2007] 1 AC 558 . . . . 341n.21, 342, 343n.28, 343n.32, 344n.38,
                       345–46, 345n.40, 346n.48, 347, 348–49, 348n.57, 349n.60, 380n.76
Dextra Bank v Bank of Jamaica [2002] 1 All ER Com 193 (PC) 346n.47
Dies v British and International Mining and Finance Corporation [1939] 1 KB 724 . . . . 131n.20
Donoghue v Stevenson [1932] AC 562 (HL) 26n.15, 32n.43
Donoghue v Stevenson 236–37
DPP v Ray [1974] AC 370 (HL) 144n.11
DSND Subsea Ltd v Petroleum Geo Services ASA [2000] BLR 530 (TCC) 77n.10,
                                               78, 79n.18, 81n.36
Dundee Evening Post, 20 August 1904 . . . . 8n.26
Dunlop Pneumatic Tyre Co Ltd v New Garage and Motor Co Ltd
  [1915] AC 79 (HL) 193n.2, 195n.18, 196, 197, 200, 200n.60, 201n.67, 206n.104, 207–8
Durham Brothers v Robertson [1898] 1 QB 765 . . . . .270n.32, 271n.40, 274n.62
Durham v Durham (1885) 10 PD 80 . . . . 94n.5

Earl of Aylesford v Morris (1873) 8 Ch App 484 (CA) 83n.53
East v Maurer [1991] 1 WLR 461 . . . . 56n.49
Ebrahimi v Westbourne Galleries Ltd [1973] AC 360 (HL) 18, 19n.80
Eco World—Ballymore Embassy Gardens Co Ltd v Dobler UK
  [2021] EWHC 2207 (TCC); 197 Con LR 108 . . . . 203, 203n.82
Edgar v Edgar [1980] 1 WLR 1410 . . . . 101n.58
Edgworth Capital (Luxenbourg) Sarl v Ramblas Investments BV
  [2015] EWHC 150 (Comm) 197n.37, 199n.56
Edler v Auerbach [1950] 1 KB 359 72
Edwin Hill & Partners v First National Finance Corp [1989] 1 WLR 225 . . . . 358n.47
EE & Brian Smith (1928) Ltd v Wheatsheaf Mills Ltd [1939] 2 KB 302 . . . . 312n.68
Egon Zehnder Ltd v Tillman [2019] UKSC 32, [2020] AC 154 . . . . 73n.34
El Makdessi v Cavendish Square Holdings BV [2015] UKSC 67; [2016] AC 1172 . . . . 33n.51
Else (1982) Ltd v Parkland Holdings Ltd [1994] 1 BCLC 130 . . . . 206n.110
Emmott v Michael Wilson Partners Ltd [2019] EWCA Civ 219, [2019] 4 WLR 53 . . . . . 248n.23, 248n.26
Energizer Supermarket Ltd v Holiday Snacks Ltd [2022] UKPC 16 . . . . 68n.25, 69n.26
Energy Venture Partners Ltd v Malabu Oil & Gas Ltd [2013] EWHC 2118 (Comm) 395n.83
Equitable Life Assurance Society v Hyman [2002] 1 AC 408 (HL) 459 . . . . .387n.32, 392n.63, 394–95n.80
Erlanger v New Sombrero Phosphate Co (1878) 3 App Cas 1218 (HL) 127n.6
Ertel Bieber & Co v Rio Tinto Co Ltd [1918] AC 260 (HL) 121n.83
Esso Petroleum Co Ltd v Harper's Garage (Stourport) Ltd [1968] AC 269 (HL) 73n.38
Euan Wallace & Partners v Westscot Homes plc 2000 SLT 327 . . . . 15n.65
Evening Standard Co Ltd v Henderson [1987] ICR 588 . . . . 355n.22
Eves v Eves [1975] 1 WLR 1338 . . . . 103n.75
Experience Hendrix LLC v PPX Enterprises Inc [2003] EWCA Civ 323,
  [2003] 1 All ER (Comm) 830 (CA) 179n.43, 184n.71, 184n.74
Export Credits Guarantee Department v Universal Oil Products Co
  [1983] 1 WLR 399 . . . . 194n.10, 199n.56

Ferguson v Wilson (1866) LR 2 Ch App 77 (CA) 219n.42
Fibrosa Spolka Akcyjna v Fairbairn Lawson Combe Barbour Ltd
  [1943] AC 32 (HL) 119n.62, 130, 130n.13, 131n.20, 133
Financial Conduct Authority v Arch Insurance (UK) Ltd [2021] UKSC 1 [2021] AC 649 . . . . 148n.27
Finesse Group Ltd v Bryson Products (a Firm) [2013] EWHC 3273 (TCC),
  [2013] 6 Costs LR 991 . . . . 237n.61
Firth v Hylane Ltd [1959] EWCA Civ J0211-3 (vLex); [1959] EGD 212 . . . . 390n.49
Flureau v Thornhill (1776) 2 Wm Bl 1078; 96 ER 635 . . . . 54n.43, 54n.46
Foakes v Beer (1884) 9 App Cas 605 (HL) 88n.95
Foley v Classique Coaches [1934] 2 KB 1 (CA) 164n.48
Forsikringsaktieselskapet Vesta v Butcher [1989] AC 852 . . . . 165n.54
Foster v Stewart (1814) 3 M & S 192 . . . . 360n.60

TABLE OF CASES   xxiii

Freedman v Union Group Plc [1997] EGCS 28 (CA)..................................... 88n.92
Fry v Lane (1888) 40 Ch D 312 ....6n.17, 83n.53
Fulton Shipping Inc of Panama v Globalia Business Travel SAU [2017] UKSC 43,
    [2017] 1 WLR 2581 .... 48n.27

G Percy Trentham Ltd v Archital Luxfer Ltd [1993] 1 Lloyd's Rep 25 (CA)................. 164n.49
G Scammel & Nephew Ltd v HC and JG Ouston [1941] AC 251 (HL)...... 106n.90, 164, 165n.51, 167–68
Gamerco SA v ICM/Fair Warning (Agency) Ltd [1995] 1 WLR 1226 (QBD)............... 134n.27
Gee v Gee [2018] EWHC 1393 (Ch)......................247n.20, 247n.21, 249–50, 252, 252n.50,
                                       254, 254n.64, 256n.78, 256n.81, 257n.85, 258
General Nutrition Investment Co v Holland and Barrett International Ltd
    [2017] EWHC 746 (Ch).. 270n.27
Gestmin SGPS SA v Credit Suisse (UK) Ltd [2013] EWHC 3560 (Comm);
    [2020] 1 CLC 428 .... 147n.22
Gibson's Executor v Anderson 1925 SC 774 .... 8n.26
Gilbert-Ash (Northern) Ltd v Modern Engineering (Bristol) Ltd [1974] AC 689 ... 165n.56, 166n.60
Gold Group Properties Ltd v BDW Trading Ltd [2010] EWHC 1632 (TCC)................ 87n.82
Golden Strait Corp v Nippon Yusen Kubishika Kaisha (The Golden Victory)
    [2007] UKHL 12 | [2007] 2 A.C. 353 .... 86n.79
GPP Big Field LLP v Solar EPC Solutions SL [2018] EWHC 2866 (Comm)............... 196n.22
Grand View Private Trust Co Ltd v Wong [2022] UKPC 47 .... 167n.63, 167n.65
Grange v Quinn [2013] EWCA Civ 24; [2013] 1 P & CR 18 .... 40n.6
Gray v Braid Group (Holdings) Ltd [2016] CSIH 68; 2016 SLT 1003.......... 201n.69, 202, 202n.74
Gray v Gee [1923] 39 TLR 42 .... 354n.16
Gray v Thames Trains Ltd [2009] UKHL 33, [2009] AC 1339........................ 64n.11, 66
Graysim Holdings Ltd v P & O Property Holdings Ltd [1996] AC 329 (HL) 158n.22
Great Peace Shipping Ltd v Tsavliris Salvage (International) Ltd [2002] EWCA Civ
    1407, [2003] QB 679.. 394n.76
Great Peace Shipping Ltd v Tsavliris Salvage (International) Ltd [2002] EWCA Civ
    1407, [2003] QB 679.. 117n.43
Griffith v Bymer (1903) 19 TLR 434 (KB) 118n.52
Grondona v Stoffel & Co [2020] UKSC 42, [2021] AC 540 ....62–64, 62n.8,
                                       63n.10, 65, 66, 69, 71, 73, 74

Haines v Hill [2007] EWCA Civ 1284, [2008] Ch 412 .... 88n.92
Hanson v Meyer (1805) 6 East 614 .... 307n.29
Harcus Sinclair LLP v Your Lawyers Ltd [2021] UKSC 32, [2021] 3 WLR 598................... 73
Hartley v Hymans [1920] 3 KB 475 .... 312n.77
Hayfin Opal Luxco 3 SARL v Windermere VII CMBS Plc [2016] EWHC 782 (Ch),
    [2018] 1 BCLC 118.............................. 198, 198n.44, 204n.92, 205n.97
Hazell v Hammersmith and Fulham London Borough Council and others
    [1992] 2 AC 1–47 (HL) 341n.20, 344, 346–47
Hedley Byrne & Co Ltd v Heller & Partners Ltd [1964] AC 465 .... 218n.39
Henderson v Dorset Healthcare University NHS Foundation Trust [2020] UKSC 43,
    [2021] AC 563................................ 62n.9, 64–66, 65n.12, 67, 69, 71, 73, 74
Henderson v Merrett Syndicates [1995] 2 AC 145 .... 165n.54
Hendy Lennox (Industrial Engines) Ltd v Grahame Puttick Ltd [1984] 1 WLR 485 (QBD)..... 241n.90
Heritage Travel and Tourism v Windhorst [2021] EWHC 2380 (Comm)............. 199, 199n.53
Herkules Piling v Tilbury Construction (1992) 61 BLR 107 (QBD) 119 .... 270n.27, 274n.65
Hern v Nichols (1698) 1 Salk 256, 91 ER 289... 214n.12
Herne Bay Steam Boat Co v Hutton [1903] 2 KB 683 (CA).......................118–19, 118n.53
Hivac Ltd v Park Royal Scientific Instruments [1946] Ch 169 .... 364n.72
Hoist Portfolio Holding 2 Ltd v Multiple Defendants (2018)
    [2018] EWHC 3113 (Ch).................................. 269n.24, 273n.55, 348
Holsworthy UDC v Holsworthy RDC [1907] 2 Ch 62............................... 88n.92
Holt v Heatherfield Trust Ltd [1942] 2 KB 1 .... 269n.22
Hopkins v Grazebrook (1826) 6 B & C 31; 108 ER 364............................... 54n.46

xxiv   TABLE OF CASES

Hopkins v Hopkins [2015] EWHC 812 (Fam) 102n.61
Horn v Commercial Acceptances Ltd [2011] EWHC 1757 . . . . 87n.82
Howard v Wood (1679) 2 Lev 245 . . . . 360n.57
HR & S Sainsbury Ltd v Street [1972] 1 WLR 834 . . . . 138n.35
Hughes v Pump House Hotel Co [1902] 2 KB 190 . . . . 272n.45, 280n.110
Hume v Rundell (1824) 2 S & S 174; 57 ER 311 . . . . 161n.33
Huth v Clarke (1890) 25 QBD 391 (QB) 219n.45
Hydrodam (Corby) Ltd, Re [1994] 2 BCLC 180 . . . . 10n.38

ICU (Europe) Ltd v Ibrahim [2020] SAC (Civ) 20 . . . . 17n.74
Imperial Tobacco Co (of Great Britain and Ireland) Ltd v Parslay [1936] 2 All ER 515 (HL) 205n.96
B, In Re [2015] EWCA Civ 1302; [2016] 1 WLR 2326 . . . . 200n.57
Spectrum Plus Ltd, In Re [2005] UKHL 41; [2005] 2 AC 680 . . . . 271n.41
Indigo Park Services v Watson 2017 GWD 40-610 . . . . 202, 202n.76
Interfoto Picture Library Ltd v Stiletto Visual Programmes Ltd [1989] QB 433 (CA) 32n.44
Investors Compensation Scheme Ltd v West Bromwich Building Society
        [1998] 1 WLR 896 (HL) 114n.20, 141, 141n.2, 154n.3, 155, 162–63, 162n.41

J Lauritzen AS v Wijsmuller BV (The Super Servant Two) [1990] 1 Lloyd's Rep 1 (CA) 113n.14
Jacobs v Morton (1994) 72 BLR 92 (QBD) 237n.56
Jaggard v Sawyer [1995] 1 WLR 269 (CA) 185n.78, 186n.83
James v Thomas H Kent Ltd [1951] 1 KB 551 . . . . 128n.8
Jarvis v Swan Tours Ltd [1973] QB 233 . . . . 171n.2
Johnson v Agnew [1980] AC 367 (HL) 185n.76
Johnson v Walton [1990] 1 FLR 350 (CA) 258n.91
Jones Brothers (Hunstanton) Ltd v Stevens [1955] 1 QB 275 . . . . 354n.15, 360n.56
JSC BTA Bank v Ablyazov (No 14) [2018] UKSC 19; [2020] AC 727 . . . . 252n.52, 255n.70
JSC BTA Bank v Khrapunov [2018] UKSC 19 . . . . 260n.109
Junior Books v Veitchi Ltd [1983] AC 520 (HL) 229n.14

K v K (ancillary relief: pre-nuptial agreement) [2003] 1 FLR 120 . . . . 99n.35
KA v MA (Prenuptial Agreement: Needs) [2018] EWHC 499 (Fam) 102n.61, 103n.71
Kagan v Harris [2019] EWHC 2567 (TCC) 239n.70
Kaufman v Gerson [1904] 1 KB 591 (CA) 80, 80n.23, 81n.35
Kawasaki Kisen Kaisha Ltd v James Kemball Limited [2021] EWCA Civ 33, [2021] 3 All ER 978 . . . 359n.49
Kelly v Cooper Associates [1993] AC 205 . . . . 166n.57
Kelly v Solari (1841) 9 M & W 54 . . . . 339n.5, 340–41, 346, 347, 384n.4
Kleinwort Benson Ltd v Lincoln City Council [1999] 2 AC 349 (HL) 339, 339n.6, 341n.18,
                                                342–43, 343n.28, 344n.36, 344n.37, 344n.38, 344n.39,
                                                345, 346n.48, 346n.50, 347, 348–49, 348n.59
Krell v Henry [1903] 2 KB 740 (CA) 117n.46, 118, 118n.50, 121
Kulkarni v Manor Credit (Davenham) Ltd [2010] EWCA Civ 69; [2010] 2 Lloyd's Rep 431 . . . . . 307n.30

Lady Hood of Avalon v Mackinnon [1909] 1 Ch 476–84 (ChD) 340n.15
Lakatamia Shipping Co Ltd v Su [2014] EWHC 3611 (Comm); [2015] 1 Lloyd's Rep 216 245,
                                                247nn.15–17, 248–50, 248n.30, 250n.44, 252
Lakatamia Shipping Co Ltd v Su [2021] EWHC 1907 (Comm) 245n.3, 247, 253n.56, 254n.65,
                                                256n.76, 257, 258
Lake v Bayliss [1974] 1 WLR 1073 . . . . 362n.66
Lamine v Dorrell (1705) 2 Ld Raym 1216 . . . . 360n.58
Law Debenture Trust Corpn v Ural Caspian Oil Corpn Ltd [1995] Ch 152 . . . . 250n.40
Lazarus Estates v Beasley [1956] 1 QB 702 (CA) 18n.76
Lazenby Garages v Wright [1976] 1 WLR 459 . . . . 309n.49
Lebeaupin v Crispon & Co [1920] 2 KB 714 (KB) 114n.24
Leeds City Council v Barclays Bank plc [2021] EWHC 363 (Comm),
        [2021] QB 1027 . . . . 143n.7, 144n.9, 144n.11

TABLE OF CASES XXV

LF2 Ltd v Supperstone [2018] EWHC 1776 (Ch); [2018] Bus LR 2303 . . . . 250n.39
Libyan Investment Authority v Goldman Sachs International [2016] EWHC 2530 (Ch). 16n.68
Lightly v Clouston (1808) 1 Taunt 112 . . . . 360n.59
Lindsay's Executor v Outlook Finance ltd [2020] CSOH 90,
    28 October, unreported 7n.19, 11n.44, 14, 15n.66, 16
Lindsay's Executor v Outlook Finance Ltd [2021] CSOH 82,
    12 August, unreported. 4n.8, 6–11, 8n.28, 9n.34, 11n.40, 12
Linklaters Business Services v Sir Robert McAlpine Ltd (No 2)
    [2010] EWHC 2931 (QB), 133 Con LR 211. . . . . 238n.66
Linklaters Business Services v Sir Robert McAlpine Ltd [2010] EWHC 1145 (QB),
    [2010] BLR 537 . . . . 238n.65
Lipkin Gorman v Karpnale Ltd [1988] UKHL 12, [1991] 2 AC 548 (HL) 65n.18, 178n.39,
                                                      179n.40, 370n.17
Livingstone v Rawyards Coal Co (1880) 5 App Cas 25 . . . . 173n.18, 176n.26
Lloyds Bank v Bundy [1975] 2 QB 326 (CA). 15n.66
Lloyds TSB Foundation for Scotland v Lloyds Banking Group plc [2013] UKSC 3;
    [2013] 1 WLR 366. . . . . 149n.34
Lochgelly Iron and Coal Co Ltd v M'Mullan [1934] AC 1 (HL) 222n.56
Longridge v Dorville (1821) 5 B & Ad 117; 106 ER 1136 (KBD). 88n.92
Luckwell v Limata [2014] EWHC 502 (Fam) 100n.46
Lumley v Gye (1853) 2 El & Bl 216; 118 ER 749 (QB). 245n.1, 246n.7, 249–50, 251n.46, 253–54,
                255–56, 259–60, 351, 351n.1, 352, 353, 354, 355n.21, 356, 358–59, 360, 366
Lumley v Wagner [1852] EWHC (Ch) J96 . . . . 355n.22, 363n.70
Luxury Italian KBB Co Ltd v Boutros [2021] EW Misc 5 (CC). 203, 203n.83
Lynch v DPP of Northern Ireland [1975] AC 653. . . . . 102n.62

M v M (Pre-nuptial agreement) [2002] 1 FLR 654 . . . . 99n.35
M/S Aswan Engineering v Lupdine Ltd [1987] 1 WLR 1 (CA). 227n.5, 232n.30, 236n.45
M'Culloch v M'Crackan (1857) 20 D 206. . . . . 12n.48
MacGilvary v Martin 1986 SLT 89 . . . . 13n.52
Mackay v Campbell 1966 SC 237; 1967 SC (HL) 53 . . . . 7nn.23–24
MacLeod v MacLeod [2008] UKPC 64 . . . . 99n.37
Magdeev v Tsetkov [2020] EWHC 887 (Comm) 123n.93
Mahmoud and Ispahani, Re [1921] 2 KB 716 (CA) 67n.22, 69
Mailbox (Birmingham) Ltd v Galliford Try Construction Ltd [2017] EWHC 67 (TCC);
    170 Con LR 219. . . . . 269n.21, 273nn.55–56
Majrowski v Guy's and St Thomas's NHS Trust [2006] UKHL 34, [2007] 1 AC 224 . . . . 216n.29, 254n.62
Manchester Building Society v Grant Thornton UK LLP [2021] UKSC 20, [2022] AC 783 . . . . . 165n.54
Manchester Ship Canal Co Ltd v Vauxhall Motors Ltd [2018] EWCA Civ 1100, [2019] Ch 331. . . . 197n.38
Mareva Compania Naviera SA v International Bulk Carriers SA (The Mareva)
    [1980] 1 All ER 213 (CA). 248n.25
Marex Financial Ltd v Creative Finance Ltd [2013] EWHC 2155 (Comm),
    [2014] 1 All ER (Comm) 122 . . . . 245n.6, 246, 246n.8
Marex Financial Ltd v Sevilleja [2017] EWHC 918 (Comm), [2017] 4 WLR 105. . . . . .245n.2, 247,
              250nn.43–44, 251–52, 253, 253n.54, 254–56, 257–58, 257n.83, 259–61
Marex Financial Ltd v Sevilleja [2018] EWCA Civ 1468, [2019] QB 173. . . .245, 246n.11, 247, 248–56
Marex Financial Ltd v Sevilleja [2020] UKSC 31, [2021] AC 39 . . . . 246n.12, 246n.13, 260n.100
Marks and Spencer Plc v BNP Paribas Securities Services Trust Co (Jersey) Ltd
    [2015] UKSC 72, [2016] AC 742. . . . . 388n.39, 388n.40
Marks and Spencer plc v BNP Paribas Securities Services Trust Co (Jersey) Ltd
    [2015] UKSC 72; [2016] AC 742. . . . . 118n.59, 121n.80
Matossian v Matossian [2016] CSOH 21 . . . . 12n.49, 12n.51
MBNA Europe Bank Ltd v Revenue and Customs Commissioners [2006] EWHC
    2326 (Ch), [2006] STC 2089 . . . . 267n.11
McDermid v Nash Dredging and Reclamation Co Ltd [1987] AC 906 (HL) 222n.56
Mercantile Group (Europe) AG v Aiyela [1994] QB 366 (CA) 248n.27

TABLE OF CASES

Meridian Global Funds Management Asia Ltd v Securities Commission [1995] 2 AC 500. . . . . . 219n.43
Meridian Global Funds Management Asia Ltd v Securities Commission [1995] 2 AC 500. . . . . . 222n.61
Merritt v Merritt [1970] 1 WLR 1211 (CA). 106n.97
Metropolitan Water Board v Dick Kerr & Co [1918] AC 119 (HL) 113n.10
Middleton v Fowler (1698) 1 Salk 282; 91 ER 247 (KB). 214n.10
Ministry of Defence v Ashman (1993) 66 P&CR 195 (CA). 171–72n.6, 180n.47, 181,
      181n.49, 181n.50, 181n.54, 182, 182n.57, 182n.60, 183n.61
Ministry of Defence v Thompson (1993) 25 HLR 552 (CA) 181n.49, 182n.60
MN v AN [2023] EWHC (Fam) 613. . . . . .100n.47, 100n.50, 102n.68, 103, 103n.73
Morgans v Launchbury [1973] AC 127 (HL) 215n.20
Morris-Garner v One Step (Support) Ltd [2018] UKSC 20, [2019] AC 649 (SC). 171n.1, 171n.3,
      171n.5, 172–76, 172n.8, 172n.13, 173n.17, 173n.20, 174n.23, 175n.24,
      179n.42, 182–83, 184, 184n.74, 185, 185n.75, 185nn.76–78, 186n.82,
      186n.89, 187, 187n.91, 187n.92, 188, 188n.97, 188n.100, 190–91
Mousaka Inc v Golden Seagull Maritime Inc [2002] 1 Lloyd's Rep 797 (QB) 88n.92
MSC Mediterranean Shipping Co SA v Cottonex Anstalt [2016] EWCA Civ 789,
 [2016] 2 CLC 272 . . . . 35n.60
Munich Re Capital Ltd v Ascot Corporate Name Ltd [2019] EWHC 2768 (Comm),
 [2020] BLR 140. . . . . 149n.32
Mur Shipping BV v RTI Ltd [2022] EWCA Civ 1406. . . . . 114n.19
Murphy v Brentwood District Council [1991] 1 AC 398 (HL) 228n.6, 231n.27, 234n.37,
      236n.52, 237–38, 240–41
Murray v Leisureplay plc [2005] EWCA Civ 963; [2005] IRLR 946 . . . . 200n.62
Mutual Finance Ltd v John Wetton & Sons Ltd [1937] 2 KB 389 (KBD) 16n.70, 80n.22, 81

National Carriers Ltd v Panalpina (Northern) Ltd [1981] AC 675 (HL) 112n.5
National Phonograph Co Ltd v Edison Bell Co [1908] Ch 335, 350. . . . . 366n.89
Nature Resorts Ltd v First Citizens Bank Ltd [2022] UKPC 10, [2022] 1 WLR 2788. . . . . 71n.30
Nippon Yusen Kaisha v Karageorgis [1975] 1 WLR 1093 (CA) 248n.24
Nitrigin Eireann Teoranta v Inco Alloys [1992] 1 WLR 498 (QBD). 232n.30
Northamber Plc v Genee World Limited [2023] EWHC 3562 (Ch). 254n.63

O'Neil v O'Neil [2017] 7 WLUK 30, 2017 GWD 22-361 . . . . 12n.50
OBG Ltd v Allan [2007] UKHL 21, [2008] 1 AC 1 . . . . 358n.48, 359
Ockford v Barelli (1871) 20 WR 116. . . . . 88n.92
Office of Fair Trading v Abbey National plc [2009] UKSC 6, [2010] 1 AC 69 . . . . 194n.8, 198n.43
Okedina v Chikale [2019] EWCA Civ 1393, [2019] ICR 1365 . . . . 67n.23
Omak Maritime Ltd v Mamola Challenger Shipping Co [2010] EWHC 2026 (Comm),
 [2011] 1 Lloyd's Rep 47 . . . . .45n.21, 46, 47, 47n.24, 48–51, 48n.27, 48n.28, 53n.39, 58
Optimares SpA v Qatar Airways Group QCSC [2022] EWHC 2461 (Comm). 35n.66
Outlook Finance Ltd v Lindsay [2016] SAC (Civ) 7. . . . . 9n.33
Outlook Finance Ltd v Lindsay's Executor [2016] SC LAN 58, [2016] HLR 75 . . . . 9n.33

Palmer Birch (a partnership) v Lloyd [2018] EWHC 2316 (TCC); [2018] 4 WLR 164 . . . . 246n.14
Pan Ocean Shipping Co Ltd v Creditcorp Ltd (The Trident Beauty)
 [1994] 1 WLR 161 (HL) 164 . . . . 168n.71, 391n.56
Paragon Finance plc v Nash [2001] EWCA Civ 1466, [2002] 1 WLR 685 . . . . 149n.29
Paragon Finance Plc v Pender [2005] EWCA Civ 760, [2005] 1 WLR 3412 . . . . 281n.119
Parker v Clark [1960] 1 WLR 286. . . . . 106n.95
Parnie v MacLean, 19 August 1904, unreported. 8n.26
Patel v Mirza [2016] UKSC 42, [2017] AC 467 . . . . .59–63, 59n.2, 62n.6, 64–65, 66,
      66n.19, 67–68, 67n.21, 69, 71, 72–73, 74, 122n.90, 123, 139n.42
Payne v John Setchell Ltd (2001) 3 TCLR 26 (TCC). 237n.57, 240n.84
Pell Frischmann Engineering Ltd v Bow Valley Iran Ltd [2009] UKPC 45,
 [2011] 1 WLR 2370 (PC). 173n.16, 174n.22, 185n.77, 186n.83, 186n.89, 189n.109
Penarth Dock Engineering Co Ltd v Pounds [1963] 1 Lloyd's Rep 359 (QB) 181n.52, 182n.60

TABLE OF CASES xxvii

Peninsula Securities Ltd v Dunnes Stores (Bangor) Ltd [2020] UKSC 36, [2021] AC 1014 . . . . 73n.36
Performing Right Society Ltd v London Theatre of Varieties [1924] AC 1 . . . . 273n.52
Permavent Ltd v Makin [2021] EWHC 467 (Ch), [2021] FSR 26 . . . . .201n.69, 203,
203n.85, 205, 205n.99
Peter Cassidy Seed Co Ltd v Osuustukkukauppa IL [1957] 1 WLR 273 (Com Ct). 122n.89
Peter Pan Manufacturing Corp v Corsets Silhouette Ltd [1964] 1 WLR 96 (Ch) 189n.107
Petromec Inc v Petroleo Brasileiro SA [2005] EWCA Civ 891;
[2006] 1 Lloyd's Rep 121 . . . . 33n.50, 37n.72
Philip Head & Sons Ltd v Showfronts Ltd [1970] 1 Lloyd's Rep 140. . . . . 308n.36
Philips Electronique Grand Public SA v BSkyB Ltd [1995] EMLR 472 (CA) 394–95n.80
Phipps v. Boardman [1967] 2 AC 46. . . . . 166, 188n.95
Pierburg v Pierburg [2022] EWHC 2701 (Fam) 100n.46
Planché v Colburn (1831) 8 Bing 14; 131 ER 305 . . . . 131n.21, 135n.29
Pluczenik Diamond Co NV v W Nagel (A Firm) [2018] EWCA Civ 2640,
[2019] 1 Lloyd's Rep 36 . . . . .149nn.31–32
Prenn v Simmonds [1971] 1 WLR 1381 (HL). 154n.4
Prescott v Potamianos (Re Sprintroom) [2019] EWCA Civ 932, [2019] BCC 1031. . . . . 70, 70n.28
Prest v Petrodel Resources Ltd [2013] UKSC 34, [2013] 2 AC 415. . . . . 17n.72, 17n.74,
18n.75, 18n.76, 18n.77, 20
Priyanka Shipping Ltd v Glory Bulk Carriers Pte Ltd [2019] EWHC 2804 (Comm) (QBD) 184,
184n.68, 184n.74, 185n.76
Proform Sports Management Ltd v Proactive Sports Management Ltd
[2006] EWHC 2903 (Ch); [2007] 1 All ER 542 . . . . 252n.48
Progress Bulk Carriers Ltd v Tube City IMS LLC (Progress Bulk Carriers)
[2012] EWHC 273 (Comm); [2012] 2 All ER (Comm) 855 . . . . 80n.27, 83, 88n.89, 90, 91
Promontia (Oak) Ltd v Emanuel [2021] EWCA Civ 1682; [2022] 1 WLR 1682 . . . . 279n.100
Prudential Assurance Co Ltd v McBains Cooper (a firm) [2000] 1 WLR 2000 (CA) 2008 . . . . 250n.42

Quinn v Leathem [1901] AC 495 (HL) 537 . . . . 256n.75

R (on the application of AR) v Chief Constable of the Greater Manchester Police
[2018] UKSC 47, [2018] 1 WLR 4079 . . . . 70n.28
R v Clarkson [1971] 1 WLR 1402 . . . . 213n.6
R v Gregory (1867) LR 1 CCR 77 . . . . 213n.7
R v Tyler and Price (1838) 8 Car & P 616; 173 ER 643 (QB) 213n.5
Radmacher v Granatino [2010] UKSC 42 . . . . 100, 100n.41, 100n.48, 101–2, 101n.54, 101n.57
Raiffeisen Zentralbank Österreich AG v Five Star General Trading LLC
[2001] EWCA Civ 68, [2001] QB 825. . . . . 273n.55
Rainy Sky SA v Kookmin Bank [2011] UKSC 50, [2011] 1 WLR 2900 . . . . 161n.34
Raja v McMillan [2021] EWCA Civ 1103 . . . . 257n.87
Ralli Bros v Compañia Naviera Sota y Aznar [1920] 2 KB 287 (CA) 123n.95, 123n.97
Reardon Smith Line Ltd v Yngvar Hansen-Tangen [1976] 1 WLR 989 (HL) 154n.4
Republic of Haiti v Duvalier [1990] 1 QB 202 (CA) 248n.28
Rice (t/a Garden Guardian) v Great Yarmouth BC (CA 30 June 2000) 35n.66
Richards v IP Solutions Ltd [2016] EWHC 1835; [2017] IRLR 133 . . . . 199, 199n.50
Roberts v Gill & Co [2010] UKSC 22; [2011] 1 AC 240 . . . . 273n.56
Robinson v Harman (1848) 1 Ex 850 . . . . 171n.2
Robinson v Harman (1848) 1 Ex 850; 154 ER 363 . . . . 46n.22, 54n.46, 56–57
Robophone Facilities v Blank [1966] 1 WLR 1428 (CA) 200n.61
Rockliffe Hall Ltd v Travelers Insurance Co Ltd [2021] EWHC 412 (Comm),
[2021] Bus LR 656 . . . . 149n.28
Royal Bank of Scotland Plc v Etridge (No 2) [2001] UKHL 44; [2002] 2 AC 773 . . . . 80n.29
Royal Devon and Exeter NHS v ATOS [2017] EWHC 2196; 174 Con LR. 58n.53
RTS Flexible Systems Ltd v Molkerei Alois Müller GmbH [2010] UKSC 14;
[2010] 1 WLR 753. . . . . 164, 164n.50
Rugg v Minett (1809) 11 East 210 . . . . 307n.28

xxviii   TABLE OF CASES

Ruxley Electronics and Construction Ltd v Forsyth [1996] AC 344 (HL) 171n.2
RV Ward v Bignall [1967] 1 QB 534 . . . . 308n.36

Said v Butt [1920] 3 KB 497 (KBD) 253n.59, 254, 257–58
Salam Air SAOC v Latam Airlines Groups SA [2020] EWHC 2414 (Comm) 119n.63
Salomon v A Salomon & Co Ltd [1897] AC 22 (HL) 13n.55
Scally v Southern Health and Social Services Board [1992] 1 AC 294 (HL) 392n.63
Scott v Pattinson [1923] 2 KB 723 . . . . 128n.8
Seager v Copydex Ltd [1967] 1 WLR 923 (CA) 189n.108
Secretary of State for Health v Servier Laboratories Ltd [2021] UKSC 24,
   [2022] AC 959 . . . . 257n.89
Secretary of State for Trade and Industry v Hollier [2006] EWHC 1804 (Ch);
   [2007] Bus LR 352 . . . . 10n.38
Secretary of State for Trade and Industry v Tjolle [1998] 1 BCLC 333 . . . . 10n.38
Sheffield City Council v E [2004] EWHC 2808 (Fam) 94n.5
Shirlaw v Southern Foundries (1926) Ltd [1939] 2 KB 206 (CA) 386n.23
Sigma Finance Corp, Re [2008] EWCA Civ 1303, [2009] BCC 393, [2009] UKSC 2,
   [2010] BCC 40 . . . . 160, 160n.29, 161n.35, 169n.73
Signia Wealth v Vector Trustees [2018] EWHC 1040 (Ch) 199, 199n.52, 202–3, 202n.80
Sim Swee Joo Shipping Sdn Bhd v Shirlstar Container Transport Ltd [1994] CLC 188 . . . . 273n.55
Sinclair v Brougham [1914] AC 398 (HL) 370n.17
Singularis Holdings Ltd v Daiwa Capital Markets Finance Ltd [2019] UKSC 50,
   [2020] AC 1189 . . . . 71n.29
Skelwith (Leisure) Limited v Alan Armstrong [2015] EWHC 2830 (Ch),
   [2016] Ch 345 . . . . 270n.32, 273n.56
Slowikowska v Rogers [2021] EWHC 2729 (Ch) 205, 205n.101
Solle v Butcher [1950] 1 KB 671 (CA) 117n.42
Somerville v 1051 GWR Ltd [2019] CSOH 61, [2019] HLR 66 . . . . 10n.38
Soteria Insurance (formerly CIS) v IBM UK Ltd [2022] EWCA Civ 440; 202 Con LR 1 . . . . 58n.53
SR Projects Ltd v Rampersad [2022] UKPC 24 . . . . 68n.25
St Albans City & District Council v International Computers Ltd [1997] FSR 251 . . . . 315n.94
St Albans v International Computers [1997] FSR 251 . . . . 316n.96
Staffordshire Area Health Authority v South Staffordshire Waterworks
   [1978] 1 WLR 1387 . . . . 96n.24
Standard Chartered Bank v Pakistan National Shipping Corporation (No 4)
   [2001] QB 167 (CA); [2002] UKHL 43; [2003] 1 AC 959 . . . . 211n.1
Stark v Walker [2020] EWHC 562 (Ch) 105, 105n.85, 106–7
Steel Wing Co Ltd, Re [1929] 1 Ch 345 . . . . 269n.23, 273n.53, 275n.71
Stobart Group Ltd v Elliott [2013] EWHC 797 (QB) 260n.108
Stocks v Dobson (1853) 4 De G M & G 11; 43 ER 411 . . . . 270n.27
Stoke-on-Trent City Council v W & J Wass Ltd [1988] 1 WLR 1406 (CA) 179n.40, 183n.62,
                                                                                     183n.65, 185n.79, 188n.99
Strand Electric and Engineering Co Ltd v Brisford Entertainments Ltd
   [1952] 2 QB 246 (CA) 171–72n.6, 176n.27, 176n.29, 178n.36,
                                                                              178n.38, 179n.41, 182n.56, 182n.60
Stubbs v Holywell Ry (1867) LR 2 Ex 311 . . . . 132n.23
Suisse Atlantique Société d'Armement Maritime SA v NV Rotterdamsche Kolen Centrale
   [1967] AC 361 . . . . 303n.7
Sumpter v Hedges [1898] 1 QB 673 . . . . 128n.10, 130, 131
Supershield Ltd v Siemens Building Technologies FE Ltd [2010] EWCA Civ 7,
   [2010] 1 Lloyd's Rep 349 . . . . 49n.30
Sutherland v Montrose Fishing Co Ltd (1921) 37 Sh Ct Rep 239 . . . . 3n.3, 15n.64
Sutton v Mishcon de Reya and Gawor & Co [2003] EWHC 3166 (Ch) 103n.74
Swordheath Properties Ltd v Tabet [1979] 1 WLR 285 (CA) 181n.51, 182n.60

Takhar v Gracefield Developments Ltd [2019] UKSC 13; [2020] AC 450 . . . . 252n.49
Tamplin SS Co Ltd v Anglo-Mexican Petroleum Co [1916] 2 AC 397 (HL) 404 . . . . 394n.75
Tancred v Delagoa Bay and East Africa Railway Co (1889) 23 QBD 239 . . . . 268n.14

TABLE OF CASES xxix

Tanner v Tanner [1975] 1 WLR 1346 . . . . 103n.75
Taylor v Caldwell (1863) 3 B & S 826, 122 ER 309. . . . . 115n.31, 117–18, 117n.45, 121
Technocrats International Inc v Fredic Limited [2004] EWHC 692 (QB). 269n.25
Test Claimants in the FII Group Litigation v HMRC [2012] UKSC 19; [2012] 2 AC 337 . . . . . 349n.60
Test Claimants in the Franked Investment Income Group Litigation and others v
    Commissioners for Her Majesty's Revenue and Customs (1) and (2) [2020] UKSC 47;
    [2020] 3 WLR 1369). 339n.2, 342n.23, 342n.24, 342n.26, 343n.27, 343n.29, 343n.30,
        343nn.32–35, 344, 345, 345n.45, 345n.46, 346, 346nn.51–52, 347, 348–49, 348nn.57–59
The Office of Fair Trading v Ashbourne Management Services Ltd and others
    [2011] EWHC 1237 (Ch). 97n.31
The Orjula [1995] 2 Lloyd's Rep 395 (QBD) 401. . . . . 232n.30, 237n.59, 241–42
The Rebecca Elaine [1999] 2 Lloyd's Rep 1 (CA). 241n.92
Thomson v Humphrey [2009] EWHC 3576 (Ch). 104n.83, 106–7
Thomson v Warwick [2022] SC INV 31, 2021 WL 09541562 . . . . 13n.54, 14, 15
Thorne v Motor Trade Association [1937] AC 797 (HL). 82n.39, 82n.44
Three Rivers DC v Bank of England (No.1) [1996] QB 292. . . . . . 273n.56, 276n.74, 276n.75, 276n.78,
        276n.79, 276n.80, 277n.82, 277n.85, 279n.98, 280n.114
Times Travel (UK) Ltd v Pakistan International Airline Corp
    [2017] EWHC 1367 (Ch). 5n.9, 19n.81, 76n.4, 77n.11, 79n.19, 89n.101, 90, 90n.105, 91
Times Travel Ltd v Pakistan International Airline Corp [2021] UKSC 40, [2023] AC 101,
    [2021] 3 WLR 727. . . . . .4–6, 4n.6, 5n.11, 5–6nn.16–17, 16–21, 16n.70, 32n.44, 33n.49,
        37n.69, 75n.1, 76–89, 78n.17, 80n.25, 82n.42, 82n.47, 83n.50, 84n.56, 84n.57,
        85n.70, 86n.75, 87n.85, 89n.96, 89n.101, 90n.103, 102n.63, 102n.64
Times Travel v Pakistan International Airline Corporation [2019] EWCA Civ 828,
    [2020] Ch 98 . . . . 5n.10, 78n.16, 82n.41, 87n.88, 89n.100
Touton Far East Pte Ltd v Shri Lal Mahal Ltd [2016] EWHC 1765 (Comm). 248n.23
Transco plc v Stockport MBC [2003] UKHL 61, [2004] 2 AC 1 . . . . 259n.95, 259n.98
Transfield Shipping Inc v Mercator Shipping Inc (The Achilleas) [2008] UKHL 48;
    [2009] 1 AC 61 . . . . 49n.30, 56
Travelport Ltd v Wex Inc [2020] EWHC 2670 (Comm) 114n.26
Triple Point Technology Inc v PTT Public Co Ltd [2021] UKSC 29, [2021] AC 1148 . . . . 114n.21
Tsakiroglou & Co Ltd v Noblee Thorl GmbH [1962] AC 93 (HL) 120n.75
TSB Private Bank International SA v Chabra [1992] 1 WLR 231 (Ch D) 248n.27
TSB v Balloch 1983 SLT 240 . . . . 14n.58

Uddin v Choudhary & Ors [2009] EWCA Civ 1205. . . . . 107n.104, 108
Union Eagle Ltd v Golden Achievement Ltd [1997] AC 514 (PC) 519 . . . . 36n.68
Union Traffic Ltd v Transport and General Workers' Union [1989] ICR 98 (CA). 253n.55, 256n.77
United Scientific Holdings Ltd v Burnley BC [1978] AC 904 . . . . 312n.73
Universal Cargo Carriers Corp v Citati (No 1) [1957] 2 QB 401. . . . . 312n.74
Universe Tankships Inc of Monrovia v International Transport Workers Federation
    [1983] 1 AC 366 (HL). 81n.37, 82n.43
UTB LLC v Sheffield United Ltd [2019] EWHC 2322 (Ch). 34n.59

Vatcher v Paull [1915] AC 372 (PC) 167n.62
Vedanta Resources plc v Lungowe [2019] UKSC 20, [2020] AC 1045 . . . . 259n.94
Vercoe v Rutland Fund Management Ltd [2010] EWHC 424 (Ch) 189n.106
Versteegh v Versteegh [2018] EWCA Civ 1050. . . . . 102n.59
Vivienne Westwood Ltd v Conduit Street Developments [2017] EWHC 350 (Ch),
    [2017] L&TR 23 . . . . 201n.69

Wade v Simeon (1846) 2 CB 548; 135 ER 1061 . . . . 88n.94
Walford v Miles [1992] 2 AC 128 (HL) 33n.46, 37n.70, 164n.47
Walter & Sullivan Ltd v J Murphy & Sons Ltd [1955] 2 QB 584 . . . . 269n.23, 275n.70, 275n.72,
        276–77, 276n.76, 278n.91, 279n.100
Warner Bros. Records Inc v Rollgreen Ltd [1976] QB 430. . . . . 277n.81
Warner Brothers Pictures Inc v Nelson [1937] 1 KB 209 . . . . 355n.22

xxx TABLE OF CASES

Warren v Mendy [1989] 1 WLR 853. . . . . 355n.22
Watson Laidlaw & Co Ltd v Pott Cassels & Williamson 1914 SC (HL) 177n.33, 183n.61, 183n.64,
189n.103, 190n.110
Waugh v Morris (1872–73) LR 8 QB 202 (KB) 122n.87
WC v HC (Financial Remedies Agreements) [2022] EWFC 22 . . . . 102, 102n.60, 103
Weddell v JA Pearce & Major [1988] Ch 26. . . . . 273n.52, 274n.60
Wells v Devani [2019] UKSC 4; [2020] AC 129 . . . . 106n.92, 165n.52, 167–68
Welsh Development Agency v Export Finance Co Ltd [1992] BCC 270 (CA) 289 . . . . 254n.61
Westdeutsche Landesbank Girozentrale v Islington London Borough Council
[1996] 2 WLR 802 (HL). 370n.17
Wheelans v Wheelans 1986 SLT 164 . . . . 12n.50
Whincup v Hughes (1871 LR 6 CP 78 . . . . 129n.11, 139
White and Carter (Councils) Ltd v McGregor [1962] AC 413 . . . . 308n.40, 308n.42, 312n.66
White v Jones [1995] 2 AC 207 . . . . 165n.55
Whitwham v Westminster Brymbo Coal and Coke Co [1896] 2 Ch 538 (CA). 177n.32, 183n.63
Willers v Joyce [2016] UKSC 44; [2018] AC 843. . . . . 296n.115
William Brandt's Sons & Co v Dunlop Rubber Co Ltd [1905] 2 AC 454 (HL) 269n.25, 272n.48,
273n.52, 273n.54, 279n.102
Williams v Bayley (1866) LR 1 HL 200 (HL) 79n.21, 80n.30, 81
Williams v Natural Life Health Foods Ltd [1998] 1 WLR 830. . . . . 219n.47
Wilmington Trust SP Services (Dublin) Ltd v Spicejet Ltd [2021] EWHC 1117 (Comm) 119n.67
Wilson v Merry & Cunningham (1868) LR 1 HL Sc 326 . . . . 165n.54
Wilsons & Clyde Coal Co Ltd v English [1938] AC 57 (HL) 222n.56
Winchester v Fleming [1958] 1 QB 259 (appeal allowed on other grounds:
[1958] 3 All ER 51). 354n.17
Winsmore v Greenbank (1745) Willes 577 . . . . 354nn.16–17
WL Thompson Ltd v Robinson (Gunmakers) Ltd [1955] Ch 177 . . . . 309n.48
Wolfson v Edelman 1952 SLT (Sh Ct) 97 . . . . 15n.63
Wood v Capita Insurance Services Ltd [2017] UKSC 24, [2017] AC 1173 . . . . .155–56, 155n.6,
155n.8, 160, 160n.30, 161, 162–63, 162n.41
Woodland v Swimming Teachers Association [2013] UKSC 66, [2014] AC 537 . . . . 221n.55, 222n.57
Wrotham Park Estate Co Ltd v Parkside Homes Ltd [1974] 1 WLR 798 (Ch). 172–73, 172n.11,
179n.43, 186n.81, 186n.84, 186n.90
WW v HW [2015] EWHC 1844 (Fam) 103n.72

Yam Seng Pte Ltd v International Trade Corp Ltd [2013] EWHC 111 (QB),
[2013] 1 Lloyd's Rep 526 . . . . 336n.62
Yam Seng Pte v International Trade Corp [2013] EWHC 111 (QB);
[2013] 1 Lloyd's Rep 526 . . . . 23n.3, 27n.16, 34n.55, 87n.83
Yoo Design Services Limited v Iliv Realty Pte Limited [2021] EWCA Civ 560. . . . . 388n.39
Young v Matthews (1866-67) LR 2 CP 127 . . . . 307n.28

Z v Z (No 2) [2011] EWHC 2878 (Fam). 102n.69
Zavarco plc v Nasir [2021] EWCA Civ 1217; [2022] Ch 105. . . . . 254n.67
Zurich Insurance Co plc v Hayward [2016] UKSC 48, [2017] AC 14. 89n.99

EUROPEAN UNION

Aziz v Caixa d'Estalvis de Catalunya, Tarragona i Manresa (Catalunyacaixa) (C-415/11)
EU:C:2013:164; [2013] 3 CMLR 5 . . . . 196n.23, 304n.12
Metallgesellschaft Ltd v Inland Revenue Commissioners, Hoechst AG v Inland Revenue
Commissioners (Joined Cases C-397 and 410/98), [2001] ECR I-01727,
[2001] Ch 620–669 (ECJ) 341n.22, 343, 344–45, 346–47, 348–49, 348n.57
Test Claimants in the FII Group Litigation v Inland Revenue Commissioners
(Case C-446/04) [2006] ECR I-11753, [2012] 2 AC 436–471 (ECJ). 342n.25, 344
UsedSoft GmbH v Oracle International Corp (C-128/11) EU:C:2012:407. . . . . 316n.98

TABLE OF CASES xxxi

NATIONAL CASES

Australia

AMEV-UDC Finance Ltd v Austin [1986] HCA 63, (1986) 162 CLR 170. . . . . 194n.10
Andrews v Australia and New Zealand Banking Group Ltd [2012] HCA 30,
 (2012) 247 CLR 205 . . . . 193n.7, 194n.11
Andrews, Ringrow Pty Ltd v BP Australia Pty Ltd [2005] HCA 71,
 (2005) 224 CLR 656 . . . . 194n.10, 197–98, 197n.35, 200n.59, 204n.90
Australian Securities and Investments Commission v Kobelt [2019] HCA 18,
 (2019) 267 CLR 1 . . . . 83n.54
Blomley v Ryan (1954) 99 CLR 362 . . . . 5n.15
Bugge v Brown [1919] HCA 5, (1919) 26 CLR 110. . . . . 214n.13, 217n.34
Cafe Du Liban Ltd v Bespoke Garage Pty Ltd [2017] NSWSC 779. 200n.60
Commonwealth Bank of Australia v Kojic [2016] FCAFC 186, (2016) 249 FCR 421 . . . . 222n.62, 223
Commonwealth of Australia v Amann Aviation (1991) 174 CLR 64. . . . . 53, 53n.37
Construction, Forestry, Maritime, Mining and Energy Union v Personnel
 Contracting Pty Ltd [2022] HCA 1, (2022) 96 ALJR 89. . . . . 213n.8
GE Crane Sales Pty Ltd v Commissioner of Taxation (1971) 46 ALJR 15 . . . . 270n.29
Giddings v Australian Information Commissioner [2017] FCAFC 225 . . . . 221n.52
Hollis v Vabu Pty Ltd [2001] HCA 44, (2001) 207 CLR 21 . . . . 216n.28
Hospital Products Ltd v United States Surgical Corporation [1984] HCA 64,
 (1984) 156 CLR 41 . . . . 166n.59
IAC (Leasing) Ltd v Humphrey [1972] HCA 1, (1972) 126 CLR 131. . . . . 194n.10
IL v The Queen [2017] HCA 27, (2017) 262 CLR 268 . . . . 217n.32
Kable v New South Wales (2012) 293 ALR 719. . . . . 216n.27
Kondis v State Transport Authority [1984] HCA 61, (1984) 154 CLR 672 . . . . 221n.53, 222n.59
Leichhardt Municipal Council v Montgomery [2007] HCA 6, (2007) 230 CLR 22 . . . . 221n.54
McLean v Westpac Banking Corporation [2012] WASCA 152. . . . . .279nn.103–4
McRae v Commonwealth Disposals Commission (1951) 84 CLR 377 (HCA). 117n.43
New South Wales v Ibbett [2006] HCA 57, (2006) 229 CLR 638 . . . . 216n.25
Northern Land Council v Quall [2020] HCA 33, (2020) 271 CLR 394 . . . . 220n.51
O'Brien v Dawson [1942] HCA 8, (1942) 66 CLR 18. . . . . 219n.42
O'Dea v Allstates Leasing System (WA) Pty Ltd [1983] HCA 3, (1983) 152 CLR 359 . . . . . 193–94n.10
Paciocco v Australian and New Zealand Banking Group Ltd [2016] HCA 28;
 (2016) 258 CLR 525 . . . . .194n.11, 200n.60, 204n.90
Parker v The Commonwealth [1965] HCA 12, (1965) 112 CLR 295 . . . . 216n.24
Pavey & Matthew Pty Ltd v Paul [1987] HCA 5, (1987) 162 CLR 221 . . . . 128n.8
Pioneer Mortgage Services Pty Ltd v Columbus Capital Pty Ltd [2016] FCAFC 78,
 (2016) 250 FCR 136 . . . . 217n.31
Plaintiff M61/2010E v The Commonwealth [2010] HCA 41, (2010) 243 CLR 319 . . . . 219n.46
Prince Alfred College Inc v ADC [2016] HCA 37, (2016) 258 CLR 134 . . . . 217n.36
R v See Lun (1932) 32 SR (NSW) 363. . . . . 213n.7
Rendell v Associated Finance Pty Ltd [1957] VR 604. . . . . 241n.90
Roxborough v Rothmans of Pall Mall Australia Ltd [2001] HCA 68; 208 CLR 516 . . . . . .384n.13, 385,
     385n.18, 386n.24, 386n.26, 387, 388–89, 391–92, 392n.61, 392n.68, 393, 394–96
Roxborough v Rothmans of Pall Mall Australia Ltd [2001] HCA 68, (2001) 208 CLR 516. . . . . 128n.9
The State of New South Wales v Lepore [2003] HCA 4, (2003) 212 CLR 511 . . . . 214n.16
Treadwell v Hickey [2009] NSWSC 1395. . . . . 272n.49
Walsh v Sainsbury [1925] HCA 28, (1925) 36 CLR 464, 477. . . . . 213n.7
Walton's Stores (Interstate) v Maher [1988] HCA 7, (1988) 64 CLR 387 . . . . 209n.109
Westpac Banking Corporation v Mason [2011] NSWSC 1241, (2011) 80 NSWLR 354 . . . . . 279n.103

Canada

Bazley v Curry (1999) 2 SCR 534 . . . . 217n.35
Bowlay Logging Ltd v Domtar Ltd [1978] 4 WWR 105. . . . . 42n.10, 44, 44n.15, 46, 47, 52
Bowlay Logging Limited v Domtar Limited, 1982 CanLII 449 (BC CA). 52n.35

xxxii   TABLE OF CASES

Deglman v Guaranty Trust Co of Canada and Constantineau [1954] SCR 725,
[1954] 3 DLR 785 . . . . 128n.8
Garland v Consumers' Gas Co [2004] 1 SCR 629, (2004) 237 DLR (4th) 385 (SCC). 380n.73, 380n.74
Hall v Hebert [1993] 2 SCR 159 . . . . 61n.5
Hou v Westpac Banking Corporation [2015] VSCA 57 . . . . 279n.103
Lobb v Vasey Housing Auxiliary [1963] VR 38. . . . . 134n.27
R v Kupferberg (1918) 13 Cr App R 166 (CA) 213n.6
Regina Chevrolet Sales Ltd v Riddell [1942] 3 DLR 159 (Sask CA) 242n.98
Timbercorp Finance Pty Ltd v FTM Nominees Pty Ltd [2015] VSC 498. . . . . .279n.103,
279nn.105–6, 279n.108, 280, 281n.118
Uber Technologies Inc v Heller 2020 SCC 16 . . . . 83n.54
Winnipeg Condominium Corp No 36 v Bird Construction Co
[1995] 1 SCR 85 (SCC). 229n.10, 229n.13

China

Dai Mingan v Yang Tao, Xiaogan IPC, 25 March 2015, (2015) E Xiao Gan Zhong
Min Er Zhong Zi No 63 Civil Judgment 379n.71
Guangdong Zhenrong Energy Co Ltd v Zhangjiakou Qintong Industrial Co Ltd,
SPC, 19 Dec 2017, (2017) Zui Gao Fa Min Zai No 114 Civil Judgment 371n.29
Jiangnan Branch, Rural Credit Cooperatives Union of Meijiang District, Meizhou
City v Luo Yuanling, Meizhou IPC, 15 Dec 2009, SPC Gazette,
2011, Issue 1 . . . . 377n.63, 379, 380n.76
Jiangsu Bright Trading Co Ltd v Zhang Yuehong, Dongtai People's Court,
14 Nov 2016, SPC Gazette, Issue 5, 2018 . . . . .372n.36, 377n.65, 378n.69, 379, 380n.76
Korean Samyung Co v Panjin Qingdao Clothing Co Ltd, Dalian Maritime Court,
6 May 1996, SPC Gazette, Issue 4, 1997 . . . . 373n.38
Li Xinfu v Chengdu Public Transport Group Co Ltd, Chengdu IPC, 25 July 2005,
[2005] Cheng Min Zhong Zi No 1561 Civil Judgment 378n.66
Liu Zhongyou v Nanchang City Municipal Construction Co Ltd and Jiangxi Province
Fuzhen Road & Bridge Construction Co Ltd SPC, 27 Dec 2017, (2017) Zui Gao
Fa Min Zai No 287 . . . . 370n.20, 371n.27, 372n.36, 374nn.49–50
Lu Qiujie v Sun Jian, SPC, 21 Nov 2013, (2013) Min Shen Zi No 1639 Civil Ruling. 375n.54
Meiyan v Shiyan People's Road Branch, Industrial and Commercial Bank of China,
SPC, 29 Nov 2017, (2016) Zui Gao Fa Min Shen No 2681 Civil Ruling 374n.46
Qingdao Honghai Investment Co Ltd v Weifang Branch, Agriculture Bank of China,
SPC, 15 Nov 2013, (2013) Min Shen Zi No 1631 Civil Ruling. 374n.46
Shanghai Quncan Construction Materials Business Department v TBEA Co Ltd, SPC,
16 Dec 2016, (2016) Zui Gao Fa Min Zhong No 223 Civil Judgment. 375n.54
Shanghai Xinhong Freight Service Co Ltd v Liu Yang Zhengzhou IPC, 19 Mar 2011,
(2011) Zheng Min Er Zhong Zi No 236 Civil Judgment 371n.24
Shenzhen Hongye Investment Holdings Group Co Ltd v Wang Xiaoling et al SPC,
21 July 2017, (2016) Zui Gao Fa Min Zai No 153 Civil Judgment. 370n.20, 374n.49
Shenzhen Siruiman Fine Chemicals Co Ltd v Shenzhen Kengzi Water Supply Co Ltd and
Shenzhen Kangtailan Water Treatment Equipment Co Ltd, SPC Gazette, 2014, Issue 5 . . . . . 372n.34
Shi Jianwei v Xu Xiuying, Shanghai No 2 IPC, (2009) Hu Er Zhong Min Yi (Min)
Zhong Zi No 1221 Civil Judgment 373n.43
Shilin County Branch, China Construction Bank v Yang Fubin, Kunming IPC,
8 Nov 2002, SPC Gazette, Issue 6, 2003 . . . . 375n.53
Sun Wei v Nantong Baichuan Flour Co Ltd, Hai'an County People's Court,
15 July 2014, SPC Gazette, Issue 7, 2015 (No 225) 378n.67, 379
Ulanqab Branch, CNPC (China National Petroleum Co) v Fengzhen City Yifeng
Petrochemical Co Ltd et al, affirmed on other ground by Ulanqab IPC,
24 May 2018, (2018) Nei 09 Min Zhong No 302 Civil Judgment 373n.39
Wang Chunlin v Yinchuan Aluminum Materials Factory, Ningxia HPC,
27 March 1995, SPC Gazette, Issue 4, 1995 . . . . 376n.57, 378n.69, 379, 380n.76

Wang Liangqun v Shenzhen Fuyuan School et al, Shenzhen Baoan District Court, 20 March 2009, (2009) Shen Bao Fa Min Yi Chu Zi No 420 Civil Judgment. 370n.22

Xin Lianhua v Xingang Commercial Ban, Tianjin No 2 IPC, 23 Feb 2004, SPC Gazette, Issue 5, 2005. . . . . 375n.53

Xu Jinliang v Wang Zhonghai, Antu County People's Court of Jilin Province, SPC Gazette, 1996, issue 2 . . . . 373n.38

Yu Shanlan v Xuanwu Branch and Beijing Branch, Industrial and Commercial Bank of China, Beijing No 1 IPC, 1 January 2005, SPC Gazette, Issue 6, 2005 . . . . 376n.60, 377, 378–79, 380n.76

Zhang Peiyao, Hui Deyue and Jiangsu Funing County Dust- Cleaning Equipment Factory v Suzhou City Nanxin Cement Co Ltd, SPC, 6 Nov 2000, (2000) Zhi Zhong Zi No 3 Civil Judgment 374n.47

Zheng Xiang v Hong Yeshan, SPC, 28 Dec 2017, (2016) Zui Gao Fa Min Zai No 39 Civil Judgment. 375n.54

Georgia

Vulcan Materials Co v Driltech Inc 306 SE 2d 253 (Ga 1983) 229n.12

Hongkong

Law Ting Pong Secondary School v Chen Wai Wah [2021] HKCA 873 . . . . .196n.22, 199, 199n.55, 203–4, 203n.86

Phillips Hong Kong Ltd v Attorney General of Hong Kong (1993) 61 BLR 41 (PC) 200n.61, 204n.91

Wing v Xiong DCCJ/2832/2003 (Hong Kong District Court) 120n.69

Ireland

Sheehan v Breccia & Ors [2018] IECA 286 . . . . 206n.105

Israel

Adras v Harlo and Jones 37(4) PD 225. . . . . 362n.66

Netherlands

Baris v Riezenkamp HR 15 November 1957, NJ 1958 67. . . . . 34n.52

New Zealand

127 Hobson Street Ltd v Honey Bees Preschool Ltd [2020] NZSC 53 . . . . 203, 203n.81

Commissioner of Inland Revenue v Chesterfields Preschools Ltd [2013] 2 NZLR 679 (NZ CA) 220n.49, 220n.50

New Zealand Netherlands Society 'Oranje' Inc v Kuys [1973] 1 WLR 1126 (PC) 166, 166n.58

Wilaci Pty Ltd v Torchlight Fund No 1 [2017] NZSC 112 . . . . 202, 202n.78

Singapore

Denka Advantech Pte v Seraya Energy Pte [2020] SGCA 119, [2021] 1 SLR 631. . . . . .194n.13, 197n.28, 197n.39, 206n.106, 206n.108, 207n.115

Quoine Pte Ltd v B2C2 Ltd [2020] SGCA (I) 02 . . . . 224n.72, 225–26

Turf Club Auto Emporium Pte Ltd v Yeo Boong Hua [2018] SGCA 44, [2018] 2 SLR 655 (SGCA) 171n.3

United States

American Broadcasting Co v Wolf [1980] 430 NYS 2d 275 (App Div) 355n.23

Calloway v City of Reno 993 P 2d 1259 (Nev 2000) 1268. . . . . 239n.73, 240n.78

D & F Estates, East River Steamship Corp v Transamerica Delaval Inc 106 S Ct 2295 (1986). 230n.18, 236n.48, 236n.50, 239

xxxiv   TABLE OF CASES

Developers Three v Nationwide Ins [1990] 582 NE 2d 1130, 1135 . . . . 361n.61
Federal Sugar Refining Co v US Sugar Equalization Board [1920] 268 F 575 . . . . 362n.68
King v Hilton- Davis 855 F 2d 1047 (3rd Cir 1988) 1051 . . . . 240n.83
Kodiak Electric Association Inc v DeLaval Turbine Inc 694 P 2d 150 (Alaska 1984) 229n.13
Mid Continent Aircraft Corp v Curry County Spraying Service Inc 572 SW 2d 308
    (Tex 1978) 313 . . . . 231n.25
National Merchandising Corp v Leyden [1976] 348 NE 2d 771 . . . . 362n.67, 364n.73
Nicor Supply Ships Associates v General Motors Corp 876 F 2d 501 (5th Cir 1989) 241n.85
Northern Power & Engineering Corp v Caterpillar Tractor Co 623 P 2d 324
    (Alaska 1981) 330 . . . . 240n.82
Pennsylvania Glass Sand Corp v Caterpillar Tractor Co 652 F 2d 1165 (3rd Cir 1981) 229n.13
Saratoga Fishing Co v JM Martinac & Co 117 S Ct 1783 (1997) 233n.36, 234n.39, 239n.74
Sea-Land Service Inc v General Electric Co 134 F 3d 149 (3rd Cir 1998) 232n.31, 233n.33
Shipco 2295 Inc v Avondale Shipyards Inc 825 F 2d 925 (5th Cir 1987) 239n.75, 239n.77,
                                                                                    240–41, 240n.83, 241n.85
Smiley v Citibank (South Dakota) NA 517 US 735 (1996) 198n.43
Texaco Inc v Pennzoil Co [1986] 784 F2d 1133, 1157 [2d Cir 1986], rev'd,
    107 S Ct 1519 [1987] 357n.44
Transport Corporation of America Inc v International Business Machines Inc
    30 F 3d 953 (8th Cir 1994) 957 . . . . 239n.73
TruGreen Companies v Mower Brothers [2008] 199 P3d 929 . . . . 361n.61
United States v Bank of New England NA (1987) 821 F (2d) 844 . . . . 223n.63
United States v TIME-DC Inc (1974) 381 F Supp 730 . . . . 223n.63

Table of Legislation

UNITED KINGDOM

Statutes

Administration of Justice Act 1982
  s 2(a)............................ 355n.25
Apportionment Act 1870
  s 2............................. 132n.24
  s 5............................. 132n.24
Companies Act 2006
  ss 170–77....................... 17n.71
  s 250........................... 14n.62
  s 251........................... 14n.62
Consumer Credit Act 1974 3–4
  s 75............................... 307
Consumer Protection Act 1987............241
  s 5(2)........................... 241n.87
Consumer Rights Act 2015 .... 85, 304–6,
                     304n.15, 314, 316, 317
  Pt 1............................. 34n.57
  Pt 1, Ch 3......................... 315
  Pt 2........................... 195n.15
  s 20............................ 313n.81
  s 23............................ 310n.52
  s 24(5).......................... 314n.85
  s 24(8).......................... 314n.86
  s 24(10)......................... 314n.86
  s 29............................ 308n.35
  s 31............................ 34n.57
  s 39(3)(b)....................... 316n.100
  s 39(6).......................... 316n.100
  s 47............................ 34n.57
  s 57............................ 34n.57
  s 58............................ 310n.52
  s 62............................ 97n.31
  Sch 2 Pt 1, para 9.................. 97n.31
Contract (Rights of Third Parties)
    Act 1999....................... 353n.7
Criminal Law Act 1977 67
Criminal Justice Act 1993
  s 52............................ 60–61
Divorce, Dissolution and Separation
    Act 2020.................... 94, 366n.87
Divorce Reform Act 1969 ....94, 96–97
Employment Relations Act 1999....... 365n.78
Employment Rights Act 1996 .... 85n.64
Equality Act 2010
  s 57............................ 365n.78
Family Law Act 1996 .... 97n.25
Forfeiture Act 1982...................... 64

Homes (Fitness for Human Habitation)
    Act 2018...................... 85n.65
Immigration, Asylum and Nationality
    Act 2006
  s 15.............................. 68
  s 21.............................. 68
Income and Corporation Taxes
    Act 1988........ 341–42, 345–46, 347–48
Infants Relief Act 1874................... 139
Insolvency Act 1986
  s 122(1)(g)...................... 19n.80
  Sch B1
    para 14....................... 267n.13
    para 14(3) 267n.13
    para 37....................... 267n.13
Insurance Act 2015
  s 14(3)(a) 31n.40
Law of Property Act 1925
  s 136 ..... 268–69, 270–71, 272, 273n.55, 279
  s 136(1)(a) 268n.17
  s 136(1)(b)...................... 268n.17
  s 136(1)(c) 268n.16
Law of Property (Miscellaneous
    Provisions) Act 1989
  s 3............................. 54n.47
Law Reform (Frustrated Contracts)
    Act 1943................125, 130, 138–39
  s 1(1)............................ 132
  s 1(2).......... 132, 133, 133n.25, 134, 137,
                 137n.33, 138, 139
  s 1(3)........134, 135, 136, 137, 137n.33, 139
  s 1(3)(b) 135
  s 2(4)......................133, 134, 135
Law Reform (Miscellaneous Provisions)
    Act 1970
  s 2............................ 366n.89
  s 5............................ 355n.25
Limitation Act 1980
  s 5.............................. 342
  s 32(1)........................... 347–48
  s 32(1)(c) 339, 341, 342–44, 345, 349
Local Government Act 1972 341
Lord Cairns' Act 1858..... 171n.3, 172, 173–74,
                 175, 185–87, 190
  s 2 .... 172n.10, 185n.76
Marine Insurance Act 1906
  s 17............................ 31n.40
Married Women's Property Act 1882
  s 12.............................. 215

xxxvi TABLE OF LEGISLATION

Marriage Act 1949 107
Matrimonial Causes Act 1923. . . . . 94n.8
Matrimonial Causes Act 1937. . . . . . . 94n.8, 101
Matrimonial Causes Act 1973
  s 3(1). 94n.10
  s 25 101–2
  s 25(1). 101n.53
Minors Contracts Act 1987 139
Proceeds of Crime Act 2002 . . . . 388n.35
Sale and Supply of Goods Act 1994
  s 1 . . . . 311n.57
  s 2 . . . . 314n.83
  s 4 . . . . 311n.62
  s 14 304–5
Sale of Goods Act 1979. . . . . 301–2, 306,
                         312, 315–16, 318
  s 6 116–17
  s 7 116–17
  s 10(1). 312n.78
  s 12 116
  s 13–15. 311
  s 13 311
  s 14 116
  s 14(2). 311
  s 14(2B) 311n.59
  s 15A. 311–13
  s 18 . . . . .306–7, 308
  s 18B. 307n.31
  s 18B(3) 307n.31
  s 18B(4) 307n.31
  s 20 308
  s 28 . . . . 116n.39, 307n.32
  s 30(1). 138n.36
  s 34 . . . . 314n.83
  s 35 . . . . 314n.83
  s 48(3). 312n.76
  s 49 308–9
  s 49(1). 308
Sale of Goods Act 1893. . . . . 116–17, 116n.36
Senior Courts Act 1981
  s 50 . . . . 172n.10, 185n.76
Supply of Goods and Services Act 1982 . . . 316–17
  s 15(1). 389–90
Supply of Goods (Implied Terms)
    Act 1973. 316–17
Tenant Fees Act 2019 . . . . 85n.65
Trade Disputes Act 1906 . . . . 365n.82
Trade Union Act 1871 . . . . 365n.82
Trade Union Reform and Employment
    Rights Act 1993. . . . . 365n.83
Unfair Contract Terms Act 1977. 3–4
  s 2 . . . . 304n.10
  s 3 . . . . 304n.10
  s 3(2)(b)(i) 304n.14
  s 6 . . . . 304n.10
  s 7 . . . . 304n.10

Statutory Instruments

Business Contract Terms (Assignment of
    Receivables) Regulations 2018. . . . . . .267n.12
Civil Procedure Rules 1998 (SI 1998/3132)
  Pt 14
    r 14.1(4) 251n.45
  Pt 16
    r 16.2(3) 281n.116
  Pt 17 . . . . 281n.119
  Pt 19
    r 19.7A 274n.66
    r 19.7A(1) 274n.66
    r 19.7A(2) 274n.67
  Pt 40
    r 40.7(1) 250n.41
    PD 40A. 256n.80
Consumer Contracts (Information,
    Cancellation and Additional Charges)
    Regulations 2013 (SI 2013/3134)
  Pt 3 . . . . 309n.46
Criminal Procedure Rules 388, 395
Insolvency Rules 1986
  r 5.21. . . . . 277n.87
  r 5.23(4)(c). 278n.92
Insolvency Rules 2016
  r 8.22. . . . . 277n.87
Law Applicable to Contractual
    Obligations and Non-Contractual
    Obligations (Amendment etc)
    (EU Exit) Regulations 2019
    (SI 2019/834). 123n.96
Supreme Court Rules 1965
  Ord. 6, r 3(1)(a). 276, 281n.116
  Ord 15, r 14(1). 274n.66
  Ord 15, r 14(2). 274n.67
Unfair Terms in Consumer Contracts
    Regulations 1999 (SI 1999/2083). 196, 336
  reg 5(1). 195

EUROPEAN UNION

EC Treaty
  Art 43 341–42
  Art 56 342

Directives

EU Directive on payment services 293
Directive 93/13/EEC of 5 April 1993
  on unfair terms in consumer
  contracts, OJ L95/93, 29
  Art 3(1) 304
Directive 1999/44/EC Consumer
  Sales Directive. 310n.54
Directive 2011/83/EU Consumer
  Rights Directive
  Art 20 . . . . 308n.35

TABLE OF LEGISLATION   xxxvii

Directive 2019/770/EU of the European
Parliament and of the Council of
20 May 2019 on certain aspects
concerning contracts for the supply
of digital content and digital services
of 22 May 2019, OJ L136 316

Regulations

Proposal for a Regulation of the European
Parliament and the Council on the
law applicable to contractual
obligations (Rome I), COM/2005/0650
final, 2005/0261 (COD)
Art 3(2) 286n.21
Regulation (EC) No 593/2008 of the
European Parliament and of the
Council of 17 June 2008 on the law
applicable to contractual
obligations (Rome I)
Art 3 . . . . 286n.21
Art 9(3) 123–24

INTERNATIONAL LEGISLATION

Convention on International Interests
in Mobile Equipment (2001, Cape
Town Convention) 320n.9, 323, 324,
328–29, 330–31, 332, 333–34, 335–36
Aircraft Protocol 323, 324, 328–29,
330, 331, 332, 333–34, 335–36
Convention on the Use of Electronic
Communications in International
Contracts 287–88, 293, 294n.102
Geneva Conventions for Bills of
Exchange and Promissory Notes
and for Cheques (1930) . . . 293, 320n.11–21
Hague Convention of 5 July 2006 on the
Law Applicable to Certain Rights
in Respect of Securities Held With
an Intermediary
Art 4 . . . . 326n.30
Art 5 . . . . 327n.31
Hague Convention on Choice of Court
Agreements (2005) 330
Hague Convention on the Law Applicable
to Agency (1978) 323
Hague Convention on the Law Applicable
to Certain Rights in Respect of
Intermediated Securities
(2002) 323, 324, 325
Hague Uniform Laws on International
Sales of Goods (1964) 293
HCCH, Principles on Choice of Law in
International Commercial
Contracts (2015) 287, 293
Art 3 285

ICC Rules of Arbitration (2021) 322n.16
ICC Uniform Rules for Contract
Guarantees 329
ICC Uniform Rules for Demand
Guarantees (1992) 329, 330
OHADA Uniform Act Relating to
General Commercial Law of the
Organization for the Harmonization
of Commercial Law in Africa (1997) 292,
294n.102, 320–21
Patent Co-operation Treaty (1970) 320n.9
Principles of European Contract
Law 321n.13, 336
Art 9:506 . . . . 315n.91
Art 9:507 . . . . 315n.93
UN Convention for the International
Sale of Goods 283n.1
UN Convention on Contracts for the
International Sale of Goods 1980 285,
287–88, 292, 293, 294, 296, 297,
314–15, 320n.10, 322–23, 330
Art 7(1) 297
Art 7(2) 297
Art 75 . . . . 315n.90, 315n.93
Art 76 . . . . 315n.93
UN Convention on the Assignment of
Receivables (2001) 327–28
UN Convention on the Recognition and
Enforcement of Foreign Arbitral
Awards (1958, New York Convention) 330
UN Convention on the Rights of
the Child (1989) 330n.43
UNCITRAL Arbitration Rules (2021) 322n.15
UNCITRAL Convention on the Limitation
Period in the International Sale
of Goods 286–88, 292, 293, 294, 330n.44
UNCITRAL Model Law on Cross-Border
Insolvency (1997) 321–22, 323, 330
UNCITRAL Model Law on International
Commercial Arbitration (1985) 321–22
UNCITRAL Model Law on International
Credit Transfers (1992) 293, 294n.102
UNCITRAL Model Law on Secured
Transactions (2016) 327–28
UNCITRAL Uniform Rules on Contract
Clauses for an Agreed Sum Due
upon Failure of Performance (1983) 292,
293, 294n.102
UNIDROIT Convention on Agency
in the International Sale of
Goods (1983) 323, 327n.32
UNIDROIT Convention on International
Financial Leasing (1988) 323, 328
UNIDROIT Convention on Stolen or
Illegally Exported Cultural
Objects (1995) 330

TABLE OF LEGISLATION

UNIDROIT Convention on
Substantive Rules for
Intermediated Securities (2009) . . . 323, 329
UNIDROIT International Factoring
Convention (1988) 327–28
UNIDROIT Model Law on
Leasing (2008). 321–22
UNIDROIT Principles of International
Commercial Contracts (2016) 285–86,
287, 293, 294, 297, 321n.13
Ch 10 294
Art 2.1.19(2) 296, 298
Art 7.4.5 . . . . 315n.91
Art 7.4.6 . . . . 315n.93
UNIDROIT Uniform Law on
Contracts for the International
Sale of Goods (1964) 322–23
Art 2 . . . . 323n.22
Art 3 . . . . 323n.22
UNIDROIT Uniform Law on
International Sales (1964) 322–23
Vienna Convention on the Law of
Treaties (1969)
Art 33(1) 333
Art 61(1) 333n.56

NATIONAL LEGISLATION

Australia

Acts Interpretation Act 1901 (Cth)
s 34AB(1) (c) 221
Frustrated Contracts Act 1959 . . . . 138n.39
Law Reform (Vicarious Liability)
Act 1983 (NSW) 216
Native Title Act 1993 (Cth)
s 203B(3) 220
Trade Practices Act 1974 (Cth).
s 51AB 222–23
s 51AC 222–23

Belgium

loi of 28 April 2022 (in force from
1 January 2023) 25n.12

China

Chinese Civil Code. 367, 369–81
Ch 29, Pt 3 .367, 369–70
Art 122 . . . . .367n.3, 368–69, 370, 375
Arts 985–988 367
Arts 986–988 371
Art 985 . . . . .370, 375
Art 985(1) 370
Art 986 371

Art 987 371
Art 988 371
General Principles of Civil Law 1986
Art 92 . . . . 368–69, 370–71, 372, 378–79
General Rules of Civil Law of the
People's Republic of China 2017 368–69

France

la bonne foi (Code civil (C civ) 28
Art 1104 . . . . 27n.19
Art 1104(1) 28n.24
Art 1104(2) 28n.26
Art 1134 . . . . 28n.23
Art 1222 . . . . 310n.53
Art 1225 . . . . 35n.67
Art 2272 . . . . 27n.19
Loi no 2018-287 of 20 April 2018
(in force from 1 October 2018) 25n.12
Ordonnance n° 2016-131 of 10 February
2016 (in force from 1 October 2016) 25n.12

Israel

Civil Wrongs Ordinance
s 62(b) 366n.88, 366n.90
Contracts (Remedies for Breach) Law 1971
s 2(2). 356n.31

Germany

Bürgerliches Gesetzbuch (BGB)
§ 242 . . . . 27n.18, 28n.27, 30
§ 311(2) 34n.52
§ 323 . . . . 313n.79
§ 323(1) 35n.67
§ 812(1) 369n.11, 370n.19, 375
§ 818(3) 371n.26
§ 822 371
§ 932 . . . . 27n.18
Gesetz zur Modernisierung des
Schuldrechts (Modernization of
the Law of Obligations Act) of
26 November 2001, in force from
1 January 2002. . . . . 30n.35
Zivilprozessordnung (ZPO)
§ 887 . . . . 310n.53

Netherlands

Dutch Civil Code (Burgerlijk
Wetboek, BW 1992) 27n.18, 29–30
art 3:11 . . . . 27n.18
art 3:12 . . . . 27n.18, 29.30
art 3:118 . . . . 27n.18
art 6:2 . . . . 27n.18
art 6:2.1 . . . . 29n.30

TABLE OF LEGISLATION

art 6:2.2 .... 29n.31
art 6:248.2 .... 29n.32
art 6:258.1 .... 29n.33

New Zealand
Frustrated Contracts Act 1944 .... 138n.38

Spain
buena fe (Código civil)
art 7.............................. 27n.19
art 464 .... 27n.19

Trinidad and Tobago
Companies Act
ss 56–57 71–72
s 517 72
Petroleum Act........................68–69
s 6(2)................................69

United States
Restatement (Second) of
   Contracts (American Law
   Institute 1981)................. 90n.103
§ 205............................ 28n.22
Restatement of the Law (Third) of Torts:
   Product Liability (1998)
§ 21, cmt e 239n.73
Restatement (Third) of the Law
   of Restitution
§ 39............................. 361n.65
§ 44.................................361
§ 44(1) 361
§ 44(2) 361
Uniform Commercial Code 314–15
§1-304 .... 28n.22
§2-508(2)....................... 312n.67
§2-712 .... 309n.49
§2-713 .... 315n.93

List of Contributors

Hugh Beale FBA
Hugh Beale is Senior Research Fellow in the Commercial Law Centre at Harris Manchester College, Oxford and Emeritus Professor at the University of Warwick Law School.

The Rt Hon Lord Burrows
Andrew Burrows is a Justice of the UK Supreme Court, a member of the Oxford Law Faculty, and Quondam Fellow of All Souls College.

John Cartwright
John Cartwright is Emeritus Professor of the Law of Contract at the University of Oxford and Emeritus Student of Christ Church.

Mindy Chen-Wishart
Mindy Chen-Wishart is Professor of the Law of Contract and Dean of the Faculty of Law at the University of Oxford.

Nili Cohen
Nili Cohen is Emeritus Professor at the Buchmann Faculty of Law, Tel Aviv University.

William Day
William Day is a barrister at 3 Verulam Buildings and Fellow of Downing College, Cambridge.

Tim Dodsworth
Tim Dodsworth is Senior Lecturer in Law at Newcastle University.

The Hon Justice Edelman
James Edelman is a Justice of the High Court of Australia and Adjunct Professor, Universities of New South Wales, Queensland and Western Australia.

Jodi Gardner
Jodi Gardner is College Lecturer in Law and Fellow of St John's College, Cambridge.

Sir Roy Goode CBE KC FBA
Roy Goode is Emeritus Professor of Law in the University of Oxford and Emeritus Fellow of St John's College, Oxford.

James Goudkamp
James Goudkamp is Professor of the Law of Obligations and Fellow of Keble College, Oxford and a barrister at 7 King's Bench Walk.

Louise Gullifer KC (Hon) FBA
Louise Gullifer is Rouse Ball Professor of English Law at the University of Cambridge and a Fellow of Gonville and Caius College, Cambridge.

Roger Halson
Roger Halson is Emeritus Professor of Contract and Commercial Law at the University of Leeds.

xlii LIST OF CONTRIBUTORS

Andrew Hamilton FRS
Andrew Hamilton is President of New York University.

Adam Kramer KC
Adam Kramer is a barrister at 3 Verulam Buildings.

The Rt Hon Lord Leggatt
George Leggatt is a Justice of the UK Supreme Court.

Qiao Liu
Qiao Liu is Professor at the School of Law, City University of Hong Kong and Honorary Professor at the TC Beirne School of Law, University of Queensland.

Hector L MacQueen
Hector L MacQueen is Emeritus Professor of Private Law at the University of Edinburgh.

Ali Malek KC
Ali Malek is a barrister and Chair of Chambers at 3 Verulam Buildings.

Donal Nolan
Donal Nolan is Professor of Private Law in the University of Oxford and Francis Reynolds and Clarendon Fellow and Tutor in Law at Worcester College, Oxford.

Edwin Peel
Edwin Peel is Professor of Law and Clarendon Harris Fellow in Law at Keble College, Oxford and an Arbitrator at One Essex Court, London.

Rebecca Probert FBA FAcSS
Rebecca Probert is Professor of Law at the University of Exeter.

The Rt Hon Lord Sales
Philip Sales is a Justice of the UK Supreme Court.

Helen Scott
Helen Scott is Regius Professor of Civil Law at the University of Cambridge.

Robert Stevens
Robert Stevens is Herbert Smith Freehills Professor of English Private Law at the University of Oxford.

Richard Taylor
Richard Taylor is Emeritus Professor of English Law, University of Central Lancashire.

Stefan Vogenauer FBA
Stefan Vogenauer is Director at the Max Planck Institute of Legal History and Legal Theory.

Sarah Worthington DBE KC (Hon) FBA
Sarah Worthington is Professor of Law, LSE, and Downing Professor Emeritus of the Laws of England, Cambridge.

PART I
CONTRACT

1

Facility, Circumvention, Economic Duress, and the Corporate Veil

HECTOR L MacQUEEN

I. Introduction

My interaction with Ewan McKendrick began at Edinburgh University's Law Faculty in the Contract Law (Honours) class that I co-taught for the first time with Stephen Woolman (later Lord Woolman of the Inner House of the Court of Session) in academic session 1980–81. Ewan was a leading member of what Stephen and I have always recalled as an exceptionally able class, setting high standards that were hard for their successors to match and pushing their teachers to their intellectual limits and perhaps beyond.[1] In the 1990s it was a pleasure to invite Ewan to take up the role of external examiner of the Contract Honours class which, by then, I taught alone, while in the early 2000s we were again reunited as members of the coordinating committee of the Study Group on a European Civil Code. So our conversations about contract law in particular have gone on for more than forty years and it is a privilege indeed to contribute something on that subject to this collection in his honour.

It is however a matter of great personal regret that since Ewan left his alma mater in order to undertake the Oxford BCL, he has not more often ventured back into the law north of the border. Scots law's loss has been English law's gain. In 1985, however, Ewan contributed two papers on economic duress to Scottish law journals, both aimed primarily at the courts and legal practitioners in Scotland.[2] At that time (and indeed ever since) there had been almost no opportunity for modern Scottish courts to say whether or not the traditional ground of challenge to a contract known as 'force and/or fear' extended to the exertion of pressure by purely economic means during pre-contractual negotiations.[3] The English courts had begun to recognize the possibility but had exhibited a degree of confusion as to whether the basis for this was the 'overborne will' of the pressurized party, or the unacceptability of the conduct of the pressurizing party, or some middle position such as the lack of reasonable

---

[1] One other member became the distinguished academic employment lawyer Douglas Brodie (now Dean of Humanities and Social Sciences and Associate Principal at the University of Strathclyde). Several other class members went on to outstanding practitioner careers.

[2] Ewan McKendrick, 'Economic Duress—A Reasonable Alternative?' [1985] SLG 54; Ewan McKendrick, 'Economic Duress A Reply' [1985] SLT 277 (hereafter McKendrick, 'Economic Duress A Reply') (the latter a response to Andrew Thompson, 'Economic Duress' [1985] SLT 85). A little later Ewan produced 'Specific Implement and Specific Performance—A Comparison' [1986] SLT 249.

[3] William W McBryde, *The Law of Contract in Scotland* (3rd edn, W Green/Scottish Universities Law Institute 2007 (hereafter McBryde, *Contract*) [17.06] notes two pre-1800 cases and one early twentieth-century one in which 'economic pressure did affect obligations'. The last of these, *Sutherland v Montrose Fishing Co Ltd* (1921) 37 Sh Ct Rep 239 (hereafter *Sutherland v Montrose*), is a sheriff court decision taking a hostile view of trade union activity that might not be permissible today; it is discussed further at n 64. See also JE Du Plessis, *Compulsion and Restitution* (Stair Society vol 51 2004) (hereafter Du Plessis, *Compulsion and Restitution*) 68–70.

Hector L MacQueen, *Facility, Circumvention, Economic Duress, and the Corporate Veil* In: *Shaping the Law of Obligations.*
Edited by: Edwin Peel and Rebecca Probert, Oxford University Press. © Hector L MacQueen 2023.
DOI: 10.1093/oso/9780198889762.003.0001

4 FACILITY, CIRCUMVENTION, ECONOMIC DURESS, CORPORATE VEIL

alternatives open to the pressurized party. Ewan argued that when the Scottish courts did come to the question, they too should recognize the possibility of economic pressure being a basis for the invalidation of a contract, but should do so on the basis of whether or not the pressure applied had been 'legitimate'. That however could not be limited to unlawful conduct; it might extend to lawful conduct being exerted towards an unlawful end such as blackmail. Pressure arising from undue influence should also be brought within the doctrine thus delineated. The relevance of the victim's consent would be limited to showing that the pressure had been a cause of their entering the contract. This 'two-tier' approach would bring the Scots law of duress 'out of the dark ages'[4] and could be used to unify not only the doctrines of force and fear and undue influence but also facility and circumvention (of which more anon). But, Ewan emphasized, if the courts were to look at the fairness or otherwise of the bargain struck as a result of the pressure, they would be overreaching themselves. They should confine themselves to cases of 'procedural' rather than 'substantive' unfairness, ie, to unfair ways of obtaining a particular contract. On the substantive side, it is for Parliament to regulate the outcomes of the exercise of economic power, not the judges (except insofar as authorized by Parliament, as, for example, in the Unfair Contract Terms Act 1977 and the Consumer Credit Act 1974).

These arguments about economic duress can still be found in Ewan's textbooks on contract law, applied of course to English law.[5] In many ways such arguments have now definitively prevailed in England with the decision of the UK Supreme Court in *Times Travel Ltd v Pakistan International Airline Corp*,[6] which is considered in section II of this chapter. The aim of this chapter is however not to undertake a detailed review of the *Times Travel* case and the differing views expressed therein by Lords Burrows and Hodge,[7] but rather to take a narrower approach and consider the possible implications for the application of the majority approach of a more or less contemporaneous Scottish first instance decision, *Lindsay's Executor v Outlook Finance Ltd*.[8]

II. *Times Travel Ltd v Pakistan International Airline Corp*

In *Times Travel* the Supreme Court held that economic or 'lawful act' duress can only be pleaded where the threat made is 'illegitimate' and that commercial pressure to achieve a change to a contract is not generally illegitimate. One of the parties (PIAC) was a global corporation, the other (TT) a small, family-owned travel agency business based in Birmingham and directed by a father-and-son team, Asrar and Ismail Ahmad. TT's business was almost exclusively the sale of PIAC flight tickets between the UK and Pakistan. Under the original agreement between PIAC and TT, the former made a fortnightly allocation of 300 tickets

---

[4] McKendrick, 'Economic Duress A Reply' (n 2) 280. For the history of force and fear see Du Plessis, *Compulsion and Restitution* (n 3) chs 3 and 4.

[5] See eg Ewan McKendrick, *Contract Law* (15th edn, Bloomsbury 2023) ch 17.

[6] [2021] UKSC 40, [2023] AC 101, [2021] 3 WLR 727 (hereafter *Times Travel*).

[7] For summary of which see later in the chapter, at 5–6; and for discussion the contribution of Mindy Chen-Wishart and Jodi Gardner to the present collection; also William Day, 'Duress and Uncertainty' (2022) 138 LQR 194; Jonathan Morgan, 'The Thin End of the Wedge: Morality, Contract Law and Lawful Act Duress' (2022) 81 CLJ 17; Hector L MacQueen, 'European Contract Law in the Post-Brexit and (Post?) Pandemic United Kingdom' (2022) 30 ERPL 3, 24–6; Oliver Jackson, 'Unconscionability, Uncertainty and Lawful Act Duress' [2021] JBL 701.

[8] [2021] CSOH 82, 12 August, unreported (Lady Wolffe) (hereafter *Lindsay's Executor v Outlook*).

to the latter, with TT entitled to commission on the price of tickets sold at a rate of 9 per cent plus an overriding commission as an incentive related to total sales. A dispute about the commissions payable broke out between PIAC and its various UK agents, including TT. A group of the agents, which TT did not join, raised an action against PIAC for payment of the claimed commission. PIAC then sent a notice of termination of appointment to TT and all the other agents, together with terms of reappointment under which not only were quite different remuneration terms set out but PIAC was also released from all claims to remuneration or commission under any other agreement. PIAC also subsequently notified TT that its fortnightly allocation of tickets would be reduced to sixty, which would make TT's business unsustainable. TT's directors therefore felt under severe pressure to sign the reappointment agreement in order to regain their allocation of 300 tickets and acted accordingly. There was no suggestion that PIAC's conduct was in any way in breach of contract or had otherwise gone beyond what the law allowed. TT's later challenge to the reappointment agreement as procured by 'lawful act' economic duress was successful at first instance before Warren J[9] but this was overturned in the Court of Appeal,[10] with that decision being upheld on different grounds by the Supreme Court.

The members of the Supreme Court were unanimous on the result but differed about the basis upon which the duress exerted by an otherwise lawful act might be held illegitimate. Lord Burrows held that the test was one of the subjective bad faith of the party applying the pressure. PIAC would have failed this test had it not genuinely believed that it did not owe the commission that was being claimed by its agents. This approach was however strongly rejected by the majority, for whom Lord Hodge was the spokesman. He articulated instead a test based on the identification of 'morally reprehensible behaviour which in equity was judged to render the enforcement of a contract unconscionable in the context of undue influence'.[11] Unconscionability is not however an overarching criterion, since that would make judges 'arbiters of what is morally and socially acceptable'.[12] It was necessary instead to identify specific contexts calling for judicial intervention to protect a weaker party. One was undue influence 'where two persons have a relationship in which A has acquired influence or ascendancy over B and A takes unfair advantage of its influence or ascendancy'.[13] Another was the doctrine of unconscionable bargains, applied where B is at a serious disadvantage relative to A through 'poverty, or ignorance, or lack of advice or otherwise' so that circumstances existed of which unfair advantage could be taken; A exploited B's weakness in a morally culpable manner; and the resulting transaction was not merely hard or improvident but overreaching and oppressive.[14]

Lord Hodge went on to provide further examples of unconscionable bargains: one from an Australian case 'in which A knowingly negotiates an agreement with B while B is elderly, unwell and intoxicated'[15] and an English one 'where a poor, illiterate and unwell person is induced to enter into a disadvantageous transaction without advice and in great haste'.[16] He also cited *Fry v Lane* for the proposition that a seller's circumstances of poverty, ignorance,

---

[9] [2017] EWHC 1367 (Ch).
[10] [2019] EWCA Civ 828, [2020] Ch 98.
[11] *Times Travel* (n 6) [2].
[12] ibid [23].
[13] ibid [23].
[14] ibid [24].
[15] ibid. The Australian case is *Blomley v Ryan* (1954) 99 CLR 362.
[16] *Times Travel* (n 6) [24], citing *Clark v Malpas* (1862) 4 De G F & J 401, 45 ER 1238 (Ch).

6 FACILITY, CIRCUMVENTION, ECONOMIC DURESS, CORPORATE VEIL

and lack of independent advice impose on the purchaser the burden of showing that the purchase was fair, just, and reasonable.[17] Finally, Lord Hodge stressed that mere inequality of bargaining power between the parties without more was insufficient to invalidate the contract.

We may note at this point that Lord Hodge's approach goes some, although not all, of the way towards Ewan McKendrick's argument that duress and undue influence should be unified, before turning to *Lindsay's Executor v Outlook Finance Ltd*.

III. *Lindsay's Executor v Outlook Finance Ltd*

A. The Action

This case concerned three deeds granted by Euan Lindsay in the autumn of 2009, less than two years before his death aged 59 on 3 June 2011. The first deed, dated 3 October, was an 'all-sums due' standard security (mortgage) in favour of Outlook Finance (based at Stourport in Worcestershire) over Euan's farm, Harperfield in Lanarkshire, which had replaced an earlier grant restricted to the sum of £275,000. The second and third deeds, both dated 29 September, were loan facilities from Outlook to Metal Bridge Farm Ltd (MBL), both of which included a personal indemnity from Euan covering all the obligations in the loan agreements. MBL had been incorporated in June 2008, bringing together various dairy and cattle-breeding businesses operated at Metal Bridge Farm in Cumbria by Euan's nephews (Rodger and Kerr) and his sister-in-law (Helen, wife of Euan's brother James).[18] A charge in English form (mortgage) had been granted over Metal Bridge Farm in favour of Outlook some time previously and this was called up later in October 2009, with Metal Bridge Farm and its stock and machinery being sold and Outlook taking the proceeds. Outlook claimed, however, that this did not fully satisfy its claims against MBL; hence its interest in procuring payment under Euan's indemnities.

The action was for (i) reduction of the first two deeds on the grounds of Euan's facility; Outlook's circumvention through its director and controlling mind, Derek Fradgley; and lesion (loss) resulting to Euan and (ii) declarator that the third deed was similarly obtained. There were also conclusions based on fraudulent misrepresentations by Outlook through its agent, Mr Fradgley, and the bad faith of Outlook as creditor in misleading Euan as cautioner (ie guarantor) as to the indebtedness of MBL. The reason for seeking declarator in relation to the third deed rather than reduction was that its subject matter had been transferred to a third party in good faith and for value, making reduction of the deed pointless, but a declarator, if granted, might be relevant to and be taken into account in the overall assessment of what might be due to Euan's estate from Outlook if any or all of the various grounds of

---

[17] *Fry v Lane* (1888) 40 Ch D 312, cited in *Times Travel* (n 6) [24].

[18] The unusual name Metal Bridge was coined after the 1820 erection over the nearby River Esk of a three-span cast-iron bridge designed by Thomas Telford and the development on the south bank beside it of a small settlement (including an inn). Telford's bridge was taken down and replaced just before the First World War. The site of the original bridge was close to where the modern bridge carries the M6 over the river. See further Institute of Civil Engineers, 'Glasgow to Carlisle Road (1825)', https://web.archive.org/web/20160304203642/http://www.engineering-timelines.com/scripts/engineeringItem.asp?id=1239, accessed 30 November 2022.

action were established.[19] This approach is consistent with the established approach to the declarator,[20] which is not strictly a discretionary remedy in Scotland.[21]

B. Facility and Circumvention as a Ground of Invalidity

The judge (Lady Wolffe) granted the remedies sought by Euan Lindsay's executor (another nephew, William). The primary ground on which she held the contracts to be voidable was 'facility and circumvention'. This became established as a ground of challenge, not only to contracts and written deeds but also to wills, in the course of the nineteenth century. Like the Scottish reception of 'undue influence' from English law in the same period, the doctrine was a by-product of the contemporary narrowing of the long-established concept of fraud.[22] The essence of facility and circumvention is the protection of an individual who transacts while subject to weakness such as mental or physical illness but without having been deprived altogether of capacity to contract (or, in the case of wills, to test). The invalidity arises if the other contracting party (or a beneficiary of the will) has in some way taken unfair advantage (circumvention) of the weakened party's condition (facility) to obtain a benefit which also causes 'lesion' (loss or harm) to that weakened party through its exorbitant nature. Deception, whether intentional or not, is usually involved. The victim's weakness means that he or she is unable to look after their interests effectively and the other party has taken advantage of this to their own benefit: hence the voidability of the transaction. The three elements are interrelated: 'if substantial lesion is averred, relatively weak averments of circumvention may be compensated for by strong and circumstantial averments of weakness and facility.'[23] But if one of the elements is missing, the claim fails.[24] Thus lesion, or an unfair outcome, is an essential element of this form of challenge to the contract.

A further crucial point about the doctrine was established by dicta of Lord Justice-Clerk Hope in the early case of *Clunie v Stirling* when, in the course of his opinion, he said:

> The actual mode or particular acts of circumvention may not be discoverable or easily proved. But the result may demonstrate that the party was really circumvented ... when he was led into the transaction under challenge; and then the nature of that transaction, the mode in which, and the party by whom it was carried through, and the object apparent on the face of it, for which, if palpably disadvantageous, it was huddled up without proper inquiry, and without the individual receiving the aid he ought to have received, all bear on the ... question, whether the party had been circumvented ... [I]t was contended that we must find some positive fact proved which amounts in itself to a distinct act or piece of circumvention; some trick, some particular practising on the mind of the party at a particular

---

[19] See the earlier opinion of Lady Wolffe following a relevancy debate: *Lindsay's Executor v Outlook Finance ltd* [2020] CSOH 90, unreported, 28 October, [13].

[20] *Laws of Scotland: Stair Memorial Encyclopaedia Reissue* (Lexis Nexis 2000) 'Remedies', [4].

[21] Lord Eassie, 'The Action of Declarator in Scotland' in Jeremy Woolf, *Zamir & Woolf: The Declaratory Judgment* (4th edn, Sweet & Maxwell 2011) [8.40–8.41].

[22] McBryde, *Contract* (n 3) [14.10–14.12], [16.04–16.10]. See further Dot Reid, 'Fraud in Scots Law' (University of Edinburgh PhD thesis, 2012) especially at 68–92, 132–68.

[23] *Mackay v Campbell* 1966 SC 237, 249 (Lord Justice-Clerk Grant); repeated almost verbatim by Lord Guest when the same case reached the House of Lords: 1967 SC (HL) 53, 61.

[24] In *Mackay v Campbell* (n 23) the averments of facility were held to be insufficient and the claim accordingly failed.

time,—some details, in short, as to the acts and practices which the general term circumvention includes; and that if one cannot lay one's hand on distinct instances, detected and proved, of particular acts and practices amounting to circumvention, there is no ground for supporting the verdict ... The correct view of the matter is quite different ... [T]he inference of fraud may be drawn from the whole case, although no one act can be pointed out as in itself a direct instance of the practice of deceit.[25]

The significance of this was underlined in a characteristically succinct but unreported dictum of Lord Kyllachy which was picked up in subsequent reported case law on circumvention: 'It is not necessary that there should be deceit. It is enough that there should be solicitation, pressure, importunity, even in some cases, suggestion.'[26]

C. The Facts of *Lindsay's Executor v Outlook Finance Ltd*

The facility of Euan Lindsay as established by the evidence reviewed by Lady Wolffe consisted in his long-term ill-health (a condition colloquially known as 'farmer's lung' which affected him from about 1975[27]) alongside growing concerns about the finances of his family and himself. In 2000 he was forced to give up working on his farm at Harperfield and move to Halltown (three miles from Metal Bridge Farm) to live there with his brother James and his sister-in-law Helen. Harperfield was left under the management of his nephew William, with whom Euan had previously conducted the farming business there in partnership under the firm name D M Lindsay. By 2008 Euan required a permanent oxygen supply and was 'tethered to an oxygen tank',[28] which, however, he was unable to carry himself, making him 'effectively housebound'.[29] In that state, 'he liked to sit in the room used as an office beside the fax machine and to read faxes received'.[30] Euan also regularly required hospitalization to treat his condition. He 'suffered from low mood and anxiety'[31] and was on anti-depressants, the side effects of which included painful ulcers and nausea; he also thought he might be suffering from stomach cancer.

Euan was deeply emotionally engaged in the success or otherwise of all the Lindsay businesses, including those run by his sister-in-law and nephews at Metal Bridge Farm, which from 2000 he could observe more or less at first hand. But in the period between 2000 and 2008 these various businesses got into significant financial difficulties thanks to the

---

[25] *Clunie v Stirling* (1854) 17 D 15, 17–18.
[26] *Parnie v MacLean*, 19 August 1904, unreported, cited approvingly in *Gibson's Executor v Anderson* 1925 SC 774, 788 (Lord Blackburn); and *Anderson v The Beacon Fellowship* 1992 SLT 111, 113 (Lord McCluskey). *Parnie* was a civil jury trial in which it was alleged that the defender had allowed his wife (the pursuer's sister) to drink herself to death, but not before getting her to make a will in his favour. The jury found that the wife had been capable of testing but her will should be reduced for the facility created by her alcoholism and her husband's circumvention. The defender's motion for a retrial was given up in January 1905: see National Records of Scotland, Warrants of the Register of Acts and Decreets 5th series [Extracted Processes] CS46/1905/1/73. The case received extensive press coverage: see eg *Dundee Evening Post*, 20 August 1904, and for the settlement *The Scotsman*, 12 January 1905. I am grateful for these references to those who answered my Twitter inquiry about the case, especially Jennie Findlay and Calum M Ross.
[27] See further <https://www.webmd.com/lung/farmers-lung-facts>, accessed 30 November 2022.
[28] *Lindsay's Executor v Outlook* (n 8) [24].
[29] ibid [24].
[30] ibid [25].
[31] ibid [24].

foot-and-mouth epizootic[32] of 2001, followed by an outbreak of TB in their herd of dairy cattle early in 2008 requiring their destruction, and later that same year defeat in a litigation which led to bankruptcy orders in England against Euan's nephews Rodger and Kerr and—slightly later, early in 2009—his sister-in-law Helen (hereafter collectively 'the Metal Bridge Lindsays').

It was in the context of the difficulties following the foot-and-mouth outbreak that the Metal Bridge Lindsays first came into contact with Outlook and its director and controlling mind, Derek Fradgley. The Metal Bridge Lindsays initially formed a strong and trusting relationship with Mr Fradgley as Outlook provided significant finance for the reconstruction and development of their businesses after 2001. He seemed to understand their needs and plans and brought documents in person for them to sign once he had explained their effects, thereafter keeping these originals but leaving copies with the family. Otherwise he communicated mainly by fax. The Metal Bridge Lindsays generally did not read the documents that they signed. But Euan, tethered to his oxygen machine beside the fax machine, did read the faxes sent by Mr Fradgley.

The crisis of 2008 and the bankruptcies of the Metal Bridge Lindsays led to a change in the attitude and approach of Mr Fradgley, whose own company (Outlook) had also become very exposed financially. It was at this point that the Metal Bridge Farm businesses were incorporated as MBL at Mr Fradgley's initiative, with him as company secretary and sole signatory on company cheques. The company's registered office was at Outlook's Stourport office, and the company's bank statements were sent there. Euan and his brother James were appointed as directors, with Mr Fradgley explaining that the more obviously capable Metal Bridge Lindsays were ineligible thanks to their bankruptcies. He got the Lindsays to sign the incorporation and other documents without explaining their effects, and then took them away without leaving copies. He also took away all the copy agreements he had previously left with the Lindsays and began to press them aggressively on repayment of their business debts, saying that Outlook itself was subject to similar pressure from its bank in respect of its debts. This last, as Mr Fradgley admitted in a 2014 witness statement given for the purposes of other litigation between the parties in England, was untrue.[33] But this could not now be put to Mr Fradgley in the instant case, as he had died in July 2017.

Lady Wolffe accepted that these untrue statements had been used as 'an effective instrument of oppression, because it led the Lindsays (including Euan) to believe that Outlook or Derek Fradgley had no leeway and that Outlook was powerless in the face of a third party bank pressing it for repayment'.[34] Lady Wolffe also held that the subsequent minutes of MBL board meetings, taken by Mr Fradgley, had been falsified 'to give an impression which did not accord with the reality and to protect Derek Fradgley's interests—if his dealings ever came under scrutiny'.[35] The minutes as recorded had a 'cumulative effect amounting to an elaborate contrivance to give the appearance that the Metal Bridge Lindsays were in control of MBL, and that Derek Fradgley was at arms' length—when the reverse was true'.[36] There

---

[32] The word denotes a disease that is temporarily prevalent and widespread in an animal population.

[33] Searches on Lexis and Westlaw have failed to bring up these English cases. Earlier stages in the Scottish litigation between the parties not so far noted are *Outlook Finance Ltd v Lindsay* [2016] SAC (Civ) 7 and *Outlook Finance Ltd v Lindsay's Executor* [2016] SC LAN 58, [2016] HLR 75.

[34] *Lindsay's Executor v Outlook* (n 8) [148].

[35] ibid [149(1)–(2)].

[36] ibid [149(4)].

10 FACILITY, CIRCUMVENTION, ECONOMIC DURESS, CORPORATE VEIL

were other instances of actions by Mr Fradgley 'redolent of the kind of conduct creditors engage in when their debtor is verging on insolvency (as the Metal Bridge Lindsays were in May and June 2008),'[37] possibly amounting to unfair preferences. All this was to the benefit of Outlook in limiting its financial exposure through the prior insolvencies of the Metal Bridge Lindsays. Finally, the extent to which Mr Fradgley in fact controlled MBL made him a *de facto* director of the company, making him subject to duties to the company and to avoid conflicts of interest.[38]

At around the same time (June 2008), Mr Fradgley became aware of Euan's ownership of Harperfield and that this large farm, which made Euan a man of substantial capital worth, was unencumbered by any security.[39] After discussion with nephew William (still managing Harperfield), Euan was initially persuaded to grant a standard security (ie mortgage) over the farm in favour of Outlook, supposed to be restricted to £200,000 but actually in the final document of October 2008 limited to £275,000. This was however finally replaced by the all-sums standard security executed on 3 October 2009. It will be recalled that just a few days earlier (29 September) Euan had signed his personal indemnities to Outlook in respect of the other obligations in loan agreements between MBL and Outlook.

All this had been preceded by a surprise visit to Euan by Mr Fradgley in late August 2009. This was to persuade Euan to enter the subsequent arrangements outlined above. The meeting had left Euan in considerable distress. This was probably because, according to evidence given by brother James, who had overheard part of the conversation, during it Mr Fradgley told Euan that he owed Outlook £2.6 million and threatened him with bankruptcy and the loss of Harperfield. Thanks to his reading of Mr Fradgley's faxes to the other Lindsays, Euan was already well aware of and deeply worried about the state of the family's finances, but had still thought his personal liability was no more than £200,000. Prior to June 2008 he had never burdened his own farm with securities, having a real horror of indebtedness which had also extended to the ways in which he did business before his retirement to Halltown. Nor did he understand what an indemnity was. Although the standard security of October 2009 had been drawn up by Euan's Scottish solicitors, they had only been implementing their client's instructions to fulfil what were understood to be his existing agreements with Outlook. They did not offer advice on a proposed transaction, although concern was expressed at the level of indebtedness involved.

D. The Decision

These findings of fact left Lady Wolffe in no doubt that, given Euan's facility, his agreement to the various documents in favour of Outlook was procured by circumvention and that he had thereby suffered lesion, making the agreements under review voidable. The Lindsays,

---

[37] ibid [150].

[38] On this point Lady Wolffe cites (ibid [152]) the 'classic *dicta* from *Secretary of State for Trade and Industry v Hollier* [2006] EWHC 1804 (Ch); [2007] Bus LR 352 [61] (Etherton J); *Re Hydrodam (Corby) Ltd* [1994] 2 BCLC 180, 183A–C; and *Secretary of State for Trade and Industry v Tjolle* [1998] 1 BCLC 333, 343–4'. She modestly omits to cite a previous opinion of hers on the point: *Somerville v 1051 GWR Ltd* [2019] CSOH 61, [2019] HLR 66, [27]–[30].

[39] Harperfield was originally a small country estate near Lanark which became a dairy farm in the ownership of the Lindsay family in 1946: see the Community Action Lanark website <https://www.communityactionlan.org/history-archaeology/item/glorious-gardens-harperfield>, accessed 30 November 2022.

including Euan, had 'reposed complete trust' in Mr Fradgley,[40] but he had engaged in 'a prolonged and elaborate circumvention to a very high degree'.[41] There had been 'deceit, solicitation and pressure', with the deceit 'taking many forms' at a time 'when there was a high degree of facility'.[42] There was no need in such circumstances to invoke the dogma that 'where the degree of facility and lesion is great, the easier it will be to infer circumvention and vice versa'.[43] In this case, the levels of both facility and circumvention were high, while there was also substantial lesion to Euan. He did not receive value from Outlook upon his execution of the indemnities and the all-sums standard security, the loss to him amounting to more than £700,000 as well as the detriment of having granted a security for an unrestricted amount.

Lady Wolffe also found that the documents in question were reducible for fraudulent misrepresentation,[44] while the indemnity agreements could also be struck down for breach of the duties of good faith owed by a creditor to a cautioner under which the former must not mislead the latter whether by positive representation or silence.[45] The stress laid on facility and circumvention in the case is probably because many of the other potentially invalidating actions had been directed more at the Metal Bridge Lindsays than at Euan. It was also not clear exactly what had passed directly between Euan and Mr Fradgley in relation to the documents signed by the former. It therefore made sense to deploy a doctrine of which a key feature was the lack of a need to show a specific act or acts of deceit; circumvention could be inferred from the whole circumstances of the case, including statements made to closely connected third parties (the Metal Bridge Lindsays) of which Euan was well aware. By these deceptive means Outlook had achieved a substantial benefit to the significant detriment of Euan. The context of the business travails of Euan's close family and his awareness of the pressure being placed upon them by Mr Fradgley was a relevant dimension on top of Euan's own obvious vulnerability, of which Mr Fradgley was clearly well aware from his interactions with the family over an extended period.

IV. Force and Fear, Undue Influence, and Facility and Circumvention in Scots Law

There is no sign in Lady Wolffe's opinion that arguments based on either force and fear or on undue influence were advanced before her. Force and fear would probably have been difficult to argue given the lack of authority on economic duress in Scots law. Mr Fradgley's threats were ones that, as a creditor's representative, he was entitled to make, and they did not involve any physical dimension that could amount to 'force'. He was simply exploiting the economic pressure under which the Lindsays in general, and Euan in particular, felt they were labouring. So far as undue influence is concerned, Scots law does not have exclusive

---

[40] *Lindsay's Executor v Outlook* (n 8) [236].
[41] ibid [248].
[42] ibid [247].
[43] Hector L MacQueen and Joe Thomson, *Contract Law in Scotland* (5th edn, Bloomsbury Professional 2020) [5.20]; see also McBryde, *Contract* (n 3) [16.12].
[44] *Lindsay's Executor v Outlook* (n 8) [265].
[45] ibid [259]–[264]. A further argument invoking the principle of mutuality of contract under which a party in breach of contract cannot enforce the obligations of the other party to the contract (ibid [259]) was not pursued in Lady Wolffe's opinion.

categories of relationships to which the doctrine is applied. The Metal Bridge Lindsays had placed a high degree of trust in Mr Fradgley in dealing with their affairs. However, Euan had, to at least some extent, been outside that trusting relationship until 2008, and the evidence about his transactions from that time with Mr Fradgley did not suggest a relationship in which the latter was exercising undue influence rather than simple intimidation.

Lindsay's Executor v Outlook Finance Ltd is unusual, possibly unique, in applying the doctrine of facility and circumvention in a business context. As already noted, the doctrine emerged in the nineteenth century and the cases then are often concerned with issues about the provision of appropriate care for the person suffering from facility. Thus, in the critical case of *Clunie v Stirling*[46] in 1854, the facile person (C) was an army officer forced to retire after suffering a series of paralyzing strokes which left him unable to read; his superior officer (S1), acting while C was unconscious following his second stroke, sold his commission, the proceeds of which were then used (to C's knowledge) to purchase an annuity from S1's son (S2) on terms more advantageous to the latter than to C. After C's death, his brother, as executor-dative and residuary legatee of his estate, successfully sought reduction of the transaction on the grounds of C's facility and S2's circumvention.[47] Three years later, *M'Culloch v M'Crackan*[48] was a dispute about an agreement dividing a deceased's estate between various claimants, giving the elderly and paralyzed pursuer far less than she should have been entitled to. Reduction of the settlement was granted, the circumvention consisting in the aggressive (but false) assertions of another party's solicitor in a meeting the day after the deceased's funeral that his clients were the deceased's heirs and that they would sue to establish that, if it was not accepted by the others. The pursuer had been neither present nor represented at the meeting, although her daughter was there.

Many of the subsequent cases are about wills and trust settlements taking effect after the truster's death and involve intra-familial tensions often resulting from 'the undignified spectacle of a family feud',[49] a pattern that has continued down to the present. Cases about contracts are relatively rare but tend to be of a similar nature. Thus, in *Wheelans v Wheelans*[50] a facile mother transferred her house to one of her sons and left it to him in her will, in a transaction that was successfully challenged on grounds of facility and circumvention by another of her sons after her death. A similar, more recent case is *Matossian v Matossian*.[51] There an elderly lady who was suffering from self-neglect, malnourishment, and poor memory, while also taking strong pain medication, transferred two of her three properties to each of two of her three sons for no consideration while also similarly transferring her whole title, right, and interest in the third property to one of those two sons, she retaining a liferent to let her live there until her death. The transaction took place in the presence of a solicitor who was instructed by one of the sons and who gave the lady no advice. A few days later she executed a will before a different solicitor in which she left a property to each of the three sons, also appointing the third as her executor. The solicitor this time was acting for the third son but did give the lady advice outwith her son's presence.

---

[46] (1854) 17 D 15.

[47] The case is also notable for a judicial expression of horror at the thought that S2 might be taken to have committed fraud: ibid 19–20 (Lord Justice-Clerk Hope).

[48] (1857) 20 D 206.

[49] *Matossian v Matossian* [2016] CSOH 21 [31] (Lord Uist).

[50] 1986 SLT 164. For an unsuccessful claim of this kind see also *O'Neil v O'Neil* [2017] 7 WLUK 30, 2017 GWD 22-361 (Glasgow Sheriff Court).

[51] [2016] CSOH 21.

After the lady's death more than three years later, the third son was able to have the *inter vivos* transfers to his brothers struck down on grounds of their circumvention of his facile mother. Although the transfers had taken place in the presence of a solicitor, he was not the lady's solicitor and had failed to advise her appropriately in the situation. In *MacGilvary v Martin*[52] a widow succeeded in striking down a sale of her home to her daughter made shortly after the death of the former's husband. At the time of the transaction the widow had been in a weak physical and mental state following her bereavement and it was accepted that this could amount to facility. Lord McDonald also stressed that actual deceit by the daughter was not required for there to be circumvention, which could be inferred from the circumstances of the case.

There are some modern non-family cases as well. But these too do not usually involve business transactions or relations. Instead, they tend to concern the befriending of vulnerable individuals by others who then take substantial control of their lives. In *Anderson v Beacon Fellowship*[53] the owner (A) of a hotel which included a hall rented, then sold, the hall to a religious fellowship. A suffered from a manic-depressive illness for which he was taking medication. During the period between the conclusion of the contract for the sale of the hall and its transfer to the fellowship, A received a number of visits from its pastor and other members, during which they engaged in religious practices with him, purported to heal him, preached to him that money was valueless, and exhorted him to renounce all of his possessions. A then made donations to the fellowship totalling £23,100. It was held that these averments were sufficient to support a claim for reduction of the donations on the grounds of facility and circumvention. Lord McCluskey emphasized that there was no need to show actual deceit to establish circumvention. In *Thomson v Warwick*[54] a farm owned by three elderly brothers, all in deteriorating health and at least one suffering from dementia, had been transferred to the defenders for no consideration. The defenders had befriended the brothers and gradually taken control of their affairs, including receiving appointment as attorneys for them. The documentation for the transfer of the farm was prepared by a solicitor who had previously acted for the defenders and had been appointed earlier to replace the brothers' long-standing solicitor, with the latter receiving no explanation for this. Sheriff Matheson held that the transfer should be struck down on the grounds of the two brothers' facility and the defenders' circumvention, plus their undue influence in relation to the third brother.

An obvious reason why facility and circumvention cases do not concern business or commercial relationships is because the doctrine is concerned with interpersonal relations of one sort or another between human beings. Business relations on the other hand are typically between companies, the personality of which is to be distinguished from that of their members, their employees, or anyone else involved in their activities. The principle was famously stated by Lord Chancellor Halsbury in *Salomon v A Salomon & Co Ltd*: a company 'must be treated like any other independent person with its rights and liabilities appropriate to itself . . ., whatever may have been the ideas or schemes of those who brought it into existence'.[55] So just as a company cannot commit criminal offences of which it is incapable

---

[52] 1986 SLT 89.
[53] 1992 SLT 111.
[54] [2022] SC INV 31, 2021 WL 09541562.
[55] *Salomon v A Salomon & Co Ltd* [1897] AC 22 (HL), 30-1.

14 FACILITY, CIRCUMVENTION, ECONOMIC DURESS, CORPORATE VEIL

as an entity, or marry, or adopt children, or make a will, or experience emotion,[56] it seems impossible that a company as such could ever suffer from facility; and this whether or not that is the condition of any of the individuals connected with it, even those who constitute its ruling mind.

What would the position have been if Euan and William Lindsay had formed a company to own and manage the farm at Harperfield rather than the partnership D M Lindsay which simply managed the farm? The evidence in the case shows that Euan consulted William before committing to the grant of the standard security over Harperfield. Suppose that that had happened as a decision of the directors of the company; would it then have been possible for the company to plead Euan's facility to escape the commitment? The answer would seem to be clearly no. Likewise if the partnership had owned the farm. By virtue of the separate personality it enjoys under Scots law,[57] a partnership decision to encumber its property would not be open to challenge on the basis that one of the partners had been facile and subject to relevant third-party circumvention at the time, since that partner is not the contracting party.[58] *Thomson v Warwick*, it may be noted in this connection, does not seem to have involved any question of partnership property; the brothers were simply co-owners of the farm. The position might be different, however, where a director or a partner was acting individually and within their authority as an agent of the company or firm. Then questions about their position in relation to the third parties with whom they dealt could be relevantly raised.[59] In partnership, likewise, the partners' mutual fiduciary duties might require one subject to similar pressure to disclose that when involved in a partnership's business decision.[60]

In the light of this, it may also be asked whether a company or a partnership as such can be a victim of undue influence or force and fear. In Scots law undue influence stems from the natural affection or trust which one person places in another rather than from any mental or physical weakness from which that person suffers. Herein lies the distinction of undue influence from facility and circumvention.[61] The Scottish case law does not show any examples of companies or partnerships as such being subject to undue influence in this sense. A third party who takes factual control of a company's affairs without having the legal authority to do so as a director may however be found to be a shadow or *de facto* director, as with Mr Fradgley in *Lindsay's Executor v Outlook Finance*, and have the fiduciary and other duties of a director placed upon him as a result.[62] This looks like a more than adequate substitute for the doctrine of undue influence.

---

[56] Hector L MacQueen and Lord Eassie (eds), *Gloag & Henderson: The Law of Scotland* (15th edn, W Green 2022) (hereafter MacQueen and Eassie, *Gloag & Henderson*) [46.07]; Neil MacCormick, *Institutions of Law: An Essay in Legal Theory* (OUP 2007) (hereafter MacCormick, *Institutions*) 95.

[57] MacQueen and Eassie, *Gloag & Henderson* (n 56) [45.11–45.22]. See further MacCormick, *Institutions* (n 56) 81; Laura Macgregor, 'Partnerships and Legal Personality: Cautionary Tales from Scotland' (2020) 20 JCLS 237; Jonathan Hardman, 'Reconceptualising Scottish Limited Partnership Law' (2020) 20 JCLS 1; Peter Hemphill, 'The Personality of Partnerships in Scotland' [1984] JR 208.

[58] Third-party pressure on a contracting party may invalidate a resultant contract: see eg *TSB v Balloch* 1983 SLT 240.

[59] Thus, for example, the actions of Mr Fradgley in relation to the Lindsays could be attributed to Outlook Finance as his principal. The agent cannot however be treated as invariably the principal's *alter ego*: see Laura Macgregor, *The Law of Agency in Scotland* (W Green/Scottish Universities Law Institute 2013) [2.04]–[2.05]. See further text accompanying n 69.

[60] MacQueen and Eassie, *Gloag & Henderson* (n 56) [45.23].

[61] McBryde, *Contract* (n 3) [16.33].

[62] MacQueen and Eassie, *Gloag & Henderson* (n 56) [46.64]; Companies Act 2006 ss 250, 251. See text accompanying n 38.

Regarding force and fear, the terminology of 'fear' is as difficult as 'facility' to apply to a partnership or a company as an entity; but if the concept is instead expressed as 'extortion', 'compulsion', or, perhaps, 'duress', the difficulty is at least considerably reduced, if not removed altogether. But there have not been many cases where a company was held able to escape a contract on this ground.[63] One is *Sutherland v Montrose Fishing Co Ltd*,[64] where it was held that trade union pressure on a company as an employer amounted to force and fear, invalidating a resultant contract. *Euan Wallace & Partners v Westscot Homes plc*[65] was a case between a partnership (EWP) and a company (WH) whose managing director (EW) was also a partner in the firm. The question however was whether force and fear had led to the repayment of a fee paid to EWP by WH for professional services rendered by EW in his partnership capacity. The company board had not authorized payment of the fee, having assumed that EW's services had been rendered in his capacity as managing director rather than as a partner. The question of possible breaches of the Companies Act was raised at a subsequent meeting of the directors along with the possibility of reporting the matter to the local procurator fiscal. EW, as a partner in EWP, agreed to make the repayment following this meeting. It subsequently emerged that the initial payment to EW was not unlawful and he was not liable to criminal charges. It was held that EWH's repayment was not made subject to force and fear. Since the payment had not been properly authorized in the first place, WH was entitled to its reimbursement. The threats at the meeting had been made in good faith and were legitimate in the circumstances. The judge thus did not need to decide whether it was EWP or EW who had been subjected to force and fear but seemed to accept that EWP could make the challenge under that head.

Facility and circumvention could be invoked in *Lindsay's Executor v Outlook Finance* because, although a number of the family members involved in the various farming businesses had made use of corporate vehicles for those purposes, the circumvention victim Euan owned the land over which the security was granted and his nephew William had never been more than a partner in the business the two men ran on the farm. Although clearly Euan was intellectually and emotionally involved in all the Lindsay family businesses, he was throughout a separate person who nonetheless at a moment of crisis provided the finance which enabled MBL to keep going at that time. The pressure under which the businesses laboured fell upon Euan as well, but in his own right, so to speak, and in that right after his death his executor could also undo its adverse results for him and his estate. A somewhat similar situation arose in *Thomson v Warwick* and it is perhaps no coincidence that a farming business was involved there as well, albeit the transactions in question were not the product of any specific business concern for the three brothers.[66] Their concern was about how they might be cared for in their declining years, with perhaps additionally an element of worry over succession planning in the farm.

---

[63] Du Plessis, *Compulsion and Restitution* (n 3) 69 draws attention to *Wolfson v Edelman* 1952 SLT (Sh Ct) 97, where threats from a creditor to have a company's transactions examined, bring it into bankruptcy, and hold its directors personally liable induced a director to make payments to the creditor. The former's (rather than his company's) later attempt to have the payments reduced on the grounds of force and fear failed.

[64] *Sutherland v Montrose* (n 3).

[65] 2000 SLT 327.

[66] Compare the factual background in this case and *Lindsay's Executor v Outlook Finance* with *Lloyds Bank v Bundy* [1975] 2 QB 326 (CA) (elderly farmer mortgages farm to support son's business indebtedness to their common bank; undue influence by bank through its representative who knew that the farmer would do as he was asked).

V. Concluding Thoughts on the *Times Travel* Case

We may now reflect on *Times Travel Ltd v Pakistan International Airline Corp* in the light of these Scottish cases and in particular *Lindsay's Executor v Outlook Finance*. First, and following the immediately preceding discussion, *Times Travel* makes clear (as do all the preceding cases on economic or lawful act duress) that the English courts have no difficulty in holding that a company may be a victim of such duress. Indeed, as Jonathan Morgan remarks, 'economic duress has largely developed in commercial cases'.[67] This reflects a shift (as long ago suggested by Ewan McKendrick) away from a focus on the victim's consent as the basis for such a plea to look instead at the behaviour of the other party and whether that induced the victim's subsequent action in entering the contract. But companies as such are rarely if ever direct victims of duress of the person or, indeed, of undue influence, actual or presumed.[68] This seems almost to follow from the nature of the doctrines as mainly if not exclusively applicable to human rather than artificial persons. The same surely applies to the doctrine of unconscionable bargains as outlined by Lord Hodge. This makes it very doubtful whether any of these doctrines can be usefully deployed to tell us whether lawful acts pressurizing another non-human person in a commercial relationship are illegitimate. The analogies involved are simply inappropriate or even inapt. Accepting for the purposes of the argument here that Lord Burrows' test of the perpetrator's subjective bad faith leads to too much uncertainty to be acceptable either, it seems that we have to look still further for solutions to the problem of lawful act economic duress.

The law of business entities—companies, partnerships, and agents—might perhaps be deployed instead in at least some cases. As suggested above for Scots law, where a director was acting individually but within their authority as an agent of the company and was subjected to personal duress or undue influence in that role, that might conceivably affect the validity of the resultant contract as binding the company.[69] An English example is *Mutual Finance Ltd v John Wetton & Sons Ltd*.[70] Here a director of a family company acting within his authority signed on behalf of the company a guarantee under the threat that his brother (who had previously been a director) would be prosecuted in respect of a forged signature on an earlier guarantee. The first director signed because he feared the ill effects that the shock of a prosecution would cause to his father, who was already in bad health. It was held that the company could set the guarantee aside on the grounds of undue influence; duress was in the judge's view confined to threats to the person, which was not applicable to the circumstances of the case.

The directors who sit on the board when it makes decisions about contracts are also under statutory and common law duties to the company and the body of shareholders which may provide a way of tackling the scenario where the board (in whole or in part) has

---

[67] Jonathan Morgan, *Great Debates in Contract Law* (3rd edn, Palgrave Macmillan 2020) (hereafter Morgan, *Great Debates*) 218.

[68] Edwin Peel has alerted me to *Libyan Investment Authority v Goldman Sachs International* [2016] EWHC 2530 (Ch), in which the court rejected the authority's claim that it made certain trades in 'synthetic derivatives' on a 'put option' and a 'forward' basis subject to the defendant company's undue influence and that the trades were unconscionable bargains. Rose J held that the parties' relationship 'did not go beyond the normal cordial and mutually beneficial relationship that grows up between a bank and a client [and that] Goldman Sachs did not become a trusted adviser or a "man of affairs" for the LIA' ([427]).

[69] See text accompanying n 59.

[70] [1937] 2 KB 389 (KBD), cited by Lord Hodge and Lord Burrows in *Times Travel* (n 6) [7], [89].

laboured under non-economic duress or undue influence from a third party with whom the contract is to be made. The relevant duties include promoting the company's success, exercising independent judgement, avoiding conflicts of interest, and not accepting benefits from third parties. Any contract where the directors failed to declare their interests may be challengeable.[71] All this seems inconsistent with a director keeping quiet about being subject to inappropriate pressure from an outside source when the board is deciding whether or not to enter contracts.

There is a lack of either English or Scottish precedent for all this, however, and once more we are faced with the problem of uncertainty. A merit of Lord Hodge's approach is that uncertainty is reduced by the existence of a body of precedent on the issues; the problem that remains is the need to reason by inappropriate or inapt analogies of companies (or partnerships) with the human individuals involved in these precedents. That difficulty might be resoluble, however, if the doctrines could be applied in this context not to the business entity itself, but to the human beings who are in fact the entity's controlling minds. In the *Times Travel* case, this would be the Ahmads, who owned and ran TT. When otherwise could the tests provided by undue influence and unconscionable bargains be relevant to a non-human contracting party unless such an inquiry into the people behind the corporate veil is permitted? The Supreme Court was admittedly concerned not to allow too much room to lawful act duress; but it also did not wish to exclude altogether the possibility of its being a ground of challenge to a commercial transaction. That being so, it seems that the law is still in need of some development.

A starting point may be the question whether the circumstances are such as to justify piercing the corporate veil to look at the true facts behind it. But the leading case on veil-piercing, *Prest v Petrodel Resources Ltd*,[72] suggests that this may only take place in very limited circumstances and where it is necessary because no other remedy is available. Lord Sumption justified the survival of such a doctrine on the basis that 'the recognition of a limited power to pierce the corporate veil in carefully defined circumstances is necessary if the law is not to be disarmed in the face of abuse'.[73] He defined the power thus:

> I conclude that there is a limited principle of English law which applies when a person is under an existing legal obligation or liability or subject to an existing legal restriction which he deliberately evades or whose enforcement he deliberately frustrates by interposing a company under his control. The court may then pierce the corporate veil for the purpose, and only for the purpose, of depriving the company or its controller of the advantage that they would otherwise have obtained by the company's separate legal personality. The principle is properly described as a limited one, because in almost every case where the test is satisfied, the facts will in practice disclose a legal relationship between the company and its controller which will make it unnecessary to pierce the corporate veil.[74]

---

[71] For the foregoing see Companies Act 2006 ss 170–77; and further Paul L Davies, Sarah Worthington, and Christopher Hare, *Gower's Principles of Modern Company Law* (11th edn, Sweet & Maxwell 2021) ch 10.

[72] [2013] UKSC 34, [2013] 2 AC 415 (hereafter *Prest v Petrodel*).

[73] ibid [27].

[74] ibid [35]. For application of *Prest v Petrodel* in the Scottish courts see *Ashley v The Scottish Football Association Ltd* [2016] CSOH 78 [30] (Lord Brodie) and *ICU (Europe) Ltd v Ibrahim* [2020] SAC (Civ) 20.

18 FACILITY, CIRCUMVENTION, ECONOMIC DURESS, CORPORATE VEIL

Our problem, however, is not that of a person using the company to evade or frustrate an obligation which would otherwise fall upon him or her. It is rather one where the corporate veil hides the extent to which one or more of the persons directing the company has been subject to improper third-party pressure of one kind or another in order to bring about a contract between the third party and the company.

The problem would also not seem to fall readily within a second category of case identified by Lord Sumption, namely those where the interposition of a company or companies conceals the identity of the 'real actors'; as he noted, this

> will not deter the courts from identifying them, assuming that their identity is legally relevant. In these cases the court is not disregarding the 'façade', but only looking behind it to discover the facts which the corporate structure is concealing.[75]

This may be referred to as 'lifting' rather than 'piercing' the veil (although Lord Sumption does not use this terminology). Again, the focus is on the manoeuvres of the 'real actors' in the company who are acting with the intention of concealing their identity behind the company façade. That was not the position with the Ahmads and TT, however, or indeed of the Lindsays with their various companies (and partnerships) at Metal Bridge and Harperfield. But we may wonder whether, as a result of this limitation, the law is still being potentially disarmed in the face of abuses behind the corporate veil. In this context Lord Denning's famous dictum, 'fraud unravels everything', is quoted by Lord Sumption;[76] but our problem does not necessarily involve fraud, at least in the narrow sense in which that term is now understood in modern English and Scots law.

In *Prest v Petrodel* Lord Mance expressed some caution in adopting Lord Sumption's narrow definition of when the corporate veil might be pierced, noting that '[i]t is however often dangerous to seek to foreclose all possible future situations which may arise and I would not wish to do so'.[77] Lord Neuberger, while doubtful of the concept of piercing the veil, stated that it 'represents a potentially valuable judicial tool to undo wrongdoing in some cases, where no other principle is available'.[78] Lord Walker of Gestingthorpe thought that 'piercing the veil' was not a doctrine of law at all but rather 'simply a label . . . to describe the disparate occasions on which some rule of law produces apparent exceptions to the principle of the separate juristic personality of a body corporate'.[79] These admittedly slender threads may still leave the door open for the courts to recognize the potential relevance of the position of the 'real actors' who, far from using corporate form to hide themselves or perpetrate reprehensible activities without personal liability, are by it left unable to bring into court personal factors which have had a bearing on the conclusion of a contract between the company and a third party.

Finally worth remembering is a dictum of Lord Wilberforce in *Ebrahimi v Westbourne Galleries Ltd*, made about the court's statutory power to wind up a company if was 'just and equitable' to do so but, it is suggested, capable of a wider application:

---

[75] *Prest v Petrodel* (n 72) [28].
[76] *Lazarus Estates v Beasley* [1956] 1 QB 702 (CA), 712; *Prest v Petrodel* (n 72) [18]. See also Lord Neuberger, ibid [83].
[77] *Prest v Petrodel* (n 72) [100]. Lord Clarke of Stone-Ebony agrees with this statement (ibid [103]).
[78] ibid [80].
[79] ibid [106].

[A] limited company is more than a mere legal entity, with a personality in law of its own: there is room in company law for recognition of the fact that behind it, or amongst it, there are individuals, with rights, expectations and obligations inter se which are not necessarily submerged in the company structure . . . The 'just and equitable' provision . . . does, as equity always does, enable the court to subject the exercise of legal rights to equitable considerations; considerations, that is, of a personal character arising between one individual and another, which may make it unjust, or inequitable, to insist on legal rights, or to exercise them in a particular way.[80]

Despite the emphasis of the majority in the *Times Travel* case on the tests of unconscionable conduct found in undue influence and unconscionable bargains as the basis for a finding of lawful act duress holding lawful act duress illegitimate, there was nothing before the Supreme Court that would have allowed consideration of the Ahmads' personal states of mind at the time they transacted with PIAC. The courts below made no exploration of the personal effects upon the Ahmads of PIAC's behaviour; Warren J merely accepted that PIAC's reduction of the ticket allocation caused both men, in their own words, 'immense stress'.[81] We learn nothing about their age or health, or the ways in which the stress manifested itself before the decision was made to accept the new contract. The first instance judgment tells of Asrar Ahmad's initial meeting with a local representative of PIAC in Birmingham (Mr Shah) at which it was stated that failure to sign the new agreements would have consequences over which the representative had no control; that is, they would flow from decisions made at a higher level in PIAC's management hierarchy. Asrar was not allowed to take away from that meeting a copy of the new agreement in order to discuss it with his son and seek legal advice.[82] A further meeting took place some days later at the TT office involving not only Mr Shah but also his successor in office, a more senior PIAC manager (Mr Baber). The threats made previously were repeated and this time the Ahmads, already aware that their business was being seriously damaged by the much reduced supply of tickets from PIAC, bowed to the pressure and signed the agreement.[83] It may be observed parenthetically that the representatives' conduct is reminiscent in some ways of Mr Fradgley's behaviour towards the Lindsays from 2008 on, except that the statements about what PIAC's senior management would decide in the event of the Ahmads not signing the new agreement were most likely true. On the face of it, however, the Ahmads' behaviour in response to the pressure from the PIAC was entirely rational; if they wished to continue in business, there was no practical alternative beyond submission and taking what was on offer from PIAC. But what could have been relevant inquiries into their states of mind had the law allowed them were never made.

It is not suggested here that *Times Travel* was wrongly decided on its known facts. But the case does exemplify the very exposed position of small businesses (by any definition) dealing and contracting with much larger ones. That may be a matter of legitimate public

---

[80] *Ebrahimi v Westbourne Galleries Ltd* [1973] AC 360 (HL), 379. The current provision on just and equitable winding-up is Insolvency Act 1986 s 122(1)(g).

[81] *Times Travel (UK) Ltd v Pakistan International Airline Corp* [2017] EWHC 1367 (Ch) [59]–[60].

[82] ibid [62].

[83] ibid [63]–[66], [108]–[121]. Warren J also accepted allegations about what was said at the second meeting with regard to the incentive commissions that PIAC would pay to agents like TT for sales made after the new agreement was signed. I do not deal with these here, although they were probably a factor inducing TT to sign and may have involved deceptive behaviour.

concern. The All-Party Parliamentary Group on Fair Business Banking (hereafter 'APPG') was allowed to intervene in the case.[84] The Supreme Court judgments make no direct reference to that intervention but the commentary on the decision made later by the APPG's legal team reveals that the intervenor's argument was based on a requirement of good faith in bargaining.[85] The commentary notes:

> Members of the APPG had long been concerned about the way in which banks sometimes exploit the strength of their bargaining position as against small and medium-sized business customers. In particular, banks have often pressured customers to sign away claims and complaints, or to enter into new and more onerous terms, or both, as the price of avoiding enforcement action and enjoying continued banking support.

It then adds:

> Many will find it disappointing the Court has given parties a licence to make bad faith demands backed up by lawful threats when, in the banking context, there is such an inequality in parties' contractual positions.

The commentary concludes: 'This reinforces the case for bank customers to have fuller and more robust protection, especially SMEs who are in vulnerable positions, yet largely outside the FCA's regulatory perimeter.'[86] The comment might well be extended beyond bank customers to small businesses dealing with much larger ones in general.[87] There is another All-Party Parliamentary Group on Small and Micro Businesses which does not yet seem to have taken an interest in this specific issue. But its existence does further demonstrate a concern across the political spectrum about the difficult positions in which small businesses frequently find themselves in dealing with more economically powerful organizations.

The suggestion made here is that in this regard more could be made of the Supreme Court's founding of lawful act economic duress on the doctrines of unfair bargaining. They are after all founded on cases about individuals, not companies, and small businesses are often little more than people working for themselves in corporate form. The courts ought to consider whether the personal circumstances of these human beings fit into these doctrines in order to apply them in a corporate context. If this requires any development of the law on piercing or lifting the corporate veil, dicta in *Prest v Petrodel* might allow that, or at least not prevent it. If it was so, the law in both Scotland and England would be a little better armed against abuse of power in commercial relationships.

Another element of reform might be a return to Ewan McKendrick's suggestion about drawing together the doctrines of duress, undue influence, unconscionable bargains, and (in Scotland) facility and circumvention under a head such as pre-contractual procedural unfairness or perhaps, as in other common law jurisdictions, unconscionability. In the light

---

[84] For more on the APPG see its website: <www.appgbanking.org.uk/>, accessed 30 November 2022.

[85] See <www.hausfeld.com/en-gb/what-we-think/perspectives-blogs/supreme-court-curtails-the-scope-of-economic-duress/>, accessed 30 November 2022. I was first alerted to this note by Hugh Beale.

[86] The FCA is the Financial Conduct Authority.

[87] For example, standard practice in franchise agreements makes renewal dependent on the franchisee's waiver of all and any extant/prior claims: see John Pratt, *Franchising: Law and Practice* (Sweet & Maxwell 2021) [9.092] (clause 3.2.10 of a model franchising agreement). The author notes that 'This clause can work unfairly for the Franchisee who may have to decide whether to sue for antecedent breaches or to renew'.

of the discussion above, however, we might wish to keep the unfairness of the result achieved by the pressure exercised as at least an adminicle of evidence in justifying the court's invalidation of the contract.[88] It clearly is a substantive requirement in facility and circumvention.[89] In Scotland consideration might alternatively be given to bringing undue influence and facility and circumvention back within the embrace of a doctrine of fraud no longer confined to intentional conduct on the part of the fraudster. Whether either approach could be achieved judicially as part of common law development in England and Scotland must be doubted; but, so unified, they might perhaps be more readily applied to business entities. On the other hand, the intense focus upon particular kinds of facts and relationships under the law's present fragmented structures may be thought even more worthwhile to keep if they are to be a basis for undoing corporate transactions.[90]

---

[88] See also the arguments on this of Mindy Chen-Wishart, 'Undue Influence: Vindicating Relationships of Influence' (2006) 59 CLP 231; 'Undue Influence: Beyond Impaired Consent and Wrongdoing towards a Relational Analysis' in Andrew Burrows and Lord Rodger of Earlsferry (eds), *Mapping the Law: Essays in Memory of Peter Birks* (OUP 2006) ch 11; see also Morgan, *Great Debates* (n 67) 232–34 (summarizing academic discussion of the topic).

[89] See text between nn 23 and 24.

[90] In defence of the existing structures see eg Rick Bigwood, *Exploitative Contracts* (OUP 2003) chs 6, 7, and 8.

2

Good Faith in English Contract Law: Lessons from Comparative Law?

JOHN CARTWRIGHT

I. Introduction

The place of good faith within English contract law is a topic which Ewan McKendrick has explored in his published writing over the years, not only in his own general works on contract law,[1] but also in lectures, articles, and his contributions to other books.[2] As I have re-read his writing on the subject, I have been reminded not only of Ewan's masterful communication of the nuances of English law, but also of his sensitivity in considering the role that comparative law might play in assessing, criticizing, and even developing a controversial issue within national law.[3] This should not of course, be surprising. Trained first in another system—Scots law—which (at least in its law of contract) is grounded in the civil law tradition, before he then devoted his career principally to the study of English law, Ewan has a natural sensitivity to the significance of differences not just in the detail of the legal rules in different legal systems, but also—and more important—in *mentality* between systems of different traditions. In this chapter I should like to discuss further the general question of the role that comparative law can play in any potential development of good faith within English contract law. In this discussion, much of what I say will reflect ideas that Ewan has already set out in his own work, and I should say at the outset that I am in very general agreement with his writing.

---

[1] Ewan McKendrick, *Contract Law* (15th edn, Bloomsbury 2023) [12.10]; Ewan McKendrick, *Contract Law: Text, Cases and Materials* (10th edn, OUP 2022) ch 15.

[2] See eg Ewan McKendrick, 'Good Faith: A Matter of Principle?' in Angelo DM Forte (ed), *Good Faith in Contract and Property Law* (Hart Publishing 1999) (hereafter McKendrick, 'Good Faith: A Matter of Principle'); Ewan McKendrick, 'Good Faith in the Performance of a Contract in English Law' in Larry DiMatteo and Martin Hogg (eds), *Comparative Contract Law: British and American Perspectives* (OUP 2016) (hereafter McKendrick, 'Good Faith in Performance'); Ewan McKendrick and Qiao Liu, 'Good Faith in Contract Performance in the Chinese and Common Laws' in Larry DiMatteo and Lei Chen (eds), *Chinese Contract Law: Civil and Common Law Perspectives* (CUP 2018).

[3] See, in particular, McKendrick, 'Good Faith in Performance' (n 2) 198–99, discussing *Yam Seng Pte v International Trade Corp* [2013] EWHC 111 (QB); [2013] 1 Lloyd's Rep 526 (hereafter *Yam Seng*) ('The present case illustrates the important role which comparative law can play in the development of the law within national legal systems. Where a legal system finds itself significantly out of line with the experience of other legal systems, a recognition of the existence of that difference may encourage that legal system to re-examine its own position. This is not to say that legal systems should blindly follow the views of the majority of nation states: there may be good reasons for a particular legal system to adopt its own distinctive legal rule, but that difference should be justified, not simply asserted').

John Cartwright, *Good Faith in English Contract Law: Lessons from Comparative Law?* In: *Shaping the Law of Obligations.*
Edited by: Edwin Peel and Rebecca Probert, Oxford University Press. © John Cartwright 2023.
DOI: 10.1093/oso/9780198889762.003.0002

II. Learning from Comparative Law—in General

Before considering whether comparative law can teach us anything about how to re-think the place of good faith within English contract law, we should first consider in general terms the appropriate role for comparisons with other systems when we are assessing particular doctrines or rules within our own system. This is not the place to engage in a broad discussion of the functions and aims of comparative law,[4] but we can note that comparison of law and legal systems takes different forms, and may be undertaken by different legal actors and for different legal purposes. It may, for example, be purely scientific research undertaken for its own sake, or it may be designed to map similarities and differences between legal systems to be used as a tool for others, such as legislators in deciding how to form, or re-form, rules in their own systems.[5] Comparative study may be undertaken with a view to facilitating grand long-term aims of producing a harmonization of legal systems, or even their unification into a single legal framework.[6] However, for our purposes, we need to focus on a narrower, more particular, context in which comparative law may be useful: where the legal actors[7] within one system may draw on the experience of other systems in order to assess a particular legal rule or doctrine within their own system and, if appropriate, recommend or implement its reform.

There is a long tradition of legal systems learning from the experience of others in their development of particular rules. Indeed, the interaction between legal systems throughout history is a story of the development of individual systems, with the benefit of the experience of others, to the extent that even though we may try to categorize legal systems into groups, or 'families', at least for the purpose of creating order for the manageable study of the mass of individual legal systems,[8] this is at most a rough-and-ready solution, and some would say that it hides the underlying reality that legal systems are not as individual, internally unified, and independent as is commonly thought.[9]

---

[4] A great deal has been written on this. For a classic discussion, see K Zweigert and H Kötz, *An Introduction to Comparative Law* (Tony Weir tr, 3rd edn, OUP 1998) (hereafter Zweigert and Kötz, *Introduction*) ch 2. There is also much useful material in Mathias Reimann and Reinhard Zimmermann (eds), *The Oxford Handbook of Comparative Law* (2nd edn, OUP 2019) (hereafter Reimann and Zimmermann, *Oxford Handbook*); Mauro Bussani and Ugo Mattei (eds), *The Cambridge Companion to Comparative Law* (CUP 2012); Esin Örücü and David Nelken, *Comparative Law: A Handbook* (Hart 2007).

[5] Mapping the law is the aim of the *Common Core of European Private Law* project: Mauro Bussani and Ugo Mattei, 'Preface: The Context' in Mauro Bussani and Ugo Mattei, *The Common Core of European Private Law* (Kluwer Law International 2003) 1–2. For the first published volume of this project, see Reinhard Zimmermann and Simon Whittaker (eds), *Good Faith in European Contract Law* (CUP 2000) (hereafter Zimmermann and Whittaker, *Good Faith*).

[6] See eg the very significant comparative studies undertaken by the Commission on European Contract Law, the Study Group on a European Civil Code and the Research Group on EC Private Law (Acquis Group) with a view to possible harmonization or unification of private law in Europe: Ole Lando and Hugh Beale (eds), *Principles of European Contract Law, Parts I and II* (Kluwer Law International 2000); Ole Lando, Eric Clive, André Prüm, and Reinhard Zimmermann (eds), *Principles of European Contract Law, Pt III* (Kluwer Law International 2003); Christian von Bar and Eric Clive (eds), *Principles, Definitions and Model Rules of European Private Law: Draft Common Frame of Reference (DCFR)* (Sellier 2009) (hereafter von Bar and Clive, *DCFR*).

[7] This may include those charged with considering possible law reform (such as the Law Commission in England and Wales), as well as those with power to implement reforms (such as legislators in any legal system, as well as judges to the extent that their legal system empowers them to develop the law).

[8] Zweigert and Kötz, *Introduction* (n 4) 63–64. Authors differ about how to categorize legal 'families': eg Zweigert and Kötz, *Introduction* (n 4) ch 5; René David, Camille Jauffret-Spinosi, and Marie Goré, *Les grands systèmes de droit contemporains* (12th edn, Dalloz 2016).

[9] James Gordley, 'Comparative Law and Legal History' in Reimann and Zimmermann, *Oxford Handbook* (n 4) 761–62.

The reform of internal rules within one legal system in light of the rules of another legal system can take different forms. The most extreme form may appear to involve a straightforward borrowing of a rule from another system, either to fill a gap[10] or to replace an existing internal rule which is perceived to be unsatisfactory. Such borrowings are sometimes referred to as legal 'transplants',[11] a metaphor which is helpful in warning of the associated risks. Before a medical transplant can be undertaken, careful checks must be undertaken to ensure that the recipient body can properly—safely—receive the donor organ. The same is true of a legal rule borrowed from another system: legal systems have their own, individual organic structures which may be compatible with some transplants but not others. One significant role for comparative law is to assess such compatibilities: understanding the place of the proposed legal rule in the context of its own ('donor') legal system, to see whether it will fit into the other ('recipient') legal system—or, at least, what the implications would be for the recipient system if it were to be incorporated. In reality, direct transplantation of legal rules is rarely appropriate, even between donor and recipient systems that appear to have very similar foundations, or even a direct common heritage. When systems become independent, they start to develop differently. An example within the civil law systems is the contract law of France and Belgium, which originally shared a common text, the *Code Napoléon*, although the judicial interpretation of the text was not identical and over the years there were some (different) legislative amendments in each jurisdiction. Recently, however, both systems have reformed their contract law in fundamentally different ways.[12] Similarly, systems which share the common law tradition cannot be assumed to be so similar that legal rules can be borrowed and transplanted without at least some adaptation to the particular circumstances of the recipient system. Although common law systems share, in broad terms, a common methodology in the judicial development of the law to the extent that it has been received independently of legislative intervention, there are differences between the systems—not only in their substantive legal rules, which in some common law jurisdictions may have been developed by the courts or by legislation in very different directions and for different reasons, but also in their legal frameworks, which may set different constraints not only on the courts but even on the legislator in their freedom to develop the law.[13] The comparative study of common law is an important subject in itself. But for our purpose, we should note that the reference to how any other legal system—even a common law system—deals with a legal rule under study in our own system has to be made with caution, remembering that there may be questions of compatibility of the legal rule within our own system.

[10] Legal systems may consider borrowing in order to fill gaps during their more formative periods, such as in the nineteenth century in the case of English contract law: David Ibbetson, *A Historical Introduction to the Law of Obligations* (OUP 2001) ch 12; AWB Simpson, 'Innovation in Nineteenth Century Contract Law' (1975) 91 LQR 247.

[11] Alan Watson, *Legal Transplants: An Approach to Comparative Law* (2nd edn, University of Georgia Press 1993); Michele Graziadei, 'Comparative Law, Transplants, and Receptions' in Reimann and Zimmermann, *Oxford Handbook* (n 4) ch 16.

[12] The reform of the French law of contract was effected by *Ordonnance* n° 2016-131 of 10 February 2016 (in force from 1 October 2016), with certain revisions made by *Loi* n° 2018-287 of 20 April 2018 (in force from 1 October 2018). The reform of the Belgian law of contract was effected by a *loi* of 28 April 2022 (in force from 1 January 2023).

[13] The constitutional framework of a legal system (civil law or common law) may be more or less relevant to the development of private law, including contract law; see Luca Siliquini-Cinelli and Andrew Hutchison (eds), *The Constitutional Dimension of Contract Law: A Comparative Perspective* (Springer 2017).

26 GOOD FAITH IN ENGLISH CONTRACT LAW

If we cannot expect simply to borrow rules from even closely related systems of our own tradition, it should be obvious that there are even greater difficulties in borrowing rules from systems of a different tradition—such as in English law borrowing rules in the form developed within a civil law jurisdiction. There are significant differences in the ways in which common lawyers and civil lawyers reason in finding the law, and even in the ways in which common law systems and civil law systems state the law. Again, not all civil law systems are identical in this; but the tendency in civil law systems is to state the law in broad, general principles rather than in more particular detail, and their courts are apparently comfortable in starting from such general statements of principle in order to reason to the particular case. English law, by contrast, is more inclined to state rules of law, and develop new rules, in more concrete terms. Legislation is often more detailed and specific than the equivalent text found in a codified civil law system.[14] And at least in relation to rules originating in the common law case law, rather than in a legislative text, the English judges' process of reasoning finds the answer to a new case through existing, individual cases which have individual authority, but within the limits of their own individual context (most notably, the facts of the case). Even where the English judges appear to build a general principle out of the existing case law, this is seen as the exception, and sometimes even an illusion.[15]

This is not, of course, to deny the valuable role that the study of other legal systems can play in helping the legal actors in any system to decide whether to reform their own legal rules, and (if so) how to do so. The lesson, though, is that it has to be done with care, working out which rules of another system can be considered relevant at all for the purpose, and then realizing that the context of the rule within that other system is crucial to understanding whether it is appropriate to adopt the rule and (even if it is appropriate) to understanding how it can be adapted so as to fit. In relation to potential legal transplants, the application of comparative law requires an understanding of the methodology, as well as the substantive detail, of both the donor and the recipient systems. Of course, whether the legal actor considering the potential reform is a reform body, the court, or the legislator, the key question is how the new rule will fit with its own (recipient) system, which will be fully understood by the actor in question. But this inevitable familiarity with the recipient system can be misleading: if the inspiration for reform is the internal rule of another system, it is necessary to seek to understand what it is that is being proposed to be transplanted, and this requires an understanding about the place of the rule within the donor system, to understand fully what might be involved in its transplant. This is particularly so if the justification for the reform is not purely internal and domestic, but to bring some degree of harmony in the relations between the legal systems. This now takes us naturally to think about the particular topic of this chapter: the role of good faith within English contract law, where some, at least, of the impetus for reform appears to be the view that English law should accept a more significant role for a general principle of good faith for the reason that many other legal systems already do so. Or, as Leggatt J said in 2013, if English law refuses to recognize a general obligation of

---

[14] For an illustration of different legislative provisions on third party rights in contract, see John Cartwright, *Contract Law: An Introduction to the English Law of Contract for the Civil Lawyer* (4th edn, Hart 2023) 48–50 (although note that the French provisions referred to there were replaced in 2016: see n 12).

[15] cf McKendrick, 'A Matter of Principle?' (n 2) 46 ('English lawyers generally, and English contract lawyers in particular, have a deep-seated distrust of general principles . . . Perhaps it is not too much of an exaggeration to conclude that one of the reasons why all English law students know about *Donoghue v Stevenson* [1932] AC 562 is because it is atypical: it is a rare example of a judge seeking to deduce a general principle from what had hitherto been a wilderness of single instances').

good faith, it 'would appear to be swimming against the tide'.[16] The fact that we appear to be doing things differently from how others do them is often the starting point for considering reform, particularly in areas where we would naturally expect a degree of convergence rather than divergence. However, it can only be a starting point. A legal system cannot simply be carried along by the tide of other legal systems, and must work out whether such a reform makes sense in itself—and, if it does, what form such reform should take within its own framework.

III. Learning from Comparative Law—in Particular

In order to consider the introduction into English contract law of a general obligation of good faith—or, at least, a greater general acceptance of obligations of good faith—by analogy with the approach to good faith taken in the contract law of other legal systems, we need to begin by seeing how such other systems have dealt with this question. There is a wealth of material across many jurisdictions on which we could draw, but we shall here just mention some common general themes, illustrated by some individual systems of the Western legal tradition.

The codified civil law systems on the European continent, as well as those around the world that have drawn their inspiration from the European systems, are well acquainted with the idea that there is a principle of good faith within contract law. This is drawn from a development and generalization, through the medieval period and into the modern law, of the ancient Roman law notion of *bona fides*,[17] although within each of the modern systems the content of such a principle, and its general scope, have also been further developed and refined. Systems have recognized the need to separate two different meanings: *subjective* and *objective* good faith. The former is essentially a matter of honesty, or actual or constructive lack of knowledge of impropriety; the latter is a norm of conduct, setting a standard for the parties' behaviour in relation to the contract. Some legal systems have developed separate terminology to make this distinction clear;[18] others refer to them by the same general term,[19] although internally they distinguish the two meanings. It is the second meaning (objective good faith) that concerns us here. In saying that there is a general principle, or obligation, of good faith in contract law, legal systems are not simply saying that

---

[16] *Yam Seng* (n 3) [124], referring to 'the general principle of good faith . . . recognised by most civil law systems—including those of Germany, France and Italy' as well as in EU Directives and proposals for harmonization of the contract law of EU member states.

[17] Zimmermann and Whittaker, *Good Faith* (n 5) 16–18; Jan Peter Schmidt, 'Historical Antecedents' in Nils Jansen and Reinhard Zimmermann (eds) *Commentaries on European Contract Laws* (OUP 2018) 108–11.

[18] eg in the reform of the Dutch Civil Code (*Burgerlijk Wetboek*, hereafter BW, in force from 1992) the opportunity was taken to revise the terminology: the new term for objective good faith in contract law is *redelijkheid en billijkheid* (reasonableness and fairness: BW art 6:2) by contrast with *goede trouw* (subjective good faith, applied in the context of acquisition of property: BW art 3:118): AS Hartkamp, 'Law of Obligations' in Jeroen Chorus, Ewoud Hondius, and Wim Voermans (eds), *Introduction to Dutch Law* (5th edn, Wolters Kluwer 2016) (hereafter Chorus, Hondius, and Voermans, *Introduction*) 174; and definitions at BW arts 3:11 (*goede trouw*) and 3:12 (*redelijkheid en billijkheid*). The Draft Common Frame of Reference, drawing principles, definitions, and model rules within European contract law, also makes the distinction between (subjective) 'good faith' and (objective) 'good faith and fair dealing': von Bar and Clive, *DCFR* vol 1, 72. German law uses *Treu und Glauben* for objective good faith (eg *Bürgerliches Gesetzbuch* (hereafter BGB) §242), but *guter Glaube* for subjective good faith (eg BGB §932).

[19] eg French law: *la bonne foi* (*Code civil* (hereafter C civ) art 1104: objective good faith; art 2272: subjective good faith); Spanish law: *buena fe* (*Código civil*, art 7: objective good faith; art 464: subjective good faith).

parties must be honest in their conduct and dealings with each other; it goes significantly beyond that, and imposes general, positive duties of proper behaviour.

Acceptance of some form of general obligation of good faith is not confined to the civil law systems. Some common law systems appear to be more open to good faith than English law:[20] perhaps most notably, the American law of contract has accepted circumstances in which the parties can undertake an agreement to negotiate in good faith[21] and an implied obligation to perform and enforce contracts in good faith, a general obligation which is found in the Restatement (Second) of Contracts and in the Uniform Commercial Code.[22] However, even there the scope of the duty is significantly more limited than in the civil law systems. Civil law systems such as France and Germany began by articulating an obligation of good faith in the performance of contracts, but in the modern law this has been extended significantly to impose a general obligation throughout the whole life of the contract, from precontractual negotiations to the operation of remedies for non-performance. For example, the original text of the French civil code in 1804 provided that 'contracts . . . must be performed in good faith',[23] but the role of good faith in contracts was developed very significantly by the case law in the later twentieth century, and the new text of the civil code on the law of contract, reformed in 2016, provides that 'contracts must be negotiated, formed and performed in good faith'.[24] Good faith is seen as one of the fundamental principles of French contract law and, balanced against two other fundamental principles, contractual freedom and the binding force of contracts, the duty of good faith is an expression of contractual balance, or fairness—*la justice contractuelle*.[25] Indeed, the French code now goes so far as to say that the newly stated obligation of good faith in contracts is a matter of public policy[26]—that is, it is mandatory, and cannot be excluded by agreement between the parties. The general obligation of good faith has in practice formed the basis of development of a number of specific duties between contracting parties, but it also remains an underlying general obligation.[27]

---

[20] cf Michael Furmston and JW Carter, 'Good Faith in Contract Law: A Commonwealth Survey' in *Eppur si muove: The Age of Uniform Law, Essays in Honour of Michael Joachim Bonell to Celebrate his 70th Birthday* (UNIDROIT 2016) 988, discussing Australia, Canada, England and Wales, New Zealand, and Singapore, and concluding at 1033 that 'the one thing that is clear is that the position is unclear'.

[21] E Allan Farnsworth, *Farnsworth on Contracts* (4th edn with updates by Z Wolfe, Wolters Kluwer 2019) (hereafter Farnsworth, *Contracts*) §§3.09, 3.34. The American courts have not, however, been unanimous in their willingness to enforce such agreements: Farnsworth, *Contracts* §3.35.

[22] Restatement (Second) of Contracts (American Law Institute 1981) §205 ('Every contract imposes upon each party a duty of good faith and fair dealing in its performance and its enforcement'); Uniform Commercial Code §1-304 ('Every contract or duty within the Uniform Commercial Code imposes an obligation of good faith in its performance and enforcement'). See Farnsworth, *Contracts* (n 21) §7.20.

[23] C civ (old) art 1134: 'Les conventions . . . doivent être exécutées de bonne foi.'

[24] C civ (new) art 1104, para 1: 'Les contrats doivent être négociés, formés et exécutés de bonne foi.' For general discussion of the development of good faith in French law, see Solène Rowan, *The New French Law of Contract* (OUP 2022) (hereafter Rowan, *French Law*) 35–42.

[25] This was stated explicitly in the Report to the President of the Republic from the Ministry of Justice explaining the reform of contract law in 2016, published at www.legifrance.gouv.fr/eli/rapport/2016/2/11/JUSC1522466P/jo/texte. See also Philippe Malaurie, Laurent Aynès, and Philippe Stoffel-Munck, *Droit des Obligations* (12th edn, LGDJ 2022) (hereafter Malaurie, Aynès, and Stoffel-Munck, *Obligations*) 259–65.

[26] C civ (new) art 1104, para 2: 'Cette disposition est d'ordre public.'

[27] Rowan, *French Law* (n 24) 36–41. The German civil code, in force from 1900, also contained a specific obligation to perform in good faith: BGB §242; this remains, but it has formed the basis of a broad generalization by the courts of the obligation of good faith and the development of new specific rules within German contract law based on good faith: Zimmermann and Whittaker, *Good Faith* (n 5) 18–32; Basil Markesinis, Hannes Unberath, and Angus Johnston, *The German Law of Contract* (2nd edn, Hart Publishing 2006) (hereafter Markesinis, Unberath, and Johnston, *German Contract*) 119–33.

The acceptance of a general obligation of good faith within a legal system involves a value judgement about the relationship between the parties to a contract, and the scope of operation of the obligation within a legal system tells us about the reach of this value judgement. Although the European civil law jurisdictions have developed their own general principles of good faith within contract law, they are not identical, and the different ways in which they are articulated, and the ways in which the courts employ them in different systems, indicate the possible range of uses of good faith. We cannot here discuss any of the systems in detail, but the approaches taken by three systems will be mentioned to illustrate the point.

We have already seen that the French system now declares a general, fundamental, non-excludable obligation of good faith in the negotiation, formation, and performance of contracts. It should be added that, either under the label of good faith or under a related label ('abuse of right': *abus de droit*), a similar principle extends to the operation by the parties of their rights arising under the contract, such as the invocation of remedies.[28] Naturally, the operation of the general obligation of good faith depends on the context—both the context of the stage in the life of the contract that is in issue (what constitutes a breach of the duty in negotiations may be different from a breach of the duty in performance of the contract) as well as the factual context of the case itself and the particular relationship of the parties (standards of good faith expected between commercial parties may not be the same as when dealing with consumers, for example). But even before the French reform of 2016 gave us the new articulation of the obligation of good faith, it was clear that the courts themselves had found ways of dealing with all these cases, and had no difficulty in finding the lines to draw between conduct which does and conduct which does not satisfy the duty to act in good faith, whether in negotiation, formation, performance, or the invocation of remedies.[29]

Dutch law has a different formulation which appears more extreme, at least if read literally. In its general part of the law of obligations, the Dutch Civil Code states a general, positive duty on parties to obligations to act in accordance with the requirement of reasonableness and fairness.[30] However, the Code goes further in providing that a rule binding on the parties (whether by law, usage, or a juridical act such as a contract) does not apply to the extent that it would be unacceptable according to the standards of reasonableness and fairness.[31] And there are similar, specific provisions relating to contracts: disapplying provisions of the contract that would be unacceptable according to standards of reasonableness and fairness,[32] and giving the court the power to modify or set aside a contract in the event of a change of circumstances where the other party cannot (on the basis of reasonableness and fairness) expect the contract to be maintained in its original form.[33] In practice, these provisions may not be invoked lightly by the courts.[34] But the very broad way in which

---

[28] Rowan, *French Law* (n 24) 42–44; Malaurie, Aynès, and Stoffel-Munck, *Obligations* (n 25) 69–71, 513.

[29] Rowan, *French Law* (n 24) 36–44; Malaurie, Aynès, and Stoffel-Munck, *Obligations* (n 25) 259–65. In relation to negotiations between commercial parties, the Cour de cassation (the French supreme court) had been able to determine what constituted a failure to comply with the rules of good faith in commercial relations: Com 22 April 1997, D 1998 J 45 ('la société Iveco avait rompu brutalement et unilatéralement des négociations très engagées, et avait manqué aux règles de bonne foi dans les relations commerciales').

[30] BW art 6:2.1. BW art 3:12 provides that, in determining what is required by reasonableness and fairness, account must be taken of generally recognized principles of law, legal beliefs prevailing in the Netherlands, and the societal and personal interests involved in the case.

[31] BW art 6:2.2.

[32] BW art 6:248.2.

[33] BW art 6:258.1.

[34] Chorus, Hondius, and Voermans, *Introduction* (n 18) 174–76.

the general obligation of reasonableness and fairness is articulated, and the powers that are given to the courts to control the contract on the basis of that principle, are notable.

German law, by contrast, has some specific provisions imposing an obligation of good faith—notably §242 of the BGB (the duty to perform obligations according to the requirements of good faith, taking customary practice into consideration), which has been applied not only in its own terms but also as a springboard for the development of obligations of good faith in other contexts, some of which have later been introduced into the code as new, independent doctrines.[35]

Just looking in outline at these three examples, we can see that there are various different techniques that can be adopted by a legal system to state and implement an obligation of good faith in contract law. The obligation may be very general, or aimed at particular stages in the life of the contract. It may or may not be made explicitly mandatory, and it may be required to be interpreted and implemented by the courts within a broader balance of interests in the contract—balancing the good faith obligation against, for example, the principles of party autonomy and the binding force of contract. In practice, any implementation by a court of a general principle of good faith is going to involve such a balancing of interests. But we can also see that the obligation of good faith, however articulated, constitutes an open norm—a statement of general principle which leaves significant scope for interpretation and application by the court. There are here two particular points to consider when reflecting on how, if at all, English judges could follow their European counterparts in accepting and applying a general obligation of good faith in contract law. First, it involves by its very nature a general principle, and reasoning from general principles in particular cases is more the technique of the civil lawyer than the common lawyer. Second, it involves an open-textured test which places a certain power into the hands of the court, and thereby appears to give the court a power over the contract that goes beyond that to which English judges are accustomed—or, indeed, beyond that with which they may feel comfortable. We shall consider these points in the following sections of this chapter. First, however, we need to consider in more detail the extent to which English law already accepts the notion of good faith, and whether this can open a way to extending its recognition.

IV. Good Faith in English Contract Law: The Past and the Present

'Good faith' is a well-established term within English private law, so one might wonder why it has become such a controversial issue in modern English contract law. However, the ways in which good faith is used within English law are significantly different from the modern approach to good faith in contract law in systems of other traditions, particularly the European civil law systems, with the result that we cannot simply assume that there can be, or should be, a parallel development in English contract law.

We can first set aside one area in which English law uses good faith, and which does indeed find close parallels in civil law jurisdictions: property law, where a defect in the rights

---

[35] eg provisions on impossibility and change of circumstances introduced into the BGB by the *Gesetz zur Modernisierung des Schuldrechts* (Modernization of the Law of Obligations Act) of 26 November 2001, in force from 1 January 2002: Markesinis, Unberath and Johnston, *German Contract* (n 27) 120–22; Reinhard Zimmermann, *The New German Law of Obligations: Historical and Comparative Perspectives* (OUP 2005) 45–46.

transferred may be cured if the transferee takes the property (inter alia) in good faith. The doctrine of the bona fide purchaser[36] is a cardinal principle of property law, in the very particular way in which the English courts of Equity developed it,[37] but it has resonance with similar principles in civil law jurisdictions, where the language of good faith is also used. That, however, is *subjective* good faith,[38] which does not concern us here. What we need to consider is the extent to which English law uses *objective* good faith as a general principle of contract law.

There is one context in which 'good faith' has been used explicitly as an objective standard within English contract law, and which is instructive: the category of contracts said to be based on *uberrima fides*—'utmost good faith'. This terminology is well established but of questionable utility, not only because there has been debate over the years about which contracts form part of this category, and the significance for those contracts of such categorization,[39] but also because the one clear example of a contract *uberrimae fidei*—the contract of insurance—has now been reformed by legislation in such a way as to remove the significance of the categorization.[40] However, before this reform, the categorization gave rise to mutual duties of disclosure on the parties to the insurance contract, thus imposing an objectively definable standard of conduct on the parties during their negotiations for the contract.[41] The fact that this was seen as a specific obligation on insurers and insureds, within the context of a particular contract (insurance), is indicative of the general approach of the English common law: not relying on a general principle, but on specific, detailed rules designed to solve particular problems. There is a certain irony here: the origin of the duties of disclosure in insurance contracts was said by Lord Mansfield in the eighteenth century to be the general principle of good faith between contracting parties:

> The governing principle is applicable to all contracts and dealings.
>
> Good faith forbids either party by concealing what he privately knows, to draw the other into a bargain, from his ignorance of that fact, and his believing the contrary.
>
> But either party may be innocently silent, as to grounds open to both, to exercise their judgment upon . . .
>
> The reason of the rule which obliges parties to disclose, is to prevent fraud, and to encourage good faith. It is adapted to such facts as vary the nature of the contract; which one privately knows, and the other is ignorant of, and has no reason, to suspect.[42]

Lord Mansfield derived the particular duty (a defined duty of disclosure) for a particular category of contracts (insurance contracts) from a general principle (good faith) which

---

[36] Maitland's 'Equity's "darling"': HAL Fisher (ed), *The Collected Papers of Frederick William Maitland* (CUP 1911) vol III, 350.

[37] In the context of land law, see EH Burn and John Cartwright (eds), *Cheshire and Burn's Modern Law of Real Property* (18th edn, OUP 2011) 78–91.

[38] Text to nn 18, 19.

[39] John Cartwright, *Misrepresentation, Mistake and Non-Disclosure* (6th edn, Sweet & Maxwell 2022) (hereafter Cartwright, *Misrepresentation*) [17-03].

[40] Marine Insurance Act 1906, s 17, as amended by Insurance Act 2015, s 14(3)(a), now reads simply 'A contract of marine insurance is a contract based upon the utmost good faith' without any stated consequence of this categorization.

[41] For details of the duties of disclosure, see Cartwright, *Misrepresentation* (n 39) [17-08] to [17-20].

[42] *Carter v Boehm* (1766) 3 Burr 1905, 1910; 97 ER 1162, 1164–65. See further Cartwright, *Misrepresentation* (n 39) [16-08].

32   GOOD FAITH IN ENGLISH CONTRACT LAW

he said applied to all contracts. This is an illustration of the approach of the courts where, even if they identify a general underlying principle in order to answer a new case, they still conclude by laying down a specific legal rule, rather than seeing the answer to the case as simply the operation of the general principle.[43] However, the reasoning of Lord Mansfield, starting from a general principle of good faith in order to find a new, particular duty owed by one contracting party to another, has not survived. Rather, the modern judges see the particular duties owed between contracting parties as making up a patchwork covering the same ground as might be covered by a general principle of good faith, but created pragmatically rather than in order to implement the general principle. Bingham LJ said:

> In many civil law systems, and perhaps in most legal systems outside the common law world, the law of obligations recognises and enforces an overriding principle that in making and carrying out contracts parties should act in good faith. This does not simply mean that they should not deceive each other, a principle which any legal system must recognise; its effect is perhaps most aptly conveyed by such metaphorical colloquialisms as 'fair', 'coming clean' or 'putting one's cards face upwards on the table.' It is in essence a principle of fair and open dealing . . .
>
> English law has, characteristically, committed itself to no such overriding principle but has developed piecemeal solutions in response to demonstrated problems of unfairness.[44]

One might read this as suggesting that the outcome is similar (fairness between contracting parties) even if the reasoning is different (a patchwork of particular rules rather than the application of a general principle). This would be an application of the functional method of comparative law,[45] finding functional equivalence between the very different rules of the separate legal systems. However, such a rather broad conclusion cannot be justified, not only because one cannot assume that a patchwork of particular rules (as in the common law) is as complete as a general principle (as in the civil law), but also—more fundamentally— because there are some very significant differences in outcomes when we compare cases in the different systems. Here comparative law is important again. It is not simply a matter of asking whether the rules, or the outcome of cases applying those rules, in two systems are the same or different. Rather, we ask *why* there are such similarities or differences. And where we find differences in outcomes, we may most clearly see that there are differences between the legal systems, either in their method of reasoning, or reflecting differences of principle or policy in the underlying rules of law.

In the context of good faith in contract law, three areas can be mentioned briefly which illustrate the reasoning of the English judges that evidences a particular approach to the nature of the contract and the relationship between the parties to a contract, and which may

---

[43]   cf Lord Atkin's reasoning in *Donoghue v Stevenson* [1932] AC 562 (HL): text to n 15.

[44]   *Interfoto Picture Library Ltd v Stiletto Visual Programmes Ltd* [1989] QB 433 (CA) 439. This reasoning has recently been approved by the Supreme Court, which noted that some common law systems (such as Canada and the United States) have begun to recognise a general requirement of good faith in contract, but English law does not do so: *Pakistan International Airline Corp v Times Travel (UK) Ltd* [2021] UKSC 40, [2021] AC 101 (hereafter *Times Travel*) [27], [37]–[39]; see the assessment of this decision in the chapters 'Facility, Circumvention, Economic Duress and the Corporate Veil' and 'Schrödinger's Lawful Act Duress: Dead or Alive?' in this volume.

[45]   Zweigert and Kötz, *Introduction* (n 4) 34–35; R Michaels, 'The Functional Method of Comparative Law' in Reimann and Zimmermann, *Oxford Handbook* (n 4) ch 13.

GOOD FAITH IN ENGLISH CONTRACT LAW: THE PAST AND THE PRESENT   33

explain something of the difference between English law and the law of those jurisdictions which are more open to accepting a general principle of good faith.

First, contractual negotiations. It is here that English law has traditionally—and most clearly—had difficulties with the suggestion that there is a general principle, or a general duty, of good faith. There are specific duties, such as (defined, limited) duties of disclosure; and defined forms of (mis)conduct are sanctioned, such as misrepresentation. But there is no general, positive duty of proper conduct during negotiations. The leading authority today is still the decision of the House of Lords in *Walford v Miles*, where Lord Ackner identified two objections to a general duty to negotiate in good faith: that its meaning is uncertain; and that it is 'inherently repugnant to the adversarial position of the parties when involved in negotiations'.[46] The question of uncertainty, which has also been raised as an objection by other judges,[47] may be debated, and judges in other legal systems have not had the same difficulty in giving meaning to a duty to negotiate in good faith, for example in deciding that one party has broken off negotiations contrary to good faith.[48] The second objection, however, is one of principle: it is simply not the court's role to control the negotiations, which are—and should be—a matter for the parties themselves. This general approach, linking the rejection of a general principle of good faith in contracting with the similar rejection of a general doctrine of inequality of bargaining power, has recently been reaffirmed by the Supreme Court in order to limit the scope of another doctrine—economic duress—in English law, demonstrating a consistent approach of policy to party freedom in negotiations within the (judge-made) common law.[49] This is not, however, to say that the parties should not be free to *impose on themselves* the duty to negotiate in good faith, which is fundamentally different from the *law imposing on the parties* a general obligation of good faith in negotiations. The latter is an approach which defines as a matter of policy the nature of contractual negotiation, imposing positive duties on the parties. If, however, the parties choose to undertake a duty to negotiate in good faith, the denial of effectiveness of such an express provision engages another principle: freedom of contract.[50] Of course, this freedom may be limited by other policies within contract law,[51] and if Lord Ackner's objection based on uncertainty is sound, then even an express agreement to negotiate in good faith may be

---

[46] *Walford v Miles* [1992] 2 AC 128 (HL) 138.

[47] eg *Courtney & Fairbairn Ltd v Tolaini Brothers (Hotels) Ltd* [1975] 1 WLR 297 (CA) 301 (hereafter *Courtney & Fairbairn*) (Lord Denning MR: 'No court could estimate the damages because no one can tell whether the negotiations would be successful or would fall through: or if successful, what the result would be').

[48] It is not surprising that civil law systems have no such difficulty: eg n 29 (French law). But common law systems, too, can give meaning to a duty to negotiate in good faith: eg in the United States, Farnsworth *Contracts* (n 21) §3.34 describes Lord Denning's statement in *Courtney & Fairbairn* (n 47) as a 'non sequitur', although, as Farnsworth notes at §§3.09, 3.34, in the US there is a broader recognition of the validity of an agreement with 'open terms' (ie, where certain terms are left open, implying a duty of fair dealing as regards the agreement of the terms left open), as well as an acceptance of circumstances in which the parties can undertake an agreement to negotiate in good faith.

[49] *Times Travel* (n 44) [44] (Lord Hodge: 'A commercial party in negotiation with another commercial party is entitled to use its bargaining power to obtain by negotiation contractual rights which it does not have until the contract is agreed'). There are of course *specific* rules which may come into play, notably statutory protections for weaker parties such as consumers: Jack Beatson, Andrew Burrows, and John Cartwright, *Anson's Law of Contract* (31st edn, OUP 2020) 400–04.

[50] cf *Petromec Inc v Petroleo Brasileiro SA* [2005] EWCA Civ 891; [2006] 1 Lloyd's Rep 121 [121] (express obligation to negotiate variation in good faith; Longmore LJ: 'It would be a strong thing to declare unenforceable a clause into which the parties have deliberately and expressly entered').

[51] cf the (unsuccessful) argument before the Supreme Court that the parties' freedom of contact should override the long-accepted rule against penalty clauses, in *El Makdessi v Cavendish Square Holdings BV* [2015] UKSC 67; [2016] AC 1172.

rejected. However, if the real objection is the principle that negotiations are inherently self-serving and should not be controlled by the court, it is not obvious that the parties should be denied the chance to waive the protection that such a principle offers, by expressly agreeing to be bound to such a duty.

The second area, performance of the contract, appears at first sight less problematic. Once the parties have passed from the stage of negotiations (pre-contract, which is not, in the eyes of English law,[52] a relationship defined and protected by general rules of law) to the stage of concluding the contract, they have crossed the line and have undoubtedly created a relationship which is governed by law, and which the courts will regulate. To say that if I enter into contractual obligations, the law expects me to meet a certain objective standard in the performance of those obligations, does not seem so controversial. We have already noted that other legal systems, both civil law[53] and common law,[54] have found less difficulty with the duty of good faith in performance than in negotiations. This is also an area where the English courts appear to be more open to developing the law on good faith in contract, although the scope of such a development is still rather limited.

The most significant steps so far were taken by Leggatt J in *Yam Seng Pte v International Trade Corp*[55] and later cases[56] which have taken the lead from *Yam Seng*. That decision did not go so far as to say that English law recognizes a general obligation on parties to perform their contract in good faith, but it rejected the idea that 'good faith' is inherently unworkable, or too uncertain for an English judge to apply; and it held that a term may be implied in a contract to the effect that the parties shall perform in good faith. The cases appear to be moving to acceptance of a term of the contract, implied and not confined to the express agreement of the parties, that they shall perform in good faith. This begins to look more like a general obligation. But it is very different from the civil law model of good faith, and is instead consistent with the English way of thinking about contractual obligations: the source of the obligations is the parties' agreement; unless there is some overriding policy, typically found in legislation,[57] terms may normally be implied only if there is no contrary express provision; and they are not implied into all contracts, but only into contracts where either the facts[58] or the particular type of contract[59] justify the implication. To an English lawyer,

---

[52] This is a key difference from some civil law systems, which see the entering into negotiations as entering into a legally protected relationship, governed by good faith: eg Dutch law: *Baris v Riezenkamp* HR 15 November 1957, NJ 1958 67; German law: BGB §311(2).

[53] French law and German law began by stating a general duty of good faith in performance, before later extending this to the negotiations: text to nn 23, 35.

[54] eg American law: text to n 22.

[55] [2013] EWHC 111 (QB); [2013] 1 Lloyd's Rep 526. *Yam Seng* is a case on which Ewan McKendrick has commented several times: eg McKendrick, 'Good Faith in Performance' (n 2).

[56] See especially *Al Nehayan v Kent* [2018] EWHC 333 (Comm), [2018] 1 CLC 216 [167]–[176] (Leggatt LJ) (hereafter *Al Nehayan v Kent*); *Bates v Post Office Ltd* [2019] EWHC 606 (QB) [702]–[721] (Fraser J) (hereafter *Bates v Post Office Ltd*).

[57] Such as statutory (implied) terms in certain consumer contracts, which cannot be excluded or restricted by an express term of the contract: eg Consumer Rights Act 2015 Part 1, ss 31, 47, 57.

[58] Terms implied 'in fact': E Peel, *Treitel on the Law of Contract* (15th edn, Sweet & Maxwell 2020) (hereafter *Treitel*) [6-051] to [6-066].

[59] Terms implied 'in law' either by statute or at common law: *Treitel* (n 58) [6-067] to [6-072]. In *Al Nehayan v Kent* (n 56) [174] Leggatt LJ said that the duty of good faith was implied into the relational contract either in fact (essential to give effect to the parties' reasonable expectations, and satisfying the business necessity test) or in law ('on the basis that the nature of the contract as a relational contract implicitly requires (in the absence of a contrary indication) treating it as involving an obligation of good faith'); cf *Bates v Post Office Ltd* (n 56) [711] (Fraser J, assuming that an obligation of good faith is implied in all relational contracts, ie by law). cf *UTB LLC v Sheffield United Ltd* [2019] EWHC 2322 (Ch) [203]–[204] (Fancourt J); *Treitel* (n 58) [6-076].

it is strange and superfluous to say that all parties who undertake obligations by contract impliedly also undertake to perform those obligations in good faith. There is a risk that such an implication will undercut the strength of the expressly undertaken obligations.[60] There are situations where the nature of the contract can carry such an additional implied obligation, just as we can see that the nature of the contract and/or the relationship between the parties entering into the contract can impose on one or both of them additional obligations in relation to the formation of the contract—such as duties of disclosure.[61] It is not, then, surprising that the courts have had little difficulty in finding that parties to a contract which creates a long-term, collaborative relationship (a 'relational contract'[62]) should be held to have implied mutual duties of good faith during its performance. It has long been accepted that this is an inherent feature of a contract of partnership;[63] it is not a great step from that to a (commercial) joint venture or another long-term collaborative contractual relationship. But it is quite another thing to say that this should apply to all contracts.

The third area which illustrates the approach of the English courts to contractual good faith—by contrast with civil law systems, in particular—is in relation to the invocation of remedies for breach of contract. Again, we see a general reluctance on the part of the English judges to build general limitations on the availability of remedies by reference to the good faith of the claimant, although there may be (targeted) exceptions. Some remedies have in-built judicial discretion which may allow matters such as the parties' good faith to be taken into account—notably equitable remedies such as specific performance.[64] And the courts have, for example, developed limitations on the enforceability of express contractual rights of termination and forfeiture, where the forfeiture will deprive the wrongdoing party of proprietary or possessory rights.[65] The operation of a termination clause will, of course, depend on its construction within the context of the contract as a whole.[66] But there is no general judicial control of termination clauses—not even a requirement for a party to serve a reminder notice, or to give extra time, before invoking a termination clause by reason of the other party's late performance.[67] This was made clear by Lord Hoffmann, emphasizing the importance of certainty in the application of an express termination clause, but also speaking more generally:

---

[60] *Compass Group UK and Ireland Ltd v Mid Essex Hospital Services NHS Trust* [2013] EWCA Civ 200, [2013] BLR 265 [154] (Beatson LJ); *MSC Mediterranean Shipping Co SA v Cottonex Anstalt* [2016] EWCA Civ 789, [2016] 2 CLC 272 [45] (Moore-Bick LJ).

[61] Text to n 41.

[62] *Al Nehayan v Kent* (n 56) [167] (Leggatt LJ: a 'category of contract in which the parties are committed to collaborating with each other, typically on a long term basis, in ways which respect the spirit and objectives of their venture but which they have not tried to specify, and which it may be impossible to specify, exhaustively in a written contract').

[63] R l'Anson Banks, *Lindley & Banks on Partnership* (21st edn, Sweet & Maxwell 2022) [16-01], although this is not only a general duty of good faith, but also a fiduciary duty between partners: ibid, [16-09]. A joint venture or a 'relational contract' do not in themselves give rise to fiduciary duties between the parties: *Al Nehayan v Kent* (n 56) [166], [167].

[64] *Treitel* (n 58) [21-031], [21-033], [21-035].

[65] *Treitel* (n 58) [18-079], [18-080].

[66] See eg *Rice (t/a Garden Guardian) v Great Yarmouth BC* (CA 30 June 2000), discussed by Simon Whittaker, 'Termination Clauses' in Andrew Burrows and Edwin Peel, *Contract Terms* (OUP 2007) 253; *Optimares SpA v Qatar Airways Group QCSC* [2022] EWHC 2461 (Comm).

[67] Civil law systems more commonly treat *late* performance differently from other breaches of contract, requiring the creditor to give a reminder notice or even a second chance for performance before exercising termination rights: C civ art 1225 (France); BGB § 323(1); Markesinis, Unberath, and Johnston, *German Contract* (n 27) 426–27.

The principle that equity will restrain the enforcement of legal rights when it would be unconscionable to insist upon them has an attractive breadth. But the reasons why the courts have rejected such generalisations are founded not merely upon authority (see per Lord Radcliffe in *Campbell Discount Co Ltd v Bridge* [1962] AC 600, 626) but also upon practical considerations of business. These are, in summary, that in many forms of transaction it is of great importance that if something happens for which the contract has made express provision, the parties should know with certainty that the terms of the contract will be enforced. The existence of an undefined discretion to refuse to enforce the contract on the ground that this would be 'unconscionable' is sufficient to create uncertainty. Even if it is most unlikely that a discretion to grant relief will be exercised, its mere existence enables litigation to be employed as a negotiating tactic. The realities of commercial life are that this may cause injustice which cannot be fully compensated by the ultimate decision in the case.[68]

V. Good Faith in English Contract Law: The Future?

The purpose of this chapter is not to answer the question whether English contract law should develop a broader, general principle of good faith, but to consider the role that comparative law can play in deciding upon any such development. As we have seen, there is a tendency to assume that, since other legal systems have accepted such a general principle, English law could—and, perhaps, should—do likewise.

However, what we can learn from comparative law is that such reasoning can be dangerous if it is not accompanied by a careful understanding of the role played by good faith in the context of other systems, and how this might translate to the English system of contract law. Any development of a general principle of good faith in English contract law must fit the English model. There are features of other systems—particularly the continental civil law systems—which are very different from English law and therefore highlight the difficulties of adopting a similar good faith principle directly. As we have seen in the earlier sections of this chapter, systems which have adopted a general principle of good faith differ in their detail and in how they apply it but, in broad terms, the continental model sees good faith as a general (even mandatory) principle of contract law, and as imposing by law a positive duty of behaviour on the contracting parties. The approach taken by the English judges, however, is not to reason from general principles but to prefer specific rules; not to impose general standards of behaviour by law on contracting parties but to focus on giving effect to what the parties themselves have agreed; and generally to be reluctant to intervene in the contract (except where one party has committed a definable wrong), basing this approach on the contracting parties' freedom to act in their own interests and the uncertainty that would be engendered by a broad judicial power of intervention to give effect to an apparently broad principle such as 'fairness' or 'good faith'. This idea was expressed recently by Lord Burrows in the context of an argument about the possible development of economic duress:

---

[68] *Union Eagle Ltd v Golden Achievement Ltd* [1997] AC 514 (PC) 519.

I do not think that this is an appropriate case in which to rely on a general principle of good faith dealing in so far as that would require a court to try to apply a standard of what is commercially unacceptable or unreasonable behaviour. That would be a radical move forward for the English law of contract and the uncertainty caused by it seems unlikely to be a price worth paying. In my view, the better strategy, at this stage in the law's development, is to try to set out a limited but clear and workable boundary for the concept of lawful act economic duress in the context of the facts with which this case is concerned.[69]

The pressure for further development of the scope of a duty of good faith in English contract law will, no doubt, continue. What is necessary, however, is to give effect to any such development within the context of the English model of contract law. The development of good faith so far has been along the lines we might expect: not applying a broad general principle directly, but finding an implied term in the contract, either on the particular facts of the case, or for specific categories of contract for which a particularized general duty of good faith can properly be devised and managed. And not by imposing on the parties a general legal obligation to act in good faith, but giving precedence to the terms of the parties' contract as the context for any such duty.

This is not to suggest that the English courts might not go further in the development of good faith duties; and, indeed, there is one area in which they could do so, in giving greater effect to express contractual agreements to act in good faith. The reluctance of the courts to allow parties effectively to agree to negotiate, or renegotiate, their contract in good faith[70] could be solved by their deciding that the content of such a duty is not too uncertain—and, indeed, it would be possible for them to appeal to evidence from other jurisdictions, both civil law and common law,[71] to find ways of defining for the purposes of English law what constitutes a failure to comply with the rules of good faith in commercial relations. It would also give a better effect to the parties' own intentions, which presently seem to be frustrated by such a strong rule against the duty to negotiate in good faith.[72] But such a (limited) development would still be consistent with the English model of contract: it would not impose positive duties by law on the parties but give effect to their own intentions, furthering certainty in contracting rather than risking uncertainty; and it would be a specific solution, not an application of a general principle.

---

[69] *Times Travel* (n 44) [95].
[70] *Walford v Miles* (n 46).
[71] cf French law (n 29).
[72] cf *Petromec Inc v Petroleo Brasileiro SA* (n 50) [121].

3

Rethinking Reliance Damages for Breach of Contract

RICHARD TAYLOR

I. Introduction

Looking back—they say you should never look back—but nevertheless, looking back, it was one of the best of times. A tale of a few cities when quite a young Ewan, from a very old city, Edinburgh, spent his first year in a full-time academic post in a much newer city, Preston,[1] shortly after completing his BCL in Oxford.[2] It was a great pleasure and privilege to have Ewan on our contract team during that all-too-short year, to try out our pet theories on him, and to absorb his penetrating, but always patient and polite, observations about them. Theorizing about the role of reliance in the law of contract and in the assessment of damages was all the rage back then. Other questions are perhaps now higher on the agenda but it is probably still worthwhile, after the passage of nearly forty years, to revisit the reliance question to see how much, or perhaps how little, may have changed. In doing so I implicitly trust, just as is undoubtedly the case with Ewan's penetrating scholarship, that his unwarranted patience and politeness will also be among those things that happily are still much the same.

On the face of it, the reliance interest in contract damages[3] has had an increasingly hard time, to the extent that some commentators have even expressed the view that it is redundant[4] or that 'the interest in getting the promised performance is the only pure contractual interest'.[5] The core criticism of the reliance interest in contract damages, neatly reversing much of what Fuller and Perdue said about the expectation interest, is that it is really the expectation interest in disguise; that is, that reliance damages are recoverable only because they are a part of what the innocent party expected to receive from performance. They are

---

[1] Belatedly granted city status in 2001, Preston has always been a popular staging post for talented Scots (like Ewan) on the way south, a not totally irrelevant example being the Scottish professional footballers who enabled Preston North End to become the inaugural 'Invincible' league and cup double winners of 1889. They were known as the 'Scotch Professors' on account of the more intelligent brand of football played by them (as compared with the unsophisticated English game). See eg Kevin McKenna, 'Who Gave English Football Its Mass Appeal? The "Scotch Professors"' *The Observer (Scotland)* (8 March 2020).

[2] Another quite old city, apparently.

[3] At this stage I have retained the terminology from the article which appropriated the adjective 'seminal': LL Fuller and William R Perdue Jnr, 'The Reliance Interest in Contract Damages' (1936) 46 Yale LJ 52, 373 (hereafter Fuller and Perdue, 'The Reliance Interest'). For reasons which will subsequently become more apparent, I have preferred in my title the arguably less generic expression 'reliance damages for breach of contract', Fuller and Perdue concerning themselves with a much wider range of questions about the protection of reliance in a much broader 'contractual' context.

[4] David McLauchlan, 'The Redundant Reliance Interest in Contract Damages' (2011) 127 LQR 23.

[5] Daniel Friedmann, 'The Performance Interest in Contract Damages' (1995) 111 LQR 628, 629 (hereafter Friedmann, 'The Performance Interest').

Richard Taylor, *Rethinking Reliance Damages for Breach of Contract* In: *Shaping the Law of Obligations*. Edited by: Edwin Peel and Rebecca Probert, Oxford University Press. © Richard Taylor 2023. DOI: 10.1093/oso/9780198889762.003.0003

thus said to be not recoverable to the extent that the contract was a bad bargain whereby the reliance would not have been recouped had the contract been performed. Reliance damages, on this view, are merely a convenient substitute which can be awarded where there is a lack of evidence (often due to the breach) about what the position would have been if the contract had been performed. They are based on a working assumption or presumption that the innocent party would have at least recouped its expenditure—subject therefore to the crucial proviso that it is open to the party in breach to prove (rarely achieved[6]) that the expenditure (or at least some of it) would not have been recouped. The reliance interest on this view is thus not a true alternative to the expectation interest because it is not protected in the situation where the claimant would have most reason to opt for it, that is, where it produces a better result for the claimant than the expectation interest. The main rationale for denying the reliance interest protection in this scenario is that the loss in such a case is not caused by the breach but by C's decision to enter into a bad bargain from which C should not be allowed to escape.

The above crude summary of the current attitude towards the reliance interest in contract damages might be termed the current orthodoxy.[7] It is certainly much more firmly entrenched than it was forty years ago, when the relationship between reliance and expectation, and whether the latter limited the former, was rather more of a moot point. The curious thing, however, is that the case law on which the orthodoxy is said to rest is rather thin and not at all at the highest level (at least in this jurisdiction). Moreover, on examination, the case law is not necessarily supportive of all that is claimed for it and deserves, at the least, closer scrutiny and analysis. It will also be argued that some of the theoretical constructs underpinning it are not as sound as they are assumed to be—for example, the identification of the reliance position with the position as if the contract had not been entered into, which is not logically the correct hypothesis for post-contractual reliance on the contractual promise.

II. Some Propositions

It may be helpful to set out in advance some propositions which, it will subsequently be argued, can be seen to emerge from an analysis of the case law.

A. *Pre-contractual* wasted expenditure is not incurred in reliance on the contractual promise and it is logical that *this* type of expenditure is only recoverable if it is within the

---

[6] *Ampurius Nu Homes v Telford Homes* [2012] EWHC 1820 (Ch); 144 Con LR 72 is a very rare, arguably genuine, example at first instance (Roth J) which however was overturned on other grounds (no termination) in the Court of Appeal ([2013] EWCA Civ 577; [2013] 4 All ER 377). *Grange v Quinn* [2013] EWCA Civ 24; [2013] 1 P & CR 18 is an interesting example in which three judges in the Court of Appeal were split on whether the reverse burden had been discharged or whether that would preclude recovery (Arden LJ concluding it had been discharged, Gloster J that it had not been and Jackson LJ that it was not relevant.) Interestingly, even Gloster J ([108]) contemplated the possibility that 'even where the defendant has discharged the burden of demonstrating that the contract was a bad bargain, the Claimant is entitled to recovery of the wasted purchase price or premium. The simplicity of this approach has considerable attraction'.

[7] Andrew Burrows, *Remedies for Torts, Breach of Contract, and Equitable Wrongs* (4th edn, OUP 2019) (hereafter Burrows, *Remedies*), calls it the 'preferable' view (at 76) and accepts it, while clearly harbouring some unease about the presumption of recoupment 'in so far as it is thought helpful' which he later acknowledges (at 81) 'may at first sight appear puzzling'. See further the discussion of the musical performer example at III.G.

expectation interest. This however is irrelevant to the correct treatment of expenditure in-curred *after* entering the contract in *reasonable reliance* on the contractual promise.

B. Such genuine reliance expenditure should be independently recoverable provided it is reasonable and foreseeable and provided it is legitimate in the circumstances to infer that the promisor can be taken to have assumed responsibility for it, should the promisor re-pudiate or wrongfully terminate the contract. This will particularly be the case where the termination occurs before the promisor has rendered any substantial performance to offset the reasonable reliance of the other party.

C. Reliance damages are designed to compensate for post-contractual reliance on the promise (as though the reliance had not been made) and are not designed to put the claimant in the position as though the contract had not been entered into (even though they may sometimes have that effect) as the latter aim is the aim of compensation for pre-contractual reliance on, for example, misrepresentations, not post-contractual reliance on contractual promises.

D. Great care should be taken before assuming that a contract constituted a bad bargain (either at the time of contracting or at the time for performance) and, in any event, the more relevant question is whether the reliance on the contractual promise was reasonable and whether the promisor can be taken to have assumed responsibility for it, if it is wasted due to the promisor's repudiation of the promise.

III. Some Case Law

A. A Too Readily Presumed Bad Bargain Involving Expenditure That Was Pre-Contractual

C & P Haulage v Middleton[8] is a key early case for the reliance interest sceptics, as one might call them. It is regularly cited as a good example of the correct denial of the recovery of re-liance damages in a bad bargain scenario. However, the facts, while well known, deserve more detailed consideration. The appellant (counterclaimant) was in business as a car re-pairer. He was originally working out of a garage at his own home but the local authority had given him notice to desist so he urgently needed to find other premises. He entered into a six-month renewable licence agreement to use the respondents' yard and had spent £1,767 making it suitable for his purposes (including building an enclosing wall, putting in electricity, etc). It was a term of the agreement that any fixtures put in were to be left at the end of the licence. All went well for six months and the licence was effectively renewed for a second six months in June 1979. In October 1979 there was a dispute and the appellant was ejected without notice. In the difficult circumstances in which he found himself, the local authority compassionately allowed him to resume working (for a further year) from his home garage. The appellant was sued for money said to be owing to the respondents but he counterclaimed for the £1,767 expenditure on the yard. The Court of Appeal upheld the County Court judge's decision that the appellant had suffered no loss and awarded nominal

---

[8] [1983] 1 WLR 1461.

damages for the admitted breach by the respondents. A number of different but related reasons were referred to in the judgments.

Ackner LJ considered that damages would put the appellant in a better position than if the contract had been performed because he had not suffered any loss of profits as he had been allowed to return to carry on business in his own garage. Indeed, he had not had to pay the rent for the remaining ten weeks of the licence but was able to use his own premises rent free. The case was different from the wasted expenditure awarded in *Anglia TV v Reed*[9] because Lord Denning MR in that case had not been contemplating a 'bad bargain' case. Ackner LJ then referred approvingly to the then relatively recently decided Canadian case of *Bowlay Logging* where Berger J had said that '[t]he law of contract compensates a plaintiff for damages resulting from the defendant's breach; it does not compensate a plaintiff for damages resulting from his making a bad bargain.'[10] The claimant, Ackner LJ concluded, is not 'entitled to be put in a position in which he would have been in if the contract had never been made.'[11]

Fox LJ gave a brief concurring judgment, noting that

> whilst it is true that the expenditure could in a sense said to be wasted as a result of the breach of contract, it was equally likely to be wasted if there had been no breach because [the respondents] wanted to get [the appellant] out and could terminate the licence at quite short notice. A high risk of waste was from the very first inherent in the nature of the contract, breach or no breach. The reality of the matter is that the waste resulted from what was, on the defendant's side, a very unsatisfactory and dangerous bargain.[12]

There are a number of observations which can be made about the above collection of reasons. First, there was no thorough investigation into whether this was truly a 'bad bargain' case. Given the situation the appellant found himself in when first told to leave his home garage, to know whether it was a bad bargain to spend £1,767 on premises of which he might only have the use for six months rather depends on how much income he was going to generate in those six months and what his other costs would be. He would only need to generate £300 income per month (less than £75 per week) to more than cover the 'premises costs'. We simply do not know (since the question was never asked) how much more than that he would need to cover his other costs and break even or make a profit and we do not know how much he did or could generate. So we really have no accurate information as to whether, even just for the first six months, it was a bad bargain or not (or to what extent). It may well have been touch and go[13] in terms of a minimum term of only six months, but depending on the limited alternatives available, it may have been a perfectly prudent enterprise not involving any actual loss.

---

[9] [1972] 1 QB 60.

[10] *Bowlay Logging Ltd v Domtar Ltd* [1978] 4 WWR 105, 117 (hereafter *Bowlay Logging*).

[11] [1983] 1 WLR 1461, 1468. See Section III.D for the argument that this is not the relevant comparison for post-contractual reliance on the promise, as opposed to pre-contractual reliance on a pre-contractual statement in order to enter the contract.

[12] ibid 1468.

[13] The average weekly wage for men over 21 in 1979 was £101.30 (HC Deb 10 February 1983 vol 36 cols 422-3W). Turnover for a self-employed person would have to be considerably higher to generate an income of £100 or more and thus £75 a week premises costs may not have been totally out of the question or disproportionate.

SOME CASE LAW   43

Second, following on from that, in relation to the contractual promise broken—that is, the agreement in June to give a second six-month licence—the £1,767 premises cost was not reliance damages in any event. The money on the premises had already been spent. In relation to the second six-month licence, it was pre-contractual expenditure. The appellant had already had the benefit of that expenditure for the minimum six-month period for which he had signed up in the previous December. An argument in favour of *reliance* is unlikely, on the face of it at least, to justify the recovery of expenditure incurred *before* the (subsequently broken) promise. *C & P Haulage* on this view is not a reliance claim at all. In fact, like *Anglia TV v Reed*, it is a pre-contractual wasted expenditure case which, since the expenditure was not incurred in reliance on the promise, is much more difficult to justify being compensated on a reliance basis (and indeed should not be justified on that basis as it confuses the issue about true reliance cases). Pre-contractual expenditure recovery is best (or at least most easily) explained as straightforward expectation recovery, money that would have been recouped if the contract had been performed, and of course in that case it is beyond question that it is limited by the expectation interest because it is the expectation interest. The fact that many (or most) cases of reliance on a promise are constituted in whole or in part by wasted expenditure does not mean that all cases of wasted expenditure are reliance cases. This is particularly true in relation to pre-contractual wasted expenditure, which can hardly be said to have been incurred in reliance on the promise.

The third point is that the award of only nominal damages in *C & P Haulage* depends partly on the accident that the appellant was able to return to his own garage rent free (and that this was not treated as a collateral benefit conferred by a third party[14]). Again, this is nothing to do with reliance as such. It seems clear from Ackner LJ's judgment that, if the appellant had been unable to carry on in business for the remaining ten weeks of the licence, he would have been entitled to loss of profits. If in the alternative he had been able to carry on in business by obtaining substitute premises at a higher rent, he would presumably have been entitled to the difference in rent. Neither of those losses materialized because he could use his own premises again, rent free. Even if the benefit of working free from home is properly brought into account, should not some allowance have been made for the fact that his own garage was now tied up in his business and was therefore not available for domestic use? However, even if such allowance were made, it would probably be less than the rent under the licence which had been saved, so again no net loss incurred.

In summary, one can say that the decision to award nominal damages was overall correct but that the best reasons for not allowing recovery on a reliance damages basis are that reliance damages were (a) not relevant because the expenditure was pre-contractual and not made in reliance on the broken promise and (b) not substantial in any event, *not because it was a bad bargain*, but because the appellant had already received, during the first six months, the minimum benefit he contracted for in return for the expenditure—so the expenditure was not wasted.

Point (b) above prompts the observation that reliance damages are typically most relevant and likely to be claimed where D fails outright to perform, or to substantially perform, the promise; that is, cases where D commits a repudiatory breach before D has rendered

---

[14] See Richard Taylor, 'Contract: *C & P Haulage v Middleton* (CA)' (1984) 18 *The Law Teacher* 217, 218 for the argument that it should have been regarded (and therefore ignored) as a collateral benefit.

much if any substantial performance.[15] Suppose that the respondents in *C&P Haulage* had thrown the appellant out just days into the first six-month licence, and let us suppose also that the appellant had already incurred the expenditure by then. Suppose further that the appellant is allowed to return to his home garage by the local authority. Expectation damages may still be nil if the appellant can still make the same revenues from the business carrying on at his home premises. But he has needlessly spent £1,767 in reliance on the contractual promise (the breach of which has deprived him of substantially the whole benefit of D's promise). If he had known that the respondents were going to immediately repudiate the agreement, he would not have spent the £1,767, which has not benefited him in any way. This needlessly spent amount, it will be argued, should be recoverable[16] to the extent that the expenditure was reasonable and foreseeable,[17] on which basis D can and ought normally be taken to have assumed responsibility for it being wasted in the event that D totally fails to perform.[18]

B. The Rebuttable Presumption that Reliance Expenditure Would Be Recouped (and the Mis-Characterisation Once More of Pre-Contractual Expenditure as Reliance)

CCC Films v Impact Quadrant Films[19] came hard on the heels of *C & P Haulage* and is treated as establishing the related rule that reliance damages are not recoverable if D can rebut the normal presumption (a presumption effectively ignored in *C & P Haulage*) that the claimant would at least have recouped the reliance expenditure. Hutchison J, in a thorough and detailed judgment, relied substantially on Berger J in *Bowlay Logging*, just as the Court of Appeal had done in *C & P Haulage*. Hutchison J however expressly addressed the issue, which was conveniently overlooked in *C & P Haulage*, of who had the burden of proving whether or not the expenditure would have been recouped and followed Berger J in saying the burden was on the defendant.

There are however three problems with attaching too much weight to *CCC Films*. First, it is only a High Court decision (albeit very carefully considered), in which the relevance of reliance damages was a late argument. Second, to the extent that it precludes recovery of reliance losses in bad bargain cases, it is technically obiter because the actual decision was that the purported reliance losses were recoverable as there was no evidence that this was a bad bargain or that the expenses would not have been recouped. Third, and most importantly, it is arguably, again, not a reliance interest case at all since, rather like *C&P Haulage* (and *Anglia TV v Reed* in relation to the bulk of the expenditure), the expenditure was pre-contractual, that is, incurred prior to entering into the contract which was broken, and thus not incurred in reliance on it. The claimants in *CCC Films* had already paid the $12,000 for

---

[15] Contrast the facts of *Bowlay Logging* (n 10) where there had been several months of performance and the alleged breach was arguably a qualitative breach (of warranty) rather than repudiatory.

[16] Possibly with some deduction for rent saved.

[17] Both qualities should be required but if it satisfies one (eg reasonableness) it is likely to be foreseeable as well, though this will not always be true.

[18] One is tempted (not for long!) to say that there has been a total failure of consideration but that would only muddy the waters and it is not conceded anyway that reliance damages should *only* be available in what is the paradigm case of total failure to perform.

[19] [1985] 1 QB 16.

the licence to exploit the films, they had consequently become entitled to the licence, and the physical tapes had already been handed over. The breach by the defendants was of a subsequent subsidiary contract whereby they retook possession of the tapes and agreed to post them to Munich. When the tapes failed to arrive in Munich there were further subsidiary contracts to deliver replacement tapes to the claimants, but again no such deliveries were made and the defendants were in breach of these contracts too. Hutchison J's conclusions in the penultimate paragraph of his judgment are worth quoting:

> I therefore find: (1) that the foreseeable result of the breach of their obligations imposed by one or more of the subsidiary contracts to deliver any of the tapes was that the expenditure incurred by the plaintiffs in acquiring the licence to exploit the tapes would be wasted; (2) that in the event that expenditure was wasted because, given that the receipt of the tapes was a necessary prerequisite to any exploitation, the plaintiffs were, by the breaches of the subsidiary contracts, prevented from undertaking any sort of exploitation of the rights for which they had paid $12,000; (3) that the onus of proving that, had the tapes been received, the plaintiffs would not have succeeded in recouping their expenditure, i.e., the $12,000 and any other exploitation expenditure, lay on the defendants and has not been discharged; (4) that accordingly the plaintiffs are entitled to judgment for $12,000.[20]

It can be seen from the quoted text that: (i) the $12,000 expenditure was all pre-contractual as far as the subsidiary contracts were concerned; (ii) Hutchison J's conclusions do not mention reliance at all (and indeed reliance is hardly mentioned in the whole judgment other than in quotations or in the arguments of counsel); and (iii) (just as with *C & P Haulage* and *Anglia TV*) the case is not really concerned with the recovery of reliance damages for breach of contract properly understood, that is, loss incurred as a result of relying on a contractual promise. Rather, it is concerned with pre-contractual expenditure which the appellant cannot prove would have been recouped but which the defendant cannot prove would not have been recouped. If this is not a true case of the reliance interest, it is not surprising that the expectation measure should be the limit, albeit subject to a burden on D, since this is in truth the protection of the expectation interest, not the reliance interest. The decision does not necessarily dictate that the protection of a genuine reliance interest must also be limited to the expectation interest in quite the same way or that the recovery of the reliance interest, as opposed to the recovery of pre-contractual expenditure, is the recovery of the expectation interest in disguise.

Nevertheless, notwithstanding the above observations, *C & P Haulage* and *CCC Films* became accepted as the pair of leading cases illustrating the principles governing the recovery of reliance damages for breach of a contractual promise (whether or not on the facts that is what they were actually concerned with). Reliance damages for breach were however just about still alive and well (and recoverable) even if subject to a potentially mortal qualification if D could discharge the burden of proof. Then came the case of *Omak Maritime Ltd v Mamola Challenger Shipping Co*[21] to deliver what in some quarters has been interpreted as the inevitable and timely fatal blow, but which closer analysis may show is only an illustration of the adage that what does not kill you only makes you stronger.

---

[20] ibid 40.
[21] [2010] EWHC 2026 (Comm), [2011] 1 Lloyd's Rep 47 (hereafter *Omak*).

C. The Subtle Shift from Bad Bargains to Mitigated Losses and Overall Expectations

The problems raised by *Omak* are due in large part to the unusual fact that this was a case where the charterers (OM) repudiated a five-year charterparty even though the market price had risen dramatically compared to the contract price. The hire payable under the charterparty was $13,700 per day whereas the market rate at the time for performance (January 2007) was $21,347. The vessel was ultimately intended to be sub-chartered. The Nigerian charterers had only entered into the agreement because Nigerian regulations required a local Nigerian company to be involved but the Nigerian authorities ultimately refused to give the necessary approval for the sub-charter. Given the rise in the market rate, there was no expectancy/net profit loss as the owners, Mamola Shipping (MS), stood to make about $7,500 more per day than they would have made under the charterparty. However, MS were required under the contract to make some alterations to the vessel, including the installation of a crane, and had incurred expenditure in pursuit of this obligation, commencing with the removal of the crane from another vessel which they owned. It is important to bear in mind throughout that this expenditure had no residual value for the owners, did not result in any improvement to the vessel, and thus had no impact whatsoever on the increase in market rate. MS claimed their expenses wasted in reliance on the contract and the arbitral tribunal awarded them $86,534, notwithstanding the very large sums they would now be able to earn at the market rate. OM appealed on the basis that the damages put MS in a better position overall than if the contract had been performed and that this was contrary to the principle going back to *Robinson v Harman*.[22] It was also argued by OM that contractual damages are not designed to put the claimant in the position as though it had never entered the contract (citing *C & P Haulage*) and, furthermore, the benefit flowing from the breach (the opportunity to benefit from a 50 per cent increase in the market rate) had to be taken into account in assessing damages, applying the principles in *British Westinghouse v Underground Electric Railways*.[23]

Teare J accepted most of these arguments and allowed the appeal, conscientiously reviewing a wide range of authorities. One of the key authorities on which he relied was our old friend *Bowlay Logging* and the more substantial passage often quoted from Berger J, where it was said:

> The law of contract compensates a plaintiff for damages resulting from the defendant's breach; it does not compensate a plaintiff for damages resulting from his making a bad bargain. Where it can be seen that the plaintiff would have incurred a loss on the contract as a whole, the expenses he has incurred are losses flowing from entering into the contract, not losses flowing from the defendant's breach. In these circumstances, the true consequence of the defendant's breach is that the plaintiff is released from his obligation to complete the contract—or, in other words, he is saved from incurring further losses.
>
> If the law of contract were to move from compensating for the consequences of breach to compensating for the consequences of entering into contracts, the law would run contrary to the normal expectations of the world of commerce. The burden of risk would be

---

[22] (1848) 1 Ex 850; 154 ER 363.
[23] [1912] AC 673.

shifted from the plaintiff to the defendant. The defendant would become the insurer of the plaintiff's enterprise.[24]

One problem with relying on these dicta on the facts (as has similarly been seen already with *C & P Haulage*) is that while *Bowlay Logging* was on its facts demonstrably a bad bargain case, no explanation or analysis was undertaken to show that *Omak Maritime* was a bad bargain case in the sense used in *Bowlay Logging* (although to be fair to Teare J, this point does not seem to have been specifically put to him). MS had, on the tribunal's figures, spent $86,000 in pursuit of installing a crane at the request of OM under a charterparty that was to earn ithem $13,000 a day for five years. There could really be no question of them not recouping their $86,000 expenditure (or whatever extra costs would have been incurred to complete the installation) over the course of the charterparty, so the bargain was not bad in this sense.[25]

Disallowing the requested expenditure, which was necessary to be able to perform the contract, is not good policy where it is the defendant that has rendered that expenditure pointless and wasted. If the owners had engaged in greater brinksmanship in preparing to transfer the crane, and had not even started the process (eg had not started to remove it from their other ship) before they were sure that the charterers would perform, the position as between the parties would have been unaffected but the owners would have been better off as they would not have incurred any, or as high an amount of, expenses. Disallowing their claim in a perfectly reasonable profitable venture does nothing to encourage reasonable and timely reliance and has a tendency to discourage it, which is a strong argument in favour of allowing recovery of reasonable and necessary reliance.[26]

Of course, if the expenses needed to modify the ship to the charterers' specifications had been excessively large compared to the hire rate so that the venture could be proved by the charterers to be a loss-making one for the owners, disallowing the expenses (or part thereof) would be perfectly understandable. However, rather than basing this on a presumption of recoupment and a reverse burden, this could equally well (or better) be explained as based on non-recovery of reliance that is not reasonable (and for which D cannot be expected to assume responsibility), as opposed to reliance that is eminently reasonable and foreseeable in a profitable (or break-even) venture (for which D can be expected to have assumed responsibility). In any event, on the facts of *Omak* there was no evidence, from either side, that the modification expenses were anywhere near being excessively large or that the bargain was a bad one in that sense, and the *Bowlay Logging* dicta, insofar as they relate to bad bargains at least, does not logically lead to denial of recovery of the reliance expenses.

The preceding discussion illustrates the fact that the real issue in *Omak* is not the prima facie recoverability of the reliance expenditure, especially as the contract is not actually loss-making in the normal bad bargain sense, but is rather the rules on mitigation, avoided loss, and collateral benefits. Essentially, a genuine reliance loss was disallowed in *Omak* because

---

[24] *Omak* (n 21) [28].

[25] It may have been 'non-optimum' in the light of the even better bargain that might have later been available given the rise in the market but that does not make it a bad bargain for present purposes.

[26] Furthermore, if they had not yet (but ought to have) incurred the expenditure by the time the charterers repudiated, it seems inconceivable that they could have been liable in damages for failing to do so or that this could have been a ground for allowing the charterers to terminate as it would be unlikely to be regarded as a breach depriving the charterers of substantially the whole benefit of a five-year charter.

the innocent party was not allowed (citing *British Westinghouse*) to end up better off *overall* than if the contract had been performed. The putative contractual position is used as a cap on the reliance expenditure, notwithstanding that the reliance was reasonable when incurred and it is the other party who is in fundamental repudiatory breach. To this denial of recovery based on the *overall* position of the claimant it might be responded that it is not the reliance damages that would be putting the owners in a better position than the contractual one (since the amount of the reliance damages would have been more than recovered if the contract had been performed); rather, it is the market hire increase which is putting them in a better overall position. That better position, it can be argued, is caused by their existing ownership of the ship with an increased market hire rate just as much as it is caused by D's breach (the latter being a 'but for' cause but not necessarily the legal cause).[27]

Moreover, the reliance by Teare J on *British Westinghouse* can be queried on another basis. Teare J relies on that case in a number of respects, not least in suggesting that

> damages for breach of contract are intended to compensate for loss suffered and the Owners have, as a result of their own efforts to mitigate their loss, suffered no loss. To ignore the benefits received by the Owners as a result of their action to mitigate their loss would be contrary to the principles established by *British Westinghouse*.[28]

In *British Westinghouse*, the central issue was whether the respondents (London Underground) could claim the £78,000 spent on new vastly superior turbines (the Parsons machines) to mitigate the much greater losses in coal consumption and the like which they would have suffered if they had continued to use the defective machines supplied by Westinghouse for the remaining years of the alleged twenty-year life of the machines. The new Parsons machines were so superior, however, that

> even if the appellants had delivered to the respondents machines in all respects complying with the conditions of the said contract, it would yet have been to the pecuniary advantage of the respondents to have replaced at their own cost the machines supplied to the respondents by Parsons machines so soon as the latter could be obtained.[29]

As is well known, the respondents were not allowed in this situation to recover the £78,000 as it saved them more than the cost of the Parsons machines and they were, by a margin of more than that sum, better off than if the original Westinghouse machines had been up to specification. And yet they were allowed to keep the damages awarded by the arbitrator for the extra costs of running the Westinghouse machines in the years *before* the Parsons replacements were purchased, even though it seems that these extra costs were also wiped out by the savings made by using the Parsons machines. So, the *Westinghouse* case itself was not one where the damages were reduced in full so as to reflect the *overall* financial

---

[27] See *Fulton Shipping Inc of Panama v Globalia Business Travel SAU* [2017] UKSC 43, [2017] 1 WLR 2581 for an illustration in the Supreme Court of how policy factors can effectively impinge on the question of whether a benefit should be taken into account. It is accepted that there were factors in *Globalia* not applicable in *Omak*, not least that the ship could have been sold in *Globalia* even if there had been no termination, but supporters of the overall position cap find it difficult to accept, even in *Globalia*, that the beneficial decision to sell the ship was not 'caused' by the breach.

[28] *Omak* (n 21) [59].

[29] [1912] AC 673, 676.

position the claimant would have been in had the contract been performed. The damages for the extra costs during the first few years of the contract before the purchase of the new machines (plus the benefits of the new machines) effectively put them in a better position than if the contract had been performed. On a strict application of Teare J's analysis, the extra costs already incurred should not have been compensated any more than the cost of the reliance expenses already incurred in *Omak* should have been—and vice versa—just as in *Westinghouse* the claimants were allowed to keep the damages for the extra costs already incurred, the reliance expenses already incurred in *Omak* ought to be recoverable notwithstanding the rise in the market wiping out the separate head of net loss of profit.

D. Rethinking Reliance Losses—Assumptions of Responsibility and the Distinction Between Post-Contractual Reliance on the Promise and Pre-Contractual Reliance in Entering into the Contract

It has already been intimated that a better way of looking at reliance cases such as *Omak* would be to ask whether D can reasonably be taken to have assumed responsibility for various types of loss.[30] It is submitted that in a case like *Omak*, where D agrees to charter a ship from C and specifies items which require expenditure, in the absence of express exclusion or denial, D can be reasonably taken to have assumed responsibility for reimbursing C if D repudiates the contract after C has incurred the expenditure which is now wasted and of no value. D also assumes responsibility for lost net profits if the market price falls and C has to hire out the ship for less than the rate under the contract. This is the simple formula of reliance expenditure plus lost net profits, which is well recognized as a safe way of assessing contractual losses.[31] An increase in market hire rates means there are no lost net profits but the reliance expenditure, for which D has taken responsibility, has still been incurred. If the increase in market hire can be used to reduce or wipe out the reliance loss, then one is in effect saying that D assumes responsibility for the expenditure but only to the extent that the market does not turn significantly in C's favour. This does not appear to be the natural qualification to be made to the assumption (and thus would need to be expressed) especially as one would not normally be contemplating breach where there is a rising market. Furthermore, as has already been pointed out, it would reduce the incentive for C to incur the expenditure before the very last moment when C is sure that D is going to perform, whereas one of the main benefits of a contract should be to encourage and promote timely reliance. If there were a liquidated damages clause in the contract saying that the charterers, if they repudiate, are liable for the reliance costs already incurred at the date of repudiation plus any net profits (x-y) that also

---

[30] When Lord Hoffmann based his decision in *Transfield Shipping Inc v Mercator Shipping Inc (The Achilleas)* [2008] UKHL 48; [2009] 1 AC 61 on assumption of responsibility and risk and said '[i]t seems to me to be logical to found liability for damages upon the intention of the parties (objectively ascertained) because all contractual liability is voluntarily undertaken' ([12]), he was speaking in the context of remoteness rules limiting the amount of recoverable loss. However, the logic of his approach (which of course is a matter of controversy) can equally be applied to the initial identification of the types of loss for which a party assumes responsibility. Certainly, within the remoteness context it seems to be accepted that the assumption of liability approach can have inclusionary as well as exclusionary effects—see *Supershield Ltd v Siemens Building Technologies FE Ltd* [2010] EWCA Civ 7, [2010] 1 Lloyd's Rep 349.

[31] See David Campbell and Roger Halson, 'Expectation and Reliance: One Principle or Two?' (2015) 32 JCL 231.

may be lost (where x = contract price less costs, y = market price at the relevant date less costs), there would be presumably be no objection to the award of the reliance costs even though the market price has risen, not fallen. No one would be arguing that this is not a genuine pre-estimate of loss (on the grounds that, in the light of the market rise, it puts the owners in a better position than if the contract had been performed) because the clause reflects explicitly the risks and responsibilities assumed by the parties, that is, the bargain they have struck. The question then in the absence of such a clause is whether such a bargain can be implied. Suppose that, just before committing the reliance expenditure, the owners should contact the charterers and ask: before we spend this money in reliance on your promise, are you still committed to the charter? If the answer would be yes, is it not reasonable to imply an assumption of responsibility for the expenditure if the charterers should repudiate the charter before it even commences (especially bearing in mind the desirability of encouraging timely and reasonable reliance)? Would not the reasonable bystander come to the same conclusion?

A crucial issue in this analysis is that the reliance is actually incurred *after* the promise and *after* entering the contract and not *in* entering the contract. A significant factor that seems to have been influential in *Omak*, linked to the capping of damages by reference to the position had the contract been performed, is that the court is concerned that it should *not* be putting C in the contrasted position as though C had never entered into the contract. The answer to this, however, is that protecting reasonable reliance on the promise is not the same as putting C in all respects back in the original position before the contract was entered into. In particular, it does not protect reliance that is not reasonable, including where the contract is clearly from the outset going to be loss-making. D would not normally be expected to assume responsibility for unreasonable reliance expenditure. In contrast, damages aimed at putting C back in the position as though C had never entered the contract do clearly cover losses incurred in bad bargains, including those which were bad from the outset. Damages for misrepresentation are the most obvious example. The complaint is that the misrepresentation induced the contract and if it is a loss-making one (whether because of the misrepresentation or not), those losses are normally recoverable. There has been a tendency[32] to equate reliance damages for misrepresentation with reliance damages for breach of contract, and certainly there are similarities and points of cross-over. But there are clearly crucial differences which have to be kept in mind. In misrepresentation, the complaint is that D misled C into entering the contract on the basis of a statement which was untrue at the time. In breach of contract, the complaint is that D made a promise on which C subsequently reasonably relied to his or her detriment, either in performing C's own side of the contract (essential reliance) or in reasonable reliance on D's promise to perform (consequential reliance). The breaking of the promise has rendered the reliance wasted for which reliance D assumed responsibility at the time of making the promise. If there has been no post-contractual reliance on the promise, there are no reliance losses *for breach of contract* to be compensated. There is no question of *aiming* to put C back in the original position in all respects *before* the contract was entered into. The aim is merely to put C in the position as though the reasonable reliance had not taken place, that is, the position before the post-contractual reliance on the promise, not

---

[32] From which I do not claim immunity—see Richard Taylor, 'Expectation Reliance and Misrepresentation' (1982) 45 MLR 139.

the position before the entry into the contract. Of course, in some, perhaps many, cases this will have the same *effect* as putting C back in his original position before the contract, but this is not the aim. It is well recognized that it is often the case that different measures of damage with totally different aims end up on the facts giving C the same award; for example, in an executed sale of defective goods where, if the market price of the goods as promised is the same as the contract price, the contractual and tortious measures will produce the same result.

E. The Fuller and Perdue Soft-Shoe Shuffle

The above exposure of the misconception about the precise aim of reliance damages for breach of contract also points to a subtle shift (whether intentional or not[33]) at an early stage in the original Fuller and Perdue analysis where they explain the reliance interest thus: 'the plaintiff has in reliance on the promise of the defendant changed his position . . . Our object is to put him in as good a position as he was in before the promise was made.'[34]

There seems to be a non-sequitur here, in that if it is C's reliance on the promise which constitutes C's change of position, one would expect the object to be to put C in as good a position as C was in before C relied on the promise, not the position C was in before the promise was made. Now in practice, these two positions may often amount to the same thing, but this is not necessarily so.

The *Omak* decision arguably illustrates the point. In *Omak* the owners' cross-appeal, against the tribunal's refusal to award reliance costs beyond the crane costs, was based on the enhanced market hire which could have been earned in the three weeks during which the vessel did not earn any hire at all as it was held at port due to the uncertainty of whether the charterers were going to perform. Teare J indicated that if (contrary to his actual decision on the main appeal) reliance damages should be awarded, they would include this loss (which was the subject of the unsuccessful cross-appeal by the owners). This is consistent with the repeated assertion in the judgment that while contractual expectation damages are not concerned with putting the claimant back in the position as though the contract had never been entered into, contractual reliance damages are designed to do this. The reluctance to award reliance damages on the facts of *Omak* is perhaps then attributable to a misapprehension that to award reliance damages would mean having to go the whole hog and put C in the position as though the contract had never been entered into (the misrepresentation measure, which *would* cover the lost opportunity of three weeks hire at the increased market rate) rather than the more limited and nuanced measure of contractual reliance damages covering only reasonably foreseeable reliance on the contractual promise *after* entering the contract.

The arguments against the reliance measure thus often wrongly assume there are only two potential 'positions' in which damages can seek to put the claimant—as if the contract

---

[33] The reason may perhaps be because they were discussing a wider range of situations where they contended that reliance should be protected, including where the reliance on the promise creates the contract (as in unilateral contracts, so that the reliance and the entering into the contract might be thought of as one and the same thing) and they also discussed misrepresentation, where the reliance on a prior statement consists of entering the contract.

[34] Fuller and Perdue, 'The Reliance Interest' (n 3) 54.

had been performed or as if the contract had not been entered into. The argument presented here, however, is that there is a third position which is the correct one for reliance damages for breach of contract: the position as if the contractual promise had not been relied on (*after* entering the contract).

A similar point can be made about *Bowlay Logging*. The claim for reliance losses was rejected on the grounds that it amounted to putting the claimant back in the position as if the (inevitably loss-making) contract had not been entered into, which, as we have seen, is not and should not be the aim (or even one of the aims) of damages for breach of contract. If the court had focused more on the question of post-contractual reliance on the contractual promise rather than going back to the pre-contract position, while it still would not have granted the full amount claimed, it may have awarded more than nominal damages. The argument for this turns on the fact that Berger J clearly found that the defendant (Domtar) had committed breaches of contract (not providing sufficient lorries to transport the cut timber), which meant that Bowlay, the claimant, had lost about a week and a half's payments. Most of the failure to recoup the reliance expenditure was found to be due to the inefficiency of the claimant in how it went about cutting the timber to be transported (so arguably the bargain was not inevitably bad from the outset but became bad because of the way the claimant went about performing it). To the extent however that D's breaches meant that C did not recover expenditure incurred, that part of the expenditure surely ought to have been recoverable.

This point, or something very similar, does appear to have been argued on appeal from Berger J's decision, but was dismissed on the facts rather summarily in the following terms:

> The appellant argues that the trial judge ought to have taken into account that some of the work was done under circumstances made more difficult by the breach. I think that the judge was justified in rejecting that contention. The evidence does not indicate that the excessive costs were brought about or even significantly contributed to by the breach.[35]

This dismissal has to be seen in the light of the immediately preceding paragraph of the appeal court's decision, in which it was noted that

> the appellant offered no evidence of a loss. It simply showed the expenditures it had incurred and the revenue it had received. It then claimed the balance as the loss incurred when it was obliged by the respondent's breach to abandon the project.[36]

In other words, the appellant's (claimant's) argument was the misconceived one (ultimately, it has to be said, derived from Fuller and Perdue) that it should be put back in the position as though the contract had never been entered into rather than compensated for those parts of its expenditures which were wasted by the breaches of the respondents, as opposed to those parts which were wasted due to its own inefficiencies.

---

[35] Seaton JA in *Bowlay Logging Limited v Domtar Limited*, 1982 CanLII 449 (BC CA) [5].
[36] ibid [4].

F. Reliance Damages in Australia—Another Case of Failure to Prove the Elusive Bad Bargain

In the course of his judgment in *Omak*, Teare J referred to the Australian High Court decision in *Commonwealth of Australia v Amann Aviation*[37] which is another case often cited by reliance sceptics[38] as showing that so-called reliance damages are really only expectation damages in disguise. The decision is complicated by the variety of different judgments delivered and the differences in reasoning even among the majority. It follows the *Bowlay Logging* line about reliance damages being recoverable subject to a reverse onus and one of the main issues left unclear is just when such reverse onus applies and what sort of onus it should be exactly. Treitel, as acknowledged by Teare J in *Omak*, was critical of the decision to the extent that it supports the line that reliance is merely part of expectation and was adamant that there are two contractual measures, attributing the single-measure reasoning to some form of 'verbal trick'.[39] It would be presumptuous and fruitless for me to attempt inadequately to supply further reasons for Treitel's views beyond those expertly articulated in his own writings.[40] What is undeniable, however, is that the court did uphold an award of substantial reliance damages and looked in a commendably careful and sceptical way at the contention that the contract in *Amann* was a bad bargain. The very large outlays on purchasing and modifying aircraft in order to perform the contract were held not to be evidence of a bad bargain once one realized that their value (see Gaudron J in particular) at the end of the contract would not simply be their write-down value but the value they would represent, given their specialist nature, for the next surveillance contract, for which they would be likely to put the claimant in a virtually insuperable position.

Amann is in fact a very good illustration of the fact that contractual parties do not only have the expectation interest of making a profit in their minds.[41] They are often equally concerned not to incur reliance expenditure losses should the other party decline to perform, which is why Amann waited until it had a signed contract with the state (six months prior to the first date for performance) before it commenced purchasing and adapting the planes needed for performance. That was why it did not have quite all the planes ready on the first day for performance, thereby giving the state the opportunity to immediately repudiate[42] the contract (wrongfully, as it was held). There is an echo here of the earlier point about encouraging a party to do what is necessary to perform or prepare to perform in good time by allowing recovery of that reasonable reliance expenditure if the other party repudiates. The other party can be taken to assume responsibility for that reasonable expenditure which is contemplated or, *a fortiori*, is necessary for the contract.

---

[37] (1991) 174 CLR 64.

[38] David McLauchlan in particular has discussed this case in detail: see eg 'Reliance Damages for Breach of Contract' [2007] NZLR 417, 430–40.

[39] *Omak* (n 21) [50].

[40] As to which see GH Treitel, 'Damages for Breach of Contract in the High Court of Australia' (1992) 108 LQR 229.

[41] Contrast Friedmann, 'The Performance Interest' (n 5).

[42] Again, the case is one of total failure to perform in the face of significant reasonable reliance already incurred by the innocent party.

G. Counter-Examples to the Current Orthodoxy

The case law discussed so far is that on which the reliance sceptics habitually rely since, at first sight at least, it can be interpreted as seeming to support their view of reliance as expectation in disguise. Given rather less attention are cases and examples where post-contractual reliance expenditure is agreed to be recoverable without reference to the promised expectation. The rule first established in *Flureau v Thornhill*[43] and upheld in *Bain v Fothergill*[44] is a historic example which is conveniently put to one side[45] as a now redundant anomaly but it is a clear illustration, at the heart of English (and Anglo-American) law for many decades, of damages being awarded on what looks like a reliance basis.[46] The rule applied to contracts for the sale of land and precluded loss of bargain damages for failure to complete due to a defect in title, and only allowed the purchaser to recover the wasted costs of investigating title and a limited range of other reliance expenses. The current orthodoxy would possibly reply that those reliance expenses were merely part of the expectancy, the full expectancy being denied because, inter alia, of the difficulties in investigating title in the days before improvements in real property law and land registration. A better explanation of the rule, however, is that in the context of the then existing problems of showing title, the vendor cannot be expected to assume responsibility for the 'fancied loss of bargain' if the sale cannot be completed due to a defect in title but can be expected to assume responsibility for the purchaser's wasted reliance expenditure in investigating title. There is, crucially, no suggestion, as far as one is aware, that this liability was dependent on any assumption that the (irrecoverable) bargain would have been good enough to at least recoup the expenditure or that the vendor could escape liability for the expenses by showing that the purchaser would anyway have made a loss on the transaction.

The *Bain v Fothergill* rule, while no longer current since its abrogation in 1989[47] in the light of improvements in land registration and related conveyancing practice, can be seen as a significant illustration of the relationship between the recoverable measure of damages for breach of contract and the responsibilities and risks which a party can be taken to have assumed in the context of the contract entered into.

A more contemporary and arguably starker example of reliance damages is to be found in *A Restatement of the English Law of Contract*:

> A enters into a contract with B, a musician, for B to perform at a concert to be held in memory of a friend of A's. A incurs expenses of £2,000 for the hire of a hall. In breach of contract B fails to turn up. In seeking to put A into as good a position as if the contract had

---

[43] (1776) 2 Wm Bl 1078; 96 ER 635.

[44] (1874) LR 7 HL 158.

[45] Although it is acknowledged and discussed by Burrows, *Remedies* (n 7) 76.

[46] There is no little irony in the fact that *Robinson v Harman* was a case allowing expectation damages because the facts fell under an exception to the *Flureau v Thornhill rule*, ie the exception established in *Hopkins v Grazebrook* (1826) 6 B & C 31; 108 ER 364 where D knew that his title was defective, which exception was itself overruled subsequently in *Bain v Fothergill* itself.

[47] Law of Property (Miscellaneous Provisions) Act 1989, s 3.

been performed, A is entitled to 'reliance' damages of £2000. This is so even though one cannot sensibly talk of A recouping those expenses had the contract been performed because this is a non-commercial contract.[48]

This is very difficult to square with reliance damages being part of the expectation interest in disguise since, as the example concedes, A never expected to recoup the expenses, at least in financial terms. A no doubt did expect to gain the satisfaction of having a concert in memory of a friend and one might therefore argue that the expenditure of £2,000 which A was prepared to make shows the minimum monetary value of that lost satisfaction. But this is highly artificial and opens up the question of whether B can attempt to show that the satisfaction would have been worth much less than £2,000, which is fraught with all sorts of difficulties. It is not clear from the example whether the contract is regarded as one for relief of distress/provision of enjoyment. If it were to be taken as such an example (which does not seem to be the case), damages for the disappointment/loss of enjoyment could be awarded directly and there appears to be no reason to claim the wasted expenditure as a proxy for this. If, as seems more likely, the contract is not regarded as falling within the distress/enjoyment category, there is surely no room for a presumption that the reliance damages are awarded in lieu of an unrecoverable type of loss. The presumption that they are no more than the expectation loss would really be a fiction in this case, and we all know where fictions in contractual remedies can lead.

In truth, the example appears, on the face of it at least, to be lacking in logical coherence in saying 'in seeking to put A into as good a position as if the contract had been performed, A is entitled to reliance damages of £2,000'. If the performer (B) had repudiated at an earlier stage when the hall had not yet been booked and, say, only £500 had been spent, for example on advance advertising, would one still say the (smaller amount of) reliance damages of £500 are also designed to put A in as good a position as if the contract had been performed? The frank answer is that they are not designed to do this and a more coherent explanation for the award (whether of the £2,000 or the £500) is that B, in agreeing to perform, assumed responsibility for reasonably foreseeable expenses that A was likely (or required) to incur in reliance on B performing, and would compensate A if those expenses were wasted as a result of B failing to perform. The limiting factor on the damages for which B assumes responsibility is whether they are reasonable/reasonably foreseeable rather than equal to or less than the difficult-to-quantify (and possibly not legally protected) level of satisfaction that A expected to get. The aim is to compensate A for the wasted reliance expenditure which the law of contract is designed to encourage so that the contractual performance can take place in a suitable venue which has to be hired in advance. It is in both parties' interests that the venue should be hired so that the contractual performance can take place as envisaged in an appropriate setting, and this supports the inference that B would voluntarily assume responsibility for that reliance expenditure if B's repudiation renders it wasted. This is surely much more satisfactory a basis for the liability than a fiction of recoupment. If it is a better basis for this example, is it not a better basis for contracts more generally?

---

[48] Andrew Burrows, *A Restatement of the English Law of Contract* (1st ed, OUP 2016) 124, s 20(7) Example 4. The example first appeared in the first edition of the *Restatement* (and is still retained in the 2nd edition) and was subsequently discussed by Burrows, *Remedies* (n 7) 76. One can detect a certain amount of scepticism about the cogency of the recoupment explanation.

The argument herein for the recovery of reliance damages (especially in termination cases, which provide most of the case law) is that A is encouraged to make the appropriate expenditure in reliance on B's contractual promise (A having refrained from incurring the expenditure until after the contract is formed) and the aim is to compensate A for the reliance on the promise incurred after the promise was made. The aim is therefore *not* to put A back in the position as if the contract had not been entered into (even though it may appear also to have this effect) but rather to put A back in the position, *after* A had entered into the contract, but *before* A had relied on the promise. This can perhaps best be illustrated by reference to two aspects of the musical performer example. If B repudiates before any expenditure is incurred by A, there would be no reliance award as there has been no reliance on the promise. There may still be a change of position by A as compared to A's position before the contract was entered into (A may, before contracting with B, have had other musicians in mind who are no longer available once B repudiates) but this would not normally be recoverable in damages for breach of this contract because B would not normally be taken to have assumed this responsibility (unless perhaps he was made specifically aware of this risk). If there had been an actionable misrepresentation by B, for example that B intended to perform when B knew that was not the case, that would give rise to damages for misrepresentation, which *are* designed to put the innocent party back in the position before the contract was made and which may well include compensation for other contracts foregone.[49] The law can impose such liability, historically for fraud and now for negligence, independently of any responsibility assumed by B, but it would not normally be reasonable for B to be taken to have assumed such responsibility (for the (un)availability of other musicians) simply for breach of the contract with A. Another way to put it would be to say, as per *The Achilleas*, that the loss of other available musicians is too remote as it is not something that one can reasonably expect B to be concerned with, or advert to, or assume responsibility for. In contrast, the waste of reasonable and foreseeable expenses is much more obviously something for which B can be expected to assume responsibility. Of course, if A spends an inordinate amount in the circumstances, such as £200,000 rather than just £2,000, on preparations for the concert, that would normally—depending of course on the scale of the event and perhaps the fee to be paid to the performer—be unreasonable, and B can only be expected to assume responsibility for reasonable expenditure.[50]

IV. Conclusions

The *Robinson v Harman*/expectation aim of contractual damages is not disputed to be the most obvious distinguishing feature or principal aim of such damages, but that does

---

[49] See *East v Maurer* [1991] 1 WLR 461.

[50] It would be wrong not to admit that there is of course a relationship between the amount of reliance which is reasonable and the position which it is *contemplated* the parties would be in had the contract been performed and the overall context in which the contract is entered into. The expenditure will not normally be reasonable if it is not proportionate to this *contemplated* position in that context. But apparent proportionality in general terms at the time the expenditure is to be incurred is not the same as making the recoverability of the expenditure dependent on the breaching party not being able to show in precise financial terms with hindsight that the expenditure (or some of it) would in fact not have been recouped.

not mean it is necessarily the only aim.[51] We know that the expectation interest does not generally involve rendering full performance and is qualified in all sorts of ways in the interests of economy and efficiency. In particular, in the current context, it does not give full (gross) expectation revenues but rather net expected profits. D is liable for these (if they are reasonably foreseeable) because by making the promise in this context D can be taken to assume responsibility for the net profits. This is even the measure of recovery in a totally executory contract and it is the justification for this which Fuller and Perdue's article was seeking to explain (paradoxically by reference to the other net profits which C has foregone on other contracts). If the contract is partially performed (sometimes called essential reliance) or reasonably acted on (sometimes called incidental reliance), in addition to the net profits, D is also taken to assume responsibility for the expenditure so incurred. D is thus liable for the combination of the reasonably foreseeable reliance expenditure actually incurred plus the reasonably foreseeable net profit (in calculating which profit, the full putative reliance expenses will have been deducted). Most of this is non-controversial. The further contention here is that whether the contract is a bad bargain or not (which we have seen is often difficult to ascertain or prove, and which indeed is very rarely proven) and who has the burden of proof on this (which brings with it complications as to the precise nature of this burden) are not necessarily the crucial or relevant questions as to whether actual reliance expenditure ought to be recovered. A better approach is to ask whether the reliance on the promise is reasonable and foreseeable and whether, in the context in which the contract was made, D can be expected to have assumed responsibility for it.

Thus, rather than reliance being part of the expectation interest, reliance can be seen as one of the potential slices of loss for which D is taken to assume responsibility. The aim of contractual damages still includes putting C in as good as the (net) position that C would have been in if the contract had been performed but it also includes giving C the actual reasonable reliance losses for which D has also assumed responsibility if the repudiation[52] comes after there has been actual reliance on the promise. If no reliance has taken place before the repudiation, the damages are the net expected profits, which involves *deducting* expected outgoings in performing or exploiting the contract from gross expected revenues. If there have already been outgoings by the time of repudiation, these are then added back in as reliance expenses. Damages are therefore net expectation + reliance. It is helpful to put them this way round since initially, in an executory contract at least, they are simply net expectation. One only needs to add in reliance once there has been reliance expenditure. The promisor assumes the responsibility for net profits (expectation) and also for reasonable reliance expenditure should it be incurred. Once D becomes aware of a difficulty in being able to perform, it is in D's interest to repudiate (or at least communicate the difficulty) sooner rather than later so that it is only net profits that D will be responsible for rather than any reasonable reliance. If there are no net lost profits to claim, D should still remain liable for any reasonable reliance which has already taken place.

---

[51] The existence of a principal aim does not preclude the existence of other aims. The fact that damages aim where possible to put C in as good as (or arguably, no worse) a position than if the contract had been performed does not necessarily involve that, having entered the contract (which D has wrongfully terminated), C has entered a hypothetical parallel universe in which C's position is always limited by that overall hypothetical contractual position irrespective of C's reasonable detrimental reliance on the broken contractual promise.

[52] As has already been noted, reliance claims tend to arise and be significant in repudiation or termination cases.

Applying this to *Omak*, which we have seen in any event is not really a bad bargain case, the charterers can be reasonably expected to assume responsibility for the expenditure on the crane (which they not only foresaw but requested) and for any lost net profits. There were no lost net profits but they should still be liable for the wasted reliance expenditure. The actual decision was that not only was there no lost net profit, given the market price rise, but that the benefits of the market price rise also wiped out any reliance loss notwithstanding that the charterers had requested the expenditure. The decision depends more on the applicability or otherwise of the *Westinghouse* avoided loss rule for expectation loss (inappropriately applied, it has been argued, to already incurred reliance expenditures) rather than on the nature of reliance losses and whether they are simply part of the expectation loss.

While the above analysis of reliance damages for breach of contract may not answer all the questions which may arise in its application[53] and may not be sufficiently persuasive to change the views of all those who subscribe to what I have called the orthodox consensus, it is hoped that enough issues have been raised about the leading cases[54] to encourage the revisiting of at least some of the current underlying assumptions, including the misleading comparator of the position as if the contract had not been entered into. In particular, it is hoped that a legitimate question has been raised as to whether *Omak Maritime*, as a first instance decision in which not all the points discussed above were argued, can really be considered to settle finally the question of whether, or in what sense or on what basis, reliance damages can be regarded as an independently recoverable or separately justified head of damages for breach of contract[55] rather than simply seen as expectation damages in disguise.

---

[53] That would be a much larger task than could ever be attempted here. An interesting set of issues arose in the exemption clause cases of *Royal Devon and Exeter NHS v ATOS* [2017] EWHC 2196; 174 Con LR and *Soteria Insurance (formerly CIS) v IBM UK Ltd* [2022] EWCA Civ 440; 202 Con LR 1 where the devotion to the orthodox theory, of reliance damages as expectation damages in disguise, forced the judges in both cases, at various levels, into inventive contortions in order to hold that exemption clauses referring to inter alia 'loss of profits' were not effective to restrict or exclude wasted expenditure reliance damages.

[54] Hardly any of which can be said to be proven cases of 'bad bargains' and many of which have also been shown on full analysis to be cases of pre-contractual expenditure rather than post-contractual reliance.

[55] Particularly for repudiatory breach.

4

The Illegality Defence in the Courts Today

ANDREW BURROWS

I. Introduction

I first met Ewan at the annual conference of the Society of Public Teachers of Law (now the Society of Legal Scholars) in the mid-1980s. I can clearly recall being very impressed by the helpful comments he made on a paper I was presenting, which revealed his almost un-rivalled ability to cut straight through to the heart of any legal issue. A few years after that, I sat on the board that appointed him to a Law Fellowship at St Anne's College, Oxford, and later we co-authored *Cases and Materials on the Law of Restitution*. Subsequently, we became friends and colleagues in Oxford. We both share long-lasting academic interests in contract, tort, and unjust enrichment and, throughout the past thirty-five years, I have learned a great deal from reading Ewan's work or talking to him about legal questions. His book *Contract Law* remains my first port of call if I want a clear, accurate, succinct, and up-to-date analysis of the law and of the controversies surrounding it. It is a classic work of practical legal scholarship and is an invaluable resource for students, academics, practi-tioners, and judges alike.

Towards the end of his chapter on illegality in *Contract Law*, Ewan writes: 'It is clear that the Supreme Court in *Patel* [*v Mirza*] has set the law on a new track but it is not entirely clear where it will lead.'[1] This observation reflects the fact that, if one were to compile a list of the legally most significant decisions of the Supreme Court since its creation in 2009, *Patel v Mirza*[2] would be at the top or very close to the top of that list. It is rare for a single decision to transform the approach taken by the common law in a particular area. Yet that is what *Patel v Mirza* did, and this chapter assesses how, in consequence, the defence of illegality is operating in the courts today.

II. *Patel v Mirza*

Before I go on to consider how *Patel v Mirza* is operating in the courts today, I first need to explain, by way of lengthy introduction, the background to, and the decision in, that case.

---

[1] Ewan McKendrick, *Contract Law* (15th edn, Bloomsbury 2023) 346.
[2] [2016] UKSC 42, [2017] AC 467 (hereafter *Patel v Mirza*).

Andrew Burrows, *The Illegality Defence in the Courts Today* In: *Shaping the Law of Obligations*. Edited by: Edwin Peel and Rebecca Probert, Oxford University Press. © Andrew Burrows 2023. DOI: 10.1093/oso/9780198889762.003.0004

A. Background

Before *Patel v Mirza* the conventional approach to the illegality defence required the courts to apply various Latin maxims. So when I studied illegality as a student, I learned that much of the relevant law stemmed from the ideas that *ex turpi causa non oritur actio* ('no action arises from a disgraceful cause') and *in pari delicto potior est conditio defendentis* ('where both parties are equally in the wrong the position of the defendant is the stronger'), and that there is a *locus poenitentiae* ('time for repentance'). We were also taught that there was a 'reliance rule' so that illegality would be a defence where the claimant had to rely on the illegality to establish or to plead its cause of action. In addition, in the context of contract, rules developed from the Latin maxims tended to draw distinctions between illegality in formation and illegality in performance. And in the realm of tort, illegality became linked with particular rules of causation. But there were also exceptions to these rules. The truth is that the common law in this area had become a nightmarish mess that was not only complex and unclear but also produced a mode of reasoning that did not appear to reflect the underlying issues that, standing back from the detail, one would have expected to be relevant.

Not surprisingly, therefore, there were calls for reform, and this led to extensive work over several years by the Law Commission. I was the Law Commissioner in charge of this project in its early days. During my time it was thought that the common law had become so entrenched that the only way forward would be legislative reform and, in the first consultation paper, our provisional recommendation was for legislation to introduce a statutory discretion under which the traditional unsatisfactory rules would be swept away and the courts would be required to take into account various factors in deciding whether illegality should be a defence.[3] But subsequently in its report (widened to include tort as well as contract and trusts), and no doubt influenced by the lack of governmental enthusiasm for legislative reform of this area of the common law, the Law Commission changed tack so that, while still favouring a range-of-factors approach, the strategy became one of largely calling on the courts to implement the necessary reform.[4]

There then followed a series of cases in the Supreme Court which revealed an underlying split of view between those Justices who thought that the existing rules were basically fine, albeit needing some refinements, and those who thought that the only satisfactory way forward was to abandon the conventional rules in favour of a policy-based or range-of-factors approach along the lines recommended by the Law Commission. In this way the scene was set for the showdown in the Supreme Court in *Patel v Mirza*, heard by a panel of nine Justices.

B. The Decision

Mr Patel, the claimant, paid sums totalling £620,000 to Mr Mirza, the defendant, pursuant to an agreement under which the defendant agreed to use the money to bet on the movement of shares using inside information. The use of inside information to deal in shares (as, for

---

[3] Law Commission, *Illegal Transactions* (Law Com CP No 154, 1999).
[4] Law Commission, *The Illegality Defence* (Law Com CP No 189, 2009), *The Illegality Defence* (Law Com No 320, 2010).

example, by betting on their movement) constitutes the offence of insider dealing contrary to section 52 of the Criminal Justice Act 1993. This was therefore a contract for the commission of a crime. In the event, the agreement could not be carried out because the expected inside information was not forthcoming. When that became clear, the claimant sought repayment of the £620,000 as restitution of an unjust enrichment. Applying the normal rules of unjust enrichment, the claimant would be entitled to restitution of the £620,000 because the money had been paid for a consideration that had totally failed, that is the claimant had obtained nothing in return for his £620,000 and equally the defendant had obtained £620,000 for doing nothing. However, the defendant argued that the defence of illegality meant that the claim should fail so that he did not have to repay the money. The illegality defence succeeded before the trial judge, applying the reliance rule that the claimant had to rely on the illegality to make out the claim, but failed before the Court of Appeal, which applied the *locus poenitentiae* doctrine. The defendant then appealed to the Supreme Court.

The Supreme Court unanimously dismissed the appeal—that is the defence of illegality failed—but for different reasoning than that of the Court of Appeal. By a majority of 6–3, the Supreme Court favoured a new policy-based approach to the illegality defence which drew on the work of the Law Commission. Lord Toulson (who had been Chair of the Law Commission for part of the time that the illegality project was ongoing) gave the leading judgment with whom Lady Hale, Lord Kerr, Lord Wilson, and Lord Hodge agreed (as did Lord Neuberger, albeit with some differences). In contrast, Lords Sumption, Mance, and Clarke favoured retaining the traditional rules, with some tweaking, and—rather ironically, given the state of the common law—feared that the new approach would create unacceptable uncertainty.

In his leading judgment, Lord Toulson explained that, at a high level of generality, a court in deciding on the defence of illegality should seek to avoid inconsistency in the law, thereby maintaining the integrity of the legal system,[5] and that a 'trio of necessary considerations' should be taken into account in achieving that high-level goal. These were, first, the purpose of the illegality in question; second, any conflicting relevant policies; and third, the need to avoid a result that was disproportionate. In deciding on whether the result was disproportionate, a number of factors might be relevant, including the seriousness of the illegal conduct, its centrality to the claim, whether the conduct was intentional, and whether there was a marked disparity in the blameworthiness of the parties' conduct.

In Lord Toulson's words:

[O]ne cannot judge whether allowing a claim which is in some way tainted by illegality would be contrary to the public interest, because it would be harmful to the integrity of the legal system, without (a) considering the underlying purpose of the prohibition which has been transgressed, (b) considering conversely any other relevant public policies which may be rendered ineffective or less effective by denial of the claim, and (c) keeping in mind the

---

[5] This was Justice McLachlin's phrase in her influential judgment in the Supreme Court of Canada in *Hall v Hebert* [1993] 2 SCR 159. This is the same idea as not 'stultifying the law', which was the language used by Lord Radcliffe in *Boissevain v Weil* [1950] AC 327(HL). Non-stultification has also been emphasized by academics, most influentially Ernest Weinrib, 'Illegality as a Tort Defence' (1976) 26 UTLJ 28 (favouring a narrow scope for illegality in relation to tort) and Peter Birks, 'Recovering Value Transferred under an Illegal Contract' (2000) 1 Theo Inq L 155–204; Peter Birks, *Unjust Enrichment* (2nd edn, OUP 2005) 247–53.

possibility of overkill unless the law is applied with a due sense of proportionality. . . . That trio of necessary considerations can be found in the case law.[6]

And he later summarized the correct approach in similar terms:

> The essential rationale of the illegality doctrine is that it would be contrary to the public interest to enforce a claim if to do so would be harmful to the integrity of the legal system . . . In assessing whether the public interest would be harmed in that way, it is necessary (a) to consider the underlying purpose of the prohibition which has been transgressed and whether that purpose will be enhanced by denial of the claim, (b) to consider any other relevant public policy on which the denial of the claim may have an impact and (c) to consider whether denial of the claim would be a proportionate response to the illegality, bearing in mind that punishment is a matter for the criminal courts. Within that framework, various factors may be relevant, but it would be a mistake to suggest that the court is free to decide a case in an undisciplined way. The public interest is best served by a principled and transparent assessment of the considerations identified, rather by than the application of a formal approach capable of producing results which may appear arbitrary, unjust or disproportionate.[7]

III. Subsequent Decisions

With that by way of introduction, I want to go on to explore how the defence of illegality is operating in the courts today and, in particular, how Lord Toulson's approach in *Patel v Mirza* has subsequently been interpreted and applied in the courts. In doing so, I shall be referring to two important Supreme Court cases that were heard before I joined the Court and in relation to which I therefore had no input. They were heard within a short time of each other and the judgments were plainly crafted to provide further clarity to the practical application of Lord Toulson's approach. These cases were *Grondona v Stoffel & Co*[8] and *Henderson v Dorset Healthcare University NHS Foundation Trust*.[9] In the former, the illegality defence failed. In the latter, it succeeded.

A. *Grondona v Stoffel & Co*

This was a professional negligence claim, brought in contract and tort, against a firm of solicitors retained to carry out conveyancing. Ms Grondona had participated with a Mr Mitchell in a mortgage fraud whereby, inter alia, a lender (Birmingham Midshires) had been deceived into lending money for the purchase of a lease of a flat by Grondona from Mitchell. By the negligence of the solicitors, the lease of the flat was not registered in

---

[6] *Patel v Mirza* (n 2) [101].
[7] ibid [120].
[8] [2020] UKSC 42, [2021] AC 540.
[9] [2020] UKSC 43, [2021] AC 563.

Grondona's name. In her claim for negligence against them, it was not in dispute that, if there were no defence of illegality, the claim would succeed, entitling Grondona to damages of £78,000 plus interest. But the solicitors argued that the illegal conduct of Grondona—she and Mitchell were guilty of conspiracy to commit a mortgage fraud—meant that there was a defence of illegality to her claim. It was held by the Supreme Court, upholding the decision of the lower courts, that, applying *Patel v Mirza*, illegality was not here a defence.

In an important passage, Lord Lloyd-Jones (giving the sole judgment, with which Lord Reed, Lord Hodge, Lady Black, and Lady Arden agreed), after referring to Lord Toulson's 'trio of necessary considerations', said the following:

> [The] evaluation of policy considerations, while necessarily structured, must not be permitted to become another mechanistic process. In the application of stages (a) and (b) of this trio a court will be concerned to identify the relevant policy considerations at a relatively high level of generality before considering their application to the situation before the court. In particular, I would not normally expect a court to admit or to address evidence on matters such as the effectiveness of the criminal law in particular situations or the likely social consequences of permitting a claim in specified circumstances. The essential question is whether to allow the claim would damage the integrity of the legal system. The answer will depend on whether it would be inconsistent with the policies to which the legal system gives effect. The court is not concerned here to evaluate the policies in play or to carry out a policy-based evaluation of the relevant laws. It is simply seeking to identify the policies to which the law gives effect which are engaged by the question whether to allow the claim, to ascertain whether to allow it would be inconsistent with those policies or, where the policies compete, where the overall balance lies. In considering proportionality at stage (c), by contrast, it is likely that the court will have to give close scrutiny to the detail of the case in hand. Finally, in this regard, since the overriding consideration is the damage that might be done to the integrity of the legal system by its adopting contradictory positions, it may not be necessary in every case to complete an exhaustive examination of all stages of the trio of considerations. If, on an examination of the relevant policy considerations, the clear conclusion emerges that the defence should not be allowed, there will be no need to go on to consider proportionality, because there is no risk of disproportionate harm to the claimant by refusing relief to which he or she would otherwise be entitled. If, on the other hand, a balancing of the policy considerations suggests a denial of the claim, it will be necessary to go on to consider proportionality.[10]

Four particularly important points may be said to emerge from this paragraph:

(i)   At a high level, the goal in applying the illegality defence is to avoid inconsistency within the legal system.
(ii) The identification and assessment of the relevant policies in play normally falls within the competence of judges to carry out without the need for expert evidence.
(iii) That process of identifying and assessing the relevant policies should be flexible and should not become too mechanistic.

---

[10] *Grondona v Stoffel* [2020] UKSC 42, [2021] AC 540 [26].

64 THE ILLEGALITY DEFENCE IN THE COURTS TODAY

(iv) One may not need to move on to consider proportionality where it is clear from the first two of Lord Toulson's trio of considerations (ie stages (a) and (b)) that the defence of illegality should not be allowed.

Applying this approach to the facts, Lord Lloyd-Jones considered that allowing the defence would not seriously deter mortgage fraud. On the other hand, denying the defence would undermine the good reasons why the law imposes duties of care on solicitors, would tend to increase the prospect of reducing mortgage fraud, would on the facts help to protect other victims of fraud (ie the lenders who could pursue Grondona if she succeeded in recovering compensation), and would recognize that Grondona had a valid property interest (that could be registered). Although considered later in the judgment, it was also thought relevant that what Grondona was here seeking was compensation for loss.

Given that the policies clearly favoured denying the defence, there was no need to go on to consider proportionality. But if one did so, to allow the defence would be a disproportionate response because the illegality was not at all central to the negligence of the solicitors; or, put another way, the negligence of the solicitors was conceptually entirely separate from the illegality.

The defence of illegality was therefore held to be inapplicable and the claim for professional negligence succeeded.

B. *Henderson v Dorset Healthcare Foundation Trust*

In this case, the claimant stabbed her mother to death while suffering a psychotic episode. She was convicted of manslaughter by reason of diminished responsibility. The defendant health authority admitted negligence in failing to have the claimant returned to hospital. The claimant brought an action in the tort of negligence against the health authority in which she claimed as damages the loss she had suffered consequent on having killed her mother, which included damages for her loss of liberty and the loss of her share of her mother's estate by reason of the Forfeiture Act 1982. The sole issue was whether the defendant had a defence of illegality to the claim for negligence. The Supreme Court held that it did have that defence.

In contrast to *Stoffel*, a complication in this case in applying *Patel v Mirza*—and it was for this reason that a panel of seven Justices heard the case—was that there was a previous decision of the House of Lords in *Gray v Thames Trains Ltd*[11] which, on somewhat similar facts, had allowed the defence of illegality. Although the negligence in that case had been very different—it concerned negligence in relation to a train accident in which the claimant had suffered PTSD—the essential similarity was that, as a consequence of the negligence, the claimant had killed someone and had been convicted of manslaughter, by reason of diminished responsibility, for that death.

The leading judgment in *Henderson* was given by Lord Hamblen (with whom Lord Reed, Lord Hodge, Lady Black, Lord Lloyd-Jones, Lady Arden, and Lord Kitchin agreed). In

---

[11] [2009] UKHL 33, [2009] AC 1339.

relation to the application of *Patel v Mirza*, Lord Hamblen made a number of important points. I here mention six of them:

(i) Although this was implicit in *Stoffel*, he explicitly stated[12] that the policy-based approach of *Patel v Mirza* applies across civil law and is not confined to claims in unjust enrichment or contract. It applies as in *Stoffel*, and in this case to torts but also to claims based on property law.

(ii) As was also made clear in *Stoffel*, Lord Hamblen was of the view that usually evidence as to the policy considerations would be unnecessary.[13]

(iii) He clarified that the consideration of policies at stages (a) and (b) requires one to consider all the relevant policies in favour of applying the defence (ie denying the claim) at (a) and then all the relevant policies for denying the defence (ie allowing the claim) at (b).[14] At (a), one should not merely consider, as Lord Toulson's wording might have been thought to indicate, the purpose of the prohibition.

(iv) As was said in *Stoffel*, Lord Hamblen was of the view that, where the balancing of policy considerations comes down clearly against applying the defence of illegality, there is no need to go on to consider proportionality.[15]

(v) Lord Hamblen made clear that *Patel v Mirza* was concerned with what can be labelled common law illegality and not statutory illegality.[16] I will return to this point later.

(vi) As regards precedent, the adoption of the new policy-based approach in *Patel v Mirza* did not wipe away existing precedent.[17] *Patel v Mirza* did not represent 'year zero'. The exercise was one of checking whether past precedents were '*Patel*-compliant'.[18]

Applying all this to the case at hand, Lord Hamblen identified a number of policies supporting denial of the claim (ie that the defence of illegality should apply). These included avoiding inconsistency in the legal system (ie while recognizing diminished responsibility, criminal law treated the defendant as guilty of, and hence responsible for, the death), the close connection between the crime and the claim, and the general deterrence of crimes. The polices going the other way—such as upholding duties of care and providing compensation to the victims of torts—were plainly outweighed by the former policies. As the policies favoured allowing the defence, one needed to move on to the third stage, and here the denial of the claim would not be disproportionate taking into account, for example, the centrality of the conduct to the claim and the criminal guilt of the defendant in that she knew what she was doing and that it was legally and morally wrong. Applying the approach in *Patel v Mirza*, therefore, the defence of illegality should succeed.

---

[12] *Henderson* (n 9) [76].
[13] ibid [115].
[14] ibid [116]–[122].
[15] ibid [123].
[16] ibid [74]–[75].
[17] ibid [77]–[78].
[18] ibid [145]. A useful analogy might be drawn with the recognition of the law of unjust enrichment in *Lipkin Gorman v Karpnale Ltd* [1991] 2 AC 548. It is not suggested that that decision at a stroke wiped away all the decisions in past cases based on the rejected 'implied contract' approach to restitution. Rather, after that decision, the courts should strive to arrive at the same decisions as bound them before but applying an unjust enrichment analysis.

Furthermore, this policy-based analysis was consistent with the decision and most of the reasoning of the House of Lords in *Gray*, albeit that there had been no consideration of proportionality by their Lordships. This meant that *Gray* was '*Patel*-compliant' and should be followed in this case.

It should be realized that the facts of *Henderson* and *Gray* may be considered somewhat exceptional. In *Patel v Mirza*, the tenor of the majority judgments was that, at least in restitution of unjust enrichment cases—because one is seeking to restore the pre-illegality position rather than to enforce a contractual obligation upholding an illegal position—there is a very strong argument for applying normal civil law rules unaffected by illegality and leaving the criminal law to deal with the criminality involved. The same may be said of claims in tort, and this derives support from *Stoffel*. But *Henderson* and *Gray* show that there are limits to that approach.[19]

Taken together, *Stoffel* and *Henderson* in the Supreme Court have served to clarify and indeed simplify the application of the trio of considerations laid down in *Patel v Mirza*. With the overall aim of avoiding inconsistency, one must identify and weigh the relevant policies for and against the illegality defence and then, if the former outweigh the latter (ie the policies favour allowing the defence), one must go on to consider whether allowing the defence would be a disproportionate response.

Having said all that, in the light of these two cases, I do have some lingering concerns as to whether the attempt made in *Patel v Mirza* to structure the analysis through a trio of considerations is to be preferred to an approach which would have allowed the courts more freely to consider and articulate a range of factors in arriving at their decision. There is some danger of the courts being unnecessarily straitjacketed into a mechanical approach when it may have been preferable to have permitted them to consider all relevant factors and to articulate those considered important in applying or rejecting the illegality defence in the particular case. Not least because of the requirement, as far as possible, to respect precedent, I doubt whether courts needed the structure provided by the trio of considerations in order to marshal the relevant factors or to ensure sufficient certainty. This links to the further point that, rather than viewing the overall aim as being to avoid inconsistency in the legal system, one might regard that policy as merely one of the relevant policies in play which will more obviously have a central role to play in some cases than in others. Similarly, proportionality might have been best treated as one relevant factor to be considered because, again, it may have greater resonance in some cases than others.

It is important to add that the new policy-based approach should ensure that, in contrast to the old unsatisfactory rules, new rules on the illegality defence can in time be formulated that are fit for purpose and reflect sound underlying policies. Those new rules need to be sufficiently flexible to allow the relevant policy factors to be taken into account but also, so far as possible, should be consistent with past decisions.

---

[19] For a different approach to tort cases after *Patel v Mirza*, see the interesting article by Liron Shmilovits, 'When Is Illegality a Defence to a Tort?' (2021) 41 LS 603 proposing a guiding principle that 'If the claimant's harm is the ordinary result of the claimant's wrongdoing, the claim fails for illegality'.

IV. Statutory Illegality and Common Law Illegality

A further point made by Lord Hamblen in the *Henderson* case is that *Patel v Mirza* was concerned with what he referred to as 'common law illegality rather than statutory illegality'.[20] He continued: 'Where the effects of the illegality are dealt with by statute then the statute should be applied.' And, as Lord Toulson said in *Patel*, 'The courts must obviously abide by the terms of any statute.'[21]

This relationship between statutory and common law illegality is not straightforward. However, it must be stressed that it is in no sense a new issue created by *Patel v Mirza*.

What can cause initial confusion is that the terms common law and statutory illegality are not here referring to the source of the illegality but to its effects on the claim in question. In most cases, at least those involving crimes, the source of the illegality is statutory. That is, the crime is laid down in statute rather than by common law. Indeed, that is true of *Patel v Mirza* itself, whether one regards the relevant crime as the statutory offence of insider dealing or the statutory offence of conspiracy to commit insider dealing (the common law offence of conspiracy having been made a statutory offence under the Criminal Law Act 1977). With statutory illegality, one is concerned with applying whatever the statute lays down, expressly or impliedly, as to the effects of the illegality. This is determined by ordinary statutory interpretation. Common law illegality is applied where the effects of the illegality have not been laid down, expressly or impliedly, in the statute, that is the statute has not dealt with the effects of the illegality. With common law illegality, one is concerned to determine the effects of the illegality at common law, and this is where *Patel v Mirza* applies.

Where the source of the illegality is statutory, one must first therefore consider whether the effects of the illegality are dealt with, expressly or impliedly, in the statute. Where the statute does not deal, expressly or impliedly, with the effects on the claim in question, one must go on to consider common law illegality and *Patel v Mirza*. Another way of expressing this—given that a statute is enacted against the background of the common law on illegality—is that the common law on illegality will apply unless it has been ousted, expressly or impliedly, by the statute in question.

Perhaps the best-known case where a statutory illegality defence succeeded was *Re Mahmoud and Ispahani*.[22] Here a wartime order, made by delegated legislation, prohibited the purchase or sale of linseed oil without a licence from the Food Controller. The claimant (who had a licence) contracted to sell linseed oil to the defendant, who did not have a licence, although the claimant was told by the defendant that he did have a licence. The defendant refused to accept the oil but the claimant's action for damages for non-acceptance failed because the contract was prohibited by the legislation and was therefore, by necessary implication, unenforceable by either party. The statute therefore comprehensively dealt with the effects of the illegality and there was no role for common law illegality.

Two post-*Patel* cases can be usefully looked at to exemplify this relationship between statutory illegality and common law illegality. In *Okedina v Chikale*,[23] the claimant employee had been employed by the defendant as a live-in domestic worker for more than

---

[20] *Henderson* (n 9) [74].
[21] *Patel v Mirza* (n 2) [109].
[22] [1921] 2 KB 716 (CA).
[23] [2019] EWCA Civ 1393, [2019] ICR 1365.

68   THE ILLEGALITY DEFENCE IN THE COURTS TODAY

18 months after her visa ran out. When she was summarily dismissed, and ejected from the home, she brought actions for unfair and wrongful dismissal, including for significant sums owed by reason, for example, of minimum wage regulations. Her claims succeeded because there was no statutory illegality defence and nor was there a common law illegality defence.

In an excellent judgment, Underhill LJ (with whom Nicola Davies and Davis LJJ agreed) said the following:

> The essential starting point is to recognise that there are two distinct bases on which a claim under, or arising out of, a contract may be defeated on the ground of illegality. These are nowadays generally referred to as 'statutory' and 'common law' illegality. Put very briefly:
>
> (1) Statutory illegality applies where a legislative provision either (a) prohibits the making of a contract so that it is unenforceable by either party or (b) provides that it, or some particular term, is unenforceable by one or other party. The underlying principle is straightforward: if the legislation itself has provided that the contract is unenforceable, in full or in the relevant respect, the court is bound to respect that provision. That being the rationale, the knowledge or culpability of the party who is prevented from recovering is irrelevant: it is a simple matter of obeying the statute.
>
> (2) Common law illegality arises where the formation, purpose or performance of the contract involves conduct that is illegal or contrary to public policy and where to deny enforcement to one or other party is an appropriate response to that conduct. The nature of the rule has long been controversial, but the controversy has been resolved by the decision of the Supreme Court in *Patel v Mirza* [2017] AC 467. The majority of the court adopted an approach based on an assessment of what the public interest requires in a particular case, having regard to a range of factors.[24]

As regards a statutory illegality defence, Underhill LJ decided that, as a matter of statutory interpretation, the relevant legislative provisions on employing an illegal immigrant (sections 15 and 21 of the Immigration, Asylum and Nationality Act 2006; section 21 has subsequently been amended) neither expressly nor impliedly rendered the contract of employment unenforceable by the employee, albeit that she did not have a visa and so was being employed contrary to those provisions. As regards common law illegality, applying *Patel v Mirza*, the ultimate crucial factor—in contrast to most of the reported cases involving illegality in the employment field—was that the employee had no knowledge of the illegality. Rather than concealing her immigration status from the employer, she had been falsely led to believe by her employer that a new visa was being arranged for her and she left these matters entirely in her employer's hands.

The other case is the decision of the Privy Council, in which I gave the judgment of the Board, in *Energizer Supermarket Ltd v Holiday Snacks Ltd*.[25] A principal issue in the case was whether an equitable easement allowing a gas pipeline to run under the land of the defendant, in favour of the claimant, was unenforceable by the claimant because of illegality in that no licence for the pipeline had been obtained by the claimant (or its predecessors in

---

[24] ibid [12].
[25] [2022] UKPC 16. The relationship between statutory and common law illegality was also examined in the Privy Council in *SR Projects Ltd v Rampersad* [2022] UKPC 24.

title) contrary to the Petroleum Act in Trinidad and Tobago. It was held that there was no illegality defence, whether statutory or common law.

There was no statutory illegality defence because, in contrast to *Re Mahmoud and Ispahani*, the relevant statute, the Petroleum Act, on its proper interpretation, did not prohibit the granting of the easement and did not impliedly render the easement unenforceable. In other words, the statute had not dealt with the effects of the illegality.

Turning to common law illegality, then, applying *Patel v Mirza*, as clarified in *Stoffel* and *Henderson*, the policies in favour of the illegality defence were clearly outweighed by the policies favouring denying the illegality defence, and we set out the relevant policies in some detail:

> [W]hile denying the enforcement of the easement might be said to offer some general support to the licensing regime, it is the Board's view that the more significant policies favour upholding the easement (ie denying the defence of illegality) . . . Upholding the easement recognises the merits of the certainty given by applying normal property law principles; and there is no inconsistency between enforcement of the easement and the licensing regime because the two are separate and one is not here enforcing an obligation to lay a gas pipeline against a party who was unlicensed to do so . . . [T]he safety and efficiency purposes of the licensing regime under the Petroleum Act are not undermined in any way by upholding parties' agreements for gas pipeline easements. Moreover, there is nothing to indicate that, over and above the criminal sanctions laid down, denying the enforcement of the easement will serve to deter others from not obtaining the necessary licence; and although under section 6(2) of the Petroleum Act the criminal offence is a summary only offence, the sanctions are potentially severe with the maximum fine being a very significant sum which, if the offence is continuing, may be increased on a daily basis. It is also a relevant policy consideration that . . . the owner of the pipeline was NGC, a state-owned utility service provider: the illegality of failing to comply with a state licensing scheme may be said to be mitigated to some extent when the State itself owns the pipeline in question. We therefore conclude that the policies clearly favour denying an illegality defence.[26]

It followed that it was unnecessary to go on to consider proportionality, but in the Board's view, it would be

> a disproportionate response to the illegality to deny enforcement of the easement in this case for at least three reasons. First, the conduct in failing to obtain a licence is separate from, and certainly not central to, the transaction. Secondly, although the potential fines are significant, the offence is summary only and one is not here dealing with serious criminal wrongdoing. Thirdly, the easement has proved important to the businesses supplied with gas.[27]

To conclude on this issue, it is worth stressing, lest the link between statutory illegality and common law illegality is made to seem more complex than it really is, that in the vast majority of cases the effect of illegality on the claim in question has not been laid down

---

[26] *Energizer Supermarket Ltd v Holiday Snacks Ltd* [2022] UKPC 16 [43].

[27] ibid [44].

(expressly or impliedly) in the relevant statute (even though, as will usually be the case, the relevant illegality is a statutory offence). In other words, the statute usually leaves open the question of the effect of illegality. The effect of illegality will therefore normally be determined by applying the common law. Another way of viewing this is to say that common law illegality is the default position subject to the effect of the illegality being fully dealt with by statute.

V. Standard of Review by an Appellate Court

One of the questions that has perplexed me most since starting on the Supreme Court is the standard of review that the Supreme Court should be applying to the decisions of the lower courts in the particular case. One might have expected that, as permission to appeal is granted only in respect of arguable points of law of general public importance, the standard of review should be one of correctness—that is, the lower courts have either been correct on the law or wrong on the law; it is for the Supreme Court to determine which; and, insofar as the decision below was incorrect on the law, that error should be rectified. In contrast, appeals to the Supreme Court are not permitted on findings of fact, so that the deference that is required to be shown to the first instance judge in respect of findings of fact—because that judge has had the benefit of seeing all the relevant evidence and hearing from witnesses— does not arise.

In practice, matters are less clear-cut and more complex than this. One reason is that errors of law can arise in relation to findings of fact (ie the wrong approach may have been taken in making those findings). However, of far greater importance is that the question to be decided may be one of mixed law and fact, or, as it may otherwise be termed, the question may require an evaluative judgment or the application of a legal standard. An obvious example is whether the standard of care in the tort of negligence has been complied with. In respect of such questions, there appears to be no simple answer to the standard of review (whether correctness or showing deference). On the contrary, the variety of situations suggests that courts may have to assess on a case-by-case basis what standard of review is appropriate, which in turn will depend on the extent to which the question is one which the first instance judge was in a better position to decide. But even if the question is one on which deference should be shown to the first instance judge (eg a decision as to whether a child should be made subject to a care order taking that child away from its parents), an appeal court may still intervene—and may send the decision back to be reconsidered at first instance—where the judge's reasoning is clearly flawed. Hence, speaking of an evaluative judgment on which an appeal court should defer to the first instance judge, the Court of Appeal (McCombe, Leggatt, and Rose LJJ) in *Prescott v Potamianos (Re Sprintroom)* said:

> the appeal court does not carry out a balancing task afresh, but must ask whether the decision of the judge was wrong by reason of some identifiable flaw in the judge's treatment of the question to be decided, 'such as a gap in logic, a lack of consistency, or a failure to take account of some material factor, which undermines the cogency of the conclusion'.[28]

---

[28] *Prescott v Potamianos (Re Sprintroom)* [2019] EWCA Civ 932, [2019] BCC 1031 [76] citing Lord Carnwath's judgment in *R (on the application of AR) v Chief Constable of the Greater Manchester Police* [2018] UKSC 47, [2018] 1 WLR 4079.

How does all this apply to the illegality defence after *Patel v Mirza*?[29] It is clear that the question whether illegality is a defence is a question of law. The standard of review by the appellate courts, including the Supreme Court, is one of correctness. There is no good reason for showing deference to the first instance judge on this question. Although the decision now rests on an evaluation of policy considerations and not on the application of unsatisfactory rules, such as the reliance rule, it is clear that the policies in question are ones that a first instance judge has no particular advantage in assessing over an appellate court. Applying the normal hierarchy on matters of law, an appeal court should overrule a lower court if satisfied that its own view of that assessment is to be preferred to that of the lower court. This includes if the analysis involves proportionality at the third stage. Although a balancing of factors is required, it is the appellate court's balancing that should count, not that of the first instance judge.

Of course, this is not to say that one ignores the decision of the first instance judge. As ever, courtesy and respect require that appellate judges look carefully at what the first instance judge has decided. But if the appellate court is satisfied that the first instance judge has made an incorrect decision on the illegality defence, it is duty bound to reverse that decision.

It follows that, just as the question whether illegality was a defence was in the past a question of law, the same applies after *Patel v Mirza*. This explains why, in a case such as *Henderson* (which, unlike *Stoffel*, was decided at first instance *after Patel v Mirza*), the Supreme Court considered the policies afresh in the light of precedent and did not consider that particular deference should be shown to the views of the first instance judge (or Court of Appeal).

VI. Court Taking the Point on Its Own Initiative

In general, the issues raised by the parties in civil litigation are a matter for them. However, as an exception to the general position, the defence of illegality is one that the courts should raise and, if necessary, decide on their own initiative. This is because there is a public interest in play that overrides the interests of the parties.

Nevertheless, there are limits to how far the courts can enter the arena to deal with a difficult question of illegality. This was explored in a recent case in the Privy Council, *Nature Resorts Ltd v First Citizens Bank Ltd*,[30] on an appeal from Trinidad and Tobago. The primary issue in the case concerned whether a deed of mortgage over land owned by the claimant company (NRL) in favour of the defendant bank, to secure a loan made by the bank to a third party, was voidable for undue influence exerted by a solicitor over NRL's managing director (Mr Dankou). It was held that there was no such undue influence.

A secondary issue in the case was whether the mortgage was in any event unenforceable by the bank against NRL on the basis of statutory (or common law) illegality in that the loan might be said to be illegal under the relevant legislation in Trinidad and Tobago (sections 56–57 of the Companies Act of Trinidad and Tobago) as constituting financial assistance

---

[29] This question was explicitly left open by the Supreme Court in *Singularis Holdings Ltd v Daiwa Capital Markets Finance Ltd* [2019] UKSC 50, [2020] AC 1189 [21].

[30] [2022] UKPC 10, [2022] 1 WLR 2788.

72 THE ILLEGALITY DEFENCE IN THE COURTS TODAY

by a company with the purchase of its shares. This had not been a point taken by the parties until it was raised by the Privy Council prior to the hearing. Ultimately, however, the Board decided (Lady Arden dissenting) that it would be inappropriate to decide the case on this basis, essentially because the question of illegality turned on difficult questions of statutory interpretation and to some extent also turned on factual questions. Yet the Board did not have the benefit of the local lower courts' views on the issues of statutory interpretation and the bank had not had the opportunity to address the factual controversies before the first instance judge. The Board (with the judgment being given by Lord Briggs and myself) summarized its reasons for not deciding the illegality issue as follows:

> We accept that, where there are proceedings before a court relating to a contract involving conduct that appears to be illegal, the court must consider whether the contract or term is unenforceable or void even if not raised by the parties. But the authorities indicate that the court must be satisfied that it has sufficient legal and factual material to deal with the illegality question: see, eg, *Edler v Auerbach* [1950] 1 KB 359, 371: *Chitty on Contracts,* 34th ed (2021), para 18-264. The Board considers that it does not have sufficient factual material before it to resolve the dispute between the parties as to the operation of sections 56 and 57; and that the issues of legal interpretation are far from straightforward and are legal issues which the Board is reluctant to resolve without the benefit of the views of the Trinidad and Tobago Court of Appeal. The impact of *Patel v Mirza* may also need to be considered and has not been the subject of any submissions (and the same may be said of section 517 of the Companies Act [to the effect that civil remedies are unaffected by the act or omission being an offence under the Companies Act]). Moreover, in the Board's view, it would be procedurally unfair to the Bank now to rest the decision in this case on sections 56-57.[31]

VII. Restraint of Trade

I have not said anything so far about what constitutes illegality for the purposes of the defence of illegality. The modern approach is to focus on the type of illegal conduct in question (ie crime or civil wrong or conduct contrary to public policy) and then to consider the effect of illegality on the particular claim in question. On this approach, reference to a contract being illegal is avoided, although one might talk of a contract or contract term being rendered void or unenforceable by reason of illegality.

However, the most legally significant area of conduct being contrary to public policy—that dealing with restraint of trade—is almost inevitably tied to contract. Hence one commonly refers to 'contracts in restraint of trade'. However, whatever the terminology, the important substantive point is that the long-established common law on restraint of trade has not been reformed or amended by the approach in *Patel v Mirza*. With the exception of severance, that area of law has long been regarded as self-contained and distinct from the rest of the law of illegality. Moreover, it has not been thought in need of fundamental reform, in the sense that the relevant law has not been based on the unsatisfactory rules that

---

[31] ibid [42].

have so bedevilled the rest of the law on illegality and has already required the consideration of relevant policies by the courts.

In our joint judgment in the Supreme Court restraint of trade case of *Harcus Sinclair LLP v Your Lawyers Ltd*,[32] Lord Briggs, Lord Hamblen, and I said the following:

> One might think that the recent series of Supreme Court cases analysing the law on illegality (*Patel v Mirza* [2017] AC 467, *Henderson v Dorset Healthcare University NHS Foundation Trust* [2021] AC 563, *Grondona v Stoffel & Co* [2021] AC 540) is also relevant. This is not least because, in the contract textbooks, illegality is usually closely linked with public policy so that, for example, contracts involving crimes are usually examined alongside contracts that are contrary to public policy, such as contracts involving sexual immorality or contracts interfering with the administration of justice or contracts in restraint of trade. But the principles governing contracts in restraint of trade are well-established and (with the exception of the rules on severance) self-contained and already reflect the type of flexibility that *Patel v Mirza* [2017] AC 467 has brought to the law on contracts affected by illegality. It seems preferable, therefore, to treat the law on the enforceability of contracts in restraint of trade as being separate from, albeit similar to, the law on the enforceability of contracts affected by illegality as laid down in *Patel v Mirza*.[33]

Given that, prior to 2019, the highest court had not decided a case on the restraint of trade doctrine for forty-five years, it is rather remarkable that there have been three recent cases in which the Supreme Court has considered the doctrine.

In *Egon Zehnder Ltd v Tillman*,[34] the power to sever the offending restraint of trade clause from the rest of the contract was explored and a previously leading case, *Attwood v Lamont*,[35] was overruled. In *Peninsula Securities Ltd v Dunnes Stores (Bangor) Ltd*,[36] the court examined what Lord Wilson described as the 'outer reaches'[37] of the restraint of trade doctrine. It was held that a restrictive covenant over land, given by a developer of a shopping centre, preventing the presence of a rival shop to that of the claimant (who was an 'anchor tenant') did not engage the doctrine; and the central reasoning of the majority of the House of Lords in *Esso Petroleum Co Ltd v Harper's Garage (Stourport) Ltd*[38] favouring a 'pre-existing freedom' test was departed from in favour of applying a 'trading society' test.

In *Harcus Sinclair* itself the dispute was between two law firms as to who should act for claimants in respect of group litigation claims arising out of diesel emissions from Volkswagen vehicles. One law firm, the defendant, had given a non-compete undertaking to the other. The question was whether that non-compete undertaking was unenforceable as an unreasonable restraint of trade.

In deciding on reasonableness, it was explained that there were two applicable principles. The first, which was for the promisee to establish, was that the non-compete undertaking was reasonable as between the parties. To satisfy this burden, the promisee had to show,

---

[32] [2021] UKSC 32, [2021] 3 WLR 598.
[33] ibid [45].
[34] [2019] UKSC 32, [2020] AC 154.
[35] [1920] 3 KB 571 (CA).
[36] [2020] UKSC 36, [2021] AC 1014.
[37] ibid [1].
[38] [1968] AC 269 (HL).

first, that the non-compete undertaking protected legitimate interests of the promisee and, second, that the non-compete undertaking went no further than was reasonably necessary to protect those interests. It was also suggested that there was a third element, namely that the promisee needed to show that the restriction was commensurate with the benefits secured to the promisor under the contract.

If the promisee succeeded in establishing that the non-compete undertaking was reasonable as between the parties, the second principle was that the burden shifted to the promisor to establish that the undertaking was unreasonable as being contrary to the public interest.

The difficulties in this case concerned the first principle only. Within that, the Supreme Court laid down crucially that, in determining whether the promisee had legitimate interests to protect, a court could consider not only the contractual provisions themselves but also, assessed at the time the contract was made, the parties' non-contractual intentions or what they contemplated would occur as a consequence of entering into the contract. That mattered on the facts because it was important to know whether one could take into account the promisee's legitimate interests on the basis that the parties intended or contemplated that they would collaborate informally. Once one took into account that informal collaboration, the promisee did have legitimate interests to protect by the non-compete undertaking.

VIII. Conclusion

Illegality as a defence raises many fascinating issues. In this essay in honour of Ewan, I have principally sought to explain and evaluate the decisions of the Supreme Court in *Stoffel* and *Henderson* which have simplified and clarified the new approach to illegality laid down in *Patel v Mirza*. I have also explored the relationship between common law and statutory illegality, explained that the illegality defence is a question of law that is subject to a correctness review by the appellate courts, and looked at the extent to which a court should deal with illegality on its own initiative. Finally, I have touched on the restraint of trade doctrine, not least to clarify that, because the principles were already flexible and enabled the relevant policies to be evaluated, that area is unaffected by *Patel v Mirza*.

5

Schrödinger's Lawful Act Duress: Dead or Alive?

MINDY CHEN-WISHART AND JODI GARDNER

I. Introduction

Ewan McKendrick's rapid rise to the highest echelons of both academia and university administration was inevitable. He is supremely talented, hard-working, humble, understated (although utterly compelling when lecturing), encouraging, kind, and excellent with people. One of these authors has known him for thirty-two years and it is clear that his goodness is not just surface-deep, but goes all the way to his core. He generates so much trust and goodwill that it is impossible not to want to be his friend, work with him, employ him, promote him. Those of us who have managed to do or be any one of these things are blessed indeed. Both of this chapter's authors have variously relied on his academic writing in our teaching and own writings, co-taught with him, moved in the same professional circle as him; it is our great pleasure to honour Ewan by this contribution.

In *Times Travel v Pakistan International Airline Corporation*,[1] the Supreme Court unanimously recognized the category of lawful act duress in English contract law.[2] But their Lordships left the content inside the closed box of lawful act duress doubtful; like Schrödinger's cat, it may be dead or alive. We make three arguments. First, the judgments of Lord Hodge for the majority and Lord Burrows in the minority appear to leave no content for this category that is not already covered elsewhere in contract law. The majority decision recognizes that there are 'to date two circumstances in which the English courts have recognised' lawful act duress.[3] The first is the exploitation of knowledge of criminal activity, which is already relieved by several other grounds of invalidity. The second is the use of 'illegitimate means to pressure the complainant into waiving a claim against the threatening party'; as interpreted by the majority, this adds little if anything to economic duress. Lord Burrows adds a third category, that of bad faith demand. But, as his Lordship effectively equates it with fraud or deceit, it adds nothing to that existing ground of invalidity. Inside the recognized box of lawful act duress, the cat is dead, dead, and thrice dead.

Second, the practical result of this legal position is normatively undesirable. As we will show, it produces the moral hazard of permitting, and indirectly encouraging, a stronger party to renege on pre-existing contractual liabilities where the counterparty needs to continue the contractual relationship. Since all their Lordships found no lawful act duress or any other invalidity on the facts of *Time Travel*, this is indeed what happened.

Third, if we are serious about the substance (and not just the form) of a category of lawful act duress, recent judicial and academic statements in support of a doctrine of good faith

---

[1] [2021] UKSC 40, [2021] 3 WLR 727 (hereafter *Times Travel*, Supreme Court).
[2] ibid [82–92] (Burrows) and [1] (majority).
[3] ibid [4].

Mindy Chen-Wishart and Jodi Gardner, *Schrödinger's Lawful Act Duress: Dead or Alive?* In: *Shaping the Law of Obligations.*
Edited by: Edwin Peel and Rebecca Probert, Oxford University Press. © Mindy Chen-Wishart and Jodi Gardner 2023.
DOI: 10.1093/oso/9780198889762.003.0005

76   SCHRÖDINGER'S LAWFUL ACT DURESS

repay examination. When this is combined with Warren J's finding of lawful act duress in the High Court decision in *Time Travel*, the result is a more substantive category of lawful act duress and the potential for a more just and coherent outcome, free of the moral hazard above. Schrödinger's cat may yet be alive.

II. *Times Travel v PIAC*

A. Facts

Times Travel (TT) was a small family-owned travel agency, which predominately sold return flights to Pakistan. At the relevant time, Pakistan International Airlines Corporation (PIAC) was the only provider of direct flights between London and Pakistan. TT was reliant on PIAC for 90 per cent of its sales, and therefore for its entire financial viability. The 'Original Agreement' of 2008 authorized TT to sell PIAC tickets at an agreed commission rate, with additions to incentivize total sales. Either party could terminate on one month's notice. Subsequently, the travel agents appointed by PIAC formed a union to negotiate with PIAC over dissatisfactions with the commission structure and payments. PIAC responded by stopping payments of commission to many travel agencies, including TT. In 2010 the trade union threatened PIAC with legal proceedings to reclaim the unpaid commission.

PIAC then took actions designed to prevent TT from joining the legal proceedings, including:

(i) informing TT that if it went down the legal route, PIAC would cease to provide TT with further tickets;

(ii) reassuring TT that an amicable solution would be agreed very soon and the outstanding commission would be paid;

(iii) sending to all its UK agents, including TT, a notice of termination and the terms of the 'New Agreement' on 24 September 2010;

(iv) refusing to provide TT with an earlier copy of the New Agreement to allow it to obtain legal advice;[4] and

(v) reducing TT's ticket allocation from 300 to 60 tickets per fortnight, later to 45, and stating that this would be reduced to zero unless TT signed the New Agreement by 31 October 2010.

Warren J commented:

it does not, I think on any view, reflect well on PIAC that it should [act] in the way which it did when TT was a successful, honest and reliable agent with a substantial period of loyal service. It was given no adequate period of notice to allow it to adjust its businesses; it was not allowed, even during the short period of notice, to acquire for cash its pre-existing ticket allocations.[5]

---

[4] *Times Travel v Pakistan International Airline Corporation* [2017] EWHC 1367 (Ch) (hereafter *Times Travel, High Court*) [62].

[5] ibid [123].

PIAC's actions caused TT 'immense stress'.[6] TT met PIAC on 17 October 2010 to express its discontent at the pressure it felt that PIAC had exerted due to the reduction in ticket stocks to TT, and to ask how it would benefit from the New Agreement. Warren J accepted TT's evidence that PIAC had made representations along the lines of:[7]

> I know it is unfair but if you sign the new 2012 agreement [it] will continue from 2013 onwards and the ticket stock will increase. This [is] my promise to you and you have my word that we will look after you and also give such high incentive that you will forget the court case. You will make more money over these incentives over what the court will award you on conclusion of this case which is not even guaranteed.[8]

In fact, the New Agreement provided for a lower commission to TT which was, moreover, only payable after specific sales targets were met, and it was initially only for six months (although PIAC orally represented that it would run 'well into the future'). Critically, it also released PIAC from all claims to unpaid commission or remuneration arising out of the Original Agreement, which totalled approximately £1.2 million.

TT later sought rescission of the New Agreement on grounds, including lawful act economic duress, to invalidate the waiver clause and recover the outstanding commission of £1.2 million.

B. High Court Finds Lawful Act Duress

In the High Court, Warren J concluded that PIAC's actions ((i)–(v) above) amounted to illegitimate pressure sufficient to conclude that there had been duress. His judgment made the following points about lawful act duress. First, he relied on academic literature and case law for the proposition that 'lawful conduct can in some circumstances amount to economic duress'.[9] He referenced *DSND Subsea Ltd v Petroleum Geo Services ASA*[10] in outlining the necessary ingredients of: (a) the defendant's illegitimate pressure, (b) which induces the claimant's submission to the contract, and (c) the claimant's lack of practical choice but to submit.

Second, he found that PIAC was in breach by refusing to pay to TT the commission that was due on the Original Agreement, stating 'I feel confident that summary judgment would have been given'.[11]

Third, he noted that PIAC, in offering TT the New Agreement in the same letter as the notice of termination, was making 'in reality a threat that, unless the Claimants gave up those claims, their agency would come to an end'.[12] He concluded that

---

[6] ibid [59].
[7] ibid [139].
[8] ibid [123].
[9] ibid [251].
[10] [2000] BLR 530 (TCC) [131].
[11] *Times Travel*, High Court (n 4) [262].
[12] ibid [260(iii)].

the pressure put on TT, in the light of all of the matters which I have identified and in the light of the factors listed by Dyson J [in *DSND*], was illegitimate . . . The New Agreement . . . may represent a possibly adequate reward for future services; but . . . cannot be seen as compensating TT in an adequate way for its forced waiver of its existing claims.[13]

Finally, he was not applying the test of good faith, but commented:

Whether PIAC has acted in good faith or bad faith is moot. The Claimants have not estab-lished that there was bad faith but nor has PIAC established good faith. It is clear to me that the whole basis on which the Notice was served and the terms of the New Agreement were formulated was to ensure that agents would lose their claims to *accrued rights* in a situation where *some of those rights . . . were clear*. Indeed [PIAC] accepted that this was the motiv-ation for the Notice. Whether this demonstrates bad faith is a matter on which different minds might take different views.[14]

There is an apparent paradox here. On the one hand, Warren J stated that PIAC wrongly, but genuinely, believed that TT's *commission had ceased to be payable*.[15] On the other hand, he never said that PIAC honestly believed that TT's *claim* was unwarranted. Indeed, the reverse is indicated, given that he stated that TT would have successfully obtained sum-mary judgment. In addition, his finding that PIAC's conduct ((i)–(v) above) constituted illegitimate pressure entitling TT to rescind the New Agreement shows that he must have believed that PIAC did not have such a genuine belief; that PIAC acted in bad faith. We will say more about this tension later.

C. Court of Appeal Finds No Duress

PIAC accepted Warren J's fact-finding on causation and no practicable alternative, but ap-pealed his finding of illegitimate pressure. The Court of Appeal's judgment can be summar-ized as follows.

First, it changed the applicable test from that of illegitimate pressure to that of bad faith demand. That is, if the threatened action is lawful (such as PIAC's threat to reduce TT's ticket allocation in the New Agreement), the issue becomes whether the demand is made in good or bad faith. Here, the focus is on whether the demand (that TT waive its claim to commission) was made honestly, as opposed to reasonably.

Second, the Court of Appeal referred to Warren J's brief obiter comment that TT had not established bad faith[16] to mean that 'there was no such bad faith'.[17] This interpretation is highly questionable. Warren J's entire discussion of duress covered only 24 of the 281 paragraphs of his judgment, and he said nothing about good and bad faith beyond citing

---

[13] ibid [263].

[14] ibid [262].

[15] ibid [260(i)].

[16] *Times Travel v Pakistan International Airline Corporation* [2019] EWCA Civ 828, [2020] Ch 98 [111] (here-after *Times Travel*, Court of Appeal).

[17] Summarized by Lord Burrows in *Times Travel*, Supreme Court (n 1) [115].

DSND[18] and the quote above,[19] since it was not central to his ratio. Warren J's statement that TT had not established PIAC's bad faith does *not* exclude bad faith in PIAC's demand.

With respect, the Court of Appeal should have engaged in a more detailed consideration of PIAC's state of mind, commensurate with making bad faith the *key* issue in the case. Given Warren J's finding of illegitimate pressure, unfair tactics, and TT's right to obtain summary judgment for PIAC's unpaid commission, there was clearly ample evidence for finding that PIAC demanded TT's waiver in bad faith.[20] Instead, the Court of Appeal merely equated Warren J's statement that PIAC had a genuine (but incorrect) view that commission was *no longer payable* with a conclusion that the *demand* was made honestly and so in good faith.

This overlooks a critical distinction between two forms of 'honesty'. The first is *substantive honesty*, where the threatening party (A) honestly believed that the threatened party's (B) claim was unwarranted and so demanded B's waiver in good faith. The second can be termed *procedural honesty*, where A knows that B has a *valid* basis for its claim, but nevertheless demands B's waiver because the law permits it as the price to B of making a new contract with A. In the second scenario, A cannot be said to demand B's waiver of its claim in good faith. A is only honest in the sense that A knows that the current law will allow A to get away with this bad faith demand.

The relevant test should be that of substantive honesty, for the reasons we will discuss at D.3(a)(i) below. Accordingly, while PIAC may have been procedurally honest in believing it could lawfully coerce TT in the context of a new contract, there was no substantive honesty because there was no genuine belief that B's substantive claim was unwarranted. This distinction would clear a pathway to a finding of lawful act duress.

D. The Decision of the Supreme Court

Two judgments were delivered, one by Lord Hodge for the majority and the other by Lord Burrows. Both confirmed the existence of the category of lawful act duress, and both found no lawful act duress by PIAC, but for different reasons.

The majority recognized two categories of lawful act duress. Neither adds anything to the existing law, rendering this doctrine redundant.

1. *First category of lawful act duress*
This occurs where the defendant exploits its knowledge of criminal activity to obtain a contractual benefit from the claimant. Lord Hodge cited three cases where the defendant made a threat (explicit or implicit) to prosecute a member of the claimant's family unless its terms were agreed.

In *Williams v Bayley*,[21] a son had forged his father's signature at the expense of a bank, and the bank pressured the father to repay the money, on threat of prosecuting the son for forgery. The father's agreement to pay the bank was avoided both on the grounds that

---

[18] [2000] BLR 530 (TCC) [131].
[19] *Times Travel*, High Court (n 4) [262(ii)].
[20] See discussion at II(A).
[21] (1866) LR 1 HL 200 (HL).

80 SCHRÖDINGER'S LAWFUL ACT DURESS

a contract to stifle prosecution was illegal and that there was actual undue influence. The same conclusion was reached in *Mutual Finance Ltd v John Wetton and Sons Ltd*,[22] where a threat was made to prosecute the contracting party's brother, with the knowledge that their father's ill health might be dangerously exacerbated by such a prosecution. In *Kaufman v Gerson*[23] a wife agreed to repay the sum that her husband had misappropriated, on threat that he would otherwise be prosecuted. While the agreement was not illegal (it was valid under the law of France where the parties were domiciled), the court set aside the contract, because of the impact of threatening 'a wife with the dishonour of her husband and children'.[24]

Lord Hodge noted that that these cases were previously seen as examples of undue influence, but are now better interpreted as examples of lawful act duress.[25]

a) Category 1 is really undue influence
There is no doubt that the Supreme Court has reconceived these cases, originally decided under the rubric of actual undue influence, as ones of lawful act duress. The basis for this is the presence of (explicit or implicit) threats, and the fact that an earlier Court of Appeal (*CTN Cash and Carry Ltd v Gallaher Ltd*[26]) and High Court (*Progress Bulk Carriers Ltd v Tube City IMS LLC (Progress Bulk Carriers)*[27]) had reclassified these cases as lawful act duress.[28]

With respect, this relabelling is not only unnecessary, but also obscures the gist of their pathology; namely, the exploitation of a *personal relationship between the claimant and the third party* who is threatened by the defendant. This is a variant of the classic protected 'relationship of influence', where there is 'trust and confidence, reliance, dependence or vulnerability on the one hand and ascendancy, domination or control on the other'.[29] The three cases cited as examples of this category all involve threats to loved ones. In *Williams v Bayley*, the threat to prosecute the claimant's son carried the additional danger of 'transportation for life' to Australia.[30] In *Mutual Finance Ltd v John Wetton and Sons Ltd*, the claimant was worried that the threat to prosecute his brother would exacerbate the condition of their seriously ill father. In *Kaufman v Gerson* the wife was concerned about her husband being imprisoned, and the resulting 'disgrace' of her children. The third party family member threatened is someone whom the victim loves, supports, has common cause with, or relies on, or any combination thereof. That renders the victim vulnerable to the threat, whereas the absence of such a relationship would deprive the threat of any significance. I care if my son, father, husband, brother may be harmed, even if they may be wrongdoers. I care much less if someone else's son, father, husband, brother may be harmed by prosecution. Indeed, I may welcome it.

---

[22] [1937] 2 KB 389 (KBD).
[23] [1904] 1 KB 591 (CA).
[24] ibid 597.
[25] *Times Travel*, Supreme Court (n 1) [8].
[26] [1994] 4 All ER 714 (CA), 718 (hereafter *CTN*).
[27] [2012] EWHC 273 (Comm); [2012] 2 All ER (Comm) 855, 864 (hereafter *Progress Bulk Carriers*).
[28] This is now regarded as the standard position in Hugh Beale, *Chitty on Contracts* (34th edn, Sweet & Maxwell 2022) [10-058-1062A] (hereafter *Chitty*). Indeed, *Chitty* goes so far as to say that it can amount to duress of the *person* (the strongest form of duress) since 'the threat of violence need not be directed at the claimant: a threat of violence against the claimant's spouse or near relation suffices' [10-017].
[29] *Royal Bank of Scotland Plc v Etridge (No 2)* [2001] UKHL 44; [2002] 2 AC 773 [11].
[30] (1866) LR 1 HL 200 (HL), 211.

Thus, the crux of the three cases discussed by the Supreme Court is the victim's *relationship* with their threatened loved ones,[31] and not the lawful threat to prosecute the latter. The latter is bereft of significance without the former and is an entirely proper response to the third party's wrongdoing. It is only objectionable when the threat is made against someone in a relationship of influence with the third party. The relationship is the gist, not the threat.[32] These cases should therefore remain examples of the single category of undue influence, actually proved. To reclass them as lawful act duress is unnecessary and obscures rather than enlightens.

b) Category 1 is really duress to the person or illegality
Alternatively (or additionally), these cases can be viewed through the lens of illegality.[33] There is a rich line of authority that regards these cases as 'consistent both with the proper scope and purpose of the law on illegality'.[34] The agreements in *Williams v Bayley* and *Mutual Finance Ltd v John Wetton and Sons Ltd* were both explicitly held to be invalid on the grounds of illegality as it is unlawful to stifle a criminal prosecution.[35]

c) Conclusions on first category
The exploitation of knowledge of criminal activity to obtain a contractual benefit is already dealt with, and appropriately so, by existing doctrines. The majority decision of the Supreme Court in *Times Travel* focused on the *threat* made against the wrong party. It is submitted that the more salient features of such cases were rightly the defendant's attempt to stifle a prosecution or to exploit the claimant's *relationship* with the threatened party. There was no need to reclassify this line of cases, and it is obfuscating to do so.

2. Second category of lawful act duress
The use of illegitimate means to manoeuvre a claimant into a position of weakness and to waive their claim against the defendant is the majority's second category of lawful act duress. At first glance this seems promising, but more detailed analysis shows that it is defined so narrowly as to make resort to lawful act duress redundant, again. This is done in three moves: merging the 'nature of the demand' with the 'nature of the threat'; requiring reprehensible means; and referring to unconscionability.

a) First move—redefining the 'nature of demand'
It is well accepted that duress requires proof of (i) illegitimate pressure, (ii) that causes the clamant to submit, and (iii) the absence of any practicable alternative.[36] Where the threat is independently unlawful, it is presumed to be illegitimate; where the threat is lawful, it is presumed to be legitimate. But it is not always so. In particular, where the threat is to do something lawful, *The Universe Sentinel*[37] directs the focus towards the nature of the

---

[31] For further discussion, see Mindy Chen-Wishart, 'The Nature of Vitiating Factors in Contract Law' in Gregory Klass, George Letsas, and Prince Saprai, *Philosophical Foundations of Contract Law* (OUP 2014) 294.

[32] Mindy Chen-Wishart, 'Undue Influence: Vindicating Relationships of Influence' (2006) 59 CLP 231.

[33] See Iona Branford and Jodi Gardner, 'Reconceiving Wrongdoing in Lawful Act Duress' (2023) 139 LQR 629 (hereafter Branford & Gardner, 'Reconceiving Wrongdoing').

[34] ibid 650.

[35] *Kaufman v Gerson* was more complicated as the contract in question was valid in French law.

[36] *DSND Subsea Ltd v Petroleum Geo Services ASA* [2000] BLR 530 (TCC) [131]; *Chitty* (n 28) [10-003].

[37] *Universe Tankships Inc of Monrovia v International Transport Workers Federation* [1983] 1 AC 366 (HL), 401 (*The Universe Sentinel*).

demand made to the victim. As Lord Scarman comments, 'what one has to justify is not a threat, but the demand'.[38] In another case, Lord Atkin explains:

> The ordinary blackmailer normally threatens to do what he has a perfect right to do—namely, communicate some compromising conduct to a person whose knowledge is likely to affect the person threatened. Often indeed he has not only the right but also the duty to make the disclosure, as of a felony, to the competent authorities. *What he has to justify is not the threat, but the demand of money*. The gravamen of the charge is the demand without reasonable or probable cause.[39]

Thus, it is the nature of the demand that makes an otherwise lawful threat *illegitimate*. 'Demand' here would naturally mean the *substance* of the impugned agreement, in contrast to the *process* of negotiating the contract.[40] This is supported by the Court of Appeal in *Times Travel*,[41] Lord Burrows' judgment,[42] *The Universe Sentinel*,[43] *Thorne v Motor Trade Association*,[44] Leggatt J (as he then was) in *Al Nehayan v Kent*,[45] and academic analysis.[46] So far, so good.

Lord Hodge, however, goes on to redefine 'the demand' to include, in effect, the *process* of concluding the contract, thus redirecting the focus back onto the 'nature of the threat'. His Lordship held that

> the court in focusing on the nature and justification of the *demand* ... has regard to, among other things, the *behaviour* of the threatening party including the nature of the pressure which it applies, and the circumstances of the threatened party ... [M]orally reprehensible *behaviour* which in equity was judged to render the enforcement of a contract unconscionable in the context of undue influence has been treated by English common law as *illegitimate pressure* in the context of duress.[47]

If all these factors are part of the '*demand*', then we move away from the unique inquiry for lawful act duress, and merge it with the approach already adopted for unlawful threats (to the person, to property, and of economic duress) by focusing on the *threat*. It becomes harder to see how lawful act has independent existence. The next step kills the category stone dead.

b) Second move—requirement of reprehensible means
To find lawful act duress, Lord Hodge held that, when making 'the demand', the stronger party must have also used 'reprehensible means', in the sense of acting in a way that

---

[38] ibid 401.
[39] *Thorne v Motor Trade Association* [1937] AC 797 (HL), 806–07 (emphasis added).
[40] Ewan McKendrick, 'The Further Travails of Duress' in Andrew Burrows and Alan Rodger (eds), *Mapping the Law: Essays in Memory of Peter Birks* (OUP 2006) 189, 193 (hereafter McKendrick 'The Further Travails of Duress').
[41] *Times Travel*, Court of Appeal (n 16).
[42] *Times Travel*, Supreme Court (n 1) [96].
[43] *The Universe Sentinel* (n 37) 401.
[44] [1937] AC 797 (HL), 806–07.
[45] [2018] EWHC 614 (Comm); [2018] 1 CLC 216 [188].
[46] See, eg, McKendrick, 'The Further Travails of Duress' (n 40) 189.
[47] *Times Travel*, Supreme Court (n 1) [1]–[2] (emphasis added).

increases the claimant's vulnerability. Refusing to contract or re-contract is insufficient, and something 'more' is needed. Hiw Lordship relies on two cases to illustrate the content of the 'more' required for a plea of lawful act duress.[48]

The critical factors in the finding of economic duress in *Borrelli v Ting*[49] were the defendant's *prior unlawful* conduct in refusing to cooperate with the liquidators of the company of which he was a director, as required under the relevant statute, as well as multiple breaches of his fiduciary duties, forgery, and provision of false evidence. Likewise, *Progress Bulk Carriers* involved a past breach of contract, a variation of contract, and then a threatened breach of the varied contract. In *Times Travel* Lord Burrows conceded that the judgment in that case 'may be interpreted as categorising the duress as unlawful, rather than lawful act, duress'.[50] Thus, the Supreme Court's conception of lawful act duress requires proof of prior unlawful acts—a seeming oxymoron. Alternatively, the Supreme Court seems to have wrongly categorized these decisions as instances of *lawful* act duress.

c) Third move—equating with unconscionability

Lord Hodge went on to say that, in *Borrelli v Ting*, the court treated 'illegitimate' as a synonym for 'unconscionable',[51] and that a claimant needs to show 'morally reprehensible behaviour' which renders the contract 'unconscionable'. Indeed, 'unconscionability' was referred to forty-two times in the Supreme Court judgments.

If 'unconscionable behaviour' here equates to what would suffice to trigger the doctrine of unconscionable bargains, then lawful act duress would again be redundant. However, it is hard to see how illegitimate demands for waiver of claim would qualify under the English unconscionable bargain doctrine.[52] The latter rests on the claimant's bargaining impairment in the form of *personal or cognitive* weaknesses,[53] while *Times Travel*, *Borrelli v Ting*, and *Progress Bulk Carriers* involved economic disadvantage per se. In contrast, if the test of relief includes situational disadvantage (as in Canada) or involves a broader statutory basis (as in Australia), such cases may be potentially within the scope of unconscionability.[54]

Unconscionable conduct and lawful act duress rest on different rationales even if they may overlap.[55] The former is concerned with the exploitation of a claimant (by obtaining an uneven contractual exchange) who is known not to have the normal personal capability to self-protect, even if they are not incapacitated in law. The latter does not involve such claimants; its focus should remain the use of lawful threats to make an illegitimate or unfair demand. Therefore, by 'unconscionable', Lord Hodge would seem to mean no more than 'reprehensible conduct'. If so, it suffers from the same fatal error of being linked to *previous* breaches of duties that is already covered by the *illegitimate* pressure demanded of economic duress cases. It therefore adds nothing to the development of the concept of lawful

---

[48] ibid [10]. See also Branford and Gardner, 'Reconceiving Wrongdoing' (n 33); Paul Davies and William Day, ' "Lawful Act" Duress' (2018) 134 LQR 5.

[49] [2010] UKPC 21, [2010] Bus LR 1718 [19], [27], [32].

[50] *Times Travel*, Supreme Court (n 1) [111].

[51] ibid [17].

[52] Although we note previous calls for the expansion of this doctrine: see Jodi Gardner, 'Being Conscious of Unconscionability in Modern Times: *Heller v Uber Technologies*' (2021) 84 MLR 874.

[53] *Earl of Aylesford v Morris* (1873) 8 Ch App 484 (CA), *Fry v Lane* (1888) 40 Ch D 312, *Cresswell v Potter* [1978] 1 WLR 255 (Ch D).

[54] See, for example, *Uber Technologies Inc v Heller* 2020 SCC 16, *Australian Securities and Investments Commission v Kobelt* [2019] HCA 18, (2019) 267 CLR 1.

[55] Branford and Gardner, 'Reconceiving Wrongdoing' (n 33).

act duress. If it means something more, with the potential to give independent content to this category, the judgment does not tell us what this might be.

d) Conclusions on second category

The majority's decision in *Times Travel* asserts that (a) lawful act duress exists and (b) there needs to be further certainty and clarity in this area.[56] Insofar as the judgment succeeds in respect of (b), it does so by defining lawful act duress out of existence, hence contradicting (a).

3. Lord Burrows' test of bad faith demand

Lord Burrows' minority decision adopts a bad faith approach to lawful act duress. Accordingly, to succeed in lawful act duress, the threatening party must make the demand for, either (a) what is claimed to be owing or (b) a waiver of an existing claim 'in bad faith in the sense that the threatening party does not genuinely believe that it is owed what it is claiming to be owed or does not genuinely believe that it has a defence to the claim being waived by the threatened party'.[57] This approach has the *potential* to give content to lawful act duress over and above that which is already covered by existing doctrines, and so beyond that prescribed by the majority judgment.

a) Majority's criticisms of bad faith demand

Before analysing Lord Burrows' bad faith approach, we need to respond to the majority's rejection of it.

i) Inequality of bargaining power

Lord Hodge states that it 'is not in dispute that there is in English common law no doctrine of inequality of bargaining power in contract'.[58] After surveying some cases and academic materials, his Lordship concludes:

> Against this commercial background the pressure applied by a negotiating party will very rarely come up to the standard of illegitimate pressure or unconscionable conduct. It will therefore be a rare circumstance that a court will find lawful act duress in the context of commercial negotiation.[59]

This stance is regarded as the concomitant of the primacy of freedom of contract underlying English common law of contract.[60] The freedom was never absolute and has been increasingly challenged, particularly by modern statutes.[61] Given this, courts are hesitant to intervene in an agreement because of vague notions of 'justice' and the inequality of power

---

[56] *Times Travel*, Supreme Court (n 1) [49]–[51].
[57] *Times Travel*, Supreme Court (n 1) [102].
[58] ibid [26].
[59] ibid [30].
[60] As stated by Benson, 'the common law conception of contract gives individuals an unfettered liberty to do as they please': Peter Benson, 'The Unity of Contract Law' in Peter Benson (ed), *The Theory of Contract Law* (CUP 2001) 200. This is clearly an exaggeration.
[61] Patrick Atiyah, 'Contracts, Promises and the Law of Obligations' in Patrick Atiyah (ed), *Essays on Contract Law* (OUP 1990) 11.

between the parties.[62] The exploitation of a superior bargaining power must be allowed to a large extent in a capitalist society, and doing so should not be considered 'bad faith'.

In truth, the law shows clear regard for inequality of bargaining power in contractual relations. First, the majority judgment merely states that inequality of power is—*in and of itself*—insufficient to justify avoiding a contract; it may be relevant in combination with other factors. Second, Lord Hodge admits that inequality 'may be a relevant feature in some cases of undue influence'.[63] Third, the concept clearly operates in many other aspects of contract law—including incapacity and unconscionability, and in statutory regulations such as the Consumer Rights Act 2015, and in the enhanced statutory protection for employees[64] and tenants.[65] Wherever possible the law should develop coherence not just between different causes of action, but also between common law and statute.[66] The relationship between inequality of bargaining power and lawful act duress therefore deserves consideration, and not out-of-hand rejection.

Finally, normative justifications exist for the relevance of unequal bargaining power, such as the protection of parties' future autonomy, market failure, and the state's legitimate refusal to subsidize exploitation. Contract law is a facilitative institution; it helps us to engage more easily in the valuable activity of contracting. As such, it should follow practices that command a 'large measure of social consensus'.[67] This includes concern for the welfare of every person, including those with weak bargaining power; 'people want the law to move with the times'.[68] Writing extra-judicially, Lord Hodge states that the 'English law of contract seeks to protect the reasonable expectations of honest people when they enter into contracts'.[69]

ii) <u>Common law regulation of monopolies</u> Lord Hodge also rejected the test of bad faith demand for lawful act duress because monopolies should not be regulated by contract law, but solely by legislation. His Lordship rejected the notion that the 'lawful act doctrine could be extended to a circumstance in which, without more, a commercial organisation exploits its strong bargaining power or monopoly position to extract a payment from another commercial organisation by an assertion in bad faith of a pre-existing legal entitlement which the other organisation believes or knows to be incorrect'.[70] Lord Burrows' extension of the doctrine to cover these situations is rejected.

However, courts have given relief where salvage contracts are unfair even though the situation is merely one where a 'commercial organisation exploits its strong bargaining power or monopoly position to extract a payment'.[71] The common law provided a level

---

[62] Jodi Gardner, *The Future of High-Cost Credit: Rethinking Payday Lending* (Hart Publishing 2022) esp ch 3; Jack Beatson and Daniel Friedman, 'Introduction: From "Classical" to Modern Contract Law' in Jack Beatson and Daniel Friedman (eds), *Good Faith and Fault in Contract Law* (OUP 1997) 8–9.

[63] *Times Travel*, Supreme Court (n 1) [26].

[64] Employment Rights Act 1996.

[65] Homes (Fitness for Human Habitation) Act 2018; Tenant Fees Act 2019.

[66] Kit Barker, 'Private Law as a Complex System: Agendas for the Twenty-First Century' in Kit Barker et al (eds), *Private Law in the 21st Century* (Hart Publishing 2017); Andrew Burrows, 'The Relationship Between the Common Law and Statute in the Law of Obligations' (2012) 128 LQR 232; Jodi Gardner and John Murphy, 'Concurrent Liability in Contract and Tort: A Separation Thesis' (2021) 137 LQR 77.

[67] Joseph Raz, *The Morality of Freedom* (Clarendon Press 1986) 419, 427.

[68] Jane Stapleton, *Three Essays on Torts* (OUP 2021) (hereafter Stapleton, *Three Essays*) 10.

[69] Lord Hodge, 'The Scope of Judicial Law-Making in the Common Law Tradition' (2020) 84 *Rabels Zeitschrift für ausländisches und internationals Privatrecht* 211, 222.

[70] *Times Travel*, Supreme Court (n 1) [52].

[71] ibid [52].

of protection until statute was developed.[72] The details of contract law will not command the same priority in parliamentary time as, say, terrorism, asylum seekers or fiscal policy. Courts working at the coalface must fill in the gaps as they find them. As Beatson observes, 'there are examples of statutory regimes which express a policy from which a principle can be derived, being used analogically in developing the common law'.[73] If Parliament is not regulating private law problems, courts should fill the gap.[74]

Lord Burrows identified just such a gap on the facts of *Times Travel*. He said:

> there are at least two features of the facts that take this case outside the realm of the mere use of monopoly power. First, Warren J found that PIAC was in breach of contract by failing to pay £1.2m of past commission owing to TT (exclusive of interest). Secondly, PIAC then went further by, for example, suddenly cutting TT's normal ticket allocation from 300 to 60 which increased TT's particular vulnerability which PIAC was then able to exploit by making the demand for the waiver.[75]

The majority's approach seems an abdication of power.

iii) <u>Bad faith and uncertainty</u> Lord Hodge criticized Lord Burrows' bad faith demand approach on the basis that 'it would be difficult to anchor the extension in any recognised legal principle'[76] and 'the extension of lawful act duress in this way would create unwanted uncertainty'.[77]

Much can be said on the other side. First, while certainty is important in law, it is overrated. It is not the be-all and end-all of contract law, or indeed private law in general.[78] Moreover, the importance and achievability of legal certainty is often overstated. As Lord Scott said in *The Golden Victory*: 'Certainty is a desideratum and a very important one, particularly in commercial contracts. But it is not a principle and must give way to principle. Otherwise incoherence of principle is the likely result.'[79] A rule that invalidates the contracts of people below a certain height would be (relatively) certain, but in no way fair or indeed useful. It is important to balance the desire for certainty with that for fairness.

Second, uncertainty, to varying extents, is a feature of *all* rules and of all aspects of the legal system.[80] Let's say a generic rule: $a + b + c =$ legal result X. A large part of the enterprise of law is to determine the precise scope of a, b, c, and even X. If it were easy, (certain) lawyers would be largely redundant; a computer program would do.

---

[72] Jodi Gardner, 'Does Lawful Act Duress Still Exist?' (2019) 78 CLJ 496.

[73] Jack Beatson, 'The Role of Statute in the Development of Common Law Doctrine' (2001) 117 LQR 247, 299. See also Stapleton, *Three Essays* (n 68) 29–31.

[74] John Murphy, 'Judicial Gap-Filling in the Law of Torts and the Rule of Law' in Jodi Gardner, Amy Goymour, Janet O'Sullivan, and Sarah Worthington (eds), *Politics, Policy and Private Law: Tort, Land & Equity* (Hart Publishing 2023).

[75] *Times Travel*, Supreme Court (n 1) [113].

[76] ibid [49].

[77] ibid [51].

[78] Rick Bigwood and Joachim Dietrich, 'Uncertainty in Private Law: Rhetorical Device or Substantive Legal Argument?' (2021) 45 MULR 60.

[79] *Golden Strait Corp v Nippon Yusen Kubishika Kaisha (The Golden Victory)* [2007] UKHL 12 | [2007] 2 A.C. 353 [38].

[80] See, eg, Tim Endicott, *Vagueness in Law* (OUP 2000) ch 5.

Third, important qualitative standards that are quantitatively uncertain (such as 'reasonableness', 'proximity', and 'foreseeability') are deployed in many areas of English contract law without fatally destabilizing them.

Fourth, even commercial parties, who are thought to care most about legal certainty, recognize the necessity of agreeing quantitatively uncertain obligations such as to 'cooperate', use 'best endeavours', or even 'act in good faith'.[81] Courts are increasingly required to interpret expressly agreed good faith duties,[82] which, as Leggatt J observed in *Yam Seng*,[83] involves 'no more uncertainty than is inherent in the process of contractual interpretation'.[84]

Finally, the majority approach is itself open to the accusation of uncertainty. Lord Burrows expressed his concern that

> without any focus on the 'bad faith demand' requirement, defined in the specific sense that I have set out, and with instead the essential guide being that the defendant's conduct must be 'reprehensible' or 'unconscionable' or using 'illegitimate means' (which is, by definition, distinct from unlawful means), one will be permitting lawful act economic duress to create considerable uncertainty in the realm of commercial contracts.[85]

iv) <u>Waiver versus new contract</u> This last objection to Lord Burrows' bad faith demand approach warrants special attention. Lord Hodge stated that a defendant's demand for a waiver is in principle 'no different' from a demand of money as a precondition to entering into a contract,[86] and since the defendant is perfectly entitled to demand the latter, they can also legitimately demand the former. This is the main Achilles heel of the majority's reasoning. Of course, a party can demand money as a precondition of entering a contract. But to demand a waiver of a valid claim is different, for a number of reasons.

First, a waiver is in effect a demand that the victim surrenders an entitlement under a valid pre-existing contract; if this is permitted, the defendant is allowed to breach a contract with impunity so long as the victim needs to renew the contract.[87] Indeed, the majority's approach *encourages* such breaches by turning the defendant's substantively bad faith demand into one made in procedural good faith.[88] The latter is allowed to take priority over the former although the defendant knows that they have no reasonable basis to dispute their victim's valid claim. This reasoning allows defendants to breach their contracts and avoid validly accrued liability whenever the counterparty needs to re-contract with them. It rewards the party who behaves not only badly, but also, in fact, unlawfully.

---

[81] See *Chitty* (n 28) [1-053-54A], [2-123], [2-146] for a detailed discussion of such terms, and references therein. See also Mary Arden, 'Coming to Terms with Good Faith' in Mary Arden, Common Law and Modern Society: Keeping Pace with Change (OUP 2016) 29.

[82] For example, *Berkeley Community Villages Ltd v Pullen* [2007] EWHC 1330 (Ch); [2007] 3 EGLR 101; *Gold Group Properties Ltd v BDW Trading Ltd* [2010] EWHC 1632 (TCC); *CPC Group Ltd v Qatari Diar Real Estate Investment Company* [2010] EWHC 1535 (Ch), [2010] CILL 2908; *Horn v Commercial Acceptances Ltd* [2011] EWHC 1757; *Re Compound Photonics Group Ltd* [2022] EWCA Civ 1371.

[83] *Yam Seng Pte Ltd v International Trade Corp Ltd* [2013] EWHC 111 (QB), [2013] 1 Lloyd's Rep 526.

[84] ibid [152].

[85] *Times Travel*, Supreme Court (n 1) [133].

[86] ibid [54].

[87] For further discussion, see Branford and Gardner, 'Reconceiving Wrongdoing' (n 33).

[88] See our discussion of the Court of Appeal's decision in *Times Travel* at II(C).

Second, this approach is at odds with the key cases relied upon by both the majority and Lord Burrows in their approval of lawful act duress. In both *Borrelli v Ting* and *Progress Bulk Carriers*, the nub of the finding of defendants' lawful act duress lies in the defendants' demands that their victims waive their previous claims accrued from the defendants' prior breaches of duty. In *Borrelli v Ting*, the defendant failed to cooperate with the liquidators as he was obliged to do. *Progress Bulk Carriers*, in particular, is on all fours with the facts of *Times Travel*. There, the claimant chartered the Cenk K to carry scrap metal to sell to purchasers in China on a fixed date. The owners, in repudiatory breach, chartered the Cenk K to another party but assured the claimant that they would provide a substitute vessel and compensate for all damages resulting from their breach. Ultimately, the owners only offered a discount (far less than the loss the charterers sustained), and on condition that the charterers waive all claims for loss from the initial breach. To avoid further loss, the charterer agreed under protest. Cooke J upheld the arbitrators' reasons for avoiding the waiver agreement for economic duress: the owners had been in repudiatory breach of contract, had lulled the charterers into a false sense of security by their assurances, and had manoeuvred them into a position where, because of the passage of time, they had no choice but to accept the owners' 'take it or leave it' and hard bargain.[89] Cooke J found illegitimate pressure in the owner's creation and exploitation of the charterer's vulnerability;[90] in particular, 'a past unlawful act, as well as the threat of a future unlawful act can, in appropriate circumstances, amount to "illegitimate pressure".[91] Given the importance of these cases to the majority's decision in *Times Travel*, it seems incoherent for their Lordships to hold that a waiver is in principle 'no different' from a demand of money in entering a new contract.

Third, the majority's approach is inconsistent with the law on compromise where substantive honesty is the test. For a compromise to be valid, the party demanding the compromise must believe, *in good faith*, that it had a fair chance of success.[92] Otherwise, that party acts in bad faith; the compromise will be invalid for lack of consideration, and may also be a contravention of public policy.[93] Tindal CJ said in *Wade v Simeon*, 'it is almost *contra bonos mores* and certainly contrary to all the principles of natural justice that a man should institute proceedings against another when he is conscious that he has no good cause of action.[94] The same must go for demands of waiver. The majority's approach also jars with *Foakes v Beer*,[95] where the repayment of debts was prioritized over a variation allowing part payment. It therefore seems incongruous to allow a debtor to renege and the creditor's rights be negated simply because the creditor needs to make a subsequent contract with the debtor.

With respect, we find the majority's four reasons for rejecting Lord Burrows' test of bad faith demand unpersuasive. The next step is to examine the scope and application of Lord Burrows' test.

---

[89] *Progress Bulk Carriers* (n 26) [40].
[90] ibid [44].
[91] ibid [36].
[92] *Callisher v Bischoffsheim* (1870) LR 5 QB 449 (QB); *Longridge v Dorville* (1821) 5 B & Ad 117; 106 ER 1136 (KBD); *Cooper v Parker* (1855) 15 CB 822, 139 ER 650; *Cook v Wright* (1861) 1 B & S 559, 121 ER 822 (QB); *Ockford v Barelli* (1871) 20 WR 116; *Holsworthy UDC v Holsworthy RDC* [1907] 2 Ch 62; *Re Cole* [1931] 2 Ch 174; *Freedman v Union Group Plc* [1997] EGCS 28 (CA); *Mousaka Inc v Golden Seagull Maritime Inc* [2002] 1 Lloyd's Rep 797 (QB), [14]; *Haines v Hill* [2007] EWCA Civ 1284, [2008] Ch 412 [79].
[93] *Chitty* (n 28) [6-054] referring to [6-052].
[94] (1846) 2 CB 548, 564, 135 ER 1061.
[95] (1884) 9 App Cas 605 (HL).

b) The scope and application of Lord Burrows' bad faith demand approach

Lord Burrows' test of bad faith involves two elements. First, the threat made must have deliberately created or increased the vulnerability of the threatened party. He found this to be present, in line with Warren J's judgment,[96] but against the majority finding.[97] Second, the defendant must have made the threat in bad faith, in the sense that they demanded that the counterparty waive its claim knowing it had no basis for challenging the claim.[98] We make three comments.

First, this is, of course, the test for the state of mind necessary for a finding of fraud or deceit. This means that, like the majority's judgment, it adds no further content to the lawful act duress category. Moreover, the effect of *Zurich Insurance Co plc v Hayward*[99] is that fraud may be found if the defendant dishonestly demands a waiver on the ostensible basis that the counterparty's claim is unwarranted, even when the claimant knows of the dishonesty but submits because it has no practicable alternative.

Second, and with respect, Lord Burrows' focus on a subjective or objective test is unnecessary and confusing. The question is not whether honesty as good faith is assessed subjectively (whether genuine belief of entitlement to demand) or objectively (whether there are reasonable grounds for such a belief). The law is clear that the test is subjective,[100] but objectivity must come into it. The real question is one of *credibility* since the defendant's self-serving declaration cannot be determinative. Thus, the more unreasonable (ie the lack of a reasonable basis for) the demand, the more it is open to a court to find, as a matter of credibility, that the defendant did not genuinely believe in its right to make it.

Third, Lord Burrows' application of this test of bad faith to the facts of *Times Travel* was, at least, questionable. He said:

> In relation to a demand for a waiver of claims, even in a situation where it can be said that PIAC deliberately increased TT's vulnerability to the demand, the 'bad faith demand' requirement is crucial for determining the illegitimacy of the lawful act threat. Had TT proved that PIAC was in bad faith in making the demand for the waiver, its claim for rescission would have succeeded in this case. *But as we have seen, the findings of fact of Warren J were to the effect that there was no such bad faith.*[101]

Lord Burrows regarded it 'as essential that, on Warren J's findings, PIAC was not acting in bad faith.'[102] As outlined above, Warren J's decision was based on whether PIAC placed 'illegitimate pressure' on TT to enter into the contract, and his answer was 'yes'. His Lordship's cursory comment on bad faith merely stated that PIAC's bad faith was not proved, but then set out ample evidence of PIAC's substantive bad faith. Thus, his Lordship was too quick to conclude that there was no bad faith on the facts. More analysis was required.

---

[96] *Times Travel*, Supreme Court (n 1) [104].

[97] ibid [57].

[98] ibid [102].

[99] [2016] UKSC 48, [2017] AC 14. It has been argued that this is not a case of misrepresentation in the sense of an induced mistake, but rather one of economic duress and lawful act duress: Kelry Loi, 'Pre-Contractual Misrepresentations: Mistaken Belief Induced by Mis-statements' [2017] JBL 597.

[100] *Times Travel*, Court of Appeal (n 16) [105].

[101] *Times Travel*, Supreme Court (n 1) [115] (emphasis added).

[102] ibid [152].

III. Concluding Thoughts: Resurrecting Lawful Act Duress

Despite the Supreme Court's clear recognition of the importance of the doctrine of lawful act duress to English common law of contract, we contend that neither the majority nor the minority judgments yield substantive content for the category beyond what is already covered by existing doctrines.

If we are serious about providing some content for this category, it would be profitable to draw from the rich literature on contractual good faith (as the mirror image of bad faith). This goes far beyond Lord Burrows' conception of bad faith as dishonesty. The case law and academic literature highlight the importance of contracting parties displaying respect for the legitimate interests of their contractual partners and for the contract itself in the forms of (a) honesty, (b) fair dealing,[103] and (c) fidelity to the contractual purpose.[104] This can provide lawful act duress with substantive content, within the confines of existing legal developments.

On (a), the focus should be on whether the threatening party can show that they acted with *substantive* honesty. On the facts of *Times Travel*, Warren J clearly doubted PIAC's honesty in demanding the waiver. He found that the outstanding commission was valid and payable, and TT would have been successful in a summary judgment against PIAC.[105] Combined with PIAC's actions designed to prevent TT from commencing legal proceedings, there is ample basis for finding that PIAC's demand for a waiver from TT was made in bad faith.[106]

On (b), the focus should be on lawful acts that are nevertheless 'illegitimate' (per Warren J) or 'reprehensible' (per Lord Hodge).[107] After all, undue influence and unconscionable bargains include just such lawful acts. Thus, Lord Hodge's restriction of the necessary 'reprehensible conduct' to instances of unlawful conduct is unwarranted. On the facts found by Warren J, PIAC dealt unfairly with TT, by the deployment of both stick (reduction in allocation of tickets, decreased commission, and threats to terminate the existing contract) and carrot (assurances given).[108]

The facts of *Times Travel* is directly comparable to *Progress Bulk Carriers*, where the shipowners gave an assurance of proper compensation to induce the counterparty's waiver of claim but later made a 'take it or leave it' offer when the counterparty desperately needed the ships. This was determined to be sufficient to find lawful act duress. It is most unfortunate that this issue was not explored further on the facts of *Times Travel*, where PIAC's conduct caused ample concern.

---

[103] In discussing the *CTN* case, Lord Burrows quoted Steyn LJ's comment that 'the aim of our commercial law ought to be to encourage fair dealing between parties': *Times Travel*, Supreme Court (n 1) [101]. And see the United States Restatement (Second) of Contracts (1981, June 2020 update), which declares that fair dealing between the parties is a relevant factor for determining whether a threat is improper.

[104] Mindy Chen-Wishart and Victoria Dixon, 'Good Faith in English Contract Law: A Humble "3 by 4" Approach' in Paul B Miller and John Oberdiek (eds), *Oxford Studies in Private Law Theory: Volume I* (OUP 2020) 187 (hereafter Chen-Wishart and Dixon, 'Good Faith in English Contract Law').

[105] *Times Travel*, High Court (n 4) [262].

[106] For a more detailed discussion of the facts, see II(A).

[107] See, eg, Chen-Wishart and Dixon, 'Good Faith in English Contract Law' (n 104) 215–17; Johan Steyn, 'The Role of Good Faith and Fair Dealing in Contract Law: A Hair-Shirt Philosophy?' (1991) 6 Denning LJ 131; Hugh Collins, 'Implied Terms: The Foundation in Good Faith and Fair Dealing' (2014) 67 CLP 297.

[108] Referred to above at II(A).

On (c), the *infidelity* to the *original* contractual purpose was clearly of importance in the finding of duress in *Progress Bulk Carriers*. Yet the Supreme Court's apparent preference for procedural over substantive honesty runs in the opposite direction. It creates the moral hazard of a supplier setting up renewable periodic contracts and then demanding a waiver of their existing liability as the price for entering into the 'new' contract. In *Times Travel*, PIAC showed infidelity to the original contractual purpose by demanding the waiver of a valid claim for £1.2 million. This is clear from Warren J's finding:

> The New Agreement was offered to the Claimants in the very letter (that is to say, the Notice) which gave notice of termination of the old agreement. There was, therefore, quite clearly no desire on the part of PIAC that Agents should in practice cease to be agents for PIAC; what PIAC wanted to achieve was simply an end to any claims by the Claimants for their outstanding commission. The Notice was in reality a threat that, unless the Claimants gave up those claims, their agency would come to an end. It of course went beyond a mere threat because, if the Claimants did not sign the New Agreement, their appointments would come to an end automatically on the expiry of the notice period.[109]

On this approach to lawful act duress as bad faith, the waiver would have been set aside for PIAC's: (a) substantive dishonesty in making the claim; (b) unfair dealing to induce TT's agreement; and (c) reneging on, and thus infidelity to, the pre-existing contract. This approach is one way, though doubtless not the only one, to resurrect lawful act duress from the zombie state left by the Supreme Court. If the Supreme Court means what it says, then lawful act duress should not simply consist of conduct that is already proscribed by other doctrines, such as undue influence, illegality, economic duress, and fraud or deceit. As such, the doctrine is a mere façade hiding a dead cat. Given the wealth of judicial statements and academic material on good (and hence bad) faith, and the findings of fact by Warren J in the High Court of *Time Travel*, there was ample basis for giving life to this category of invalidity in the Supreme Court. With the greatest of respect, this was a missed opportunity.

---

[109] *Times Travel*, High Court (n 4) [260].

6

Contracts and Relationships of Love and Trust

REBECCA PROBERT AND TIM DODSWORTH

I. Introduction

In setting out to contribute to this collection in honour of Professor Ewan McKendrick, we were united in wishing to pay tribute to his superb scholarship, his clarity of exposition, and his incisive mind. At the same time, we wondered what we *could* contribute, given that our own areas of interest are quite different from his. But since family lawyers do occasionally talk about contracts,[1] and contract lawyers occasionally talk about the domestic sphere,[2] we thought it was worth persevering. And we were able to draw inspiration from a chapter that Ewan wrote in 2002, in which he expressed his doubts about the incursion of contract law into family life.[3] As he commented:

> Where relationships are governed by love and trust, there is little or no need for a contract to regulate the relationship between the parties. This argument might appear to be undermined by the fact that the relationship between husband and wife is contractual in nature, but the modern doctrines that make up the law of contract have little application to marriage and it would be surprising if many married couples made use of the law of contract when working out their relationship. The presumption that there is no intention to create legal relations in a domestic context has in the past helped to keep contract in its place 'in the commercial sphere and out of domestic cases, except where the judges think it has a useful role to play'.[4]

In the sections that follow we reflect on three key dimensions of the relationship between contracts and relationships of love and trust. First, we explore the relationship between the idea of marriage as a contract and the possibility of its termination. As we will show, that relationship has changed over time, to the extent that we question whether it is still helpful to describe the relationship between spouses as 'contractual in nature'. Second, while there is little evidence of married couples making use of the law of contract to regulate their ongoing relationship, the past decade or so has seen important developments in the context of marital property agreements. Considering such agreements from the perspective of both contract law and family law, we suggest that to approach them as contracts risks

---

[1] See eg Sharon Thompson's excellent analysis of prenuptial agreements, *Prenuptial Agreements and the Presumption of Free Choice* (Hart Publishing 2015) (hereafter Thompson, *Prenuptial Agreements*).
[2] See eg Hanoch Dagan, 'Intimate Contracts and Choice Theory' (2022) 18 Eur Rev Contract Law 104 (hereafter Dagan, 'Intimate Contracts').
[3] Ewan McKendrick, 'The Contracting Society: A Misplaced Faith' in Paul Beaumont (ed), *Christian Perspectives on the Limits of the Law* (Paternoster Press 2002).
[4] ibid 90 (references omitted).

Rebecca Probert and Tim Dodsworth, *Contracts and Relationships of Love and Trust* In: *Shaping the Law of Obligations.* Edited by: Edwin Peel and Rebecca Probert, Oxford University Press. © Rebecca Probert and Tim Dodsworth 2023. DOI: 10.1093/oso/9780198889762.003.0006

94 CONTRACTS AND RELATIONSHIPS OF LOVE AND TRUST

misunderstanding their scope. Finally, we explore the potential use of contracts in certain familial contexts to provide a remedy where family law does not—for example, where the parties are cohabiting without having gone through any ceremony or have gone through a ceremony that is not recognized by the law—but suggest that they are something of a blunt instrument and that reforms to obviate the need to rely on contracts would be preferable.

II. When the Love Has Gone: Terminating the Contract

The idea that marriage is a contract is one that seems beyond question. Judges seeking to define the law's concept of marriage continue to describe it as such.[5] Yet, as we will show in this section, the idea that marriage is a contract is far from straightforward. It is an idea that has persisted over the centuries despite fundamental changes to both marriage and contract law. Moreover, while there are certain parallels between the evolution of the law governing divorce and the law governing the termination of contracts, there is also a long-standing reluctance to take the idea of marriage as a contract too literally in this context.

A brief sketch of the evolution of divorce law may be helpful by way of introduction. England and Wales were unique among Protestant countries in not adopting some form of divorce at the time of the Reformation.[6] A valid marriage remained indissoluble save by death. Only in the late seventeenth century was this principle modified, and then only by the extraordinary means of passing private Acts of Parliament to terminate individual marriages.[7] Not until 1857 was legislation finally passed creating a new civil court with the power to grant a divorce, and then only if one spouse could be shown to be at fault.[8] A further hundred years or so passed before the Divorce Reform Act 1969 made 'irretrievable breakdown' the sole ground for divorce and allowed such breakdown to be inferred from separation as well as from conduct,[9] and another half-century before the last vestiges of fault disappeared with the coming into force of the Divorce, Dissolution and Separation Act 2020. As the law now stands, after a couple have been married for a year,[10] either or both may apply for a divorce on the basis that the marriage has irretrievably broken down. Such breakdown no longer needs to be established by proof of any specific facts.

One influential account of these developments has traced the evolution of marriage 'from sacrament to contract'.[11] Others analyse the move to no-fault divorce as part of the shift

---

[5] See eg *Durham v Durham* (1885) 10 PD 80, 82; *Sheffield City Council v E* [2004] EWHC 2808 (Fam) [132].

[6] Henry VIII's 'divorces' were, it should be noted, actually annulments.

[7] Roderick Phillips, *Putting Asunder: A History of Divorce in Western Society* (CUP 1988).

[8] The 1857 Act allowed a divorce to be granted to a man whose wife had committed adultery, or to a woman whose husband had either compounded his adultery by cruelty, desertion, bigamy, or incest or, alternatively, had committed bestiality, sodomy, or rape. The Matrimonial Causes Act 1923 removed the need for wives to show 'aggravated' adultery, and the Matrimonial Causes Act 1937 added the grounds of cruelty, desertion for three years, and incurable insanity.

[9] The Divorce Reform Act 1969 reframed the old fault-based grounds as facts that would be evidence of irretrievable breakdown, along with separation for two years (with the consent of the other spouse) or separation for five years (without such consent): for discussion see Joanna Miles, Daniel Monk, and Rebecca Probert, '"Irretrievably Broken"? Introducing the Life-Story of the Divorce Reform Act 1969' in Joanna Miles, Daniel Monk, and Rebecca Probert (eds), *Fifty Years of the Divorce Reform Act* (Hart Publishing 2022).

[10] There remains an absolute bar on applying for a divorce within the first year of marriage: Matrimonial Causes Act 1973, s 3(1).

[11] John Witte Jr, *From Sacrament to Contract: Marriage, Religion, and Law in the Western Tradition* (Westminster John Knox Press, 2nd ed 2012).

from *status* to contract.[12] It would, however, be equally valid to frame the development of the law of divorce in terms of changing ideas about the *nature* of a contract and in particular about the possibility of termination. Modern scholars have seen the ability to exit from a marriage as intrinsic to the idea of marriage as a contract.[13] But in earlier centuries the defining feature of marriage was its very indissolubility, and yet it was nevertheless regarded as a contract. As Mary Lyndon Shanley has pointed out, prior to 1640, when writers spoke of the relationship between husband and wife being contractual in nature, all that they meant was that it was based on the consent of the parties to marry each other. The contractual nature of marriage did not enable the parties to negotiate over its terms: '[t]o contract a marriage was to consent to a status which in its essence was hierarchical and unalterable.'[14] The idea of marriage as a contract was thus used to justify its indissolubility and as an analogy for the equally unbreakable contract between the sovereign and the people.[15] Indeed, for this generation marriage was not merely a type of contract but the paradigm contract. As Tim Stretton has commented, 'prior to the late sixteenth century the language of contract was most frequently employed not in relation to law or commerce but to marriage'.[16] Of the thirty mentions of the term 'contract' in Shakespeare's plays, Stretton notes that twenty-seven relate to marriage and three to treaties relating to peace between kingdoms.

By the close of the century, however, we find the idea of marriage as a contract being used by John Locke to argue for a very different approach. His argument was that couples should be able to vary the terms of the contract as they wish, including agreeing upon its termination, as long as such agreement did not derogate from what he held to be marriage's central aim: the procreation and upbringing of children. As he put it:

It would give one reason to enquire, why this compact, where procreation and education are secured, and inheritance taken care for, may not be made determinable, either by consent, or at a certain time, or upon certain conditions, as well as any other voluntary compacts, there being no necessity in the nature of the thing, nor to the ends of it, that it should always be for life.[17]

Over the course of the eighteenth century, the idea of marriage as a 'contract' became more problematic as the term began to acquire a broader meaning in the context of commerce. Various commentators felt impelled to deny that marriage was a 'mere civil contract'.[18] While Blackstone confidently claimed that the law 'considers marriage in no other light than a civil contract', he seems to have had in mind its formation rather than any deeper claim about its meaning. As he noted, 'the law treats it as it does all other contracts; allowing

---

[12] For discussion see Elizabeth S Scott and Robert E Scott, 'Marriage as Relational Contract' (1998) 84 Va L Rev 1225 (hereafter Scott and Scott, 'Marriage as Relational Contract').

[13] Dagan, 'Intimate Contracts' (n 2); Scott and Scott, 'Marriage as Relational Contract' (n 12).

[14] Mary Lyndon Shanley, 'Marriage Contract and Social Contract in Seventeenth Century English Political Thought' (1979) 32 *The Western Political Quarterly* 79 (hereafter Shanley, 'Marriage Contract') 79.

[15] ibid. See also Tim Dodsworth, 'Agreements' in Rebecca Probert and John Snape (eds), *A Cultural History of Law in the Age of Enlightenment* (Bloomsbury 2019).

[16] Tim Stretton, 'Contract and Conjugality in Early Modern England' in Lorna Hutson (ed) *The Oxford Handbook of English Law and Literature, 1500–1700* (OUP 2017) 425.

[17] John Locke, *Two Treatises of Government: Book II* (first published 1690, ed Lee Ward, Hackett Publishing 2016) 162–63.

[18] *A Vindication of Marriage as Solemnized by Presbyterians in the North of Ireland*, by A Minister of the Gospel (1702) 15; Daniel Defoe, *A Treatise Concerning the Use and Abuse of the Marriage Bed* (1727).

it to be good and valid in all cases, where the parties at the time of making it were, in the first place, *willing* to contract; secondly, *able* to contract; and, lastly, *did* contract, in the proper forms and solemnities required by law.' His claim about marriage as a contract also needs to be contextualized in terms of his understanding of other contracts: it has been noted that his version of contract law was 'unlike the set of principles with which modern lawyers are familiar'.[19]

By the mid-nineteenth century, however, a distinct law of contract had emerged and the courts were beginning to develop the doctrine of breach. The divorce legislation that was passed in 1857 can be seen as being in line with the contractual thinking of the time, in allowing a marriage to be terminated where a central obligation of the contract had been breached. Indeed, some tried to use the language of breach of contract to argue that the grounds for divorce should be extended beyond adultery. Lords Lyndhurst and Hutchinson, for example, suggested that a divorce should be granted on the 'wilful desertion' of the other spouse, contending that '[e]ven in the most ordinary contract, the breach of it on the one side puts an end to the obligation on the other, and we see no reason why a different rule should be applied to the contract of marriage, and more especially in a case destructive of the entire objects of the union'.[20] In the early decades of the twentieth century, advocates of reform similarly used the language of breach when arguing for the grounds for divorce to be extended beyond adultery.[21]

Similarly, if we look at the position in the late twentieth century, we can find parallels between divorce law and contract law insofar as a contract may be terminated even in the absence of breach by one party and the parties cannot bind themselves forever. During the debates leading up to the passage of the Divorce Reform Act 1969, it was proposed that a couple should have the option of entering into a written agreement that their marriage would be for life.[22] This was, however, decisively rejected. As one MP argued, the vast majority of couples getting married were already convinced that they were entering into a lifelong union 'because their love, their affection, their trust is, to them, far superior to that of anyone else's'.[23] However, as he went on to note, once these elements had disappeared, preserving the marriage in name only served little purpose. In the following decade, in *Staffordshire Area Health Authority v South Staffordshire Waterworks*[24] we find the Court of Appeal similarly rejecting the idea that a contract could last forever and holding that it was necessary to infer a term making the agreement terminable on reasonable notice. The case in question involved an agreement between a local hospital which had given up its private well in return for the supply of 5,000 gallons of water for free and at a special rate for any additional amounts that would apply 'at all times hereafter'. As Lord Denning MR noted, the phrase should not be interpreted as meaning 'forever' or 'in perpetuity'. While there are

---

[19] William Cornish, Stephen Banks, Charles Mitchell, Paul Mitchell, and Rebecca Probert, *Law and Society in England, 1750–1950* (Hart 2nd ed 2019) 195.

[20] Hansard HL Deb 23 June 1857 vol 146, col 233.

[21] See eg Lord Buckmaster's speech when introducing the Separation and Divorce Bill 1918 (Hansard HL Deb 12 November 1918 vol 31 col 1192) and the speeches by Rupert De la Bère and AP Herbert in support of the Marriage Bill 1936, which proposed adding the grounds of desertion, cruelty, and incurable insanity (Hansard, HC Deb 20 November vol 317 cols 2080 and 2093).

[22] Hansard HC Deb 2 May 1969 vol 782 col 1827 (Bruce Campbell).

[23] Hansard HC Deb 2 May 1969 vol 782 cols 1834–35 (Alec Jones).

[24] [1978] 1 WLR 1387.

obvious differences between the two contexts, the response of the law was similarly pragmatic in both.

Given that the late twentieth century was a time of novel ways of thinking about how both marriages and contracts could be brought to an end, it is unsurprising that the idea of marriage as a contract continues to be invoked for very different purposes rooted in very different positions. For some, the idea of marriage as a contract still conveys the idea of a union for life. In the course of the debates on the ill-fated Family Law Bill 1996,[25] for example, we find Edward Leigh MP proclaiming that '[w]e all accept that the marriage contract should be the most solemn contract that one makes in one's life' and that it should be 'uniquely unbreakable'.[26] For others, the implication is that the contract will bind the parties unless one of them is in breach of their obligations.[27] And for yet others the idea of marriage as a contract means that the parties can agree between themselves that they no longer wish to be bound or end the contract by withdrawing their consent. As the Ministry of Justice noted in its consultation paper on reforming the legal requirements for a divorce, marriage 'works by consent': as it reasoned, just as couples must consent to be married, so too they need to consent to remain in the marriage.[28]

It is also unsurprising that it has been a common tactic for opponents of divorce reform to draw analogies between contracts that involve little commitment and proposals to introduce no-fault divorce. For example, we find claims that a marrying couple who also took out a finance agreement for twenty-four months would 'have a firmer commitment to that agreement to purchase than they have to the marriage that they are embarking on'[29] or that such a change would reduce marriage 'to the legal status of a tenancy contract—one that can be dissolved at minimal notice by either party, without any expectation of permanence or any explanation'.[30]

But when we consider these analogies more closely they are difficult to sustain beyond a very superficial level. At one level, we could draw an analogy between divorce under the 2020 Act and modern consumer contracts. As noted above, there is a bar on applying for a divorce in the first year of the marriage—what one might term a minimum commitment period. Most consumer contracts are regulated to the extent that they effectively limit the initial commitment period to twenty-four months.[31] If the parties wish to extend that contract, they can do so either by a monthly rolling contract or through renewed agreement. As with marriage, continued consent is assumed by the lack of action to end the contract, but either may take such action by providing reasonable notice. And in both contexts the

---

[25] The Family Law Act 1996 did receive Royal Assent, but the provisions that would have introduced no-fault divorce were never brought into force and were eventually repealed.

[26] Hansard HC Deb 24 April 1996 vol 276 col 454. In the same debate, John Patten MP similarly noted that 'much has been said about the importance of contracts and of not lightly entering into agreements' and saw the marriage contract as one in which 'two people decide to marry and live with each other for the rest of their lives' (col 480).

[27] Hansard HC Deb 24 April 1996 vol 276 col 454, Sir Michael Neubert, asking 'Is not the removal of fault the equivalent to saying that there is no contract, and therefore that there can be no breach of contract?'

[28] Ministry of Justice, *Reducing Family Conflict: Reform of the Legal Requirements for Divorce* (Sept 2018) 25.

[29] Hansard HC Deb 24 April 1996 vol 276 col 454 (Elizabeth Peacock).

[30] Hansard HC Deb, 8 June 2020, vol 677 col 119 (Sir John Hayes).

[31] See for example Ofcom's General Conditions C1.11; Consumer Rights Act 2015, Part 1 Sch 2(9); even if the term may in principle be acceptable, the requirement of fairness under CRA 2015 s 62 in effect limits the commitment period through restrictions on early termination fees (see eg *The Office of Fair Trading v Ashbourne Management Services Ltd and others* [2011] EWHC 1237 (Ch)); CMA Guidance on Unfair Contract Terms Guidance (2015) [5.15.4]–[5.15.7]; exceptions apply to consumer credit agreements.

parties' freedom to determine the terms of the contract and the circumstances in which it can be ended is limited: the parties cannot agree to bind themselves to maintain the contract beyond the term stipulated by the law.

Drawing such an analogy also helps us to identify the *differences* between such contracts. First, and most obviously, most couples embark on marriage in the hope and expectation that it will be for life. The greater ease of divorce does not seem to have changed this. Moreover, most marriages do in fact endure for life. For those entering into consumer contracts, both the expectations of the parties and the actual duration of their contracts are very different.

Linked to this is the fact that the limits on the initial commitment period within consumer contracts perform a very different function from the restriction on ending a marriage within the first year. The former should be seen as a *maximum*, reflecting the desire to protect consumers from committing themselves to potentially bad bargains for prolonged periods. In the consumer context, true consent by the consumer is seen to be overshadowed by three main factors: the significant imbalance in bargaining power between the business and the consumer; the information asymmetry that exists; and the consumer's psychological 'limitations' in being able to accurately and rationally predict their future. The bar on obtaining a divorce within the first year of a marriage is conceived as a *minimum* period, designed to send a message that a couple should not rush into a divorce. Its purpose, however, is largely symbolic, since it does not oblige the parties to take any positive steps during that time: indeed, there is nothing to prevent the parties from separating the day after the wedding.

So we can dismiss the idea that no-fault divorce reduces marriage to the status of a short-term consumer contract. At the same time, we question whether it resembles any other kind of contract: the parties are unable to set their own terms as to what will justify its termination, for example, or agree to be married for a particular period of time.[32]

While it might be too precipitate to abandon the idea of marriage as a contract altogether, it is clearly an analogy that needs to be applied with caution. In legal terms, perhaps the most fundamental difference between marriage and other contracts is the potential for the persistence of obligations after the contract has come to an end. Any attempt to construe post-divorce provision as a form of damages for breach of contract quickly founders on the fact that the law in this area no longer seeks to allocate responsibility for breakdown. Notwithstanding the passage of legislation encouraging the courts to consider whether the financial obligations of the parties to each other should be terminated, it still remains the case that the very fact of having been married enables an ex-spouse to bring a claim for financial provision, sometimes many years after the marriage has come to an end. That brings us on to our second topic, namely the scope for spouses to contract out of financial obligations in advance.

---

[32] Katherine O'Donovan, *Family Law Matters* (Pluto Press 1993) 59. Advocates of so-called limited term marriages (see eg EF Coppolino, 'Marriage: Bring on the Renewable Term Contract', http://members.planetwaves.net/marriage-bring-on-the-renewable-term-contract/), whereby couples agree to be married for a specific period and then either part or renew the contract, seem to assume that the alternative is being married for life and seem not to consider the very real possibility of couples separating before the specified term.

III. Contracting Out of the Obligations of Marriage: For Love or For Money?

In the past, some commentators drew parallels with commercial contracts in calling for spouses to be able to determine the financial consequences of their marriage in advance and opt out of the obligations that might otherwise be imposed upon them upon divorce. Moira Wright, writing in the 1980s, contrasted the law's limited involvement in 'the contractual relationship of buyers and sellers' with 'the wholesale drafting of the marriage contract on behalf of the parties which takes place in family law' and argued that the parties should be allowed 'to determine the nature of their relationship ab initio, preferably by entering into a contract at the time of marriage which fully reflects the intentions of the parties as to the nature of the relationship between them'.[33]

Since that time there has been a significant shift in English law in terms of the ability of the parties to enter into pre-nuptial agreements.[34] The traditional position was that a pre-nuptial agreement was void as contrary to public policy, since it anticipated the ending of the relationship before it had even begun. But from the late 1990s judges began to give greater weight to such agreements as part of 'all the circumstances of the case' that they are required to consider when deciding what orders should be made upon divorce,[35] and in *Crossley v Crossley* a pre-nuptial agreement was regarded as being of 'magnetic importance'[36] in the context of a short, childless marriage between individuals who were both independently wealthy.

The question of whether an agreement between spouses regarding post-divorce obligations was enforceable as a contract arose in the Privy Council case of *MacLeod v MacLeod*.[37] The husband and wife in that case had been born and brought up in America and had signed a pre-nuptial agreement before their wedding in Florida (where such an agreement would have been binding) in 1994. However, most of their married life was spent on the Isle of Man. By 2001 the marriage was in difficulties, and the parties entered into a further post-nuptial agreement in 2002. This made some changes to the 1994 agreement, making further provision for the wife both during the marriage and in the event of death or divorce. Subject to these variations, the parties confirmed that they still intended to be bound by the 1994 agreement 'and that in any proceedings they would request the court to adhere to its provisions'.[38] However, two years later the husband brought proceedings for divorce and the wife claimed that the agreement should be disregarded in determining what financial provision should be made. The Board held that the 2002 agreement was 'valid and enforceable', in relation both to the parties' respective rights during the marriage and the provisions setting out how assets were to be divided upon divorce. The latter, however, were 'subject to the court's powers of variation',[39] and any attempt to oust the jurisdiction of the court would be void.

---

[33] Moira Wright, 'Marriage: From Status to Contract?' (1984) 13 Anglo-Am LR 17, 18, 22.

[34] There is, it should be noted, a very different approach to pre-nuptial agreements in other jurisdictions: see eg Scott and Scott, 'Marriage as Relational Contract' (n 12); Thompson, *Prenuptial Agreements* (n 1).

[35] Under Matrimonial Causes Act 1973 s 25(1). Examples of cases where pre-nuptial agreements were taken into account include *M v M (Pre-nuptial agreement)* [2002] 1 FLR 654 and *K v K (ancillary relief: pre-nuptial agreement)* [2003] 1 FLR 120.

[36] [2007] EWCA Civ 1491 [15].

[37] [2008] UKPC 64.

[38] ibid [10].

[39] ibid [40].

As the Board emphasized, contracts in the family sphere 'are not like straightforward commercial relationships'.[40] In the 2010 case of *Radmacher v Granatino*,[41] the majority of the Supreme Court went further and held that a *pre*-nuptial agreement was not only enforceable as a contract[42] but should be given effect as long as it had been 'freely entered into by each party with a full appreciation of its implications unless in the circumstances prevailing it would not be fair to hold the parties to their agreement'.[43]

The language of 'love' and 'trust' makes frequent appearances in the case law in this area. 'Love' is noted as a reason for an individual wanting a pre-nuptial agreement. In *Radmacher*, for example, Lord Phillips described how the wife saw the pre-nuptial contract as a means of ensuring that her husband 'was marrying her for love and not for her money'.[44] This accords with the modern perception that marriage *should* be an expression of love rather than being influenced by mercenary considerations: as Elizabeth van Acker notes, 'base considerations, such as wealth, may taint the entire marriage'.[45] Unsurprisingly, then, the narrative that the less wealthy individual was marrying 'for love' rather than money is frequently met with in the case law.[46]

At the same time, articulating the suspicion, or even just acknowledging the possibility, that less wealthy party is not actuated solely by love reflects a lack of trust in them. This is presumably why Ms Radmacher emphasized that it was her father who had insisted on the pre-nuptial agreement. In the recent case of *MN v AN*, the fact that the husband had called the wife a 'gold-digger' during an argument over the proposed terms of their pre-nuptial agreement was clearly seen as reflecting badly on him rather than on her.[47]

Love also emerges as a reason for exercising caution about the enforcement of such agreements. The rationale offered by Lord Phillips in *Radmacher* for giving weight to a nuptial agreement was that there should be respect 'for autonomy' and 'to the decision of a married couple as to the manner in which their financial affairs should be regulated'.[48] However, Lady Hale, in her dissenting judgment, noted that while some might regard those about to marry 'as in all respects fully autonomous beings', others 'may wonder whether people who are typically (although not invariably) in love can be expected to make rational choices in the same way that businessmen can'.[49] The wife in *MN v AN* similarly invoked ideas of love and trust in arguing that the pre-nuptial agreement should be disregarded, noting that her future husband had 'first raised the issue of her "signing something" when she was lying in bed. She said she loved him and trusted him . . . so she just said "yes"'.[50] The intimacy of the setting underlines just how different an agreement discussed in a lover's arms is likely to be from one negotiated at arm's length between commercial parties.

---

[40] ibid [42].

[41] [2010] UKSC 42 (hereafter *Radmacher*).

[42] This point, as Lady Hale noted, was obiter: ibid [138].

[43] ibid [75].

[44] ibid [13].

[45] Elizabeth van Acker, *Governments and Marriage Education Policy: Perspectives from the UK, Australia and the US* (Palgrave Macmillan 2008) 42.

[46] *Luckwell v Limata* [2014] EWHC 502 (Fam) [12]; *Pierburg v Pierburg* [2022] EWHC 2701 (Fam) [8], [50].

[47] *MN v AN* [2023] EWHC (Fam) 613 [81] (hereafter *MN v AN*). However, Moor J excused the husband's use of this word on the basis that it was said during an argument and 'both said things that they would not normally say'.

[48] *Radmacher* (n 41) [78].

[49] ibid [135].

[50] *MN v AN* (n 47) [68].

Many scholars have echoed Lady Hale's concerns and questioned whether it is appropriate to accord respect to autonomy in a context where there may not only be inequality of bargaining power at the start of the marriage but also inequalities of opportunity during the marriage, where one spouse takes on the bulk of caring responsibilities and the other is free to pursue their career.[51] In other words, the issue is not merely that love and trust may affect the judgment of the individual at the time of entering into the agreement, but that people do things 'for love' during the course of a relationship that are not in their economic best interests.

Yet the extent to which 'autonomy' has become a central principle in family law should not be overstated. In reality, the fact that a pre-nuptial agreement is *enforceable* is of relatively limited significance.[52] The crucial point is that such an agreement is still not *binding*, in that it cannot oust the jurisdiction of the court to make orders reallocating assets between the parties upon divorce under the Matrimonial Causes Act 1973. The court is directed to take all the circumstances of the case into account in deciding what order(s) to make, with 'first consideration' being given to the welfare of any minor children.[53]

All this was spelt out in *Radmacher* itself. First, as Lord Phillips held, for a nuptial agreement to carry 'full weight', both parties would have to have entered it 'of their own free will, without undue influence or pressure, and informed of its implications'.[54] This assessment of the making of the agreement, as *Chitty* notes, 'requires consideration of a far wider range of factors than those which would vitiate a contract'.[55] However, even allowing for this expanded list, it is crucial to recognize that Lord Phillips was referring to what would be *necessary* for a pre-nuptial agreement to be given 'full weight', not what would be *sufficient* for its terms to be enforced in full.[56] As he made clear, the weight to be given to a pre-nuptial agreement will also depend on whether it achieves a fair result, taking into account the relative position of the parties at the end of their marriage. Individuals cannot opt out of obligations to their children, and factors such as the needs of one of the spouses and/or compensation for relationship-generated disadvantage may 'render it unfair to hold the parties to an antenuptial agreement'.[57] Indeed, he even accepted that it might be unfair to preclude a spouse from sharing in the assets accrued by the other during the marriage where their domestic contributions had enabled the other spouse to focus on their career. In other words, in the context of pre-nuptial agreements the question is not the binary one of whether there is a valid contract or not but the degree of weight to be given to the agreement.[58]

This cuts both ways. There may be cases where the court had concerns about the way in which the agreement was made but still takes the view that it is right to give some weight

---

[51] See eg Alison Diduck, 'Autonomy and Vulnerability in Family Law: The Missing Link' in Julie Wallbank and Jonathan Herring (eds) *Vulnerabilities, Care and Family Law* (Routledge 2013); Jonathan Herring, *Relational Autonomy and Family Law* (Springer 2014); Anne Barlow, 'Solidarity, Autonomy and Equality: Mixed Messages for the Family' [2016] CFLQ 223.

[52] See also Edwin Peel, *Treitel on the Law of Contract* (15th edn, Sweet & Maxwell 2020) [11-049] (hereafter *Treitel*), describing enforceability as a 'red herring'.

[53] Matrimonial Causes Act 1973 s 25(1).

[54] *Radmacher* (n 41) [68].

[55] Hugh Beale (gen ed), *Chitty on Contracts* (34th edn, Sweet & Maxwell 2022) [4-245] (hereafter *Chitty*), noting that the court will take into account 'the parties' emotional state at the time of their agreement, and also their age, maturity and relationship history'.

[56] This crucial qualification is not discussed in *Chitty*.

[57] *Radmacher* (n 41) [81].

[58] The same goes for separation agreements: see *Edgar v Edgar* [1980] 1 WLR 1410.

to it. In *Versteegh v Versteegh*, for example, Lewison LJ noted that a pre-nuptial agreement 'does not have to be contractually binding', with any potential unfairness in its making being a factor to take into account rather than a reason for disregarding it.[59] Similarly, in *WC v HC (Financial Remedies Agreements)*, Peel J held that since the wife had refused to sign the post-nuptial agreement it was 'not a formally arrived at agreement in the *Radmacher* sense'; however, as he went on to note, to disregard it completely would be 'contrary to the s25 requirement to take account of all the circumstances of the case'.[60] The fact that a pre-nuptial agreement does not have to be valid as a contract is also reflected in the way that key concepts are interpreted. In relation to duress, for example, the courts continue to frame the test as being whether the will of either of the spouses was overborne.[61] By contrast, in contract law it has long been accepted that it is not a question of the 'overborne' will (a matter of fact)[62] but instead a question of whether the pressure was illegitimate (a matter of law)[63] and, if so, whether the other party had any practical choice.[64]

Equally, there may be cases where there are no concerns about how the agreement was made but it is still deemed 'unfair' to hold the parties to its terms because it does not meet their needs or compensate them for relationship-generated disadvantage. Here it is worth noting that meeting a spouse's needs does not mean simply providing for bare subsistence, although different judges have different views as to how generously 'needs' should be assessed in this context.[65] By way of illustration, in *WC v HC* the wife's needs were assessed at £7.45m, which accounted for approximately 60 per cent of the assets available to the parties.[66] Moreover, the Court of Appeal noted in *Brack v Brack* that since the court remains under an obligation to take all of the factors listed in section 25 into account in deciding what award to make, its 'search for a fair outcome' may lead to an order 'which, contrary to the terms of an agreement, provides a settlement for the wife in excess of her needs'.[67]

That said, it is clear from the case law that an agreement may alter what is regarded as fair. In *MN v AN*, Moor J noted that in the absence of a pre-nuptial agreement a court might have made slightly more generous provision for the wife, but 'that is not the test'.[68] The existence of an agreement has also been held to justify matrimonial assets being divided unequally in cases where they would otherwise have been divided equally.[69] Here the idea of marriage as an equal partnership in which the assets accrued during the relationship are to be shared yields to the idea of marriage as involving two partners each equally capable of bargaining about their rights. Thus in *CMX v EJX (French Marriage Contract)*, the wife's claim that the

---

[59] [2018] EWCA Civ 1050.

[60] [2022] EWFC 22 [40]–[41].

[61] See eg *Hopkins v Hopkins* [2015] EWHC 812 (Fam) [53]; *KA v MA (Prenuptial Agreement: Needs)* [2018] EWHC 499 (Fam) [63] (hereafter *KA v MA*).

[62] See the discussion of *Lynch v DPP of Northern Ireland* [1975] AC 653 in *Chitty* [10-005].

[63] See also Lord Burrows' speech in *Pakistan International Airline Corp v Times Travel (UK) Ltd* [2021] UKSC 40 [105] ff (hereafter *Times Travel*).

[64] Lord Burrows' suggestion that the legitimacy of pressure could depend on whether it was made in bad faith alone was rejected: *Times Travel* [46].

[65] See also *Brack v Brack* [2018] EWCA Civ 2862, in which Eleanor King LJ noted the 'degree of latitude' enjoyed by the court when 'deciding on the level of generosity or frugality which should appropriately be brought to the assessment of those needs'.

[66] See also *CMX v EJX (French Marriage Contract)* [2022] EWFC 136 (hereafter *CMX*), in which the wife's needs included two properties in France as well as a house in central London.

[67] [2018] EWCA Civ 2862 [103], King LJ.

[68] *MN v AN* (n 47) [88].

[69] *Z v Z (No 2)* [2011] EWHC 2878 (Fam).

marriage involved a 'true, loving, equal partnership'[70] fell on deaf ears: the fact that she had signed a marriage contract in France opting for separate property meant that the sharing principle was inapplicable.

Of course, in thinking about the reasons why couples enter into pre-nuptial agreements, it needs to be noted that the choice facing the parties may not be between marriage with a pre-nuptial agreement and marriage without a pre-nuptial agreement but rather between marriage with a pre-nuptial agreement and no marriage at all. In *KA v MA*, for example, the wife 'knew full well' that the agreement was 'the condition precedent' to the husband agreeing to the marriage,[71] while in *WC v HC*, both parties agreed that they would not have married without a pre-nuptial agreement.[72] In *MN v AN*, Moor J confirmed that it would not be unfair or undue pressure for an individual to say that they would not marry without an acceptable agreement:

> This must be correct as the ability to apply for financial remedies after the breakdown of a relationship is entirely dependent on there having been a marriage. A wife cannot secure the right to apply for financial remedies via a marriage by signing a pre-nuptial agreement only to renounce the agreement thereafter on the basis that she only signed it because he said there would be no marriage if she did not.[73]

Given the lack of recognition of cohabiting couples, marriage with a pre-nuptial agreement is likely to offer far more protection than no marriage. This brings us to our third topic: how contracts may be used in a positive way to confer rights outside legal marriage.

IV. Contracting for Obligations Outside Legal Marriage

For couples who have not gone through a valid ceremony of marriage, entering into a contract may be a way of conferring rights, rather than limiting entitlements. In a context in which the protection offered by the general law is limited, entering into such a contract could be framed as an expression of love by the financially stronger party and as a means of providing reassurance to the financially weaker party.

It is now twenty years since Hart J explicitly accepted in *Sutton v Mishcon de Reya* that 'there is nothing contrary to public policy in a cohabitation agreement governing the property relationship between adults who intend to cohabit or who are cohabiting for the purposes of enjoying a sexual relationship'.[74] The point was, of course, technically *obiter*, since the agreement in *Sutton* in fact involved a master–slave agreement that was regarded as contrary to public policy. But the suggestion was hardly a controversial one, since the possibility of cohabiting couples entering into an agreement about their property rights had already been implicitly accepted in the context of contractual licences and constructive trusts.[75]

---

[70] *CMX* (n 66) [20].

[71] *KA v MA* (n 61) [64].

[72] See also *WW v HW* [2015] EWHC 1844 (Fam) [6] (agreement acknowledged that 'the marriage was conditional upon the agreement being executed').

[73] *MN v AN* (n 47) [60].

[74] *Sutton v Mishcon de Reya and Gawor & Co* [2003] EWHC 3166 (Ch) [22]. For discussion of how many of the older authorities dealt with different kinds of relationships—and also predated certain key developments in the law of contracts—see Rebecca Probert, 'Cohabitation Contracts and Swedish Sex Slaves' [2004] CFLQ 453.

[75] See eg *Tanner v Tanner* [1975] 1 WLR 1346; *Eves v Eves* [1975] 1 WLR 1338.

Yet Chris Barton's comment that '[t]here is rather more literature on this subject than there is law' remains valid today.[76] The fact that cohabitants can enter into a contract does not mean that they will. As one recent practitioner guide notes, cohabitation contracts are rarely encountered in practice: '[t]hose who are cohabiting, or intending to cohabit, will rarely see a solicitor for the express purpose of entering into a cohabitation agreement.'[77]

There are a range of reasons for this absence of cohabitation contracts. One is that many cohabitants do not realize that they will not be protected by the law upon the breakdown of their relationship. Surveys have established that almost half of the population continues to believe that 'couples who live together for a period of time have a common law marriage which gives them the same rights as married couples'.[78]

A second group of reasons for the absence of cohabitation contracts could be framed in terms of love and trust. One element of this is the optimism bias within relationships: couples in love do not think that they will split up, and so do not see the need to make provision for that contingency.[79] It is therefore unsurprising that one study found respondents describing cohabitation contracts as 'defeatist' and 'cold'.[80]

There are also practical considerations. Couples at the start of their relationship may not have amassed sufficient resources to make the expense of consulting solicitors worthwhile. This is all the more likely given the age of couples when they begin to cohabit and the fact that most will be living together in rented accommodation. While the subsequent purchase of a home together would be an obvious trigger for the parties to consider their financial position, various empirical studies suggest that this is not a priority for couples.[81]

Other reasons for not having a cohabitation contract can be positively combative. Many cohabitants are in 'uneven' relationships, that is, relationships in which one may have more knowledge of their legal rights and responsibilities than the other.[82] In addition, where there are significant economic disparities between the parties, each will have very different interests at stake and so different ideas about what should be in any contract. Such differences may preclude agreement being reached even where a contract was considered. Again, some of the cases in which a constructive trust was claimed provide examples: in *Thomson v Humphrey*,[83] Mr Humphrey had tried to persuade Mrs Thomson to sign a 'living together agreement' confirming that she had no interest in his property. However, Mrs Thomson

---

[76] Chris Barton, 'Contract—A Justifiable Taboo?' in Rebecca Probert (ed) *Family Life and the Law: Under One Roof* (Ashgate 2007) 78.

[77] Helen Wood, James Cook, Lisette Dupré, Ashley Murray, David Salter, and Emily Ward, *Cohabitation Law, Practice and Precedents* (LexisNexis, 8th ed 2020) 197.

[78] Anne Barlow, 'Modern Marriage Myths—The Dichotomy Between Expectations of Legal Rationality and Lived Law' in Rajnaara C Akhtar, Patrick Nash, and Rebecca Probert (eds) *Cohabitation and Religious Marriage: Status, Similarities and Solutions* (BUP 2020).

[79] The classic study is that carried out by Baker and Emery in the US, which found that those questioned were aware that 50% of marriages ended in divorce but estimated the likelihood of their own marriages ending in divorce as 0%: Lynn A Baker and Robert E Emery, 'When Every Relationship Is above Average: Perceptions and Expectations of Divorce at the Time of Marriage' (1993) 17 Law and Hum Behav 439. Such optimism is not unique to intimate relationships: consumer law is also faced with the difficulty that many consumers simply do not believe it statistically likely that unfortunate events will happen to them.

[80] Jane Lewis, Jessica Datta and Sophie Sarre, Individualism and Commitment in Marriage and Cohabitation, Lord Chancellor's Department Research Series, No 8/99, 81.

[81] Gillian Douglas, Julia Pearce, and Hilary Woodward, 'Dealing with Property Issues on Cohabitation Breakdown' [2007] Fam Law 36, 38.

[82] Anne Barlow and Janet Smithson, 'Legal Assumptions, Cohabitants' Talk and the Rocky Road to Reform' [2010] CFLQ 328.

[83] [2009] EWHC 3576 (Ch).

had refused to sign the draft and gave evidence that she had explained to Mr Humphrey that she 'would not agree to be with him if those were his terms'.[84] The different interests of the parties were also evident in *Stark v Walker*,[85] a rare example of a claim based on an alleged cohabitation contract. In this case, Ms Stark was the one pressing for an agreement that would make provision for her and their child. Her solicitor, for example, had written to Mr Walker's attorney in Boston noting that a 'source of disharmony' in their respective clients' continuing relationship was the issue of 'financial responsibility for their joint living expenses and for the support of the child' and emphasizing the importance of the parties entering into a written financial agreement.[86] Mr Walker, however, appears to have been reluctant to enter into any such agreement and the subsequent proceedings involved 'many disputed allegations' about whether any agreement had ever been reached.

A final reason for the absence of valid cohabitation contracts is that the kinds of arrangements made by couples without legal advice may simply not meet the requirements for a contract. This is of course familiar ground for contract lawyers: insofar as contract law textbooks consider cohabitation contracts, it is generally under the heading of intention to create legal relations (or, rather, the lack of any such intention). The case of *Stark v Walker* is particularly illuminating here. Ms Stark sought to argue that Mr Walker had promised to pay her an annual sum of £50,000, index-linked, plus household expenses, for the rest of her life. This was based in part on a document produced by Mr Walker in 1997—handwritten on lined paper, riddled with spelling mistakes, and consisting solely of the following:

> I WARREN R. WALKER will pay Koo Stark the Equivalent of £50,000 pounds per Anum payable quarterly—For her household expenses Rent, food, Nanni and cleaning costs. This Amount is consistently more than any legal obligation that WARREN R. WALKER is eligable for but he does this out of Kindness and love and guarantees the amount. Warren Walker.[87]

On being cross-examined about this document he explained that he had written it to ensure that he would still have 'access' to his daughter but added that 'if it had been a formal letter, he would have gone to a lawyer, he would have had the letter typed, and he would not have referred to acting out of "kindness and love".' As the judge noted, '[t]he overall tenor of his evidence was that the document was intended to provide Ms Stark with a degree of comfort, which would look to her like a binding promise, but which would not actually be binding in law'.[88] Even though the judge held that no consideration had been provided for the promise,[89] he felt compelled to also consider the status and meaning of the document in order to decide whether the parties had the requisite intention to create legal relations. The judge reiterated that, although Mr Walker had intended for the document to look like a binding contract to Ms Stark, it was only intended to be no more than a 'gentleman's agreement'. In commercial contracts, where there is a presumption that the parties do intend to create legal relations, the intention is determined objectively from the words of the

---

[84] ibid [48].
[85] [2020] EWHC 562 (Ch).
[86] ibid [31].
[87] ibid [35].
[88] ibid [38].
[89] ibid [81].

agreement[90] and the surrounding context rather than what the party had actually intended. In *Blue v Ashley*,[91] where a promise of £15 million was made over drinks to incentivize Mr Blue, the court held that the agreement lacked the requisite intention. In *Wells v Devani*[92] the court took into account a number of external factors in order to determine the intention of the parties, including the purpose of the gathering, the location, the commercial viability of the deal, and the detail of the offer in relation to the value of the deal. However, the court did not take into account the subjective intention of either of the parties.[93]

Since Mr Walker's intention *not* to enter into legal relations prevailed over any expectations that his note might have created without the need for him to have expressed those intentions, it is worth querying whether the concept of intention to create legal relations applied in the commercial setting has much in common with the concept applied in the domestic setting. One explanation for adopting a different approach where family and contract law cases overlap is the desire to avoid double recovery,[94] although this cannot explain the approach in cohabitation cases where no family law remedies are available. There might be a further dimension. The judicial assumption that these domestic agreements should (only) be enforced through 'family ties and affection'[95] also influences what might is expected of the parties' implicit understanding of each other's intentions.[96] Lord Denning MR in *Merritt v Merritt*[97] found that living together in 'harmony' contributed to the finding in *Balfour v Balfour*[98] that the parties could not have meant the court to intervene in their arrangements. The ideology of harmony and deep understanding in a domestic setting appears to have translated into a different meaning of intention. While the relationship between Mr Walker and Ms Stark was far from harmonious at the time the agreement was made, the judge seems to have expected Ms Stark to have known of Mr Walker's real intentions, presumably by reference to a time when their relationship was still intact.

The impact of such a different understanding of intention can be shown by imagining a change in the facts of *Blue v Ashley*. If evidence had been presented that Mr Ashley had attempted to make the agreement appear more formal than he had really intended (for example by presenting most of the terms in writing) then it would likely have resulted in the finding of a contract, as Mr Blue (objectively) would have been justified in relying on the appearance of Mr Ashley's intention. By contrast, the same evidence in *Stark v Walker* was used to prove that there was no intention to create legal relations and therefore no contract.

Cases such as *Stark* thus suggest that we should be cautious about the extent to which contracts *could* be an appropriate solution for cohabiting couples in the absence of wider reform of the law relating to cohabitation. Moreover, cases such as *Thomson* also raise questions about whether they *should* be. While cohabitation contracts have certainly had their

---

[90] Lord Wright in *G Scammel & Nephew Ltd v HC and JG Ouston* [1941] AC 251, 268 (HL): 'But the test of intention is to be found in the words used.'

[91] *Blue v Ashley* [2017] EWHC 1928 (Comm).

[92] [2019] UKSC 4.

[93] It would be different if the other party knew of that intention.

[94] Stephen Hedley, 'Keeping Contract in Its Place—*Balfour v Balfour* and the Enforceability of Informal Agreements' (1985) 5 OJLS 392.

[95] *Parker v Clark* [1960] 1 WLR 286, 332 (Bristol Assizes).

[96] Jeanette Ashton and Juliet Turner, 'A Contemporary Reimagining of the Intention to Create Legal Relations Doctrine' (2022) 4 JBL 283.

[97] [1970] 1 WLR 1211 (CA).

[98] [1919] 2 KB 571 (CA).

CONTRACTING FOR OBLIGATIONS OUTSIDE LEGAL MARRIAGE   107

advocates,[99] there is little advantage to the financially weaker party if the contract is used strategically to preclude potential claims, as was attempted in *Thomson*. As David McLellan has noted, '[i]n a society where power is systematically distributed asymmetrically, contract is likely to reinforce such an asymmetry'.[100]

A second context, and one where there may be more potential for a contract to play an important role, is where a couple have a religious-only marriage. Such marriages are particularly common within Muslim communities in England and Wales.[101] Here it is significant that Islam has traditionally viewed marriage as a contract rather than a sacrament, and that it is a requirement for the *nikah* ceremony to be accompanied by an agreement setting out the dowry, or *mahr*, that is to be paid to the wife in the event of the husband's death or a subsequent divorce.[102] Within English law, the significance of that agreement will depend on the status of the marriage. Where the marriage is valid—for example, where the parties complied with the required preliminaries and the *nikah* was conducted in a registered place of worship in the presence of a registrar or authorized person—the accompanying agreement will have the same status as any other marital property agreement.[103] The same is true if the marriage was void—for example, if the parties went through a ceremony in a registered place of worship but knowingly and wilfully failed to give notice—since the courts have the same powers to reallocate assets between the parties on making a decree of nullity as upon a decree of divorce. However, if the *nikah* ceremony was conducted altogether outside the framework of the Marriage Act 1949 it will be classified as non-qualifying, with the result that the court has no power to reallocate assets between the parties. In this context the agreement assumes considerable significance as the source of obligations between the parties.

This was the scenario in *Uddin v Choudhary & Ors*.[104] Mohammed Uddin and Nazim Choudhary had gone through a *nikah* ceremony that did not comply with the requirements for a valid marriage under English law. The marriage did not work out, and Nazim was granted an Islamic divorce by an Islamic Sharia Council. Burhan Uddin, the groom's father, subsequently claimed the sum of £25,500 in the county court, which he said represented the value of various items, mainly jewellery, taken by the bride. This was met with a counterclaim by Nazim for the sum of £15,000, which she said had been promised by way of dowry. The judge at first instance, HHJ Collender, rejected the claim that Nazim had taken the items in question, further holding that any gifts made had been absolute ones and were not contingent on the continuance of the marriage. However, he accepted Nazim's case that there was 'a properly agreed dowry' and found that this was a valid and enforceable contract.[105] Mummery LJ subsequently refused Mr Uddin's application for permission to appeal, noting that while '[t]here was no ceremony which was recognised by English law', it

---

[99] See in particular the body of work by Elizabeth Kingdom: 'Cohabitation Contracts: A Socialist-Feminist Issue' (1988) 15 Jo L Soc 77; '"Lawyers Will Draft Anything": Attitudes to Cohabitation Contracts', Occasional Paper No 5, University of Liverpool, Department of Sociology, Social Policy and Social Work Studies, 1994; 'Cohabitation Contracts and the Democratisation of Personal Relations' (2000) 8 Fem LS 5.

[100] David MacLellan, 'Contract Marriage—The Way Forward or Dead End' (1996) 23 Jo L Soc 234.

[101] Rebecca Probert, Rajnaara Akhtar, and Sharon Blake, *Belief in Marriage* (BUP 2023).

[102] Judith E Tucker, *Women, Family and Gender in Islamic Law* (CUP 2008) 48.

[103] For discussion see Mairead Enright, 'The Beginning of the Sharpness: Loyalty, Citizenship and Muslim Divorce Practice' (2013) 9 Int JLC 295.

[104] [2009] EWCA Civ 1205.

[105] ibid [7].

was 'a valid ceremony so far as the parties were agreed and it was valid for the purposes of giving legal effect to the agreement which had been made about gifts and dowry'.[106]

Whether the enforcement of a contractual agreement over *mahr* provides an adequate remedy will depend on the sum stipulated in the contract: it may be merely nominal, intended to ensure the validity of the marriage under Islamic law rather than to make adequate provision in the event of a divorce.[107] If anything, *Uddin v Choudhary* provides a disincentive to making any more than nominal provision, given the risk that the stipulated sum will have to be paid in circumstances where Islamic law would not require this. It is a condition of a *khula* divorce—that is, one initiated by the wife other than in pursuance of a term of the marriage contract or on the basis that her husband has acted unreasonably—that she should forfeit her right to *mahr*.[108] Similarly, the enforceability of the contract accompanying a *nikah* does not solve the broader issue as to the non-recognition of the *nikah* itself. Again, the fact that contract law provides *a* solution should not mean that it is *the* solution.

So, contracts may have a useful role to play in certain domestic contexts in default of other protection. But as Ewan identified, where the relationship is one of love and trust, couples may not perceive any need to make provision for a future in which such love and trust has vanished. In the absence of a loving and trusting relationship, contracts are more likely to be used to safeguard assets rather than to promise provision.

V. Conclusion

As we noted at the outset, what has been particularly striking for us in collaborating on this chapter is the extent of the differences between the approach of contract law and that of family law. Ewan's scepticism as to whether contract law is the right mechanism to regulate contracts characterized by love and trust inspired us to compare the reasons for the unique approach adopted in each field.

Our review of marriage as a contract identified that, although our two fields' shared vocabulary (of, for example, 'termination', 'consent', and even 'duress') might at first appear similar, the underlying functions—attributing fault and compensation on the one hand and needs-based reallocation of shared assets on the other—diverge. However, both systems have had to grapple with surprisingly similar problems, for example where relationships are envisaged to last forever or where circumstances inevitably change. The comparison unearths a radically different emphasis of underlying values. For contract lawyers autonomy is a core value, whereas for family lawyers it is a highly contentious one. Family law focuses on resolving disputes where individuals have typically relied on love and trust and not spelt out their respective obligations and rights, whereas contracts are used by individuals precisely to clarify their respective obligations and rights in advance in the absence of love and trust.

Ewan identifies that the doctrine of intention to create legal relations rightly limits the reach of contract law into family relations. Though both areas of law share a vocabulary,

---

[106] ibid [11].

[107] Shaista Gohir, *Information and Guidance on Muslim Marriage and Divorce in Britain* (Muslim Women's Network 2016), 28–29 and 31 (http://www.mwnuk.co.uk/resourcesDetail.php?id=156).

[108] Samia Bano, 'British Muslim Communities, Islamic Divorce and English Family Law' in Joanna Miles, Daniel Monk, and Rebecca Probert (eds), *Fifty Years of the Divorce Reform Act* (Hart Publishing 2022) 251.

our comparison of the different understandings of them reflects how far apart contract and family law are in what they consider to be desirable features of relationships of love and trust. Nevertheless, there is a natural complementarity between these areas where relationships of love and trust fall beyond the reach of family law, which only underscores the importance of understanding the scopes and limitations of the contract and family law spheres. Whatever the role of contracts in family law, there is a role for contract and family lawyers to compare language, values, and limitations, and for participants to better understand the relationship between their subjects.

7

Shades of Frustration

WILLIAM DAY*

I. Introduction

Through his curatorship of the relevant part of *Chitty on Contracts* since 1994,[1] his editorship of a prominent collection of essays,[2] his chapters on the topic in his enduringly popular student textbook,[3] and numerous journal articles and book chapters,[4] Ewan McKendrick is probably the most prolific and influential academic now working in the field of the law of frustration. What Ewan has been writing about for the past thirty years involves an overarching question: when will events that occur after the parties enter into a contract ('supervening events') excuse their contractual performance? The answer at a high level of generality is 'not often', and those rare cases where performance is excused in the absence of an applicable express term (such as a force majeure clause) are invariably attributed to something called 'the doctrine of frustration'.

In this chapter, I want to suggest that there is no such thing as 'the' doctrine of frustration. Nor can a clean distinction be drawn between frustration and force majeure clauses. The case law recognizes that there are various terms which may be implied into the contract that, when triggered, can discharge future performance. Those cases and force majeure clauses are two shades of the same thing: an examination of terms of the parties' bargain to see whether they objectively agreed that performance was not required in the circumstances of the supervening event. But it would also be wrong to treat these as occupying the whole field. The nature of some intervening events raises considerations of public policy. In those cases, the content of the parties' agreement is not determinative but instead forms the backdrop for a different type of analysis. An error made in the past has been to search for a single theory or doctrine to explain *the whole* of the law of frustration. The central argument developed in this chapter is that this is simply not possible. Different terms—express or implied in law or implied in fact—may be at issue in different cases, and the public policy cases form their own, further, distinct category or categories.

---

* I am very grateful to Ed Peel for comments on an earlier draft.

[1] See now Hugh Beale (ed), *Chitty on Contracts* (34th edn, Sweet & Maxwell 2021) ch 26 (hereafter *Chitty*).

[2] Ewan McKendrick (ed), *Force Majeure and Frustration of Contract* (2nd edn, Informa Law 1995) (hereafter McKendrick, *Force Majeure and Frustration*).

[3] See now Ewan McKendrick, *Contract Law* (14th edn, Macmillan 2021) (hereafter McKendrick, *Contract Law*).

[4] See eg Ewan McKendrick, 'Frustration, Restitution and Loss Apportionment' in Andrew Burrows (ed), *Essays on the Law of Restitution* (OUP 1991); Ewan McKendrick, 'Force Majeure Clauses: The Gap between Doctrine and Practice' in Andrew Burrows and Edwin Peel (eds), *Contract Terms* (OUP 2007) (hereafter McKendrick, 'Force Majeure Clauses'); Hannes Unberath and Ewan McKendrick, 'Supervening Events' in Gerhard Dannemann and Stefan Vogenauer (eds), *The Common European Sales Law in Context: Interactions with English and German Law* (OUP 2013); Ewan McKendrick, 'Frustration: Automatic Discharge of Both Parties?' in Andrew Dyson, James Goudkamp, and Frederick Wilmot-Smith (eds), *Defences in Contract* (Hart 2017); Ewan McKendrick, 'Brexit, Uncertainty and the Doctrine of Frustration' (2019) 34 JIBLR 439.

William Day, *Shades of Frustration* In: *Shaping the Law of Obligations.* Edited by: Edwin Peel and Rebecca Probert, Oxford University Press. © William Day 2023. DOI: 10.1093/oso/9780198889762.003.0007

Lord Wilberforce famously had little time for a debate about the correct theoretical basis for the law of frustration, saying that they 'shade into one another'.[5] But as Ewan has perceptively identified, the underlying explanation matters because, 'if we are not sure of the basis of the doctrine, we are unlikely to be able to predict with any degree of certainty the circumstances in which the courts will invoke it'.[6] Further, the modern approach of lumping the different categories together has obscured the relevant (and different) tests for excusing performance. This has led to an opaque approach which risks substituting judicial value judgement for proper contractual analysis. This is seen by Ewan's helpful description of the modern law in *Chitty on Contracts*:

> Rather than seek to identify a single, definitive test that can be applied in all cases, more recent authority supports a broader approach which seeks to take account of all of the facts and circumstances of the case when deciding whether or not a contract has been frustrated. This 'multi-factorial' approach has regard, among other factors to . . . [t]he terms of the contract, its matrix or context and the parties' knowledge, expectations, assumptions and contemplations, in particular as to risk, [which] have been described as 'ex ante factors', whereas the remaining factors are 'post-contractual'.[7]

The benefit of splitting the law of frustration back up into its constituent parts would be to move away from such an unattractively uncertain approach, re-aligning the rules with the underlying reasons for excusing performance, and re-introducing bright-line rules of the type which commercial parties are entitled to expect from the law of contract.

II. Force Majeure

It is now not novel to include force majeure clauses in a discussion of the law of frustration. Some fifteen years ago Ewan pointedly noted that 'force majeure clauses fare rather badly' in academic treatment in contrast to 'the analysis of the doctrine of frustration',[8] and one of his major contributions in this field has been to rebalance the focus between the two.

The existence and scope of any force majeure clause is very likely to affect an argument about frustration. On the dominant multi-factorial approach this is because, if the contract contemplates the supervening event or type of event, it may be difficult to say that the supervening event renders performance of the contract radically different from that contemplated at the time of contracting. On the implied term theory advocated in this chapter, the existence of the express term leaves 'no room' for the implied.[9] That is because it can then be said that the parties, objectively, turned their minds to that type of supervening event occurring and provided for when it might excuse performance. Such terms also provide a degree of certainty to any debate between the contracting parties over the

---

[5] *National Carriers Ltd v Panalpina (Northern) Ltd* [1981] AC 675 (HL) 693.
[6] Ewan McKendrick, 'Force Majeure and Frustration—Their Relationship and a Comparative Assessment' in McKendrick, *Force Majeure and Frustration* (n 2) 39 (hereafter McKendrick, 'Force Majeure and Frustration').
[7] *Chitty* (n 1) [26.019].
[8] McKendrick, 'Force Majeure Clauses' (n 4) 233.
[9] *Bremer Handelsgesellschaft mbH v Vanden Avenne-Izegen PVBA* [1977] 1 Lloyd's Rep 133 (Com Ct) 163. Cf McKendrick, 'Force Majeure and Frustration' (n 6) 34.

effect of a supervening event: the force majeure clause removes the difficulty of applying the multi-factorial test, and instead makes this a familiar question about the construction of contracts, albeit an area where ordinary principles of interpretation can be distorted by the *contra proferentem* principle.

In *Metropolitan Water Board v Dick Kerr & Co*,[10] the contract was to construct a reservoir within six years, but in the event of 'difficulties, impediments, obstructions, oppositions, doubts, disputes, or differences, whatsoever and howsoever occasioned' the engineer had a discretion to grant extensions.[11] The House of Lords held that, despite this clear wording, the delay caused by the First World War fell outwith the clause, and 'the interruption [was] of such a character and duration that it vitally and fundamentally change[d] the conditions of the contract',[12] such that it was discharged for frustration. Although *contra proferentem* was not expressly invoked, it is hard not to see it as an application of that doctrine, and in any event it must be the wrong construction: the words 'whatsoever and howsoever' unambiguously made the clause wide enough to encompass the impact of the war. Nonetheless, the effect of the restrictive interpretation adopted by the House of Lords was to create a gap in the express terms into which a further term could be implied that enabled discharge of the contract for frustration.[13] The reasoning therefore supports the implied term theory of frustration, even if the result on the express terms in question is somewhat suspect.

In contrast, in *Super Servant Two*,[14] the defendants contracted to transport the claimants' drilling rig from Japan to Rotterdam using either of the ships called Super Servant One and Super Servant Two. The contract contained a generous force majeure clause, permitting the defendant to 'cancel its performance' on the occurrence of a long (and not closed) list of events 'which reasonably may impede, prevent or delay the performance of this contract'.[15] The Super Servant Two sank; the claimants argued that the contract was not frustrated because the Super Servant One was available, albeit contractually committed elsewhere. The Court of Appeal considered that the force majeure clause was so generous that it could not be interpreted literally, but instead should be read down to apply only to events beyond the control of the defendant.[16] Only if it could be shown that the sinking of the Super Servant Two had not been caused by the negligence of the defendant could the force majeure clause be invoked. The Court of Appeal also went on to reject an alternative claim in frustration, on the basis that the impossibility arose from the defendant's decision to contract out the Super Servant One elsewhere. The reasoning on this latter point should have been simply that the force majeure clause left no room for the operation of an implied term. Instead, Bingham LJ said that, if the contract had only made provision for the Super Servant Two and it had sunk without negligence, 'I feel sure the contract would have been frustrated'.[17] This reasoning—albeit *obiter*—obviously poses challenges for the implied term theory of frustration advanced in this chapter, as Ewan has noted.[18]

---

[10] [1918] AC 119 (HL).
[11] ibid 124.
[12] ibid 126 (Lord Finlay LC).
[13] ibid 127–28 (Lord Dunedin), 131–34 (Lord Atkinson), and 138 (Lord Parmoor).
[14] *J Lauritzen AS v Wijsmuller BV (The Super Servant Two)* [1990] 1 Lloyd's Rep 1 (CA).
[15] ibid 4.
[16] ibid 6–8 (Bingham LJ) and 11–13 (Dillon LJ).
[17] ibid 9.
[18] McKendrick, 'Force Majeure and Frustration' (n 6) 34.

114   SHADES OF FRUSTRATION

More recently, the Court of Appeal has equivocated as to whether force majeure clauses should still be read *contra proferentem*.[19] That approach to construction might be thought to be 'old intellectual baggage',[20] or 'old and outmoded'.[21] Yet the Supreme Court has also recently reaffirmed the rule that 'clear words are necessary before the court will hold that a contract has taken away valuable rights or remedies which one of the parties to it would have had at common law'.[22] Given that force majeure clauses are typically invoked as defences to claims for damages or some other remedy for breach, it would be odd if that principle did not apply to them. Further, so long as it is kept in a subservient role to the ultimate question of what the parties meant when agreeing the words of the contract, this presumption reflects the inherent probabilities of the parties' apparent intentions.[23]

Force majeure clauses need not be labelled as such, and they have no prescribed content. The clause 'should be construed in each case with a close attention to the words which precede or follow it, and with a due regard to the nature and general terms of the contract. The effect of the clause may vary with each instrument'.[24] Ewan has identified three particular variants in his work:[25] (i) force majeure clauses 'proper', which typically provide a right to cancel or suspend performance on the occurrence of a certain event (or often a long list of events); (ii) hardship clauses, which respond where supervening events make performance more onerous or costly, and trigger a process for trying to conclude a contractual variation; and (iii) intervener clauses, which refer disputes over continued performance to a third party (such as an expert appointed by the International Chamber of Commerce).

A fourth variant is the material adverse change clause. This was recently the subject of major litigation, triggered by the start of the COVID-19 pandemic. In *Travelport Ltd v Wex Inc*,[26] the defendant entered into a $1 billion transaction to buy a payments business which primarily operated in the travel sector. The parties entered into a share purchase agreement on 24 January 2020, just as the world's attention was beginning to focus on a novel coronavirus emerging from the city of Wuhan in China. There was a substantial period between the dates of signing and completion, with one condition precedent for completion being that there had been no 'Material Adverse Effect' in the meanwhile. That was a defined term which contained a carve-out relating to 'conditions resulting from pandemics'. There was then an exception to the carve-out that applied where it could be shown that a pandemic had a disproportionate effect on the companies being sold versus other participants in their industries.[27] The detail of the litigation is, for present purposes, irrelevant.[28] The point is simply that this is yet another way in which the parties can, and do, anticipate and expressly allocate the risk of the effect of supervening events on contractual performance.

---

[19] *Mur Shipping BV v RTI Ltd* [2022] EWCA Civ 1406 [54] (Males LJ) and [71] (Arnold LJ). For Ewan's view of where the law stands, see *Chitty* (n 1) [26.067].

[20] *Investors Compensation Scheme Ltd v West Bromwich Building Society* [1998] 1 WLR 896 (HL) 912 (Lord Hoffmann).

[21] *Triple Point Technology Inc v PTT Public Co Ltd* [2021] UKSC 29, [2021] AC 1148 [111] (Lord Leggatt).

[22] ibid [106] (Lord Leggatt).

[23] See further William Day and Adam Kramer, 'Interpretation' in Mindy Chen-Wishart and Prince Saprai (eds), *Research Handbook on the Philosophy of Contract Law* (Edward Elgar forthcoming).

[24] *Lebeaupin v Crispon & Co* [1920] 2 KB 714 (KB) 720.

[25] Ewan McKendrick, 'The Regulation of Long-Term Contracts in English Law' in Jack Beatson and Daniel Friedmann (eds), *Good Faith and Fault in Contract Law* (Clarendon 1995) 323–29

[26] [2020] EWHC 2670 (Comm).

[27] ibid [140]–[144].

[28] Although it is worth noting that the parties agreed that the provision was not to be construed *contra proferentem*: ibid [134].

III. Implied Terms

Where there is no express term anticipating the supervening event, the exercise in which the parties then engage usually involves a search for implied terms. There is 'no numerus clausus, no limited class' of such implied terms;[29] instead, there are an infinite variety of terms that might be implied, and each contract may be different. For present purposes, however, it suffices to discuss a few of the principal categories.

A. Impossibility of Contractual Performance

There is no prohibition in contract law against contracting for the impossible or the unreal. This is probably because of the common law's approach to remedies:[30] there is no conceptual or policy difficulty allowing parties to promise the impossible where the default remedy in contract law is damages rather than specific performance. On the other hand, where a supervening event makes performance impossible (rather than simply more difficult), the contract may be treated as discharged 'for frustration' where that is the product of what the parties have agreed. In the absence of an express promise to keep performing in the face of impossibility, the law is willing to imply such a term given the improbability that the parties would, objectively, have agreed to do the impossible.

This follows the reasoning in the foundational case in the modern law of frustration, *Taylor v Caldwell*.[31] This was a contract

> whereby the [defendant] agree to let, and the [claimant] agree to take, on the terms hereinafter stated, The Surrey Garden and Music Hall, Newington, Surrey for the following days, viz:—Monday, the 17th June; 1861, Monday, the 15th July, 1861, Monday, the 5th August, 1861, Monday, the 19th August, 1861, for the purpose of giving a series of grand concerts and day and night fêtes at the said Gardens and Hall on those days respectively at the rent or sum of 100l for each of the said days.[32]

A fire broke out at the Music Hall on 11 June 1861; the entire structure burned down in three hours. The claimant sued the defendant in breach of contract for the losses caused from the cancellation of the events. Blackburn J dismissed the claim:

> where, from the nature of the contract, it appears that the parties must from the beginning have known that it could not be fulfilled unless when the time for the fulfilment of the contract arrived some particular specified thing continued to exist, so that, when entering into the contract, they must have contemplated such continuing existence as the foundation of what was to be done; there, in the absence of any express or implied warranty that the

---

[29] *Canary Wharf (BP4) T1 Ltd v European Medicines Agency* [2019] EWHC 335 (Ch); 183 Con LR 167 [41] (hereafter *Canary Wharf*).

[30] Edwin Peel, *Frustration and Force Majeure* (4th edn, Sweet & Maxwell 2021) [1.002] (hereafter Peel, *Frustration and Force Majeure*).

[31] *Taylor v Caldwell* (1863) 3 B & S 826, 122 ER 309. For an alternative view that the importance of this case is 'exaggerated', see Catharine MacMillan, '*Taylor v Caldwell* (1863)' in Charles Mitchell and Paul Mitchell (eds), *Landmark Cases in the Law of Contract* (Hart 2016) (hereafter MacMillan, 'Taylor v Caldwell').

[32] ibid 310.

116 SHADES OF FRUSTRATION

thing shall exist, the contract is not to be construed as a positive contract, but as subject to an implied condition that the parties shall be excused in case, before breach, performance becomes impossible from the perishing of the thing without default of the contractor.[33]

The term implied by Blackburn J appears to be one implied *in law*,[34] albeit an unusual one because it falls to be implied (subject to any contrary terms) in all contracts to deal with a particular *situation* rather than (as is usually the case) for a particular type of *contract* (eg sale of goods, employment, leases). Nonetheless, as Blackburn J noted,[35] there is a strong analogy to be drawn between this and the rule for contracts for the sale of goods, that now appears as section 7 of the Sale of Goods Act 1979: '[w]here there is an agreement to sell specific goods and subsequently the goods, without any fault on the part of the seller or buyer, perish before the risk passes to the buyer, the agreement is avoided.' While not expressed as an implied term (in contrast with, for example, sections 12 and 14 of the 1979 Act), that is unarguably the effect of section 7. It is well established that the provisions of the Act create default rules which can be disapplied or varied by agreement,[36] and section 7 should be seen no differently. So, for example, a seller of specific goods can be liable if the goods perish through a freak accident if they have given an express warranty that the goods will still exist at the time of delivery.

Rooting the result in the parties' agreement in this way has been criticized as being 'fictitious',[37] and a 'façade',[38] but there is much to commend Blackburn J's analysis. Indeed, one might get to the result without much reliance on an implied term at all. On its proper interpretation, the contract involved an exchange of concurrent conditions—payment of money in return for the availability of the Music Hall—and, in the absence of both parties being ready, able, and willing to perform, the obligations of neither party accrued.[39] The same analysis is also capable of explaining the section 7 cases.

Ewan has rightly noted that the difference between this type of frustration case and many cases of common mistake is one only of timing.[40] Section 6 of the Sale of Goods Act 1979 provides that '[w]here there is an agreement to sell specific goods and subsequently the goods, without any fault on the part of the seller or buyer, perish before the risk passes to the buyer, the agreement is avoided'. Like section 7, section 6 is best understood as creating a term implied in law. Indeed, the draftsman of the original legislation (the Sale of Goods

---

[33] ibid 312.

[34] ibid 314: 'that excuse is *by law* implied' (emphasis added).

[35] ibid 313–14. This has attracted some criticism in Peel, *Frustration and Force Majeure* (n 30) [2.023–025] and [2.029] but there is nothing much in this: see MacMillan, 'Taylor v Caldwell' (n 31) 188–89.

[36] The draftsman of the Sale of Goods Act 1893 said that 'the Act does not seek to prevent the parties from making any bargain they please. Its object is to lay down clear rules for the case where the parties have either formed no intention, or failed to express it': MacKenzie Dalzell Chalmers, *Sale of Goods Act, 1893, including the Factors Acts, 1889 & 1890* (4th edn, William Clowes & Sons 1899) ix–x. See also Michael Bridge (ed), *Benjamin's Sale of Goods* (11th edn, Sweet & Maxwell 2020) [6.031].

[37] Roy McElroy and Glanville Williams, *Impossibility of Performance* (CUP 1941) 62 (hereafter McElroy and Williams, *Impossibility of Performance*).

[38] David Ibbetson, *A Historical Introduction to the Law of Obligations* (OUP 1999) 224.

[39] See, by analogy, Sale of Goods Act 1979, s 28. See eg McElroy and Williams, *Impossibility of Performance* (n 39) 100 and John Cyril Smith, 'Contracts—Mistake, Frustration and Implied Terms' (1994) 110 LQR 400. For a recent analysis in favour of the rehabilitation of this 'failure of condition' thesis, see Jordan English, 'Discharge of Contractual Obligations' (Dphil, Oxford) ch 5.

[40] McKendrick, *Contract Law* (n 3) 281–82 and 292.

Act 1893) understood himself to be codifying the case of *Couturier v Hastie*,[41] which itself is best understood as rendering the contract 'void by reason of an implied condition precedent, because the contract proceeded on the basic assumption that it was possible of performance'.[42] It follows that a contract will not be void if the subject matter is non-existent at the time of contracting where one party has in fact expressly or otherwise warranted the existence of that subject matter.[43]

B. Impossibility of Contractual Purpose

A different term may be implied—in fact, *not* in law—where the contracting parties share a particular purpose when entering the contract. The term implied is that, if the shared or joint purpose for entering into the contract is rendered impossible by supervening events, then the contract is discharged.[44] This was recognized by the so-called Coronation Cases, which marked the next milestone in the development of the law of frustration after *Taylor v Caldwell*.[45] These cases arose out of the postponement of Edward VII's coronation from 26 June to 9 August 1902, which was announced on 24 June 1902 due to ill-health requiring the monarch to undergo an urgent operation.

Krell v Henry[46] concerned a contract for the hire of rooms on Pall Mall for the days of 26 and 27 June 1902 (but, perhaps importantly, only for the days and not overnight). Plainly contractual performance was not rendered impossible by the postponement of the coronation: unlike the Music Hall in *Taylor v Caldwell*, the rooms were still available for use, and the fee could still be paid. However, the contract was discharged because the parties shared a common purpose that the rooms were to be hired to view the coronation processions. That common purpose was not an express term of the contract, recorded in that case by two letters as those did not refer to the coronation processions at all.[47] It has been suggested recently that *Krell* therefore supports an extra-contractual approach because 'the parties had a common approach going beyond their agreement'.[48] However, it is wrong to say that the decision in *Krell* went further than the terms of the contract.[49] Rather, the case is another example of determining the terms of a contract not just by the express words but also by its implied terms, bearing in mind the context in which the express words were uttered and, in particular, the publicity for the rooms which advertised their view of the coronation processions. In *Krell* itself, Vaughan Williams LJ said the business efficacy test for implication of terms in fact was 'of importance in the present case' and that 'one must, in judging whether

---

[41] *Couturier v Hastie* (1856) 5 HLC 673. See M Chalmers, The Sale of Goods (William Clowes & Sons 1890) 10–11, commenting that the 'rule may be based either on the ground of mutual mistake, or on the ground of impossibility of performance'.

[42] *Solle v Butcher* [1950] 1 KB 671 (CA) 691 (Denning LJ).

[43] *Great Peace Shipping Ltd v Tsavliris Salvage (International) Ltd* [2002] EWCA Civ 1407, [2003] QB 679 [77]–[81] (Lord Phillips MR) approving *McRae v Commonwealth Disposals Commission* (1951) 84 CLR 377 (HCA).

[44] On appropriate facts one might imply a term in fact for something other than automatic discharge, such as suspension of performance or renegotiation of terms (although the more complicated the proposed contractual response to the supervening event, the more difficult it will be to meet the test for implication in fact). However, there is no case law on this, and unlikely to be for as long as the multi-factorial approach remains dominant.

[45] MacMillan, 'Taylor v Caldwell' (n 31) 202–03.

[46] [1903] 2 KB 740 (CA).

[47] ibid 741.

[48] *Canary Wharf* (n 29) [244], see also [36]–[38].

[49] William Day, 'Isn't Brexit Frustrating?' (2019) 78 CLJ 270, 271–72 (hereafter Day, 'Isn't Brexit frustrating?').

118   SHADES OF FRUSTRATION

the implication ought to be made, look not only at the words of the contract, but also at the surrounding facts and the knowledge of the parties of those facts'.[50] The critical point in *Krell* for the purposes of the business efficacy test was that the rooms had been advertised on the basis that they would provide a view of the coronation processions.[51] The only error in *Krell* was to treat the case as falling within the 'principle' of *Taylor v Caldwell*,[52] whereas *Taylor v Caldwell* was only relevant by way of analogy: *Krell* was actually recognizing a different implied term, both in type and in its content.

A different result had been reached a few days earlier by a similarly constituted Court of Appeal in *Herne Bay Steam Boat Co v Hutton*.[53] The defendant contracted with the claimant for use of a steamboat on 28 and 29 June 1902 to enable paying guests to see the Royal Navy Review, which had been organized as part of the coronation celebrations. The case might have been considered to make a stronger claim for frustration, given the contract expressly referred to 'the purpose of viewing the naval review and for a day's cruise around the fleet'.[54] When the coronation was postponed the review was cancelled, and the defendant refused to make payment under the contract or make use of the steamboat. However, the Court of Appeal held that the contract had no term equivalent to that in *Krell*. The defendant was liable for the outstanding sum because, on its proper construction, 'seeing the naval review or . . . going around the fleet with a party of paying guests, does not lay the foundation of the contract'.[55] Even though there was an expressly stated purpose for the contract, it was one in which the defendant was 'alone concerned';[56] it was not shared by the claimant, despite the express term, and its reference in the contract was merely 'to define more exactly the nature of the voyage'.[57]

Distinguishing *Krell* and *Herne Bay* is only possible if one treats this as an exercise of implication in fact.[58] The contract in *Krell* would lack any commercial or practical sense without an implied term,[59] because there was no other reason to contract for use of the rooms on Pall Mall for two days (excluding nights), whereas the contract in *Herne Bay* was still perfectly functional and explicable without the naval review taking place during the contracted cruise.

It is nonetheless tempting to suggest that the construction of the contract in *Herne Bay* was simply wrong, and certainly that is the view now taken of *Chandler v Webster*,[60] which involved another dispute over a room on Pall Mall taken by the claimant expressly for the purpose of watching the coronation processions.[61] The claimant had part-paid the

---

[50] *Krell v Henry* (n 46) 750.
[51] ibid 741.
[52] ibid 754–55 (Vaughan Williams LJ), 755 (Romer LJ), and 755 (Scrutton LJ). See also *Griffith v Bymer* (1903) 19 TLR 434 (KB) where rooms were taken on St James's Street to view the processions at 11am on 24 June 1902 *after* the decision to operate on Edward VII had been made but *before* it was announced. Wright J applied the 'principle' of *Couturier v Hastie*, finding that this went to 'the whole root of the matter', such that the contract was void.
[53] [1903] 2 KB 683 (CA). Vaughan Williams and Romer LJJ heard both cases; Stirling LJ was on the bench for *Herne* instead of Scrutton LJ.
[54] ibid 684.
[55] ibid 689 (Vaughan Williams LJ).
[56] ibid 690 (Romer LJ).
[57] ibid 692 (Stirling LJ).
[58] Ewan advances a similar argument in *Chitty* (n 1) [26.033–034] and *Contract Law* (n 3) 297–98.
[59] *Marks and Spencer plc v BNP Paribas Securities Services Trust Co (Jersey) Ltd* [2015] UKSC 72; [2016] AC 742 (hereafter *Marks and Spencer*) [21] (Lord Neuberger).
[60] *Chandler v Webster* [1904] 1 KB 493 (CA).
[61] ibid 493.

fee already and sued for restitution of that sum; the defendant counterclaimed for the outstanding part of the fee. The Court of Appeal accepted that the contract had been frustrated but dismissed the claim in restitution and allowed the counterclaim on the basis that the obligation to pay had fallen due before the postponement of the coronation. It is hard to see why that timing point mattered if the parties' respective obligations were simply construed as subject to implied conditionality that Edward VII's coronation proceed as scheduled.[62]

A claim for an implied term along the lines recognized in the Coronation Cases can be defeated not only by a force majeure (or similar) clause, but also by other express terms of the contract. This was the key point in the recent case of *Canary Wharf v European Medicines Agency*.[63] In that case the European Medicines Agency (EMA) unsuccessfully sought to escape a twenty-five-year lease on a London skyscraper by arguing that the lease would be frustrated when the UK ceased to be a Member State of the EU. However, the contract contemplated that the EMA's headquarters might not remain in Canary Wharf for the duration of the lease. That was because, subject to (albeit onerous) conditions, the lease expressly permitted the EMA to assign or sublet the property in part or in its entirety to some other tenant or sub-tenant. Those terms undermined the EMA's case that the parties' common purpose in respect of the lease was to provide a permanent headquarters for the EMA for twenty-five years.[64]

C. Change to the Underlying State of Affairs

It is much more difficult to advance a frustration argument beyond the narrow circumstances which engage the term implied in law as to impossibility of performance, or any term implied in fact as to impossibility of contractual purpose. This is illustrated by the well-known case of *Blackburn Bobbin Co v Allen & Sons*,[65] where a contract to sell Finnish birch timber at Hull was not frustrated by the outbreak of the First World War, making it impossible for the seller to obtain timber from Finland. As Pickford LJ observed, 'it was no concern of the buyers as to how the sellers intended to get the timber there'.[66]

Most of the cases in this residual category concern delay or obstruction. The question of whether that engages any term implied in fact may be resolved by comparing the nature of the delay or obstruction to the stipulated contractual performance. So, for example, in *Wilmington Trust SP Services (Dublin) Ltd v Spicejet Ltd*, a ten-year aircraft lease was not frustrated where the aircraft had been grounded in India for two years by the Indian civil aviation authority following fatal crashes involving similar aircraft,[67] but the court did not rule out that a longer period might constitute frustration.[68] In *Wing v Xiong*, a ten-day isolation order was imposed in 2003 in Hong Kong in reaction to the SARS outbreak, preventing

---

[62] The case was in any event overruled in *Fibrosa Spolka Akcyjna v Fairbairn Lawson Combe Barbour Ltd* [1943] AC 32 (HL).

[63] *Canary Wharf* (n 29); Day, 'Isn't Brexit Frustrating?' (n 49) 271. See also *Salam Air SAOC v Latam Airlines Groups SA* [2020] EWHC 2414 (Comm) and the even more conclusive 'hell or highwater clause' in that case.

[64] *Canary Wharf* (n 29) [217]–[219].

[65] [1918] 2 KB 467 (CA).

[66] ibid 469.

[67] [2021] EWHC 1117 (Comm).

[68] ibid [65]: 'It may be (I express no view one way or the other) that if there is still no sign of the ban being lifted in, say, three years' time, that might amount to frustration.'

120   SHADES OF FRUSTRATION

a tenant from reaching his flat.[69] The tenant alleged that this frustrated the lease and discharged him from having to pay any further rent. The court disagreed, because the lease was for two years. A ten-day exclusion from the property was insignificant in that context. (If any term were to be implied in fact it would be something much less drastic than ending the entire lease, such as suspending payment of rent for those ten days,[70] although even that implied term has now been rejected by the Court of Appeal in litigation arising from the COVID-19 pandemic;[71] the risk remains with the tenant for these supervening events.) In contrast, in *Bank Line Ltd v Arthur Capel & Co*,[72] ship-owners successfully argued for frustration of a twelve-month time charter. The vessel was requisitioned in May 1915 for the war effort but released by September 1915. This temporary unavailability was frustrating because of its 'serious effect' in the context of a one-year time party.[73]

A different result was reached in the so-called Suez Canal Cases.[74] This litigation arose from the impact on international trade of the Suez crisis, and the closure of the Canal as a shipping lane, requiring vessels instead to take the much longer journey around the Cape of Good Hope. The issue came to a head in *Tsakiroglou & Co Ltd v Noblee Thorl GmbH*,[75] where the House of Lords held that this was insufficient to frustrate the contract despite the parties contemplating that the Canal would be used at the time of contracting. However, that was a case where the goods were not perishable such that voyage time was not critical, and nor was a date (or period) for delivery fixed that presupposed access to the Suez Canal.[76] In those circumstances, no term could be implied in fact making performance conditional on the Canal being open, so as to release the sellers when the Canal was closed. But even where the contract anticipates that performance will be delivered more quickly than it transpires is possible (such as for perishable goods), that does not necessarily mean that performance will be excused. The contract has to be construed to identify to whom the risk of delay has been allocated by agreement. A well-known example is *Davis Contractors Ltd v Fareham Urban District Council*,[77] where the building contract envisaged that seventy-eight houses would be built in eight months but the work took twenty-two months to complete. As Ewan puts it in *Chitty*, a 'builder who undertook to perform such work for a definite lump sum undertook the commercial risk that delay would increase his costs'.[78]

---

[69] *Wing v Xiong* DCCJ/2832/2003 (Hong Kong District Court).
[70] As it happened, no rent abatement was claimed: ibid [24].
[71] *Bank of New York Mellon (International) Ltd v Cine-UK Ltd* [2022] EWCA Civ 1021.
[72] [1919] AC 435 (HL) (hereafter *Bank Line*).
[73] *Chitty* (n 1) [26.043]. The more difficult point in *Bank Line* is that the charterparty contained a force majeure clause, giving the charterers the option of cancellation if the ship was not delivered by a certain date or if the ship were commandeered by the government. This provision was unsurprising given the charterparty had been concluded in February 1915, while the war was ongoing. In those circumstances, the risk of the supervening event had been anticipated and expressly allocated, and so in principle should not have been impliedly reallocated. Lord Sumner construed the force majeure wording as being permissive: it provided for *some* of the legal effects that would follow requisition but not all such effects: *Bank Line* (n 72) 455. This appears to be more of the overly narrow approach to construing force majeure clauses discussed at text to nn 10–23.
[74] ibid [26.048].
[75] [1962] AC 93 (HL).
[76] ibid 114–15 (Viscount Simonds). Ewan has noted that following the Suez Canal Cases international trade contracts now regularly identify the closure of the Suez Canal as a force majeure event: McKendrick, 'Force Majeure and Frustration' (n 6) 43–44.
[77] [1956] AC 696 (HL).
[78] *Chitty* (n 1) [26.050].

D. 'Limits'

In both his student textbook and also in *Chitty*, Ewan identifies three principles that 'limit' the operation of frustration:[79] (i) the express terms of the contract; (ii) the foreseeability of the supervening event at the time of contracting; and (iii) the rule against 'self-induced' frustration. However, once the relevant cases are understood as turning on express and implied conditions, these cease to be freestanding limits on a doctrine of frustration and are simply relevant factors in a broader construction exercise. The first limit simply reflects the rule that implied terms cannot cut across what has been expressly agreed;[80] the second is relevant to an assessment of whether the officious bystander or business efficacy tests are satisfied;[81] and the third reflects the inherent probabilities of the parties' intentions, such that clear express words would be required to reach a different outcome.[82] Further, as discussed next, these 'limits' do not operate in the same way (or at all) where the supervening event raises issues of public policy. That is because those cases raise considerations going beyond the interests of the parties.

IV. Public Policy

Where the supervening event is a change in the law that renders performance illegal, the effect of the supervening event is governed by public policy rather than what the parties agreed. Indeed, public policy may well require overriding the terms of the contract. This has nothing to do with the term implied by law in cases such as *Taylor v Caldwell*, nor the term implied in fact in cases such as *Krell v Henry*. It is an entirely different doctrine.

A good example that demonstrates that difference is *Ertel Bieber & Co v Rio Tinto Co Ltd*.[83] This involved contracts by which an English company agreed to sell copper ore to German companies between 1911 and 1919. The contract made express provision in the event of war:

> If owing to strikes, war, or any other cause over which the sellers have no control, they should be prevented from shipping the ore . . . or delivering same to the buyers, the obligation to ship and/or deliver shall be suspended during the continuance of such impediment, and for a reasonable time afterwards.[84]

Towards the end of the First World War, the English company sought declarations that the contracts had been discharged rather than merely suspended in the manner agreed, such that the obligation to sell and deliver copper at pre-war prices would not resume once the hostilities ceased. The House of Lords granted the declarations sought. The contract would be void for illegality on the outbreak of war without the force majeure clause, and the force

---

[79] ibid [26.058–095] and McKendrick, *Contract Law* (n 3) 295–303.

[80] See eg *Marks and Spencer* (n 59) [18] and [28] (Lord Neuberger).

[81] Or whether, if a term excusing performance in the face of impossibility would otherwise be implied by law, whether it has been excluded by agreement. Hence why it is just one factor to take into account: *Canary Wharf* (n 29) [211].

[82] See discussion at text to nn 14–23.

[83] [1918] AC 260 (HL).

[84] ibid 270.

122   SHADES OF FRUSTRATION

majeure clause could not save the contract because it would undermine the public policy that required the interests of the state and the war effort to be put above all else. As Lord Dunedin explained, the vice of the force majeure clause was that:

> It hampers the trade of the British subject, and through him the resources of the kingdom. For he cannot, in view of the certainly impending liability to deliver (for the war cannot last for ever), have a free hand as he otherwise would. He must either keep a certain large stock undisposed of, and thus unavailable for the needs of the kingdom, or, if he sells the whole of the present stock, he cannot sell forward, as he would be able to do if he had not the large demand under the contract impending. It increases the resources of the enemy, for if the enemy knows that he is contractually sure of getting the supply as soon as war is over, that not only allows him to denude himself of present stocks, but it represents a present value which may be realized by means of assignation to neutral countries.[85]

The importance of this public policy would apply even where the contracts were otherwise governed by German law rather than English law.[86]

This is not to say that the content of the parties' agreement is irrelevant when public policy issues are raised. The first step in the analysis will always require construction of the terms of the contract to determine whether it requires performance that has been rendered illegal by the supervening event at all. So, for example, in *Waugh v Morris*,[87] a charterparty provided that a ship was to load a cargo from a port in France and deliver it to London. In London, the ship was prevented from landing the cargo by the authorities because of a fear about the spread of cattle disease from France to England. Blackburn J held that the contract was not frustrated: the charterparty required the cargo to be unloaded from alongside the vessel. Landing was not necessary: 'the performance by receiving the cargo alongside in the river without landing it at all was both legal and practicable.'[88] In those circumstances, the supervening illegality could not be relied upon to excuse performance.

The terms of the parties' agreement are even more important where a supervening prohibition builds in an element of discretion. Contract law has long been accustomed to dealing with legislation framed in this way. For instance, in an international sales contract, a licence typically must be obtained before import or export of goods or services are legal. The contract will usually be construed as being 'subject to licence' and its express or implied terms will place a duty on one party—usually reasonable or best endeavours—to obtain the licence. Responsibility for the supervening event is thus allocated: the failure to obtain the licence does not discharge the contract or render it unenforceable for illegality but instead may lead to a claim for damages if it can be shown that (for example) reasonable or best endeavours were not undertaken.[89]

After the Supreme Court's decision in *Patel v Mirza*,[90] the effect of English law illegality at the time of contracting on an English law-governed contract is now determined by asking

---

[85] ibid 275. See also 279 (Lord Atkinson) and 286–88 and 290 (Lord Sumner).
[86] ibid 293 (Lord Dunedin) 300 (Lord Atkinson) and 302–03 (Lord Parker).
[87] (1872–73) LR 8 QB 202 (KB).
[88] ibid 207 (Blackburn J).
[89] See eg *Re Anglo-Russian Merchant Traders and John Batt & Co Ltd* [1917] 2 KB 679 (CA). Cf the unusual facts in *Peter Cassidy Seed Co Ltd v Osuustukkukauppa IL* [1957] 1 WLR 273 (Com Ct), where the sellers assured the buyers that the export licence was merely a formality and the only uncertainty was timing. Devlin J considered this conduct implied a term in the contract placing an *absolute* duty on the sellers to obtain the licence.
[90] [2016] UKSC 42, [2017] AC 467.

whether it would be harmful to the integrity and coherence of the legal system or (possibly) certain aspects of public morality to allow a claim to be enforced. That assessment is conducted through a framework of a 'trio of considerations':

> it is necessary (a) to consider the underlying purpose of the prohibition which has been transgressed and whether that purpose will be enhanced by denial of the claim, (b) to consider any other relevant public policy on which the denial of the claim may have an impact and (c) to consider whether denial of the claim would be a proportionate response to the illegality, bearing in mind that punishment is a matter for the criminal courts.[91]

This is a major change, and it is not clear whether the effect of supervening English law illegality on an English law-governed contract is also now governed by the same criteria. The matter has not yet been considered at appellate level. In *Canary Wharf v European Medicines Agency*, the Court held that *Patel v Mirza* was only applicable to contracts which themselves involved a legal wrong, whereas supervening illegality in the frustration context was broader.[92] On the other hand, in *Magdeev v Tsetkov*[93] the Court held that the trio of considerations did not apply in the context of supervening foreign illegality because the public policy there was international comity rather than integrity of the legal system.[94] That may suggest that the *Patel v Mirza* test *should* apply where the supervening event is English law illegality and the governing law of the contract is English law. That is certainly the better view. There should be no difference in approach turning on the accident of timing: whether the English law illegality arises before or after contracting, the essential public policy question—that is, the impact of enforcing the claim on the integrity and coherence of the English legal system—remains the same.

Supervening foreign law illegality involves different doctrines again. There is both the rule in *Ralli Bros v Compañia Naviera Sota y Aznar*[95] and the choice of law rule in Article 9(3) of the Rome I Regulation.[96] The latter is clearly not part of the domestic law of contractual frustration: it is part of the conflict of laws or private international law. As to the former, although the judgments in *Ralli Bros* pay lip service to the doctrine of frustration,[97] as I have argued elsewhere,[98] the rule created by that case is better understood as being a public policy rule of the law of the forum (*lex fori*) which requires a court to refrain from taking a step which it would otherwise be entitled to take in its own territory out of respect for the territorial sovereignty of another state or international comity, to use the language of *Magdeev v Tsetkov*. The rule in *Ralli Bros* also does not fit the typical characteristics of a frustration claim. Its effect is to render the contract unenforceable, not to discharge it. It applies only where the contract positively requires performance in a place where it would be illegal, leaving no room for an implied term. And the only law that can be taken into account is that of the contractually stipulated place of performance (the *lex loci solutionis*), even if some

---

[91] ibid [101] and [120] (Lord Toulson).
[92] *Canary Wharf* (n 29) [170] (Marcus Smith J).
[93] [2020] EWHC 887 (Comm).
[94] ibid [331] (Cockerill J).
[95] [1920] 2 KB 287 (CA) (hereafter *Ralli Bros*).
[96] Article 9(3) of Regulation (EC) No 593/2008 as maintained after Brexit by Law Applicable to Contractual Obligations and Non-Contractual Obligations (Amendment etc) (EU Exit) Regulations 2019 (SI 2019/834).
[97] *Ralli Bros* (n 95) 291 (Lord Sterndale MR), 296–97 (Warrington LJ), and 300–04 (Scrutton LJ).
[98] William Day, 'Contracts, Illegality and Comity: *Ralli Bros* Revisited' (2020) 79 CLJ 64.

other foreign law may in practice render the performance radically different to what had been promised.

V. Conclusion

There are, of course, good pedagogical and practical reasons to group together the various different doctrines that can operate to excuse contractual performance following supervening events. However, the prevailing approach in the modern authorities goes too far in conflating the different principles into a monochrome 'doctrine' of frustration, leading in turn to the wretched 'one size fits all' multi-factorial test. We would be better served by a greater emphasis on the differences between the various principles that have developed over time. Sometimes the answer will lie in the express terms of the contract, and sometimes the relevant term may be implied by law or in fact. On occasion, the result will be dictated by considerations going beyond the terms of the contract, where the relevant public policy will vary depending on whether domestic or foreign law illegality issues are raised. We thus do the law of frustration a grave disservice by not appreciating its many different shades.

8
Repeal the Law Reform (Frustrated Contracts) Act 1943

ROBERT STEVENS

I. Introduction

The problem with the Law Reform (Frustrated Contracts) Act 1943 is apparent from its title. Although it is today common to talk of 'frustrated contracts', this is a misnomer.[1] It implies that, just as where a contract is rescinded for fraudulent misrepresentation, the entire bargain is no longer on foot and does not govern the parties' continuing relation. It is entirely 'frustrated'. This is a mistake.

Instead, what are frustrated (ie rendered incapable of performance) are particular obligations that are created by contracts. Some obligations may remain on foot and be unaffected by the frustrating event, while others may have been conditional upon the performance of the now frustrated obligation of the counterparty but are not themselves frustrated. Unlike in the case of avoidance (rescission) for fraudulent misrepresentation (or otherwise), what should continue to govern the parties' relation after the frustrating event, including any entitlement to restitution, is the still extant agreement between the parties. This was and, where still applicable, is the position at common law, at least in its final iteration.

For example:

> *P* agrees to hire a music hall from *D* for six weeks, for £10,000 per week. Three days after the agreement is entered into, the music hall burns to the ground through the fault of neither party.

D's obligation to provide the music hall for hire is frustrated: it is impossible to perform. Although in some situations it might be that *D* has undertaken to provide the music hall come hell, high water, or fire, most often the best construction of the agreement will be that the obligation is conditional upon it being possible to perform. The parties may not have expressly agreed this, but in law, as in language generally, their words are not best read as being absolute but as subject to limits. *D*'s obligation to provide the music hall is conditional upon the music hall's existence, and so is discharged or frustrated.

P's obligation to pay, by contrast, is conditional upon *D* providing the music hall for use. If *D* does not do so, *P* does not have to pay, regardless of the reason why no music hall is provided. If payment has been made in advance, it should be recoverable; in the circumstances, *D* is not entitled to it. Any payment was conditional upon the performance by the counterparty. Each parties' obligations are discharged (or more accurately, *P*'s obligation to pay

---

[1] See also JA Weir, 'Nec Tamen Consumebatur ... —Frustration and Limitation Clauses' (1970) 28 CLJ 189.

Robert Stevens, *Repeal the Law Reform (Frustrated Contracts) Act 1943* In: *Shaping the Law of Obligations*. Edited by: Edwin Peel and Rebecca Probert, Oxford University Press. © Robert Stevens 2023. DOI: 10.1093/oso/9780198889762.003.0008

fails to accrue), but for different reasons. Unlike in the case of rescission or avoidance, other agreed terms should remain unaffected.

In some situations, this ought to lead to 'partial frustration' of a contract.[2] For example:

> P agrees to hire seven music halls from D for six weeks, for £10,000 per week each. After three days, one of the music halls burns down through neither party's fault.

If P can provide the remaining six music halls, that is what he must continue to do. It may be that D is entitled to reject (ie refuse to pay for) any number lower than seven. Whether D is entitled to so reject is a matter of construction. If he is, D is under no obligation to pay for anything, but if he chooses to accept the remaining six he must pay for their use. However, in any event, P's obligation to provide the destroyed hall is frustrated, no claim for damages for breach will arise, and D's obligation to pay for it will never accrue.

This chapter builds upon Ewan McKendrick's essay on 'Frustration, Restitution and Loss Apportionment'.[3] That work has the hallmarks of the teaching Ewan had then done on the London intercollegiate LLM with Peter Birks. My approach, perhaps reflecting our different temperaments, is both less tolerant and less Whiggish.[4]

The claim of this chapter is that the Act is a badly drafted misstep. The best and most straightforward legal reform is to repeal it and to return to the common law position.

II. Two Reasons for Restitution

One of several unfortunate consequences of mediating claims for restitution through an omnibus 'unjust enrichment' framework is that this can obscure fundamental differences between different species of claim.

Four straightforward examples, side by side:

> D is employed as a lecturer in law at the University of Oxbridge on a two-year contract at a salary of £5,000 per month. After six months of employment, the University discovers that D had dishonestly misrepresented that he had a first-class degree, when in fact he possesses no academic qualifications at all. The University seeks to rescind the contract for the (fraudulent) misrepresentation.

At common law, the availability of rescission for misrepresentation, which occurs through 'self-help' without the need of a court order, is relatively restricted, and is barred where the party seeking rescission is unable to return what they have received.[5] This restricted approach to rescission was then supplemented by the availability of a claim for damages for deceit. By contrast, rescission in equity, which is court-ordered, has always been wider as

---

[2] To the contrary, see Edwin Peel, *Frustration and Force Majeure* (4th edn, Sweet & Maxwell 2022) [5-007].

[3] In Andrew Burrows (ed), *Essays on the Law of Restitution* (Clarendon Press 1991) 14. See also Ewan McKendrick, 'The Consequences of Frustration—The Law Reform Frustrated Contracts Act 1943' in Ewan McKendrick (ed), *Force Majeure and Frustration of Contract* (2nd edn, Informa Law 1995) 223 (hereafter McKendrick, *Force Majeure and Frustration*).

[4] '[T]o argue that it was a mistake to enact the 1943 Act is to overstate the case': McKendrick, *Force Majeure and Frustration* (n 3) 169.

[5] *Clarke v Dickson* (1858) EB & E 148; 120 ER 463; *Blackburn v Smith* (1848) 2 Ex 783; 154 ER 707.

the court can make an allowance for the value of what the claimant has received, in making an order for restitution from the defendant.[6] There is, however, no parallel claim for damages in equity. In this example, therefore, court-ordered rescission ought to be available, with a consequent claim for restitution of the salary paid, subject to the University making an allowance for the value of the work (if any) provided by the defendant. Each side's performance is unwound as the basis for each is removed through rescission. The approach is one of mutual restitution.

Second, and by contrast:

> D is employed as a lecturer in law at the University of Oxbridge on a two-year contract at a salary of £5,000 per month. After six months of employment at the University, D commits a gross breach of his contract of employment that justifies his dismissal, an option the University exercises.

Here, the University's obligation to cooperate with D in facilitating his performance of his work, the doing of which forms a condition precedent to his entitlement to be paid his salary, was itself conditional upon D not having committed the (repudiatory) breach that he did. Because of D's breach, the University is now justified in withholding such cooperation, so that no further obligation to pay D will accrue. In the modern, if misleading, language of the current law, the University can 'terminate for breach'. The University will also, of course, have a claim for damages for breach of the (still extant) contract.

The ability of the University to withhold further payment does not affect D's entitlement to the salary that he has already earned. Unlike in the case of rescission or avoidance, the (subsisting) agreement between the parties provides a good justification, a legal ground, for all payments that have been earned under it. 'Termination for breach' entails that the parties are discharged from future performance, but not that, without more, there ceases to be an entitlement to any performance already rendered under the agreement. No claim for restitution of those payments is therefore possible.

Third, it may be that the parties have agreed that the performance rendered by one (or both) of them is conditional. Often, but not always, that condition is counter-performance from the other party. For example.

> D contracts to supply twenty firemen *per annum* to guard P's office buildings at night, for five years, for an annual fee of £100,000 payable in advance. Three years later, P discovers that D by mistake provided no fireman in the first year but did do so in the next two years. P does not wish to 'terminate the contract' (ie he does not wish to exclude D from the premises and thereby prevent any further payments from falling due).

Regardless of any claim for damages for breach of contract, P should have a claim for restitution of the £100,000 paid for the first year. In the traditional (if, again. misleading[7]) language

---

[6] Eg *Erlanger v New Sombrero Phosphate Co* (1878) 3 App Cas 1218 (HL).

[7] Because the 'consideration' (ie reason) which may support a promise so as to render it enforceable (a promise in exchange) is not the same as the 'consideration' (ie reason) for the performance by one party to the other (usually, the counter-performance by the other party, not the promise of it). We are using the word 'consideration' to refer to two different things.

of the common law, the consideration for the payment of £100,000 (ie the reason for it (the condition), the provision of firemen to guard the building in the first year) has totally failed.

In order for P to recover the payment of £100,0000 it should not be necessary for him to rescind (ie avoid the contract *ab initio*). The basis of his claim is not that there was no justification, or legal ground, for the payment. There was: that was what the parties had contractually agreed. Rather, his claim is founded upon the agreement between the parties, under which the performance rendered had been agreed to be conditional. This does not entail that his claim is one to enforce the agreement made (ie it is not a contractual action of the form 'do what you agreed to do', or 'pay damages for failing to do what you agreed to do'). Even if the agreement is unenforceable, perhaps because of the failure to comply with a statutory formality requirement,[8] the claim for restitution is based upon the parties having agreed that the performance rendered was conditional, and that condition having failed.

Similarly, in order for P to recover the payment of £100,000 it should not be necessary to 'terminate for breach' (ie to discharge any obligation to render *future* performance).[9] The only questions are whether the payment was rendered conditionally under the agreement, and whether that condition has failed. Whether other future obligations, as yet unperformed, are discharged or remain on foot is not here determinative of this question. In our third example, therefore, restitution should follow regardless of 'termination'.

Fourth, and finally:

D employs P to paint his kitchen for a fee of £400 (the going rate), the work to be completed within six months. P commences work, completes three of the four walls, but then leaves to do better paid work elsewhere. After pressing for the work to be completed for nine months, D employs X for a fee of £100 to complete the work.

P has no contractual entitlement to payment; he has not fulfilled the condition precedent to D's obligation to pay arising: his painting the kitchen. D's work has undoubtedly left P better off than he would have been without it (he has in total paid £100 for the painting job's completion that would ordinarily have cost him £400). D has been saved the expense of paying £300 more. There is however no injustice to correct. P did the work on the condition that he would be entitled to payment if he completed the job. As he never did, the condition under which he did the work has not failed. It does not suffice to show that P has received no counter-performance in exchange for his work: that was the bargain he made. This was the result reached by the Court of Appeal in the materially identical *Sumpter v Hedges*.[10]

What if we changed the facts of the last example so that D had paid P part of the price in advance? Should this make a difference to the end result? In principle the answer is no. The builder has not earned any payment unless and until the agreed condition has been satisfied. The employer should be entitled to restitution of his payment without deduction. That

---

[8] *Scott v Pattinson* [1923] 2 KB 723; *James v Thomas H Kent Ltd* [1951] 1 KB 551; *Deglman v Guaranty Trust Co of Canada and Constantineau* [1954] SCR 725, [1954] 3 DLR 785; *Pavey & Matthew Pty Ltd v Paul* [1987] HCA 5, (1987) 162 CLR 221.

[9] *Roxborough v Rothmans of Pall Mall Australia Ltd* [2001] HCA 68, (2001) 208 CLR 516.

[10] See *Sumpter v Hedges* [1898] 1 QB 673, defended at length by Ben McFarlane and Robert Stevens, 'In Defence of *Sumpter v Hedges*' (2002) 118 LQR 569.

the payee has rendered partial performance should not enable him to resist a claim for re-payment, unless the result of such work is that the sum has been earned.[11]

By contrast, if the agreement had been that the decorator was entitled to £100 per wall, the completion of three walls would entitle him to £300 under the contract. Again, the end result should not turn upon whether any payment has been made in advance or not.

The rule in the context of the sale of goods is different. If a seller agrees to supply 500 widgets for £3,000, but only supplies 100, the buyer has a choice. He can reject the short delivery, and pay nothing. Or, if he accepts, he must pay for the 100 widgets at the contract rate (not the market rate) because he has accepted them. Here a new contract is formed: the seller offering 100 widgets (implicitly at the contract rate) which the buyer has accepted. By contrast, the expense of work incurred by the counterparty in the past (eg the painting work above) is not something that there is any possibility of now rejecting and so should not have to be paid for. That work was accepted on the basis that it would be paid for *if* completed, a condition that has not failed.

A claim for restitution following rescission or avoidance of a contract has therefore a fun-damentally different justification from a claim for restitution where there has been a 'total failure of consideration' for a payment or other performance rendered conditionally under an agreement.

In the first, the claim is independent of the now avoided agreement between the par-ties. In the second, the claim is based upon the parties' agreement that the performance sought to be reversed was rendered conditionally, and that condition having failed. In the first, there is no justification for the performance rendered by either party under the now avoided bargain, requiring the complete unwinding by way of restitution of the perform-ance rendered by each party. In the second, if the recipient is entitled, under the agreement, to any performance rendered by his counterparty, it cannot be recovered, but if such per-formance was rendered conditionally, it may be recovered if that condition has failed. This may require the reversal of the performance rendered by one party but not the other, in whole or in part.

Our dedicatee, in his usual scholarly way, once posed the question 'Total Failure of Consideration and Counter-Restitution: Two Issues or One?'[12] The answer given above is an emphatic 'two'. Whether return of a counter-performance received is impossible (so as to bar common law rescission) or should be ordered as a pre-condition of restitution of a per-formance rendered (as with rescission in equity) only arises in the context of rescission (or avoidance) of a contract, where the basis for each parties' performance is removed. Where a payment or other performance is rendered conditionally under an agreement, and that con-dition fails, restitution should follow regardless of whether the counterparty has rendered a partial counter-performance. Such counter-performance may be relevant to the anterior question of whether the condition has or has not failed, but a partial counter-performance may not suffice to constitute an entitlement to the performance received. The justification for the two kinds of claim are different, and are subject to different rules.

---

[11] But see *Whincup v Hughes* (1871 LR 6 CP 78 where a difficult to defend construction of the parties' bargain was adopted.

[12] Ewan McKendrick, 'Total Failure of Consideration and Counter-Restitution: Two Issues or One?' in Peter Birks (ed), *Laundering and Tracing* (OUP 1995).

III. The Common Law

By the time of the enactment of the Law Reform (Frustrated Contracts) Act 1943, the common law was in conformity with the above statements of general principles in the context of frustration.

In the leading decision of the House of Lords, *Fibrosa Spolka Akcyjna v Fairbairn Lawson Combe Barbour Ltd*,[13] the plaintiffs were a textile company in Poland. In July 1939 they entered into a contract with the defendant British firm for the supply of bespoke industrial machines. The overall price was £4,800, with £1,600 payable with the order, the balance payable against shipping documents. The plaintiffs paid £1,000 of the initial sum on account. On 1 September 1939 Germany invaded Poland, and, on 3 September, Britain declared war. The entitlement to the payment had been agreed to be conditional upon the machines being delivered, which could now no longer occur, and so restitution of £1,000 was awarded.

The common law position after *Fibrosa* has been subject to two criticisms,[14] but neither is justifiable. First, it is said that the supposed rule that any counter-performance at all bars recovery survives: the so-called total failure restriction. Of course, the opposite is true on the facts of *Fibrosa*. The sellers had begun manufacturing for the purpose of performance but this did not bar recovery. The only questions are whether the payment had been agreed to be conditional, and whether that condition had failed.

Second, and inconsistently, it is claimed to be problematic that the common law did not permit the payee to deduct the value of the expenditure which he had already incurred in performing. However, in principle there should be no such setting off. The payor's claim is to the return of the performance rendered, not the overall net enrichment of the payee. The payee has incurred the expenditure on the basis that he would be paid as and when he completed performance. There was no agreement in *Fibrosa* that the payee was entitled to anything for part performance, and in this respect the case is the same as the hypothetical unpaid painter, which is also the same as the unfairly maligned decision of the Court of Appeal in *Sumpter v Hedges*. Such setting off should only be permissible if there is an entitlement to be paid under the agreement for the incomplete counter-performance rendered, which there was not.

As is well known, *Fibrosa* overturned the earlier decision of *Chandler v Webster*.[15] In that case the Court of Appeal had held that unless the contract to hire rooms to see the Coronation, the purpose of which was frustrated by the King's illness, was 'wiped out altogether'[16] or 'rescinded *ab initio*',[17] money payable before the frustrating event could still be claimed, and payments already made could not be recovered.

The *Chandler v Webster* fallacy was to conflate the two reasons for restitution that we have already seen. It is true that, if a contract is 'wiped out altogether' or 'rescinded *ab initio*', any performance rendered under it is *prima facie* recoverable. It does not follow that this is the only situation in which restitution will follow. Still less does it follow, as the court also concluded, that, as a matter of construction, if the date for a payment to be made has accrued due, that means it has become unconditionally earned, regardless of any

---

[13] [1943] AC 32 (hereafter *Fibrosa*).
[14] See, for example, Hugh Beale (ed), *Chitty on Contracts* (34th edn, Sweet and Maxwell 2021), [26-103].
[15] [1904] 1 KB 493 (CA).
[16] ibid 499 (Collins MR).
[17] ibid 501 (Romer LJ).

counter-performance to be rendered in exchange for it. The court had confused the two different kinds of claim for restitution that we have identified above, seeming to exclude altogether the claim for restitution based upon the conditionality of the performance rendered, in accordance with the parties' agreement.

In relation to the recovery of the value of services rendered under a contract, the leading case at common law was (and, where applicable, still is) *Cutter v Powell*.[18] Cutter was a sailor on a voyage from Jamaica to Liverpool, who was to be paid upon arrival, but who died before the ship docked. His administratrix failed in her claim for a *quantum meruit* for the work done. Whether what is promised is to pay only upon completion, or for a proportion of the work as it is done (ie whether the obligation is 'entire') is, again, a matter of construction. On the facts, that the sailor's right to payment was conditional upon completion was clear because the agreed fee for the voyage was thirty guineas, four times the market rate payable for the time to be served.

In cases of frustration it might be argued that the logic of the entire obligation rule should not apply. Could it not be said that part of the basis upon which Cutter did the work was that he would have the opportunity to complete it, so that when he unforeseeably died his estate should have a claim for the value of what he had done? Does the frustrating event not mean that 'all bets are off', so that the agreement should no longer govern the parties' relation, as it undoubtedly does not in the context of avoidance?

The answer is that the defendant only accepted the work on the basis that they would pay if it were completed. To allow a claim for partial performance is to re-write the parties' bargain. The failure of Cutter's subjective expectations cannot justify imposing an obligation on the counterparty. Cutter's contractual obligation to *continue* to work was subject to the condition that he lived. The ship-owner's entitlement to the work *already rendered* was only subject to the condition that it was to be paid for once complete. Which it never was.

Of course, it could have been that the agreement was, on its true construction, that *Cutter* would be paid at the going rate for each day's work, *and* a reward upon completion. If this had been so, then a contractual action would have been available for each day of work completed. There would still be no claim for restitution.[19]

It might be said that (the near obsolete) *Cutter v Powell* and (the still important) *Sumpter v Hedges* create a dissonance between the restitution of payments and services. Advanced payments (that are not deposits) are recoverable by the payor when the deal is not fully executed, even where this is a result of the claimant's breach,[20] whereas the part performance of a service is not recoverable where the deal is not fully executed, save where this is a result of the defendant's breach.[21] However, the comparison is a false one. Everything turns upon the agreement the parties have made. Cases such as *Sumpter v Hedges* and *Cutter v Powell* are closer to cases of deposits. It should and does not suffice that the claimant has received nothing in return for the performance rendered. The claimant, in providing the work, does so on the agreed basis that it is only to be paid for if it is completed. Only if the reason for non-completion is that they have been denied the opportunity to do so by the defendant should any claim for restitution arise.

---

[18] (1795) 6 TR 320; 101 ER 573. See also *Appleby v Myers* (1867) LR CP 651.

[19] This issue of construction divided the Supreme Court in *Barton v Morris* [2023] UKSC 3.

[20] *Dies v British and International Mining and Finance Corporation* [1939] 1 KB 724. See also *Fibrosa* (n 13).

[21] Where the defendant is the party in breach see *Planché v Colburn* (1831) 8 Bing 14; 131 ER 305 (hereafter *Planché v Colburn*).

IV. The Law Reform (Frustrated Contracts) Act 1943

A. Payments

Section 1(1) of the Act states:

> Where a contract governed by English law has become impossible of performance or been otherwise frustrated, and the parties thereto have for that reason been discharged from the further performance of the contract, the following provisions of this section shall, subject to the provisions of section two of this Act, have effect in relation thereto.

This sub-section repeats the mistake of the title in stating that what are frustrated are contracts. The obligation of a payor will virtually never be impossible to perform or be otherwise frustrated. Rather, the payor's obligation may be (expressly) conditional upon the counterparty's performance. It is only the counterparty's obligation of performance which may be frustrated because it is (implicitly) conditional upon factual possibility.

Section 1(2) of the Act commences (emphasis added):

> *All* sums paid or payable to any party in pursuance of the contract before the time when the parties were so discharged (in this Act referred to as 'the time of discharge') shall, in the case of sums so paid, be recoverable from him as money received by him for the use of the party by whom the sums were paid, and, in the case of sums so payable, cease to be payable:

This subsection removes the common law requirement that to be recoverable the payment must have been made under a condition that has failed, and substitutes for it the rule that, as we have seen, applies in the context of avoidance of a contract.[22] *All* payments due cease to be payable, and *all* moneys paid are recoverable.

On its face, this provision leads to ridiculous results. For example:

> *D* is employed as a lecturer in law at the University of Oxbridge at a salary of £5,000 per month. After six months of employment at the University, *D* dies.

The analysis at common law would be that *D*'s obligation to work was frustrated, it being a condition of his obligation to teach that he is alive. The salary for each month completed before his death had been earned. If unpaid, it could be recovered by his estate and, if already paid, there would be no claim for restitution.[23] Under the Apportionment Act 1870, salary accrues on a daily basis, so that if only part of one month were complete, the salary for each day completed could still be claimed.[24] Nothing could be claimed for an incomplete day of work. No claim for restitution would be available.

By contrast, the Act seems to require *all* payments to be recovered, regardless of how long the previous employment had been. On its face, it requires a full unwinding of the bargain,

---

[22] See also Charles Mitchell, Paul Mitchell, and Stephen Watterson (eds), *Goff & Jones: The Law of Unjust Enrichment* (10th edn, Sweet and Maxwell 2022) [15-14].

[23] *Stubbs v Holywell Ry* (1867) LR 2 Ex 311.

[24] Apportionment Act 1870, s 2 and s 5.

THE LAW REFORM (FRUSTRATED CONTRACTS) ACT 1943   133

as if it had been avoided. It is true that an allowance could then be made, at the court's discretion, for the expense incurred by the dead man in performing his duties over the months of work,[25] but this figure may be lower than the payments received (ie the University may have made a bad deal). For the *Chandler v Webster* fallacy (that it is necessary to avoid a contract before restitution follows) another fallacy is substituted (that frustrated contracts (*sic*) should be treated as if they are avoided).

Put another way, the Act fails to distinguish between sums payable, but which will not be earned because of the frustrating event (as in *Chandler v Webster* or *Fibrosa*) and sums earned before the frustrating event, which should remain payable if unpaid, and be irrecoverable if paid.

Ridiculous results such as these may possibly be avoided by appealing to a subsequent provision. Section 2(4) states:

> Where it appears to the court that a part of the contract to which this Act applies can properly be severed from the remainder of the contract, being a part wholly performed before the time of discharge, or so performed except for the payment in respect of that part of the contract of sums which are or can be ascertained under the contract, the court shall treat that part of the contract as if it were a separate contract and had not been frustrated.

This cumbersome provision creates a judicial discretion ('appears to the court') to apply a fiction ('as if it were a separate contract') in order to deal with the overly broad starting point in section 1(2). A court may therefore conclude that each month completed (query each day?) should be treated as a separate contract, thereby achieving the (correct) result that would have been reached at common law.

Section 2(4) probably enables sensible courts to re-insert into section 1(2) a requirement that the agreed condition under which money has been paid has failed before it is recoverable (or that money unpaid remains payable where the condition of it being earned has been satisfied). We still however lack clear authority on how these provisions are to be construed.

Unfortunately, section 1(2) continues:

> Provided that, if the party to whom the sums were so paid or payable incurred expenses before the time of discharge in, or for the purpose of, the performance of the contract, the court may, if it considers it just to do so having regard to all the circumstances of the case, allow him to retain or, as the case may be, recover the whole or any part of the sums so paid or payable, not being an amount in excess of the expenses so incurred.

The proviso seems to have been enacted in order to reverse the conclusion in *Fibrosa* that the manufacturers should be entitled to no deduction for the work they had carried out in performance of the abortive deal. It is not, as has been claimed, a statutory version of the change of position defence that applies to mistaken payments,[26] as it confines its operation to expenses incurred 'in or for the performance of the contract'. Again, it seems to contemplate treating frustration as the equivalent of avoidance, where such deduction would also be possible, as we have seen.

---

[25] Under the proviso to s 1(2), discussed later.
[26] *BP Exploration Co (Libya) Ltd v Hunt (No 2)* [1979] 1 WLR 783, 800 (Robert Goff J) (hereafter *BP v Hunt*).

134 REPEAL THE LAW REFORM (FRUSTRATED CONTRACTS) ACT 1943

Again, the common law rule is the preferable one, as it respects the parties' agreement which should continue to govern their relation, including any claim for restitution. Unless there is an entitlement to be paid for the work done under the contract, there should be no payment for it. The defendant never accepted or agreed to pay anything for incomplete work. The agreed basis for it having been done has not failed.

Further, the 'proviso' does not enact a rule, but instead leaves the court with a choice to make a deduction 'if it considers it just', without further guidance. In the one English decision to actually consider the application of the proviso, *Gamerco SA v ICM/Fair Warning (Agency) Ltd*,[27] the court refused to make any deduction, reaching the same result as would have obtained at common law. The claimants were concert promoters who had paid the defendants, the corporate form of Guns N' Roses, $412,500, with a balance of $362,500 still payable, when the obligation to provide a stadium where the concert being promoted was to take place was frustrated by it being declared unsafe a few days before the scheduled performance. The money paid was recoverable under the Act, and in principle this is the right result, as the defendants were only entitled to the payment if the concert took place. By this point, the defendants had incurred expenses of $50,000, while the plaintiffs had incurred around $450,000. Garland J chose to exercise his discretion by making no deduction at all.

This is the correct result in principle, and it is to be hoped that future courts exercise their choice in the same way. The qualification 'if it considers it just' should be read as 'never'.

B. Non-Money Benefits

Even worse than the Act's treatment of payments, is the Byzantine approach it adopts in relation to non-money benefits. Unlike section 1(2), which was the product of the work of the Law Revision Committee given the task of reconsidering the mistake that was *Chandler v Webster*, section 1(3) 'was not considered by the Law Revision Committee and it was subjected to minimal Parliamentary scrutiny'.[28] Also unlike section 1(2), which with the aid of section 2(4) can be read restrictively so as to give identical results to those that would have obtained at common law, section 1(3) requires restitution to be awarded in cases in which the common law (and principled good sense) would not.

Section 1(3) of the Act provides:

> Where any party to the contract has, by reason of anything done by any other party thereto in, or for the purpose of, the performance of the contract, obtained a valuable benefit (other than a payment of money to which the last foregoing subsection applies) before the time of discharge, there shall be recoverable from him by the said other party such sum (if any), not exceeding the value of the said benefit to the party obtaining it, as the court considers just, having regard to all the circumstances of the case and, in particular,—

> (a) the amount of any expenses incurred before the time of discharge by the benefited party in, or for the purpose of, the performance of the contract, including any sums

---

[27] [1995] 1 WLR 1226 (QBD). See also *Lobb v Vasey Housing Auxiliary* [1963] VR 38.
[28] McKendrick, *Force Majeure and Frustration* (n 3) 154.

paid or payable by him to any other party in pursuance of the contract and retained or recoverable by that party under the last foregoing subsection, and

(b) the effect, in relation to the said benefit, of the circumstances giving rise to the frustration of the contract.

Again, this section on its face requires *all* valuable benefits conferred before the time of discharge to be recoverable, subject to this being the 'just sum'. In the example of the deceased academic, his estate is entitled to restitution of the value of the benefit the University obtains from the work provided over the entire course of the performance of the contract, with allowance made for the payments the University had made. If, as so often, the valuable benefit obtained by the University employer far exceeds what has been paid for the work over the months or years, can the deceased academic's estate escape from the bad bargain he has made, and recover it back? In order to avoid such ridiculous results, the court could fall back again on section 2(4), or simply state that such a sum is not 'just' and go no further.

Again, section 1(3) applies a variation on the rule that applies in the context of the avoidance of a contract. Again, the need for the relevant performance to have been rendered conditionally, and for that condition to have failed as a result of the frustrating event, is not found in the statutory language.

The Act does not apply the same approach to valuation as is adopted at common law. This ameliorates to some extent the problems that would otherwise be created. At common law, where a service has been rendered under an agreed condition that has failed, or under a contract that has been avoided, the recipient is required to repay the value of that service.[29] This is so even where that service is not, in fact, enriching to the defendant.[30] By contrast, section 1(3) looks not to the value of the service *itself*, but to the valuable benefit that *results* from that service. This operates as a cap on recovery. Further, where that consequential valuable benefit no longer exists because of the frustrating event (for example, improvements done to a building that is destroyed by fire, thereby frustrating the ability to complete performance), this is to be taken into account in quantifying the 'just sum' under section 1(3)(b). The Act seeks to reverse only the extent to which the defendant has, as a matter of fact, been left better off today as a result of the claimant's service, which is not the common law's traditional approach.

The result in *Appleby v Myers*,[31] where the claimant had contracted to erect machinery on the defendant's land but which work was destroyed by an accidental fire before completion, ought to remain the same. No claim should succeed. Although the Act's wording compels the court to require the defendant to pay for work on a basis that he never accepted it, it should not do so in a way that leaves the defendant worse off than if the contract had never been entered into.

For good or ill, the Act may be said to be more consonant with 'unjust enrichment' as its organizing idea than is the common law, where, if there is a claim to the value of a service, it is not capped by the valuable benefit resulting to the defendant. The effect of the Act is therefore to force recipients of services to pay for work on a basis upon which they never

---

[29] *Planché v Colburn* (n 21); *Brewer Street Investments Ltd v Barclays Woollen Ltd* [1954] 1 QB 428 (CA).
[30] See generally, Robert Stevens, *The Laws of Restitution* (OUP 2023) 67–70, 132–33.
[31] (1867) LR 2 CP 651.

accepted it (reversing *Cutter v Powell*), but at the least it should not make the defendant worse off as a result of having entered into the bargain.

The (very) difficult decision in *BP v Hunt*, still the only decision to consider section 1(3), may be best analysed by considering first what the result would have been at common law and second what the result would have been if the contract had been rescinded in equity, and then comparing the position reached by the court in applying the Act.

Mr Hunt obtained an oil concession from the Libyan government in 1957 but did not have the resources to exploit it himself. He entered into a contract with BP under which he gave it half the concession, and it undertook to do the exploration and, if oil was discovered, the extraction. Before it was known whether the concession was a productive field, Hunt was paid by BP in money and oil ('farm-in' contributions). Hunt was then obliged to reimburse BP half of the expenditure incurred by it, and the farm-in contributions, plus 25 per cent, from three-eighths of his share of any oil production once it came on stream.

All went well at first. A large field was discovered and went into operation in 1967. Oil and revenue flowed. However, in 1971 the Libyan government expropriated BP's interest, and subsequently, in 1973, Mr Hunt's. At that point, BP had received $63m of reimbursement oil from Mr Hunt for its expenditure. It had, in addition, also received very large sums from its half share of the concession.

It was BP's obligations of performance that were frustrated. It was unable to perform any further extraction, and if Mr Hunt had sued it for breach of contract any such claim would have failed. Mr Hunt's obligations to reimburse were always possible to perform but were conditional upon oil continuing to flow, which after expropriation it did not.

At common law, what would the position have been? Mr Hunt's transfer of half of the concession had been done on the basis that he was paid farm-in contributions in money and oil, and that BP would carry out its obligations to explore, develop, and appraise the field. This had been satisfied. BP had done the work on the basis that it was to be entitled to be reimbursed from three-eighths of Mr Hunt's share of oil production once it came on stream, which it had been. It had no entitlement to any further payments from Mr Hunt. Mr Hunt had never accepted the work on any other basis, and in this respect the case is the same as *Cutter v Powell*. There would be no recovery by either party.

By contrast, if the court were to rescind or avoid the contract *ab initio*, a calculation of the value of the performance rendered by each side would have to be made, and set off one against another. Mr Hunt would have to make restitution of all the value of the performance received from BP, but BP would have to give allowance not only for the payments received in return from Mr Hunt as the oil flowed, but also for the value of the half share of the concession that it had received from him.

Neither of these approaches was that adopted by the court, which went for a curious hybrid of the two. In quantifying the 'valuable benefit' acquired by Mr Hunt as a consequence of what BP had done, Robert Goff J reached a figure of $85m. This was calculated by taking the overall increase in Mr Hunt's cash flow from BP's work ($170m) and halving it. The halving was done on the rough and ready basis that half of Mr Hunt's enrichment was attributed to BP's work, but half was attributable to the portion of the concession that Hunt retained.[32] The market value of the work done and the payments

---

[32] See Robert Goff and Gareth Jones (eds), *The Law of Restitution* (7th edn, Sweet and Maxwell 2007) [20-075]. This explanation (which does not appear in the judgment) is presumably that of Robert Goff.

made[33] by BP was \$98m, but from this was deducted the \$63m already received from Mr Hunt in 'reimbursement oil'. As the balance of \$35m was lower than the valuable benefit (\$85m) cap, this was what was awarded.

But what of the value of the half of the concession that Mr Hunt had given to BP, from which it had been extracting oil for several years? Mr Hunt sought to recover this by way of a counterclaim against BP. Robert Goff J rejected this counterclaim in the following terms:

> Mr. Hunt has already been fully recompensed in respect of his contractual performance, whereby B.P. obtained their valuable benefit. Under the contract, Mr. Hunt had transferred to B.P. a half share in the concession, and made available to them a substantial quantity of reimbursement oil. The consideration to be furnished by B.P. under the contract was to supply the farm-in contributions in money and in oil, and to carry out such obligations as the contract placed upon them as operator in relation to the exploration, appraisal, and development of the field, the construction of the pipeline, terminal and other facilities, and bringing the field into production; in so doing, B.P. would be bringing their experience and expertise to bear upon the development of a concession in which Mr. Hunt held a half share, and taking the risk that they would not find oil in commercial quantities. Everything which was required of B.P. to be done, in return for the transfer of the half share in the concession and the availability of reimbursement oil, had been done by them.[34]

By looking at whether the consideration for the transfer of the half share of the concession had failed, Robert Goff J was reverting to the approach that would have been adopted at common law. But, as we have seen, section 1(3) (like section 1(2)) has no such condition. It simply requires valuable benefits received to be reversed, with an allowance made for expenditure in exchange. If the same common law approach had been taken in relation to the value of BP's work, no claim would have succeeded.

The result was a kind of lop-sided rescission with Mr Hunt required to reimburse BP for the market value of the work it had done, while BP kept the benefit of the half share of the concession it had obtained from him that had been profitable for four years. The result was to give BP reimbursement at a higher rate than the three-eighths share of Mr Hunt's receipts from oil production, contrary to the bargain made by the parties.

Perhaps the common law position could be reverted to by stipulating that there is only a 'just sum' to be awarded under subsection 1(3) where the condition under which the work or other benefit that has been provided has failed. This does not, however, fit with the only decision we have on the subsection's interpretation, save in relation to the counterclaim.

C. When Does the Act Apply?

By creating a bespoke (and defective) regime for the unwinding of 'frustrated contracts' (*sic*), the Act creates differences between cases that should be treated in the same way. For example:

---

[33] The \$2m 'farm-in payments' should have been recoverable under section 1(2) of the Act, rather than 1(3), but Goff J did not differentiate the two. See [1983] 2 AC 352, 370 (HL).

[34] [1979] 1 WLR 783, 833.

138 REPEAL THE LAW REFORM (FRUSTRATED CONTRACTS) ACT 1943

> *P* agrees to hire a music hall and gardens from *D* for six weeks, for £10,000 per week. Three hours before the agreement is entered into, the music hall burns to the ground through the fault of neither party.

If payment has been made, or other performance rendered, is this governed by the Act or not? On the orthodox account, this is a case of 'common mistake', not 'frustration'. The Act is stated to apply where the contract '*has become* impossible of performance or been otherwise frustrated', whereas here it was impossible to provide the music hall from the outset. If the fire occurs a few hours later, do we enter a different legal regime? Should the application of the Act be read narrowly or widely?

Similarly, are cases of 'partial' frustration examples of a contract which is 'impossible to perform', or not? For example:

> *D* contracts to sell to *P* 500 tonnes of beetroot grown on his farm in Staffordshire, for £500 per tonne. Unforeseeably, a new form of blight strikes the crop so that there are only 50 tonnes grown.

D ought to be obliged to deliver to *P* the 50 tonnes he has, even if he is excused from delivering the remaining 450 tonnes because his obligation to do so is frustrated.[35] *P* is entitled to reject any such short delivery,[36] but otherwise the seller should be under a continuing obligation to deliver what the farm produces even if it falls short of the 500 tonnes expected. Does such a case of 'partial' frustration fall within the Act? It would be unfortunate if it did as *D* should be required to pay for each tonne he accepts at the contract rate, and not be relieved of any obligation to pay under section 1(2).

Finally, are cases of subsequent illegality within the Act?[37] These are often treated as examples of frustration, and might be thought of as cases of 'legal impossibility', although the legal basis for relieving one or both from the obligation of performance is quite different from that applicable in cases of factual impossibility of performance.

Regardless of where the line is drawn, the Act creates an anomalous regime without justification.

V. Conclusion

Once enacted, legislation can seem like part of the legal furniture, impossible to dispense with. This is especially so for longstanding pieces of legislation, such as the Law Reform (Frustrated Contracts) Act 1943 which most of us took in with our basic legal education. It has formed the basis for legislative reform in New Zealand,[38] Victoria,[39] and most Canadian provinces. However, it should perhaps come as no surprise that legislation reforming private law enacted while the nation was fighting for its life in a world war is not of the highest quality. As observed by Ewan McKendrick, 'with the benefit of hindsight, we can see that

---

[35] cf *HR & S Sainsbury Ltd v Street* [1972] 1 WLR 834 (Bristol Assizes).

[36] Sale of Goods Act 1979, s 30(1).

[37] See the chapter 'Shades of Frustration' in this volume.

[38] Frustrated Contracts Act 1944.

[39] Frustrated Contracts Act 1959.

CONCLUSION   139

this piece of legislation was enacted after inadequate discussion and analysis of the relevant issues'.[40]

When we put sections 1(2) and 1(3) together, we see that the Act provides for a scheme of 'mutual restitution'.[41] This is appropriate in the context of rescission or avoidance of a contract by a court, but not that of frustration.

Although it would be possible to enact legislation more readily consonant with the general law position, there is an easier path that has been taken before. The Infants Relief Act 1874 foolishly enacted that contracts entered into by minors, except those for necessaries, were void. On its face, this meant that even where perfectly fair bargains with a child were fully executed, the parties were able to obtain restitution of any benefit conferred. In principle, incapacity to contract should ordinarily go to the enforceability against, and not the validity of, any agreement entered into by the incapacitated party. Fully executed agreements should not, without more, be subject to reversal. This had been the common law position, and it was to this that the law reverted with the passing of the Minors Contracts Act 1987 which simply repealed the Infants Relief Act. This reversion to the (general) common law position is also the best option to take with the Law Reform (Frustrated Contracts) Act 1943.

There are, unfortunately, many other examples of legislative intervention in private law that are either counterproductive, or only saved from being so by the possibility of creative interpretation by the judiciary. This does not mean, of course, that the judiciary are free from error, as *Chandler v Webster* (and *Whincup v Hughes*) showed. Ordinarily, however, the judiciary is concerned with the easier task of resolving the outcome in a particular case, rather than reforming an entire area of law.[42] Mistakes can usually therefore be distinguished away or, when it matters, be overruled. The prospects for a distracted legislature repealing its own badly drafted reform, when the problem rarely gives rise to litigation, is not great.

---

[40] McKendrick, *Force Majeure and Frustration* (n 3) 154.
[41] McKendrick, *Force Majeure and Frustration* (n 3) 154–55.
[42] An exception is the very unfortunate *Patel v Mirza* [2016] UKSC 42, [2017] AC 467.

9

Contractual Interpretation: Meaning, Intention, and Disembodied Spirits

ADAM KRAMER*

I. Introduction

I have since early in my contract law career sought to approach the interpretation of contracts from a pragmatic and practical standpoint. That fits with my current job of barrister. Indeed, it is one of the reasons I left academe for that job.[1]

The contextual approach given form by Lord Hoffmann around twenty-five years ago now[2] (although not, of course, created by him) has the strong virtue of working in practice. It provides a framework within which the points and counterpoints as to why a particular interpretation is the right one can be deployed: this provision must be read against what is normal practice in the industry, that provision sits within a section dealing with a particular type of obligation, this reading would lead to very unfair or extreme results in this common situation, that provision was agreed against a background of a particular uncertainty as to a change in taxation, this provision does not deal with the most obvious scenario (which must be deliberate), and so on. The contextual approach also allows the old cases to be understood, compared, and explained. In other words, the 'common sense' bit really works.

Ewan McKendrick is, I think, broadly in the same camp: a pragmatic moderate. His reaction to Lord Hoffmann's decision in *Investors Compensation Scheme* was not, like most judges and academics, to give their personal reaction to how it fits with their preferred worldview, but instead to survey 180 subsequent English and Welsh cases to assess pragmatically how *ICS* was being received in the law and whether it was working.[3] (Answer: the decision drew together approaches already in the authorities, there was evolution not revolution, and the law was working fine.) Similarly, his reaction to the almost intemperate debate between Lords Sumption and Hoffmann twenty years later was to draw the sting from it, pointing out that they are both largely right, and highlighting the necessary complexities of the interpretative process.[4]

---

* With thanks to George Leggatt and the editors for many useful comments on a draft.

[1] After publishing one very learned and theoretical article on contract interpretation in the *Oxford Journal of Legal Studies* at the start of my academic career (see n 15 below), of which I am still proud despite no longer fully understanding all of it, I realized it would be odd to continue as a contract academic without practising law, as I had barely seen a non-consumer contract and would have little opportunity to do so in my ivory tower.

[2] *Investors Compensation Scheme Ltd v West Bromwich Building Society* [1998] 1 WLR 896.

[3] Ewan McKendrick, 'The Interpretation of Contracts: Lord Hoffmann's Re-Statement' in Sarah Worthington (ed), *Commercial Law and Commercial Practice* (Hart Publishing 2003).

[4] Ewan McKendrick, 'Interpretation' in William Day and Sarah Worthington (eds), *Challenging Private Law* (Hart Publishing 2020).

Adam Kramer, *Contractual Interpretation: Meaning, Intention, and Disembodied Spirits* In: *Shaping the Law of Obligations.* Edited by: Edwin Peel and Rebecca Probert, Oxford University Press. © Adam Kramer 2023.
DOI: 10.1093/oso/9780198889762.003.0009

142 MEANING, INTENTION, AND DISEMBODIED SPIRITS

And, perhaps due to temperament, or to a desire to justify my daily toil, I too am a believer rather than a sceptic when it comes to the agreement-centred project of English contract law. I think there is a right answer that judges strive for, that is, a single (best) meaning of the contract. I don't, for example, think the process of asking what the reasonable person would have understood is a fig-leaf for policy or discretionary decisions as to what a fair contract or outcome would be.

But, on reflection, what do I mean by the meaning of the contract that judges strive for? In what sense is an intended meaning intended? To what extent do the words of a contract breathe on their own? When are there gaps?

It is in an attempt to be rigorous and not woolly about these questions that I here try to unpick what it is that those of us who interpret contracts in chambers, offices, and courts are actually doing.

II. The Objective Principle Is Not Itself a Problem, But Nor Is It an Answer

It is, of course, a fundamental part of human communication that we can't read minds. And so we have to communicate through words or conduct. We have to use shared norms and conventions (what does a word mean; how do people normally choose what to say and what not to say; what would be normal in this situation if unsaid, etc). Communication only works if we both get this right; if we both assess the norms correctly; if we both take into account only the apparently shared information to which the communicator can be expected to be referring. Each communicator must try to get it right, and take responsibility for getting it wrong. So, of course, a person can be taken to mean what they reasonably appear to intend to mean. So in everyday communication, so also in contracts. We call this the objective principle.[5]

This is the core of communication. For me, it does not itself provide a serious challenge to the concept of meaning. It merely shifts over the question of meaning of the speaker to one of apparent meaning of the speaker.

But, by the same token, it also does not answer the question at the heart of this chapter. It dictates that it is not right to ask what the speaker actually meant (subjectively; in their head), but instead it is necessary to ask what the speaker appears to have meant. But this still raises the question of what a human *can* mean when he or she says or writes something, because it is necessary to understand that in order to understand what a human *appears* to have meant. The promisor is not a superhero with perfect foresight, and the reasonable person will know that and must be realistic. No human could have held all of the possible contents and applications of what he or she said in their mind at the time of saying it.

What are the limits on what a speaker could have (subjectively) intended/contemplated, and what are the implications of those limits when considering what it is reasonable to think the speaker meant?

---

[5] As this includes shared norms and mutual context, this is the objective principle in the second of the three senses identified by Lord Leggatt in 'Making Sense of Contracts: The Rational Choice Theory' (2015) 131 LQR 454 (hereafter Leggatt, 'Making Sense of Contracts') 475.

The criticism 'the court is just making the contract up because the promisor clearly never intended that' is one that accepts the objective principle but still asks what is realistic. It has force to the extent that it is saying that a reasonable person would not understand the promisor to have intended something because it would be clear to the audience that the promisor did not think of it. The answer to that question, where there is one, relates to whether people need to read particular written terms, or consciously foresee circumstances, in order to intend a result in relation to them. The short answer is—to my mind—that they don't, although there are limits, of course.

III. You Don't Have to Think It to Mean It

We need to be careful when we use terms such as 'think', 'contemplate', 'intend', or 'crossed the speaker's mind'. Perhaps the first point to make is that we should be careful when we say that things can't be meant or intended unless they were foreseen or thought of (and so also when we say the reasonable person can't understand something to have been meant or intended because it was unlikely to have been foreseen and thought of by the promisor).

The first sense in which we need to be careful about this is a psychological one. It is wrong as a matter of the science of the brain, so far as I understand it. A favourite lawyers' example for this is the bedless hotel. I book a hotel room and go up in the lift and get to the room and find it has no bed. Is that a breach of contract? Of course it is. Although bed was never expressly specified, the reasonable person in my position would understand that a hotel offering a room is offering a room with a bed unless it says otherwise, because that is the normal purpose of a hotel room booking. It goes without saying/is implied. And, relevantly for present purposes, when I asked for a hotel room I meant a room with a bed *even though it did not at the moment of the booking (and of using the words 'hotel room') cross my mind that the hotel must have a bed or might not have a bed.*

I said in the previous paragraph that it did not cross my mind, but the concept of what crosses a person's mind is highly problematic. Works such as Kahneman's *Thinking, Fast and Slow*[6] have shown us that (on his schema), as well as directed, effortful, calculating, conscious 'system 1' thinking there is also a lot more fast, automatic, unconscious 'system 2' thinking. My modest efforts have not revealed to me learning in the field on how this applies to meaning and communication in particular, but, perhaps surprisingly, the point has been considered by that cutting-edge thinktank of psychology that is the English High Court in a pair of cases about reliance on tortious misrepresentations.

Briefly, in *Leeds City Council v Barclays Bank plc*[7] and *Crossley v Volkswagen AG*[8] the defendants sought to strike out deceit claims based on implied representations on the basis that the claimants cannot have relied on or been induced by the misstatements—reliance/inducement being a necessary element of the tort of deceit and indeed of negligent misstatement also—unless they were consciously aware of the misstatements, that is, unless the claimants consciously brought to mind that the implications of the defendants' conduct

---

[6] Daniel Kahneman, *Thinking, Fast and Slow* (Penguin 2012).
[7] [2021] EWHC 363 (Comm), [2021] QB 1027 (hereafter *Leeds*).
[8] [2021] EWHC 3444 (QB) (hereafter *Crossley*). Full disclosure: I acted for the claimants in this one. I cited Kahneman in the written skeleton argument, although he did not get a mention in the High Court's judgment.

were that the defendants were representing those particular things. (The representations were: in *Leeds* that LIBOR rates were being set honestly, in the context of the sale of LIBOR-pegged loans; and in *Crossley* that the cars were lawful to drive, in the context of the marketing and distribution by the defendant manufacturer of those vehicles for sale.)

Opposite results were reached in the two cases (and both have settled without appeals). In *Leeds*, it was held that the claimant must have had 'conscious' 'awareness' of the representation (although that awareness could be 'quasi-automatic'),[9] hence the claim was struck out. In *Crossley*, a strict awareness requirement was thought to be inconsistent with the prior cases and problematic. And an important point that was brought out in *Crossley* was the strangeness of the position *if* the law accepts that the implied representations had been made (which was not challenged in the strike-out, and as to which there is some support in prior cases as regards the LIBOR-rigging representation), but the law then does not accept that they could have been relied upon.[10] For the purposes of determining whether the representations had been made impliedly by the defendants' conduct, it was necessary that the reasonable person would understand them to have been intended (the objective test for all communications inside and outside the law of contract). So the law as applied to the speaker seems to have no problem with something apparently being intended without apparently consciously crossing the speaker's mind, whereas the law as applied to the recipient would (eg under the approach in *Leeds*) say something does not affect a person's decision unless it consciously crossed their mind.

The answer is that there is no need for something to cross one's mind for it to be intended or to affect a decision (and so some of the comments in *Leeds* go too far).[11] The hotel agent in the above example is correctly understood to represent that the hotel room will have a bed whether or not it is likely that the hotel employee who marketed or sold the room consciously thought about that, and the guest's decision to book the hotel is induced by the statement that there is a bed whether or not that guest consciously thought about there being or not being a bed. Conscious thought is not needed for intention, because as a matter of psychology we act without it (on both sides of the communication), by reference to various norms known, and heuristics applied, that get us through the world without our brains exploding due to having too much to process.[12]

So, we can mean many things that do not cross our mind. So, therefore, we can be reasonably understood to mean many things that it is unlikely ever crossed our mind. And contract interpretation must allow for that.

---

[9] *Leeds* (n 7) especially [146] to [148], but as to 'quasi-automatic' see [113] and [148].

[10] *Crossley* (n 8) [97].

[11] See also the useful example of *DPP v Ray* [1974] AC 370 (HL), considered in detail in both *Leeds* (n 6, see especially [112]–[113]) and *Crossley* (n 8, see especially [60]–[63] and [92]). A student goes to a Chinese restaurant fully intending to pay, sits down, eats, then decides not to pay and leaves. The House of Lords confirmed there had been commission of the crime of obtaining a pecuniary advantage by deception. By sitting down and ordering, Mr Ray had represented that he intended to pay. The waiter had relied on that representation, although not consciously. Lord Morris in *Ray* noted that 'He induced the waiter to believe that that was his intention' and 'the waiter . . . proceeded on the basis that an ordinary customer would pay his bill before leaving' (386).

[12] That sentence is shorthand for 'I don't fully understand how we do communicate and make decisions and would welcome psychologists and behavioural economists explaining this to me better'. But see for example Dan Sperber and Deirdre Wilson, 'Pragmatics' in Frank Jackson and Michael Smith (eds), *Oxford Handbook of Contemporary Philosophy* (OUP 2007), who describe pragmatic inferential elaborations of meaning as 'performed automatically and unconsciously during comprehension'. Sperber and Wilson are probably the leading modern academics in the pragmatics field, as the successors to Paul Grice (see further Deirdre Wilson and Dan Sperber, *Meaning and Relevance* (CUP 2012).

IV. Delegating, Appointing, Out-sourcing, Shortcuts

Another sense in which we should be careful when we say that things can't be meant or intended unless they were foreseen or contemplated (and therefore the reasonable person can't understand something to have been meant or intended because it was unlikely to have been foreseen and contemplated) is that we need to take account of the frequent possibility of speakers intending without foreseeing or contemplating something. To me, this is a group of situations under the umbrella of delegation, appointment of an agent or authority, out-sourcing, and so on, as explored in the following sections.

A. I Agree the Terms, Whatever They Are

Contracts of adhesion/standard form contracts provide a challenge for contract law because the agreement to them typically does not involve reading them, although still involves expressing consent knowing that they exist. When I myself am agreeing to such a contract, that is because I see such a standard form and think 'I am aware that, where competition has not operated to protect me, there is unfair contract terms legislation to protect me against unfair terms and that will do the bargaining for me (through regulation or private disputes)'. Lawyers can be strange like that. Most people probably have the more usual reaction of 'I want the goods or service and have to agree to this to get it and these terms probably don't matter'.

Either way, the signatory/clicker of the 'I agree' button does not know what the terms are, but has still agreed to them anyway. The specific terms haven't crossed my mind when I sign or click but that is my problem—I know there are terms and can read them if I want to.[13] I am taking the risk. This is a bit like agreeing to (and to pay for) whatever wine the sommelier thinks will suit my meal, or agreeing to be bound by an expert's determination. I don't need to know what wine the sommelier will choose or what the expert will determine to have agreed to it. I have delegated the authority, or perhaps waived the right to say I haven't agreed.[14] Or at least it is reasonable to understand me to have done so.

B. All Agreements Are Like This

I think every written agreement is like an unread boilerplate contract. Commercial parties, at least, may well read at least a significant portion of their written contract (although not the standard terms at the end which they typically trust their lawyers to have checked and/ or wouldn't understand), but they know that the words are intended to be binding going forward irrespective of what they subjectively thought and what the counterparty subjectively thought because the written contract is the only source of the obligations. There are a few basic features of this.

---

[13] But contrast eg Robin Bradley Kar and Margaret Jane Radin, 'Pseudo-Contract and Shared Meaning Analysis' (2019) 132 Harv L Rev 1135, who see boilerplate terms as not contracted (only 'pseudo-contract'), nor assented to, and not common meaning.

[14] As Lord Leggatt points out, a principle of personal responsibility underlies cases holding parties to contracts because of their signature whether or not they have read the contracts: Leggatt, 'Making Sense of Contracts' 474.

First, contracting parties know that the written contract is not merely evidence of what the promisor intended; it is the record of the agreement and it lives independently.

Second, contracting parties know that the written contract must be taken to have a single meaning, even though it derives from two or more consciousnesses reaching agreement, which may have had two or more understandings of what was being agreed.[15] The reasonable interpreter also knows this, and must identify what reasonably appears to have been the single meaning intended by both parties. But it is intended in the sense that the interpreter knows that the contracting parties know that they have committed to a single meaning, not in the sense that the single meaning was thought of or apparently thought of by the parties. This gives primacy and further independent vitality to the text of the contact.

Third, contracting parties intend their contracts to be binding in future situations. That is part of the purpose of the agreement, especially where it (like many contracts) deals with relationships, long-term obligations, and executory promises. For the contract to govern, it is necessary that the agreed text provides a single answer to what happens in future situations, but (unless perhaps if the parties say otherwise) it is *not* necessary that the parties have foreseen or could have foreseen those situations. I return to unforeseen circumstances presently, as they in particular shine a light on interpretation.

Relatedly, and prosaically, it is in the nature of words that they are general. Communication with a manageable shared vocabulary[16] requires the use of general words, in combination (ie in sentences), and using their context to add meaning.[17] We know that and accept it. It means that the word (and so the sentence) might mean more than we mean by it. It also means that we use words without consciously (or, I think, even unconsciously) thinking of all the things that can fall within the meaning of the word or even being aware of them. And we do so knowing that the word's shared meaning is inevitably fuzzy, such that at the edges of the word's meaning people will disagree as to whether the word covers the particular instance (because people learned the words' meanings inductively through use rather than through the memorizing of common single exhaustive definitions). By using words, we know that they will go further in the meaning reasonably ascribed to them than we intend them to, and that the audience will not know when that has happened. To an extent I have delegated some meaning to the agents I employ—the words I use—even without thinking about all of the elements, examples, or edges of that meaning.

All of this means that by agreeing to a contract the parties are agreeing to something that has a life of its own, and something that can mean things that the parties did not themselves consider, foresee, or indeed specifically mean. The individual parties intend to be bound to what the contract means because they have committed/delegated/waived by entering into that contract (at least in the case of written contracts where the parties know they

---

[15] Adam Kramer, 'Common Sense Principles of Contract Interpretation (and How We've Been Using Them All Along)' (2003) 23 OJLS 173, 195 (hereafter Kramer, 'Common Sense Principles'); Ryan Catterwell, *A Unified Theory of Contract Interpretation* (Hart 2020) [4-20] to [4-21].

[16] Native speakers of a language might expect to share a vocabulary in the low tens of thousands of words. Speaking in an idolect made up of bespoke words created exactly for my situation has the advantage of *precisely* saying what I want to convey without fear of being misunderstood. It, however, has the substantial drawback of there being no prospect of my being understood either, because the words are not common to others. Perhaps paradoxically, the only way to communicate with perfect clarity may be to do so with oneself in one's head.

[17] To convey something without any context, if possible at all, would require an impractically huge amount of text.

are binding themselves). They send the contractual document out into the world to govern their arrangements.

C. What Does This Mean for the Interpreter?

This means the interpreter of a written contract has a licence to interpret the contract, seeking to derive a meaning but with the following in mind.

First, the drafters apparently intended a single meaning fixed for all time through the text that they have chosen and knowing it will be and must be interpreted objectively and divorced from their individual, that is, actual intentions. As Lord Sales puts it, 'They have legislated for themselves.'[18] This means the intention to be derived is necessarily of a notional constructed single mind, rather than what either of the drafters actually thought. That single mind must still be assumed to be communicating through the shared norms of communication and of society by reference to a shared factual matrix including their prior trading and communications,[19] but it is a notional mind, not either of the drafters'.

Second, the drafters apparently intended the contract to govern across all of its natural scope and without restriction to what they actually considered or foresaw at the date of contracting, especially where the contract is intended to operate into the future. This means that the meaning to be derived does not require consideration of what even the notional single mind foresaw or specifically intended (the *intention* being that the words and contract govern—have *meaning*—even in situations not specifically contemplated).[20]

V. Lord Leggatt's 'Rational Choice Theory'

Lord Leggatt, in characteristically direct and perceptive fashion, traversed much of this ground in an article in 2015,[21] confirming (if confirmation was needed) his position as successor to Lord Hoffmann as philosopher-judge in this field (or, perhaps, 'psychologist-judge'[22]).

One of the main points Leggatt makes is that the objective principle requires us to apply pragmatic maxims to determine meaning, and these maxims, which he calls 'rational choice theory', assume or presume rationality and an intention to communicate. These assumptions are an elucidation of Grice's maxims, or of Sperber and Wilson's relevance and other maxims. Leggatt's discussion of these points provides a useful exposition of what it means to take a speaker to be participating in the game of communications, and of the norms that the

---

[18] Philip Sales, 'Contractual Interpretation: Antinomies and Boundaries', in this volume (hereafter Sales, 'Contractual Interpretation') page ref.

[19] Subject in contract interpretation to any policy-driven rules of law restricting the admissibility of such evidence, eg the restriction in English law to the admissibility of evidence of pre-contractual negotiations. McKendrick is right to criticize this rule of English law: 'Interpretation of Contracts and the Admissibility of Pre-contractual Negotiations' (2005) 17 SAcLJ 248.

[20] In this way the approach to interpretation becomes objective in Lord Leggatt's third and strongest sense: Leggatt, 'Making Sense of Contracts' (n 5) 475.

[21] Leggatt, 'Making Sense of Contracts' (n 5).

[22] Cf his very influential judgment when a High Court judge in *Gestmin SGPS SA v Credit Suisse (UK) Ltd* [2013] EWHC 3560 (Comm); [2020] 1 CLC 428 as to the limitations on human memory and therefore on witness evidence at trial.

speaker is fairly assumed to be employing,[23] but do not of themselves touch on the fundamental questions of what meaning is and the nature of the task of interpretation.

Leggatt's more important points for the purposes of this chapter are that (in line with the points made above) parties intend contracts to govern their rights and obligations, often agree contracts without reading them, and intend contracts to be binding in unforeseen circumstances, all of which give licence to the courts to deem a hypothetical speaker and interpret the contract *as if it were intended by* that hypothetical person.[24]

David McLauchlan responds to Leggatt with a detailed defence of Hoffmannian interpretation.[25] I (perhaps like McKendrick when he was responding to the Sumption/Hoffmann debate) see less between Leggatt and Hoffmann than McLauchlan does (and, perhaps, than Leggatt himself does). Leggatt's title, 'rational choice theory', sounds radical, but that refers mainly to the pragmatic process of attributing normative compliance (reasonableness, relevance, etc) to the speaker when interpreting—the basic objective test. The more important part of Leggatt's article for me is the recognition that parties intend things without them crossing their mind, intend a single meaning although the parties have multiple minds, and intend their contract to have a life of its own and to cover situations they have not foreseen. That gives licence to do what the courts already do under the Hoffmannian approach, such as apply contracts to unforeseen circumstances. But there is no change to the approach itself[26] (and, I would hazard, no need to call what we do 'rational choice theory').

VI. The Frustrations of Unforeseen Circumstances

The question of drafter intention is raised particularly acutely in the application of contracts to unforeseen events and circumstances.

First, an easy case. If an insurer agrees to make payments in the event of a notifiable disease (a disease that is added by regulators to a national list of contagious diseases the occurrence of which must be notified so that outbreaks can be spotted and controlled), it agrees to make payments for all future diseases that are made notifiable even though it, of course, cannot foresee those diseases specifically.[27]

Clearly, by referring to the open category of notifiable diseases, the insurer is deliberately referring to unknowns: anything that is made a notifiable disease in the future. No

---

[23] See further Kramer, 'Common Sense Principles' (n 15). See also William Day and Adam Kramer, 'Interpretation' in Mindy Chen-Wishart and Prince Saprai (eds), *Research Handbook on the Philosophy of Law* (Edward Elgar 2023 forthcoming).

[24] Leggatt, 'Making Sense of Contracts' (n 5) 462 and 474. See also Philip Sales, 'In Defence of Legislative Intention' (2019) 48 ABR 6, making similar points as to the necessarily fictional 'legislature' whose intention is inferred when construing legislation despite the particular legislators no doubt having differing, overlapping, incomplete views, and whose intention is also inferred to include gap-filling and extrapolation to what they would have intended had they thought about the circumstances that have arisen.

[25] David McLauchlan, 'A Better Way of Making Sense of Contracts?' (2016) 132 LQR 577 (hereafter McLauchlan, 'A Better Way').

[26] I leave aside the separate question of rectification, with which Leggatt, 'Making Sense of Contracts' (n 5) and McLauchlan, 'A Better Way' (n 25) both engage, but which is outside the scope of this article.

[27] Cf the COVID-19 business interruption insurance litigation and 'disease clauses' in *Financial Conduct Authority v Arch Insurance (UK) Ltd* [2021] UKSC 1 [2021] AC 649, although that dispute was not about what counted as a notifiable disease.

insurer would dispute that. It is essentially delegating a decision as to its coverage to those regulators.[28]

I wonder whether even this has limits—what if the approach of the regulators changes so that they make notifiable not only contagious diseases but also other diseases, such as coronary disease? Or what if the regulators even took the step of making coronary disease a notifiable disease deliberately to make sure they trigger these very notifiable disease insurance policies?[29] The insurer can then make a reasonable case that this falls outside what the parties would have expected could ever be made notifiable, and that they would not intend the policy to respond in this case. (This is, the insurer might say, a bit like the converse of a contract providing for payments to the council pegged to the amount of the Social Housing Grant, where that grant is later abolished. The contract was construed as requiring a payment as if the Social Housing Grant had continued.[30]) But what is the insurer really saying here? How can they make this argument within the context of construction and what the contract means?

The given here is that 'the parties did not foresee' the situation.[31] Two outcomes may obtain where parties did not foresee the situation (ignoring for a moment that it is totally irrelevant whether the *parties* foresaw the situation). The first is that the contract can still apply. In that case the court must decide and apply 'what they must have been taken to have intended in relation to the events which have arisen which they did not contemplate'.[32] It must 'promote the purposes and values which are expressed or implicit in its wording, [...] to reach an interpretation which applies the . . . wording to the changed circumstances in the manner most consistent with them'[33] and, as Mance LJ (as he then was) explained, work out 'how its language best operates in the fundamentally changed and entirely unforeseen circumstances in the light of the parties' original intentions and purposes'.[34]

The second possible outcome is that the contract is frustrated, where the change of circumstances is not something the parties can have intended to have covered by the terms of the contract and neither of them has impliedly assumed the risk of the change. In *Davis Contractors Ltd v Fareham UDC* the test was formulated as one of circumstances being radically different to what had been promised so that 'It was not this that I promised to do' or it was something 'which the contract did not contemplate'.[35] Similarly, a force majeure clause

---

[28] In contrast, if the insurer uses a closed exhaustive list, then it delegates nothing to the possible evolution of the concept of notifiable diseases, as in *Rockliffe Hall Ltd v Travelers Insurance Co Ltd* [2021] EWHC 412 (Comm), [2021] Bus LR 656.

[29] Cf the example of a bank exercising its right to alter a particular borrower's mortgage interest rate because it thought that borrower was a nuisance in *Paragon Finance plc v Nash* [2001] EWCA Civ 1466, [2002] 1 WLR 685 [31] (Dyson LJ).

[30] *Council of the City of York v Trinity One (Leeds) Ltd* [2018] EWCA Civ 1883. This is the example used for an unexpected change of circumstances in Kim Lewison, The Interpretation of Contracts (7th edn, Sweet & Maxwell 2021) [2.121].

[31] *Pluczenik Diamond Co NV v W Nagel (A Firm)* [2018] EWCA Civ 2640, [2019] 1 Lloyd's Rep 36 [31] (Leggatt LJ) (hereafter *Pluczenik*).

[32] *Bromarin AB v IMD Investments Ltd* [1999] STC 301, 310 (Chadwick LJ), *Pluczenik* (n 31) [33] (Leggatt LJ); *Munich Re Capital Ltd v Ascot Corporate Name Ltd* [2019] EWHC 2768 (Comm), [2020] BLR 140 [48] (Carr J).

[33] *Debenhams Retail plc v Sun Alliance and London Assurance Co Ltd* [2005] EWCA Civ 868, [2005] 3 EGLR 34 [27] (Mance LJ).

[34] *Lloyds TSB Foundation for Scotland v Lloyds Banking Group plc* [2013] UKSC 3; [2013] 1 WLR 366 [23] (Lord Mance).

[35] [1956] AC 696, 729 (Lord Radcliffe) and 723 (Lord Reid) (hereafter *Davies v Fareham*). See further Edwin Peel, *Frustration and Force Majeure* (4th edn, Sweet & Maxwell 2021) [13-008ff] (hereafter Peel, *Frustration and Force Majeure*) as to the many cases where it was important or decisive to the question of frustration whether the circumstances or events were within the parties' contemplation.

150 MEANING, INTENTION, AND DISEMBODIED SPIRITS

will not apply to something that falls within its literal words but 'cannot reasonably be supposed to have been in the contemplation of the parties'.[36]

In this latter situation only, that of frustration, is there found to be a true 'gap' in the contract. There is not even an implied allocation of risk. The contract has run out (it is incomplete[37]) and comes to an end.

Judges have shown more than a little discomfort in interpreting contracts in these situations, clearly being concerned that, as they are necessarily dealing with the unforeseen or unforeseeable, the interpretation is a fiction. Mance LJ has said that 'To speak even of objective intention in such circumstances involves some artificiality'.[38] Chadwick LJ agreed that, although permissible, this is 'an artificial exercise, because it requires there to be attributed to the parties an intention which they did not have (as a matter of fact)'.[39]

However, as we have seen, there is no need for judges to be squeamish or embarrassed. As we saw above, contracts are intended to provide for situations that are not contemplated, and are intended to live separately from the contractors and their minds. That being the case, the interpretive task is a legitimate one, but Mance LJ and Chadwick LJ are right that the 'intention' being identified is that putative intention of the contract, not the actual or even apparent intention of any particular person, and that the intention encompasses the interpolation of an answer from the contractual material (of contractually declared intentions in other situations, apparent commercial purposes, etc[40]) using rather more detective work than is necessary for most cases of construction. As Gerard McMeel puts it:

> [T]he courts will attempt to find a solution in the interstices of the contract, having regard to its overall nature and purpose, the other terms, and the context. The contract is the governing instrument and must be made to yield a solution.[41]

The judicial slide from describing the construction task as identifying intentions, the usual way of talking about construction, to describing it as identifying 'what parties must have been taken to have intended'[42] is a reflection not of a fundamentally different task being performed, but that in these sorts of cases the shorthand (and, sometimes, even fiction) of talking about the parties' intentions has become unworkable. Talking about parties' intentions is ordinarily harmless, although still misleading, as in all cases we are really talking about the contract's intention.

It may be for this reason that the courts have traditionally resisted attempts (including through the 'implied term' theory) to assimilate the frustration question into construction. Guenter Treitel explained that the implied term theory ceases to be focused on intention when it looks not at what the parties agree but at what the parties would have agreed to,[43]

---

[36] *Bailey v De Crespigny* (1869) LR 4 QB 180 (Hannen J).

[37] Kramer, 'Common Sense Principles' (n 15) 192.

[38] *Debenhams Retail plc v Sun Alliance and London Assurance Co Ltd* [2005] 3 EGLR 34 [27].

[39] *Bromarin AB v IMD Investments Ltd* [1999] STC 301, 310.

[40] See eg Lord Neuberger's citation in *Arnold v Britton* [2015] UKSC 36, [2015] AC 1619 [22], of *Aberdeen City Council v Stewart Milne Group Ltd* [2011] UKSC 56 as seeking to apply the parties' objectives.

[41] Gerard McMeel, *The Construction of Contracts* (3rd edn, OUP 2017) [1.103]. Although to the end of this might be added 'except where it cannot sensibly be made to yield a solution and has run out'.

[42] See text to n 32.

[43] Peel, *Frustration and Force Majeure* (n 35) [16-008] (not departing from Treitel's explanation in earlier editions), although Treitel (text again retained in Peel's edition) accepts that at heart frustration is about construction at [16-012].

and Lord Radcliffe in *Davis v Fareham* said that this is replacing the parties with 'disembodied spirits'.[44]

Indeed, a similar issue arises when a dispute raises other questions not covered by express drafting. What duties of care do the parties owe to each other? What are the fetters on a discretion granted? These are the sorts of topics parties do not always cover expressly, and the doctrine of implied terms resolves them by construction. (Again, some judges are squeamish about saying that implying terms is a construction exercise, but Lord Hoffmann was surely right that it is.[45])

But in fact there is no mismatch between the approach to determining whether a contract is frustrated or whether there is an implied term on one hand, and construction more generally on the other. The confusion arises from a failure to realize that even in ordinary construction, in relation to foreseeable circumstances or expressly covered topics, the contractual intention is that of a disembodied spirit—the apparent intentions of a putative single author, or entirely ad idem multiple authors, of the contract as written. The author is a 'construct'[46] and perhaps that is why interpretation is 'construction'. It is just that when circumstances are unforeseen and unforeseeable, it is more obvious than usual that the court must look to an apparent intention of the parties derived from their having agreed that the particular contract would govern even in unforeseen circumstances.

In the particular context of frustration, this does also reveal why (as commentators observe) foreseeability of circumstances may prevent frustration,[47] but unforeseeability does not necessarily lead to frustration. If the circumstances are unforeseen it then remains to establish whether there is an implied allocation of risk—that is, whether the objectives and obligations in the contract show sufficiently clearly what the notional single author would intend to happen in the unforeseen circumstances. As we have seen, something being unforeseen or unforeseeable does not mean the contract does not cover it.

This is no more than a construction exercise, albeit a very difficult one. It may yield an answer if the circumstances fall 'in the ambit of the shared world of the contract',[48] or where in some (probably rare) cases there is not enough in the contract to point to a single answer as to what the contract and its hypothetical single author intends. After all, there must be a single salient meaning/answer that the parties (with lawyers) or third parties could have discerned at any time; this is not just about resolving the dispute that has arisen, but about doing so in a way that reflects what the contract provides and no more.

---

[44] *Davies v Fareham* (n 35) 728. Others see frustration as a doctrine of law not sourced in presumed intention or construction, eg Andrew Phang, 'The Challenge of Principled Gap-Filling: A Study of Implied Terms in Comparative Context' [2014] JBL 263, 280.

[45] See further Adam Kramer, 'The Implication of Contract Terms as an Instance of Interpretation' (2004) 63 CLJ 384.

[46] Sales, 'Contractual Interpretation' (n 18).

[47] And see *Astor Management AG v Atalaya Mining plc* [2018] EWCA Civ 2407, [2019] Bus LR 106, [40]–[42] for an example where the circumstance being within the parties' contemplation also shuts the door to an application of the 'what the parties would have intended in those unforeseen circumstances' construction approach.

[48] Sales, 'Contractual Interpretation' (n 18).

VII. Conclusion

I finished this draft shortly after Christmas, and Lord Radcliffe's talk of the meaning of a contract as being that of a disembodied spirit suggests that I should have started this article, with apologies to Dickens, as follows: 'Party intention was dead: to begin with. There is no doubt whatever about that.'

But contractual meaning, and the construction exercise, are living and well. We must simply remember that although party intention provides the justification for enforcing the contract—the parties apparently intended the contractual document to bind them and have a life of its own—party intention does not help us to the content of the agreement. That comes from the document itself, as necessarily interpreted by the reasonable reader *as if* having come from a single author, and as necessarily applied without shyness to whatever circumstances or questions have arisen (even if likely not contemplated). The agreeing of the contract—the project of entering into the contract—gives licence to the court to interpret the contract in that way at such future date as a disagreement arises, and the contextual approach that the courts have got so good at applying and talking about is rightly how the courts conduct such interpretation.

10
Contractual Interpretation: Antinomies and Boundaries

PHILIP SALES

I. Introduction

Entering into a contract is an event with profound legal consequences. The parties are bound, according to the contract's terms. The state (through the courts) will enforce it against them. Pacta sunt servanda is the rule.

By forming a contract, the parties create a shared legal world. That shared world comprises a set of legal rights and obligations which frame the way in which they are entitled to behave towards each other. They have legislated for themselves and rule of law values are taken to inform this legislated regime. Predictability and an ability to plan one's affairs with a reasonable appreciation of the boundaries of what is and is not permissible are as much values to be respected in this context as in the context of legislation passed by Parliament applicable to the general public.

These features of contract inform the approach to the interpretation of contracts. On the one hand, the legal consequences of a contract are such that a party is only to be subject to them if they have consented to be bound. Free consent is the foundation for their obligation. On the other hand, where there is a contract each party is entitled to rely on it in planning their affairs, and rule of law values concerning certainty of rights and obligations and predictability of consequences when deciding how to act are also relevant. Rule of law values mean that contractual promises are to be read as subject to reasonable interpretation. These two objectives are in tension. They are reconciled through the principle of objective interpretation of contracts.

To understand what a contractual promise means, the courts ask what a reasonable person, placed in the position of the parties, would understand the contract to mean. This principle allows for the promisor to seek to make clear exactly the extent to which they are willing to be bound, and to that extent recognizes and respects the principle of consent. But at the same time interpretation is not governed by the subjective notion of consent, but rather consent as it reasonably appears to the other party to have been given.

An analogy may be drawn with legislation promulgated by Parliament. On the one hand, it is the will of the legislature which is required to create law. On the other, it is recognized that the law brought into existence by an exercise of will also has to be read in the light of rule of law values which the legal system respects. Lord Simon of Glaisdale made this point in *Black-Clawson International Ltd v Papierwerke Waldhof-Aschaffenburg AG*:

Philip Sales, *Contractual Interpretation: Antinomies and Boundaries* In: *Shaping the Law of Obligations.* Edited by: Edwin Peel and Rebecca Probert, Oxford University Press. © Philip Sales 2023. DOI: 10.1093/oso/9780198889762.003.0010

interpretation cannot be concerned wholly with what the promulgator of a written instrument meant by it: interpretation must also be frequently concerned with the reasonable expectation of those who may be affected thereby. This is most clearly to be seen in the interpretation of a contract: it has long been accepted that the concern of the court is not so much with the subject-matter of consent between the parties (which may, indeed, exceptionally, be entirely absent) as with the reasonable expectation of the promisee. So, too, in statutory construction, the court is not solely concerned with what the citizens, through their parliamentary representatives, meant to say; it is also concerned with the reasonable expectation of those citizens who are affected by the statute, and whose understanding of the meaning of what was said is therefore relevant. The sovereignty of Parliament runs in tandem with the rule of objective law . . . if the draftsman uses the tools of his trade correctly, the meaning of his words should actually represent what their promulgator meant to say and the court of construction, retracing the same path in the opposite direction, should arrive, via the meaning of what was said, at what the promulgator meant to say.[1]

So, for a contract, one can say that consent is the foundational justification for treating a party as bound by it, but that there is a departure from a principle of pure consent in order to take account of other values as well. It is tempered by the reasonable expectation of the other party, as induced by the words (or conduct) used to make the contract with them, which is the foundation of *their* consent and willingness to be bound. It is also tempered by a principle of fairness between the parties. Since each party is subject to obligations owed to the other, neither can claim that their own subjective beliefs as to the meaning of a promise (whether given by them or to them) should govern in a dispute about that meaning. Hence the idea of an objective approach to interpretation of contracts.

This is a compromise, hallowed in doctrine and practice, between competing and incommensurable values.[2] Recognition of this allows one to understand certain puzzles. If one flexes one aspect of the compromise to give it more prominence, it potentially detracts from other aspects.

Another aspect of the interpretation of contracts where a compromise between competing values has to be struck concerns a tension between context and linguistic sense. The role played by context[3] and the factual matrix[4] in which the parties act when they make the contract is important. Given imprecision in the meaning of words, their sense has to be determined at some level by reference to the context in which they are used and the apparent object of the speaker in choosing to use the language they did in that context. If one takes a wide approach to this aspect, to bring in more rather than less context, the greater is the potential to change the apparent meaning of the words used in drafting the contract, as opposed to restricting their meaning to that given by a stricter and narrower reference to pure linguistic rules and conventions.

This poses problems in light of another feature of contract law, which is the need for meaning to be determinable by a third party unconnected with the making of the contract,

---

[1] [1975] AC 591, 645 (HL).

[2] On pluralist compromise as the foundation for legal doctrine, see Philip Sales and Frederick Wilmot-Smith, 'Justice for Foxes' (2022) 138 LQR 583 (hereafter Sales and Wilmot-Smith, 'Justice').

[3] *Investors Compensation Scheme v West Bromwich Building Society* [1998] 1 WLR 896 (HL) (hereafter *ICS*).

[4] *Prenn v Simmonds* [1971] 1 WLR 1381 (HL); *Reardon Smith Line Ltd v Yngvar Hansen-Tangen* [1976] 1 WLR 989 (HL).

namely a judge, in order to access the power of the state for the purposes of enforcement. And since access to the state in the person of a judge is a necessary condition for enforcement of a contract in the case of a dispute, the parties have to be able to have recourse to lawyers who are themselves able to predict how a judge might react. Therefore there is a need for determinacy and objectivity in the standards to be applied in working out what a contract means, as recognized by the law. It is not a simple matter of what the parties believe the contract means, but one of how strangers will read it.

A judge has ready access to the words used by the parties. Where there is uncertainty about what words were used, the judge can find the facts. But a judge will have a less ready feel for the context in which the parties found themselves when they contracted. Context is a more amorphous concept, open to a wider range of competing interpretations. In order to understand their obligations, the parties to the contract (with legal advice) need to be able to predict how a judge will interpret it. The more widely one refers to context in interpreting a contract, the greater the scope for uncertainty in knowing how the judge will perform this interpretative act. That is because different aspects of the context may point in different directions (and the more widely one brings in context, the more likely it is that different aspects of it will point in different directions) and also because, for all that context assists in understanding meaning, it can also operate in tension with linguistic meaning.

Under the pressure of these competing considerations, the courts have moved in an arc from a very narrow focus on linguistic meaning, through acceptance of the significance of the factual matrix, to a wider approach to relevant context (*ICS*), and back to a closer focus on linguistic meaning in *Arnold v Britton*[5] and *Wood v Capita Insurance Services Ltd.*[6] It is sometimes denied that there has been a significant change,[7] and in *Wood* itself Lord Hodge observed that the recent history of the law on contractual interpretation 'is one of continuity rather than change'.[8] Others, however, have emphasized the degree of change involved.[9]

The truth seems to lie somewhere between these positions. There is a strong element of continuity in the approach of the courts. Text and context have always been key factors in contract interpretation. But at the same time, something has changed as doctrine has developed over time.

Litigants argue over context, both as to what is taken to constitute it and as to its role in setting the scene for the text used, because it makes a difference to the interpretation of the words in which a contract is expressed. There are fundamental reasons why this is a feature of the arguments over contractual interpretation, to do with the nature of language and with the juristic nature of the exercise of interpretation of a contract.

Modern contractual interpretation draws on insights derived from the later work of Ludwig Wittgenstein[10] about how language works and how meaning is conveyed. Words do not have a simple correspondence with objects in the world or concepts. Language is

---

[5] [2015] UKSC 36, [2015] AC 1619 (hereafter *Arnold v Britton*).

[6] [2017] UKSC 24, [2017] AC 1173 (hereafter *Wood v Capita*).

[7] See eg David McLauchlan, 'Continuity, Not Change, in Contract Interpretation' (2017) 133 LQR 546; Ewan McKendrick, 'Interpretation' in William Day and Sarah Worthington (eds), *Challenging Private Law: Lord Sumption on the Supreme Court* (Hart Publishing 2020).

[8] [2017] UKSC 24, [2017] AC 1173, [15].

[9] See eg Gerard McMeel, *McMeel on the Construction of Contracts* (3rd edn, OUP 2017) 109; Catherine Mitchell, *Interpretation of Contracts* (2nd ed, Routledge 2018) 66.

[10] In particular, in Ludwig Wittgenstein, *Philosophical Investigations* (GEM Anscombe tr, 3rd edn, Basil Blackwell 1967) (hereafter Wittgenstein, *Philosophical Investigations*), and writers drawing on his work. See also HP Grice, *Studies in the Way of Words* (Harvard UP 1989).

autonomous, in the sense that it is detached from the world. Sense or meaning is given by the use to which it is put by the person using it.[11] This view of language necessarily involves greater recourse to context in order to explain how the words in which a contract has been expressed are being used, and with what object. How is the agent using the words, as a tool to convey the meaning he or she wishes? As Adam Kramer says, 'meaning is discovered by the recognition of the fact that the communicator intended it to be discovered'.[12] Lord Hoffmann's speech in *ICS* seems to be infused with this philosophically informed view of language.[13]

The jurisprudential tradition associated with HLA Hart emphasizes the relative indeterminacy of language and hence of the law, which depends on language.[14] Natural languages like English are 'irreducibly open-textured'.[15] As a result, law and legal rules also have an open texture.[16] We do not live in a world suitable for 'mechanical' jurisprudence, in which no choice has to be made to determine the meaning of a text or utterance which is to be given normative effect across time: 'human legislators can have no such knowledge of all the possible combinations of circumstances which the future may bring. This inability to anticipate brings with it a relative indeterminacy of aim.'[17] New and unanticipated cases arise which call for the judge to supply a specific degree of determinacy in the language and the aim of the rule, when applying it to decide the case at hand in accordance with it. As Hart put it:

> When the unenvisaged case does arise, we confront the issues at stake and can then settle the question by choosing between the competing issues in the way that best satisfies us. In doing so we shall have rendered more determinate our initial aim, and shall incidentally have settled a question as to the meaning, for the purposes of this rule, of a general word.[18]

For these purposes, where the enforcement of the rule, such as in a contract, depends on the decision of a judge, what 'best satisfies us' is what best satisfies the judge.[19] But at the same time, the linguistic formulation of the rule, since it appeals to general standards of language in relation to which there is *some* (and often a considerable) degree of settled meaning, albeit it might become questionable in marginal cases, does provide substantial guidance independent of the judgment of a judicial official.

It is not feasible to expect that words can be used with total clarity as regards their application in all future circumstances. But this feature of language does not mean that the careful use of language serves no purpose. On the contrary, language may be used in a way which clearly and adequately does serve the primary objects which the parties have in mind

---

[11] See the account in GP Baker and PMS Hacker, *Wittgenstein: Understanding and Meaning* (Blackwell 1980), in particular ch VIII ('A word has a meaning only in the context of a sentence'), ch XI ('Vagueness and determinacy of sense'), ch XVI ('Understanding and Ability'), ch XVII ('Meaning and Understanding').

[12] Adam Kramer, 'Common Sense Principles of Contract Interpretation (And How We've Been Using Them All Along)' (2003) 23 OJLS 173, 175.

[13] See also Lord Hoffmann, 'The Intolerable Wrestle with Words and Meaning' (1997) 56 SALJ 565.

[14] See HLA Hart, *The Concept of Law* (Joseph Raz and Penelope A Bulloch eds, 3rd edn, OUP 2012), ch VII, 'Formalism and Rule-Scepticism'.

[15] ibid 128.

[16] ibid 124–36.

[17] ibid 128.

[18] ibid 129.

[19] ibid 135.

when they choose it. The indeterminacy in marginal, unanticipated cases does not constitute ignorance about its meaning. It is just that, as regards those cases, 'We do not know
the boundaries because none have been drawn . . . we can draw a boundary—for a special
purpose. Does it take that to make the concept usable? Not at all! (Except for that special
purpose.)'[20] In the contractual legal context, the special purpose is the application of a legal
rule in a situation which was not immediately and clearly in the contemplation of the parties when they framed their rule, but where it is accepted that the rule has to be interpreted
both to see whether it has any application at all and, if it does, to work out what it must be
taken to mean. The parties will frame their contract by focusing on what is most directly important to them, and their choice of language will be directed to that. But since the language
is used to create a legal bond between them which has wider implications and constitutes
more of a shared world than they could readily construct in detail for themselves, which
covers more cases than they had directly in their minds, the legal solution to a dispute has to
be capable of dealing with the marginal cases which are within the ambit of the shared world
of the contract but are not its primary focus. The courts have to do this by constructing
meaning, by drawing inferences about what the parties are likely to have intended, which
really means would reasonably have intended, had they concentrated more directly on the
situation which has now occurred and given rise to the dispute.

The potential extent of legitimate disagreement about linguistic meaning is reduced further by the specification of an accepted methodology for how to address the resolution of
the cases of uncertainty at the margins of linguistic meaning. However, such a methodology
cannot wholly eliminate the uncertainty which might arise and in the ultimate analysis difficult cases can only be resolved by an exercise of judgment.

These features of language and law find expression in the cases. Exactly where within the
open-textured range of meaning of a word or sentence the precise meaning is intended to
be fixed is governed to a large extent by an understanding of the purpose for which the word
or sentence is being used. As explained by Hart, however, that purpose may itself require
elaboration by the person applying the rule which contains that language. Again, there is
no significant difference in this respect between statutory interpretation and contractual
interpretation.

Words are not regarded as having simple, fixed meanings like building blocks. As Lord
Mance put it:

> In matters of statutory construction, the statutory purpose and the general scheme
> by which it is to be put into effect are of central importance. They represent the context
> in which individual words are to be understood . . . 'the notion of words having a nat-
> ural meaning' is not always very helpful . . . , and certainly not as a starting point, before
> identifying the legislative purpose and scheme.[21]

Similarly, Lord Nicholls, discussing the meaning of the words 'occupier' and 'occupation' as
used in a statute, said:

---

[20] Wittgenstein, *Philosophical Investigations* (n 10) [69].
[21] *Bloomsbury International Ltd v Department for Environment, Food and Rural Affairs* [2011] UKSC 25; [2011]
1 WLR 1546, [10].

[T]he concept of occupation is not a legal term of art, with one single and precise legal meaning applicable in all circumstances. Its meaning varies according to the subject matter. Like most ordinary English words 'occupied', and corresponding expressions such as occupier and occupation, have different shades of meaning according to the context in which they are being used . . . In many factual situations questions of occupation will attract the same answer, whatever the context . . . the answer in situations which are not so clear cut is affected by the purpose for which the concept of occupation is being used. In such situations the purpose for which the distinction between occupation and non-occupation is being drawn, and the consequences flowing from the presence or absence of occupation, will throw light on what sort of activities are or are not to be regarded as occupation in the particular context.[22]

The juristic nature of the exercise of interpretation of a contract draws judges and litigants into an exploration of the context in which words are uttered or written with a view to making a binding contract. It follows from the objective approach to contract interpretation, which is normatively justified for the reasons given above, that both the user of the words and the recipient of them are constructs rather than real people. A contract is taken to be an exercise in joint authorship, where the subjective understanding of neither party is determinative of the intended meaning. That the recipient is a construct is made clear by the way in which the courts ask how a reasonable person, situated as the parties were, would have understood the words used. This also implies that the user is a construct, as is also brought out by commentators, who emphasize that it is assumed that the language of the contract was deliberately chosen by the parties with the shared intention of giving it a particular meaning and that the parties were acting as reasonable and rational people.[23] Since both parties are constructs (indeed, on one view, they could be seen as aspects of the same construct) and interpretation is truly an exercise in construction of meaning in that context, rather than a function of evidence about the particular subjective psychological state of either party (other than to establish what aspects of the factual matrix were known to them), some understanding of the context is in fact critical for the interpretative exercise.

Where the language used in a contract is clear as to the result for a particular case, the court can confidently proceed on the basis that this represents the joint intention of the parties for that case. Such an approach provides a good discipline for the parties to think carefully about what is important for them and to specify this clearly. The better and more precise the drafting, the less there is for the courts to do in making sense of it and the more the norm-specifying space is truly filled by the parties.[24]

On the other hand, where the contractual language is not clear, the courts have to move to identify the parties' joint intention as to meaning at a higher level of abstraction, employing a wider range of materials. Then, the inference to be drawn as to their intention is more debatable and obscure. One may be dealing with a situation to which they had given no thought at all or which, in negotiation, they left to one side as too difficult, perhaps in the hope it would never arise. Interpretation then shades into construction. This involves a

---

[22] *Graysim Holdings Ltd v P & O Property Holdings Ltd* [1996] AC 329, 334–35 (HL).

[23] George Leggatt, 'Making Sense of Contracts: the rational choice theory' (2015) 131 LQR 454, 467–68; Kim Lewison, *The Interpretation of Contracts* (7th edn, Sweet & Maxwell Ltd 2020) [1.18]–[1.19] and [2.08].

[24] Cf Philip Sales, 'The Contribution of Legislative Drafting to the Rule of Law' (2018) 77 CLJ 630, 632, making a similar point about legislation.

process of imagining how contracting parties placed as these ones were would have wished the contractual rule to be articulated and applied in this new situation.

The court is then effectively obliged to proceed by reference to what a *reasonable* combination of contracting parties would have wished to do if they had notice of the problem, and to call on a wider range of aids to interpretation which offer clues to answering that question. It is still possible to locate this constructed meaning within a framework of inference as to the parties' joint intention, operating as a sort of hybrid subject, the intention of which may be inferred in appropriate cases from these wider background factors. Writing about legislation, in a well-known formulation, Henry Hart and Albert Sacks said judges should presume legislators are 'reasonable men pursuing reasonable purposes reasonably'.[25] The same presumption applies as regards the parties to a contract, who are private legislators creating their own shared legal world.

In constructing models of the contracting parties like this, there is scope for a judge to inject an element of his or her own values and predispositions as normative content to fill out the idea of the reasonable author. What a judge thinks a reasonable person would do is likely to reflect to some degree the judge's own values and expectations. However, the principle of a contract as self-legislation by the parties requires that the inquiry should be framed as one into the presumed intention of them as agents. It is relatively simple to posit the parties as a unified person exercising their own agency, and to look for clues in the properly available evidence as to how that person would have been likely to have intended to resolve the particular case.

The available clues are the language chosen by the parties, the internal scheme of the contract, and the background factual context or matrix in which the contract was made (in so far as that casts light on the purposes the parties were trying to achieve when they made it). There is no simple metric or stated rule which can govern where the balance is struck between linguistic meaning and internal and external context. These are incommensurable ingredients, all of which are relevant for a legal solution. Certainty and predictability therefore require a high degree of regularity of approach among legal practitioners.[26] To a significant degree, this depends upon the strength of the legal culture as well as upon statements of the methodology to be used.[27]

As regards methodology, the Supreme Court has said that a court should have regard to (i) the conventional meaning of the disputed words, (ii) the consistency of rival meanings with other parts of the contract and its scheme, (iii) the overall purpose of the disputed clause and the wider contract, (iv) the context in which the contract was concluded, and (v) common sense.[28] This is helpful to a degree, in that following this methodology may sufficiently resolve a doubt about meaning, but it can be said that it also poses and does not resolve the tension which might be found to exist in more difficult cases. Similarly, the description of the process of interpretation as involving an iterative process, according to which the interpreter shuttles between linguistic meaning and how that fits with the scheme

---

[25] Henry M Hart and Albert M Sacks, *The Legal Process: Basic Problems in the Making and Application of Law* (William N Eskridge, Jr and Philip P Frickey eds, Foundation Press 1994) 1124–25.

[26] Cf Sales and Wilmot-Smith, 'Justice' (n 2) 594–95.

[27] See eg Shivprasad Swaminathan, '*Mos Geometricus* and the Common Law Mind: Interrogating Contract Theory' (2019) 82 MLR 46, 66–70; Karl N Llewellyn, *The Common Law Tradition: Deciding Appeals* (Little Brown 1960) 185–86, 202, 213–16.

[28] *Arnold v Britton* (n 5) [15] (Lord Neuberger).

160   ANTINOMIES AND BOUNDARIES

of the contract and its overall purpose as suggested by the background factual context,[29] is helpful up to a point, but does not resolve every disputed issue of interpretation.

Lord Hodge explained the position pithily in *Wood v Capita*, in a paragraph which efficiently encapsulates the approach to be adopted:

> Textualism and contextualism are not conflicting paradigms in a battle for exclusive occupation of the field of contractual interpretation. Rather, the lawyer and the judge, when interpreting any contract, can use them as tools to ascertain the objective meaning of the language which the parties have chosen to express their agreement. The extent to which each tool will assist the court in its task will vary according to the circumstances of the particular agreement or agreements. Some agreements may be successfully interpreted principally by textual analysis, for example because of their sophistication and complexity and because they have been negotiated and prepared with the assistance of skilled professionals. The correct interpretation of other contracts may be achieved by a greater emphasis on the factual matrix, for example because of their informality, brevity or the absence of skilled professional assistance. But negotiators of complex formal contracts may often not achieve a logical and coherent text because of, for example, the conflicting aims of the parties, failures of communication, differing drafting practices, or deadlines which require the parties to compromise in order to reach agreement. There may often therefore be provisions in a detailed professionally drawn contract which lack clarity and the lawyer or judge in interpreting such provisions may be particularly helped by considering the factual matrix and the purpose of similar provisions in contracts of the same type. The iterative process, of which Lord Mance spoke in *Sigma Finance Corporation* . . . assists the lawyer or judge to ascertain the objective meaning of disputed provisions.[30]

A court has to consider the contract as a whole and, depending on the nature, formality, and quality of its drafting, has to give more or less weight to elements of the wider context in reaching its view as to its objective meaning.

Lord Hodge employs the metaphor of tools, which in turn involves emphasis on the purpose for which the tool is being used. But while it is helpful to draw attention to the importance of the purpose for which language is being used and to the different weight to be given to linguistic meaning in the context of a complex and professionally drawn contract and in a more informally drawn contract, this is not a formulation which entirely resolves the underlying tensions which may exist between the different elements which constitute the process.

It is also a formulation which does not wholly capture a further aspect of the underlying clash of values which may be relevant in interpreting a contract, namely the competing claims of the need to provide certainty and the desire to ensure a fair and just outcome in a particular case, in the light of full knowledge of all the circumstances when the contractual rule falls to be applied. This important dimension in contractual interpretation, which can also be regarded as involving an aspect of the weighting of linguistic meaning against

---

[29] See *Re Sigma Finance Corp* [2008] EWCA Civ 1303, [2009] BCC 393, [98] (Lord Neuberger), approved at [2009] UKSC 2, [2010] BCC 40, [12] (Lord Mance) (hereafter *Sigma Finance*).
[30] [2017] UKSC 24, [2017] AC 1173, [13].

context, is explored in detail by Ewan McKendrick.[31] As he explains, the importance to be attached to certainty (which tends to be associated with giving greater weight to linguistic meaning, albeit that may not be sufficient in itself to provide certainty) varies, depending on the context of the particular contract. It is at its greatest in the case of a contract drafted in detail by professionals and where the parties have roughly equal bargaining power, and so have a legitimate expectation that the courts will give effect to their agreement as it has been drafted. Conversely, where contracts are concluded on an informal basis (but are agreements which are intended to have binding legal effect) or are expressed in open and flexible terms, 'the need for certainty is less obvious and it therefore weighs less heavily in the scales'.[32]

The so-called iterative approach can be regarded as an approach which is continuous with previous approaches to interpretation, as Lord Hodge was at pains to explain in *Wood v Capita*, rather than as a radical departure. But it might be said that this is because it does not tell one very much that was not already obvious, and like previous formulations does not resolve or dissolve the underlying competition of values which the courts have to determine. To speak of checking rival linguistic meanings against the other provisions and scheme of the contract is just a way of saying that a contract has to be construed as an integrated whole, which is a very basic feature of the interpretation of any legal instrument. 'In the construction of all instruments it is the duty of the court not to confine itself to the force of a particular expression but to collect the intention from the whole instrument taken together.'[33] To say that rival meanings have to be checked against the commercial context is just to say that one should have regard to the likely purposes the parties, situated as they were, had in making the contract in the first place. But these can be read widely or narrowly, as the debate about the significance of and weight to be attached to business common sense in *Rainy Sky SA v Kookmin Bank*[34] makes clear.[35]

Turning to legal culture, its importance is not always emphasized in the context of debates about the meaning of contracts, but it is real. This reflects another feature of language, on the Wittgensteinian account: 'If language is to be a means of communication there must be agreement not only in definitions but also (queer as this may sound) in judgment.'[36] Wittgenstein elaborates on this point: 'Let me ask this: what has the expression of a rule— say a sign-post—got to do with my actions? . . . I have been trained to react to this sign in a particular way, and now I do so react to it . . . A person goes by a sign-post only in so far as there exists a regular use of sign-posts, a custom.'[37]

---

[31] Ewan McKendrick, 'Commercial Contract Law: How Important Is the Quest for Certainty?' [2021] LMCLQ 72.

[32] ibid 72.

[33] *Hume v Rundell* (1824) 2 S & S 174, 177; 57 ER 311 (Leach V-C).

[34] [2011] UKSC 50, [2011] 1 WLR 2900. See also, eg, Neil Andrews, 'Interpretation of Contracts and "Commercial Common Sense": Do Not Overplay This Useful Criterion' (2017) 76 CLJ 36; Lord Hodge, 'Can Judges Use Business Common Sense in Interpreting Contracts?' in Larry DiMatteo and Martin Hogg (eds), *Comparative Contract Law: British and American Perspectives* (OUP 2015).

[35] Similarly, the divergence of view between the judiciary at all levels in *Sigma Finance* (n 29) can be regarded as a function of differences as to the weight to be attached to commercial sense against linguistic meaning. See also the difference of view in *Bank of Credit and Commerce International v Ali* [2001] UKHL 8, [2002] AC 251 (hereafter *BCCI v Ali*).

[36] Wittgenstein, *Philosophical Investigations* (n 10) [242]. See the discussion in GP Baker and PMS Hacker, Wittgenstein: Rules, Grammar and Necessity (Basil Blackwell 1985) ch V, 'Agreements in Definitions, Judgements and Forms of Life'.

[37] Wittgenstein, *Philosophical Investigations* (n 10) [198].

It has often been noted that the ability of English law to operate with a high degree of formality in the interpretation of contracts and statutes is related to the close-knit legal culture which exists among judges and practitioners:

> The homogeneity of the English judiciary (and the senior bar) is of immense importance to the whole legal culture of England; it certainly plays a part in determining how questions of law are viewed and decided . . . to the extent that judges share the same 'inarticulate major premises', traditional legal reasoning is not nearly so bogus as American realism has been credited with demonstrating.[38]

Karl Llewellyn makes a similar point about how deciding cases according to law actually works, in the context of an overall doctrinal environment which is assumed more than it is articulated. The idea of the law embraces 'the skill and the traditions of the crafts of law, the ways of seeing, thinking, feeling, doing, and duty in and into which the craftsmen—the body of craftsmen—have been reared'.[39] The law controls what a judge does 'in good part by moulding in advance his sense of "what is sense" '.[40]

Senior courts can exercise a guidance function to some degree, both by issuing statements of principle (even though, like any rule, the statements do not apply themselves) and by seeking to set the mood or tone of the culture in which the principles are applied. Thus there is the debate described above about whether there has been a change in the law regarding interpretation of contracts pursuant to recent decisions of the Supreme Court, in the form of a retreat from the approach in the *ICS* case, which appeared to emphasize background context, in the later cases of *Arnold v Britton* and *Wood v Capita*, which appeared to place greater emphasis on textual meaning.[41]

However, to ask only about the statement of the legal rules misses the cultural dimension, which is also important. Lord Sumption has described this as a matter of 'mood': 'Instinct and mood play an important role in judicial analysis, and *ICS* changed the mood among judges dealing with commercial contracts in ways which are altogether more fundamental [than any change of the rules].'[42] As he went on: 'Just as *ICS* changed the judicial mood about language and tended to encourage the view that it was basically unimportant, so the more recent cases may in due course be seen to have changed it back again, at least to some degree.'[43]

The prevailing culture or mood about the proper resolution of conflicts between incommensurable values can provide some determinacy and predictability, as is emphasized in

---

[38] PS Atiyah and Robert S Summers, *Form and Substance in Anglo-American Law: A Comparative Study of Legal Reasoning, Legal Theory and Legal Institutions* (Clarendon 1987) 355. See also Max Weber, *Economy and Society: An Outline of Interpretative Sociology*, vol 2 (Guenther Roth and Claus Wittich eds, Ephraim Fischoff tr, University of California Press 1979) 759, 794; Roger Cotterrell, *Law's Community: Legal Theory in Sociological Perspective* (OUP 1995) 170. William Scheuerman argues in *Frankfurt School Perspectives on Globalization, Democracy and the Law* (Routledge 2008) 43, that, similarly in international arbitration, where the flexible standards of the lex mercatoria may be applied, a certain amount of regularity and predictability is achieved as a result of 'the relative homogeneity of legal decision makers and the fact that arbitrators and international business share relatively similar social interests and ideological views'.

[39] Karl N Llewellyn, *The Common Law Tradition: Deciding Appeals* (1960) 185.

[40] ibid 202.

[41] *ICS* (n 3); *Arnold v Britton* (n 5); *Wood v Capita* (n 6).

[42] Jonathan Sumption, 'A Question of Taste: The Supreme Court and the Interpretation of Contracts' (2017) 17(2) OUCLJ 301, 306.

[43] ibid 314.

Llewellyn's account. The mood in the legal system provides guidance for a judge interpreting a contract, to help them decide on the proper balance between the linguistic meaning of the text and the commercial purposes the judge thinks the parties to the contract had in mind. As well as contributing to mood, or the setting of the cultural environment in which agreements fall to be interpreted, by demonstration through their own practice, senior appellate courts have a role in seeking explicitly to calibrate the mood by express statements, such as those in *ICS*, *Arnold v Britton*, and *Wood v Capita*. But these statements only provide guidance as to how the disparate elements regarded as relevant to the exercise of interpretation should be balanced, and thereby reduce the scope for dissension and unpredictability to some degree; they are not capable of eliminating the uncertainty which inheres in having to balance them in the first place.

A further puzzle related to this concerns the extent to which the interpretation of a contract should be regarded as a question of law, which an appellate court is entitled to decide afresh for itself and substitute its view for that of the first instance judge, if it disagrees with them. It is not obvious why this should be so. For many issues, the approach of an appellate court is to decline to substitute its own view of a matter for that of the judge, especially where the relevant legal principles to be applied are clear (as they are in the field of contractual interpretation) and the assessment to be made relates to the application of the principles to the particular facts of a case, in circumstances where the factual context (usually a matter for the assessment of the judge at first instance) is important.[44] The interpretation of a contract depends on a mixture of facts and a normative element, but the normative element is itself heavily informed by assessment of the evidence: how would reasonable persons placed like the parties have understood the words? So why is the meaning of a contract treated as a pure question of law, open to the unconstrained judgment of an appellate court?

In *Carmichael v National Power Plc* Lord Hoffmann explained that for historic reasons it has been determined that questions of law are 'questions which cannot be correctly answered except by someone skilled in the law', and 'questions of fact which lawyers have decided judges can answer better than juries', where the second category included the construction of documents'.[45] He said of this:

> [T]he rule was adopted in trials by jury for purely pragmatic reasons. In mediaeval times juries were illiterate and most of the documents which came before a jury were deeds drafted by lawyers. In the 18th and 19th centuries the rule was maintained because it was essential to the development of English commercial law. There could have been no precedent and no certainty in the construction of standard commercial documents if questions of construction had been left in each case to a jury which gave no reasons for its decision.[46]

However, a separate question arises regarding the role for an appellate court where reasons are given by judges at first instance, and in many situations the role of the appellate court is one of review to ensure that what the judge has done falls within acceptable parameters rather than one of substitution of its own fresh decision. Lord Hoffmann's statement implies that it is possible that, if access to appellate courts came under great pressure and had to be

---

[44] cf Philip Sales, 'Proportionality Review in Appellate Courts' (2021) 26 JR 40.
[45] [1999] 1 WLR 2042, 2048–49 (HL), citing from Lord Devlin's Hamlyn Lectures on *Trial by Jury* (1956).
[46] ibid.

164 ANTINOMIES AND BOUNDARIES

further limited to allow the court system to operate efficiently and with a minimum of delay, additional criteria might be applied in terms of pragmatic reasons to explain when an appellate court should be prepared to treat something as a question of law in relation to which it should act as primary decision-maker. It could be argued that this should only be when the issue of construction has wider ramifications than the context of the particular contract (eg because it arises in the context of standard commercial documents of the type to which Lord Hoffmann referred).

II. The Boundaries of Contractual Interpretation

Although the interpretation of contracts can appear to be a technical matter with only limited doctrinal significance, in fact the boundaries of what a court will do in interpreting a contract are of critical significance across a range of issues in the law of obligations. Those boundaries have changed over time, and this may have important implications for doctrine within and outside contract.

At the most basic level, the courts' approach to contractual interpretation governs whether a contract can be said to exist. The courts' approach to interpretation determines the extent to which a judge is authorized to fill in blanks left by the parties in order to conclude that a contract has been made, rather than some arrangement which is incomplete and hence ineffective or a mere unenforceable agreement to agree.[47]

It is often the case that crucial terms, such as the price, are not expressly agreed, and the court can imply a term that a reasonable price be paid.[48] The courts will be especially sympathetic to adopting this approach if a transaction has been carried into effect. As Steyn LJ observed in *G Percy Trentham Ltd v Archital Luxfer Ltd*, 'the fact that the transaction is executed makes it easier to imply a term resolving any uncertainty, or, alternatively, it may make it possible to treat a matter not finalized in negotiations as inessential'.[49] Lord Clarke made a similar point in *RTS Flexible Systems Ltd v Molkerei Alois Müller GmbH*:

> Even if certain terms of economic or other significance have not been finalised, an objective appraisal of [the parties'] words and conduct may lead to the conclusion that they did not intend agreement of such terms to be a precondition to a concluded and legally binding agreement.[50]

In *G Scammel & Nephew Ltd v HC and JG Ouston,* Lord Wright emphasized the connection between doing justice and the approach to interpretation:

> The object of the court is to do justice between the parties, and the court will do its best, if satisfied that there was an ascertainable and determinate intention to contract, to give effect to that intention, looking at substance and not mere form. It will not be deterred by

---

[47] See, eg, the debate regarding the enforceability of agreements to negotiate in good faith: *Walford v Miles* [1992] 2 AC 128 (HL); Alan Berg, 'Promises to Negotiate in Good Faith' (2003) 119 LQR 357; Edwin Peel, 'Agreements to Negotiate in Good Faith' in Andrew Burrows and Edwin Peel (eds), *Contract Formation and Parties* (OUP 2010).

[48] *Foley v Classique Coaches* [1934] 2 KB 1 (CA); *British Bank for Foreign Trade v Novinex* [1949] 1 KB 623 (CA).

[49] [1993] 1 Lloyd's Rep 25, 27 (CA).

[50] [2010] UKSC 14; [2010] 1 WLR 753, [45].

mere difficulties of interpretation. Difficulty is not synonymous with ambiguity so long as any definite meaning can be extracted. But the test of intention is to be found in the words used. If these words, considered however broadly and untechnically and with due regard to all the just implications, fail to evince any definite meaning on which the court can safely act, the court has no choice but to say that there is no contract. Such a position is not often found.[51]

Wells v Devani[52] provides a good recent example which illustrates the importance of the approach to interpretation in terms of identifying the doctrinal boundary, whether a contract existed or not. The claimant agreed to act as agent for the sale of the defendant's property and a dispute arose as to whether the claimant was entitled to commission on a sale which he had facilitated. At a basic level it appeared that the parties intended to make a binding contract requiring payment of commission, but the Court of Appeal said that the contract did not specify the event (whether introduction of prospective purchaser, exchange of contract, completion, or otherwise) on the basis of which it would become payable and therefore it was incomplete and ineffective. The Supreme Court allowed the appeal. It was prepared to interpret the terms used by the parties as covering the payment of commission upon completion and out of the proceeds of sale, and even had that not been possible it would have held that an equivalent term was to be implied.

Contractual interpretation is also critical for determining other doctrinal boundaries. This is because it is relevant to deciding the extent to which the courts will treat a contract as encapsulating the shared legal world which the parties wished to create for themselves. This is a function of doctrinal conceptions regarding the interaction of different areas of law, which in turn inform the interpretation of the contract. Since contract is taken to represent the will of the parties,[53] and consent of a person is taken to provide an especially strong foundation for treating them as subject to legal obligations, the usual position is that contract trumps or at least moulds obligations which have other foundations.

Accordingly, where a duty of care in tort arises out of a contractual arrangement, it will be fashioned in the light of the objective interpretation of the contract.[54]

Where a contractual arrangement also gives rise to fiduciary obligations, even if those obligations exist as something over and above the pure contractual duties, still the contract may have a moulding function. In certain paradigm situations, where one party has assumed to act in relation to the property or affairs of another, the content of the fiduciary obligations which arise will be reasonably standard and well-known,[55] and it will require very clear contract terms to depart from them. This is also true in relation to contract terms which are said to disapply ordinary rights or remedies available to a party.[56] But in other situations, the ambit of fiduciary obligations falls to be moulded around the contract the

---

[51] [1941] AC 251, 268 (HL).

[52] [2019] UKSC 4; [2020] AC 129.

[53] Albeit subject to the application of the objective approach described above (text at n 30).

[54] See eg authorities on concurrent duties of care in contract and tort: for instance *Wilson v Merry & Cunningham* (1868) LR 1 HL Sc 326, 332 (Lord Cairns LC); *Tai Hing Cotton Mill Ltd v Liu Chong Bank Ltd* [1986] AC 519; *Forsikringsaktieselskapet Vesta v Butcher* [1989] AC 852; *Henderson v Merrett Syndicates* [1995] 2 AC 145; *Manchester Building Society v Grant Thornton UK LLP* [2021] UKSC 20, [2022] AC 783.

[55] See *White v Jones* [1995] 2 AC 207, 271 (Lord Browne-Wilkinson) (HL).

[56] *Gilbert-Ash (Northern) Ltd v Modern Engineering (Bristol) Ltd* [1974] AC 689, 717 (Lord Diplock) (HL) (hereafter *Gilbert-Ash*).

166   ANTINOMIES AND BOUNDARIES

parties have made, and equity takes care not to distort their bargain by importing an exces-sive degree of obligation over and above this.[57]

So, for example, the existence and scope of the fiduciary obligations of agents depends upon the terms on which they are acting. In *New Zealand Netherlands Society 'Oranje' Inc v Kuys*, Lord Wilberforce said:

> The obligation not to profit from a position of trust, or, as it is sometimes relevant to put it, not to allow a conflict to arise between duty and interest, is one of strictness. The strength, and indeed the severity, of the rule has recently been emphasised by the House of Lords: *Phipps v. Boardman* [1967] 2 AC 46. It retains its vigour in all jurisdictions where the principles of equity are applied. Naturally it has different applications in different contexts. It applies, in principle, whether the case is one of a trust, express or implied, of partnership, of directorship of a limited company, of principal and agent, or master and servant, but the precise scope of it must be moulded according to the nature of the relationship. As Lord Upjohn said in *Phipps v. Boardman*, at p. 123: 'Rules of equity have to be applied to such a great diversity of circumstances that they can be stated only in the most general terms and applied with particular attention to the exact circumstances of each case.'[58]

In an influential judgment in the High Court of Australia in *Hospital Products Ltd v United States Surgical Corporation*, Mason J said:

> That contractual and fiduciary relationships may co-exist between the same parties has never been doubted. Indeed, the existence of a basic contractual relationship has in many situations provided a foundation for the erection of a fiduciary relationship. In these situ-ations it is the contractual foundation which is all important because it is the contract that regulates the basic rights and liabilities of the parties. The fiduciary relationship, if it is to exist at all, must accommodate itself to the terms of the contract so that it is consistent with, and conforms to, them. The fiduciary relationship cannot be superimposed upon the contract in such a way as to alter the operation which the contract was intended to have ac-cording to its true construction.[59]

This approach implies another element of uncertainty. To what extent does equity impose obligations over and above what appears from the contract? To what extent do equitable conceptions inform the content of the contract (as does the general law regarding remedies for breach of contract according to the approach in the *Gilbert-Ash* case[60])? To what extent does the contract control the impact of equity?[61]

The answers to these questions are further complicated by changing conceptions over long periods of time of the strictness with which contracts will be read in accordance with their linguistic meaning and the extent to which the courts will interpret them in a broadly purposive manner. This can be illustrated by consideration of the equitable doctrine of

---

[57] Lord Neuberger of Abbotsbury, 'The Stuffing of Minerva's Owl? Taxonomy and Taxidermy in Equity' (2009) 68 CLJ 537, 543; *Kelly v Cooper Associates* [1993] AC 205, 214–15 (Lord Browne-Wilkinson) (PC).

[58] [1973] 1 WLR 1126, 1129–30 (PC).

[59] [1984] HCA 64, (1984) 156 CLR 41, 97.

[60] *Gilbert-Ash* (n 56).

[61] For discussion, see eg Lord Briggs, 'Equity in Business' (2019) 135 LQR 567.

fraud on a power,[62] which now is characterized as a rule that a fiduciary power should be exercised for proper purposes.[63] The original doctrine developed historically as a way to control misuse of powers in circumstances in which the then applicable interpretive approach was not capable of supplying such controls, because the dominant emphasis was on the strict linguistic meaning of deeds and other instruments. But modern approaches to interpretation give greater emphasis to spelling out interpretive content according to the evident purpose of the parties.[64] Although this seems amply justified according to modern conceptions of the interpretive exercise appropriate to a wide range of legal instruments, it does have the effect of somewhat obscuring the boundary between interpretation (including of contracts) and the imposition of obligations by equity, *dehors* the instrument. This is not least because the range of matters to which it is relevant to have regard to determine the content of the proper purpose rule in equity are the same as those to which it is relevant to have regard for the purposes of interpretation, according to modern practice.[65]

In *After Virtue*, Alasdair MacIntyre analysed the state of modern moral discourse as using conceptions drawn from an Aristotelian tradition, framed in terms of virtue, which have lost their meaning or had it distorted when torn from the context of that tradition and used as part of a different conception of morality.[66] This seems to have resonance in this context as well. Concepts of equity were drawn, historically, from the Aristotelian tradition,[67] and were used against the background of a more limited approach to interpretation. Perhaps, rather than trying to give equitable doctrines in all cases the same meaning as they had hundreds of years ago, change should be contemplated. As the approach to interpretation changes and becomes more inherently equitable in nature, it is natural to expect that the boundary between contract and equity should change.

It is important to see that the positioning of this boundary is a function of the approach to the interpretation of instruments which establish the basic framework for the relevant legal relationship between the parties, including in particular contracts. A contract is the regime the parties have chosen for themselves to establish their relationship. If the practice of interpretation has expanded to accommodate wider aspects of the relationship, it is that practice and the contract itself which ought to govern, with the consequence that the distinct role of equity becomes more limited.

Frederick Schauer comments, with reference to Karl Llewellyn's theory of law, that the propositional form of law is distinct from what it actually does, in terms of how it is interpreted and applied by the courts, which is 'a function of a complex array of rules, practices, conventions, professional skills, and, at times, idiosyncrasies, most of which are devoted to trying to achieve a rule's purpose (or "reason"), rather than just following its letter'.[68] If one adopts a strong purposive approach to the interpretation of rules, the rule (in its pure linguistic from) tends towards surplusage, and the real rule is redefined as a combination of text, background and principle which together generate a just result: 'a long tradition, with

---

[62] *Vatcher v Paull* [1915] AC 372 (PC).

[63] *Grand View Private Trust Co Ltd v Wong* [2022] UKPC 47, [51]–[63].

[64] I discuss this in more detail in Philip Sales, 'Use of Powers for Proper Purposes in Private Law' (2020) 136 LQR 384.

[65] *Grand View Private Trust Co Ltd v Wong* [2022] UKPC 47, [61]–[63].

[66] Alasdair MacIntyre, After Virtue: A Study in Moral Theory (3rd edn, Duckworth 2007).

[67] See eg *The Earl of Oxford's Case* (1615) 1 Ch Rep 1; 21 ER 485.

[68] Frederick Schauer, 'Introduction' in Karl N Llewellyn, *The Theory of Rules* (Frederick Schauer ed, University of Chicago Press 2011) 7.

168 ANTINOMIES AND BOUNDARIES

Llewellyn as one of the pioneers, seeks to redefine prescriptive rules so that they incorporate what are in reality anti-rule perspectives.'[69] As Schauer notes, this is a strong tendency in US legal thought. Clearly, it is less pronounced in English law. But there is nonetheless a significant element of it in modern approaches to contractual interpretation, as cases like the *Scammel & Nephew* decision and *Wells v Divani* illustrate.

Finally under this heading, it is the practice of interpretation which is a key driving force in governing the boundary between contract and unjust enrichment. Where a contract between the parties governs the terms of their relationship, this displaces any application of the law of unjust enrichment.[70] The *Pan Ocean Shipping* case[71] concerned the right of a charterer of a ship to recover hire which proved to have been overpaid, where the charterer sought to rely on the law of unjust enrichment (restitution) in seeking recovery. Lord Goff explained that the contract contemplated that hire might have to be repaid under certain circumstances and was to be construed as governing how that should be happen, including if necessary by the implication of a term for repayment of the overpaid amount. He explained:

> All this is important for present purposes, because it means that, as between shipowner and charterer, there is a contractual regime which legislates for the recovery of overpaid hire. It follows that, as a general rule, the law of restitution has no part to play in the matter; the existence of the agreed regime renders the imposition by the law of a remedy in restitution both unnecessary and inappropriate.[72]

If, through interpretation of the contract, including the implication of terms, the relevant aspect of the parties' relationship is governed by the contractual regime, this displaces other solutions which might otherwise have been imposed as a matter of application of the general law. The justice of the case will itself inform the interpretation of express terms and whether a term should be implied, so it appears that, as with equity, while contract will displace unjust enrichment, unjust enrichment ideas are capable of informing what interpretation the contract will be found to bear.

III. Conclusion

Since contract is the pre-eminent self-chosen institution for the regulation of relations between parties, the interpretation of contracts is a subject of major importance. This is both in terms of the determination of disputes arising out of contracts and also in terms of governing the boundaries between contract law and other areas of the law of obligations. Contractual interpretation poses certain puzzles, the resolution of which depends finally on the decision actually made in a particular case. There are antinomies which arise from the necessity of balancing different, incommensurable elements within an overall practice of interpretation. There is no final a priori resolution for these antinomies. Although contract

---

[69] ibid 27.
[70] See further Edwin Peel's chapter, ch 23.
[71] *Pan Ocean Shipping Co Ltd v Creditcorp Ltd* [1994] 1 WLR 161 (HL).
[72] ibid 164 (Lord Goff of Chieveley); see also *Barton v Morris* [2023] UKSC 3; *HEB Enterprises Ltd v Richards* [2023] UKPC 7.

may displace the general law of obligations in various ways, the underlying ideas of justice which inform that general law also penetrate into contract; accordingly, the relationship between them is more reflexive than may at first appear. Ultimately, the practice of interpretation depends on what is done by courts on the ground and the judgments which individual judges are disposed to make as a result of their training and their absorption of the relevant contemporary legal culture.

The extent of the uncertainty created by these antinomies can be managed, but not fully eliminated, by the work of senior appellate courts in seeking to lead the formation of the standards arising from that culture and in attempting to calibrate those standards. But according to where they perceive their advantage to lie, parties will always seek to exploit these antinomies in argument by emphasizing the particular elements in the overall mix which happen to suit their case. In the final analysis, where, after hearing argument, there is dispute within the judiciary as to the interpretation of a contract,[73] this has to be resolved in the usual manner available to a system based on authority, by a majority decision at whatever is the relevant highest level.[74]

---

[73] See, eg, *BCCI v Ali* (n 35) and *Sigma Finance* (n 29).

[74] Which may be the Court of Appeal, in the case of a contract dispute which has no general public importance; or otherwise at the level of the Supreme Court. Cf Jeremy Waldron, *Law and Disagreement* (OUP 1999), for discussion of this issue as it arises in relation to statutory interpretation.

11

The Damage in Negotiating Damages

SARAH WORTHINGTON

I. Introduction

This chapter focuses on the crucial issue of principle left exposed in the 2018 Supreme Court decision of *Morris-Garner v One Step (Support) Ltd*.[1] The question before the Court was beguilingly simple: when can the remedy for breach of contract be assessed not by way of 'expectation damages',[2] but instead by way of 'negotiating damages',[3] being—as the label suggests—the sum which would reasonably be agreed between the parties as the price for releasing the defendant from the obligation which it failed to perform?

The Court's answer, delivered in a 30,000-word judgment, was far from simple. For the ensuing five years lawyers have struggled to unravel the judgment's key paragraphs. To provide yet another round in these debates may thus seem a poor choice for a chapter in a book titled *Shaping the Law of Obligations*. But, for good reason, the case is acknowledged to be not only difficult but also important.[4]

Unless we understand the principles underpinning different remedies, we will never properly understand the nature of the rights in issue. For all the words in *One Step*, it is still not clear exactly *when* negotiating damages will be awarded and when not, nor, more importantly, quite *why* they are awarded in some cases but not in others. This uncertainty is all the more troubling when common law damages for breach of contract are claimed not as a matter of judicial discretion but as of right, to be awarded or refused on the basis of legal principle.[5] In *One Step*, ordinary contract damages and negotiating damages are both billed as compensatory remedies for the claimant, but it seems that neither the claimant nor the court can choose freely to pursue one in preference to the other.[6]

---

[1] *Morris-Garner v One Step (Support) Ltd* [2018] UKSC 20, [2019] AC 649 (SC) (hereafter *One Step*).

[2] *Robinson v Harman* (1848) 1 Ex 850, 855 (Parke B). That typically means putting C in the same economic position as if the contract had been performed. However, if the contract is designed to provide C with non-economic benefits, those aspects can be evaluated in money and added to C's claim for compensation: *Ruxley Electronics and Construction Ltd v Forsyth* [1996] AC 344 (HL); *Jarvis v Swan Tours Ltd* [1973] QB 233.

[3] *One Step* (n 1) [3], being the majority's preferred terminology generally, although borrowed from a case concerning damages under Lord Cairns' Act; contrast the SGCA in *Turf Club Auto Emporium Pte Ltd v Yeo Boong Hua* [2018] SGCA 44, [2018] 2 SLR 655 (SGCA), preferring '*Wrotham Park* damages'.

[4] A measure of its importance can be gleaned from the number of commentators writing on it. See, eg, Andrew Burrows, 'One Step Forward?' (2018) 134 LQR 515; William Day, 'Restitution for Wrongs: One Step in the Right Direction?' (2017) 133 LQR 384; William Day, 'Restitution for Wrongs: One Step Forwards, Two Steps Back' (2018) 26 RLR 60; Adam Kramer, 'Contract Damages' in William Day and Sarah Worthington (eds), *Challenging Private Law: Lord Sumption on the Supreme Court* (2020), ch 5; Charles Mitchell and Luke Roskill, 'Making Sense of Mesne Profits: Causes of Action' (2021) 80 CLJ 130; Charles Mitchell and Luke Roskill, 'Making Sense of Mesne Profits: Remedies' (2021) 80 CLJ 552; Edwin Peel, 'Negotiating Damages after *One Step*' (2020) 35 JCL 216; Man Yip and Alvin WL See, 'One Step Away from *Morris-Garner*: *Wrotham Park* Damages in Singapore' (2029) 135 LQR 36.

[5] *One Step* (n 1) [95](12) (Lord Reed).

[6] ibid [96]–[97]. If this is what the Court meant, it is doubted. See, eg, *Strand Electric and Engineering Co Ltd v Brisford Entertainments Ltd* [1952] 2 QB 246 (CA) (hereafter *Strand Electric*); *Ministry of Defence v Ashman* (1993)

Sarah Worthington, *The Damage in Negotiating Damages* In: *Shaping the Law of Obligations*. Edited by: Edwin Peel and Rebecca Probert, Oxford University Press. © Sarah Worthington 2023. DOI: 10.1093/oso/9780198889762.003.0011

172   THE DAMAGE IN NEGOTIATING DAMAGES

II. *One Step* and the Argument Advanced in This Chapter

In *One Step* itself, the difference between the expectation damages measure and the negotiating damages measure was c.£2m, so the answer to the question before the Court was worth debating. The facts were unexceptional. C had purchased a business from D, with C's position protected by a restraint of trade covenant prohibiting D from competing for three years.[7] Less than a year later D set up in competition. Much later, well after the covenants had expired and indeed after D had sold the offending business for a substantial profit, C claimed damages for breach of contract. The proceedings at every level focused on principle, not quantification, but C's experts had assessed expectation damages (C's provable economic losses as a result of D's breaches) as c.£4m and negotiating damages (the sum for which C would reasonably have agreed to release D from the restraint of trade clause) as c.£6m.[8] The Supreme Court held that C was confined to expectation damages: neither C nor the court could elect for the more advantageous negotiating damages measure.

The majority's explanation was set out in Lord Reed's judgment.[9] Lord Reed began with a detailed assessment of the different principles underpinning damages claims in tort, in contract, under Lord Cairns' Act (LCA),[10] and in the long line of 'negotiating damages' cases that followed *Wrotham Park Estate Co Ltd v Parkside Homes Ltd*,[11] including the exceptional disgorgement remedy for breach of contract awarded in *Attorney General v Blake*.[12] He then set out the principles underpinning negotiating damages in a series of paragraphs (see especially [91]–[95]) which included the key finding that negotiating damages are available:[13]

> 92 ... *where the breach of contract results in the loss of a valuable asset created or protected by the right which was infringed, as for example in cases concerned with the breach of a restrictive covenant over land, an intellectual property agreement or a confidentiality agreement. Such cases share an important characteristic* ... The claimant has in substance been deprived of a valuable asset, and his loss can therefore be measured by determining the economic value of the asset in question. *The defendant has taken something for nothing, for which the claimant was entitled to require payment.*

This is a difficult paragraph to unravel, but that is the goal of this chapter. It may facilitate the journey to reveal my intended destination at the outset.[14]

First, the aim is not to invent new legal territory for this area. It is merely to put in place clearer signposts across the territory that already exists. Many of the present difficulties are

---

66 P&CR 195 (CA) (hereafter *MoD v Ashman*). Also contrast this with the liberty given to C to decide whether to pursue its claim for compensation by proving its expectation losses or by proving its (necessarily lower value) reliance losses, and whether to pursue only its economic losses or also its amenity damages.

   [7] And also prohibited D from soliciting C's customers or using C's confidential information.
   [8] *One Step* (n 1) [12]–[15].
   [9] With Baroness Hale PSC, Lord Wilson, and Lord Carnwath JJSC agreeing. Lord Sumption reached the same conclusion on the facts, but for different reasons.
   [10] Lord Cairns' Act 1858, s 2, now s 50 of the Senior Courts Act 1981.
   [11] *Wrotham Park Estate Co Ltd v Parkside Homes Ltd* [1974] 1 WLR 798 (Ch) (hereafter *Wrotham Park*).
   [12] *Attorney General v Blake* [2001] 1 AC 268 (HL) (hereafter *Blake*).
   [13] *One Step* (n 1) [92].
   [14] This is also my long-preferred destination: see Sarah Worthington, 'Reconsidering Disgorgement for Wrongs' (1999) 62 MLR 218.

of our own making. We have used terms such as 'use value', 'licence fee', 'hypothetical bargain', '*Wrotham Park* damages',[15] 'release fee', and now the preferred term 'negotiating damages', in quite undifferentiated ways to describe very different remedies being awarded in response to quite different legal claims. To use the same terms, without discrimination, to describe several conceptually distinct legal territories inevitably leads to analytical chaos: no route map can deal effectively with that problem.[16]

Second, the only way out of this difficulty is to unpick the distinct strands of legal analysis buried in the cases, and expose them for what they are. If that is done it will be clear that these various terms are used in five quite distinctive contexts, with only the fifth being material in *One Step*. These five contexts are, variously, the money remedy due to C by way of: (i) ordinary contract damages (assessing C's loss as a result of D's breach of contract);[17] (ii) ordinary tort damages (assessing C's loss as a result of D's tort);[18] (iii) LCA damages (assessing C's loss as a result of the court's exercise of its discretion in declining to grant C the injunction requested); (iv) disgorgement damages (stripping D of all the profits made from D's breach, in the rare cases where that is the principled response); and, finally, (v) restitution for unjust enrichment (stripping D of the unjust enrichment obtained from C by virtue of D's unauthorized use of C's property). If we are to make sense of this area, then we need different labels—different signposts—to indicate that a different legal analysis underpins each of these five different remedies.

Finally, it follows that the crucial analytical argument in this chapter is that the form of 'negotiating damages' being considered in *One Step*, and the form which all the analysis in that case is endeavouring to define and circumscribe, is an *unjust enrichment claim* advanced by C, not a claim for compensation for breach of contract. It is a claim against D because D has been unjustly enriched by the unauthorized *use* of C's property. If this is recognized, it then follows directly from the very nature of this claim that this option is not available unless D has indeed made unauthorized use *of C's property*. This is so when D makes such use of C's chair or horse or land or intellectual property;[19] it is not so when D merely breaches a term of some contractual arrangement between C and D, no matter how valuable C's contractually protected rights might be. If this is true, it follows that *One Step* negotiating damages (if recognized as an unjust enrichment claim) is straightforwardly not available for breach of a restraint of trade clause. Equally, it is suggested, it is not available for breach of an equitable duty of confidence or a contractual confidentiality agreement.[20] D's various wrongs in these circumstances do not include *D's use of C's property*.

The wider context is important, however. Even without an unjust enrichment claim, C is protected in other ways. C can of course claim ordinary contract damages. That is what

---

[15] Following *Wrotham Park* (n 11).

[16] A point made emphatically by Lord Walker in *Pell Frischmann Engineering Ltd v Bow Valley Iran Ltd* [2009] UKPC 45, [2011] 1 WLR 2370 (PC), [46] (hereafter *Pell Frischmann*).

[17] Meaning the orthodox expectation damages measure: see n 2. By way of illustration, see Lord Sumption's approach in *One Step* (n 1). Note that claims for reliance losses in contract do not provide another distinctive remedial option to C; their basis lies under the head of expectation damages: they are available only when C cannot prove expectation damages, but can at least show that those damages would exceed C's provable reliance losses. In those circumstances C can elect to claim only the latter provable sum. See the analysis in Ewan McKendrick, *Contract Law* (14th edn, Macmillan International 2021) 399–401.

[18] For the general rule, see *Livingstone v Rawyards Coal Co* (1880) 5 App Cas 25, 39 (Lord Blackburn).

[19] And any associated proof of D's contract breach or D's commission of a tort is merely to show that D's use is *unauthorized*; it is not for the purpose of claiming C's economic losses by way of ordinary contract or tort damages.

[20] Contrast *One Step* (n 1), especially [92] and [93]. Nevertheless, see section VII of this chapter.

happened in *One Step*. Tort damages may provide an alternative in some situations. But in almost all the early negotiating damages cases C could show no such loss. That was the problem. In many of those cases, however, C could nevertheless seek an injunction to protect its rights.[21] The court could then either order an injunction or, alternatively, award LCA damages to C. The LCA jurisdiction is wide: it can protect both proprietary and non-proprietary interests;[22] it is therefore not subject to the same 'asset-restrictive' limitations sought to be imposed on *One Step*-type negotiating damages.

There are hints of these various alternative claims hiding in the shadows of the principal paragraphs of *One Step* noted earlier. It is this looming presence of different remedial approaches, I suggest, that makes these paragraphs so difficult to unravel and to apply outside the contexts specifically described.

For example, in paragraph [91] Lord Reed notes:

> 91 The use of an imaginary negotiation can give the impression that negotiating damages are fundamentally incompatible with the compensatory purpose of an award of contractual damages. *Damages for breach of contract depend on considering the outcome if the contract had been performed*, whereas an award based on a hypothetical *release fee depends on considering the outcome if the contract* had not been performed but *had been replaced by a different contract*.[23]

He holds that this impression of fundamental incompatibility is misleading. Nevertheless, this observation identifies a crucial distinction in the relevant counterfactuals in assessing remedies. The latter approach describes precisely the scenario adopted in assessing LCA damages: in those cases, and those cases alone, the court assesses the price at which C would agree to a common *future* where D has been released from the contract or tort obligations it would otherwise owe C. The terminology of '*release fee*' is perfect: it is accurate and informative.

Moving on, the meat of defining negotiating damages then appears in paragraphs [92]–[95]. Taking paragraph [92], cited earlier, as illustrative, there is an evident tension between the assertion that

> The claimant has in substance been deprived of a valuable asset, and *his loss* can therefore be measured by determining *the economic value* [presumably to him] of the asset in question

and the next observation that

> The *defendant has taken something for nothing*, for which the claimant was entitled to require payment.

---

[21] Injunctions to restrain breach of negative covenants or continuing trespasses are relatively common, even where breach of the covenant or commission of the tort does not cause C provable economic loss.

[22] See *Pell Frischmann* (n 16) itself, and also Lord Walker at [46].

[23] *One Step* (n 1) [91] (emphasis added).

The former clings to the idea that it is C's economic position that is the focus. Yet so often in these cases C's economic position has been shown to be completely unaffected by D's breach: D has used assets which C was not using at all. It does not clarify or assist to insist that the compensable loss in issue is 'a loss of a different kind',[24] and yet is a loss which C cannot itself elect to pursue.[25]

By contrast, the insight that really clamours for a remedy in C's favour is that D '*has taken something for nothing*' from C. Notice four matters in this context. *First*, this clearly requires more than D simply benefiting incidentally from its breach of contract or the tort. What matters is that D has *taken* something from C. The wrong is merely in the background to explain why the *taking* is unauthorized. *Second*, where such *taking* is unauthorized, leaving it unremedied seems patently unjust. This is regardless of whether C has suffered any economic loss itself. Equally, however, and *third*, the injustice that requires a remedy only arises where D *has* taken a benefit. It is not enough, as we will see, that D's breach has simply prevented C from using its own asset. That is remedied by ordinary contract or tort damages. *Finally*, the labelling issue: this focus on D, and D's taking of an unauthorized benefit from C, is—I suggest—the key finding in all the words in *One Step*. It is this remedy that the Court sought to describe and circumscribe. And this remedy—I argue—is a remedy in unjust enrichment, not a remedy for breach of contract.

All this reinforces the need for clearer language. Negotiating damages is too broad a term to enable different contexts to be usefully distinguished. In the context of C's claims for ordinary contract or tort damages, the focus is on C's economic position. C can recover damages for all the economic losses it has suffered as a result of D's breach of contract or D's tort. This includes C being able to recover '*C's provable lost hire charges or licence fees*', being what C might otherwise have gained in the ordinary course if the assets were, as they should have been, at C's disposal. As the cases show, this means that C will have such claims where C is in the business of hiring out its equipment, leasing its land, licensing its intellectual property, but not otherwise.

By contrast, if the focus is on D's unauthorized taking of C's asset for its own use, and *if* C's claim is a claim in unjust enrichment, then the remedial focus is on D's position, not C's. C can recover the unjust enrichment in D's hands. This enrichment might best be labelled as '*D's use value*' to make the point that the focus is on the value *to D* of D's use of C's asset. That is typically the hire charge, or rental or lease charge, that D would have to pay to third party to obtain the same benefit D has obtained without authority from C.

And by further contrast, LCA damages apply in a much wider context. Hire charges, licence fees, and use value do not capture the breadth of the context, nor the approach that needs to be taken by the court. Those terms all look either at what has been lost by virtue of breaches that have already taken place, or what has been gained by unauthorized usage that has already taken place. By contrast, LCA damages look *forwards* to a reformed arrangement between the parties, and, for the reasons already noted, a '*release fee*' measure appears perfect as a description of the court's approach to the assessment before it.

But the real task of this chapter is to persuade that the core claim being discussed by the Supreme Court in *One Step* is really an unjust enrichment claim, not a claim for

---

[24] *One Step* (n 1) [30].
[25] ibid [36].

176 THE DAMAGE IN NEGOTIATING DAMAGES

compensation for breach of contract. That requires re-examination of the key cases under-pinning this jurisdiction.

III. Older Authorities: Tort Cases

Lord Reed's examination of the earlier authorities began with the tort cases. Where C's property is 'invaded' in the commission of a tort, the cases divide sharply into two groups. In the first, the invasion causes financial loss to C, typically being loss or damage to the property itself and/or lost income because D's breach prevents C's own profitable use of the property.[26] In the second group, C suffers no such financial loss because the property is not taken or damaged, and C would not have made productive use of it.

For example, in *Strand Electric and Engineering Co Ltd v Brisford Entertainments Ltd*,[27] C's chattels (electric switchboards which C hired out in its own business) were wrongfully detained by D. C sued D in detinue for return of the chattels and its lost hiring charges. Romer LJ focused on C's own economic losses.[28] He noted the surprising absence of direct authority which addressed C's tort losses arising from D's retention and use of C's chattels. Nevertheless, he followed the approach traditionally adopted in land cases and ordered D to return the chattels and pay by way of damages the lease or hiring charges C would otherwise have accrued for the whole period.

He rejected D's complaint that C should not be able to recover the full hiring value but should give allowance for the usual lay periods when C would not have been able to find a hirer, holding instead that '[i]t does not lie in the mouth of such a defendant to suggest that the owner might not have found a hirer; *for in using the property* he showed that he wanted it and he cannot complain if it is assumed against him that he himself would have [hired the chattels] rather than not . . . had the use . . . at all'.[29] The obvious inference is that, were the facts otherwise, this assumption would not be made: C would then recover losses only on its usual pattern of hiring.

Romer LJ also rejected D's related claim that it had *not* 'used' the chattels, and so was not subject to this presumption, since it had not actively operated the switchboards but simply kept them on site. Romer LJ noted that D's reason for retaining the switchboards was to make its theatre more saleable than it would otherwise have been, and held that this amounted to use of the equipment by D for its own purposes.[30] In assessing C's losses, Romer LJ also noted that it was irrelevant whether D's use had been profitable for D or not; the only point in issue in the tort claim was an assessment of C's economic losses.[31]

This is all standard fare. The more interesting question is what is to happen if C's property is *not* damaged, and C would *not* have used it productively. In those circumstances, even though a wrong has been committed, C has suffered no economic loss. The orthodox

---

[26] *Livingstone v Rawyards Coal Co* (1880) 5 App Cas 25 (HL), 39 (Lord Blackburn).
[27] *Strand Electric* (n 6).
[28] Somervell and Denning LJJ, by contrast, focused on D's benefits from its unauthorized use, as discussed in what follows.
[29] *Strand Electric* (n 6) 257 (Romer LJ).
[30] ibid 256 (Romer LJ).
[31] ibid.

response, both in contract and tort, would be to say that D's wrong has not caused C the type of harm for which the law would make D liable.

Yet there is a powerful intuition that there is something seriously deficient in a legal regime that permits D to make unauthorized use of C's property at will, with no legal consequences so long as the use does not harm C's economic position. The very suggestion goes against all common notions of property and private ownership. And so the judges found a way to provide remedies in just this these circumstances.

Looking back at the legal landscape from our present position, we might say that the judges who took this bold step were clearly not quite sure how to categorize the legal problem being addressed, nor how to describe the remedy they were awarding, but award they did, and with remarkably similar reasoning.

They recognized clearly the distinction between what they were doing in orthodox cases where C's provable economic loss was in issue and what they were doing in these cases where C had suffered no such provable loss.

Both issues arose in *Whitwham v Westminster Brymbo Coal and Coke Co*, where Lindley LJ explained:

> The plaintiffs have been injured in two respects. First, they have had the value of their land diminished; secondly, they have lost the use of their land [although this was not a loss which had caused the plaintiffs economic harm], and the defendants have had it for their own benefit. It is *unjust to leave out of sight the use which the defendants have made of this land for their own purposes*, and that lies at the bottom of what are called the way-leave cases. Those cases are based upon the principle that, if one person has without leave of another been using that other's land for his own purposes, he ought to pay for such user.[32]

The same appreciation of the two different strands of analysis is evident in *Watson Laidlaw & Co Ltd v Pott Cassels & Williamson*,[33] a patents case. Lord Shaw contrasted the traditional claim by C for the economic loss caused to C's business by D's infringement of C's patent with the different claim which C might make when D made use of the patented invention in jurisdictions where C could not have traded. He described the former as governed by the principle of '*restoration*' of C to the condition in which he would have been had he not so sustained the harm (whether by way of D's tort, breach of contract, or infringement of C's statutory rights), no matter how difficult that might be to quantify in money. This is ordinary contract, tort, or statutory damages. By contrast, the second strand was governed by the principle '*of price or of hire*' applicable 'wherever an abstraction or invasion of property has occurred':

> For wherever an abstraction or invasion of property has occurred, then, unless such abstraction or invasion were to be sanctioned by law, the law ought to yield a recompense under the category or principle, as I say, *either of price or of hire*. If A, being a liveryman, keeps his horse standing idle in the stable, and B, against his wish or without his knowledge,

---

[32] *Whitwham v Westminster Brymbo Coal and Coke Co* [1896] 2 Ch 538 (CA), 541–42 (Lindley LJ). Similarly Rigby LJ at 543.

[33] *Watson Laidlaw & Co Ltd v Pott Cassels & Williamson* 1914 SC (HL) 18 (HL Scotland) (hereafter *Watson Laidlaw*).

178 THE DAMAGE IN NEGOTIATING DAMAGES

rides or drives it out, it is no answer to A for B to say: 'Against what loss do you want to be restored? I restore the horse. There is no loss. The horse is none the worse; it is the better for the exercise.'[34]

Based on that analysis, he held that C was entitled to prove and claim its own loss in the markets in which it operated *and also* (since these were not overlapping) prove and claim a royalty for the unauthorized sale or use of every one of the infringing machines in those other markets in which C's own operations were not competing.[35]

The very same approach was adopted by the majority in *Strand Electric*. As noted earlier, Romer LJ based his conclusions on the fact that the tort had deprived C of the profit earning capabilities of its assets. By contrast, both Somervell and Denning LJ reached the same remedial quantum, but based their conclusions on D's 'use value'. As Somervell LJ put it, 'the defendants had for their own benefit the use of the plaintiffs' chattels ... The wrong is not the mere deprivation, as in negligence and possibly some detinue cases, but the *user*'.[36] Because this was a case where the goods were normally hired out commercially, he valued that user at the commercial rate.

Denning LJ was equally forthright, while also recognizing the alternative option open to C of simply claiming for C's own economic loss:

> If a wrongdoer has made use of goods for his own purposes, then he must pay a reasonable hire for them, even though the owner has in fact suffered no loss.... He cannot be better off by doing wrong than he would be by doing right ....
>
> I am here concerned with the cases where the owner has in fact suffered no loss, *or less loss than is represented by a hiring charge.*[[37]] In such cases *if the wrongdoer has in fact used the goods* he must pay a reasonable hire for them ... The claim for a hiring charge is ... not based on the loss to the plaintiff, but on the fact that the defendant has used the goods for his own purposes. It is an action against him because he has had the benefit of the goods. *It resembles, therefore, an action for restitution rather than an action of tort.*[38]

This final observation is especially prescient, given that English law was more than thirty-five years away from recognizing claims in unjust enrichment and their associated remedies of restitution of the unjust enrichment that D had obtained at C's expense.[39] Perhaps even more remarkable is that Denning LJ recognized this as the appropriate characterization

---

[34] ibid 30.

[35] ibid 32. Note that the royalty measure is apt for the latter aspect of the claim: it represents the proper 'price' D would have to pay to obtain the use it had made of C's patents in jurisdictions where C was not itself operating. By contrast, C's *own* losses, in the areas where C *was* competing, are assessed on the basis of proof of C's own losses, and these may sometimes require full disgorgement of D's profits *if* (and only if) C can prove that these profits *are* the equivalent of C's losses. This frequent equivalence between C's lost business and D's gained business in patent cases explains why the alternative approaches in calculating C's losses are so common, and are indeed reinforced by statutory provisions delivering precisely those ends. Nevertheless, it is important to recognize that the goal is to *assess C's losses* as a result of D's infringement; it is not to strip D of D's gains where there is no equivalence. Lord Shaw makes that plain: ibid 30–31.

[36] *Strand Electric* (n 6) 252 (emphasis added).

[37] This is a significant (and I think accurate) observation, the implication being that C can elect for the more advantageous option.

[38] *Strand Electric* (n 6) 254–55 (emphasis added).

[39] *Lipkin Gorman v Karpnale Ltd* [1988] UKHL 12, [1991] 2 AC 548 (HL).

OLDER AUTHORITIES: TORT CASES 179

here, even though many of the early unjust enrichment cases were concerned with D's receipt of *assets* at C's expense, not merely receipt of the *'use value'* of those assets.[40]

Several points are worth reinforcing.

First, all these judges clearly appreciated they were doing two different things: remedying the loss C had suffered as a result of D's wrongdoing was one thing; compelling D to pay a hire fee or royalties for the unauthorized use of C's assets was another. The first requires C and D to be linked by D's *wrongdoing to C* where C has suffered a resulting economic loss; the second requires C and D to be linked by D's *unauthorized use of C's assets* where D has had the benefit of use.

Second, this 'use value' approach is only available if there *is* 'use' by D. If C is simply kept out of its expected use of its own assets because D has negligently damaged those assets and cannot return them, or because D is a carrier or a warehouseman who has detained those assets for longer than expected, then the appropriate remedy is simply the ordinary remedy in tort or contract for the recovery of C's provable economic loss; it is not recovery related to D's unauthorized 'use', as there has been no such 'use' by D.[41] Put another way, in these 'use value' cases, the claim being made or the right being protected is not simply *C's* 'loss of dominion' over its assets; it is *D's* abstraction of benefit, its 'taking something for nothing' in making use of C's assets without C's consent.

Third, not one of these claims addressing D's 'use value' (here categorized as unjust enrichment claims) requires D to disgorge the profits of its beach. These are not disgorgement claims. The judges made this plain in all the cases considered so far, and that approach persists in those still to be addressed. Despite this, there is dogged discussion, even after *One Step*, which posits the question of whether negotiating damages are 'restitutionary' or 'compensatory'. 'Restitutionary' in this context refers not to restitution for unjust enrichment— far from it—but to disgorgement of the profits generated from D's wrongdoing.[42] By contrast, the analysis already laid out here, and supported in what comes later, all confirms, firmly, the view that 'use value' claims are *not* designed to strip D of all the profits generated by its unauthorized use of C's assets; they are not even designed to do this on some sliding scale that somehow addresses the significance of C's rights or the culpability involved in D's use of C's assets.[43]

Disgorgement is an exceptionally rare remedy in the common law. Bar the contract breach claim in *Attorney General v Blake*,[44] which was itself described as exceptional and has barely been followed since, the disgorgement remedy is restricted to fiduciaries and those in receipt of confidential information. In these two contexts the disgorgement remedy is not designed to protect C from economic harm, nor to protect C from having its property used in an unauthorized fashion; it is designed to protect these special *relationships* by discouraging self-interested behaviour by D where the nature of the relationship renders that

---

[40] Even with *Lipkin Gorman* in play, Nourse LJ predicted that the likely recognition of 'use value' as an unjust enrichment claim still lay some way into the future: *Stoke-on-Trent City Council v W & J Wass Ltd* [1988] 1 WLR 1406 (CA), 1415 (hereafter *Stoke-on-Trent CC*).

[41] *Strand Electric* (n 6) 249–50 (Somervell LJ), 254 (Denning LJ).

[42] See the comments and the cases cited in *One Step* (n 1) [11] (C's formulation of its claim), [58]–[60], [113]; also see the extended analysis in Mitchell and Roskill, 'Mesne Profits: Remedies' (n 4), which includes discussion of these cases.

[43] Much of the subsequent discussion of the remedy awarded in *Wrotham Park* (n 12) is in this vein, and yet finds no support in the judgment itself; see too *Experience Hendrix LLC v PPX Enterprises Inc* [2003] EWCA Civ 323, [2003] 1 All ER (Comm) 830 (CA) (hereafter *Experience Hendrix*), discussed below.

[44] *Blake* (n 12).

180 THE DAMAGE IN NEGOTIATING DAMAGES

a real moral hazard *and* the relationship cannot provide the protective attributes intended and inherent in it merely by focusing on remedying harm to C.[45] In these circumstances the approach is not to seek compensation from D, but to deny D the benefit of all of D's profit-making ventures that fall within the scope of the fiduciary or confidential relationship.[46]

IV. Older Authorities: Contract Cases

The preceding cases are all tort cases, but the approach to 'use value' claims in the context of contracts offers further insights. The simple facts in *Ministry of Defence v Ashman*[47] expose the remedial alternatives in play. C owned property which it leased at a concessionary rent to D2, a member of the Royal Air Force. At the outset, D2 had agreed that he was entitled to occupy the property only so long as he remained a serving member of the Royal Air Force living with his spouse (D1). Two years later, D2 moved out, leaving D1 and their two children in occupation. A month later, C gave the defendants notice to vacate within two months. However, D1 could not afford the local market rents, and did not leave until eleven months after the notice to vacate had expired, when she finally obtained local authority housing.

The issue before the court was the basis upon which C's 'damages' or 'mesne profits'[48] should be calculated. Three very different figures were suggested: the open market rental of the property (£472 pcm); the rental cost of appropriate local authority housing (£145 pcm); or the concessionary rental charge offered by C to its service personnel (£95 pcm). C claimed the proper basis was the property's open market rental; D1 and D2 claimed it was the concessionary rental. The Court of Appeal awarded the equivalent local authority housing rental. What is crucial for present purposes is how the court arrived at this conclusion.

The court's finding that the basis of C's claim in this case lay in unjust enrichment could not be more explicit. The orthodox compensatory measure in tort was an alternative route to a remedy, but the two remedies were described in terms, and on principles, that render them mutually exclusive: the former is not some special measure of compensation operating as a subset of the latter category in special cases.

Hoffmann LJ offered a pithy description of the route taken by the majority:

> A person entitled to possession of land can make a claim against a person who has been in occupation without his consent on two alternative bases. *The first is for the loss which he has suffered in consequence of the defendant's trespass.* This is the normal measure of damages in the law of tort. *The second is the value of the benefit which the occupier has received. This is a claim for restitution.* The two bases of claim are mutually exclusive and the plaintiff must elect before judgment which of them he wishes to pursue. These principles are not only fair but, as Kennedy L.J. demonstrated, well established by authority.

---

[45] Sarah Worthington, 'Fiduciaries: When Is Self-Denial Obligatory?' (1999) 58 CLJ 500.

[46] See Sarah Worthington, *Equity* (2nd edn, OUP, 2006), ch 5 (hereafter Worthington, *Equity*) (but noting the comments below at n 105). Note too that this same approach does not apply to contractual duties of confidence, where the remedies are contract damages, not disgorgement, unless the relationship can be characterized as also a relationship of confidence and the information in issue as 'confidential'.

[47] *MoD v Ashman* (n 6).

[48] ie sums of money paid for the occupation of land to a person with a right of immediate occupation, where no permission has been given for that occupation.

OLDER AUTHORITIES: CONTRACT CASES 181

It is true that in the earlier cases it has not been expressly stated that a claim for mesne profit for trespass can be *a claim for restitution. Nowadays I do not see why we should not call a spade a spade.*[49]

Kennedy LJ reached the same conclusion via the older authorities.[50] He cited from *Swordheath Properties Ltd v Tabet*[51]—another case where tenants had overstayed—and from *Penarth Dock Engineering Co Ltd v Pounds.*[52] In the latter case D had failed to remove a pontoon he had purchased from C in circumstances where C could not itself show any loss from the breach of contract and Lord Denning MR had said that:

The test of the measure of damages is *not what the plaintiffs have lost, but what benefit the defendant obtained by having the use of the berth* . . . If he had moved it elsewhere, he would have had to pay on the evidence £37–10s a week for a berth for a dock of this kind.[53]

In *MoD v Ashman*, C had elected for this unjust enrichment 'use value' remedy. It adduced no evidence of its own losses, these being irrelevant to a restitution claim. All that mattered was the value of benefit which D1 and D2 had received. Both Hoffmann and Kennedy LJJ agreed that the open market value will ordinarily be appropriate because the defendant has chosen to stay in the premises rather than pay for equivalent open market premises somewhere else. But they noted that sometimes benefits may not be worth as much to the particular defendant as to someone else, especially in circumstances where a defendant has not been free to reject the benefit. In short, special circumstances may warrant subjective devaluation.

Here there were two special circumstances: D1 had previously occupied the premises at a concessionary rent; and she now had, in practice, no choice but to stay in those premises until the local authority was willing to rehouse her. The latter context indicated an objective 'use value' to D1, valuing what she would have to pay for equivalent accommodation elsewhere as the equivalent local authority housing rental which she was unable to access immediately. But D1 could not remain in C's property, insisting on that below-market 'use value', if her earlier behaviour had indicated she valued C's property more highly than that. Here, however, she had occupied C's property at a concessionary rate below her own objective 'use value' assessment, not at a market rate.[54] She was thus entitled to subjectively devalue her 'use value' to the local authority equivalent, a value well below the market rate. All this confirms unequivocally that the court was implementing an unjust enrichment remedy, not a compensatory remedy, in favour of C: its focus was on D's use value, not C's economic loss.

Lloyd LJ was content to go along with the majority's unjust enrichment assessment, with 'damages' assessed on the basis of the benefit accruing to D1 from her unauthorized occupation.[55] Nevertheless, his preferred approach was to confine C to claiming its own losses

---

[49] *MoD v Ashman* (n 6) 200–01 (emphasis added); similarly, see *Ministry of Defence v Thompson* (1993) 25 HLR 552 (CA), with the judgment given by Hoffmann LJ. Note that the assertion is that mesne profits 'can' be a claim for restitution, with the implication that the term can also be used for other measures of 'damages'. See the comprehensive analysis in Mitchell and Roskill, 'Mesne Profits: Causes of Action' (n 4).

[50] *MoD v Ashman* (n 6) 199.

[51] *Swordheath Properties Ltd v Tabet* [1979] 1 WLR 285 (CA) (hereafter *Swordheath Properties*).

[52] *Penarth Dock Engineering Co Ltd v Pounds* [1963] 1 Lloyd's Rep 359 (QB) (hereafter *Penarth Dock*).

[53] ibid 362 (emphasis added).

[54] *MoD v Ashman* (n 6), especially 201–02 (Hoffmann LJ).

[55] ibid 204–05.

182 THE DAMAGE IN NEGOTIATING DAMAGES

only, on the orthodox compensation measure. C would thus have recovered only the concessionary rental for the entire period of D1's unauthorized occupation, although with the small concession that C would not be required to prove that it would in any event have been able to find a suitable tenant for the entire period.[56]

Lloyd LJ's reason for this restrictive view was that C had only claimed 'damages', and in any event he did not believe that a claim in unjust enrichment was legally open against a tenant holding over, instead reading all the older cases cited by the majority not as cases of restitution for unjust enrichment 'but rather as special cases where the plaintiff can apparently recover more than his loss'.[57] The oddity in categorizing these older cases as cases where C is confined to recovering its *own* compensatory losses (notwithstanding that these had been shown to be nil), but then awarding C a sum which is more than those losses, is surely not lost on anyone.

But Lloyd LJ's judgment provides one insight which merits close attention. He distinguished between tenants who hold over after the lawful termination of the tenancy, and tenants who hold over *with the consent of the landlord*.[58] With a modern eye, we might not characterize these cases as Lloyd LJ did. But the crucial point to note is that where D holds over *with C's consent*, C cannot claim damages in trespass because D has C's consent, and cannot claim restitution for unjust enrichment because the enrichment is with C's consent. What is missing is that C's consent to D's holding over has often come without an express stipulation as to the rent to be paid during that period. However, C's permission is reasonably seen as not by way of gift, and the courts will likely be quick to find a common understanding or an implied term that D was to continue to pay the earlier rent. It is only when—and if—D refuses to do so that C will terminate the arrangement, give D notice to quit if that is necessary, and then sue D for compensation *or* for restitution for unjust enrichment (precisely as in *MoD v Ashman*, including all these steps to eventual resolution).

Put more forcefully, while the contract between C and D is on foot, the risk allocation prescribed by its terms cannot be displaced by C electing to pursue what might seem to be an alternative claim for restitution for unjust enrichment rather than its claim in damages for breach of contract. The claim in unjust enrichment relating to D's use value is only available for the period when the contract has ceased to govern the parties' relationship.[59] What the contract does in all these cases where negotiating damages come into the frame is define when D is no longer authorized to use D's property. This was true in *Swordheath Properties*, *Penarth Dock*, *Strand Electric*, *MoD v Ashman*, and *MoD v Thompson*.[60]

Before closing, there is one important further point. Proper classification and characterization of the various claims advanced by C is essential if like cases are to be treated alike. The majority in *MoD v Ashman* described the 'use value' claim as a claim for restitution of D's unjust enrichment. By contrast, *One Step* describes these as claims for C's compensation. If the *One Step* characterization is correct, and the 'use value' identifies *a loss of a*

---

[56] See this similar approach to assessing C's losses in *Strand Electric* (n 6) 256–57 (Romer LJ), discussed earlier (see text at n 28).

[57] *MoD v Ashman* (n 6) 203 (Lloyd LJ).

[58] ibid 202 (Lloyd LJ).

[59] See the analysis in *Barton v Morris* [2023] UKSC 3 (SC), although in a very different context.

[60] *Swordheath Properties* (n 51) (remedies only after the tenants held over); *Penarth Dock* (n 52) (only after the end of the generous time limit the contract gave for removing the pontoon); *Strand Electric* (n 6) (see the earlier discussion at the text to n 32 to n 46); *MoD v Ashman* (n 6) (only after the end of the notice to quit); *MoD v Thompson* (n 6) (similar to *Ashman*, with Hoffmann LJ summarizing and applying the law in *Ashman*).

different type which C has suffered and for which C should be compensated, then it is difficult to see why C is not able to *add* this loss to the other heads of loss that are recoverable in the orthodox tort claim. Yet this additive approach is not possible. It is possible when C wishes to add other heads of compensatory loss together, such as adding loss of the asset, or damage to the asset, to C's provable loss of earnings. But it is not possible to add the 'use value' measure. In *MoD v Ashman*, for example, C could claim *either* D's use value, *or* C's lost hiring charge, but not both: the claims are mutually exclusive.[61] That seems right; but it also suggests the compensatory characterization of the use value claim is inapt.

V. Older Authorities: Cases Where There Is No Use of C's Property

The conclusion from these tort and contract cases—that the unjust enrichment claim, or 'use value' claim, is only available to C where D is unjustly enriched by *use of C's assets*—can be seen hiding in the weeds in the much criticized (but arguably correct) analysis in *Stoke-on-Trent City Council v W & J Wass Ltd*.[62] In this case C had the right to operate a statutory market, and D set up an unauthorized rival market within close proximity. C suffered no financial loss, but nevertheless endeavoured—unsuccessfully—to claim substantial damages based on the licence fee D would have been required to pay if it had operated lawfully.

In advancing its claim, C relied on analogies with the earlier cases already considered in this chapter. In particular, C relied on the fact that its market right was a property right, being an intangible right attached to the relevant market site. C further suggested that this right gave C a monopoly in respect of holding markets within a certain area (in this case, within a radius of 6⅔ miles of C's market site). The former invited analogies with land use cases,[63] the latter with patent cases.[64]

The court found neither analogy persuasive. The judges distinguished the land use cases because here D had not made *use of C's property right* attached to land, but had instead used land in close proximity in an unauthorized way that might have (but did not) cause economic harm to C's property.[65] The preferable analogy was with cases of nuisance, as when D blocked C's light or obstructed C's access to C's own property.[66] Equally, the judges distinguished the patent cases, where the claim is that D has made wrongful use *of the property comprised in the patent*, in breach of the patent-holder's monopoly right. Here D had not made wrongful use of C's monopoly right to operate markets anywhere within a radius of 6⅔ miles of a given site, because C did not have such a right; C merely had the right to operate its market *at the given site*, and not to be disturbed in the enjoyment of that right by other people operating markets within a radius of 6⅔ miles.[67] In short, on either analogy

---

[61] *MoD v Ashman* (n 6) 201 (Hoffmann LJ). Also see *Watson Laidlaw* (n 33) 30 (Lord Shaw).
[62] *Stoke-on-Trent CC* (n 40).
[63] Eg *Whitwham* (n 32).
[64] Eg *Watson Laidlaw* (n 33).
[65] *Stoke-on-Trent CC* (n 40) 1414–15 (Nourse LJ), 1416 (Nicholls LJ).
[66] ibid 1415 (Nourse LJ).
[67] ibid 1418 (Nicholls LJ). By contrast, Nourse LJ thought the patent cases were examples of orthodox tort claims (with the court assessing C's financial loss as a result of lost market and finding a licence fee to be the appropriate measure of a provable loss where, unlike here, real loss could be shown), and not illustrations of the 'user principle': ibid, 1413–14. Also see n 35.

184   THE DAMAGE IN NEGOTIATING DAMAGES

the court was not persuaded that this was an appropriate case for the application of the 'user principle' and the consequential award of user or licence fee damages.

This was precisely the conclusion reached by David Edwards QC in a careful judgment in *Priyanka Shipping Ltd v Glory Bulk Carriers Pte Ltd.*[68] This was also a contract case: C sold a ship to D, with the parties agreeing that the vessel was only to be used for scrap and was not to be used by D for further voyages. In breach of that agreement, D used the ship for further voyages. The court granted C an injunction to prevent further breaches, but held that, in respect of past losses, negotiating damages were not available, and LCA damages, at least in respect of past breaches, afforded no additional remedy beyond the common law quantification.[69] C had not claimed common law damages for breach of contract, these being difficult to assess and likely to be minimal/nominal. The reason for refusing negotiating damages was that, on these facts, D had not used C's property (since, after the sale, the vessel was D's), and—in trading the vessel itself—it had not taken C's right to trade the vessel, since C had lost that right on sale of the vessel.[70]

If the argument is followed so far, then the decision in *Experience Hendrix LLC v PPX Enterprises Inc*[71] may warrant revisiting. It was heavily influenced by the exceptional decision in *AG v Blake*[72] (see especially the judgment of Mance LJ[73]), and is out of line with modern analysis.[74] In *Experience Hendrix*, D was the owner of various master tapes of Jimi Hendrix recordings and also owned the copyright in those recordings. A settlement agreement between C and D obliged D not to use its property in specified ways without paying royalties to C. D breached the agreement. C sued, obtaining an undertaking from D to the court that D would comply with the contract in the future. C also sought negotiating damages or an account of profits to compensate for the harm suffered up until the undertaking was given, since it could not prove its orthodox contract damages. The court ordered negotiating damages by way of a royalty payment for past breaches, not a full account of profits as had been ordered in *AG v Blake*, even though the court found the analogies with that case compelling.

The reason this case is out of line with modern analysis is that C's contract right only prevented D dealing *with D's own assets* in particular ways, as in *Surrey CC* and in *Priyanka Shipping*. There was no appropriation or use of *C's property* by D. Accordingly, following the analysis earlier in this chapter, there is no basis for C to claim an unjust enrichment remedy for D's unauthorized use *of C's assets*. Equally, following the analysis in *One Step*, the preconditions for an award of negotiating damages are not present.

To the contrary, however, in *One Step* Lord Reed indicated the decision could nevertheless be supported:

---

[68] *Priyanka Shipping Ltd v Glory Bulk Carriers Pte Ltd* [2019] EWHC 2804 (Comm) (QBD) (hereafter *Priyanka Shipping*).

[69] ibid [141] and [169].

[70] ibid especially [195]–[197], and also [198]–[199].

[71] *Experience Hendrix* (n 43).

[72] *Blake* (n 12).

[73] Adopting the view, it seems, that a court could in appropriate circumstances—and in order to protect valuable contract rights—order remedies ranging from orthodox contract damages to negotiating damages to accounts of profits (as had been ordered in *Blake*) on a continuum that could reflect the value of the rights infringed.

[74] See the qualified comments of Lord Reed in *One Step* (n 1) [82] on *Blake* and [85] and [90] on *Experience Hendrix*; see too *Priyanka Shipping* (n 68) [198].

Notwithstanding some of the reasoning, the decision in the case can be supported on an orthodox basis. *The agreement gave the claimant a valuable right to control the use made of PPX's copyright.* When the copyright was wrongfully used, the claimant was prevented from exercising that right, *and consequently suffered a loss equivalent to the amount which could have been obtained by exercising it.*[75]

But the latter is the very loss C could not prove. Moreover, if negotiating damages are to be available every time C has a contract which requires D to deal with its own property in specific ways, then almost every contract will be open to this alternative remedy, which was precisely the outcome Lord Reed and the majority in *One Step* did not want to see.

VI. Injunctions and Lord Cairns' Act (LCA) Damages

Whatever the limitations on the availability of 'use value' claims, C's rights can often be protected by injunction or, if that is denied, by LCA damages in lieu. The terminology of 'negotiating damages' and its various equivalents is common in court assessments of the damages to be awarded in lieu of an injunction or specific performance under LCA.[76] Despite the overlapping terminology, this jurisdiction has almost nothing in common with the jurisdiction to award asset-restrictive *One Step*-type negotiating damages. For a start, the LCA jurisdiction involves injunctions and damages awards for the threatened infringe-ment of both proprietary and non-proprietary rights.[77] There is no pre-condition requiring that C has lost a valuable asset, or that D has taken something for nothing. In addition, the LCA jurisdiction operates on quite distinct principles. Most significantly, it enables the award of damages for wrongs that that have not yet been committed, as when the court awards damages in lieu of an order for specific performance or an injunction to prevent a threatened continuing wrongdoing.[78]

A wide variety of rights merit protection by injunction or specific performance. The statutory market right in *Stoke-on-Trent CC*[79] was such a right. The court recognized that C would be entitled to a permanent injunction to prevent D's wrongful interference with C's market right (ie an injunction restricted in time and in area to C's statutory entitlements to be free of interference), and, moreover, would be entitled to such an injunction without proof of loss.[80]

---

[75] *One Step* (n 1) [89].

[76] Lord Cairns' Act 1858, s 2, now s 50 of the Senior Courts Act 1981. This statutory provision allows for the award of damages 'in addition to, or in substitution for' an injunction or specific performance. The concern here is with the latter. With the former—ie damages in addition to—the rule is that if C wishes, at trial, to recover a money remedy for harms suffered before the injunction/specific performance order is granted, those damages are assessed under the ordinary common law (or equitable) rules for the assessment of remedies for harm (whether past or pro-spective) caused by a tort or breach of contract or other infringement that has already been committed: *Johnson v Agnew* [1980] AC 367 (HL) 400–01 (Lord Wilberforce, the other Law Lords agreeing). To the same effect, see *Priyanka Shipping* (n 68) [141] and [169] (David Edwards QC), after careful analysis and despite Lord Reed's com-ments in *One Step* at [47].

[77] *One Step* (n 1) [2]; *Pell Frischmann* (n 18) [46].

[78] *Jaggard v Sawyer* [1995] 1 WLR 269 (CA), 284 (Millett LJ), cited in *One Step* [43].

[79] *Stoke-on-Trent CC* (n 40).

[80] ibid 1419 (Nicholls LJ).

186 THE DAMAGE IN NEGOTIATING DAMAGES

But what is C's position if the court has jurisdiction to grant an injunction, but declines to do so? *Wrotham Park Estate Co Ltd v Parkside Homes Ltd*[81] was just such a case.[82] D had erected houses and constructed roads in breach of a restrictive covenant which bound D and any purchasers who bought these houses from D. C sought a mandatory injunction for demolition of the roads and houses. Brightman J held that there was jurisdiction to grant such an injunction,[83] but declined to do so given the economic and social waste involved.[84] He then needed to consider what damages, if any, should be awarded in the court's discretion in substitution for the injunction, as allowed under LCA.

D argued that since C had suffered no economic loss as a result of the breach—and, although this was not made explicit, would presumably suffer no further harm as a result of the continuing breach—the damages should be nil.[85] By contrast, C argued—by reference to the trespass, detinue, and patent infringement cases discussed earlier in this chapter—that substantial damages ought to be ordered, that a 'licence fee'/'negotiating damages' measure was appropriate, and that in development contexts where a landowner's property stood in the way of a development, such a fee was typically a half or a third of the development value of the land.[86]

Brightman J rejected D's argument: since the court had declined to order an injunction, for social and economic reasons, which it would not have hesitated to grant in circumstances where the social and economic costs were lower, then it would be of 'questionable fairness' to leave C with no remedy at all and D with all the fruits of its wrongdoing.[87] The judge also declined to accept C's approach, holding that the cases upon which C relied were 'a long way from the facts of the case before me',[88] and that a damages award in these circumstances needed to be *an adequate substitute for the injunction the court might otherwise have granted.*[89] This was a sum that the court calculated C might reasonably have demanded of D as the price for relaxing this particular covenant in these particular circumstances: in short, a *'release fee'.* The qualifications, although not made explicit by Brightman J, are evident in his reasoning: he awarded C only 5 per cent (£2,500) of the development value of the land on the basis that the covenant had not been inserted in order to give C a right or an asset of commercial or nuisance value; the effect of D's breach on C was insignificant and related to only a very small part of C's land; and C had known of the proposed sale of the land as development land, but had not protested and D had purchased it on that basis.[90] Clearly the 'release fee' in these cases escalates in direct proportion to the harm C suffers by the continuing infringement and the benefit D gains from the latitude in allowing it: *both* are material in any hypothetical 'release' negotiation between the parties.

---

[81] *Wrotham Park* (n 11).

[82] This case seems worth attention notwithstanding Lord Reed's assessment that it 'is a source of potential confusion because of the opacity of its reasoning, and it can now be regarded as being of little more than historical interest': *One Step* (n 1) [3].

[83] It is obvious from these brief headlines that C cannot claim LCA damages if the court has no jurisdiction to grant an injunction: the statutory power would not then exist, and the common law affords no equivalent: ibid [4] and [45]–[46], doubting *Pell Frischmann* (n 18) [48](5); also see *Jaggard v Sawyer* (n 78) 287.

[84] *Wrotham Park* (n 11) 811.

[85] ibid 812.

[86] ibid 812–15.

[87] Ibid, 812.

[88] ibid 814.

[89] ibid 815; *One Step* (n 1) [44]; *Pell Frischmann* (n 18) [48]; *Blake* (n 13) 281.

[90] *Wrotham Park* (n 12) 815–16.

It is plain that these cases are in a class of their own. They are not like cases claiming ordinary contract or tort damages, where C has to prove a loss to C *already sustained*, and is not entitled to demand a remedy for a wrong anticipated to be continuing into the future. They are also not like cases advancing unjust enrichment 'use value' or 'negotiating damages' claims, where D has made unauthorized use of C's property: these too are claims looking to the past, not the future. The critical feature of LCA damages awards is that they look *forward*, and aim to provide C with an adequate monetary substitute for the court's effective sanctioning of D's continuing breach by declining to order an injunction to prevent it. In this context, a hypothetical '*release fee*' is intended to reflect the reasonable price of putting in place a different arrangement to govern the parties' future relationship, not some backward-looking process to address past harms.[91]

Even with this limited background to LCA damages, it is difficult to agree with Lord Reed that these cases are aligned coherently with the other negotiating damages cases analysed in *One Step*, or that this might be so because the LCA damages measure 'reflect[s] the fact that the refusal of an injunction had the effect of *depriving the claimant of an asset which had an economic value*'.[92] The laudable intention in this description is to maintain alignment with other negotiating damages scenarios, where it is crucial that C does have an *asset*—some property—in the game. And yet the 'asset' in issue in LCA cases is simply a *right* of some kind, in contract or tort, which a court might protect by injunction. The language of property and 'assets' loses all discriminatory power if used as loosely as this.

The purpose of this section is not to dig deeply into the details of LCA damages, but simply to note that they are *very* different from the asset-restrictive *One Step*-type negotiating damages which the Supreme Court endeavoured to describe and define: they arise in much broader contexts, they require no asset-loss by C or asset-taking by D, their quantification is not designed to compensate C for past losses, or remedy past unjust enrichments that worked in D's favour. Instead, they aim to settle the future relationship between the parties, being a future where D will no longer owe C the duties that D threatens to breach. This is such a different starting point, a different end point, and different means of travel between them that there seems little reason to look for enlightenment delivered by way of commonalities between this form of damages and the forms of damages which were the primary target of investigation in *One Step*.

VII. More Controversial Cases: Equitable and Contractual Obligations of Confidence

This final section, on obligations of confidence, deals with one of the specific categories where the majority in *One Step* indicated that negotiating damages *will* be available. The justification for this conclusion in the context of C's right to control confidential information was set out by Lord Reed as follows:

---

[91] See Lord Reed's description in *One Step* (n 1) [91], although this was not provided by way of defining his preferred approach to LCA damages.

[92] *One Step* (n 1) [63] (emphasis added).

188 THE DAMAGE IN NEGOTIATING DAMAGES

[in this context] the contractual right is of such a kind that its breach can result in *an iden-tifiable loss equivalent to the economic value of the right, considered as an asset . . .* That is something which is true of some contractual rights, such as a right to *control* the use of land, intellectual property or confidential information, but by no means of all.[93]

This is doubted. If D discloses the confidential information, without authority, C will of course have various claims against D, but—even in the absence of proof of expectation damages—has D's breach resulted in some other form of 'an *identifiable loss equivalent to the economic value of the right*'? And is it apt to regard C as being 'deprived of a valuable *asset*'?[94] Presumably the answer to each question is 'Yes', given the Court's specific finding that negotiating damages are available for breaches of obligations of confidence. But it is difficult—perhaps impossible—to see why C's rights under a contractual non-disclosure agreement fall into this category, but C's rights under a commercial restraint of trade clause do not. Both rights are likely to have significant economic value; both rights would be pro-tected by injunction, giving some indication of the law's inclination to protect each; in both cases D's breach could 'result in an identifiable loss [presumably] equivalent to the eco-nomic value of the right'; and in neither case would we say that C's right is one giving it *control* over 'property', or an 'asset', thus making it equally hard to say that in either case D's breach has deprived C of a 'valuable asset'.[95] Both rights would seem to belong in the *same* category, not in different ones, as *One Step* holds they do.

Alternatively, perhaps the central principle underlying these breach of confidence cases is revealed by the descriptive strand, that D '*has taken something for nothing*, for which the claimant was entitled to require payment'.[96] But here too the difficulties with confidential information are no less. The '*something*' being taken must be given real meaning: taking an asset is one thing, but simply causing C 'to suffer pecuniary loss resulting from . . . wrongful competition, such as a loss of profits and goodwill, which is measurable by conventional means'[97] was held to be not enough. Breach of restraint of trade clauses was therefore put in the 'not enough' category, yet it is difficult to see why breach of an obligation of confidence escapes the same fate.

In my view, breach of confidence cases (whether the breach is of equitable or common law obligations) do not belong in the *One Step* negotiating damages canon. Confidential information is not property.[98] It is not like land or chattels or IP (think of transferring or licensing confidential information, or creating security over it, or a trust of it). It con-founds all hope of drawing defensible analogies which assist in deciding whether *One Step* negotiating damages are available to list confidential information alongside these other as-sets, and, further, to insist it sits in contrast with other legal rights to control D's activities which would seem equally valuable, such as C's right to control D's interference with C's statutory market,[99] or C's competing business.[100]

---

[93] ibid [93] (emphasis added).
[94] ibid [92] (emphasis added).
[95] Indeed, see ibid [125], where Lord Sumption describes a restraint of trade clause as closely analogous to a right of property. By contrast, information is not regarded as property. The compelling dissent of Lord Upjohn in *Boardman v Phipps* [1967] 2 AC 46 (HL), 127–29, is accepted as orthodoxy.
[96] ibid [92] (emphasis added).
[97] *One Step* (n 1) [93].
[98] See n 95.
[99] *Stoke-on-Trent CC* (n 40).
[100] *One Step* (n 1).

Equally, even in relation to confidential information, it is inappropriate to bundle together C's equitable and contractual rights to control D's use of information. The equitable duty arises regardless of any contract, when the context is right and the information is confidential.[101] The remedy for unauthorized disclosure by D is *disgorgement* of the profits D has generated by the breach.[102] By contrast, the contractual duty allows C to nominate which information is not to be disclosed (which may include information which equity would not regard as 'confidential'), and then insist D complies with the tailored terms of the parties' contractual confidentiality clause. The remedy for breach does not look to D's profitable use of the designated information (unless the equitable duty also applies and can be used to deliver those ends), but instead provides orthodox contract damages to remedy the economic harm C suffers from the breach.[103] There are contexts in which the two breaches and their remedies overlap fully,[104] but often they do not.

Care is needed in the assessment of remedies in these cases.[105] Simple labels (whether equitable or contractual) cannot be applied unthinkingly. As noted in quite different circumstances, any analysis of remedial consequences must start with a precise understanding of the obligation which has been breached and the detailed performance requirements demanded by it.[106] In duty of confidence cases, the equitable or contractual obligation may specify that D is not to use the information *at all*, or, alternatively, not to use it *without paying for it*. Context matters, of course, but that different formulation often leads to the inference that the former constraint suggests that C retains to itself the right to *all* the benefits that might derive from productive use, that is, all the profits of any lucrative venture, whereas in the latter context the inference may be that C retains the right to receive a royalty or licence fee from any use. These two different forms of constraint suggest different remedial consequences. In the equitable context, if D then breaches the obligation of confidence, it follows that the *profits* D must disgorge from the *unauthorized* use[107] are, in the former context, *all* the profits D derives, whereas in the latter context they are only a licence fee.[108] This approach ensures that, in either context, D is *only* stripped of the profits D has derived from the breach of the particular equitable obligation owed to C, but, equally, is stripped *fully* of those profits. Similarly, in the contractual context, breach of the contractual constraint will require D to compensate C for the losses C suffers as a result of the breach. In the former context, these are all the commercial profits C might have generated from its own use of the information;[109] in the latter context it is the lost royalties C would expect to obtain from

---

[101] *AG v Guardian Newspapers (No 2)* [1990] 1 AC 109 (HL); *Coco v AN Clark (Engineers) Ltd* [1968] FSR 525 (Ch).

[102] *AG v Guardian Newspapers (No 2)* (n 101).

[103] See by analogy the earlier discussion of *Watson Laidlaw* (n 33) at the text to n 33.

[104] As when certain information is regarded as confidential in equity *and* under the parties' contract, and D's profits from its unauthorized use mirror exactly the commercial benefits C has foregone because of the contractual breach. See by analogy above at n 35.

[105] And in this context my current thinking is more refined than in Worthington, *Equity* (n 46) 152–54.

[106] *AIB Group (UK) Plc v Mark Redler & Co Solicitors* [2014] UKSC 58 (SC) at many stages in the judgments, including [52], [59], [61], [64], [66], [70], [76] (Lord Toulson SCJ) and [92], [93], [138] (Lord Reed SCJ); by contrast, see the controversial decision in *Vercoe v Rutland Fund Management Ltd* [2010] EWHC 424 (Ch) holding that the court could choose the appropriate remedy for breach of confidence from a sliding scale ranging from ordinary contract damages to full disgorgement depending on the value of the right being infringed. That approach is not favoured here.

[107] eg *Peter Pan Manufacturing Corp v Corsets Silhouette Ltd* [1964] 1 WLR 96 (Ch).

[108] This may well be the best explanation of the much-criticized judgment in *Seager v Copydex Ltd* [1967] 1 WLR 923 (CA).

[109] This would seem to be the appropriate measure in *Pell Frischmann* (n 16), and may explain why the PC's assessment of damages was so much higher than that ordered by the lower courts.

190   THE DAMAGE IN NEGOTIATING DAMAGES

anyone using the information D has used without consent.[110] In the contract context, C may also have suffered other collateral damage as a result of the breach of confidence.

Finally, and more simply, in both cases C may of course seek an injunction to prevent D making unauthorized disclosures in the future in breach of either the equitable or the contractual obligation. C will generally succeed in obtaining such an order. However, if the court declines to order an injunction, it can instead order LCA damages in lieu. These are assessed on the *release fee* basis discussed earlier. This is true whether the breach in issue is breach of the equitable or the contractual duty, notwithstanding the purists who would insist that LCA only applies to common law wrongs.

In short, none of the remedies for breach of a duty of confidence in equity or in contract deliver the *One Step* form of negotiating damages, although both may deliver LCA damages if the court has jurisdiction to award an injunction but declines to do so.

VIII. Conclusion

It is a measure of the serious thought that went into the judgments in *One Step* that we are still debating the issues five years later. This contribution endeavours to unravel some of the critical strands of analysis in the judgments. A key conclusion is that we have made this area more difficult for ourselves, not by failing to treat like cases alike, but by failing to treat different cases differently, and—crucially—doing that because we have neglected to label them differently and more informatively.

One Step endeavoured to unify the analysis and provide a coherent approach to remedies in cases where C's property or valuable rights had been *invaded and used by D* without C's permission. One result was to use a single preferred term—'negotiating damages'—to describe what, when properly unwrapped, appear to be several conceptually distinct legal territories.

The argument advanced in this chapter is that we would do well to keep these different areas separate and label them accordingly. In the *One Step* context, with its focus on situations where D's wrong was to invade and use C's property or valuable rights, there are three distinctive types of claims in play. The first, and simplest, is C's ordinary compensation claim in contract or tort, where C is entitled to recover its own *provable lost hire or licence or royalty charges* because D has kept C out of the ordinary use of its own assets. Second is C's claim for LCA damages, where C seeks an injunction to prevent D's further future infringement of C's rights, and the court instead awards damages in lieu. These LCA damages are appropriately assessed by way of a *release fee*, designed to compensate C for the court's decision to vary the future arrangement between the parties by releasing C's rights and permitting D's infringements in their ongoing relationship.

Finally, and most controversially, but also most importantly, the key argument in this chapter is that the form of 'negotiating damages' of primary concern in *One Step*, the form which is the subject of all the most cited paragraphs, is an *unjust enrichment claim* advanced by C, not a claim for compensation for breach of contract. It is a claim against D because D

---

[110] Again, and only by analogy, see *Watson Laidlaw* (n 33).

has been unjustly enriched by its unauthorized *use* of C's property. This conclusion is consistent with earlier authorities.

If this recharacterization is recognized, it then follows directly from the very nature of this claim that this option it is not available unless D has indeed made unauthorized use *of C's property*. This is so when D makes such use of C's chair or horse or land or intellectual property; it is not so when D merely breaches a term of some contractual arrangement between C and D. It follows that *One Step* negotiating damages (if recognized as an unjust enrichment claim) are straightforwardly not available for breach of a restraint of trade clause. Equally, such damages are not available for breach of an equitable duty of confidence or a contractual confidentiality agreement. D's various wrongs in these circumstances do not include *D's use of C's property*.

All this reinforces the need for clearer language. Words, if used appropriately, can significantly simplify the task of treating like cases alike and different cases differently. We can then more confidently address the proper ambit of *One Step* negotiating damages.

12

The Critical Reception of *Cavendish Square Holdings v Makdessi*

ROGER HALSON

I. Introduction

In November 2015 contract lawyers in the UK received a slightly premature Christmas present in the form of the UK Supreme Court's judgment in *Cavendish Square Holding BV v Makdessi; ParkingEye Ltd v Beavis (Consumers' Association Intervening).*[1] Before this decision, the principles underlying the law relating to contractual liquidated damages and penalty clauses had not been considered by the UK's highest appellate court for more than one hundred years.[2] The breadth and scope of the decision is obvious from the very different commercial contexts of the two conjoined appeals in *Cavendish*. The first appeal, *Cavendish Square Holding BV v Makdessi* (the *Makdessi* appeal), involved a substantial commercial contract; the second, *ParkingEye Ltd v Beavis*, a low-value consumer contract (the *ParkingEye* appeal). As Lord Mance observed, the cases truly 'lie at opposite ends of a financial spectrum.'[3]

The significance of *Cavendish* was also recognized in a different way. Since its establishment in 2009 the Supreme Court has generally followed the practice of the judicial body it replaced, the appellate committee of the House of Lords, and sat with five members. When cases involve more wide-ranging issues, such as *Cavendish*, seven Justices might sit.[4] Perhaps inevitably, the result of seven senior voices addressing such a commercially important topic for the first time in a century was a lengthy report. Their review of the operation of the penalty jurisdiction and associated doctrines, including both historical and comparative perspectives, extended to over 316 paragraphs.

It seems as if the UK Supreme Court in *Cavendish* started a trend. As proof that Anglo-Australian rivalry extends beyond rugby and cricket, not to be outdone, in *Paciocco v Australian and New Zealand Banking Group Ltd*[5] the High Court of Australia applied the law of penalties to what French CJ described as 'essentially undisputed territory'[6] but took 376 paragraphs to do so! This extensive treatment was perhaps compensation (overcompensation?) for the brevity of its previous decision in *Andrews v Australia and New Zealand Banking Group Ltd.*[7] In *Andrews* the High Court had held that certain fees which banks

---

[1] [2015] UKSC 67, [2016] AC 1172 (hereafter *Cavendish*).
[2] Since *Dunlop Pneumatic Tyre Co Ltd v New Garage and Motor Co Ltd* [1915] AC 79 (HL) (hereafter *Dunlop*).
[3] *Cavendish* (n 1) [116].
[4] In 2015 the Supreme Court delivered judgments in seventy-nine cases. Of these, sixty-five (or 85%) were heard by five justices; only thirteen were heard by seven and one case, dealing with costs, was heard by a bench of three.
[5] [2016] HCA 28; (2016) 258 CLR 525 (hereafter *Paciocco*).
[6] ibid [6]. To similar effect see Keane J [253].
[7] [2012] HCA 30, (2012) 247 CLR 205 (hereafter *Andrews*).

Roger Halson, *The Critical Reception of* Cavendish Square Holdings v Makdessi In: *Shaping the Law of Obligations.* Edited by: Edwin Peel and Rebecca Probert, Oxford University Press. © Roger Halson 2023. DOI: 10.1093/oso/9780198889762.003.0012

levied on their customers were not prevented from being penalties because the liability to pay the fees was 'triggered' by an event which was not a breach of contract.[8] It is clear that previously, as asserted in *Cavendish* by Lords Neuberger and Sumption,[9] the law in Australia had been the same as in England with its insistence upon a breach of contract as a pre-condition to the application of the penalty jurisdiction.[10] This radical[11] expansion of the law was effected in fewer than twenty pages and attracted trenchant criticism.[12] Even more recently, the Singapore Court of Appeal joined this competition in *Denka Advantech Pte v Seraya Energy Pte*,[13] where Andrew Phang Boon Leong JA delivered a thorough and reflective judgment that was four paragraphs longer than that in *Cavendish* and which is interesting for the grounds upon which the clauses in issue were upheld, as well as for the rejection of some aspects of the Supreme Court's decision in *Cavendish*.

This chapter will look at the reception that the *Cavendish* decision has received in the UK as well as overseas. Domestic cases will be examined to see how the principles laid down in *Cavendish* have been applied and sometimes refined. These cases will be presented as multiple factual applications of the new concepts and approach introduced by the UK Supreme Court. Overseas cases, including the cases referred to above, as well as other cases that can be more quickly digested, will be discussed with a focus upon the extent to which the approach of the Supreme Court in *Cavendish* has been endorsed or departed from.

A distinctive feature of the scholarship of Ewan McKendrick has been the extent to which he has made technical areas of commercial law more accessible to non-specialists. The scheme of presentation followed in this chapter is a respectful attempt to do the same. However, before commencing that analysis the facts of the conjoined appeals in *Cavendish* will be expanded and the 'new' law applicable to stipulated damages clauses summarized.

---

[8] The factual situation, so-called unauthorized borrowing from a bank, was the same one that the House of Lords examined in *Office of Fair Trading v Abbey National plc* [2009] UKSC 6, [2010] 1 AC 69 where the penalty rule was 'avoided' by careful drafting.

[9] *Cavendish* (n 1) [41].

[10] In the most recent High Court decision prior to *Andrews, Ringrow Pty Ltd v BP Australia Pty Ltd* [2005] HCA 71, (2005) 224 CLR 656, 662 (hereafter *Ringrow*), all six judges restated the traditional view that '[t]he law of penalties . . . is attracted where a contract stipulates that on breach the contract breaker will pay an agreed sum'. In the High Court see also *IAC (Leasing) Ltd v Humphrey* [1972] HCA 1, (1972) 126 CLR 131, 143 (Walsh J); *O'Dea v Allstates Leasing System (WA) Pty Ltd* [1983] HCA 3, (1983) 152 CLR 359, 390 (Brennan J); *AMEV-UDC Finance Ltd v Austin* [1986] HCA 63, (1986) 162 CLR 170, 184 (Mason and Wilson JJ citing *Export Credits Guarantee Department v Universal Oil Products Co*[1983] 1 WLR 399) and 221 (Dawson J). For an academic review of these cases see Anthony Gray, 'Contractual Penalties in Australian Law after *Andrews*: An Opportunity Missed' (2013) 18 Deakin LR 1, 9–14.

[11] cf Gageler J in *Paciocco* (n 6) [122] who rejects this characterization, stating that '*Andrews* did nothing to disturb the settled understanding in Australia'. However, this view is surely contrary to the numerous decisions, including three of the High Court itself, referred to in the previous footnote.

[12] '[T]he task which the court set itself, namely to provide a meaningful historical account of the evolution of the penalties doctrine over several hundred years within the space of a few pages seems an impossible and futile exercise': JW Carter, Wayne Courtney, Elisabeth Peden, Andrew Stewart, and GJ Tolhurst, 'Contractual Penalties: Resurrecting the Equitable Jurisdiction' (2013) 30 JCL 99, 109. In a convincing and powerful critique, the article also questions the High Court's selective citation of authority and interpretation of prior Australian decisions: 'Imperfectly reported cases, decided in contexts vastly different from those which arise under the modern law, to say nothing of fragments from a handbook of equity written in the 17th century have no bearing on the law of today' (131–32). See also Sirko Harder, 'The Relevance of Breach to the Applicability of the Rule against Penalties' (2013) 30 JCL 52.

[13] [2020] SGCA 119, [2021] 1 SLR 631 (hereafter *Denka*); see Roger Halson, 'Liquidated Damages and Penalties—A Review of the *Cavendish* Decision by the Singapore Court of Appeal' (2021) 137 LQR 375.

II. The *Cavendish* Case

The *Makdessi* appeal involved Cavendish Square Holding BV, part of the world's leading marketing communications group, and Mr Makdessi, the co-founder and co-owner of the largest advertising and marketing communications group in the Middle East. Following extensive negotiations, with both sides advised throughout by experienced commercial lawyers, Mr Makdessi agreed to sell to Cavendish approximately 47 per cent of the shares in the group he founded, with the price payable in stages. Under clause 11.2 of the sale contract, he undertook not to engage in competitive activity. He further acknowledged in clause 5.1 that if he did so compete he would lose the right to future interim and final payments and, in clause 5.6, that he could be required to sell to Cavendish the rest of his shares at a reduced price that took no account of goodwill. It was accepted that Mr Makdessi was in breach of clause 11.2 and so argument centred upon the effects of that breach.

At first instance Burton J in the Commercial Court rejected Mr Makdessi's submission that clauses 5.1 and 5.6 were penal and so unenforceable. He granted Cavendish a declaration that Mr Makdessi was not entitled to further payments and was obliged to sell his remaining shareholding at the reduced price. The Court of Appeal allowed Mr Makdessi's appeal, holding that the two clauses were not genuine pre-estimates of loss; rather, their function was to act as a deterrent, and so both were unenforceable as penalties. Cavendish appealed to the Supreme Court, contending that the clauses were not penal and further that the common law rule on penalties should be abolished or at least restricted to the extent that it should not apply to commercial transactions between parties with equal bargaining power acting on legal advice.

In the *Parking Eye* appeal, Mr Beavis had 'overstayed' in a car park for fifty-six minutes longer than the free two-hour period permitted and so, under the terms displayed at the entrance to, and throughout, the car park, became liable to a parking charge of £85 (reducible to £50 if paid within fourteen days).[14] Mr Beavis refused to pay any charge. Both Judge Maloney QC sitting in the Chelmsford County Court and the Court of Appeal rejected his argument that the £85 charge was unenforceable at common law because it was a penalty and/or was 'unfair' and so unenforceable under Regulation 5(1) of the Unfair Terms in Consumer Contracts Regulations 1999 (the 1999 Regulations).[15]

In the *Makdessi* appeal the 'primary case' of counsel for Cavendish was that the penalty rule was 'antiquated, anomalous and unnecessary' and that the Supreme Court should now take the opportunity to abolish it.[16] This invitation was rejected by all members of the Supreme Court, who chose instead to restate it.[17] All the substantive speeches delivered in *Cavendish* refer to detailed historical, and briefer comparative, analyses to support this conclusion. However, the full extent of the change in the applicable law is disguised by the fact that the previous leading authority, the *Dunlop* case,[18] was not overruled but rather was

---

[14] Interestingly, given the modest amount in dispute, Mr Beavis was represented by experienced senior counsel who were acting pro bono with the other costs of the litigation paid for by 'crowdfunding': Chloe Smith, 'Landmark £85 Parking Ticket Battle Hits Supreme Court', LS Gaz (23 July 2015), www.lawgazette.co.uk/landmark-85-parking-ticket-battle-hits-supreme-court/5050202.article (last accessed 5 January 2023).

[15] SI 1999/2083. These now revoked by Part 2 of the Consumer Rights Act 2015 which enacts similar, but not identical, provisions.

[16] *Cavendish* (n 1) [36] and [126].

[17] ibid [36]–[39] (Lords Neuberger and Sumption, Lord Carnwath agreeing), [162]–[170] (Lord Mance), [292] (Lord Toulson agreeing).

[18] *Dunlop* (n 2).

reinterpreted. The well-known statement of principle by Lord Dunedin in the *Dunlop* case was criticized for its rigidity, as a 'straightjacket'[19] of 'immutable rules of general application'.[20] Nonetheless, Lords Neuberger and Sumption appear to suggest a continuing role for those principles in relation to simple cases.[21] Subsequent examples where *Dunlop* has been applied to straightforward cases are rare,[22] perhaps because such cases are rarely the subject of reported appeals.

The Supreme Court upheld the clauses in both appeals and so reversed the decision of the Court of Appeal in the *Makdessi* case and affirmed the decision of the same court in the *Parking Eye* case. The decision was unanimous as to outcome, with the exception that Lord Toulson JSC dissented in the *Parking Eye* case on the basis that, in his view, the notice demanding extra payment was unfair under the 1999 Regulations.[23]

In summary, the Supreme Court confirmed: that a clause which provides that a payment is to be made (or other obligation performed) upon an event other than the payer's breach of contract will not fall within the 'penalty jurisdiction' (the 'breach requirement');[24] that between 'properly advised parties of comparable bargaining power' there should operate a 'strong initial presumption' of enforceability;[25] and that the penalty rule would continue to apply to clauses requiring a party to transfer assets at undervalue as much as to those requiring a payment to be made.[26]

More controversially, the Supreme Court said that the definition of a penalty stated by Lord Dunedin in the *Dunlop* case, that is, as a clause that provided for the payment of a sum that was greater than a genuine pre-estimate of loss, will no longer apply generally;[27] that the proper test for a penalty now places emphasis upon the justifying legitimate interest of the party seeking to enforce the clause (the 'legitimate interest requirement'); and that the sum or detriment stipulated must be proportionate to the protection of the legitimate interest (the 'proportionality requirement').

The breach, legitimate interest, and proportionality requirements will now be discussed in more detail.

---

[19] *Cavendish* (n 1) [225] (Lord Hodge).

[20] ibid [31] (Lords Neuberger and Sumption).

[21] ibid [22], [32] (Lords Neuberger and Sumption).

[22] *GPP Big Field LLP v Solar EPC Solutions SL* [2018] EWHC 2866 (Comm) and *Blu-Sky Solutions v Be Caring Ltd* [2021] EWHC (Comm) are examples. This 'residual' role for the old *Dunlop* approach has been approved by the Hong Kong Court of Appeal in *Law Ting Pong Secondary School v Chen Wai Wah* [2021] HKCA 873.

[23] *Cavendish* (n 1) [315]. This was on the basis that the other Justices had applied the wrong test to determine whether there had been a significant imbalance in the parties' rights and obligations as developed in *Aziz v Caixa d'Estalvis de Catalunya, Taragona I Manresa (Catalunyacaixa)* (Case C-415/11) EU:C:2013:164; [2013] 3 CMLR 5.

[24] *Cavendish* (n 1) [43] (Lords Neuberger and Sumption, Lord Carnwath agreeing), [130] (Lord Mance), [258] (Lord Hodge), [291] (Lord Clarke agreeing), [292] (Lord Toulson agreeing with Lords Mance and Hodge).

[25] ibid [35] (Lords Neuberger and Sumption, Lord Carnwath agreeing).

[26] ibid [35] (Lords Neuberger and Sumption, Lord Carnwath agreeing), [157], [170], [183] (Lord Mance), [226], [230] (Lord Hodge), [291] (Lord Clarke agreeing), [292] (Lord Toulson agreeing).

[27] ibid [25], [35] (Lords Neuberger and Sumption, Lord Carnwath agreeing, suggesting that it may continue to apply in 'straightforward' cases), [225] (Lord Hodge), [292] (Lord Toulson agreeing). It is also implicit in the speech of Lord Mance ([145]).

III. The Breach Requirement: 'Engaging' the Penalty Rule

The facts of the conjoined appeals in *Cavendish* (like those of *Dunlop* before it) involved payments (in *Dunlop* and the *Parking Eye* appeal) or other onerous obligations (the *Makdessi* appeal) which were treated in the judgments as if 'triggered' by a breach of contract. As a result, the jurisdiction to review the clause as potentially penal was applicable. The Justices of the Supreme Court used different words and metaphors to express this conclusion: Lords Neuberger and Sumption speak of the penalty rule being 'engaged'[28] while Lord Mance preferred the 'trigger' analogy[29] and elsewhere spoke of the penalty doctrine being 'potentially applicable'.[30] Although the judgments in *Cavendish* did not directly raise the question whether the penalty jurisdiction is applicable to contractual clauses which are 'triggered' by an event other than a breach of contract,[31] the issue was discussed after a more radical proposal by counsel for Cavendish[32]—that is, that the penalty rule should be abolished altogether—was rejected.[33] The further submission of counsel for Makdessi that 'as an alternative to confirming or abrogating [the Supreme Court] could extend it so that it applied more generally'[34] was also rejected. The Supreme Court declined to follow the *Andrews* case[35] where the High Court of Australia had addressed this question 'head-on'[36] and concluded that breach of contract is *not* an essential pre-requisite for the application of the penalty doctrine. The Supreme Court in *Cavendish* acknowledged that the insistence upon a breach of contract inevitably meant that its application could be avoided by 'clever drafting'.[37] A number of techniques are available to contract drafters to outflank the traditional penalty rule, one of which is to draft the contractual clause in a way that ensures that the payment or other benefit arises upon the happening of an event that is not a breach of contract.

The breach requirement now marks a major divergence between the law of England and Wales and that of Australia.[38] The Singapore Court of Appeal (SCA) in *Denka*[39] has recently endorsed the approach to this issue taken in *Cavendish*, as opposed to *Andrews*. In *Denka* the SCA acknowledged that '[t]he removal of the breach requirement appears attractive at first blush', but declined to extend the jurisdiction in this way.[40] The approval of this aspect

---

[28] ibid [12] 'In what circumstances is the penalty rule engaged?', copying the language of the single judgment of the High Court of Australia in *Andrews* (n 8): 'It has been established at least since the decision of Lord Macclesfield in *Peachy v Duke of Somerset* that the penalty doctrine is not engaged if...'

[29] ibid [171].

[30] ibid [193].

[31] ibid [130] (Lord Mance).

[32] ibid [36] (Lords Neuberger and Sumption, Lord Carnwath agreeing), [162] (Lord Mance).

[33] ibid [39] (Lords Neuberger and Sumption, Lord Carnwath agreeing), [130] (Lord Mance: 'I do not see the distinction between situations of breach and non-breach as being without rational or logical underpinning'), [291] (Lord Toulson agreeing).

[34] ibid [40] (Lords Neuberger and Sumption, Lord Carnwath agreeing).

[35] *Andrews* (n 8).

[36] *Cavendish* (n 1) [129] (Lord Mance).

[37] ibid [43] (Lords Neuberger and Sumption, Lord Carnwath agreeing). Lord Hodge ([258]) refers to 'careful' rather than 'clever' drafting. See also *Edgeworth Capital (Luxenbourg) Sarl v Ramblas Investments BV* [2015] EWHC 150 (Comm) [59] (Hamblen J) (hereafter *Edgeworth*). See also *Ahuja Investments Ltd v Victorygame Ltd* [2021] EWHC 2382 (Ch) [132], where it was noted that 'the drafting in the present case is not sufficiently "clever" to circumvent the rule'.

[38] For discussion of a further divergence in relation between these systems in an analogous area of law see the discussion of relief from forfeiture in *Manchester Ship Canal Co Ltd v Vauxhall Motors Ltd* [2018] EWCA Civ 1100, [2019] Ch 331, [53] (further appeal to the SC dismissed at [2019] UK SC 46).

[39] *Denka* (n 14) [82].

[40] ibid [92].

of the *Cavendish* decision was justified by the commercial uncertainty that the Australian approach would create, which would 'permit the courts to review a wide range of clauses on *substantive* (and *not* merely procedural) grounds' and so constitute 'a general, uncertain and significant legal incursion into the *freedom of contract*'.[41] The SCA endorsed the concern, expressed by Lord Neuberger and Lord Sumption in the *Cavendish* case,[42] that *Andrews* '[transforms] a rule for controlling remedies for breach of contract into a jurisdiction to review the content of the substantive obligations which the parties have agreed'.

The SCA further acknowledged that the breach limitation created the opportunity for contractors 'to circumvent [the jurisdiction] by clever drafting', as illustrated in the UK by the litigation in the *Office of Fair Trading v Abbey National plc*,[43] which, like the Australian case of *Andrews*, involved the enforceability of terms in banks' contracts with customers levying charges for so-called unauthorized borrowing.

A. Breach Requirement: Illustrations

1. *Hayfin Opal Luxco 3 SARL v Windermere VII CMBS Plc*

Hayfin Opal Luxco 3 SARL v Windermere VII CMBS Plc[44] involved a commercial mortgage-backed securitization structure. The court had to consider whether there had been a historic underpayment of interest to an investor. Snowden J said (obiter dicta[45]) that *if* there had been any underpayment, a clause under which the investor would ostensibly become entitled to further interest payments calculated on a different basis would not be subject to the penalty jurisdiction. This was because it was part of an 'elaborate mechanism'[46] to determine the amount that would be payable overall on the notes and that the contractual clause 'for the avoidance of doubt'[47] expressly provided that any non-payment of an amount otherwise due shall not constitute a 'default'.[48]

2. *Brown's Bay Resort Ltd v Pozzoni*

The Privy Council held in *Brown's Bay Resort Ltd v Pozzoni*[49] that a clause which specified a penalty fee payable by the tenant of commercial premises if he caused an interruption to the lease could not be reviewed as a penalty. Rather, the fee was a part of the consideration payable if normal performance was interrupted, and so was not a sum payable in lieu of common law damages.

---

[41] ibid [82] (all emphases in original).

[42] *Cavendish* (n 1) [42].

[43] [2009] UKSC 6, [2010] 1 AC 696. For a further jurisdictional contrast see *Smiley v Citibank (South Dakota) NA* 517 US 735 (1996), where the US Supreme Court held that late payment fees levied by a bank on its credit card accounts were not unenforceable penalties because they could be characterized as 'interest' which the bank was entitled to charge under an old statutory provision.

[44] [2016] EWHC 782 (Ch), [2018] 1 BCLC 118 (hereafter *Hayfin*).

[45] ibid [108]. He found that there had been no historic underpayment of interest.

[46] ibid [117].

[47] ibid [118].

[48] ibid.

[49] [2016] UKPC 10.

3. *Richards v IP Solutions Ltd*

In *Richards v IP Solutions Ltd*[50] the directors of a business sold to investors were retained as employees and shareholders but were later summarily dismissed for the retention of a bonus to which they were not entitled. A 'bad leaver' clause in the company articles required a shareholder who was summarily dismissed to transfer their shares for £1. It was said (obiter dicta[51]) that the 'bad leaver' clause was not subject to the penalty jurisdiction because it was more akin to a primary than a secondary obligation.

4. *Signia Wealth v Vector Trustees*

The High Court in *Signia Wealth v Vector Trustees*[52] held that the penalty rule was not applicable to 'bad leaver' provisions in a director's contract regulating the compulsory transfer of company shares when none of the transfer events had anything to do with a breach of contract.

5. *Heritage Travel and Tourism v Windhorst*

In *Heritage Travel and Tourism v Windhorst*,[53] the claimants provided large short-term loans to the defendant. Following the defendant's default, a settlement agreement was entered which included an 'acceleration clause' whereby further default entitled the claimants to serve notice that full payment was due as well as a daily 'lump sum' while sums remained outstanding. Such 'provisions . . . are not a trigger . . . so as to attract the operation of the rule against penalties, but simply define the period during which [sums] become due'.[54]

6. *Law Ting Pong Secondary School v Chen Wai Wah*

A schoolteacher had failed to take up the appointment he had accepted under a contract that required the teacher to give three months' notice or make an equivalent payment for early termination. Applying *Cavendish*, the Hong Kong Court of Appeal in *Law Ting Pong Secondary School v Chen Wai Wah*[55] found that the termination provision did not engage the penalty jurisdiction because this provision was in fact a primary obligation under the contract. Consequently, the school was claiming from the teacher a contractual debt and not damages payable upon the teacher's breach of contract.

7. *In re B*

The breach requirement restated by the UK Supreme Court in *Cavendish* is that the breach of contract which is the 'trigger' for the stipulated payment (or other detriment) must be a breach of a contractual duty owed by the contemplated payer. A breach of a contractual duty owed to any other party does not come within the penalty jurisdiction.[56] This aspect

---

[50] [2016] EWHC 1835; [2017] IRLR 133.
[51] It was held that the directors' conduct, though wrongful, did not in fact justify summary dismissal.
[52] [2018] EWHC 1040 (Ch); (hereafter *Signia Wealth*).
[53] [2021] EWHC 2380 (Comm).
[54] ibid [90].
[55] [2021] HKCA 873 (hereafter *Law Ting Pong*).
[56] *Export Credits Guarantee Department v Universal Oil Products Co* [1983] 1 WLR 399 (HL). See also *Edgeworth* (n 37), upheld at [2016] EWCA 412 except for the method of calculating the fee payable where a clause providing for the payment of a €150m fee for services in connection with the raising of a large sum of money to purchase an extensive office complex was said to constitute part of the remuneration payable to a lender and so could not be a penalty even though the fee only became payable when there was a default upon a separate loan. This was because the default which made the fee payable was a breach of a different contract and not that between the contemplated payer and payee.

of the breach requirement was applied by the Court of Appeal in an unusual context. *In re B*[57] a mother wanted to relocate, with her children and new husband, to Abu Dhabi. An order was made permitting relocation subject to, inter alia, the new husband executing a second charge on London property exercisable immediately upon the breach of undertakings about access and future care of the children. The father of the children challenged the order, inter alia on the ground that the charge might be unenforceable as a penalty. The Court of Appeal found that the father's fear was 'understandable, but misplaced'.[58] This was because the £250k charge became payable upon the breach of the court order by either the mother or her new husband; it did not become payable upon breach of any contractual duty owed by the person liable to make the payment.

IV. Legitimate Interest Requirement

A. Applying the Test for a Penalty

If the penalty rule is engaged,[59] the next step is to apply the appropriate test to ascertain whether the provision being examined is an unenforceable penalty. It is with respect to the ascertainment and application of the test for a penalty that *Cavendish* effected the greatest change to our previous understanding of the law. The magnitude of this change should not be disguised by the fact that the previous leading authority, *Dunlop*, was not formally overruled[60] but was rather reinterpreted.

This reinterpretation built upon the struggle of modern judges prior to the decision in *Cavendish* to apply the principles stated in *Dunlop* by Lord Dunedin in a way that did not frustrate the reasonable expectations of commercial transactors. A typical statement is that of Lord Woolf in *Phillips Hong Kong Ltd v Attorney General of Hong Kong*: 'the court has to be careful not to set too high a standard and bear in mind that what the parties have agreed should normally be upheld. Any other approach will lead to undesirable uncertainty especially in commercial contracts.'[61]

More recently, this approach was put more succinctly by Arden and Buxton LJJ in *Murray v Leisureplay plc*,[62] where they described the 'generous margin' that should be accorded to parties before a provision is considered penal. The different formulations for the appropriate test proffered by the Justices in *Cavendish* will be examined in this section and illustrations of their application given thereafter.

---

[57] [2015] EWCA Civ 1302; [2016] 1 WLR 2326 (hereafter *In re B*).

[58] ibid [65].

[59] *Cavendish* (n 1) [12] and see the High Court of Australia in *Andrews* (n 8).

[60] Indeed, a residual role for the application of the previously accepted understanding of Lord Dunedin's judgment in *Dunlop* was expressly preserved by Lords Neuberger and Sumption (*Cavendish* (n 1) [22], as noted above in section II). Interestingly, the proposition that *Dunlop* should continue to apply to simple cases was also made by Nettle J, the dissentient, in *Paciocco* (n 12) [322]. See also the decision of the Supreme Court of New South Wales in *Cafe Du Liban Ltd v Bespoke Garage Pty Ltd* [2017] NSWSC 779, applying *Paciocco* (n 12) and referring to Nettle J's statement but without any reference to the *Cavendish* decision.

[61] (1993) 61 BLR 41, 59 (PC) (hereafter *Phillips*). See also *Robophone Facilities v Blank* [1966] 1 WLR 1428, 1477 (CA) (Diplock LJ).

[62] [2005] EWCA Civ 963; [2005] IRLR 946, [43] and [114], relied upon in *Cadogan Petroleum Holdings Ltd v Global Process Systems* [2013] EWHC 214 (Comm); [2013] 2 Lloyd's Rep 26 [36].

According to Lords Neuberger and Sumption, the test is 'whether the impugned provision is a secondary obligation which imposes a detriment on the contract-breaker out of all proportion to any legitimate interest of the innocent party in the enforcement of the primary obligation'.[63]

According to Lord Mance:

> What is necessary in each case is to consider, first, whether any (and if so what) legitimate business interest is served and protected by the clause, and, second, whether, assuming such an interest to exist, the provision made for the interest is nevertheless in the circumstances extravagant, exorbitant or unconscionable.[64]

According to Lord Hodge, 'the correct test for a penalty is whether the sum or remedy stipulated as a consequence of a breach of contract is exorbitant or unconscionable when regard is had to the innocent party's interest in the performance of the contract'.[65]

The different formulations each appear to comprise two elements, though perhaps only Lord Mance separates them expressly.[66] First, the party seeking to enforce the clause must have a 'legitimate interest' in its enforcement. Second, there must be a certain proportionality between the legitimate interest and the sum (or other sanction) stipulated. Both of these matters must be judged at or relative to a particular point in time. The older law on penalties laid down in *Dunlop*[67] turned on whether or not a term was a genuine pre-estimate of loss and was judged at the time of contracting. The same approach to timing is taken with the new test introduced in the *Cavendish* case. It would seem to be implicit[68] in the requirement of a legitimate interest that this must exist at the time its protection is planned, that is, at the time of contracting. It then follows that the requirement of proportionality between the sum (or other detriment) specified and the legitimate interest it serves to protect should be judged at the same time. That the enforceability of any clause subject to the penalty jurisdiction is to be judged by reference to the time of contracting was confirmed in one of the first cases to apply the new approach propounded in *Cavendish*, the judge also remarking that this was the only matter upon which the parties could agree.[69] In this respect the penalty jurisdiction[70] has developed differently in the UK than in the United States, where 'the modern trend' is to assess the reasonableness of the clause either at the time of contract formation or at the moment of breach.[71]

---

[63] *Cavendish* (n 1) [35].

[64] ibid [152].

[65] ibid [255].

[66] ibid [152].

[67] *Dunlop* (n 2). See *Commissioner of Public Works v Hills* [1906] AC 368, 376, repeated in *Dunlop*, 86–87.

[68] Though see Lord Hodge, who expressly said that 'the court . . . approaches the matter as a question of construing the particular contract at the time when it was made' ([221]).

[69] *Hayfin* (n 44) [137]; *Vivienne Westwood Ltd v Conduit Street Developments* [2017] EWHC 350 (Ch), [2017] L&TR 23, most recently confirmed in *Permavent Ltd v Makin* [2021] EWHC 467 (Ch), [2021] FSR 26 (hereafter *Permavent*). In *Gray v Braid Group (Holdings) Ltd* [2016] CSIH 68 (Court of Session) [35], Lord Malcolm warned against making inferences based upon market movements that post-dated the agreement being construed.

[70] For a comparison between the penalty jurisdiction and relief from forfeiture see Roger Halson, Liquidated Damages and Penalty Clauses (Oxford University Press, 2018) paras 5.02–5.31, especially at 5.21 for a discussion of the different times by reference to which the respective tests for validity are applied.

[71] Lon Fuller, Melvin Eisenberg, and Mark Gergen, *Basic Contract Law* (9th edn, West Academic Publishing, 2013) 352.

202 CRITICAL RECEPTION OF *CAVENDISH SQUARE HOLDINGS V MAKDESSI*

B. The Legitimate Interest: Illustrations

1. *The Makdessi appeal*

It was emphasized that Cavendish, the purchaser of Mr Makdessi's business, had a 'very substantial and legitimate interest in protecting the value of the company's goodwill. This protection was effected by giving the sellers a strong financial incentive to remain loyal'.[72] Lord Mance added the clauses were fairly designed to protect against competition that was difficult to detect.[73]

2. *Gray v Braid Group (Holdings) Ltd*

In *Gray v Braid Group (Holdings) Ltd*,[74] a company director complicit in 'bribery offences' challenged a provision in the company's Articles of Association which obliged him to sell his £20.6m shareholding back to the company for under £2,500. This 'bad leaver' provision was upheld because of the company's legitimate interest in removing a fraudulent employee as soon as possible, and requiring the sale of his shareholding at a low price was justified because fraud could destroy the company and the shareholders chose this mechanism as the most effective way to protect honest shareholders.[75]

3. *Indigo Park Services v Watson*

In a case similar to the *ParkingEye* appeal, *Indigo Park Services v Watson*,[76] it was held that a parking management company had a legitimate interest to protect sufficient to justify a £40 parking fee as well as, in this case, the recovery of £96 costs, because fraud could destroy the company and this mechanism was chosen as the most effective way to protect honest shareholders. It was not clear in the *Indigo* case that the company's business model was premised upon a high turnover of short-term visitors as in *ParkingEye*.[77]

4. *Wilaci Pty Ltd v Torchlight Fund No 1*

In *Wilaci Pty Ltd v Torchlight Fund No 1*,[78] a sixty-day commercial loan of AU$37m was made with AU$320,000 interest, an AU$5m arrangement fee, and weekly additional interest of AU$500,000 for late payment. The New Zealand Court of Appeal held that the additional interest was not 'out of all proportion to the legitimate interests of [the lender]', including the 'exceptionally high' level of risk involved in lending money to a debtor who was 'unbankable' elsewhere.[79]

5. *Signia Wealth v Vector Trustees*

The High Court in *Signia Wealth*[80] noted obiter (because the penalty rule was not in fact 'engaged') that 'bad leaver' provisions regulating shareholdings held by former employees

---

[72] *Cavendish* (n 1) 274 (Lord Hodge). See also Lords Neuberger and Sumption ([75]).
[73] ibid [172].
[74] [2016] CSIH 68; 2016 SLT 1003.
[75] ibid [44].
[76] 2017 GWD 40-610 (Sherriff Court).
[77] *Cavendish* (n 1) [286] (Lord Hodge). See also Neuberger and Sumption ([99]) and Lord Mance ([193]).
[78] [2017] NZSC 112.
[79] ibid [101] and [93]; cf *Ahuja Investments Ltd v Victorygame Ltd* [2021] EWHC 2382 discussed in the next section for a default interest provision which was considered to be a penalty.
[80] *Signia Wealth* (n 52).

protected a legitimate interest in ensuring that shareholdings were held by a small cohort directly involved with the development of the company.

6. *127 Hobson Street Ltd v Honey Bees Preschool Ltd*

In *127 Hobson Street Ltd v Honey Bees Preschool Ltd*[81] a childcare company leased premises in a multistorey building served by a single lift. The owners undertook to install a second lift and agreed to an extensive indemnity provision if this obligation was breached. Applying *Cavendish*, the Supreme Court of New Zealand held that the indemnity protected the tenant's legitimate interest in the provision of a second lift which, with concentrated traffic at 'pick up' and 'drop off' times, was essential to the operation and planned expansion of their business.

7. *Eco World—Ballymore Embassy Gardens Co Ltd v Dobler UK*

A liquidated damages clause in a construction contract was held to be valid in *Eco World—Ballymore Embassy Gardens Co Ltd v Dobler UK*[82] where the employer had taken over part of the works as completed even though the contract made no provision for reducing the sum payable. The term was clear and certain and so 'operable', and the claimant had a legitimate interest in enforcing the defendant's primary obligation to compete the works as a whole by the completion date.

8. *Luxury Italian KBB Co Ltd v Boutros*

In *Luxury Italian KBB Co Ltd v Boutros*,[83] a property refurbishment contract had been entered into where both parties were aware of the performer's thin profit margin—there was 'no fat to burn'.[84] In these circumstances the performer was protecting a legitimate interest when stipulating onerous payment default provisions which required the payment of more than £114k interest on a contract price of just over £64k.

9. *Permavent v Makin*

Permavent Ltd v Makin[85] involved an agreement between former business partners whereby one assigned, and undertook not to in future assert, IP rights in roofing products in exchange for purchase of his shares for £620k. These products represented 60 per cent of the company's gross profits. When the assignor breached the agreement, it was held that the assignee had a legitimate interest in enforcing provision requiring repayment of £620k and the forfeiture of his entitlement to royalties upon the sale of the relevant products.

10. *Law Ting Pong Secondary School v Chen Wai Wah (2021)*

In *Law Ting Pong*,[86] the Hong Kong Court of Appeal said that if the termination provisions in the teacher's contract were subject to the penalty rule the provision was still enforceable, as it protected a legitimate interest of the school. This was identified as protecting against

---

[81] [2020] NZSC 53.
[82] [2021] EWHC 2207 (TCC); 197 Con LR 108.
[83] [2021] EW Misc 5 (CC).
[84] ibid [85].
[85] *Permavent* (n 69).
[86] *Law Ting Pong* (n 55). For the facts see text at n 55.

204 CRITICAL RECEPTION OF *CAVENDISH SQUARE HOLDINGS V MAKDESSI*

the difficult task of securing adequate teaching capacity at short notice close to the beginning of the school term.

V. The Proportionality Requirement

Differing expressions were used by the Justices in *Cavendish* to describe the required relationship between the sum (or other detriment) stipulated and the justifying interest it serves to protect. Lords Neuberger and Sumption said it must be 'out of all proportion',[87] Lord Mance that it must be 'extravagant, exorbitant or unconscionable',[88] and Lord Hodge that it must be 'exorbitant or unconscionable'.[89] All seem to permit a broad margin of error before the clause will become unenforceable.

The principle was expressed pithily by the High Court of Australia in a decision that post-dated *Cavendish*: 'It is not enough that it should be lacking in proportion. It must be "out of all proportion".'[90] In this respect the degree of latitude inherent in these statements of the requirement of proportionality may be regarded as an implementation of the previous oft-repeated refrain that courts should not be over-zealous in their approach to 'policing' penalty clauses.[91]

In one of the first cases applying the post-*Cavendish* law on penalties, the High Court considered the application of the proportionality requirement[92] in a dispute arising from a complex commercial mortgage-backed securitization scheme which involved the acquisition of loans secured on income generating commercial property. The purchase of these loans was funded by the issue of notes to investors who were entitled to interest payable. At issue in the case was the correct method for the calculation of interest and whether, if there had been a historic underpayment of interest, the claimants were entitled to rely upon a further provision which levied interest on the unpaid amount, or whether that provision was unenforceable as a penalty. Having noted the focus of the penalty doctrine 'on the lack of proportionality between the amount of the secondary liability imposed and the innocent party's legitimate interest in performance of the primary obligation',[93] Snowden J said (obiter[94]) that if a contractual provision provided for the payment of further interest that would constitute 'a multiplication of the unpaid amount by a very sizable factor' and so result in 'a sum many times the amount that would adequately compensate the innocent party for being kept out of his money', such a provision would breach the proportionality requirement, as it would be 'regarded as exorbitant (if not extortionate)'.[95] Such a provision is not saved from being penal by the fact that the party in breach of contract is 'so rich' he will not

---

[87] *Cavendish* (n 1) [32].

[88] ibid [152].

[89] ibid [255].

[90] In *Ringrow* (n 11) 669, quoted with approval by Gageler J in *Paciocco* (n 12) [156].

[91] See the discussion in section IV, 'Applying the Test for a Penalty', and the discussion of Lord Woolf's statement in *Phillips* (n 61).

[92] *Hayfin* (n 44).

[93] ibid [142].

[94] Snowden J held that there had been no historic underpayment of interest but that if there had been the clause was not reviewable as a penalty because it was expressly provided that such non-payment shall not constitute a contractual 'default', ie breach ([108]). Indeed, he prefaced his further 'brief' ([130]) examination of the penalty jurisdiction with the express reservation that he did 'not finally have to decide this point' ([140]).

[95] ibid [140].

be bothered by the lack of proportionality.[96] Nor can the contract breaker do so by under-taking to limit his claim to specified funds if the extent of those funds would still constitute 'a wholly disproportionate amount'.[97]

A. Proportionality: Other Illustrations

1. *Cargill International Trading Pte Ltd v Uttam Galva Steels Ltd*

In *Cargill International Trading Pte Ltd v Uttam Galva Steels Ltd*,[98] a case involving the sale of steel, a default rate of interest of one-month LIBOR plus 12 per cent pa was specified. It was held that the default rate was not disproportionate to the increased credit risk of the defaulting party when compared to rates for unsecured loans in the Indian market.

2. *Permavent v Makin*

In *Permavent*, a provision in a settlement agreement that required repayment of the £620k share purchase price as well as the suspension of 5 per cent commission was described as 'ex-tremely harsh' but still 'not out of all proportion'[99] to the claimant's legitimate business interests.

3. *Ahuja Investments v Victorygame Ltd*

In *Ahuja Investments v Victorygame Ltd*,[100] the High Court dismissed a claim for default interest of 12 per cent compounded monthly. The Court acknowledged that there was some justification for increasing the rate of interest as a defaulting buyer was a higher credit risk. Nonetheless, a four-fold increase from 3 per cent to 12 per cent, and the introduction of compounding, was considered too great and to constitute a penalty.

4. *Slowikowska v Rogers*

In *Slowikowska v Rogers*[101] the High Court held that there was at least a triable issue that a 65 per cent rate of interest applicable to an unpaid loan was disproportionate to any legitimate interest.

5. *Blu-Sky Solutions v Be Caring Ltd*

In *Blu-Sky Solutions v Be Caring Ltd*[102] a company sought to cancel a contract for 800 new mobile phones prior to connection. The contract provided for a cancellation charge of £225 per connection (£180k total). The charge was almost eight times the amount of

---

[96] ibid [142] echoing the classic statement of Lord Wright in *Imperial Tobacco Co (of Great Britain and Ireland) Ltd v Parslay* [1936] 2 All ER 515, 523 (HL) that 'A millionaire may enter into a contract in which he is to pay li-quidated damages, or a poor man may enter into a similar contract with a millionaire, but in each case the question is exactly the same, namely whether the sum stipulated as damages for the breach was exorbitant or extravagant' (quoted in *Cavendish* (n 1) [34] (Lords Neuberger and Sumption) and [257] (Lord Hodge).

[97] *Hayfin* (n 44) [142].

[98] [2019] EWHC 476 (Comm).

[99] *Permavent* (n 69) [77] and [78]. See also text at n 101.

[100] [2021] EWHC 2729 (Ch).

[101] [2021] EWHC 192 (Ch).

[102] [2021] EWHC 2619 (Comm) (hereafter *Blu Sky*).

206 CRITICAL RECEPTION OF *CAVENDISH SQUARE HOLDINGS V MAKDESSI*

claimant's actual loss of profit[103] and so 'out of all proportion to any legitimate interest of the claimant'.[104]

VI. Conclusion

The survey of post-*Cavendish* UK law has revealed that the Supreme Court's restatement of the law applicable to agreed remedies has been applied many times. Perhaps surprisingly, the new concepts and approach introduced in the case do not appear to have resulted in any insuperable problems of application. Inevitably, however, such a major reformulation of commercial law has been subject to a more throughgoing examination in overseas juris-dictions, where the judgments of the UK's senior appellate court have only persuasive value. Table 12.1 below summarizes the different approaches discussed in this chapter which these jurisdictions have taken.[105]

One major common law jurisdiction is of course absent from both the earlier discussion and Table 12.1. The approach of Canadian courts to liquidated damages clauses 'stands apart' from the other major common law jurisdictions.[106] The distinguishing feature of Canadian jurisprudence in this area has been an emphasis upon demonstrated oppression as a pre-condition of intervention. Both the Supreme Court in *Cavendish*,[107] as well as the Singapore Court of Appeal in *Denka*[108] rejected, it is suggested correctly, the commercial uncertainty that would result from incorporating unconscionability into the law of stipu-lated damages.

The discussion and Table 12.1 below reveal a high degree of convergence in common law jurisdictions with regard to the so-called breach requirement, with Australia as the 'outlier'. This divergence has already been observed in other areas of contract law, particu-larly promissory estoppel, where the High Court of Australia abandoned the restriction on the operation of the doctrine that a promissory estoppel cannot, of itself, create a cause of action.[109] These divergences may reflect the greater importance attached to certainty and predictability in commercial dealings in the jurisdictions that continue to emphasize the breach requirement.

The Supreme Court's acceptance in *Cavendish* of the breach requirement means that the application of the jurisdiction may sometimes turn upon what Hoffman LJ has described as 'somewhat formal distinctions'.[110] However, acceptance of restriction is necessary to avoid a larger category of contractual clauses becoming subject to the review of the courts under the guise of the penalty jurisdiction. The need to limit the ambit of the doctrine follows

---

[103] Reference to 'actual loss' seems to be unnecessary to the application of the *Cavendish* test for a penalty, as op-posed to that in *Dunlop*.

[104] *Blu Sky* (n 102) [125].

[105] Ireland has been added for comparison though not discussed above as the Supreme Court of Ireland has not yet considered the applicability of *Cavendish* in Ireland. The summary in the chart is based upon the Irish Court of Appeal decision in *Sheehan v Breccia & Ors* [2018] IECA 286.

[106] See *Denka* (n 14) [136].

[107] A typical statement is that of Lord Mance ([169]).

[108] See *Denka* (n 14) [97].

[109] *Walton's Stores (Interstate) v Maher* [1988] HCA 7, (1988) 64 CLR 387. For a discussion and justification of the position in the UK see Roger Halson, 'The Offensive Limits of Promissory Estoppel' (1999) LMCLQ 256.

[110] *Else (1982) Ltd v Parkland Holdings Ltd* [1994] 1 BCLC 130, 145 quoted in *Cavendish* (n 1) [43] (Lords Neuberger and Sumption); see also [258] (Lord Hodge).

Table 12.1 International overview of the breach requirement

	Breach requirement	Legitimate interest (including proportionality) requirement
UK	YES	YES
Australia	NO	YES
Hong Kong	YES	YES
Ireland	YES	NO
New Zealand	YES	YES
Singapore	YES	NO

inevitably from the higher-level commitment to freedom of contract which guarantees to contractors the maximum autonomy to fashion their own contractual obligations. The general principle of laissez faire guarantees to transactors the maximum degree of contractual self-determination; the rule against penalties is a specific, and so necessarily restrictively defined, derogation from it.[111]

This more circumscribed approach also fits with the general character of the English common law of contract which more readily justifies intervention in the private ordering of rights through contract when there is a demonstrated incidence of procedural, as opposed to substantive, unconscionability.[112] The challenge of defining a clear limit upon the power to review penalty clauses has been grappled with when any reform of the doctrine has been considered.[113] In *Cavendish*, the Supreme Court endorsed the breach limitation while at the same time acknowledging its necessarily arbitrary operation, both reflected in Lord Mance's slightly hesitant comment that he did 'not see the distinction between situations of breach and non-breach as being without rational or logical underpinning.'[114]

With respect to the major innovation introduced in *Cavendish*, the legitimate interest (and associated proportionality) requirement, the careful judgment of Andrew Phang Boon Leong JA in *Denka* represents the most reflective rejection of it.[115] Proceeding from a respect for contractors' autonomy and the principle of freedom of contract, we have already noted the conclusion of the SCA, justified by the maintenance of commercial certainty, that the penalty jurisdiction should not apply to payments 'triggered' by non-breach events. However, the rejection of the restatement of the law in *Cavendish* (and the retention of the old *Dunlop* test) is justified in a parallel argument. The merit of incorporating into the test

---

[111] See *Cavendish* (n 1) [257] (Lord Hodge) and [33] (Lords Neuberger and Sumption).

[112] For a discussion of these issues in the context of a theoretical approach to contract law see Stephen Smith, *Contract Theory* (OUP 2004) 340–64.

[113] See eg the English Law Commission's discussion of the issue in *Penalty Clauses and Forfeiture of Monies Paid* (Law Com CP No 61, 1975) [22]. Their proposal to abandon the requirement of breach and replace it with one that applied the rules as to penalties 'wherever the object of the disputed contractual obligation is to secure the act or result which is the true purpose of the contract' was never implemented.

[114] *Cavendish* (n 1) [130].

[115] See *Denka* (n 14).

for the validity of a liquidated damages clause an express reference to a broader range of justifying, that is, legitimate interests is rejected when any uncertainty created by such a new test would surely be of a very different order from that which would result if non-breach events were brought within the rule. Although the result of many cases would be the same whichever test is applied, as the SCA admits, this would not always be the case; the SCA acknowledges that the second appeal in *Cavendish*, involving a charge for overstaying in a retail car park, would be decided differently.[116] In such cases it is suggested, contrary to the view of the SCA, that there is merit, and little detriment, in examining the full range of circumstances that might justify the clause in question, as the *Cavendish* test directs. Indeed, this intuition has been fully corroborated by the discussion of the subsequent experience of UK courts applying the Cavendish principles.

[116] ibid [181].

PART II
TORT

13

Direct and Vicarious Liability of Corporations

JAMES EDELMAN

I. Introduction

A little more than twenty years ago, sitting at lunch with Ewan McKendrick at Lady Margaret Hall, our discussion turned to a recent decision of the Court of Appeal which had held that an employee was not liable for a deceitful statement that was made on behalf of his corporate employer.[1] We considered the puzzle of whether an employee, being a natural person, should be personally responsible for acts done on behalf of a corporation. We later co-authored a note related to this issue.[2] At the conference for the Society of Public Teachers of Law later that year, over a heated but highly enjoyable discussion with several colleagues which lasted well past midnight, Ewan and I conceded that our note had been written partly just to test the waters; to provoke thought about what it means in law to act for another. But even when he is not testing the waters, everything Ewan writes provokes thought. For that reason, in this chapter in his honour, I will return to the topic we broached more than two decades ago, but from the opposite perspective. I will focus upon the manner in which a corporation can be responsible based on acts or liability of a natural person and, just perhaps, where acts might truly be said to have been done by the corporation.

This chapter is not concerned with the myriad of particular statutory rules for the attribution of acts or the attribution of liability from a natural person to a corporation. Nor is it concerned with the particular rules for when a corporation will be held responsible for another's action. The focus is instead to provide a broad taxonomy of the ways in which a corporation can be held responsible. The take-home message is this: there are three long-established ways in which a corporation might be held responsible and a fourth may be slowly emerging.

II. The Four Categories in Summary

First, a corporation can be held vicariously liable based upon the attribution of the *liability* of its officers or employees to the corporation itself. The rules for when that liability will be attributed are not yet fully developed.

Second, a corporation can be held liable based upon the attribution of the *acts* of its officers or employees. Whether or not the officer or employee is *liable*, the *act* and any mental state is attributed from the officer or employee to the corporation. The act and the mental

---

[1] *Standard Chartered Bank v Pakistan National Shipping Corporation (No 4)* [2001] QB 167 (CA), later overturned [2002] UKHL 43; [2003] 1 AC 959.

[2] Ewan McKendrick and James Edelman, 'Employee's Liability for Statements' (2002) 118 LQR 4.

James Edelman, *Direct and Vicarious Liability of Corporations* In: *Shaping the Law of Obligations.* Edited by: Edwin Peel and Rebecca Probert, Oxford University Press. © James Edelman 2023. DOI: 10.1093/oso/9780198889762.003.0013

state become the act of the corporation, for which responsibility can be imposed if the attributed conduct of the corporation is wrongful.

Third, a corporation can be held liable for its own non-delegable duty or based upon the attribution of the acts of natural persons to whom actions have been *delegated* by the corporation. A delegate is a person who acts for themself. Hence, a non-delegable duty is a label that describes a duty that cannot be discharged by delegating it. It is either discharged by the corporation or not. Conversely, where a natural person or a corporation has a duty which is delegable, then the natural person or corporation will not be liable for any wrongful performance by a reasonably chosen delegate. The delegate's actions are usually personal unless legislation provides for the acts of a delegate to be attributed to the delegator.

These three categories are well established in theory, although they have been often confused in practice. This has led to uncertainty as to how principles of responsibility should be applied. I will deal with each category in turn before turning to a fourth way in which the law might develop to hold a corporation responsible. Indeed, some statutes have already taken steps in this direction. The fourth way is for a corporation to be directly liable if it can be said that the corporation *itself* had performed an action with the required intention. Stated in this way, it can immediately be seen that this is a controversial proposition. Since a corporation does not exist as a physical entity in the world, how is it possible for a corporation itself to perform an action or to form an intention? I do not seek to provide any firm answers to this question, only to raise it for future consideration.

III. Broader Application

Although this chapter is focused upon the civil responsibility of corporations, the principles of direct and vicarious liability of others are of wider application. First, rules of direct and vicarious liability can be seen in criminal law as well as civil law. One of the greatest sources of confusion in the criminal law is the conflation of different attribution rules. In 2020, the Australian Law Reform Commission published an important report on corporate criminal responsibility.[3] At the start of a key chapter of the report concerning corporate attribution, the Commission quoted an observation of Professor Fisse that the 'attribution of criminal liability to corporations is an intractable subject: indeed, it is one of the blackest holes in criminal law'.[4]

Second, the rules of attribution are not limited to attribution of acts and liability from a natural person to a corporation. They extend also to attribution of acts and liability from one natural person to another. In broad terms: the first category, commonly described as vicarious liability, is secondary liability which applies across civil and criminal law to make both corporate and natural persons liable for the liability of others; and the second category is really just the rules of agency, which also apply across civil and criminal law to make corporate and natural persons liable, as primary actors, for the acts of others.

The breadth of operation of these rules can be illustrated by reference to the common law rules of criminal responsibility. At common law, a person could be criminally liable for

---

[3] Australian Law Reform Commission, *Corporate Criminal Responsibility* (Report 136, April 2020).

[4] ibid 217 [6.1], quoting Brent Fisse, 'The Attribution of Criminal Liability to Corporations: A Statutory Model' (1991) 13 Syd LR 277, 277.

wrongdoing either by primary liability or by secondary liability. Primary liability, known as liability in the first degree, was where the accused person was found to have committed the act themselves or where the act was committed by another and attributed to the accused person. Secondary liability, known as liability in the second and third degrees, was where the accused person was found to have been involved in the offence of another, so that the liability of that other person could be attributed to the accused.

The rules of primary liability—liability in the first degree—were the rules of personal action or agency. In general terms, agency operated so that where two parties had a common agreement or understanding, then the acts of one of them, in furtherance of that agreement, would be attributed to the other. It did not matter if the person acting was incapable of being criminally responsible, for example due to insanity.[5] The attribution upon which criminal responsibility was based was of the person's acts, not of the person's liability.

On the other hand, secondary liability—liability in the second degree or, somewhat curiously named, in the third degree—was the criminal liability of a person that was based on the criminal liability of another. A principal in the second degree was a person who was present at the scene of a crime and encouraged the perpetrator but did not physically participate. If the perpetrator was criminally liable, then so was the principal in the second degree.[6] A principal in the third degree, or 'accessory before the fact', was a person who aided and abetted in the commission of the crime, but who was not present at the scene of the crime. Again, the liability of the accessory before the fact was derivative of, or dependent upon, the criminal responsibility of the person who was aided and abetted.[7] For secondary liability, the person who committed the crime need not be identified or convicted, but it was necessary to prove that the offence had been committed.

IV. The Four Categories in Detail

A. Vicarious (Secondary) Liability Distinguished from Primary Liability

There is a basic confusion that must be avoided. This confusion is between attributing *liability* to a corporation and attributing *acts* to a corporation. The literal language of vicarious liability suggests the former. It requires someone to be liable and then for that liability to be attributed to the corporation. By contrast, the attribution of acts says nothing about the liability of the person whose actions are attributed. But, as Kiefel CJ, Keane J, and I said in *Construction, Forestry, Maritime, Mining and Energy Union v Personnel Contracting Pty Ltd*,[8] the term 'vicarious liability' is commonly used to describe both types of attribution: attribution of liability and attribution of acts. It might be better for clarity if the term 'vicarious liability' were used only to describe true vicarious liability—that is, liability for the liability of another.

---

[5] *R v Tyler and Price* (1838) 8 Car & P 616, 618–19; 173 ER 643, 644 (QB).

[6] *R v Kupferberg* (1918) 13 Cr App R 166, 168 (CA); *R v Clarkson* [1971] 1 WLR 1402 (Courts Martial Appeal Court).

[7] *R v Gregory* (1867) LR 1 CCR 77, 79; *Walsh v Sainsbury* [1925] HCA 28, (1925) 36 CLR 464, 477; *R v See Lun* (1932) 32 SR (NSW) 363, 364.

[8] [2022] HCA 1, (2022) 96 ALJR 89, [82].

214 DIRECT AND VICARIOUS LIABILITY OF CORPORATIONS

On one view of the older authorities,[9] the central focus was primary liability, that is, liability based on the attribution of another's acts. In *Middleton v Fowler*, Holt CJ said that when a servant 'acts in execution of the authority given by [their] master ... then the act of the servant is the act of the master'.[10] And in *Ackworth v Kempe*, Lord Mansfield said that 'the act of the sheriff's bailiff is the act of the sheriff'.[11] In today's language we would say that the acts of an agent that are authorized by actual or ostensible authority are attributed to a principal. When a principal authorizes an agent to act, the acts of the agent will be attributed to the principal by whose authority the acts were performed.

But from at least the seventeenth century an employer could also be held responsible for the wrongs of another, despite the acts being committed without authority. In *Hern v Nichols*, Holt CJ held that responsibility for unauthorized deceit of an employee arose for reasons of policy: 'somebody must be a loser by this deceit, it is more reason[able] that [the person] that employs and puts a trust and confidence in the deceiver should be a loser, than a stranger'.[12] In *Bugge v Brown*,[13] Isaacs J relied on the decision of Holt CJ in *Hern v Nichols* for the proposition that the responsibility of a master for the wrongful act of their servant does not depend upon any authority, whether express, implied, or ostensible. Rather, the reason for attribution of liability was said to be that 'it is more just to make the person who has entrusted [their] servant with the power of acting in [their] business responsible for injury occasioned to another in the course of so acting, than that the other and entirely innocent party should be left to bear the loss'.[14]

The approach of holding an employer liable when the employee was acting in the employer's business was famously expressed by Salmond as involving a requirement that the employee be acting 'in the course of [their] employment', which was not merely where the act was authorized, but also where it was 'a wrongful and unauthorised *mode* of doing some act authorised by the [employer]'.[15] The problem with Salmond's formulation was that although it was clear that it was the employee's act that was attributed to the employer when it was done with authority, it was not clear whether it was the employee's act or the employee's liability that was attributed to the employer when the wrongful act was done without authority but in the course of the employer's business, or, as Salmond put it, as 'an unauthorised mode of an authorised act'.

The formulation by Salmond was a very clever slide of language. Acts are either authorized or they are not. The Salmond formulation permitted some unauthorized acts to sound like they were authorized and therefore an ordinary application of agency. As Gummow and Hayne JJ said in *The State of New South Wales v Lepore*,[16] in the context of considering whether a school could be liable for sexual assaults committed on its students, '[t]he notion of an unauthorised mode of doing an authorised act has evident difficulties in application', especially in the context of conduct that amounts to a criminal offence. That might have

---

[9] But compare Warren Swain, 'A Historical Examination of Vicarious Liability: "A Veritable Upas Tree"?' (2019) 78 CLJ 640, 643.
[10] (1698) 1 Salk 282, 282; 91 ER 247, 248 (KB).
[11] (1778) 1 Dougl 40, 42; 99 ER 30, 31 (KB).
[12] (1698) 1 Salk 256, 91 ER 289.
[13] [1919] HCA 5, (1919) 26 CLR 110.
[14] ibid 117.
[15] John Salmond, *The Law of Torts* (Sweet & Maxwell 1907) 83.
[16] [2003] HCA 4, (2003) 212 CLR 511, [226].

been a polite way of saying that a sexual assault on a student is simply incapable of being characterized as an unauthorized manner of performing a teacher's authorized duties.

The nature of vicarious liability was confronted directly in Australia in *Darling Island Stevedoring and Lighterage Co Ltd v Long*.[17] In that case, an employee was injured due to a hatch being left unsecured on his employer's ship. Commonwealth regulations imposed responsibility for securing the hatch on the 'person-in-charge', which was relevantly defined as the person in control of loading or unloading. Kitto J (with whom Taylor J agreed) held that although the acts of the person-in-charge could be attributed to the employer, the Commonwealth regulations only imposed liability on the person-in-charge. Therefore, although the act of the person-in-charge could be attributed to the employer, there was no liability because that act was not a tort when committed by the employer.

Kitto J observed that the term 'vicarious liability' was claimed to have been coined by Sir Frederick Pollock, whose full expression was 'vicarious liability for a servant's act'.[18] In other words, as Kitto J explained, it was really 'liability for vicarious acts'; the liability exists 'not because the servant is liable, but because of what the servant has done'.[19] The principle of vicarious liability is, on this view, only one of agency, which will be discussed in the next section of this chapter. It was this sense of vicarious liability that Lord Wilberforce used in *Morgans v Launchbury*,[20] when he said that agency is 'merely a concept, the meaning and purpose of which is to say "is vicariously liable"'.

An example given by Kitto J to illustrate his point in *Darling Island Stevedoring and Lighterage Co Ltd* was *Broom v Morgan*.[21] In that case, Mrs Morgan was the owner of a pub in Hampstead. She employed Mr and Mrs Broom to manage the pub. Mr Broom negligently left open a trap door at the pub and Mrs Broom fell through it. Mrs Broom sued Mrs Morgan for negligence, claiming that Mrs Morgan was vicariously liable for the negligence of Mr Broom. Mrs Morgan's defence was that Mr Broom was not liable because of a rule of spousal immunity contained in section 12 of the Married Women's Property Act 1882, which disabled a wife from suing her husband for a tort. Therefore, Mrs Morgan argued, she could not be vicariously liable. That argument was rejected. As Kitto J explained in *Darling Island Stevedoring and Lighterage Co Ltd*, the liability of the master exists 'not because the servant is liable, but because of what the servant has done'. It results 'from attributing to the master the conduct of the servant'.[22]

The approach of Kitto J in *Darling Island Stevedoring and Lighterage Co Ltd* contrasted starkly with that of Fullagar J in the same case. Fullagar J said of vicarious liability that the 'liability is a true vicarious liability: that is to say, the master is liable not for a breach of a duty resting on him and broken by him but for a breach of duty resting on another and broken by another'.[23] Although at common law the doctrine of vicarious liability permitted an employee's liability to be attributed to an employer, where the liability was statutory—and the question was one of breach of statutory duty—the issue was one of statutory

---

[17] [1957] HCA 26, (1957) 97 CLR 36.
[18] ibid 60.
[19] ibid 61.
[20] [1973] AC 127, 135 (HL).
[21] [1953] 1 QB 597 (CA).
[22] [1957] HCA 26, (1957) 97 CLR 36, 61.
[23] ibid 57.

interpretation. The Commonwealth regulations did not contemplate attributing the liability of the person-in-charge to the employer.

In expressing his preference for the view that vicarious liability involved only true attribution of liability and not attribution of acts, Fullagar J did not explain how that approach could be reconciled with the decision in *Broom v Morgan*. But an explanation was offered by Windeyer J in *Parker v The Commonwealth*.[24] Windeyer J adopted the view of true vicarious liability, that is, liability for the liability of another, and said that *Broom v Morgan* was simply an exception where the employer could not take advantage of the immunity of the employee.

The issue reached the High Court of Australia in *New South Wales v Ibbett*.[25] In that case, two plain-clothed police officers trespassed onto Mrs Ibbett's property at 2 a.m. in pursuit of her son for a driving offence. One officer drew a gun in Mrs Ibbett's presence. The State of New South Wales admitted vicarious liability for the tortious conduct of the police officers. The question before the High Court was whether the state was liable for exemplary damages. On the theory that vicarious liability is the attribution of acts, it is simple to see why the state should be required to pay exemplary damages for the conduct directly attributed to it. But on the theory that it is the attribution of liability, there may be questions as to whether the attributed liability to pay compensation should be extended to an attributed liability to pay exemplary damages. Nevertheless, in a unanimous judgment—recognizing the availability of exemplary damages—the High Court took the view that the vicarious liability provided for in the Law Reform (Vicarious Liability) Act 1983 (NSW) had been based upon the approach of Fullagar J in *Darling Island*, and thus it was the liability of the police officers that was attributed to the state, rather than their actions.[26] This led Allsop P in the New South Wales Court of Appeal in *Kable v New South Wales*[27] to suggest that the view of Fullagar J appeared to have prevailed. The policy-based approach of Fullagar J was favourably compared with the agency approach in *Hollis v Vabu Pty Ltd*,[28] where five members of the High Court said that Fullagar J had 'expressed the view, surely correctly, that the modern doctrine respecting the liability of an employer for the torts of an employee was adopted not by way of an exercise in analytical jurisprudence but as a matter of policy'. So too, in the House of Lords in *Majrowski v Guy's and St Thomas's NHS Trust*,[29] Lord Nicholls said that the approach taken in *Hollis v Vabu* in Australia was also now 'settled law' in England: 'The employee's wrong is imputed to the employer.' His Lordship added that the contrary view had been 'firmly discarded'.[30]

So where does this leave the approach of Kitto J? Could it really be said that any principal, including a corporation, can have the acts of an agent attributed to it, but that an employer corporation could not have the acts of an employee attributed to it even where the employee is acting as an agent? The best understanding of the law is that an employer, or a corporation, can be liable by *either* means. In other words, either the *acts* of an agent or employee can be attributed to the corporation or employer, subject to the rules of agency, or the

---

[24] [1965] HCA 12, (1965) 112 CLR 295, 301.
[25] [2006] HCA 57, (2006) 229 CLR 638.
[26] ibid [6], [56].
[27] (2012) 293 ALR 719, [52]–[53] (NSW CA).
[28] [2001] HCA 44, (2001) 207 CLR 21, [34].
[29] [2006] UKHL 34, [2007] 1 AC 224, [15].
[30] ibid [15].

liability of an agent or employee can be attributed to the corporation or employer, subject to the rules of vicarious liability.

In *Pioneer Mortgage Services Pty Ltd v Columbus Capital Pty Ltd*,[31] the first appellant company was a mortgage originator for mortgages funded by the first respondent. An employee of the appellant company stole funds from the accounts of clients who had taken mortgages with the first respondent. The respondent claimed against the appellant company on the basis of *vicarious liability* for the liability of the employee and, in the alternative, on the basis of the *attribution of acts* of the employee. The Full Court of the Federal Court of Australia held that the appellant company was liable on both bases: attribution of the acts of the employee and attribution of the liability of the employee. In *IL v The Queen*, Kiefel CJ, Keane J, and I described these two methods of attribution—of acts and of liability—as, respectively, primary liability (ie liability for one's own acts) and derivative liability (ie liability derived from another's liability).[32] In the words of Glanville Williams, 'the law may recognise both vicarious responsibility in the proper sense of the term and also a doctrine of vicarious conduct'.[33] But clarity of thought would be advanced by eschewing the language of 'vicarious liability' for attribution of acts and instead treating the attribution of acts as governed by agency and its associated rules.

The term 'vicarious liability' should be used only to describe the doctrine concerned with the circumstances in which an employer—usually, and relevantly for the purposes of this chapter, an employer corporation—is liable for the liability of a third-party employee for acts done in the course of employment.

In the many cases where the wrongdoing of the third party involves a breach of some statutory duty, whether that breach of duty should be attributed to the corporate employer will be a question of statutory interpretation. But in the rare cases where the wrongdoing involves purely common law liability, any increased precision in the test for 'scope of employment' or a close connection to employment may depend upon the justification for vicarious liability.

It suffices to say that one modern enunciation of the policy underlying the test for vicarious liability, developing the approach of Isaacs J in *Bugge v Brown*,[34] has not yet found favour in Australia. That approach was adopted by McLachlin J in *Bazley v Curry*, who reasoned from policy (that an employer who introduced a risk to advance their own interests should be liable for the losses caused by the introduction of that risk) to a conclusion that the employer is liable due to 'a significant connection between the creation or enhancement of a risk and the wrong that accrues therefrom'.[35] In *Prince Alfred College Inc v ADC*, five members of the High Court of Australia said of the policy justification that 'the requirement of connection might be based on what had been said by Salmond. . . . However, the risk-allocation aspect of the theory is based largely on considerations of policy, in particular that an employer should be liable for a risk that its business enterprise has created or enhanced. Such policy considerations have found no real support in Australia or the United Kingdom'.[36] But no other justification of policy has yet been advanced in Australia.

---

[31] [2016] FCAFC 78, (2016) 250 FCR 136, [57].
[32] [2017] HCA 27, (2017) 262 CLR 268, [34].
[33] Glanville Williams, 'Vicarious Liability: Tort of the Master or of the Servant?' (1956) 72 LQR 522, 544.
[34] [1919] HCA 5, (1919) 26 CLR 110, 116–17.
[35] (1999) 2 SCR 534, [41].
[36] [2016] HCA 37, (2016) 258 CLR 134, [59].

B. Primary Liability by Attribution of Acts Performed by an Agent

The operation of the rules of agency was neatly explained by Denning LJ in *Cassidy v Ministry of Health*.[37] Mr Cassidy was a labourer who was suffering from a contraction of two of his fingers. He was diagnosed and operated upon by the assistant medical officer at a Liverpool hospital. For two weeks after the operation, while Mr Cassidy's arm was in a splint, he was under the care of the assistant medical officer, as well as the house surgeon and the nursing staff of the hospital. When the splint was taken off, Mr Cassidy's two fingers were badly damaged, together with the other two good fingers on the same hand. The effect was that Mr Cassidy's entire hand had become useless. One issue in the case was whether Mr Cassidy was required to identify which staff member of the hospital was responsible. A related issue was whether the hospital, and therefore the Ministry of Health, would be liable. The trial judge held that Mr Cassidy had failed to identify which person was responsible and therefore the hospital, and hence the Ministry of Health, could not be liable.

The Court of Appeal allowed Mr Cassidy's appeal and held the hospital, and therefore the Ministry of Health, liable. The starting point was that the hospital owed Mr Cassidy a duty of care. As Denning LJ explained: 'authorities who run a hospital, be they local authorities, government boards, or any other corporation, are in law under the selfsame duty as the humblest doctor; whenever they accept a patient for treatment, they must use reasonable care and skill to cure him of his ailment.'[38] The point that Denning LJ was making was that the hospital—the corporation itself—was directly liable because it had, as described in *Hedley Byrne & Co Ltd v Heller & Partners Ltd*,[39] assumed responsibility for Mr Cassidy.

How was it possible to say that the hospital was negligent, rather than its staff members? Denning LJ continued:

> The hospital authorities cannot, of course, do it by themselves: they have no ears to listen through the stethoscope, and no hands to hold the surgeon's knife. They must do it by the staff which they employ; and if their staff are negligent in giving the treatment, they are just as liable for that negligence as is anyone else who employs others to do his duties for him.[40]

In other words, the hospital was liable because the acts of the staff were attributed to the hospital. Mr Cassidy had gone into hospital with two stiff fingers. The actions of the hospital, through its staff, left him with a useless hand. As Denning LJ concluded, the hospital had

> nowhere explained how it could happen without negligence. They have busied themselves in saying that this or that member of their staff was not negligent. But they have called not a single person to say that the injuries were consistent with due care on the part of all the members of their staff.[41]

The point that Denning LJ was making is a hornbook principle of agency law. Sometimes it is misunderstood because it is expressed in Latin: *qui facit per alium facit per se* (who acts

---

[37] [1951] 2 KB 343 (CA) (hereafter *Cassidy*).
[38] ibid 360.
[39] [1964] AC 465, 529.
[40] *Cassidy* (n 37) 360.
[41] ibid (n 37) 366.

through another, acts themself). But the point is simple. As Starke J had said in Australia nearly a decade earlier, since a company '"cannot act in its own person for it has no person" . . . it must of necessity act by directors, managers, or other agents'.[42] Provided that the person acts with actual or implied authority, or ostensible authority, the person's acts will be attributed to the corporation.

In his valuable contribution to this area of the law in *Meridian Global Funds Management Asia Ltd v Securities Commission*,[43] Lord Hoffmann, delivering the advice of the Judicial Committee of the Privy Council, described the general rules of agency as rules of attribution that complement the company's primary rules of attribution from its constitution. Lord Hoffmann described the primary rules of attribution as being rules such as 'the decisions of the board in managing the company's business shall be the decisions of the company'.[44] Strictly, these primary rules of attribution are also rules of agency. Both also derive from the constitution. The difference is simply that general agency rules—such as that the CEO has power to engage in an ordinary transaction on behalf of the company—are usually implied in the constitution, and specific rules—such as when the company is bound by decisions of the board or the shareholders in a general meeting—are usually expressed. In either case, subject to legislation, it is always open to the company to amend the rules in its constitution.

There are, however, two possible further additions to Lord Hoffmann's taxonomy of how corporations can be made liable. The first addition is that in some circumstances corporations can be liable for acts of delegates or duties that cannot be delegated as well as for the acts of agents. The second, and contentious, possible addition is that in some circumstances corporations can be directly liable for their own acts. Each of these matters is explained in what follows.

C. Primary Liability by Attribution of Acts Performed by a Delegate

The attribution of acts of an agent to a corporation is often confused with the attribution of acts of a delegate to a corporation. In 1890, Wills J erroneously said that 'the word "delegate" means little more than an agent'.[45] That statement has been the cause of an enormous amount of misunderstanding. There is, in fact, a very important difference between delegates and agents. Unlike an agent, who acts for another, a delegate acts for themselves.[46] This distinction can have important consequences, which can be illustrated by a comparison of two cases.

In *Williams v Natural Life Health Foods Ltd*,[47] Mr Mistlin was the managing director and principal shareholder of Natural Life Health Foods. Mr Mistlin had played a prominent part in preparing detailed financial projections which Natural Life Health Foods sent to two people who were enticed to enter a franchise agreement. The franchise proved to be a disaster and they sued Natural Life Health Foods for negligence in the preparation of the

---

[42] *O'Brien v Dawson* [1942] HCA 8, (1942) 66 CLR 18, 32, quoting *Ferguson v Wilson* (1866) LR 2 Ch App 77, 89 (CA).

[43] [1995] 2 AC 500, 506.

[44] ibid.

[45] *Huth v Clarke* (1890) 25 QBD 391, 395 (QB).

[46] *Plaintiff M61/2010E v The Commonwealth* [2010] HCA 41, (2010) 243 CLR 319 at 350 [68].

[47] [1998] 1 WLR 830.

detailed financial projections. Natural Life Health Foods was wound up, so they sued Mr Mistlin. The House of Lords held that Mr Mistlin was not liable. In the leading judgment, Lord Steyn said:

> Whether the principal is a company or a natural person, someone acting on his behalf may incur personal liability in tort as well as imposing vicarious or attributed liability upon his principal. But in order to establish personal liability . . . [t]here must have been an assumption of responsibility.[48]

Mr Mistlin had acted only as an agent of Natural Life Health Foods in providing the financial projections. He had not assumed any personal responsibility. The responsibility was assumed by Natural Life Health Foods.

The position would have been different if Mr Mistlin had provided the financial projections as a delegate of Natural Life Health Foods. The result can be compared with *Commissioner of Inland Revenue v Chesterfields Preschools Ltd*.[49] That case involved allegations of misfeasance in public office against the Commissioner of Taxation and various individuals. Delivering the judgment of the New Zealand Court of Appeal, Stevens J accepted the Commissioner's submission that the individuals were delegates of the Commissioner, not agents. The acts of the individuals could not be attributed to the Commissioner. As he explained:

> Once a delegate has been delegated a power they exercise that power as their own. They do not exercise the delegator's power through the delegator; they exercise their own delegated power under their own name. The delegate must exercise their own independent discretion in the exercise of their delegated power.[50]

An example of the confusion between agents and delegates can be seen in *Northern Land Council v Quall*.[51] The question in that case was whether the Northern Land Council had the power to delegate its function of certifying an application for registration of an Indigenous Land Use Agreement. Kiefel CJ and Gageler and Keane JJ held that there was such a power of delegation. Nettle J and I held that there was not. But, for present purposes, the relevant point about the case is a misunderstanding in the way that it was argued in the courts below.

Judicial review had been sought on the basis that the Northern Land Council did not have the power to delegate its certification function to the Chief Executive Officer. There was considerable force in this submission: section 203B(3) of the Native Title Act 1993 (Cth) expressly provided that a representative body, which included the Northern Land Council, could not make an arrangement with another person for the performance of the Council's functions. It was assumed that if the Northern Land Council had no power to delegate the certification function, then the certification by the Chief Executive Officer must be invalid.

But the Chief Executive Officer had not purported to certify the application as a delegate. He purported to certify it *as* the Northern Land Council. The certification began as

---

[48] ibid 835.
[49] [2013] 2 NZLR 679 (NZ CA).
[50] [2013] 2 NZLR 679, [61].
[51] [2020] HCA 33, (2020) 271 CLR 394.

follows: 'This document is the certification by the Northern Land Council.' It contained the statement 'the NLC hereby certifies . . .'. One might immediately ask: how was the Northern Land Council to act if not through a natural person such as the Chief Executive Officer? To reiterate Denning LJ's point made earlier: the Northern Land Council had no hands to sign a certification and no voice to issue instructions to certify. It could only act through individual *people*. Provided that the Chief Executive Officer had authority to certify the application *on behalf of* the Northern Land Council, and it would be very surprising if the Chief Executive Officer did not, then the case ought to have been a very simple application of the rules of agency.

Although the actions of a delegate are usually personal and are not attributed to a corporation, there are two exceptions. First, legislation can require a delegate's actions to be attributed to another. An example of such a statutory exception in Australia is section 34AB(1)(c) of the Acts Interpretation Act 1901 (Cth), which provides that, subject to contrary intention, where 'an Act confers a power on a person or body (in this section called the *authority*) to delegate a function, duty or power . . . a function, duty or power so delegated, when performed or exercised by the delegate, shall, for the purposes of the Act, be deemed to have been performed and exercised by the authority'. The effect of section 34AB(1)(c) is that where a delegate makes a decision adverse to an applicant, the applicant cannot then make a fresh application to the delegator who has not exercised any power.[52] But by attributing the delegate's acts to the delegator, section 34AB(1)(c) may also have the consequence that the delegator can become liable if the acts were wrongful.

Second, there are some duties which are non-delegable. A corporation that owes a non-delegable duty is personally responsible for the discharge of that duty. The corporation cannot avoid the responsibility for proper discharge of the duty by attempting to delegate the duty to perform to a person who would then act only for themselves. The duty of proper performance remains that of the corporation. The most common instance in which a non-delegable duty will arise is where the corporation assumes responsibility for the personal performance of the duty: the corporation has 'undertaken the care, supervision or control of the person or property of another or is so placed in relation to that person or [their] property as to assume a particular responsibility . . . in circumstances where the person affected might reasonably expect that due care will be exercised'.[53] Then, as Gleeson CJ has explained, echoing Lord Blackburn, 'the circumstance that the third party is an independent contractor [rather than an agent] does not enable the defendant to avoid liability'.[54]

An example of a case involving a non-delegable duty is the decision of the Supreme Court of the United Kingdom in *Woodland v Swimming Teachers Association*.[55] In that case a school student suffered a severe brain injury during a swimming lesson. The Supreme Court held that the school was responsible for the negligence of an independent contractor to whom the school had delegated the function of teaching swimming during school hours. Lord Sumption gave various examples of non-delegable duties where a natural person or corporation assumes responsibility to ensure that care will be taken, rather than merely assuming responsibility to take reasonable care. One is an employer who assumes responsibility for a

---

[52] *Giddings v Australian Information Commissioner* [2017] FCAFC 225, [29]–[30].

[53] *Kondis v State Transport Authority* [1984] HCA 61, (1984) 154 CLR 672, 687 (hereafter *Kondis*).

[54] *Leichhardt Municipal Council v Montgomery* [2007] HCA 6, (2007) 230 CLR 22, [9]. See also *Dalton v Angus* (1881) 6 App Cas 740, 829 (HL).

[55] [2013] UKSC 66, [2014] AC 537 (hereafter *Woodland*).

222 DIRECT AND VICARIOUS LIABILITY OF CORPORATIONS

safe system of work.[56] Another may be a hospital which assumes responsibility for treating a patient.[57] Notably, in *Cassidy v Ministry of Health*,[58] Denning LJ said that the attribution to a hospital of the conduct of its employees extended also to the conduct of its independent contractors: the acts are attributed 'when hospital authorities undertake to treat a patient . . . whether the contract under which [the doctor or surgeon] was employed was a contract of service or a contract for services'. This reasoning was approved by Mason J (with whom Deane and Dawson JJ agreed) in *Kondis v State Transport Authority*.[59]

D. Primary (Direct) Liability by Systems of Action

So far, the concepts that I have been discussing concerning the attribution of responsibility to a corporation are all well-established, although often misunderstood, categories: (i) vicarious liability, (ii) attribution of acts of an agent, and (iii) non-delegable duties or attribution of acts of a delegate. Each of these categories involves making the corporation responsible based upon the acts or the liability of another. The question that I now turn to is whether it is possible for a corporation to be directly liable without any attribution.

Traditionally, the answer to this question has been 'no'. In his 1793 *Treatise on the Law of Corporations*, Stewart Kyd remarked: '[a] corporation being merely a political institution, it can have no other capacities than such as are necessary to carry into effect the purposes for which it was established; it cannot therefore be considered as a moral agent subject to moral obligation.'[60] Two hundred years later, Lord Hoffmann said, in *Meridian Global Funds Management Asia Ltd v Securities Commission*:[61]

> There is in fact no such thing as the company as such, no ding an sich, only the applicable rules. To say that a company cannot do something means only that there is no one whose doing of that act would, under the applicable rules of attribution, count as an act of the company.

In *Commonwealth Bank of Australia v Kojic*,[62] I questioned whether this principle is always correct. In that case, the primary judge in the Federal Court of Australia had held that the Commonwealth Bank had acted unconscionably in contravention of section 51AB or 51AC of what was then the Trade Practices Act 1974 (Cth). The case was pleaded and argued as a case of attribution of the acts of bank employees, not as a case of attribution of their liability. The primary judge concluded that the bank had acted unconscionably by aggregating the knowledge of two of the bank's employees, neither of whom individually had sufficient knowledge to have acted unconscionably. In the Full Court of the Federal Court of Australia, Allsop CJ concluded, with the agreement of the two other justices (including me), that even with the aggregation of knowledge the bank had not acted unconscionably. But

---

[56] ibid [13], citing *Wilsons & Clyde Coal Co Ltd v English* [1938] AC 57 (HL); *Lochgelly Iron and Coal Co Ltd v M'Mullan* [1934] AC 1 (HL); *McDermid v Nash Dredging and Reclamation Co Ltd* [1987] AC 906 (HL).
[57] *Woodland* (n 55) [14]–[16].
[58] [1951] 2 KB 343, 362.
[59] *Kondis* (n 53) 685–86.
[60] Stewart Kyd, *A Treatise on the Law of Corporations* (1793) vol 1, 70–71.
[61] [1995] 2 AC 500, 507.
[62] [2016] FCAFC 186, (2016) 249 FCR 421, [153].

the Court also considered whether it was possible to aggregate the knowledge of individual officers of the bank.

One controversial decision of the First Circuit Court of Appeals in 1987 had held that a bank had committed a felony by acting wilfully even though its officers had been acquitted. Delivering the opinion of the court in that case, Bownes J said this:

> [A] corporation cannot plead innocence by asserting that the information obtained by several employees was not acquired by any one individual employee who then would have comprehended its full import. Rather, the corporation is considered to have acquired the collective knowledge of its employees and is held responsible for their failure to act accordingly.[63]

In *Commonwealth Bank of Australia v Kojic*, I concluded that there was no place for such a controversial principle in section 51AB or 51AC of the Trade Practices Act 1974 (Cth). However, I accepted that there might be instances where a corporation acts unconscionably, and wrongfully, even though no individual had done so. The example I gave was where a corporation had put procedures into place which were intended to ensure that no individual could have knowledge sufficient for an act to be unconscionable. There was no suggestion that this was the case in *Commonwealth Bank of Australia v Kojic*.

Elise Bant has recently advanced a sophisticated model of how a corporation might be directly liable based upon its systems or procedures, or what she described as 'systems intentionality'.[64] As more corporations engage systems involving computerized decisions, and even artificial intelligence, there may be a need for the law to develop such a model of primary liability for corporations. Bant has argued that just as a corporation might be said to act by some electronic process that is not the direct product of some human interaction, so too a corporation might be said to manifest a state of mind based upon the purpose or design of its systems. She quoted Peter French, who argued that a corporate act that is consistent with corporate policy can be described as corporate intention.[65]

Eva Micheler adopts a similar approach, referring to 'real entity' theory. She borrows from institutional economics to distinguish between 'brute facts' and 'social facts'. The latter can apply to corporations or 'firms', which have two characteristics:

> First, the members intend to act not as individuals but as part of the firm. Second, non-members take part in this collective intention because they too agree that the members of the firm are together and constitute a social fact. This consensus makes firms real. The firm is something that, by consensus, is treated by 'everyone' as an 'active social unit'.[66]

---

[63] *United States v Bank of New England NA* (1987) 821 F (2d) 844, 856, quoting *United States v TIME-DC Inc* (1974) 381 F Supp 730, 738.

[64] See Elise Bant, 'Culpable Corporate Minds' (2021) 48 UWAL Rev 352 (hereafter Bant, 'Culpable Corporate Minds'); Elise Bant and Jeannie Marie Paterson, 'Systems of Misconduct: Corporate Culpability and Statutory Unconscionability' (2021) 15 J Eq 63.

[65] See Bant, 'Culpable Corporate Minds' (n 64) 381–82, quoting Peter French, *Collective and Corporate Responsibility* (Columbia University Press 1984) 44.

[66] Eva Micheler, *Company Law: A Real Entity Theory* (OUP 2021) 21.

224 DIRECT AND VICARIOUS LIABILITY OF CORPORATIONS

To speak of a corporation as having purposes and intentions is not a fiction of law. A fiction of law, as Jeremy Bentham explained, involves a 'wilful falsehood'.[67] It is a conscious deeming of something to be that which it is not.[68] It would, of course, be a fiction if we were to speak of the subjective intentions of a corporation as though they were identical to those of a natural person. But when we speak of corporate purposes and corporate intentions, we are speaking of the operation of the objective construct of a corporation. That construct operates in the same way as a polity, a Parliament, or even a sports team.

We can attribute intentions and purposes to the construct of a corporation, just as we attribute them to a polity, a Parliament, or a sports team. We can say 'Australia's goal is to lead the world in engineering'. Or we could say 'Parliament's purpose of the new law is to protect the privacy of individuals'. That statement of purpose will be valid even if none of the members of Parliament who voted in favour of the Bill had read the Bill or formed any subjective purpose. Again, we might say 'Fremantle scored a record number of goals and fulfilled their purpose of winning the football game'. As John Finnis explained, that statement is valid even if the subjective intention of many team members was to lose:[69]

> The purpose of the team is to win. Individual members have many other purposes, some, at times, more or less sharply at odds with winning. To understand the game as a social act, one must bear in mind the social purpose, and not be distracted by the irrelevant aspects of the individual players' purposes. Conceivably, every member of the team, for personal reasons, may secretly wish to lose the game (without being too obvious about it). Even so, the social act of the team's play retains its purpose: to win.

So too, it may be that we can say 'the corporation intended to protect the environment', independently of the intentions of the directors of the corporation. The simplest way in which the corporation's intention might be discerned is from its 'purposes' as provided in its constitution. However, this exercise might often be difficult because a modern trend, lamented by Lord Wrenbury in 1918 in *Cotman v Brougham*,[70] is the expression of corporate purposes in such broad terms, or, as in *Cotman v Brougham* itself, not expressing them at all, so that it is impossible to state the corporation's purposes with any specificity relevant to particular action. More often the intention might need to be discerned, as Bant has argued, by 'its corporate systems, policies and patterns of behaviour'.[71]

Just as corporate intention might, arguably, be identified as directly held by a corporation, the same might be said of corporate acts. A case that illustrates the boundaries of the attribution of acts of natural persons to a corporation and the possibility of direct acts by a corporation through its systems is *Quoine Pte Ltd v B2C2 Ltd*.[72] That case concerned cryptocurrency trades that were executed, by automated trading algorithms, by B2C2 and its counterparties on a trading platform operated by Quoine. B2C2 executed a trade which Quoine priced at 250 times the current market rate in B2C2's favour. The

---

[67] Jeremy Bentham, 'A Fragment on Government' in John Bowring (ed), *The Works of Jeremy Bentham* (William Tait 1843) vol 1, 243.

[68] John Burton, 'Introduction to the Study of Bentham's Works' in John Bowring (ed), *The Works of Jeremy Bentham* (1843) vol 1, 41.

[69] John Finnis, *Intention and Identity* (OUP 2011) 87.

[70] [1918] AC 514, 523 (HL).

[71] See Bant, 'Culpable Corporate Minds' (n 64) 355.

[72] [2020] SGCA(I) 02.

CONCLUSION 225

reason for this pricing was that a change in passwords for critical systems on Quoine's platform prevented its program from accessing data from external exchanges necessary to calculate an accurate market price. When Quoine's Chief Technical Officer realized what had occurred he purported to reverse the trade. The Court of Appeal of the Republic of Singapore, sitting with international judges, held by majority that this was a breach of contract. A central issue, and the point on which the court divided, was whether a mistake had been made by Quoine sufficient to render the contract void or voidable at common law or in equity, to be assessed as at the time that the contract was made.

In his dissenting judgment, Mance IJ said that it is 'by definition impossible' to assess the actual state of mind and conduct of parties in the making of a contract between computers programmed by humans.[73] But he accepted that there 'was a fundamental mistake, in that Quoine's system operated . . . in a way that was not conceived as possible'.[74] The approach he took was to ask what a natural person in the circumstances *could or would have known or believed*, if they had known of the circumstances which actually occurred.[75] That approach effectively treated Quoine, through its computers and systems that executed the transaction, as having made a sufficiently serious mistake in equity so that the contract was voidable. By contrast, the majority considered whether any mistake by a human being could be attributed to Quoine. The only relevant human beings were the programmers. Their mistake, the majority held, 'if anything, was in the way that the [computer platform] had operated as a result of Quoine's failure to make certain necessary changes to several critical operating systems'.[76] That was not a sufficient vitiating mistake.

V. Conclusion

Most of the discussion in this chapter is a distillation of the fundamental underlying principles concerning the different ways in which a corporation can be held responsible for wrongdoing and an emphasis on the importance of keeping those principles distinct. Any assertion that a corporation is responsible for something can be hopelessly confused unless it is made clear whether that responsibility is based upon (i) attributing the *liability* of a natural person to the corporation, (ii) attributing the *acts* of an agent of the corporation to the corporation, or (iii) based either on the breach of a duty that cannot be delegated or, if it can be delegated, by attributing the acts of a delegate of corporate power to the corporation. Another difficult issue of principle that courts may need to confront in the future is whether a fourth way of holding a corporation responsible should be recognized. Putting aside specific legislation, can it ever be legitimate to treat a corporation—through its systems—as having acted or formed intentions *itself* without those acts or intentions being attributed from natural persons? The decision of the majority of the Court of Appeal of the Republic of

---

[73] ibid [185].
[74] ibid [183].
[75] ibid [194].
[76] ibid [98], [114].

Singapore managed to decide the *Quoine* case without altering the conventional paradigm in the context of a contract involving algorithms. But would the same conclusion have been reached if the case had involved what has been described as 'strong' artificial intelligence, intelligence, and learning abilities in an area which can approximate those of humans? That is just the sort of difficult question that Ewan McKendrick so often confronted in his writing. And, as his technique always revealed, the proper resolution of such questions requires a clear understanding of basic principles.

14

Damage to 'Other Property': Exploring the Boundary Between Property Damage and Pure Economic Loss

DONAL NOLAN

I. Introduction

Although Ewan McKendrick is best known as a contract and commercial law scholar, he also made many valuable contributions to scholarship on the law of tort. In this chapter, I explore an issue which connects Ewan's interests in product liability,[1] negligence recovery for economic loss,[2] and fundamental questions of personal property.[3] The issue concerns the dividing line between property damage and pure economic loss, and specifically what amounts to damage to 'other property' for the purposes of the law of tort. This question is best understood as one relating to the element of damage, and in particular what the law recognizes as damage to property of the claimant. It ought therefore to be considered alongside connected issues, such as what amounts to 'damage' to an item of property, and who has standing to sue for property damage.[4]

A brief outline of the problem under discussion will help to situate what follows. As we shall see, it has been held in cases involving defective chattels or structures that there is an important distinction between damage to the chattel or structure itself (which is treated as a form of pure economic loss) and damage to other property of the claimant (which is treated as property damage). To take a simple example, if you buy a defective toaster, and it catches fire but destroys only itself, you are said to have suffered only pure economic loss. But if the fire spreads and destroys other things of yours, such as your kettle and your kitchen table, then any claim in respect of those things is said to be for property damage. The difficulty arises when it comes to more complex chattels and structures, where one component of the chattel or structure causes damage to the rest of it. Suppose, for example, that you buy a car and one of the tyres on the car explodes and destroys the rest of the car. Is this a case where 'the car' has simply damaged itself, so that your loss is purely economic, or is it a case where one item of property (the tyre) has damaged another (the rest of the car), so that it gives rise to a property damage claim?

This issue has given rise to a steady stream of case law since it was first adverted to by the English courts in *M/S Aswan Engineering v Lupdine Ltd*.[5] Nor is its practical significance in

[1] Norman Palmer and Ewan McKendrick, *Product Liability in the Construction Industry* (LLP 1993).
[2] Ewan McKendrick, '*Pirelli* Re-examined' (1991) 11 LS 326 (hereafter McKendrick, '*Pirelli* Re-examined').
[3] Norman Palmer and Ewan McKendrick (eds), *Interests in Goods* (LLP 1998).
[4] For a discussion of the issue which does consider it in this way, see Nicholas J McBride and Roderick Bagshaw, *Tort Law* (6th edn, Pearson 2018) 142–52.
[5] [1987] 1 WLR 1 (CA) (hereafter *Aswan Engineering*). For a summary of that case and the subsequent authorities, see text following n 45.

Donal Nolan, *Damage to 'Other Property': Exploring the Boundary Between Property Damage and Pure Economic Loss* In: *Shaping the Law of Obligations*. Edited by: Edwin Peel and Rebecca Probert, Oxford University Press. © Donal Nolan 2023.
DOI: 10.1093/oso/9780198889762.003.0014

228   DAMAGE TO 'OTHER PROPERTY'

doubt. Shortly after *Aswan Engineering*, the House of Lords in *Murphy v Brentwood District Council*[6] held that (with one or two possible exceptions that need not concern us here) a person who suffers pure economic loss as a result of acquiring a defective product or premises is not owed a duty of care by the party responsible for the defect, whereas such a duty is generally owed in respect of personal injury and damage to other property. The drawing of such a sharp line between pure economic loss and property damage at the duty of care stage naturally elevates the significance of the boundary itself, at least as compared with its importance in common law systems which take a more liberal approach to recovery of pure economic loss. (It is probably no coincidence that the vast majority of the case law dealing with the problem of damage to other property is from the United Kingdom and the United States, the two most prominent common law countries to recognize a general bar on pure economic loss recovery.) Despite the importance of the issue, however, it has not yet been the subject of sustained analysis by the English courts at the appellate level. Furthermore, the point is sometimes missed entirely, as in a recent Privy Council decision where it was simply assumed that the destruction of an aircraft caused by defective landing gear was property damage in respect of which a duty of care was owed by the manufacturer of the landing gear to the owner of the aircraft.[7] By contrast, the issue has been explored more fully by the courts in the US and by commentators in England,[8] sources which will be drawn upon in the analysis that follows.

The question of what amounts to damage to other property is a complex one, to which there are no easy answers.[9] It is therefore important to emphasize at the outset that the aims of this chapter are modest, and that my principal goals are to set out as clearly as possible the nature of the problem and the response of the courts to it on both sides of the Atlantic, and to put forward some tentative suggestions as to the best way forward for English law.

Before I begin my exploration of the problem, three further points should be made. The first is that one sometimes comes across the notion that the question of what amounts to damage to other property can somehow be ignored, perhaps on the basis that a policy-based

---

[6] [1991] 1 AC 398 (HL) (hereafter *Murphy*).

[7] See *Bahamasair Holdings Ltd v Messier Dowty Inc* [2018] UKPC 25, [2019] 1 All ER 25. Since the claimant had bought the aircraft with the defective landing gear fitted to it, this would seem (on the authorities discussed herein) to have been a case of the aircraft damaging itself, and hence of pure economic loss. However, both the courts in the Bahamas and the Privy Council appear to have treated it as a property damage case, which raised only the questions of fact that were the subject of the appeal to the Council.

[8] The most sustained academic treatments of the point are Andrew Tettenborn, 'Components and Product Liability: Damage to "Other Property"' [2000] LMCLQ 338 (hereafter Tettenborn, 'Components and Product Liability') and William Kitchen, 'Beyond Physical Integration: Distinguishing "Other Property" from the "Thing Itself"' [2022] Oxford Univ Undergraduate LJ 129 (hereafter Kitchen, 'Beyond Physical Integration'). Other useful discussions are Richard Townshend-Smith, 'Property Damage and Economic Loss After *Murphy v Brentwood District Council*' [1991] Sing J Legal Stud 447 (hereafter Townshend-Smith, 'Property Damage and Economic Loss'); Robert Stevens, *Torts and Rights* (OUP 2007) 26–30 (hereafter Stevens, *Torts and Rights*); and Duncan Fairgrieve and Richard Goldberg, *Product Liability* (3rd edn, OUP 2020) paras 16.55–16.74 (hereafter Fairgrieve and Goldberg, *Product Liability*). For reasons of space it has not been possible for me to subject the arguments of Tettenborn and Kitchen to detailed consideration. However, I draw on their excellent contributions throughout this chapter, and I do not think that my conclusions are substantially at odds with either analysis, though there are certainly differences of emphasis.

[9] See Townshend-Smith, 'Property Damage and Economic Loss' (n 8) 463 ('an impossible question', the answer to which cannot be based on 'logical criteria'); Tettenborn, 'Components and Product Liability' (n 8) 339 (the point is 'awkward, because in many situations there is no obviously correct way to answer it'); Stevens, *Torts and Rights* (n 8) 26 ('not always an easy question to answer'); Michael A Jones (ed), *Clerk & Lindsell on Torts* (23rd edn, Sweet & Maxwell 2020) para 10-22 (hereafter *Clerk & Lindsell*) (a 'question which it is hard to answer logically').

analysis to the question of recovery is to be preferred.[10] Such a suggestion must be rejected. Any legal system that distinguishes between property damage and pure economic loss for the purposes of tort claims needs to be able to draw the distinction between them.[11] If desired, the location of the boundary line can be informed by policy considerations, but the courts cannot simply refuse to mark out the boundary at all. The second point is that, although useful connections can be made between the question of damage to other property and doctrines in the law of property concerned with the relationship between things—such as the doctrine of accession—the principles underlying those doctrines were devised to deal with a different set of problems, and hence they cannot simply be imported wholesale into the tort analysis. And finally, the chapter is concerned with the boundary between property damage and pure economic loss, rather than with the consequences of that classification. It follows that there is no discussion in what follows of cases in other jurisdictions where it was (or would now be) accepted that the loss was purely economic, but recovery was nonetheless allowed on the ground that, say, it was the result of a 'sudden and calamitous event',[12] or that the defect which caused the loss was a dangerous one, which could have caused damage to other property or personal injury.[13]

II. Damage to the Property Itself

It will be helpful to begin with a brief exploration of why damage to the property itself is classified as pure economic loss, and why the English (and, generally, American) courts have held that such economic loss is not usually recoverable in tort. There appears now to be pretty much universal acceptance that damage to the defective property itself is a form of pure economic loss. In England the importance of the distinction between damage to the property itself and damage to other property seems first to have been accepted judicially by Lord Brandon (dissenting) in *Junior Books v Veitchi Ltd*,[14] but it was more thoroughly expounded by the House of Lords in *D & F Estates Ltd v Church Commissioners for England*.[15] According to Lord Bridge in *D & F Estates*, if the hidden defect in a chattel was 'the cause of personal injury or *of damage to property other than the chattel itself*', then the manufacturer would be liable, but if it was discovered before any such damage occurred, then the chattel would be merely defective in quality and the resultant economic loss recoverable only in contract.[16] Similarly, Lord Oliver observed that 'in no other context has it previously been suggested that a cause of action in tort arises in English law for the defective manufacture of

---

[10] For a possible example, see *Winnipeg Condominium Corp No 36 v Bird Construction Co* [1995] 1 SCR 85 (SCC) [15] (La Forest J).

[11] See also Fairgrieve and Goldberg, *Product Liability* (n 8) para 16.57 ('the need to decide what precisely has been damaged by what . . . must exist where a legal system is prepared in principle to compensate in some such cases whilst stopping short of compensating whenever a loss is suffered through the acquisition [of a defective product]').

[12] See, eg, *Vulcan Materials Co v Driltech Inc* 306 SE 2d 253 (Ga 1983).

[13] See, eg, *Pennsylvania Glass Sand Corp v Caterpillar Tractor Co* 652 F 2d 1165 (3rd Cir 1981); *Kodiak Electric Association Inc v DeLaval Turbine Inc* 694 P 2d 150 (Alaska 1984); *Winnipeg Condominium* (n 10). This is also true of the decision in *Anns v Merton London Borough Council* [1978] AC 728 (HL) (hereafter *Anns*), where liability was limited to cases where there was an imminent danger to the health and safety of the occupiers of the premises.

[14] [1983] AC 520 (HL) 549. See also at 536 (Lord Keith).

[15] [1989] 1 AC 177 (HL) (hereafter *D & F Estates*).

[16] ibid 206 (emphasis added).

230 DAMAGE TO 'OTHER PROPERTY'

an article which causes no injury *other than injury to the defective article itself*.[17] The same distinction was drawn by the US Supreme Court in a case decided shortly before *D & F Estates*, *East River Steamship Corp v Transamerica Delaval Inc*.[18]

Why is damage to the property itself not treated by the courts as a form of property damage? The answer generally given is something along these lines. Where the claimant acquires property which is already defective, the manifestation of that defect in physical changes to the product cannot amount to an invasion of the claimant's property right in the product, since the claimant only ever had a right to a defective thing in the first place. It is worth pausing to note that this conclusion is not quite so obviously correct as it is often assumed to be. It can readily be accepted that there is no invasion of the claimant's property rights simply by virtue of the continuing existence of a defect within the property from the moment at which the claimant acquired their right in it (as where the claimant buys a television that never works). But it does not necessarily follow that the same is true where a pre-existing defect causes deleterious physical changes to the product during the period of the claimant's ownership. It is not stretching the notion of 'damage' particularly far to claim that, say, a television with a faulty connection which triggers a fire that destroys the set has suffered 'damage' as a result—indeed, that very assumption underlies talk of '*damage* to the property itself'. Furthermore, if that damage is the result of the negligence of the defendant, it is not entirely clear why it cannot be characterized as a violation of the claimant's property right in the television.[19] Indeed, the German courts—who are more accustomed to thinking in terms of violations of property rights in this context than are common law courts—have consistently upheld the idea that there *is* a violation of property rights in such a case, even if the primary driver of this doctrine of *Weiterfresserschäden* seems to have been to circumvent perceived deficiencies in contract law, such as short limitation periods that may expire before the claimant has even had the chance to discover the problem.[20]

However, although there are occasional examples of common law courts adverting to a distinction between an inherent defect and damage to the defective property caused by that defect,[21] the tendency has been to elide the two, thereby forestalling any argument along the lines set out in the previous paragraph. Consider, for example, the somewhat conclusory assertion by Deane J of the High Court of Australia that a defectively constructed building cannot 'be said to have been subjected to "material, physical damage" merely by reason of the inadequacy of its foundations since the building never existed otherwise than with its

---

[17] ibid 211 (emphasis added).

[18] 106 S Ct 2295 (1986) (hereafter *East River*). See, eg, at 2300 (Blackmun J) ('In this case, there was no damage to "other" property. Rather, [it is claimed that] each supertanker's defectively designed turbine components damaged only the turbine itself').

[19] Note that, unlike in the case of the television that never worked, here the set is much less valuable after the fire than it was beforehand, regardless of whether one assumes that before the fire (1) the fault was not known about (and so did not affect its value), or (2) the fault was known about and could easily be fixed.

[20] For discussion of this doctrine in English, see Gerhard Wagner, 'The Development of Product Liability in Germany' in Simon Whittaker (ed), *The Development of Product Liability* (CUP 2010) 130–31 (hereafter Wagner, 'Product Liability in Germany'); and John Bell and André Janssen, *Markesinis's German Law of Torts* (Hart Publishing 2019) 470–80 (including translated extracts from key cases). Following on from the point made in the previous footnote, it is a condition of this doctrine's application that the value of the property after the occurrence of the damage is less than its value before that time (taking account of the presence of the defect): see BGH 14 May 1985, NJW 1985, 2420; Ingeborg Schwenzer, 'Product Liability and Property Damages' (1989) 9 Tel Aviv U Stud L 127, 134–35 (hereafter Schwenzer, 'Product Liability').

[21] See, eg, *D & F Estates* (n 15) 211 (Lord Oliver) (distinguishing 'damage' to the defective structure from a case where the structure is 'inherently defective and dangerous ab initio without any deterioration between the original construction and the perception of risk').

foundations in that state'. By equating the defect (the foundations) with the damage, Deane J rules out the possibility of analysing the physical changes brought about by the defective foundations (eg cracks in the walls) as 'damage', and then characterizing this as damage to property of the claimant on the basis that the building did previously exist in a state in which those physical changes had not yet occurred. And while admittedly this distinction tends to collapse where the physical changes in question were inevitable and unavoidable, that is not necessarily the case where the defect could have been corrected had it been discovered before any such changes took place.[22]

What this all seems to me to suggest is not that the common law courts have been wrong to classify damage to the property itself as pure economic loss, but that the classification is the result of a choice as to what counts as property damage, and not an application of some immutable notion of property rights. It is important to bear this in mind when we turn to the question of what amounts to damage to 'other property'. It is also important when considering that question to bear in mind *why* the courts have chosen to treat damage to the property itself as pure economic loss. One reason is no doubt the simplicity of the common law solution when compared to the inevitable complexity that attaches to the more nuanced German doctrine, which has been strongly criticized by German scholars for drawing unworkable distinctions. And the other reason seems to be that contract law is considered to provide adequate protection to the purchaser of a defective product, even where the defect has the effect of destroying the product entirely. A number of considerations are thought to point to the conclusion that such cases ought to fall within the exclusive purview of the law of contract. The first is that, were the product to be completely valueless by virtue of a defect from the moment of acquisition, the only remedy would be in contract, and it is not clear why the owner should be in a better position where the value of the product is destroyed after acquisition by the 'spreading' of a defect that was present from the start. This point is often expressed by saying that the gist of the claimant's complaint in cases of damage to the product itself is their failure to receive the benefit of their bargain.[23] Another, related, consideration thought to justify limiting the claimant to contractual avenues of redress for damage to the product itself is that (with the exception of possible consequential losses) the value of the product 'forms a natural cap on liability',[24] as is also the case in most contractual warranty claims.[25] And finally, allowing tort claims for damage to the product itself would have the effect of creating transmissible warranties of quality,[26] which (it is said) would 'undermine, to an unacceptable degree, established contractual principles'.[27]

---

[22] This therefore being a condition of the German *Weiterfresserschäden* doctrine, which applies only where the product 'suffers from an isolated defect that is easy and cheap to cure if detected at the time of delivery or subsequently' (Wagner, 'Product Liability in Germany' (n 20) 130).

[23] See, eg, Schwenzer, 'Product Liability' (n 20) 137 ('It is hard to see any difference between the two cases; in either case the buyer has not received what he bargained for'). This is a persistent theme of the American case law: see, eg, *East River* (n 18) 2300, 2302.

[24] Tettenborn, 'Components and Product Liability' (n 8) 341.

[25] See *Mid Continent Aircraft Corp v Curry County Spraying Service Inc* 572 SW 2d 308 (Tex 1978) 313 (loss of use and cost of repair are only expenses incurred by purchaser where product damages itself).

[26] To see why this is, see Kitchen, 'Beyond Physical Integration' (n 8).

[27] McKendrick, '*Pirelli* Re-examined' (n 2) 331. The desire to avoid creating such transmissible warranties was central to the analysis of the House of Lords in *Murphy* (n 6).

III. Three Timing Issues

In this section of the chapter I consider the implications for the damage to other property issue of the time at which the component part which damages the remainder of a complex chattel or structure was fitted to the composite item. I look first at cases where the component was fitted to the composite item after ownership or possession of that item had passed to the claimant, before going on to look at cases where it was fitted before the transfer of ownership or possession. After dealing with this issue, I then turn to the problem of the commingling of ingredients to make a finished product which is flawed because of a defect in one of the ingredients. I argue that in this scenario the loss is purely economic, and that the explanation for this also lies in questions of timing.

A. Component Added After Transfer of the Property to the Claimant

Commentators are agreed that there is damage to other property of the claimant (and hence a property damage claim) where the component part which causes the damage was added to the composite item when that item was already in the claimant's hands.[28] Hence, if the claimant replaces a tyre on their car with a defective tyre negligently manufactured by the defendant, which explodes and damages the car, the claimant has a claim against the defendant for the damage to the car (but not for the destruction of the new tyre). The reason that this does not amount to 'damage to the property itself' (and hence to pure economic loss) is that the claimant had a property right in a perfectly sound car before that car was damaged as a result of the defendant's negligence. And note that in this case the justifications for the refusal to treat damage to the property itself as property damage have no force: the rule is a simple one to apply; it cannot be claimed that the gist of the claimant's complaint is that they have not received what they bargained for; the loss suffered is not capped by the value of the item purchased (ie the tyre);[29] and allowing recovery does not have the effect of creating a transmissible warranty of quality.

Although the English courts regard it as clear-cut that there is property damage in this scenario,[30] some American courts have rejected this analysis in a sub-set of cases where the replacement part was manufactured by the producer of the composite item and its use was contemplated at the time of the original bargain pursuant to which the claimant acquired the composite item.[31] It is, however, hard to square this approach with any sensible theory of property rights and the nature of property damage, and it is respectfully suggested that this is an unnecessary complication of what should be a simple enough point.[32] These decisions seem to be driven by the idea that in cases within the sub-set the claimant's complaint

---

[28] Tettenborn, 'Components and Product Liability' (n 8) 345–46; Stevens, *Torts and Rights* (n 8) 27; Fairgrieve and Goldberg, *Product Liability* (n 8) para 16.56; *Clerk & Lindsell* (n 9) para 10-23; Kitchen, 'Beyond Physical Integration' (n 8) 149.

[29] This final point is emphasized by Tettenborn, 'Components and Product Liability' (n 8) 346.

[30] An example is *Nitrigin Eireann Teoranta v Inco Alloys* [1992] 1 WLR 498 (QBD) (replacement tubing fitted to chemical plant by claimant owner damaging plant). See also *Aswan Engineering* (n 5) 21 (purchase of empty pails example); *The Orjula* [1995] 2 Lloyd's Rep 395 (QBD) 401 (hereafter *The Orjula*).

[31] The leading case is *Sea-Land Service Inc v General Electric Co* 134 F 3d 149 (3rd Cir 1998) (hereafter *Sea-Land*) (pure economic loss where replacement connecting rod caused damage to engine because its use as a replacement was contemplated at the time the engine was purchased).

[32] See also Tettenborn, 'Components and Product Liability' (n 8) 346.

is essentially contractual in nature,[33] and the error into which the courts in question have fallen here shows the perils of adopting a purely functional approach to the question of damage to other property, without reference to property rights analysis.

B. Component Added Before Transfer of the Property to the Claimant

Where the defective component was already incorporated into the composite item when the claimant acquired that item, whether damage the component causes to the rest of the item amounts to damage to 'other property' should be determined by the principles that will be discussed in the next section. This is true regardless of whether the component was present in the property from the beginning or was added by a previous owner. Again, this seems straightforward enough when it is recalled that the reason why damage to the property itself is treated as pure economic loss is that the claimant never owned the property in an undefective (and hence 'undamaged') state. If the component and the composite item are considered to be one thing then that thing was defective/damaged when it came into the claimant's hands. The fact that at some earlier time it was undefective/undamaged is irrelevant as far as the claimant's property rights are concerned, which is of course what matters (since the claimant must establish damage to *the claimant's* property).[34] Nor does that fact make any difference when it comes to the rationales for excluding tort claims for damage to the product itself. As Andrew Tettenborn says, the gist of the claimant's complaint here is that 'he has bought useless goods' and his loss is capped at their value, so 'there is no good reason to compensate him other than through contract'.[35]

Again, however, an overly functional analysis can cause difficulties in this regard. This is illustrated by the decision of the US Supreme Court in *Saratoga Fishing Co v JM Martinac & Co*[36] to define equipment added to a fishing vessel as 'other property' for the purposes of a tort claim against the vessel's manufacturer simply because the equipment had been added by a previous user after the vessel had left the initial distribution chain. According to Breyer J (who gave the majority opinion), for the extent of a manufacturer's liability to diminish on resale of the product made no sense from a deterrence perspective, while the buyer of a second-hand product was unlikely to have the same level of contractual protection as a buyer direct from a manufacturer or dealer. With respect, these arguments are weak—*any* second-hand buyer is likely to have weaker contractual protection, for example, regardless of whether an intermediate user has made changes to the product—and the dissenting opinion of Scalia J is to be preferred. Scalia J (with whom O'Connor and Thomas JJ agreed on this issue) would have affirmed the judgment of the Ninth Circuit Court of Appeals, which had held that, since the additional equipment was part of the ship when it was acquired by the plaintiff, it was part of the product that itself caused the harm, and hence no distinction should be made for tort purposes between damage to the added equipment and damage to the rest of the vessel.

---

[33] See, eg, the reliance on the 'object of the bargain' test in *Sea-Land* (n 31) at 153–54.
[34] See also Stevens, *Torts and Rights* (n 8) 28 (in this scenario, the claimant 'would, from the moment of acquisition, only have one right to a single asset ... which is never free from the defect').
[35] Tettenborn, 'Components and Product Liability' (n 8) 347.
[36] 117 S Ct 1783 (1997) (hereafter *Saratoga*).

234   DAMAGE TO 'OTHER PROPERTY'

Although there is no English authority on this question, surprisingly the editors of *Clerk & Lindsell on Torts* express tentative agreement with the majority approach in *Saratoga*, arguing that 'it would be anomalous' if, in the case of a car destroyed because of defective brakes, the liability of a brake manufacturer 'were to depend on the fortuitous circumstance of whether the brakes were last replaced before or after' the claimant bought the car.[37] But from a property rights perspective there is nothing 'anomalous' about this at all, and in any case if it *were* anomalous then it is hard to see why the same would not be true of the distinction between defective brakes fitted to the car on manufacture and replacement brakes fitted by the claimant or a previous owner (a distinction on which *Clerk & Lindsell* relies[38]). Besides, the *Saratoga* approach gives rise to anomalies of its own, since it distinguishes between changes made to the property by persons in the product distribution chain (such as car dealers) and those made by previous 'users' of the product. It follows that, if a car dealer adds a defective tyre to a car, then whether the tyre is 'other property' or not in the hands of a later owner depends on whether the dealer then used the car as a demonstration model or not.[39] This makes little sense.

The discussion of these timing issues demonstrates the importance of considering the 'other property' question from the perspective of the claimant, and of keeping the issue of the claimant's property rights front and centre of the analysis. When courts and commentators lose sight of this, and switch to looking at these questions from a purely functional perspective, or from the point of view of the defendant's liability exposure, they tend to over-complicate what are in fact relatively straightforward issues and to draw distinctions that are difficult to defend on any rational basis.

C. Commingling of Ingredients to Produce a Flawed Final Product

Property rights analysis is also useful when it comes to resolving another issue on the borderline between property damage and pure economic loss (and centrally concerned with issues of timing), namely the commingling of ingredients to produce a final product flawed because of a defect in one ingredient. Suppose that the claimant is a producer of port wine, which is made by combining table wine and brandy. And suppose that the brandy which the claimant buys to make a batch of port was contaminated with copper during distillation, which renders the final product worthless. Has the claimant suffered property damage or pure economic loss?

In *Bacardi-Martini Beverages Ltd v Thomas Hardy Packaging Ltd*,[40] the Court of Appeal held on analogous facts (benzene contamination of carbon dioxide used to make alcoholic drinks) that the loss was purely economic. To see why that was correct, it is helpful to focus again on the claimant's property rights. The port wine in the example has not been damaged

---

[37] *Clerk & Lindsell* (n 9) para 10-25. See also Kitchen, 'Beyond Physical Integration' (n 8) 152–54 (who does not consider this question from the perspective of the claimant's property rights, despite claiming that his analysis is rights-based). In *Murphy* (n 6) Lord Oliver seems to have assumed that a replacement tyre added to a car by a previous owner would be 'other property' for the purposes of a claim by the current owner (see at 211), but it is hard to know how much weight to put on what seems to have been a throwaway remark.

[38] *Clerk & Lindsell* (n 9) paras 10-23–10-25.

[39] See *Saratoga* (n 36) 1790 (Scalia J).

[40] [2002] EWCA Civ 549, [2002] 2 Lloyd's Rep 379 (hereafter *Bacardi-Martini*).

by the copper but was 'merely defective from the moment of its creation'.[41] Hence from the time at which the claimant acquired property rights in the port (which was the time at which it came into being), the port was defective and valueless. But what if the claimant seeks to shift the focus from the port to the table wine, and to claim that the copper in the brandy damaged the wine? The problem with this argument is that the wine was never damaged by the copper, because at the very moment that it came into contact with it, the wine was deliberately being transformed by the claimant into something else, namely port.[42] Hence there was no violation of the claimant's property rights in the *port* because the port never existed *without* the copper, and no violation of the claimant's property rights in the *wine* because the wine never existed *with* it.[43]

In the example given the solution is straightforward because there is no question that the process of making port transforms the table wine used in that process into something else entirely. And the same would be true where, for example, a contaminated egg is used to bake a cake. Conversely, one can posit scenarios where the principal ingredient retains its identity, such that the addition of a contaminant *can* be said to have 'damaged' it, for example where vanilla syrup laced with arsenic is added to a cup of coffee. Doubtless it is also possible to imagine intermediate scenarios, where it may be more difficult to say whether the principal ingredient has retained its identity or not. However, this in itself does not cast doubt on the value of property rights analysis in approaching this problem. As Robert Stevens says, when it comes to the divisibility of property rights, 'difficult cases on the margin are inevitable'.[44]

IV. The Core Question

We can now turn to the core question of distinguishing between damage to the property itself and damage to other property in a case where the claimant acquired the composite item with the defective component already incorporated in it. At this point, property rights analysis no longer provides a complete answer, and a more functional or pragmatic approach is required. I begin my analysis of this question by discussing the English case law, before briefly considering the American jurisprudence, and then subjecting the question to critical analysis.

A. The English Case Law

The English authorities on the issue of damage to other property divide into some early appellate decisions in which the question was discussed at a relatively high level of generality

---

[41] *Bacardi-Martini* (n 40) 386 (Mance LJ). The same analysis is employed by the German courts: see Schwenzer, 'Product Liability' (n 20) 138.

[42] See *Bacardi-Martini* (n 40) 383 (Mance LJ) (the other ingredients 'ceased . . . to exist . . . at the moment of admixture'). It is important to say '*deliberately* being transformed *by the claimant*' because if a third party were to pour brandy into the claimant's wine unasked then that would clearly amount to property damage, regardless of whether the brandy was defective or not. On the potential subjectivity of 'property damage' see Donal Nolan, 'Damage in the English Law of Negligence' (2013) 4 JETL 259, 277.

[43] Kitchen, 'Beyond Physical Integration' (n 8) 150–51 disagrees with the *Bacardi-Martini* decision, but his objections are not convincing.

[44] Stevens, *Torts and Rights* (n 8) 29.

236 DAMAGE TO 'OTHER PROPERTY'

and later decisions (almost all at first instance) in which the court was faced with a specific problem, resolution of which was generally determinative of the outcome of the case. And although much of the focus has been on the dicta in the early cases, it is suggested that the decisions in the later cases are more useful when it comes to identifying the underlying principles in this area.

A brief summary of the early appellate authorities will nevertheless be useful. As we have seen, the first case in which the question of damage to 'other property' was mentioned was *Aswan Engineering*,[45] where the claimant had bought pails of a water-proofing compound called Lupguard. The pails, which had been made by the defendant, melted in the heat of a Kuwaiti dockside, and the Lupguard was lost. Although it was not necessary to decide the question, Lloyd LJ's 'provisional view' appears to have been that this was damage to other property (the pails having damaged the Lupguard), and that the same would be true where a tyre burst and damaged the car to which it was fitted, or a defective cork rendered wine undrinkable.[46] Similarly, Nicholls LJ thought that, as a matter of 'strict legal analysis', the Lupguard and the pails were different items of property, although a manufacturer's duty of care probably did not extend to faulty packaging in this way.[47]

In *D & F Estates*,[48] the issue was first considered at the highest level. According to Lord Bridge, a possible explanation for the decision in *Anns v Merton London Borough Council* that there was 'material physical damage'[49] in an acquisition of defective premises case was that the house in question was a 'complex structure' in which 'damage to one part of the structure caused by a hidden defect in another part . . . may qualify to be treated as damage to "other property"'.[50] Lord Oliver agreed that damage to the walls of a house caused by defective foundations (as in *Anns*) could perhaps be treated as damage to other property on a 'complex structure' analysis.[51] Nevertheless, on the facts of *D & F Estates*, the cost of re-plastering a flat in which defective plaster had fallen from the walls and ceilings was clearly pure economic loss, since it arose solely out of damage to the plaster itself.

In the later *Murphy* decision Lords Bridge and Oliver backtracked somewhat on the 'complex structure' theory. According to Lord Bridge:[52]

> The reality is that the structural elements in any building form a single indivisible unit of which the different parts are essentially interdependent . . . It is quite artificial . . . to treat a defect in an integral structure, so far as it weakens the structure, as a dangerous defect liable to cause damage to 'other property'.

Lord Oliver agreed with Lord Bridge on this point, as did Lord Keith and Lord Jauncey in cases where the entire building had been erected and equipped by the same contractor, although they thought that the position might be different where, for example, a

---

[45] *Aswan Engineering* (n 5).
[46] ibid.
[47] ibid 28–29.
[48] *D & F Estates* (n 15).
[49] *Anns* (n 13) 504–505 (Lord Wilberforce).
[50] *D & F Estates* (n 15) 207.
[51] ibid 212, 214.
[52] *Murphy* (n 6) 478.

sub-contractor had installed defective electric wiring which caused a fire.[53] Lord Bridge also considered that a distinction should be made between a part of a complex structure which posed a danger only because it did not perform its proper function of sustaining the other parts 'and some distinct item incorporated in the structure which positively malfunctions so as to inflict positive damage on the structure in which it is incorporated', such as a defective boiler that explodes and damages a house, or a defective electrical installation which malfunctions and sets the house on fire.[54] Lord Jauncey agreed that in the case of such 'ancillary equipment' a claim would lie on ordinary *Donoghue v Stevenson* principles.[55]

The distinctions drawn in *Murphy* were not explained and have not generally been applied by the lower courts in such a way as to generate liability. An exception is *Jacobs v Morton*,[56] where a piled raft foundation under the claimant's house constructed during the ownership of a predecessor in title had failed. It was held that the engineers who had designed the foundation and supervised its installation owed the claimant a duty of care that extended to the cost of the demolition and rebuilding of the house necessitated by the failure of the earlier work. According to the judge, the claimant had suffered property damage applying the complex structure theory as expounded in *Murphy*, since the defective raft foundation (1) was designed and built by persons with no responsibility for any other part of the building; (2) had inflicted positive harm on the rest of the house; and (3) had been installed some eight years after the house had been built. It is respectfully suggested that the decision and reasoning in this case is incompatible with later decisions and that on these facts a different result could be expected today. In *Payne v John Setchell Ltd*,[57] for example, HHJ Humphrey Lloyd QC gave short shrift to a complex structure argument where the inadequate foundations of two adjoining cottages required underpinning work to be carried out on the properties. It was necessary, he commented, 'to avoid any artificiality and to be realistic' when considering the 'other property' issue.[58]

Another one of those later decisions is *The Orjula*,[59] where Mance J rejected a submission that seventy-two drums of hydrochloric acid stowed in a container should be treated as separate items for the purposes of a tort claim by the charterer of a vessel on which the container was being carried. Even if (because of the inadequate stow) some of the drums had damaged other drums, it would be contrary to the 'spirit and reasoning' of *Murphy* for the charterer as bailee of the container to be able to recover for that as damage to other property.[60] The only other post-*Murphy* case concerning defective chattels is *Finesse Group Ltd v Bryson Products (a Firm)*,[61] where defective adhesive caused demonstration panels to separate from the stands to which they were attached. Akenhead J very much doubted that the adhesive and the panels and stands could be construed as anything other than part of a single 'structure', such that the delamination was simply damage to the defective thing itself. It was 'fanciful' to suggest, for example, that if the heel of a shoe fell off because the

---

[53] ibid 470.
[54] ibid.
[55] ibid 497.
[56] (1994) 72 BLR 92 (QBD).
[57] (2001) 3 TCLR 26 (TCC) (hereafter *Payne*).
[58] ibid [41].
[59] *The Orjula* (n 30).
[60] ibid 401 (Mance J).
[61] [2013] EWHC 3273 (TCC), [2013] 6 Costs LR 991.

238   DAMAGE TO 'OTHER PROPERTY'

glue attaching it to the sole was defective, the owner would have a claim against the glue manufacturer.[62]

Turning to defective premises, four further cases should be mentioned. The first is *Bellefield Computer Services Ltd v E Turner & Sons Ltd*,[63] where part of the claimant's dairy burned down due to deficiencies in an internal firewall for which the defendant was to blame. According to Schiemann LJ:[64]

> [I]n the present case the whole of the dairy was built at the same time by the builders, marketed as a unit, bought as a unit to be used as a unit and was used as a unit. I have no doubt that any holding either that (1) the rooms on one side of the wall should be treated for present purposes as constituting a different building from the rooms on the other side of the wall, or that (2) the wall should be treated as constituting a different building from the rooms on one side of it, would be a thoroughly undesirable approach to the issues before us.

Tuckey LJ said that the fact that different parts of the dairy were used for different purposes within its overall function as a dairy did not mean that it ceased to be a single building and expressed his agreement with the reasoning of the judge below, who had emphasized that the wall was an integral part of the dairy as originally built.

The second case is *Linklaters Business Services v Sir Robert McAlpine Ltd*, where it was alleged that defects in the fitting of insulation material for chilled water pipes during the renovation of an office building had caused the pipework to corrode. Akenhead J refused to strike out a claim for contribution by the main contractors for the renovation work against the sub-contractors who had fitted the insulation material, holding that it was arguable in the light of *Murphy* that their negligence had caused the claimant lessees of the building property damage.[65] However, when the case came to trial before the same judge, it was held that on closer analysis the claimants had suffered only pure economic loss.[66] The insulated chilled water pipework was essentially one 'thing' for tort purposes, not least because one would never have the pipework without the insulation.

Akenhead J was again faced with the damage to other property issue in *Broster v Galliard Docklands Ltd*,[67] where he held that there was no realistic prospect of establishing that the builder of a row of six terraced houses was liable in tort to purchasers of the properties when alleged deficiencies in the common roof caused it to lift and fall back during a storm, damaging the rest of the houses. According to the authorities, it was necessary 'to consider the structure as a whole and to avoid any artificiality in practically considering the structure',[68] and in the instant case:[69]

> It would be wholly artificial to argue that the segment of the roof over each individual terraced unit was to be considered as separate from the whole roof or indeed that the roof as

---

[62] ibid [29].
[63] (2000) 2 TCLR 759 (CA).
[64] ibid 773.
[65] *Linklaters Business Services v Sir Robert McAlpine Ltd* [2010] EWHC 1145 (QB), [2010] BLR 537.
[66] *Linklaters Business Services v Sir Robert McAlpine Ltd (No 2)* [2010] EWHC 2931 (QB), 133 Con LR 211.
[67] [2011] EWHC 1722 (TCC), [2011] PNLR 34.
[68] ibid [11] (Akenhead J).
[69] ibid [16] (Akenhead J).

a whole was to be considered as separate from the walls of the units below. It follows that there is damage to 'the thing itself'.

Finally, in *Kagan v Harris*,[70] pipes installed under the floor of a renovated kitchen had leaked, causing damage to the floor slab above. Edwards-Stuart J refused to give summary judgment for the defendant on the householder's claim against the sub-contractor responsible for the pipes, since there was not enough evidence to determine whether the pipes were separate from the floor itself or whether the floor and the pipes should be 'regarded as the same bit of property' for tort purposes.[71]

B. The American Jurisprudence

Although the American case law on the core question is far more extensive than the English authorities, it is also fairly consistent, which makes it easier to summarize it briefly. With the exception of cases concerning asbestos contamination in buildings, which have their own separate line of authority,[72] the two general principles that apply in most US jurisdictions are: (1) that 'when a product or system is deemed to be an integrated whole', damage caused by a component part to the rest of the product or system is treated as harm to the product or system itself;[73] and (2) that whether a product or system is regarded as an integrated whole for these purposes is primarily based on the subject-matter of the transaction pursuant to which the plaintiff acquired the thing in question.[74] In *Shipco 2295 Inc v Avondale Shipyards Inc*,[75] for example, the buyer of an oil tanker could not recover in tort from the builder of the vessel or the designer of its steering mechanism for damage which a defect in that mechanism caused to other parts of the ship. According to Davis CJ, in attempting to identify the 'product', the court should ask what the object of the purchase contract was. In the instant case, the answer was the completed tanker, since the buyer had not bargained separately for individual components of the vessel. It followed that the vessel must be considered 'the product' for tort purposes and not the components that made it up. The focus on the 'object of the bargain' in the US case law reflects the influence of the *East River* decision, and in particular the argument made there that recovery is denied for damage to the product itself because in such cases the buyer's essential complaint is that they have not received the benefit of their bargain, which is a matter for contract not tort.[76] Hence in *Shipco* it was said that giving the buyer a tort remedy would undermine a 'central objective' of *East River* in confining plaintiffs in cases of this kind to contractual avenues of redress.[77]

---

[70] [2019] EWHC 2567 (TCC).
[71] ibid [30] (Edwards-Stuart J).
[72] See Richard C Ausness, 'Tort Liability for Asbestos Removal Costs' (1994) 73 Or L Rev 505.
[73] See *Restatement of the Law (Third) of Torts: Product Liability* (1998) § 21, cmt e. See also *East River* (n 18) 2300 (Blackmun J) (turbine supplied 'as an integrated package' properly regarded as 'a single unit'); *Transport Corporation of America Inc v International Business Machines Inc* 30 F 3d 953 (8th Cir 1994) 957 (McMillian CJ) ('damage to other components integrated into a single unit are not considered damage to other property'); *Calloway v City of Reno* 993 P 2d 1259 (Nev 2000) 1268 (Young J) (both 'an airplane's engine and a building's heating and plumbing system are necessary and integrated parts of the greater whole').
[74] See, eg, *Saratoga* (n 36) 1791 (Scalia J).
[75] 825 F 2d 925 (5th Cir 1987) (hereafter *Shipco*).
[76] See n 23 and accompanying text.
[77] *Shipco* (n 75) 928 (Davis CJ).

240   DAMAGE TO 'OTHER PROPERTY'

Although most of the American authorities on damage to the property itself have been defective product cases, a similar approach has been taken in the defective premises context. In *Calloway v City of Reno*,[78] for example, the Supreme Court of Nevada held that damage to townhouses caused by allegedly defective framing was damage to the properties themselves, and so pure economic loss. The alleged defects had merely deprived the houseowners of 'the benefit of their bargains'.[79] The court cited a raft of decisions from other US jurisdictions to similar effect and made it clear that the same analysis would apply if, say, the heating and plumbing system of an apartment complex caused damage to the rest of the complex.[80]

C. Analysis

Finally, how *ought* the English courts to approach the question of the distinction between damage to the thing itself and damage to other property in cases where the claimant acquires the product or premises with the defective element already present?

The first point that should be made is that whether the component part was manufactured or installed by a party different from the party responsible for the composite item is a complete irrelevance and should have no bearing on the damage to 'other property' question. The nature of the loss or damage suffered by the claimant cannot rationally depend on whether, for example, a boiler in the claimant's house was installed by the main contractor responsible for the construction of the building or a sub-contractor.[81] The idea that it can originates in the speeches of Lord Keith and Lord Jauncey in *Murphy*, but their Lordships did not explain why they considered this to be significant, and no explanation has been given in the subsequent case law. Nor, with one or two exceptions,[82] have the American courts accorded any weight to this consideration. In the *Shipco* case, for example, the Court saw 'no rational reason' to give a buyer greater rights to recover for a defect in a product 'because the component is designed, constructed, or furnished by someone other than the final manufacturer'.[83] Commentators have also been dismissive of the idea.[84] Two further observations should be made in this connection. One is that, since virtually no premises or products of any complexity are today built or produced solely by one party, were the courts to attach much weight to the 'separate contractor' idea the exception would potentially swallow up the rule. The other observation is that the damage to other property issue cuts both ways, so that if the component is regarded as 'other property' then not only is

---

[78] 993 P 2d 1259 (Nev 2000).

[79] ibid 1269 (Young J).

[80] ibid 1268.

[81] '[T]he nature of the plaintiff's loss is the same in both cases, and the would-be policy of confining him to his contractual remedy, if any, is equally pertinent': John G Fleming, The Law of Torts (9th edn, LBC Information Services 1998) 550–51.

[82] See, eg, *Northern Power & Engineering Corp v Caterpillar Tractor Co* 623 P 2d 324 (Alaska 1981) 330 and cases there cited.

[83] *Shipco* (n 75) 929 (Davis CJ). See also *King v Hilton-Davis* 855 F 2d 1047 (3rd Cir 1988) 1051.

[84] See, eg, Andrew Grubb and Alastair Mullis, 'An Unfair Law for Dangerous Products: The Fall of Anns' [1991] Conv 225, 231 (Grubb and Mullis, 'An Unfair Law') (no 'logical or practical basis'); Duncan Wallace, '*Anns* Beyond Repair' (1991) 107 LQR 228, 237 (anomalous and unworkable in the construction context). In *Payne* (n 57) the judge described the idea that a sub-contractor would be liable when a main contractor would not as 'absurd'.

damage done *by* the component to the rest of the thing property damage, but so is damage done *to* the component by the rest of the thing.[85] And it is very hard to see why the right of a houseowner to recover for the destruction of a boiler when a wall collapses should depend on who installed the boiler when the house was built.

The second point is that considerable weight should be given to the degree of the physical integration of the component and the composite item. The more closely integrated the component is, the less realistic it is to regard it as 'other property', and one point on which the English courts have been consistent since *Murphy* is the need to avoid making artificial distinctions in this context.[86] Attaching weight to this consideration also achieves some symmetry with the position under the Consumer Protection Act 1987, where there is no liability for damage caused to the defective product itself or to a product which has been supplied with the defective product 'comprised in it',[87] language suggestive of some degree of physical attachment.[88] Although in general physical integration should only be a weighty consideration, where the component cannot be removed from the composite item without damaging one or other of the two then this should be regarded as determinative, since on a property rights analysis it no longer makes sense to think of them as separate items of property.[89] A useful analogy can be drawn here with the doctrine of accession in personal property law, where it has been held that an item incorporated into a chattel will lose its identity as a separate item of property if it cannot be removed without causing damage.[90]

Although the degree of physical integration of the component part is an important consideration when assessing whether it is 'other property' for tort purposes, it only provides a complete answer to the issue where the component cannot be removed without damage resulting. In other cases, additional factors may need to be taken into account. In particular, the 'damage to the property itself' rule would be emasculated if any removable component were to be considered 'other property',[91] and this would also be inconsistent with the English authorities. In *The Rebecca Elaine*,[92] for example, it was assumed that damage caused by defective pistons to the engine of a fishing vessel was pure economic loss, even though the pistons could have been removed. It is therefore suggested that two other criteria should be considered in addition to physical integration.

The first of these additional considerations is what might be described as a 'commercial reality' test. In assessing whether there is damage to property, significance should be attached to the way in which one would expect the parties to the transaction pursuant to which the claimant obtained ownership or possession of the composite item to have characterized the subject-matter of the transaction. In *The Orjula*, for example, the bailees would

---

[85] See, eg, *Nicor Supply Ships Associates v General Motors Corp* 876 F 2d 501 (5th Cir 1989) (time charterer of ship could recover in tort when fire caused by allegedly defective engine damaged seismic equipment charterer had added to vessel); *Saratoga* (n 36).

[86] See also Fairgrieve and Goldberg, *Product Liability* (n 8) para 16.72 ('the courts will not make artificial distinctions' in such cases).

[87] Consumer Protection Act 1987, s 5(2).

[88] See Tettenborn, 'Components and Product Liability' (n 8) 344.

[89] See also Grubb and Mullis, 'An Unfair Law' (n 84) 232 (no damage to 'other property' in such a case).

[90] *Hendy Lennox (Industrial Engines) Ltd v Grahame Puttick Ltd* [1984] 1 WLR 485 (QBD) (property in diesel engines did not pass when incorporated into generator sets as they could be removed). See also *Rendell v Associated Finance Pty Ltd* [1957] VR 604 (Full Ct); *Thomas v Robinson* [1977] 1 NZLR 385 (SC). In the light of the accession cases, Kitchen's claim ('Beyond Physical Integration' (n 8) 139–40) that focusing on physical integration is 'unprincipled' is hard to fathom.

[91] For a convincing argument to this effect, see Kitchen, 'Beyond Physical Integration' (n 8).

[92] [1999] 2 Lloyd's Rep 1 (CA).

242 DAMAGE TO 'OTHER PROPERTY'

doubtless have thought that they were taking possession of a container packed with drums of acid, rather than a container, seventy-two drums of acid, and some staging. The commercial reality test has the advantage of tapping into ordinary intuitions about the divisibility of property—people think they buy a 'car', for example, not a collection of car parts.[93] It can also be defended on functional grounds, since focusing on the subject-matter of the transaction chimes with one of the reasons why damage to the property itself is not generally actionable in tort, namely that contract law is thought to give adequate protection in such cases.[94] It would however be a mistake to elevate this 'object of the bargain' idea into the sole test of the divisibility of property, as the American courts have sometimes done. The functional approach adopted in the US can give rise to analytical errors if divorced entirely from some basic underlying conception of property rights,[95] and there is clearly a legitimate role for other considerations, most obviously the degree of physical integration of the component and composite item.

The other additional consideration to which some weight should be attached is what has been termed the 'functional distinctness' of the component part,[96] or the 'interdependence' between it and the composite item.[97] In particular, a component which is unlikely to be used separately from the composite item is less likely to constitute 'other property', and the same is true of a component which is essential to the proper functioning of the larger unit of which it is a part.[98] To give a simple example, since a cork in a bottle of wine is made only for the purpose of sealing such bottles and is essential to the proper functioning of the bottle of wine (at least until it is opened), this final consideration would militate against treating the cork and the wine as separate items of property for the purposes of the damage to other property rule, even though the cork can be removed without damaging the wine. As this example shows, there is likely to be a degree of congruence between the 'commercial reality' test and the 'functional distinctiveness' consideration, since the greater the interdependence between the component and the composite item the more likely it is that the parties to a transaction involving the latter will regard it as a single thing (in this case a 'bottle of wine').

V. Conclusion

In this chapter I have considered the question of what amounts to damage to 'other property' for the purposes of the law of tort, with particular reference to cases where a defective component causes damage to the composite item of which it forms a part. The main conclusions of my analysis are as follows:

---

[93] See also Tettenborn, 'Components and Product Liability' (n 8) 344 ('people's general understanding of the nature of a "product" . . . is clearly a useful guide').

[94] See text following n 22.

[95] See text following n 30 and n 35.

[96] Clerk & Lindsell (n 9) para 7-148.

[97] Kitchen, 'Beyond Physical Integration' (n 8) passim.

[98] See also Tettenborn, 'Components and Product Liability' (n 8) 344. Like physical integration, these factors are also relevant in the doctrine of accession. In Regina Chevrolet Sales Ltd v Riddell [1942] 3 DLR 159 (Sask CA), for example, it was held that tyres added to a truck became the property of the truck's owner because they had no real value except for such use and were essential to the proper working of the vehicle.

1. There is damage to other property of the claimant where the component was added to the composite item when that item was already in the claimant's hands.
2. Where the component was already incorporated into the composite item when the claimant acquired that item, whether damage the component causes to the rest of the item constitutes damage to other property should be determined by the principles set out hereafter. This is true regardless of whether the component was present in the item from the start or was added by a previous owner.
3. Whether the component was made or installed by a party different from the party responsible for the production or construction of the composite item should have no bearing on the damage to 'other property' question.
4. When deciding whether there is damage to 'other property', considerable weight should be given to the extent of the physical integration of the component and the composite item, and if the component cannot be removed from the composite item without causing damage then the two should be regarded as a single piece of property for tort purposes.
5. In cases where the component can be removed from the composite item without causing damage, account should also be taken of (a) the way in which one would expect the parties to the transaction pursuant to which the claimant obtained ownership or possession of the item to have characterized the subject-matter of the transaction; and (b) the 'functional distinctness' of the component part, or the 'interdependence' between it and the composite item.

15

Procuring Wrongs

JAMES GOUDKAMP[*]

I. Introduction

In certain circumstances, private law imposes liability for facilitating wrongs committed by other persons. One illustration of this, found in the law of equity, lies in the rules regarding knowingly assisting a breach of trust. Another example, drawn from the law of torts (or from the law of contract according to some writers), concerns the cause of action recognized in *Lumley v Gye*.[1] Private law is gradually adding to the list of circumstances in which it imposes liability for facilitating wrongdoing. This chapter examines one such extension, which was developed in *Marex Financial Ltd v Sevilleja*.[2] The wrong recognized in that case consists, in outline, in knowingly and intentionally inducing a violation of rights embodied in a judgment. Its existence was recently confirmed by, in particular, *Lakatamia Shipping Co Ltd v Su*.[3] The creation of the *Marex* tort has been heralded as an important development. For example, the Commercial Court in its *Report 2020–2021* singled out the wrong's recognition as one of its 'highlights' for that year.[4] Similarly, the authors of *Civil Fraud* write that the tort's acknowledgement is a 'significant practical development'.[5] This chapter examines the process by which the *Marex* tort was recognized (section II) and its scope (section III). It then considers the tort's significance (section IV) before turning, finally, to examine some wider issues that the wrong raises regarding the law of torts (section V).

II. Development of the *Marex* Tort

In *Marex*, the claimant company obtained a US$5m judgment against two corporate defendants for breach of contract.[6] A few weeks later, when a freezing order was made against the defendants in support of enforcement, it transpired that they had almost no assets. This prompted the claimant to issue proceedings against their alleged owner, Mr Sevilleja, and to apply for permission to serve him with the claim form out of the jurisdiction. The claimant contended that, following the circulation of the draft judgment as well as after judgment had been entered, Mr Sevilleja had transferred to his own control money that had been

---

[*] I am grateful to John Murphy for his comments on a draft of this chapter. I also acknowledge the considerable benefit derived from reading his draft paper 'Inducing Others' Wrongs: A Nascent or Needless Tort?'

[1] *Lumley v Gye* (1853) 2 El & Bl 216; 118 ER 749 (QB).

[2] *Marex Financial Ltd v Sevilleja* [2017] EWHC 918 (Comm), [2017] 4 WLR 105 (hereafter *Marex*).

[3] *Lakatamia Shipping Co Ltd v Su* [2021] EWHC 1907 (Comm) (hereafter *Lakatamia*).

[4] *The Commercial Court Report 2020–2021* (Judicial Office 2022) 10.

[5] Thomas Grant and David Mumford, *Civil Fraud: Law, Practice & Procedure* (Sweet & Maxwell 2018) [3.022B] (hereafter Grant and Mumford, *Civil Fraud*).

[6] *Marex Financial Ltd v Creative Finance Ltd* [2013] EWHC 2155 (Comm), [2014] 1 All ER (Comm) 122.

James Goudkamp, *Procuring Wrongs* In: *Shaping the Law of Obligations*. Edited by: Edwin Peel and Rebecca Probert, Oxford University Press. © James Goudkamp 2023. DOI: 10.1093/oso/9780198889762.003.0015

held in the companies' bank accounts. The claimant said that this prevented the companies from dealing with it in accordance with their obligations and that Mr Sevilleja had hence committed the tort of causing loss by unlawful means. The claimant also contended that Mr Sevilleja had acted tortiously in inducing the companies to violate its rights under the judgment, that is to say, that he had committed what is now known as the *Marex* tort.

For his part, Mr Sevilleja challenged the court's jurisdiction to determine the claims that had been brought against him. He did so on various grounds, including that there was no such wrong as the *Marex* tort. He argued that the non-payment of a judgment debt was not itself an actionable wrong with the result that it was not tortious to induce a judgment debtor to fail to discharge a judgment debt. Various additional points were made, including that it was unnecessary to recognize the *Marex* tort in view of the jurisdiction to make a freezing order post-judgment, which was an unmeritorious submission given that such an order had been made shortly after judgment had been entered but had failed to prevent (some of) the damage alleged. Conversely, the claimant maintained that the *Marex* tort was within the principles that had been established by *Lumley v Gye*.[7] The basic idea that the claimant advanced was that since it is a wrong intentionally to induce a breach of contract, it must also be a wrong intentionally to induce a breach of rights embodied in a judgment that vindicated the rights that had been created by the contract concerned. It was said, in effect, that a right cannot be made less valuable on account of its having been novated by a judgment.

In brief reasons, Knowles J, drawing on cases concerned with the enforcement of foreign judgments, held that a failure to pay a judgment debt was an actionable wrong.[8] This led him to conclude that the claimant had 'the better argument for the existence of the tort',[9] which he seemed to regard, together with the tort of inducing a breach of contract, as a sub-species of a more general wrong of inducing a violation of others' rights.[10] For this reason, as well as for other reasons that are not presently relevant, he rejected Mr Sevilleja's jurisdictional challenge. The Court of Appeal refused Mr Sevilleja permission to appeal as regards whether it was sufficiently arguable that the *Marex* tort existed,[11] but granted him permission to appeal on the ground that the claims against him were barred by the doctrine of reflective loss (on the logic that the claimant's alleged loss was simply a manifestation of that which the companies had suffered). The Court of Appeal held that that doctrine barred around 90 per cent of the claim. Its decision was reversed on a further appeal to the Supreme Court.[12] However, neither the Court of Appeal nor the Supreme Court engaged directly with what Knowles J had said regarding the *Marex* tort.[13] Accordingly, its status was left in a certain amount of doubt. Its existence was supported only by the view that had been expressed at first instance that it arguably formed part of English law.[14] (It is unclear what became of the proceedings following the Supreme Court's decision.)

---

[7] *Lumley* (1853) 2 El & Bl 216; 118 ER 749 (QB).
[8] *Marex* (n 2) [20]. See also at [45].
[9] ibid [28].
[10] ibid [18]–[19].
[11] *Marex Financial Ltd v Sevilleja* [2018] EWCA Civ 1468, [2019] QB 173 [6].
[12] *Marex Financial Ltd v Sevilleja* [2020] UKSC 31, [2021] AC 39 (hereafter *Marex* (SC)).
[13] Although see the remarks of Lord Sales at [199] of the Supreme Court's judgment, which seemingly approve of Knowles J's analysis regarding the existence of the *Marex* tort.
[14] While the appeals in *Marex* were unfolding, Knowles J's remarks were the subject of passing comment in *Palmer Birch (a partnership) v Lloyd* [2018] EWHC 2316 (TCC); [2018] 4 WLR 164 [172].

There matters stood for several years until the decision in *Lakatamia Shipping Co Ltd v Su*.[15] In that case, the claimant had obtained two judgments against a Mr Su for breach of contract. The combined sum owed thereunder was around US$47m,[16] which Mr Su failed to pay. In the course of its enforcement efforts, the claimant discovered that Mr Su had owned two properties and a private airplane. Those assets had been sold and the funds thereby realized transferred to Mr Su's mother, who was known as Madam Su, and dissipated. Bryan J found that Madam Su had thereby committed both the *Marex* tort and the tort of unlawful means conspiracy.[17] The judge said:

> The Marex tort finds a close, and I consider compelling, analogy with the tort of inducing a breach of contract. There would seem to be no compelling reason why, in circumstances where the law protects against intentional interference by third parties with contractual rights it should not equally protect against intentional interference with rights established by judgments.[18]

He added:

> I can see no reason why the law should protect against third-party interference with contractual rights but not against such interference with contractual rights that have been novated by judgment. Absent such protection, the law would perversely diminish the protection that it affords to a victim of a breach of contract where the victim has had those rights vindicated by the courts.[19]

Accordingly, *Lakatamia* confirmed the existence of the *Marex* tort. It is true, of course, that *Lakatamia* is a first instance decision like the decision in *Marex* itself. The High Court is not bound by it. But as a practical matter, the High Court is very unlikely not to follow the decision, especially given the exceptionally comprehensive nature of Bryan J's judgment and the fact that it was entered, unlike that in *Marex*, following a trial.

Thus, in *Gee v Gee*,[20] the court took it as read that that which had been said in *Lakatamia* as regards the *Marex* tort represented the law. The claimant had succeeded in a proprietary estoppel claim against his father and brother in respect of the family farm.[21] He then alleged that the defendants had breached the order consequent upon the judgment. Specifically, it was said that a lease pertaining to part of the farm had been surrendered to the lessor (Christ Church, Oxford) in contravention of the order. On the basis of these allegations, the claimant applied for further orders. The case raised various procedural issues, some of which are explored below. However, the important point for present purposes is that HHJ Paul Matthews proceeded on the basis that the *Marex* tort had been vouchsafed a position in tort law and that the claimant was entitled to claim in respect of it.[22]

---

[15] *Lakatamia* (n 3).
[16] *Lakatamia Shipping Co Ltd v Su* [2014] EWHC 3611 (Comm); [2015] 1 Lloyd's Rep 216.
[17] *Lakatamia* (n 3) [822].
[18] ibid [120].
[19] ibid [121].
[20] *Gee v Gee* [2022] EWHC 1369 (Ch) (hereafter *Gee*).
[21] *Gee v Gee* [2018] EWHC 1393 (Ch).
[22] ibid [14].

A proper understanding of the *Marex* tort requires an appreciation not only of the cases that established its existence but also of the policy context in which it was cultivated. Over the course of the past few decades, the courts have increasingly emphasized the public interest in the enforcement of judgments.[23] This emphasis has catalysed numerous innovations. However, by far the most significant is the development, commencing with the foundational decisions in *Nippon Yusen Kaisha v Karageorgis*[24] and *Mareva Compania Naviera SA v International Bulk Carriers SA (The Mareva)*,[25] of the power to make freezing orders. That jurisdiction, which exists to protect claimants against the risk that defendants will dissipate their assets with a view to stultifying any judgment that is ultimately obtained against them, has since been steadily enlarged. Thus, freezing orders can be awarded post-judgment and regardless of whether or not one was made pre-judgment.[26] They can be made in relation to persons against whom the claimant has no claim but who hold assets for the defendant.[27] They can be awarded against foreign defendants who have no assets within the jurisdiction.[28] And they can be made in support of claims over which only foreign courts have jurisdiction.[29] The advent of the *Marex* tort is very closely connected with the power to grant freezing orders, as is discussed further below. Its recognition is another manifestation of the courts striving to promote the policy in favour of the enforcement of judgments.

III. Scope of the *Marex* Tort

In *Lakatamia*, Bryan J said that the elements of the *Marex* tort 'stand to be identified by analogy'[30] with the tort of inducing a breach of contract. He then enumerated the elements of the *Marex* tort as follows:

> (1) The entry of a judgment in the claimant's favour, (2) Breach of the rights existing under that judgment, (3) The procurement or inducement of that breach by the defendant, (4) Knowledge of the judgment on the part of the defendant, and (5) Realisation on the part of the defendant that the conduct being induced or procured would breach the rights owed under the judgment.[31]

Bryan J also made it clear that various rules that govern the tort of inducing a breach of contract extend to the *Marex* tort. Thus, he observed that as is the case with the tort of inducing a breach of contract, '[t]he defendant does not need also to intend . . . to damage the claimant'[32] or to have acted maliciously.[33] Similarly, just as it is unnecessary for a defendant

---

[23] 'It is the policy of English law that English judgments should be paid' (*Touton Far East Pte Ltd v Shri Lal Mahal Ltd* [2016] EWHC 1765 (Comm) [3] (Males J)); 'the policy of the law [is to] weigh . . . heavily in favour of the enforcement of judgments' (*Emmott v Michael Wilson Partners Ltd* [2019] EWCA Civ 219, [2019] 4 WLR 53 [44] (Gross LJ) (hereafter *Emmott*)).

[24] *Nippon Yusen Kaisha v Karageorgis* [1975] 1 WLR 1093 (CA).

[25] *Mareva Compania Naviera SA v International Bulk Carriers SA (The Mareva)* [1980] 1 All ER 213 (CA).

[26] Relevant cases are discussed in *Emmott* (n 23) [40]–[44].

[27] *TSB Private Bank International SA v Chabra* [1992] 1 WLR 231 (Ch D); *Mercantile Group (Europe) AG v Aiyela* [1994] QB 366 (CA).

[28] *Republic of Haiti v Duvalier* [1990] 1 QB 202 (CA).

[29] *Broad Idea International Ltd v Convoy Collateral Ltd* [2021] UKPC 24, [2023] AC 389.

[30] *Lakatamia* (n 3) [125].

[31] ibid [126].

[32] ibid [127(1)].

[33] ibid [127(5)].

to a claim for inducing a breach of contract to have known the detailed terms of the agreement, it is inessential, in order for liability to arise in the *Marex* tort, that the defendant have been conscious of the 'contents of the judgment'.[34] And as with the rule that a defendant will be taken to know of a contract if they are wilfully blind to its existence, 'blind-eye knowledge is sufficient' for the *Marex* tort.[35] Bryan J's judgment in *Lakatamia* thus gives a significant amount of detail regarding the scope of the *Marex* tort. However, several important issues arise regarding its parameters, and it is to these that attention is now turned.

A. The Nature of the Underlying Obligation

In the wake of the decisions in *Marex* and *Lakatamia* it might, perhaps, have been thought that the *Marex* tort was limited to protecting rights in judgments that novate contractual obligations. After all, the underlying judgments in both cases had been entered in respect of contractual duties that had been breached. And in both cases the court considered that the *Marex* tort was an extrapolation from the tort of inducing a breach of contract. However, any such limitation would have been very difficult, if not impossible, to justify.[36] Intentionally inducing a violation of rights established by judgments is not any less objectionable simply because the judgment is not based on a breach of contract. Happily, *Gee* confirms that the *Marex* tort is not concerned only with judgments that are entered in respect of a breach of contract. Although the claimant in that case had obtained judgment on a proprietary estoppel claim, HHJ Paul Matthews considered that there was no difficulty with his seeking a remedy for the *Marex* tort. Admittedly, the judge did not specifically engage with the fact that the judgment had not been entered as regards a claim for breach of contract. But the case is nevertheless authority in support of the proposition that the *Marex* tort is not limited to judgments entered in respect of claims for breach of contract. Properly understood, the protection afforded by the *Marex* tort extends to all judgments.

B. Entry of a Judgment

In each of *Marex*, *Lakatamia*, and *Gee*, judgment had actually been entered in favour of the claimant. One interesting issue that arises is whether the *Marex* tort protects (or should protect) rights in claims which have not yet crystallized into a judgment. It might be argued, for at least two reasons, that the *Marex* tort can have no application unless and until a judgment is entered. The first reason is based on an analogy with the tort of inducing a breach of contract. That tort cannot be committed unless a contract has actually been formed.[37] Consistent with the general principle of the law of contract that a party can withdraw from

---

[34] ibid [127(2)].

[35] ibid [127(3)].

[36] A view apparently shared by Grant and Mumford, *Civil Fraud* (n 5) [3.022].

[37] Consider Paula Giliker, 'A Role for Tort in Pre-Contractual Negotiations? An Examination of English, French and Canadian Law' (2003) 52 ICLQ 969, 974–75; Jesse Max Creed, 'Integrating Preliminary Agreements into the Interference Torts' (2010) 110 Columbia Law Rev 1253.

250 PROCURING WRONGS

pre-contractual negotiations without incurring any liability,[38] the *Lumley v Gye* tort provides no protection at all against conduct that causes a party to walk away from such negotiations. By parity of reasoning, it might be suggested that the *Marex* tort similarly requires that the claim have matured into a judgment. However, there is, of course, an crucial difference between a party to pre-contractual negotiations and a party who has a claim against another: the former has nothing but a mere expectation of acquiring rights whereas the latter actually has a potentially valuable asset.[39]

The second argument builds upon certain remarks that the courts have made concerning freezing orders. It is often said that unless and until a person is restrained from dissipating their assets by an injunction, there is no restriction on their disposing of their assets even if they do so in order to render worthless a claim that has been brought against them. Thus, in *Law Debenture Trust Corpn v Ural Caspian Oil Corpn Ltd*, Sir Thomas Bingham MR said that 'the defendant violates no legal right of the plaintiff if he makes himself judgment-proof by dissipating his assets before he is enjoined from doing so'.[40] If it is not wrongful for a person who is not subject to a freezing order to dispose of their assets in order to prevent any judgment that is ultimately entered against them from being enforced, it might be thought that it cannot be a tort to procure a defendant against whom liability has not yet been established to dispose of their assets. However, this thought appears to be incorrect since the inducer may well be liable for (at least) the tort of lawful means conspiracy.

At the bare minimum, there are three pre-judgment situations to which one would expect the *Marex* tort to extend. The first situation concerns the period between the date on which a draft judgment is circulated to the parties' legal representatives and the date on which judgment is entered. Although judgments only take effect upon their being entered,[41] and although the court retains a discretion to reconsider its judgment until the moment that it is entered,[42] it is difficult to see why a claimant who has obtained a judgment subject only to the formality of its being entered should not have their position protected. Indeed, the *Marex* tort arguably already extends to this situation. In *Marex* itself, the claimant alleged that the defendant had dissipated the assets of the companies in question including during the period between the draft judgment being made available and judgment being entered,[43] and Knowles J considered that it was sufficiently arguable for the purposes of establishing jurisdiction that this amounted to the *Marex* tort.[44] However, to the extent that this is not already the law, extending the scope of the *Marex* tort so that it protects the claimant's

---

[38] For discussion, see Ewan McKendrick, 'Negotiations "Subject to Contract" and the Law of Restitution' (1995) 3 RLR 100.

[39] 'A claim which is arguably viable, is a potential asset': *LF2 Ltd v Supperstone* [2018] EWHC 1776 (Ch); [2018] Bus LR 2303 [65] (Morgan J). The precise nature of the asset is a matter of significant debate among scholars. Some contend that a wrongdoer immediately owes the claimant a duty of repair upon their committing a wrong. Others argue that a wrongdoer is merely subject to a liability and that no duty to repair will arise unless and until the claimant obtains judgment. For discussion, see Stephen A Smith, 'Duties, Liabilities and Damages' (2012) 125 Harvard L Rev 1727 (favouring the former view); Sandy Steel and Robert Stevens, 'The Secondary Legal Duty to Pay Damages' (2020) 136 LQR 283 (favouring the latter understanding). See also John Murphy's paper referenced in the opening footnote of this chapter.

[40] *Law Debenture Trust Corpn v Ural Caspian Oil Corpn Ltd* [1995] Ch 152 (CA) 166 (hereafter *Law Debenture Trust*).

[41] See CPR Part 40.7(1).

[42] *Prudential Assurance Co Ltd v McBains Cooper (a firm)* [2000] 1 WLR 2000 (CA) 2008.

[43] See in particular *Marex* (n 2) [9].

[44] cf Bryan J's view of the elements of the *Marex* tort in *Lakatamia*, which identifies entry of a judgment in the claimant's favour as one of the ingredients of the wrong. See the text accompanying n 33.

position pending the entry of judgment would, it is suggested, be a merely incremental step. The second situation is where the defendant has admitted the claim. If the defendant admits a claim in which the only remedy sought is the payment of money, the claimant would be entitled to enter judgment against them.[45] It is difficult to see why the protection that the *Marex* tort affords should not be extended to a claimant who has a right to enter judgment without more ado. The third situation concerns default judgment. If a claimant has a right to enter default judgment against the defendant, obtaining judgment is essentially a formality. It might be said that it would elevate form over substance if the *Marex* tort did not secure the position of such a claimant.

What about instances where the entry of judgment in the claimant's favour is not a foregone conclusion? Since tort law protects contractual rights from intentional third-party interference, it would be surprising if it did not protect claims for breach of such rights from such interference.[46] Why should a person whose contractual rights have been (at least allegedly) violated and who has needed to sue in order to vindicate them be placed into a worse position as concerns third-party interference than one who has not sued? However, if the *Marex* tort should protect claims for breach of contract, it is difficult to see why it should be confined to safeguarding such claims. There is no obvious reason for protecting only claims for breach of contract as opposed to claims for breaches of other obligations. And consistent with this, the *Marex* tort, in the post-judgment universe, secures the judgment creditor's interest in rights established by judgments irrespective of the source of the underlying obligation.[47]

If and to the extent that the *Marex* tort secures rights in claims that have not yet matured into judgments, a question arises as to what, specifically, the defendant's knowledge needs to relate. It might well be that the defendant would simply need to be conscious of the fact that the claimant has a claim against another person. If so, they would not need to know or believe that the claim is well founded or likely to succeed. However, there is, admittedly, no definite authority one way or the other in this regard. If and to the extent that the *Marex* tort extends only to the three specific pre-judgment situations addressed previously, it is doubtful that the defendant would need to know that a draft judgment had been made available, that the claim had been admitted, or that the claimant is entitled to enter default judgment.

---

[45] CPR Part 14.1(4).

[46] cf Sir Thomas Bingham MR's remark in *Law Debenture Trust* (n 40) 165 that 'I would not be willing to hold that interference with a secondary right to a remedy (as opposed to a primary right to performance) could never attract the application of the *Lumley v. Gye* principle. For example, if, following default by the principal debtor, a third party induced a guarantor to dishonour his secondary obligation to pay the creditor, I would need much persuasion that the third party was not liable in tort. But it does not seem to me to follow that a third party is necessarily liable in tort for any interference with any right properly regarded as secondary, particulary [sic] where that right is contingent'. For illuminating discussion, see David Foxton, 'How Useful Is Lord Diplock's Distinction between Primary and Secondary Obligations in Contract?' (2019) 135 LQR 249, 268–70. Foxton makes the powerful point that it would be 'unappealing' for tort law to protect primary contractual rights as well as secondary rights that have merged in primary obligations derived from judgments but not the secondary rights prior to such merger.

[47] See the text accompanying n 41.

C. Type and Status of the Judgment

In *Marex*, *Lakatamia*, and *Gee*, the judgments in issue had been entered following a trial. It might be queried, therefore, whether the *Marex* tort safeguards rights in summary and default judgments. There is no authority on the point but there is no obvious reason why the protection afforded by the *Marex* tort should be limited to particular types of judgment. Further, if a defendant induces a breach of rights established by a judgment, it presumably makes no difference that the judgment concerned was, at the relevant time, being appealed (even if the appeal is subsequently allowed) or subject to a stay of execution. The tort of inducing a breach of contract cannot be committed where the contract breaker has a right to rescind the agreement.[48] A parallel rule presumably applies to the *Marex* tort. In particular, if, exceptionally, a judgment is rescinded because it was obtained by fraud,[49] it will be incapable of forming the basis of a claim based on the decision in *Marex*.

D. Orders

One noteworthy feature of the decision in *Gee* is that the judge repeatedly spoke of the *Marex* tort as protecting rights established by orders rather than rights enshrined in judgments.[50] It might be suggested that nothing turns on this given that the order in issue in *Gee* was an order consequent upon a judgment. However, the distinction between judgments and orders[51] will make a difference for present purposes when, as is typical on *ex parte* applications, the court makes an order without delivering a judgment. Suppose that C applies *ex parte* for an interim injunction against D1 restraining him from carrying out some activity on his land that, if undertaken, would damage property belonging to C. If the court grants the injunction, it is unlikely to hand down any judgment and will simply make an order that sets out what D1 must not do. If D2 procures a breach by D1 of the injunction resulting in C's suffering damage, has D2 committed the *Marex* tort? D2 will, of course, likely be liable for the tort of unlawful means conspiracy.[52] But whether or not this is so, the question remains whether D2 has committed the *Marex* tort. Given that the courts have recognized the *Marex* tort, it is difficult to identify any compelling reason for restricting it to rights established by judgments. Indeed, it might well be that, properly understood, the *Marex* tort in fact applies only to rights created by orders in circumstances where orders are instruments that require one or both of the parties to do something whereas, strictly speaking, judgments do not themselves oblige anyone to do anything.[53]

---

[48] *Proform Sports Management Ltd v Proactive Sports Management Ltd* [2006] EWHC 2903 (Ch); [2007] 1 All ER 542 [33].

[49] Regarding the power to rescind judgments obtained by fraud, see *Takhar v Gracefield Developments Ltd* [2019] UKSC 13; [2020] AC 450.

[50] *Gee* (n 20) [10]–[15].

[51] As to the distinction, see Adrian Zuckerman, *Zuckerman on Civil Procedure: Principles of Practice* (4th edn, Sweet & Maxwell 2021) [23.6].

[52] Contempt of court constitutes unlawful means for the purposes of the tort of unlawful means conspiracy: *JSC BTA Bank v Ablyazoz (No 14)* [2018] UKSC 19; [2020] AC 727 [16].

[53] Consider Stephen Smith, *Rights, Wrongs, and Injustices: The Structure of Remedial Law* (OUP 2020) 21: 'Judgments at Law are not strictly orders, as they do not state that the defendant or anyone else must do something.... A Judgment for damages does not say that the defendant has a legal duty to pay a sum of money, or that the defendant owes the claimant a sum of money, or even that the defendant should pay the claimant the sum of money. Nor does it transfer ownership in money or other property to the claimant'.

E. Mere Omissions

In *Marex*, the defendant was alleged to have dissipated the judgment debtors' assets. He argued that this did not constitute the *Marex* tort and that nothing short of steps taken to prevent the judgment debt from being discharged was required. Rightly, Knowles J gave this submission short shrift. He said that 'dissipation and . . . non-payment were two sides of the same coin'.[54] However, by this he did not mean that a mere failure to take steps to cause a judgment debtor to discharge a debt will suffice to establish liability. Just as mere omissions will not amount to the tort of inducing a breach of contract,[55] they will not constitute the *Marex* tort. Rather, Knowles J's point was that the dissipation of a judgment debtor's assets which thereby renders the judgment debtor incapable of discharging the liability owing under the judgment is itself a positive step taken to prevent the debt from being discharged. Any such active step will, if done with the requisite mental element, constitute the *Marex* tort.[56]

F. The Need for an Actual Breach

Although none of the cases decided to date regarding the *Marex* tort says so in terms, it is clear that the defendant must procure an actual violation of the claimant's rights established by the judgment in issue in order for liability to arise. This follows by analogy with the tort of inducing a breach of contract. According to the current orthodoxy, that tort, and as Ewan McKendrick explains, 'is an example of accessory or secondary liability'.[57] That is to say, it is actionable only where there is an actual breach of contract. The logic is that since the tort is a form of derivative liability, there is no possibility of its being committed unless the wrong on which it is parasitic—a breach of contract—exists.[58]

G. The Rule in *Said v Butt*

Pursuant to the rule in *Said v Butt*,[59] an employee (or director) will not be liable for inducing their employer (or company) to breach a contract provided that the employee (or director) acts *bona fide* within the scope of their authority. In the eponymous case, McCardie J explained the logic on which the rule rests as follows:

> [the employee's] acts are in law the acts of his employer. In such a case it is the master himself, by his agent, breaking the contract he has made, and in my view an action against the

---

[54] *Marex* (n 2) [25].

[55] cf *Union Traffic Ltd v Transport and General Workers' Union* [1989] ICR 98 (CA) 106 (mere presence sufficient).

[56] *Lakatamia* (n 3) [127(4)].

[57] Ewan McKendrick, *Contract Law* (14th edn, Red Globe Press 2021) 158. For criticism of the accessory liability theory and doubts regarding the extent to which the law actually embraces it, see John Murphy, *The Province and Politics of the Economic Torts* (Hart Publishing 2022) ch 3.

[58] '[O]ne cannot be liable for inducing a breach unless there has been a breach. No secondary liability without primary liability': *OBG Ltd v Allan* [2007] UKHL 21; [2008] 1 AC 1 [44] (Lord Hoffmann) (hereafter *OBG*). See also at [189].

[59] *Said v Butt* [1920] 3 KB 497 (KBD).

agent under the *Lumley* v *Gye* principle must therefore fail, just as it would fail if brought against the master himself for wrongfully procuring a breach of his own contract.[60]

'Grave reservations' have been expressed regarding the rule in *Said v Butt*.[61] Doubts about its status are magnified given that the courts have rejected the theory that an employee's acts are attributed to the employer in the context of vicarious liability,[62] to which theory McCardie J clearly subscribed. However, as things presently stand, it remains part of the law governing the tort of inducing a breach of contract.[63] Does the rule apply also to the *Marex* tort? In *Gee*, HHJ Paul Matthews proceeded on the basis that it does, although he considered that it was well arguable that its requirements were unsatisfied on the facts of the case.[64]

H. Defences

As we have seen, the courts have accepted that the *Marex* tort finds a close analogy with the tort of inducing a breach of contract. The latter tort is subject to the defence of justification. In *Lakatamia*, Bryan J held that the analogy broke down in this regard. He considered that the *Marex* tort is not qualified by that defence. He said:[65]

[w]hilst there may be limited circumstances in which it is reasonable to induce a breach of a contractual right (a right which by its very nature is a right created by contract) in the furtherance of, by way of example, a moral obligation, I cannot see any room for an equivalent defence in relation to rights established by due process and enshrined in a judgment.

The authors of *Civil Fraud* disagree with Bryan J. They write that his claim that justification is not a defence to the *Marex* tort 'is considered too broad a proposition'.[66] They then observe that Bryan J's view entails 'a judgment elevating the status of the claimant's right vis-à-vis the inducer beyond that given to him by the contract, a conclusion which is difficult to support'. With respect, however, Bryan J's position is readily supportable and, indeed, is correct. It is true that it involves elevating rights established by judgments above rights owing under contracts. But this is consonant with authority. Thus, in *Zavarco plc v Nasir* Sir David Richards observed that when judgment is entered, the claim against the defendant merges in and is replaced by 'an obligation of a higher nature'.[67] A further significant point in favour of Bryan J's view lies in the fact that there is an established mechanism for challenging judgments, namely, the appellate process. In view of the system for appeals, it would make no sense to permit persons to induce judgment debtors to disregard their obligations on the basis that doing so is justified. Leaving aside exceptional situations (such as, for example,

---

[60] ibid 505–06.
[61] *Welsh Development Agency v Export Finance Co Ltd* [1992] BCC 270 (CA) 289 (Dillon LJ).
[62] See, eg, *Majrowski v Guy's and St Thomas's NHS Trust* [2006] UKHL 34, [2007] 1 AC 224 [15].
[63] The rule was recently considered in *Antuzis v DJ Houghton Catching Services Ltd* [2019] EWHC 843 (QB), [2019] Bus LR 1532 and *Northamber Plc v Genee World Limited* [2023] EWHC 3562 (Ch).
[64] *Gee* (n 20) [16]–[17].
[65] *Lakatamia* (n 3) [131].
[66] Grant and Mumford, *Civil Fraud* (n 5) [3.002A] (footnote omitted).
[67] *Zavarco plc v Nasir* [2021] EWCA Civ 1217; [2022] Ch 105 [37].

instances in which judgments can be rescinded), the only way in which it is proper to challenge rights established by judgments is for the judgment debtor to appeal.

Before moving on, it is worth considering in more detail precisely why the defence of justification is unavailable as regards the *Marex* tort. Some torts are not subject to a defence of justification because the absence of justification is built into their elements. John Gardner called such wrongs 'fault-anticipating'.[68] A good example of such a tort is that of negligence. Since it is an element of that tort that the defendant engaged in unreasonable conduct, it is conceptually impossible for it to be subject to defences that are premised on the defendant's conduct being reasonable.[69] The idea of justified negligence is oxymoronic. Another example of a fault-anticipating wrong is that of unlawful means conspiracy. Because the ingredient of unlawful means is satisfied only by conduct that is both unjustifiable and unexcused,[70] it follows that there is no logical room for any plea of justification. Conversely, a given tort might not admit of any (or certain) justification-type defences not because its elements require proof of unreasonable conduct but because the law simply does not care about the defendant's reasons (or certain of them) for committing it.[71] They are simply afforded no weight by virtue of the law's authority.[72] It appears from Bryan J's remarks quoted earlier that the *Marex* tort falls into the latter category. The absence of justification is not an ingredient of the tort. Rather, the courts simply refuse to give any weight to reasons that a defendant might have had for committing it, since doing so would be inconsistent with the authority by which judgments are underpinned and incompatible with the existence of the appellate system.

I. Remoteness

What remoteness test applies to the *Marex* tort? Unfortunately, it is not possible to glean any guidance by analogy to the tort of inducing a breach of contract in this regard because it appears, rather surprisingly, that there is no authority as regards the remoteness rule applicable to that wrong.[73] Hazel Carty writes with reference to the *Lumey v Gye* tort that '[a]ll intended damage will be recoverable, as will non-remote consequences',[74] but this simply invites the question when a consequence is non-remote. In considering the position as concerns the *Marex* tort, it is important to observe that it cannot be committed without an intention to induce a violation of the claimant's rights established by the judgment in issue. This being the case, there is a firm basis for supposing that a claim for the *Marex* tort is not subject to any remoteness restrictions since, as Lord Lindley put it in *Quinn v Leathem*, '[t]he intention to injure the plaintiff negatives all excuses and disposes of any question of

---

[68] John Gardner, *Offences and Defences: Selected Essays in the Philosophy of Criminal Law* (OUP 2007) 151 (hereafter Gardner, *Offences and Defences*).

[69] This has not deterred some judges from trying to fashion such defences: see James Goudkamp, *Tort Law Defences* (Hart Publishing 2013) 53–54.

[70] *JSC BTA Bank v Khrapunov* [2018] UKSC 19; [2020] AC 727 [10] (hereafter *JSC BTA Bank v Khrapunov*).

[71] This is presumably how Donal Nolan understands the rule in *Rylands v Fletcher* given his view that it is not subject to any justification-type defences: Donal Nolan, 'The Distinctiveness of Rylands v Fletcher' (2005) 121 LQR 421, 436 (hereafter Nolan, 'The Distinctiveness of Rylands v Fletcher').

[72] For discussion in a different context, see Gardner, *Offences and Defences* (n 68) 147–48.

[73] Although in *Boxfoldia Ltd v National Graphical Association (1982)* [1988] ICR 752 (QBD) 760 Saville J proceeded on the assumption that the relevant test was one of reasonable foreseeability of the kind of damage.

[74] Hazel Carty, *The Economic Torts* (2nd edn, OUP 2010) 44.

256 PROCURING WRONGS

remoteness of damage'.[75] It is true that an intention to violate rights enshrined by a judgment is not precisely the same thing as an intention to injure. However, for practical purposes a defendant who intends to induce a violation of a claimant's rights in a judgment debt will intend to injure the latter. The two are co-extensive.

J. Remedies

Damages for the *Marex* tort are assessed by reference to the same rules which apply to the tort of inducing a breach of contract.[76] As concerns injunctive relief, there is no reason why the courts should not be able to injunct a person from procuring a violation of rights embodied in a judgment. Since an injunction can be obtained to prevent a person from inducing a breach of a future contract,[77] one would expect the same principle to obtain as regards the *Marex* tort.

K. Procedure

Does a claimant who sues in respect of the *Marex* tort need to issue separate proceedings, or can he or she seek a remedy in the litigation in which the judgment was handed down? In *Gee*, HHJ Paul Matthews said that '[i]n principle, I can see no reason why it should be necessary to start a fresh claim in respect of a wrong done by procuring a breach of an order when the court is already seised of the original proceedings and may in any event be asked to make other orders in respect of the execution of that order'.[78] He considered that the position was *a fortiori* where, as in *Gee*, the persons said to have committed the *Marex* tort were already parties to the original proceedings.[79] The judge added that the court could make appropriate orders in the extant proceedings regarding pleadings, disclosure, and evidence pursuant to the power to direct an inquiry as to any claim.[80] He also held that it was no impediment to the claimant advancing a claim in the existing proceedings that the order consequent upon the judgment did not contain a liberty to apply. The logic was that

> such a liberty is implied for the purposes of enabling the party having the benefit of the order to complain that the party with obligations to perform under the order has not performed them, and to have the order modified to take account of what the performing party has done or not done since the order was made.[81]

---

[75] *Quinn v Leathem* [1901] AC 495 (HL) 537. Consider also the remarks of Lord Denning MR in *Doyle v Olby (Ironmongers) Ltd* [1969] 2 QB 158 (CA) 167. For further discussion of this point, see James Goudkamp and Eleni Katsampouka, 'Punitive Damages and the Place of Punishment in Private Law' (2021) 84 MLR 1257, 1271–77.

[76] *Lakatamia* (n 3) [949].

[77] *Union Traffic Ltd v Transport and General Workers' Union* [1989] ICR 98 (CA) 106, 111.

[78] *Gee* (n 20) [15]. See also [24].

[79] ibid [15].

[80] See CPR Practice Direction 40A.

[81] *Gee* (n 20) [21].

IV. What Does the *Marex* Tort Add?

What is the practical utility, if any, of the *Marex* tort? Although its arrival on the scene was greeted with a certain amount of fanfare,[82] it might be thought that it is in fact of little importance. Knowles J seemed to suggest as much in *Marex* itself. He 'question[ed] whether the facts of the present case are widespread so that the tort would be invoked more widely'.[83] Perhaps more significantly, it might be contended that it does not add much to other torts, particularly the torts of unlawful means conspiracy and causing loss by unlawful means. It might also be argued that its goals are already sufficiently secured by the court's jurisdiction to make freezing orders. Contrary to the foregoing, in this section it is argued that the *Marex* tort has the potential to move the needle.

A. Relationship with Other Torts

In *Marex*, Knowles J's conclusions regarding the *Marex* tort made no difference to his decision since the claimant also established that the court had jurisdiction to try its claim for the tort of causing loss by unlawful means, which claim was based on the same factual allegations as the claim for the *Marex* tort.[84] Similarly, the claim in respect of the *Marex* tort added nothing to the proceedings in *Lakatamia*, since the conduct that underpinned that tort also constituted the tort of unlawful means conspiracy. And in *Gee*, although it appears that the claimant only expressed an intention to pursue a remedy in the *Marex* tort, remarks that the court made regarding the coordination between the defendants[85] leave little room to doubt that the claimant could have also advanced a credible claim for the tort of unlawful means conspiracy. All of this suggests that, as a practical matter, the *Marex* tort does not add anything. Having said that, there are certain ways in which the *Marex* tort has the potential to make a difference.

The *Marex* tort's sphere of influence is larger than that of the tort of unlawful means conspiracy insofar as the latter, but not the former, requires there to be a combination. A person who induces a judgment debtor to breach rights embodied in a judgment by making threats against the latter will be liable for (at least) the *Marex* tort,[86] but they will presumably not be liable for the tort of unlawful means conspiracy. The threats made will be inconsistent with the existence of a combination. Relatedly, whereas it might be impossible for the *alter ego* of a company to conspire with the latter,[87] there is no impediment, subject to possible arguments regarding the rule in *Said v Butt*,[88] to such a person inducing the company to act contrary to the rights enshrined in a judgment to which it is subject. Similarly, the *Marex* tort's ambit is wider in certain respects than that of the tort of causing loss by unlawful means.[89]

---

[82] See the text accompanying nn 4–5.

[83] *Marex* (n 2) [27].

[84] ibid [36].

[85] *Gee* (n 20) [12].

[86] Consider the position in this regard as concerns the tort of inducing a breach of contract: see *Clerk & Lindsell on Torts* (23rd edn, Sweet & Maxwell 2020) [23.38] (hereafter *Clerk & Lindsell on Torts*).

[87] The Court of Appeal has left open the question of whether the *alter ego* of a company can conspire with it: *Raja v McMillan* [2021] EWCA Civ 1103.

[88] See the text accompanying nn 65–70.

[89] For recent consideration of the boundaries of the unlawful means tort at the ultimate appellate level, see *Secretary of State for Health v Servier Laboratories Ltd* [2021] UKSC 24, [2022] AC 959.

258   PROCURING WRONGS

The unlawful means tort requires proof that the defendant used unlawful means against a third party which interfered with the latter's ability to deal with the claimant. By contrast, the commission of the *Marex* tort is not conditional upon the inducement constituting unlawful means against the judgment debtor.

B. Freezing Orders

What does the *Marex* tort add to the court's jurisdiction to make freezing orders? Both the *Marex* tort and freezing orders have the same end in view. They are both directed at preventing a claimant from being unjustly deprived of the fruits of a judgment. Freezing orders do this by enjoining respondents, usually before judgment has been entered but sometimes after judgment has been delivered[90] as in *Marex* itself, from dissipating their assets. The *Marex* tort aspires to protect interests in rights embodied in judgments by preventing third parties from intentionally inducing a violation of those rights. It follows that the *Marex* tort and freezing orders are intimately connected with each other. However, there are also some significant points of distinction. Freezing orders are backed up by the court's power to punish for contempt persons who breach them or who assist others to do so. That jurisdiction is not, however, compensatory.[91] Persons who suffer damage because of a contempt of court, including a breach of a freezing order, cannot, at least as the law presently stands, invoke that jurisdiction to obtain redress for the loss sustained. By contrast, the *Marex* tort sounds, of course, in damages. Another difference lies in the fact that the only conduct that will breach a freezing order, relevantly, is steps taken to dissipate assets outwith the scope of any exceptions to which the order is subject. Although each of *Marex*, *Lakatamia*, and *Gee* concerned the dissipation of assets, the *Marex* tort can be committed wherever rights established by a judgment are violated and regardless of whether the conduct induced involves the dissipation of assets. For example, if C sues D for defamation and obtains a final injunction restraining republication of a defamatory statement and T intentionally induces D to breach that injunction, T will have committed the *Marex* tort.

V. Wider Issues

This section addresses two associated issues. The first is whether the *Marex* tort is in fact a new tort. The second is whether the line of authority that descends from *Marex* supports the recognition of a tort of contempt.

---

[90] See the text accompanying n 31.
[91] 'Proceedings for contempt of court are always in a rather special category because they are intended to uphold the authority of the court and to make certain that its orders are obeyed. They are not intended to provide solace or compensation to the plaintiff. If the plaintiff wants compensation, she must seek it in other forms': *Johnson v Walton* [1990] 1 FLR 350 (CA) 353 (Lord Donaldson MR); cf the remarks of Lord Mance in *Customs & Excise Commissioners v Barclays Bank plc* [2006] UKHL 28, [2007] 1 AC 181 [101], who seemed to consider that compensation is among the purposes of the contempt jurisdiction.

A. Is the *Marex* Tort a Discrete Tort?

To this point, we have assumed, as the foundational cases have generally done, that the *Marex* tort is a novel tort. But is this assumption correct? Perhaps the decisions recognizing the *Marex* tort, properly understood, merely expand the boundaries of the tort of inducing a breach of contract such that that tort also protects against third-party interference with rights established by judgments. Before addressing this issue, it is first worth considering whether anything turns on how it is resolved.[92] In *Chocosuisse Union des Fabricants Suisse de Chocolat v Cadbury Ltd*, Laddie J asserted that it was 'a matter of semantics' whether one is dealing with a 'separate and new tort' or 'merely a new branch of an existing tort'.[93] He presumably held this view on the basis that that which ultimately matters is whether the defendant's conduct concerned is tortious. However, Laddie J's view is difficult to support for at least two reasons. First, the fact that a tort is novel means that claims in respect of it should be largely impervious to being disposed of without a trial, at least absent its already having been authoritatively decided that the tort does not exist. That is because it is well established that the power to enter summary judgment or to strike out a claim should be exercised sparingly, if at all, where the claim is based on a developing area of jurisprudence.[94] Of course, it might be said that this principle extends also to a new limb of an extant tort. But one would expect the rule to apply with particular force where one is dealing with a novel tort.

Second, if a particular liability rule is simply an appendage of another tort, rules applicable to the latter will prima facie extend to the former. An excellent but certainly not the only illustration of the courts' employing this reasoning concerns the rule in *Rylands v Fletcher*. The courts consider that that rule is simply an appendage of the tort of private nuisance.[95] It is said to be 'essentially concerned with an extension of the law of nuisance to cases of isolated escape'.[96] This offshoot thesis[97] has prompted the courts to hold that at least certain principles that govern the tort of private nuisance extend to the rule in *Rylands v Fletcher*.[98] For example, because the tort of private nuisance is a tort to land and hence does not afford a remedy for personal injuries, the same has been said to be true of the rule in *Rylands v Fletcher*.[99] In short, if one is concerned with an offshoot of an existing tort, it is likely that it will inherit at least some of the latter's traits. Conversely, novel torts are unlikely, or at least less likely, to be subject to certain principles that are peculiar to other wrongs.

Is, then, the *Marex* tort a freestanding head of liability? It is, on any view, very closely associated with the tort of inducing a breach of contract. Its elements are nearly identical to those of the latter. Moreover, the courts have made it clear that the *Marex* tort is extrapolated from that of inducing a breach of contract. These circumstances suggest that the

---

[92] The issues here are explored in greater detail in James Goudkamp, 'New Torts' in David Rolph, John Eldridge, and Timothy Pilkington (eds), *Australian Tort Law in the 21st Century* (Federation Press 2023) (forthcoming).

[93] *Chocosuisse Union des Fabricants Suisse de Chocolat v Cadbury Ltd* [1998] RPC 117 (Ch D) 127.

[94] See, eg, *Vedanta Resources plc v Lungowe* [2019] UKSC 20, [2020] AC 1045 [48].

[95] 'The rule in *Rylands v Fletcher* is a sub-species of nuisance': *Transco plc v Stockport MBC* [2003] UKHL 61, [2004] 2 AC 1 [9] (Lord Bingham) (hereafter *Transco*).

[96] *Cambridge Water Co v Eastern Counties Leather plc* [1994] 2 AC 264 (HL) 304 (Lord Goff).

[97] For compelling criticism of the view that the rule in *Rylands v Fletcher* is an offshoot of the tort of private nuisance, see John Murphy, 'The Merits of Rylands v Fletcher' (2004) 24 OJLS 643 and Nolan, 'The Distinctiveness of Rylands v Fletcher' (n 71). For argument that the rule in *Rylands v Fletcher* might in fact be an extension of cattle trespass, see Percy Winfield, 'The Foundation of Liability in Tort' (1927) 27 Colum L Rev 1, 7.

[98] See, eg, *Transco* (n 95) [9].

[99] ibid.

260   PROCURING WRONGS

Marex tort is not truly a discrete wrong. Consistent with this, in *Marex* Lord Sales repeatedly referred to the cause of action for inducing a violation of rights in the judgment as 'the *Lumley v Gye* claim'.[100] Similarly, the authors of *Civil Fraud* deal with the *Marex* tort within a chapter concerned with the tort of inducing a breach of contract.[101] The authors of *Clerk & Lindsell* likewise address the *Marex* tort within a section of text relating to the latter wrong.[102] Conversely, several of the *Marex* tort's characteristics support the conclusion that it is in fact a freestanding rule. As we have seen,[103] liability in the *Marex* tort is not subject to the defence of justification, unlike the tort of inducing a breach of contract.[104] Furthermore, the *Marex* tort has no necessary connection with contractual obligations. It can be committed even though the judgment in issue was entered other than for a breach of contract.[105] Only time will tell, but the better view might be that the *Marex* tort is a discrete wrong.

B. A Tort of Contempt of Court?

The *Marex* tort is, in all but name, a tort of contempt of court. That is because a third party who commits it will have deliberately interfered with the course of justice and hence be in contempt.[106] Since the *Marex* tort cannot be committed without the tortfeasor being in contempt, it might be suggested that its recognition supplies impetus for the establishment of a tort of contempt. In *Chapman v Honig*,[107] a landlord issued a tenant with a notice to quit in retaliation for the latter giving evidence against the landlord's interests in a case to which the landlord had been a party. That was a contempt of court. A majority of the Court of Appeal held that it was not actionable in tort, principally on the logic that the contemnor had a contractual right to do what he did. Although the majority did not rule out the possibility of recognizing a tort of contempt, they were inclined against the creation of a new wrong in this regard. Subsequent courts have since proceeded on the footing that contempt is not a tort.[108] However, and significantly, in *JSC BTA Bank v Khrapunov*,[109] Lord Sumption and Lord Lloyd-Jones left the door ajar in this regard. It might well be that the recognition of the *Marex* tort will supply the leverage needed for it to be opened.

---

[100] *Marex* (SC) (n 12) [111], [141], [199] and [213].

[101] Grant and Mumford, *Civil Fraud* (n 5) ch 3.

[102] *Clerk & Lindsell on Torts* (n 86) para 23.26.

[103] See the text accompanying nn 71–77.

[104] For consideration in a different context of whether a distinctive defences regime supports the conclusion that one is dealing with a discrete cause of action, see Lionel Smith, 'Defences and the Disunity of Unjust Enrichment' in Andrew Dyson et al (eds), *Defences in Unjust Enrichment* (Hart Publishing 2016).

[105] See the text accompanying n 41.

[106] 'In general, it is a contempt of court for anyone, whether party to the proceedings or not, deliberately to interfere with the due administration of justice': *Attorney General v Punch Ltd* [2002] UKHL 50, [2003] 1 AC 1046 [66] (Lord Hope).

[107] *Chapman v Honig* [1963] 2 QB 502 (CA).

[108] See, eg, *Stobart Group Ltd v Elliott* [2013] EWHC 797 (QB) [108] (HHJ Pelling QC): 'There is no tort of "Contempt of Court".'

[109] *JSC BTA Bank v Khrapunov* (n 70) [22].

VI. Conclusion

The decision to welcome the *Marex* tort into the hall of wrongs is a testament to the vitality of the law of torts and affirmation of Hoffmann J's remark in *Associated Newspapers Group plc v Insert Media Ltd* that tort law 'is not static' and 'that new forms of tort may develop'.[110] It also evinces a growing tendency for private law to attach liability to the facilitation of others' wrongs. This chapter has sought to chart the boundaries of the *Marex* tort and to understand it against the backdrop of the policy in favour of the enforcement of judgments. It is too soon to tell whether it will make a meaningful difference in terms of the outcome of cases. However, the most important consequence of the *Marex* tort's recognition might lie in its supplying impetus for the creation of other civil wrongs.

[110] *Associated Newspapers Group plc v Insert Media Ltd* [1988] 1 WLR 509 (Ch D) 514.

PART III
COMMERCIAL

16

Who Can Sue the Obligor When Receivables Are Financed?

LOUISE GULLIFER

I. Introduction

I have had the pleasure of knowing, and working with, Ewan since we taught commercial law together at Oxford in the early 1990s. Over the years since then I have benefited enormously from his help and advice as a colleague and friend, as well as from his superb publications in the areas of contract and commercial law. Although he is rightly thought of as an academic giant in the field of contract law, Ewan's writing on contract law is largely from the perspective of contract law's place in commercial transactions. His commercial astuteness, to which his practice at the Bar from 3VB (my own set of chambers) contributed, characterizes his conception of many parts of contract law, such as interpretation, frustration, and remedies. Moreover, Ewan has significantly contributed to both domestic commercial law, in his editorship of the seminal work by Professor Sir Roy Goode,[1] and to transnational commercial law, in his co-editorship of two editions of the book from which it originated as a distinct teaching subject.[2] I hope, therefore, that this chapter, on a point of commercial law of significance to receivables financing, will be a fitting tribute to a wonderful and generous friend, colleague, and commercial lawyer.

Receivables (debts owed to a business, usually as a result of the operation of that business) are often the most valuable asset of that business. A provider of finance to that business, therefore, is likely to want some kind of proprietary interest in the receivables of a business as protection against the credit risk of that business. While there are a number of models for finance provided in this way, the proprietary protection usually takes the form of either of an outright purchase of receivables, or a mortgage or charge, over the receivables securing a loan. The legal techniques used in these transactions are novation, assignment, and (if not an assignment) a charge. While in some financing models, the person who owes the receivable (the obligor) is notified of the financier's proprietary interest from the outset so that the financier collects on the receivable, in many situations the obligor is not notified and, in the normal course of events, deals entirely with, and pays, the business. In these situations, one of the main characteristics of the arrangement is that it is confidential, in that the obligor (typically the customer of the business being financed) does not know of the arrangement. In such a situation, if the obligor does not pay and the receivable has to be

---

[1] Roy Goode and Ewan McKendrick, *Goode and McKendrick on Commercial Law* (6th edn, LexisNexis Butterworths 2020).

[2] Roy Goode, Herbert Kronke, Ewan McKendrick, and Jeffrey Wool, *Transnational Commercial Law: Text, Cases and Materials* (1st edn, OUP 2007); Roy Goode, Herbert Kronke, and Ewan McKendrick, *Transnational Commercial Law: Text, Cases and Materials* (2nd edn, OUP 2015).

enforced by action, the question arises as to who is the person who can bring such an action. More specifically, from a business point of view, the question is whether the business can enforce the debt without revealing the existence, and interest, of the financier.

This chapter examines this question in the context of various financing models: outright sale of the receivables, a loan secured by a mortgage over the receivables, and a loan secured by a charge over the receivables. Much of the case law and academic discourse examines the situation where it is the financier who wants to be able to enforce against the obligor. Less attention has been paid to where it is the business who wishes to enforce the receivable, particularly where the enforcement takes place without the obligor having been notified of the arrangement,[3] and it is this which is the chief focus of this chapter.

The argument made in this chapter is that where the financing arrangement is not effected by a statutory assignment,[4] the assignor is entitled to sue the obligor, and the determining factors as to whether the assignee needs to be joined in that action are, first, whether notice has been given to the obligor of the assignment or charge, and, second, whether there is a need to have any parties before the court other than the party primarily entitled to sue.

II. Financing Models

There is a distinction, both legal and practical, between receivables finance based on sale of the receivables, and that based on a loan secured on receivables. The latter is used in many situations, including as part of an asset-based lending package,[5] as a traditional bank debenture where fixed and floating charges are taken over all the assets of the business, and in other, more specialist, financing, such as project finance. The former is found in a number of iterations,[6] of which the two main categories are factoring (also called notification financing) and invoice discounting (also called non-notification financing). A similar structure is also used in securitizations, where receivables are sold to a special purpose vehicle.

A. Factoring

A factoring arrangement is one in which the financier purchases the receivables, and the obligors are notified of the purchase and instructed to pay the financier.[7] The financier collects in the receivables itself and the business has no further contact with the obligor in relation to each receivable, although it may, of course, have an ongoing commercial relationship

---

[3] That is, the outright assignment, the mortgage, or the charge.

[4] Or novation, but this is very rarely used.

[5] Asset-based lending, a model much used in the US but also becoming prevalent in the UK, is where advances are made against specific categories of client assets, such as receivables, stock, and machinery. The value of each category is calculated (called a 'borrowing base') and a percentage of this amount is advanced, with a security interest being taken over the relevant category of assets. See, for example, the BVCA Guide to Asset Based Lending, available at https://www.bvca.co.uk/Portals/0/library/documents/ABL%20Guide/ABL%20Asset-Based%20Lending-Apr15-web.pdf.

[6] For a more detailed breakdown, see Simon Mills and Noel Ruddy (eds), *Salinger on Factoring* (6th edn, Sweet & Maxwell 2020) paras 1.43 to 1.62 (hereafter Mills and Ruddy, *Factoring*).

[7] In relation to present receivables, the obligors are notified immediately after the conclusion of the financing arrangement and, in relation to future receivables, they are notified when those receivables arise, often within the invoice itself.

with the obligor as a customer. This form of financing tends to be used by businesses at the lower end of the receivables financing market in the UK, partly because smaller businesses have less ability to manage the collection of their receivables and partly because non-notification financing (such as invoice discounting), as it is more risky for the financier, is often only offered to larger businesses. While a large number of businesses are financed by factoring, the aggregate amount financed is far less than that financed by invoice discounting arrangements.[8]

B. Invoice Discounting

An invoice discounting arrangement is one in which the financier purchases the receivables but the obligors are not notified of the arrangement. The arrangement, therefore, is 'confidential' and all dealings with the obligors are carried out by the financed business, who collects in the receivables and pays the proceeds into a bank account to be held in trust for the financier (typically, the bank account is in the name of the business to retain confidentiality).[9] One of the main reasons for this type of arrangement is that businesses frequently do not want their customers to be aware of their financing arrangements, and, particularly, are concerned if their customers have to deal directly with invoice financiers. In these arrangements, the financier will have the right, under the financing agreement, to give notice to the obligor under certain circumstances, typically when there is an event of default under the financing agreement or the financed business enters insolvency proceedings.[10] A similar procedure applies to securitizations: here the originator collects the debts and notice to the obligors is often seen a last resort.[11]

C. Security Interests

It is harder to generalize about the use of security interests over receivables to secure an obligation to repay loan finance, since the variety of uses is so wide. Some receivables financiers take a fixed charge (or, if that is inappropriate, a floating charge) over all receivables of the business in addition to purchasing the business's receivables: this is to cover 'non-vesting debts', particularly those subject to an effective anti-assignment clause.[12] They may also take fixed and floating charges over all the assets of the business in order to be a 'qualifying chargeholder' if the business were to become insolvent.[13] If the financing agreement is a

---

[8] In relation to financiers who are members of UK Finance, in Q3 2021 the number of businesses financed by factoring was 11,107 (total sales £4.5bn), while 13,505 were financed by invoice discounting (total sales £62bn) (UK Finance, Invoice Finance and Asset Based Lending Tables Q3 2021 (personal communication)).

[9] Mills and Ruddy, *Factoring* (n 6) 3–23.

[10] ibid.

[11] *MBNA Europe Bank Ltd v Revenue and Customs Commissioners* [2006] EWHC 2326 (Ch), [2006] STC 2089 [59]; Louise Gullifer and Jennifer Payne, Corporate Finance Law: Principles and Policy (3rd edn, Hart Publishing 2020) 483.

[12] If the financed business is a small or medium-sized business, it is likely that any anti-assignment clause will be ineffective under the Business Contract Terms (Assignment of Receivables) Regulations 2018.

[13] A qualifying chargeholder (defined in para 14(3) of Sch B1 of the Insolvency Act 1986) can appoint an administrator out of court (para 14) and can also apply to the court to appoint an administrator if the financed business is already in liquidation (para 37).

factoring agreement, it is likely that notice will be given to the obligors of the charged receivables. In other situations where a lender takes security over receivables, it is much less likely that notice will be given.[14] The secured lender will, typically, have the right under the security agreement to give notice to the obligors if there is a default on the part of the financed business, so as to enable it to enforce its security by collecting from the obligors. Until that point, the financed business will continue to collect in the receivables owed to it, and will operate its relationship with the obligors in exactly the same way as it would in the absence of the secured loan.

The following section analyses how these commercial consequences are achieved under English law.

III. Legal Techniques to Achieve the Commercial Consequences

A. Statutory Assignment/Novation

Where the business being financed is content for its obligors to know about the financing arrangement from the outset, two legal techniques can be used to transfer the receivables to the financier: novation and statutory assignment under section 136 of the Law of Property Act 1925. These techniques can be used to effect either an outright transfer (for example, in a factoring arrangement) or a transfer by way of security, that is, a legal mortgage.[15] Novation requires consent from the obligor (mere notice will not suffice), and for this reason it is rarely used in the type of financing discussed in this chapter. It gives the financier strong protection, in that the obligor can only obtain a good discharge by paying the financier, since, after novation, the obligor owes the obligation to the new creditor and, if the obligor does not pay, the financier is the only person who can sue the obligor, its contractual counterparty.

For an assignment to be a statutory assignment, express notice in writing must be given to the obligor and similar consequences to novation apply. The obligor can only obtain a good discharge by paying the financier,[16] and the statutory assignee is the only person who can sue the obligor for non-payment.[17] It can, thus, be seen that in both these techniques three features align: notice to the debtor (so that the debtor knows to pay the financier); the exclusive ability of the financier to give a good discharge on payment; and the exclusive ability of the financier to sue the obligor. The alignment of these features makes logical sense: after notice the obligor is left in no doubt as to who to pay and who can sue it.

---

[14] See, for example, Joanna Lilley, David Metzger, and Kate Wild, 'Drafting Security over Contractual Right in Project and Real Estate Finance' (2019) 34 JIBFL 738 (hereafter Lilley, Metzger, and Wild, 'Drafting security').

[15] A legal mortgage takes effect by an absolute statutory assignment with a condition for reconveyance, which would need to take place by another assignment. See *Tancred v Delagoa Bay and East Africa Railway Co* (1889) 23 QBD 239 and Roy Goode and Louise Gullifer, *Goode and Gullifer on Legal Problems of Credit and Security* (7th edn, Thomson Reuters 2023) 3-09(a) (hereafter *Goode and Gullifer*). For the practical disadvantages of a legal mortgage of receivables, see Marcus Smith, 'Assignments of Intangibles as Security: Some Unlitigated Pitfalls' (2015) 9 JIBFL 558, 559 (hereafter Smith, 'Unlitigated Pitfalls').

[16] Law of Property Act 1925, s 136(1)(c): a statutory assignment passes and transfers to the assignee 'the power to give a good discharge for the [receivable] without the concurrence of the assignor'.

[17] Law of Property Act 1925, s 136(1)(b): a statutory assignment passes and transfers to the assignee 'all legal and other remedies for the same'. The meaning of s 136(1)(a), the assignee is transferred 'the legal right to such debt or thing in action' is more contentious.

The requirements of section 136 support this alignment: uncertainty is reduced (or perhaps eliminated) by the requirement of writing for both the assignment and the notice and by the fact that notice rendering the assignment statutory cannot be given of a future debt, that is, one that arises under a contract not yet made.[18] Moreover, situations in which there could be doubt as to who to pay, such as an assignment of part of a debt or where the assignment is by way of charge,[19] cannot be the subject of a statutory assignment.

B. Equitable Assignment

1. *General*

Where no notice is to be given immediately to the obligor, any assignment cannot be statutory and therefore takes effect as an equitable assignment. This technique is therefore used for invoice discounting arrangements, and also, if a loan is to be secured, by an equitable mortgage, which is an absolute assignment in equity of the receivables with a condition for reconveyance on repayment of the secured obligation.[20] If the assignment meets the other requirements set out in section 136 (apart from that of written notice to the obligor), then it has the potential to become a statutory assignment if notice is given:[21] this can take place at any time, even long after the equitable assignment has taken place, as long as it is before proceedings are brought to enforce the receivable.[22] It is only if the section 136 requirements are not otherwise met that the assignment remains equitable after notice is given to the obligor. One example of this is where it is of part of a debt,[23] another is where the original assignment is oral[24] (or otherwise fails to comply with the formality requirements in section 136[25]), and a third is where the subject matter of the assignment is future receivables (although these will, eventually, become present receivables in respect of which notice can then be given which will convert the assignment into a statutory one[26]). As mentioned above, notice would typically be given in an invoice discounting arrangement when there is a default by the financed business, raising doubts about its ability to collect in the receivables and hold them on trust for the financier. In respect of an equitable mortgage, the right to notify the obligor would typically be exercised as a precursor to the mortgagee enforcing the mortgage by collecting in the receivables.

---

[18] *Colonial Bank Ltd v European Grain & Shipping Ltd* [1988] 3 WLR 60, 67 (CA).

[19] See Section III.C.

[20] See *Goode and Gullifer* (n 15) 3-09(b).

[21] An example of this is *Mailbox (Birmingham) Ltd v Galliford Try Construction Ltd* [2017] EWHC 67 (TCC); 170 Con LR 219 [42] and [43] (hereafter *Mailbox v Galliford*).

[22] *Holt v Heatherfield Trust Ltd* [1942] 2 KB 1, 4.

[23] For example, *Re Steel Wing Co Ltd* [1929] 1 Ch 345 (hereafter *Steel Wing*); *Walter & Sullivan Ltd v J Murphy & Sons Ltd* [1955] 2 QB 584 (hereafter *Walter & Sullivan*).

[24] For example, *Hoist Portfolio Holding 2 Ltd v Multiple Defendants* (2018) [2018] EWHC 3113 (Ch) (hereafter *Hoist Portfolio*).

[25] The assignment must be in writing under the hand of the assignor. Examples of where this was not the case are *William Brandt's Sons & Co v Dunlop Rubber Co Ltd* [1905] 2 AC 454 (HL) (hereafter *Brandt's v Dunlop*), and *Technocrats International Inc v Fredic Limited* [2004] EWHC 692 (QB).

[26] This follows from the wording of s 136 (notice must be given to 'a debtor'); see *Goode and Gullifer* (n 15) 3–11 and CH Tham, *Understanding the Law of Assignment* (CUP 2019) 440–44 (hereafter Tham, *Assignment*).

2. No notice to the obligor

If notice to the obligor has not been given, then the obligor will pay the financed business and will be able to obtain a good discharge by doing so.[27] This position is justified on conceptual, policy, and practical grounds. The receivable is a legal chose in action, and can therefore be discharged by payment to the person to whom the sum is owed in law. It is, of course, entirely impractical for an obligor to pay someone of whom he has no knowledge, and, moreover, without notice the conscience of the obligor cannot be affected by the assignment.[28] As a matter of policy, it must surely be right that the position of the obligor should not be changed by the assignment, of which he has had no notice. Moreover, in a non-notification financing arrangement, this position reflects the agreed position between the financier and the financed business. An invoice discounter's protection comes from the fact that the business usually holds the proceeds of the collected receivable on trust for it. This trust is either express (if the financing agreement so provides) or constructive.[29] An equitable mortgagee's protection is that the proceeds are also subject to the equitable mortgage: this is likely to be expressly provided for in the mortgage instrument, but would in any case follow from the creation of the equitable mortgage over the receivables.[30]

3. Notice to the obligor

Once notice has been given to the obligor, either the assignment becomes statutory (in which case only the assignee has the power to give a good discharge) or it does not because the criteria for a statutory assignment are not met. In that (quite rare) case, there are two possibilities. The first is that the assignment is of the whole debt, but the formal requirements of section 136 were not met in relation to the assignment itself or the notice given, or that the notice was given at the time when the debt was a future debt, and notice has not been given since it became a present debt.[31] In any of these situations, the assignee can give a good discharge (in that the obligor who pays the assignee will no longer be obliged to pay the assignor[32]) and the obligor cannot,[33] on the grounds that the conscience of the obligor is affected by the notice, and he cannot pay contrary to the information given by the notice.[34]

---

[27] *Stocks v Dobson* (1853) 4 De G M & G 11; 43 ER 411; *Herkules Piling v Tilbury Construction* (1992) 61 BLR 107 (QBD) 119 (hereafter *Herkules v Tilbury*); *General Nutrition Investment Co v Holland and Barrett International Ltd* [2017] EWHC 746 (Ch) [67].

[28] Greg Tolhurst, *The Assignment of Contractual Rights* (2nd edn, Bloomsbury Publishing 2016) [8.06] (hereafter Tolhurst, *Contractual Rights*).

[29] *GE Crane Sales Pty Ltd v Commissioner of Taxation* (1971) 46 ALJR 15 (hereafter *Crane v Federal Commissioner*); *Barclays Bank Ltd v Willowbrook International Ltd* [1987] 1 FTLR 386. Cf Marcus Smith and Nico Leslie, *The Law of Assignment* (3rd edn, OUP 2018) [26-20]–[26-22] (hereafter Smith and Leslie, *Assignment*).

[30] *Goode and Gullifer* (n 15) 3–35. An alternative view is that the proceeds belong absolutely to the mortgagee (see Bruce Johnston, 'When Security Assignments Don't Work' [2019] JIBLR 161, 163 (hereafter Johnston, 'Security Assignments') but this view relies on *Crane v Federal Commissioner* (n 29), a case about an absolute equitable assignment rather than an equitable mortgage. In the absence of specific agreement, it is likely that the parties intended the proceeds to be subject to the mortgage, which is therefore created by the mortgage instrument (see *Goode and Gullifer* (n 15) 3–35). A similar argument applies to the proceeds of receivables subject to a fixed charge.

[31] Until it becomes a present debt no question of payment arises.

[32] *Brice v Bannister* (1878) 3 QBD 569. See also *Skelwith (Leisure) Limited v Alan Armstrong* [2015] EWHC 2830 (Ch), [2016] Ch 345 [66] (hereafter *Skelwith v Armstrong*) where the judge indicated that express empowerment in the assignment agreement for an equitable assignee to be able to give a good discharge (from *Durham Brothers v Robertson* [1898] 1 QB 765, 770 (hereafter *Durham v Robertson*)) was no longer required.

[33] Although the latter proposition is contentious; see Tham, *Assignment* (n 26) ch 11; cf Tolhurst, *Contractual Rights* (n 28) [8.06].

[34] Tolhurst, *Contractual Rights* (n 28) [8.06]; *Deposit Protection Board v Dalia* [1994] 2 AC 367, 381 (hereafter *Deposit Protection v Dalia*). This proposition depends on the notice being sufficiently precise to affect the conscience of the obligor.

The second is that the assignment is of part of a debt. Here, the position is particularly difficult, as there is a single debt, and so neither the assignor or the assignee can give a good discharge until they are both paid.[35]

C. Charge

The difference between a charge over the receivables and an equitable mortgage is that a charge is an appropriation of the receivables to the satisfaction of the obligation,[36] while an equitable mortgage entails an absolute equitable assignment.[37] Ownership of the receivables, therefore, remains with the chargor. Despite this difference, which is important conceptually, some legal consequences are the same. For example, the rule in *Dearle v Hall*[38] applies in the same way to a charge and an equitable mortgage, as does the rule that independent set-offs arising after notice to the obligor cannot be asserted against the assignee.[39] However, there are some important differences, such as that the charge cannot be converted into a statutory assignment merely by giving notice to the debtor, since section 136 of the Law of Property Act expressly excludes an assignment 'purporting to be by way of charge only'. This is because, in the case of a charge, it is defeasible on the payment of the secured obligation, and so whether the debt is owed to the assignee or the assignor will depend on the state of account between those parties.[40] It is therefore inappropriate for the consequences of section 136 to apply.

As with invoice discounting and equitable mortgages, it will normally be envisaged that the chargor will operate the business, including all relationships with its obligors, itself during the currency of the secured loan. No notice, then, will be given to the obligors. In this situation, the obligor will obtain a good discharge on paying the chargor. Whether the chargor can dispose of the proceeds of the receivable will depend on whether the charge is fixed or floating: in order to be fixed, the chargor must not be entitled to dispose of the proceeds without the leave of the chargee.[41]

If (and when) notice of the charge is given to the obligor, the effect will depend on the terms of the notice. If the obligor is required to continue to pay the chargor, arguably only the chargor can give a good discharge: not only does it still own the receivable but this is compatible with the intentions of both the chargor and the chargee, while payment to the

---

[35] *Deposit Protection v Dalia* (n 34). For criticism, see Tolhurst, *Contractual Rights* (n 28) [8.06].

[36] This describes a fixed charge, or a crystallized floating charge.

[37] For discussion of the relationship between assignment and charge, see Michael Bridge, Louise Gullifer, Kelvin Low, and Gerard McMeel, *The Law of Personal Property* (3rd edn, Sweet & Maxwell 2021) [22-011]–[22-013] (hereafter Bridge et al, *Personal Property*).

[38] *Dearle v Hall* (1828) 3 Russ 1. The rule is that priority between assignments is prima facie governed by the order of notice to the obligor, subject to the proviso that a person taking a second assignment with notice of the first assignment cannot obtain priority by being the first to give notice. For the application of this rule to charges and mortgages, see Hugh Beale, Michael Bridge, Louise Gullifer, and Eva Lomnicka, *The Law of Security and Title-Based Financing* (3rd edn, OUP 2018) [4.12]–[4.14] (hereafter Beale et al, *Security*).

[39] In relation to a floating charge, the cut-off point for independent set-offs is when there is notice to the obligor and the charge has crystallized: see *Business Computers Ltd v Anglo-African Leasing Ltd* [1977] 1 WLR 578.

[40] *Durham v Robertson* (n 32).

[41] *In Re Spectrum Plus Ltd* [2005] UKHL 41; [2005] 2 AC 680. If the charge is fixed, the proceeds will be subject to the fixed charge: see n 30.

272   WHO CAN SUE THE OBLIGOR WHEN RECEIVABLES ARE FINANCED?

chargee would not be. If, however, the obligor is required by the notice to pay the chargee, payment to the chargee must be required for a good discharge, for the reasons given earlier.[42]

IV. Who Can Bring an Action Against an Obligor

A. Introduction

These discussions of equitable assignment and charge have focused on who can give a good discharge for payment. It is argued in this chapter that this also determines whether the assignee needs to be joined in an action brought by the assignor. This argument is developed in the next section, which focuses on who can sue the obligor for non-payment and in what circumstances, and argues that where no notice has been given to the obligor, the assignee does not need to be joined to an action by the assignor.[43]

Once an assignment has become a statutory assignment (which could be at the point the assignment took place, or later on[44]), there is no doubt that the correct person to sue the obligor for non-payment is the assignee and not the assignor.[45] Any uncertainty, therefore, only exists where an assignment is equitable at the time action is taken. An assignment will be equitable at the time when action is taken only if no notice has been given to the obligor or, if notice has been given, if one of the reasons set out previously[46] apply, namely, a failure to comply with the formal requirements of section 136 or that the assignment is of part of a debt. In the typical receivables financing arrangement, these reasons are unlikely to be the case[47] and the main reason why an assignment would be equitable would be that notice of assignment has (deliberately) not been given to the obligor. None of the cases cited in section IV.B of this chapter—except conceivably the case of *William Brandt's Sons & Co v Dunlop Rubber Co Ltd*,[48] which was decided in 1905—concerned the enforcement of a debt in the course of a straightforward receivables financing arrangement. In such a situation, either the assignee sues as a statutory assignee[49] or, because the financing arrangement is confidential, the assignor wishes to sue as legal owner of the debt.

---

[42] Section III.B.3. Although this payment would have the effect of destroying the chargor's equity of redemption: see Roy Goode, 'Contractual Prohibitions against Assignment' [2009] LMCLQ 300, fn 52 (hereafter Goode, 'Contractual Prohibitions'). However, the chargee, in this situation, would hold any surplus value in the proceeds on trust for the chargor, and the discharge obtained by the obligor is necessary because otherwise the obligor would be disadvantaged if it had to challenge the payment instruction, if necessary, by interpleading.

[43] See Bridge et al, *Personal Property* (n 37) [22-050].

[44] Section III.B.1.

[45] For the inability of the assignor to sue if the assignment has become statutory, see *Hughes v Pump House Hotel Co* [1902] 2 KB 190 (hereafter *Hughes v Pump House*).

[46] Section III.B.1.

[47] The financier, who is almost always a repeat player, is very likely to comply with the formal requirements and will typically be financing the whole of the business's debts.

[48] *Brandt's v Dunlop* (n 25).

[49] By the time the assignee commences proceedings, it is very likely to have given notice to the obligor in, for example, a letter before action. Service of proceedings may well be sufficient notice of assignment to render the assignment statutory, although this does not mean that the proceedings are brought by a statutory assignee (*Compania Colombiana de Seguros v Pacific Steam Navigation Co* [1965] 1 QB 101, 126; *Treadwell v Hickey* [2009] NSWSC 1395 [79]).

B. The Assignee's Right to Sue

Despite the rarity of this situation in the receivables financing context, the bulk of the case law has focused on the circumstances in which an equitable assignee can enforce the debt. The overall effect of the case law can be summarized as that, while an assignee can sue the obligor, in most cases it must join the assignor to the action. There are two explanations for this requirement. The first is substantive: the equitable assignment is a trust or is sufficiently trust-like for the cause of action to be vested in the assignor, who must therefore be before the court.[50] The second is that joinder is a procedural requirement[51] which applies if there is a good reason for the assignor to be before the court,[52] and that in almost all cases where an assignment is equitable, and the assignee wishes to bring an action, such good reasons will exist. For example, if the assignment is for part of a debt there is a danger that the assignor will also sue in a separate action and the results might conflict,[53] and if the formal requirements of section 136 are not fulfilled, there could be a dispute about the existence or validity of the assignment. Until fairly recently, even the procedural view was expressed as a rule of practice requiring joinder with very rare and extremely limited exceptions.[54] However, more recently, the courts articulated the position in terms that joinder could be waived if there was no reason for the assignor to be joined.[55] Building on this reasoning, judges in a number of cases have conceptualized the assignee's right to sue as substantive.[56] For example, in *Charnesh Kapoor v National Westminster Bank*,[57] Etherton LJ summarized the 'consistent line of authority' as showing that 'the equitable assignee of a debt, and not the equitable assignor, has the substantive legal right to sue for the assigned debt'.[58] This conceptualization of the equitable assignee's right to sue appears to have led to a correlative

---

[50] James Edelman and Steven Elliott, 'Two Conceptions of Equitable Assignment' (2015) 131 LQR 128 (hereafter Edelman and Elliott, 'Two Conceptions').

[51] For explanations of the basis of the assignee's right to sue if joinder is a procedural requirement (based on the idea that the assignor sues in equity and not at law), see Smith and Leslie, *Assignment* (n 29) [11.55]–[11.84], Tolhurst, *Contractual Rights* (n 28) [4.21]–[4.25] and CH Tham, 'Joinder of Equitable Assignors of Equitable and Legal Choses in Action' [2017] LMCLQ 537.

[52] *Brandt's v Dunlop* (n 25) 462; *Performing Right Society Ltd v London Theatre of Varieties* [1924] AC 1, 14 (Viscount Cave); *Weddell v JA Pearce & Major* [1988] Ch 26, 40 (hereafter *Weddell v Pearce*).

[53] *Steel Wing* (n 23). See also *Deposit Protection v Dalia* (n 34) 381 (Simon Brown LJ) on the avoidance of multiple actions.

[54] The only exception cited by the earlier cases was *Brandt's v Dunlop* (n 25), where the defendant obligor disclaimed any desire to have the assignor before the court.

[55] *Central Insurance Co Ltd v Seacalf Shipping Corporation (The Aiolos)* [1983] 2 Lloyd's Rep 25, 33–34 (hereafter *The Aiolos*); *Sim Swee Joo Shipping Sdn Bhd v Shirlstar Container Transport Ltd* [1994] CLC 188, 190 (this is a rule of practice, which will not be insisted upon where there is no need, in particular if there is no risk of a separate claim by the assignor); *Raiffeisen Zentralbank Österreich AG v Five Star General Trading LLC* [2001] EWCA Civ 68, [2001] QB 825 [60]; *Hoist Portfolio* (n 24) [9]–[11]. *Mailbox v Galliford* (n 21) is an example of a case where the assignor was not required to be joined (the relevant assignment was a re-assignment to the original assignor and was equitable because notice to the debtor was not given until after the adjudication proceeding had commenced) and *Hoist Portfolio* (n 24) is an example of a case where the need to join the assignor was waived on condition that the assignor confirmed by letter (shared with the court) that it had no further interest in the relevant debts (the relevant assignment was equitable because it did not comply with the formal requirements of s 136).

[56] *Three Rivers DC v Bank of England (No.1)* [1996] QB 292, 303, 308, 315 (hereafter *Three Rivers*); *Deposit Protection v Dalia* (n 34) 386, 387–88; *Charnesh Kapoor v National Westminster Bank* [2011] EWCA Civ 1083, [2012] 1 All ER 201 [40], [43] (hereafter *Kapoor v NWB*); *Roberts v Gill & Co* [2010] UKSC 22; [2011] 1 AC 240 [67] (Lord Collins), [127] (Lord Clarke); *Bexhill UK Limited v Abdul Razzaq* [2012] EWCA Civ 1376 [58] (hereafter *Bexhill v Razzaq*); *Skelwith v Armstrong* (n 32) [66]; *Mailbox v Galliford* (n 21) [50].

[57] *Kapoor v NWB* (n 56).

[58] ibid [43].

reduction in the circumstances in which an equitable assignor can sue without joining the equitable assignee.[59]

In practical terms, however, the failure to join an assignor to proceedings brought by the assignee is, under current law, unlikely to be fatal to the action. Commencement of proceedings without joining the assignor is not a nullity[60] and is effective for the purposes of commencing proceedings within the limitation period.[61] The assignee can, therefore, always join the assignor as a defendant at a later date if required, and the only adverse consequence to the parties is likely to be some quite minimal costs.[62] The obligor will, at the latest, be aware of the assignee at the point when proceedings are commenced, and the joinder of the assignor is unlikely to change the relationship between the assignor and the obligor. However, where the existence of the financing relationship is confidential, a requirement of joinder of the assignee to a suit brought by the assignor against the obligor could be commercially adverse to the financed business and its operating relationship with its customers. The next section examines whether, and when, an equitable assignor can sue an obligor without joining the assignee to the proceedings.

C. The Assignor's Right to Sue

1. Introduction

Cases considering the circumstances in which an equitable assignor can sue the obligor are far fewer than those considering the right of the assignee to sue. This may well be because, in many situations, it is assumed that, at least where no notice of assignment had been given to the obligor, the assignor could sue the obligor without joining the assignee to the action, with the proceeds of the action being held on trust for the assignee,[63] and, knowing nothing of the assignment, the obligor does not object to the identity of the claimant.[64] This analysis follows from the view that the assignor holds the debt on trust for the assignee, and is therefore the legal owner of the debt.[65] A trustee can bring an action in respect of trust property without joining any beneficiaries[66] (although subject to the power of the Court to order joinder where appropriate[67]), and if an equitable assignment were a trust, or trust-like, one might expect the same analysis to apply. On this view, the trustee joinder is a procedural rather than a substantive requirement, and only required where there is a good reason for the assignee to be before the court. However, the view, discussed above, that the equitable

---

[59] See IV.C.3.

[60] *Weddell v Pearce* (n 52), see especially 41.

[61] *The Aiolos* (n 55).

[62] It seems very unlikely that, in a modern case, a claimant would find itself in the position of the assignee plaintiff in *Durham v Robertson* (n 32), whose claim failed for non-joinder without, it seems, having been given the opportunity to join the assignor.

[63] See III.B.2.

[64] Indeed, as long as the obligor obtains a good discharge for payment to the assignor/claimant, it is hard to see what interest it has in objecting to the identity of the claimant.

[65] See, for example, *Herkules v Tilbury* (n 27), in which the decision and reasoning seem to presuppose this view.

[66] CPR 1998/3132 r 19.7A(1); see also Supreme Court Rules 1965 Ord 15 r 14(1); Lynton Tucker, Nicholas Le Poidevin QC, and James Brightwell (eds), *Lewin on Trusts* (20th edn, Sweet & Maxwell 2022) [47-001]; White Book CPR Rule 19.7A.

[67] CPR 1998/3132 r 19.7A(2); see also Supreme Court Rules 1965 Ord 15 r 14(2)

assignee has 'the substantive legal right' to sue the obligor appears to have led to some expansive dicta in recent cases requiring joinder of the assignee in all circumstances.[68]

2. Notice to the obligor

Where notice of the assignment has been given to the obligor there can be no objection, except conceivably as a matter of costs, to the equitable assignee being required to be joined in an action brought against the obligor by the assignee. Post-notice, as mentioned above,[69] the obligor must pay the assignee and the assignee can give a good discharge, and it thus makes good sense for the assignee to be before the court. This conclusion mirrors that of the Court of Appeal in *Walter & Sullivan v Murphy*.[70] In that case, the relevant assignment was equitable because it was of part of a debt. Notice had been given to the obligor. The assignor sued the obligor for the whole debt, and the obligor alleged that no claim lay without the joinder of the assignees. This issue was heard as a preliminary issue. The Court of Appeal unanimously held that the assignees should be joined in the action on two connected grounds. Since the assignment was of part of a debt, both the assignor and assignee should be before the court: this was clear from the authority of *Re Steel Wing*.[71] The Court of Appeal also stressed the importance of joining the assignee if notice had been given to the obligor. Parker LJ (giving the judgment of the court) said:

> In the present case, however, it is the assignor who is seeking to recover, and in his own right, and it is strongly urged that he is entitled to do so without joining the assignee. We think that that is an impossible contention. *The whole object of the notice to the debtor is to protect the assignee. After receipt of that notice the debtor pays the assignor at his peril.*[72]

3. No notice to the obligor

Where there is no notice to the obligor, the position is different. The obligor does not know about the assignment, and is therefore dealing entirely with the assignor. It will pay the assignor, and can obtain a good discharge, and, apart from giving notice, the assignee cannot prevent this. The assignee's interest will then (usually) shift to the proceeds of the payment.[73] This analysis applies in the same way to a payment obtained through litigation, and the assignee is similarly protected. Where the assignee has agreed not to give notice, for reasons of confidentiality, the case for not requiring joinder of the assignee is even stronger: it would upset the whole operation of the financing arrangement. Further, as discussed below, if joinder were required, parties in a confidential arrangement would have to make complicated arrangements to avoid the requirement.

The basis of the view that joinder of the assignee is necessary whenever an assignor sues (irrespective of notice or other good reason) seems to emanate from the case of *Three Rivers*

---

[68] The dicta are discussed in the text that follows. As a result of these dicta, some commentators take the view that the assignee must always be joined (Smith and Leslie, *Assignment* (n 29) [11.87]; Ying Khai Liew (ed), *Guest on the Law of Assignment* (4th edn, Sweet & Maxwell 2021) 3-22) or even that only the assignee can sue (Johnston, 'Security Assignments' (n 30) 163, 164).

[69] III.B.3.

[70] *Walter & Sullivan* (n 23).

[71] *Steel Wing* (n 23) and see text to n 53.

[72] *Walter & Sullivan* (n 23) 588 (emphasis added).

[73] See III.B.2.

DC v Bank of England (No.1).[74] The circumstances in that case were unusual, and far removed from confidential receivables financing. A large number of depositors in a failed bank (BCCI) were suing the Bank of England for failure to supervise BCCI properly. Before the depositors brought the action, they had made equitable assignments of their rights against the Bank of England to BCCI, but (initially) BCCI was not joined in the action, although it later was by an amendment with language making it clear that its claim was made as assignee in the name of the assignors. The issue raised in the pleadings, however, and addressed by the court, was whether the assignors still had a cause of action, despite the equitable assignment of their claims.[75] The Court of Appeal held that they did, relying mainly on *Walter & Sullivan v Murphy*[76] and on the cases about whether and when an equitable assignee could sue an obligor.[77] While no appeal was made from the order of the judge that the proceedings should be stayed pending the joinder of the assignee, the Court of Appeal stated that they agreed with that order, and therefore took the view that the assignee should be joined in the action. The judgment of Peter Gibson LJ gives most support to the view that joinder of the assignee is necessary whenever the assignor sues. He said, referring to the authorities on suits by equitable assignees:

> These authorities, in my judgment, clearly establish that the equitable assignee can be regarded realistically as the person entitled to the assigned chose and is able to sue the debtor on that chose, but that save in special circumstances the court will require him to join the assignor as a procedural requirement so that the assignor might be bound and the debtor protected. *If, unusually, the assignor sues, he will not be allowed to maintain the action in the absence of the assignee.*[78]

There are, however, some reasons for this seemingly unequivocal statement to be qualified in the situation where no notice of the assignment has been given to the obligor. Earlier in his judgment, Peter Gibson LJ said:

> An assignor, *if the assignment is known*, will not be allowed to sue in his own name for himself. He may sue as trustee for the assignee if the assignee so wishes, but in that event he should reveal his representative capacity (R.S.C., Ord. 6, r. 3(1)(a)) and if he attempts to recover for himself, even if, for example, only part of the debt has been assigned, he will be required to join the assignee.[79]

The words in italics (arguably) qualify the entire sentence and indicate that what Peter Gibson LJ is addressing is a situation where the obligor knows of the assignment. Moreover, Peter Gibson LJ's (and Staughton LJ's) reliance on *Walter & Sullivan v Murphy*, as establishing the requirement for the assignee to be joined,[80] must be qualified by the dual

---

[74] *Three Rivers* (n 56).
[75] *Three Rivers* (n 56) 299.
[76] *Walter & Sullivan* (n 23).
[77] Discussed in IV.B.
[78] *Three Rivers* (n 56) 313 (emphasis added). Note, in addition, that counsel in *Three Rivers* agreed that practice (exemplified in the rules referenced in n 66) whereby trustees could normally sue third parties without joining the beneficiaries was different in respect of actions by assignors or assignees.
[79] *Three Rivers* (n 56) 308.
[80] *Three Rivers* (n 56) 301, 310–11.

WHO CAN BRING AN ACTION AGAINST AN OBLIGOR 277

facts in that case (acknowledged by both Lord Justices) that notice had been given to the obligor, and that the assignment was of part of a debt. In addition, Peter Gibson LJ distinguished *Warner Bros. Records Inc v Rollgreen Ltd*,[81] a case in which an equitable assignee of rights under an agreement was held to be unable to exercise an option in the agreement, on the basis that that case concerned a situation where no notice of the assignment had been given to the grantor of the option (the obligor).[82]

Three Rivers also seems to be the genesis of the idea that the procedural rules on an action brought by a trustee[83] do not apply to an action brought by an assignor.[84] It is true that Peter Gibson LJ did say that the practice was different, but this was on the basis of an agreement by counsel,[85] and no reasons were given for the difference in application.

Two recent cases appear to give greater support to the view that, when an assignor sues, the assignee must always be joined to the action. One is *Kapoor v National Westminster Bank*,[86] a case in which the issue was whether an assignee of part of a debt (necessarily an equitable assignment) was the creditor entitled to vote in relation to the approval of an individual voluntary arrangement.[87] In deciding that the assignee was a creditor and could vote, Etherton LJ said that the following propositions emerged clearly from the authorities:

[A]n equitable assignee of debt is entitled in its own right and name to bring proceedings for the debt. The equitable assignee will usually be required to join the assignor to the proceedings in order to ensure that the debtor is not exposed to double recovery, but that is a purely procedural requirement and can be dispensed with by the Court. By contrast, the assignor cannot bring proceedings to recover the assigned debt in the assignor's own name for the assignor's own account. The assignor can sue as trustee for the assignee if the assignee agrees, and, in that event the claim must disclose the assignor's representative capacity. In any other case, the assignor must join the assignee, not because of a mere procedural rule but as a matter of substantive law in view of the insufficiency of the assignor's title.[88]

In addition, as a summary, he said:

There is no good reason of policy or principle for the courts to refuse to recognise the title of the undisputed equitable assignee of part of a debt, and every good reason for the courts to refuse to recognise the bare legal title of the assignor, except where the assignor is a trustee for the assignee and expressly suing as such or the assignee joins in the proceedings.[89]

In relation to the assignor, at least, the statements in relation to joinder were arguably obiter, in the sense that the real issue was the interpretation of the word 'creditor' in the Insolvency

---

[81] *Warner Bros Records Inc v Rollgreen Ltd* [1976] QB 430.
[82] *Three Rivers* (n 56) 315.
[83] See IV.B.
[84] See, for example, Smith and Leslie, *Assignment* (n 29) [11.87], and the implicit acceptance of this proposition in *Kapoor v NWB* (n 56).
[85] *Three Rivers* (n 56) 311.
[86] *Kapoor v NWB* (n 56).
[87] The (then) Insolvency Rules 1986 r 5.21 (now Insolvency Rules 2016 r 8.22) provided that a 'creditor' is entitled to vote by reference to the amount of the debt owed to him.
[88] *Kapoor v NWB* (n 56) [30].
[89] ibid [40].

Rules rather than any question of who should be joined in any action.[90] Moreover, the assignment in *Kapoor* was of part of a debt, in which case there is a good reason for the assignee to be joined.[91] Furthermore, it is not clear that the statements relate to a situation where no notice is given to the obligor, since this was not the case in the situation before the court. In *Kapoor* the assignor was a family trust of the obligor's family and 'an associate'[92] of the obligor, and the purpose of the assignment was to put some of the debt in the hands of a non-associate, and it appears from the evidence that the obligor suggested the assignment in the first place.[93] In these circumstances, the question of whether notice of the assignment was specifically given was not investigated either at first instance or in the Court of Appeal, but the argument at first instance made on behalf of the assignee included the following propositions, taken from Halsbury's Laws of England, which appear to be limited to where notice has been given:

2. An assignor, *if the equitable assignment is known*, will not be allowed to sue in his own name for himself. He may sue as trustee for the assignee, but only if the assignee so wishes.

3. A debtor *with notice of the equitable assignment* who pays the assignor without the consent of the assignee will have to pay the assignee again.[94]

The other case is *Bexhill UK Limited v Abdul Razzaq*,[95] and is one of the few cases in which an assignor's right to sue was actually in issue. The obligor was the guarantor of a debt owed by a company of which he was a director (RSA) to the assignor, who had lent money to RSA. The obligor granted the assignor a charge over a commercial property he owed as security for his obligations under the guarantee. The assignor's rights under the charge fell within an assignment previously made to the assignee bank to secure a financial facility. The case therefore concerned a type of receivables financing arrangement. On default by RSA, the assignor commenced proceedings to obtain possession of the property. The obligor raised as a defence the argument that the assignor had no right to sue because all its rights under the charge had been assigned to the assignee. The assignment was equitable, because, at the time of the assignment, the rights under the charge were a future 'thing in action': no express notice of the assignment of this particular right was given to the obligor, so it appeared to be uncontested that the assignment remained equitable.[96]

The main issues considered by the Court of Appeal were whether the assignment was an absolute one or by way of charge, and whether the assignor was suing as agent for the assignee. The issue as to joinder was not contested: counsel for the assignor accepted the analysis of counsel for the obligor that 'if there ha[d] been an "absolute" assignment which [took] effect in equity and [the assignor] could not act as agent for [the assignee] in pursuing the claim, then [the assignee] had to be joined for the claim to be able to continue'.[97]

---

[90] For criticism of the case on these lines, see PG Turner, 'May the Assignee of Part of a Debt Vote at a Creditors' Meeting?' (2012) 71 CLJ 270.

[91] *Walter & Sullivan* (n 23) 589.

[92] For the purposes of Insolvency Rules 1986 r 5.23(4)(c).

[93] *Kapoor v NWB* (n 56) [61]–[64].

[94] ibid [105] (emphasis added).

[95] *Bexhill v Razzaq* (n 56).

[96] ibid [57].

[97] ibid [37].

Therefore, since the Court of Appeal held that the assignment was absolute and that the assignor did not act as agent in bringing the action, despite an obligation to collect receivables in the ordinary course of trading as agent for the assignee, the need for joinder was assumed without argument.[98] The Court of Appeal made it clear that the assignor could apply to the trial judge to join the assignee to the action.[99]

To what extent, then, is the *Bexhill* case authority for the proposition that the assignee must always be joined in an action by an equitable assignor, even when no notice has been given to the obligor?[100] Arguably, the obligor did have notice in the *Bexhill* case. Although there was no express notice of the assignment, he knew about it. As director of RSA, he had signed the finance agreement between RSA and the assignor which expressly notified RSA of the assignment.[101] The requirement for notice of an equitable assignment is not strict: it is enough that 'the debtor should be given to understand that the debt has been made over by the creditor to some third person'.[102] Further, as mentioned above, the need for joinder was assumed without argument. On this basis, at best the *Bexhill* case is weak authority for the proposition.

Unlike the English case law, there is some specifically relevant case law in Australia. There have been a series of cases in which the right to sue an obligor of an assignor who has securitized its receivables has been challenged on the grounds that the debt has been equitably assigned (that is, without notice to the obligor).[103] Most of these challenges foundered on the speculative nature of the evidence of securitization, but in *McLean v Westpac Banking Corporation*[104] Newnes JA in the Western Australia Court of Appeal opined on the legal merits, saying that in the absence of a 'legal' assignment (that is, an assignment that fell within the Australian equivalent of Law of Property Act section 136), the assignor was entitled to enforce the loan as the holder of the legal title. This view was followed in *Timbercorp Finance Pty Ltd v FTM Nominees Pty Ltd*,[105] a case where the facts were fully particularized and where the legal merits were fully argued. The argument that the action should be struck out as the assignee should have been joined in the proceedings[106] was based on the dictum from *Kapoor* set out previously.[107] The judge accepted the argument of the assignor that it could sue as it had the legal title, and that there was no need for joinder of the assignee as the risk of double recovery did not arise because payment to the assignor would fully discharge the obligation.[108]

---

[98] At one point, Aikens LJ did say that, in an equitable assignment, the general rule was that the assignee had the right to sue as it is beneficially entitled to the thing in action, and that the assignor would not be allowed to sue unless the assignee were joined as a party, relying on the *Three Rivers* case (n 56).

[99] *Bexhill v Razzaq* (n 56) [68].

[100] *Bexhill v Razzaq* (n 56) does appear to have been treated as some authority for this proposition in *Promontia (Oak) Ltd v Emanuel* [2021] EWCA Civ 1682; [2022] 1 WLR 1682 [114]–[117], although the principal authority relied upon is John McGhee (gen ed), *Snell's Equity* (34th edn, Sweet & Maxwell 2020) §3-023, which in its turn relies on *Walter & Sullivan* (n 23) 588, which, as discussed previously, is entirely predicated on notice having been given to the debtor.

[101] *Bexhill v Razzaq* (n 56) [56] and [57].

[102] *Brandt's v Dunlop* (n 25) 462.

[103] See, for example, *Westpac Banking Corporation v Mason* [2011] NSWSC 1241, (2011) 80 NSWLR 354; *McLean v Westpac Banking Corporation* [2012] WASCA 152 (hereafter *McLean v Westpac*); *Hou v Westpac Banking Corporation* [2015] VSCA 57; *Timbercorp Finance Pty Ltd v FTM Nominees Pty Ltd* [2015] VSC 498 (hereafter *Timbercorp v FTM*); *Bendigo and Adelaide Bank Ltd v Pritchard* [2021] QSC 179.

[104] *McLean v Westpac* (n 103) [30].

[105] *Timbercorp v FTM* (n 103).

[106] *Timbercorp v FTM* (n 103) [3].

[107] *Kapoor v NWB* (n 56) [30]. See IV.B.

[108] *Timbercorp v FTM* (n 103) [17], [20], [27].

The emphasis in the *Timbercorp* case on the question of who can give a good discharge supports the argument made here that joinder of the assignee is not necessary where there is no notice to the obligor, since in that situation the assignor can give a good discharge. Moreover, this makes sense in the securitization context considered in the Australian cases, where the business relationship between the originator and the obligors continues, as in other forms of non-notification receivables financing.

V. Other Possibilities for the Parties

A. Charge

Despite the argument made here, a business might want to be more certain that it would be able to sue its obligors without joining the financier. In order to do this, it would need to insist on the financier's proprietary interest being by way of charge.[109] Given that a charge is an appropriation of the receivables to the satisfaction of the obligation, but that the chargor remained their owner in all senses, it would be hard to argue that the chargor could not sue the obligors, or that the chargee had a substantive right to be joined in the action. Thus, if no notice of the charge is given to the obligor, the only person who can give a good discharge is the chargor, and only the chargor can sue the obligor for non-payment.[110] However, as discussed above,[111] if notice of the charge requiring payment to the chargee is given to the obligor, so that the chargee can give a good discharge, it makes no sense for the chargor to have the right to sue the obligor without joining the chargee, since it is necessary for the protection of the obligor for the position between these parties to be definitively determined.[112] Similarly, the chargee would not be able to bring an action against the chargor without joining the chargee.

There are two practical issues with the use of a charge in this context. First, the business model may require an outright sale rather than the creation of a security interest, as with securitization. Second, a chargee is likely to want to include in the charge agreement remedies such as provision for the execution of a legal mortgage and a power of attorney to do so in the name of the chargor. In these circumstances, the charge may well actually be an equitable mortgage.[113]

B. Suit in a Representative Capacity

Another possibility suggested by the cases is that an equitable assignor need not join the assignee if it sues the obligor with the assignee's agreement, and either as trustee[114] or as

---

[109] See further, and for other advantages of a charge, Smith, 'Unlitigated Pitfalls' (n 15); Johnston, 'Security Assignments' (n 30); Lilley, Metzger, and Wild, 'Drafting Security' (n 14).

[110] *Hughes v Pump House* (n 45) 193. See also *Bexhill v Razzaq* (n 56) [37].

[111] III.C.

[112] *Ardila Investments NV v ENRC NV* [2015] EWHC 1667 (Comm); [2015] 2 BCLC 560 [23]. See also Goode, 'Contractual Prohibitions' (n 42) fn 52.

[113] See John Armour and Adrian Walters, 'Funding Liquidation: A Functional View' (2006) 122 LQR 295, 303. However, apart from the points made in the text preceding, this makes very little difference in practice: see Beale et al, *Security* (n 38) [6.57]–[6.65].

[114] *Three Rivers* (n 56) 308 and see IV.C.3: arguably this statement is qualified by the words 'if the assignment is known'; *Kapoor v NWB* (n 56) [30] and see IV.C.3.

agent.[115] In either case, it appears from the cases that the representative capacity would need to be made known on the claim form.[116]

In relation to suit as a trustee, where there is an equitable assignment it would seem very odd if a formal declaration of trust were required, since, on any view, the assignment is either a trust of some description[117] or, if seen as a transfer of equitable title, is sufficiently analogous to a trust for these purposes. The question is then whether it would always be necessary for the claim form to state the representative capacity—for example, where the obligor has not had notice of the assignment and the assignee has agreed to confidentiality (and, as argued in this chapter, where it is not necessary to join the assignee). It did not seem to be necessary in the Australian case of *Timbercorp*[118] but the position in English law seems uncertain.[119] The statements in the cases which seem to require it are arguably referring to situations where no notice has been given.[120]

The idea of suit as agent is less straightforward. It is clear from the *Bexhill* case that whether the assignor sues as agent will depend on the agreement between the parties, and an agreement that the assignor collects in the receivables as agent for the assignee in the ordinary course of business would not be construed as an appointment to act as agent in suing an obligor.[121] It also appears from the *Bexhill* case that the capacity of the claimant as agent would have to be clear from the claim form.[122]

VI. Conclusion

The question of whether, and when, an assignor can sue the obligor without joining the assignee has received relatively little attention, but is of practical importance in the context of non-notification receivables financing, including securitization. Some statements from recent cases, many of which are not strictly on the point, have led to the view that an assignee must always be joined by the assignor for proceedings to be valid. This chapter argues that joinder should not be required when an assignor can give a good discharge for payment, namely, when notice of the assignment has not been given to the debtor. This would enable a financed business to operate its relationships with its customers, even if it were necessary to sue a customer for payment of a debt, without the involvement of the financier and, maybe, even without the customer finding out about the financier's existence. On close examination, the statements in the English cases do not contradict this argument, and there is actual support for the argument in a line of Australian cases concerning actions by originators of securitization.

---

[115] *Bexhill v Razzaq* (n 56) and see IV.C.2.
[116] CPR r 16.2(3), the successor to RSC r 6(3)(1)(a).
[117] Edelman and Elliott, 'Two Conceptions' (n 50); Smith and Leslie, *Assignment* (n 29) [11.24].
[118] *Timbercorp v FTM* (n 103) [27].
[119] Cf *Paragon Finance Plc v Pender* [2005] EWCA Civ 760, [2005] 1 WLR 3412 [112], where, in a securitization arrangement, an SPV acquired equitable title to a mortgage, a failure to indicate that the originator was suing as trustee was said not to affect the validity of the proceedings (or could be cured under the court's power under CPR Pt 17).
[120] See IV.C.3.
[121] *Bexhill v Razzaq* (n 56) [61]–[66].
[122] ibid [66].

17

The 'Tripartite Guide' to Uniform Instruments in the Area of International Commercial Contracts: Background, Content, and Legal Effect

STEFAN VOGENAUER

I. Contract Law, Transnational Contract Law, and Ewan McKendrick

It is a privilege and honour to contribute to a collection building on the scholarly work of Ewan McKendrick.[1] His *œuvre* is, of course, vast and varied. Most law students will be familiar with his publications on English contract law. In fact, this is how I first encountered his writings. I distinctly remember a very cloudy Oxford afternoon down at the river at the Trinity College boathouse during Eights Week, and thus perilously close to my impending contract law exam paper, frantically revising excerpts from the second edition of his widely used contract law textbook[2] while intermittently cheering the College's First Eight (it might have been advisable to focus more on the first of these activities). Later, as a colleague in the Oxford Faculty of Law, Ewan contributed to a number of publications on European and transnational contract law which I co-edited.[3] More recently, we even co-authored an article.[4] Be it as a reader, an editor, or a co-author of his work, I never failed to be struck by the clarity of his writing. It is always authoritative, straight to the point, and—crucially, from the perspective of an editor—on time.

The latter feature is particularly remarkable, given the considerable administrative burden that Ewan carried throughout his tenure as Professor of English Private Law at Oxford. It was particularly in his capacities as Chair of Law Board (the then feeble functional

---

[1] An early version of this contribution was presented at the 7th Conference on International Arbitration and the UN Convention for the International Sale of Goods at the Faculdad de Derecho of the Universidad Panamericana, held virtually on 10 February 2022. I very much benefited from the insights of Daniel Girsberger and Ingeborg Schwenzer who acted as commentators. However, all the views expressed in this contribution are entirely mine. Most importantly, they are not to be taken to reflect the views of the three 'formulating agencies' or the joint panel of experts mentioned at nn 13 and 47. All weblinks were last assessed on 1 March 2023.

[2] Ewan McKendrick, *Contract Law* (2nd edn, Macmillan 1994) (now 15th edn, Bloomsbury 2023).

[3] Ewan McKendrick, 'Harmonisation of European Contract Law: The State We Are In' in Stefan Vogenauer and Stephen Weatherill (eds), *The Harmonisation of European Contract Law: Implications for European Private Laws, Businesses and Legal Practice* (Hart 2006) 5–29; Hannes Unberath and Ewan McKendrick, 'Supervening Events' in Gerhard Dannemann and Stefan Vogenauer (eds), *The Common European Sales Law in Context: Interactions with English and German Law* (OUP 2013) 562–80; Ewan McKendrick, 'Section 6.2: Hardship' and 'Section 7.4: Damages' in Stefan Vogenauer (ed), *Commentary on the UNIDROIT Principles of International Commercial Contracts (PICC)* (2nd edn, OUP 2015) 806–22 and 972–1032.

[4] Ewan McKendrick and Stefan Vogenauer, 'Supervening Events in Contract Law: Two Cases on the Interaction of National Contract Laws, International Uniform Law and "Soft Law" Instruments' in Christoph Benicke and Stefan Huber (eds), *Festschrift für Herbert Kronke* (Gieseking 2020) 1121–38.

Stefan Vogenauer, *The 'Tripartite Guide' to Uniform Instruments in the Area of International Commercial Contracts: Background, Content, and Legal Effect* In: *Shaping the Law of Obligations*. Edited by: Edwin Peel and Rebecca Probert, Oxford University Press.
© Stefan Vogenauer 2023. DOI: 10.1093/oso/9780198889762.003.0017

284 THE 'TRIPARTITE GUIDE'

equivalent of a Dean in a proper Law School) and University Registrar that we had frequent interactions. Unlike other distinguished scholars who move over to the dark side of university administration, he consistently acted with common sense, honesty, integrity, and decency. An appointment with him would invariably include a lengthy chat where he would show a genuine interest in the well-being of his interlocutor, going far beyond the characteristic Oxford mix of small talk and gossip.

One of Ewan's administrative promotions was responsible for my closer involvement with the branch of his scholarship that served as a point of departure for the present chapter. After his appointment as Pro-Vice-Chancellor of the University he had to give up some of his teaching, including the graduate course on 'Transnational Commercial Law' which he had delivered with Roy Goode for many years, and later with Tom Krebs. The task of finding a successor fell to the then convenor of the commercial law subject group, Andy Burrows. He discharged it by stopping on his bike when he saw me walking from the St Cross Building towards the University Parks on yet another summer afternoon. Someone would have to do it, he said, and it did not matter whether the person was a member of the subject group or not—so this was settled as far as he was concerned. When teaching the course, the student edition of the pioneering textbook that Ewan had written with Roy Goode and Herbert Kronke, aka 'the blue brick',[5] was indispensable; and so was the companion volume with primary materials in the field, aka 'the red brick'.[6]

Now in its second edition, the textbook still provides a magisterial overview of the continuously emerging field of transnational commercial law, including a discussion of two interrelated themes that are at the heart of this contribution. First, it addresses the problem of the bewildering variety of pertinent legal instruments, including but not limited to those 'intended to become legally binding', 'facultative instruments', 'contractually incorporated non-binding rules', and 'guides'.[7] It points out that, to some extent, these texts 'communicate among each other', so that there is a 'dialogue of sources': some instruments make direct reference to others, some clearly borrow from others, some are simply complementary. Yet there is no proper coordination between them, as there is no one 'systematically pulling the strings together'.[8]

Second, the book focuses on the role of the international, transnational, and intergovernmental 'organizations engaged in elaborating legislative instruments and other texts aimed at the modernization and harmonization of private and commercial law'.[9] It introduces the reader to an array of such institutions, variously referred to as 'law-formulating organization[s]',[10] 'harmonizing agencies',[11] and 'formulating agencies',[12] most importantly the Hague Conference on Private International Law (the 'Hague Conference'), the International Institute for the Unification of Private Law ('UNIDROIT'), and the United

---

[5] Roy Goode, Herbert Kronke, and Ewan McKendrick, *Transnational Commercial Law: Text, Cases and Materials* (OUP 2007)(now 2nd edn, OUP 2015, sadly, no longer blue) (hereafter Goode, Kronke, and McKendrick, *Transnational Commercial Law*); all references below are to the second edition.

[6] Roy Goode, Herbert Kronke, Ewan McKendrick, and Jeffrey Wool, *Transnational Commercial Law: Primary Materials* (OUP 2007) (now 2nd edn, OUP 2012) (hereafter Goode, Kronke, McKendrick, and Wool, *Primary Materials*).

[7] Goode, Kronke, and McKendrick, *Transnational Commercial Law* (n 5) 166–70.

[8] ibid 170–71.

[9] ibid 174.

[10] ibid 171.

[11] ibid 192, 203, 210.

[12] ibid 178.

Nations Commission on International Trade Law ('UNCITRAL').[13] Because of their overlapping spheres of interest, these main producers of transnational commercial law are structural competitors. Although there is a desire to avoid turf wars, according to the authors, two or more agencies frequently 'occupy the same field but through different kinds of instrument', or 'different agencies may address different facets of a particular activity'.[14] As a result, they argue, 'it is clear that coordination of these activities must be a matter to which the greatest priority is given'.[15]

It is the purpose of this contribution to analyse a recent effort to achieve precisely this end. This is the *Legal Guide to Uniform Instruments in the Area of International Commercial Contracts, with a Focus on Sales*, published by the three above-mentioned formulating agencies in 2021.[16] Because of its long and somewhat unwieldy title, and with a nod to the joint authorship of the three agencies, it is often simply referred to as 'the *Tripartite Guide*'. I am particularly interested in the question whether it has any legal effect. However, in order to provide an answer it is important first to describe the background, the drafting history, and the content of the document.

II. Background

The origins of the *Tripartite Guide* may be traced back to the Secretariat of UNCITRAL, the agency that prepared the adoption of the United Nations Convention on Contracts for the International Sale of Goods (the 'CISG') in 1980.[17] In the context of the thirty-fifth anniversary of the Convention, the Secretariat assessed its actual application in practice.[18] On the one hand, there were recent developments that had the potential of increasing the use of the Convention in international contracting. The Hague Conference had just approved its Principles on Choice of Law in International Commercial Contracts (the 'Hague Principles').[19] Their Article 3 encouraged States to abolish traditional restrictions with regard to choices of law in international commercial contracts. Domestic courts should be required to acknowledge party choices of 'rules of law' emanating from non-State sources, as long as these were 'generally accepted on an international, supranational or regional level as a neutral and balanced set of rules'. If States were to adopt this solution, an important barrier to the use of instruments such as the CISG would be removed: national courts would have to apply the Convention whenever the parties had designated it as governing their contract, including in such situations where it would not otherwise apply according to its own terms.[20]

On the other hand, it was no secret, in 2015, that not many States were keen on introducing such a rule. The European Union ('EU') had rejected a similar proposal a few

---

[13] ibid 171–77, 192–93.

[14] ibid 195–96.

[15] ibid 177.

[16] UNCITRAL, HCCH, and UNIDROIT, *Legal Guide to Uniform Instruments in the Area of International Commercial Contracts, with a Focus on Sales* (UNCITRAL 2021) (hereafter *Tripartite Guide*).

[17] Unless mentioned otherwise, all legal instruments mentioned in this contribution are reprinted in the second edition of Goode, Kronke, McKendrick, and Wool, *Primary Materials* (n 6).

[18] UNCITRAL Secretariat, Note by the Secretariat on 'Current trends in the field of international sale of goods law', 23 April 2015, UN Doc A/CN.9/849 (hereafter UNCITRAL, 'Current trends').

[19] HCCH, Principles on Choice of Law in International Commercial Contracts (HCCH 2015).

[20] ibid Commentary 3.5.

286 THE 'TRIPARTITE GUIDE'

years earlier.[21] The private international laws in other parts of the world were similarly restrictive.[22] Moreover, there were increasing doubts whether the CISG was still fit for purpose in the light of recent developments in trade and technology. It had not been revised since its adoption in 1980. Meanwhile, the field of international commercial contract law had become crowded with competing instruments and drafts. These included the first three editions of the UNIDROIT Principles of International Commercial Contracts (the 'PICC') at the global level, as well as the Uniform Act Relating to General Commercial Law of the Organization for the Harmonization of Commercial Law in Africa ('OHADA')[23] and a draft Regulation of the EU for a Common European Sales Law ('CESL') at the regional level. A 2012 proposal by the Swiss government for UNCITRAL to embark on a major new codification of international commercial contract law[24] had fallen flat in the face of strong resistance from some of the Contracting States, notably the USA.[25] The State Department had forcefully argued that, for the time being, no further legislative work in the field was necessary, desirable, or feasible.[26]

III. Preparatory Work

In this environment, the Secretariat of UNCITRAL looked for a way forward.[27] In a note summarizing recent developments, it highlighted the decreasing rate at which national legislators adopted the CISG and the persistently widespread practice of contractual parties opting out of the instrument.[28] It also acknowledged the difficulties resulting from the abundance of various texts in the field. Problems existed even with regard to different United Nations Conventions prepared by UNCITRAL. It was, for example, not clear to what extent a provision in the Convention on the Limitation Period in the International Sale of Goods (the 'Limitation Convention') could be employed as a general principle underlying the CISG for the purpose of supplementing the latter. There were similar 'challenges' concerning the use of the PICC when interpreting the CISG.[29] The Secretariat presented a variety of possible reactions, ranging from complete inaction to full-scale codification of international commercial law. More realistic solutions included 'the preparation of a text

---

[21] cf Art 3(2) of the Proposal for a Regulation of the European Parliament and the Council on the law applicable to contractual obligations (Rome I), COM/2005/0650 final, and Art 3 of the Regulation (EC) 593/2008 of the European Parliament and of the Council of 17 June 2008 on the law applicable to contractual obligations (Rome I) [2008] OJ L177/6.

[22] For a comprehensive overview, see Ralf Michaels, 'Preamble I' in Vogenauer, *Commentary* (n 3) paras 58–77 (hereafter Michaels, 'Preamble I'). More recently, see Organization of American States, *Guide on the Law Applicable to International Commercial Contracts in the Americas*, 21 February 2019, OAS/Ser. Q, CJI/RES. 249 (XCIV-O/19) paras 197–202.

[23] Available at <https://www.droit-afrique.com/uploads/OHADA-Uniform-Act-1997-commercial-law.pdf>.

[24] UNCITRAL Secretariat, Note by the Secretariat on 'Possible future work in the area of international contract law: Proposal by Switzerland on possible future work by UNCITRAL in the area of international contract law', 8 May 2012, UN Doc A/CN.9/758.

[25] UNCITRAL, Report of the UN Commission on International Trade Law, Forty-fifth Session (25 June–6 July 2012), UN Doc A/67/17, paras 127–132.

[26] Keith Loken, 'A New Global Initiative on Contract Law in UNCITRAL: Right Project, Right Forum?' (2013) 58 Vill L Rev 509.

[27] It appears that the initiative was taken by Mr Luca Castellani, a Legal Officer in the Secretariat: cf Representative of UNCITRAL, cited in UNIDROIT Governing Council, Report, UNIDROIT 2020—C.D. (99) B.21, November 2020, para 175 ('the initiator of the project').

[28] UNCITRAL, 'Current trends' (n 18) paras 9, 13–20.

[29] ibid paras 38 and 27 with n 26.

specifically aimed at providing guidance to legislators or at implementing, and possibly complementing, the CISG domestically' and 'additional promotional work . . . focusing on the use and application of the CISG, especially among practitioners and the judiciary'. Moreover, it was suggested 'to further highlight complementarity among various texts prepared by international organizations and to promote their adoption and use in a joint manner'.[30]

The response of the UNCITRAL annual plenary session was muted. When discussing the note of the Secretariat in the summer of 2015 it was suggested that even just amending the CISG would be 'untimely given that it remained to be demonstrated whether such work was useful or desirable'. There was, however, support for some promotional and capacity-building activities aimed at supporting the adoption and effective implementation of the Convention, but only 'within available resources'—and UNCITRAL was aware that it had no proper institutional framework in place to coordinate such efforts.[31]

Undeterred, the Secretariat reached out to the Permanent Bureau of the Hague Conference and the Secretariat of UNIDROIT before the end of the year. It suggested that the three formulating agencies should cooperate on a project for the 'creation of a roadmap to the existing texts in the area of international sales law (sales contracts) prepared by each organisation, primarily the CISG, the UNIDROIT Principles, and the Hague Principles, and providing an assessment of interactions between the texts, their actual and potential use, application, and impact, all with the goal to facilitate promotion of their appropriate use, uniform interpretation, and adoption'.[32] Discussions between the Secretariats about 'cooperating in preparing an explanatory text' led to a 'Joint Proposal' which each of them submitted to their respective governing bodies.[33]

The Joint Proposal[34] pointed out that the three formulating agencies had published or adopted a raft of uniform law texts in the field. It singled out the Hague Principles, the PICC, and a number of international treaties prepared by UNCITRAL, notably the CISG, the Limitation Convention, and the Convention on the Use of Electronic Communications in International Contracts (the 'Electronic Communications Convention').[35] The Joint Proposal acknowledged the existence of a 'substantive overlap and cross-fertilization' between these texts. This might not be a problem as such. However, there was 'insufficient awareness' of the relationship between them. This led to 'challenges' in their use, application, and interpretation. Therefore, it was suggested that 'a joint effort aimed at providing guidance on how those texts relate would be beneficial for all texts concerned'.[36] This should take the form of an 'explanatory text' outlining the coverage and basic themes of each of

---

[30] ibid paras 34, 20, 46.

[31] UNCITRAL, Report, Official Records of the General Assembly, Seventieth Session (29 June to 16 July 2015), UN Doc A/70/17, paras 333–34.

[32] UNCITRAL Secretariat, Communication of 14 December 2015, cited in UNIDROIT Secretariat, Memorandum concerning Item No 13 on the agenda: Draft Triennial Work Programme 2017–2019, April 2016, UNIDROIT 2016—C.D. (95) 13 rev, para 71.

[33] UNCITRAL Secretariat, Note by the Secretariat on a 'Joint proposal on cooperation in the area of international commercial contract law (with a focus on sales)', 24 May 2016, UN Doc A/CN.9/892, paras 4–5.

[34] UNCITRAL Secretariat, 'Joint proposal on cooperation in the area of international commercial contract law (with a focus on sales)', annexed to Note by the Secretariat (n 33) 3–5; also reproduced in UNIDROIT Secretariat, Memorandum (n 32) Annex 5 (34–36).

[35] UNCITRAL Secretariat, 'Joint proposal' (n 34) 3–4. Further instruments are mentioned in n 9 of the document.

[36] ibid 3–4 (with regard to the 'challenges', explicit reference is only made to the CISG).

288 THE 'TRIPARTITE GUIDE'

these instruments and illustrating how they interact, perhaps akin to a joint document published by the three organizations on their respective instruments on security interests in 2012.[37]

Greater clarification on the relationship between the instruments would not only further their application and uniform interpretation in particular disputes. It would also encourage legal actors to adopt and use them in the first place, given that they are all of an optional nature and require a decision of legislators to incorporate them into their national laws, or a choice of judges, arbitrators, counsel, and commercial operators to opt into or out of their application in a given scenario. The document would therefore provide these actors with 'coordinated presentation and guidance as to the content and consequences' of the options available. It would guide them 'across a range of relevant issues, from choice of law to identification, among existing texts, of those most suitable for each type of transaction'.[38] Importantly, the project 'would not require new legislative work'. It would only contribute to 'establishing clarity in the field by taking stock'. It would 'analyse existing texts, coordinate them by highlighting mutual relationships and consolidate them'.[39]

As to the process of drafting such a guide, the Joint Proposal recommended that 'a significant amount of the preparatory work' should be done by a small joint panel of experts who would represent 'different legal traditions and levels of economic development'. They were expected to provide further detail on the scope and methodology of the guide, map and arrange the relevant texts, provide a short description of their content and relevance, and finally assess their interaction. However, the Secretariats of the three formulating agencies would retain oversight of the work and provide guidance and coordination throughout. The panel of experts would make recommendations, but the final text of the guide would be determined by the three agencies.[40]

The Joint Proposal was endorsed by the other two Secretariats and approved by the governing bodies of all three organizations during 2016.[41] The decision was facilitated by a number of features: the document would have a 'non-legislative', and thus no normative, character,[42] its adoption would not be too protracted because it would not require the direct involvement of national governments,[43] and, by outsourcing much of the

---

[37] ibid 3, referring to the text discussed at n 133.
[38] ibid 4.
[39] ibid 4–5.
[40] ibid 5.
[41] HCCH Council on General Affairs and Policy, Conclusions and Recommendations of the Conference of March 2016, para 23; UNIDROIT Governing Council, Report, UNIDROIT 2016—C.D. (95) 15, June 2016, para 309 ('high priority'); UNCITRAL, Report, Official Records of the General Assembly, Seventy-first Session (27 June to 15 July 2016), UN Doc A/71/17, para 281; UNIDROIT General Assembly, Report, UNIDROIT 2016—A.G. (75) 8, December 2016, paras 33, 44.
[42] UNIDROIT General Assembly, Report 2016 (n 41) para 33: 'the project would not produce a new normative instrument but would prepare further guidance on the existing documents'; UNIDROIT Secretariat, Item No 9 on the agenda: Preparation of a guidance document, UNIDROIT 2017—C.D. (96) 8, April 2017, para 5: 'The Legal Guide would not be of normative character and would refrain from interpreting relevant rules'; it would rather 'provide basic information on existing instruments'; Interim Secretary General of UNIDROIT, quoted in UNIDROIT Governing Council, Report, UNIDROIT 2018—C.D. (97) 19, June 2018, para 160: 'a non-legislative text that would illustrate the relations between the instruments while leaving aside issues of interpretation'.
[43] Secretary General of UNIDROIT, quoted in UNIDROIT Governing Council, Report 2016 (n 41) para 276: 'a project between the three Secretariats which would not require any intergovernmental meetings'; Secretary General of UNIDROIT, quoted in UNIDROIT Governing Council, Report, UNIDROIT 2017—C.D. (96) 15, June 2017, para 111: it would not have to be 'developed through a formal intergovernmental mechanism, but could be completed through cooperation between the three Secretariats and a small group of international experts'.

preparatory work to the panel of experts, the costs for the formulating agencies would be 'minimal'.[44]

By spring 2017, the Secretariats had held further discussions, selected experts, agreed more precisely on the issues to be covered, and produced a provisional table of contents of the text. The first draft of each Section would be the responsibility of the formulating agency with the closest relationship to the relevant subject matter. A consolidated draft would then be revised and finalized by the three Secretariats, followed by formal approval by the governing bodies of the organizations.[45] In the event, each Section was assigned to an expert or a sub-group of experts.[46]

The panel of experts consisted of five legal scholars: Neil B Cohen (USA), Lauro Gama Jr (Brazil), Pilar Perales Viscasillas (Spain), Hiroo Sono (Japan), and Stefan Vogenauer (Germany). They were appointed not only for their specific expertise on one or more of the relevant instruments, but also with a view to representing different legal traditions and geographic regions.[47] However, it was made clear from the start that their contribution would be in a personal capacity.[48] The experts first met in July 2017, together with representatives of the three Secretariats: Luca Castellani (UNCITRAL), Anna Veneziano (UNIDROIT), and Ning Zhao (HCCH).[49] The representatives coordinated all the meetings. The representative of UNCITRAL normally tabled an agenda, yet discussions unfolded in a collegial and informal atmosphere. Only two meetings were held in person; otherwise the panel worked via email exchanges and videoconferences.[50] Feedback on interim results was sought at the Annual Conference of the International Bar Association ('IBA') in October 2018.[51] A first, non-consolidated draft was produced in February 2019 and continuously revised until October of the same year. At that stage, the Secretariats agreed upon the text of the introductory Chapters I and II of the document, as well as on Chapter III which covers questions of private international law. Chapters IV and V, dealing with the substantive law of international commercial contracts, were still work in progress.[52]

---

[44] HCCH Council on General Affairs and Policy, Conclusions 2016 (n 41) para 23; cf UNIDROIT Governing Council, Report 2016 (n 41) para 306: 'low or no cost projec[t]'. This remained a recurring theme, cf UNIDROIT Governing Council, Report 2017 (n 43) para 112: 'keep the budget as low as possible'; Deputy Secretary General of UNIDROIT, quoted in UNIDROIT Governing Council, Report, UNIDROIT 2019—C.D. (98) 17, June 2019, para 131: 'no funding was allocated to the project'; HCCH Permanent Bureau, Prel. Doc. 16 of January 2020, prepared for the Council of General Affairs and Policy, para 6.

[45] UNIDROIT Secretariat, Item No 9 (n 42) paras 4–8, with 'Draft Outline' in the Annex, 4-5.

[46] UNIDROIT Secretariat, Item No 5 on the agenda: Adoption of the Work Programme, UNIDROIT 2019—A.G. (78) 3, November 2019, para 48.

[47] HCCH Permanent Bureau, Preliminary Document No 6 of December 2017, prepared for the Council of General Affairs and Policy, para 6; UNIDROIT Secretariat, Item No 10 on the agenda: International Sales Law, UNIDROIT 2018—C.D. (97) 10, February 2018, para 3.

[48] UNIDROIT Secretariat, Item No 9 (n 42) para 6.

[49] UNIDROIT Secretariat, Item No 10 (n 47) para 4.

[50] UNIDROIT Secretariat, Item No 8 on the agenda: International Sales Law, UNIDROIT 2019—C.D. (98) 8, March 2019, para 1.

[51] HCCH Permanent Bureau, Prel. Doc. 16 of January 2020 (n 44) para 5.

[52] UNIDROIT Secretariat, Item No 3 on the agenda: International Sales Law, UNIDROIT 2020—C.D. (99) A.5, April 2020, para 6.

IV. Institutional Approval and Publication

Finalizing the document was complicated by the fact that each of the three formulating agencies has its own consultation and approval mechanisms. As a result, there was no streamlined and single procedure for securing feedback from the respective Member States and governing bodies, nor was it possible to take a joint and simultaneous vote on the final draft. The exact manner of proceeding had thus been uncertain right from the start.[53] However, in light of 'the complexities inherent in the nature of multi-partite approval processes for joint projects', the agencies ultimately came up with a pragmatic 'tripartite approval process'.[54]

As a first step, the draft of October 2019 was shared with the HCCH membership, whose feedback was sought on the first three chapters, that is, those parts that concerned HCCH instruments and issues of private international law more broadly.[55] The advice received was incorporated in a consolidated draft of January 2020.[56] This document also contained the final draft of Chapters IV and V, as agreed by the Secretariats. It was made available to the governing bodies of the three agencies.[57] In March of the same year, the first three chapters of the consolidated draft were approved at the annual meeting of the Council on General Affairs and Policy of the Hague Conference, which was attended by sixty-eight of the HCCH Member States.[58] Meanwhile, the Secretariats of UNIDROIT and UNCITRAL had also canvassed, received, and implemented feedback from their respective stakeholders.[59] On this basis, the Governing Council of UNIDROIT unanimously approved the full final draft in May 2020, 'subject to such minor adjustments' as might be introduced at the subsequent annual plenary session of UNCITRAL.[60]

At this session, held in July, UNCITRAL considered both the draft and a note by its Secretariat that proposed twenty further 'adjustments' in the light of suggestions it had received.[61] It appears that most of these were based on 'last minute comments sent by the CISG Advisory Council',[62] a private and independent body of self-appointed experts with observer status at UNCITRAL meetings.[63] All the amendments had been agreed between the three Secretariats prior to the session.[64] One of them had even been proposed by the

---

[53] Secretary General of UNIDROIT, quoted in UNIDROIT Governing Council, Report 2017 (n 43) para 121.

[54] HCCH Permanent Bureau, Prel. Doc. 16 of January 2020 (n 44) paras 1, 8.

[55] ibid paras 2, 7.

[56] ibid para 7 (the draft is reproduced in the Annex).

[57] UNCITRAL Secretariat, Note by the Secretariat on the 'Legal Guide to Uniform Instruments in the Area of International Commercial Contracts (with a focus on sales)', 3 January 2020, UN Doc A/CN.9/1029; HCCH Permanent Bureau, Prel. Doc. 16 of January 2020 (n 44) para 7 and Annex; UNIDROIT Secretariat, Item No 3 (n 52) paras 6–7 and Annex I.

[58] HCCH Council on General Affairs and Policy, Conclusions and Decisions of the Conference of March 2020, paras 1, 42.

[59] UNIDROIT Secretariat, Item No 3 (n 52) para 9, with Comments in Annex 2.

[60] UNIDROIT Governing Council, Report, UNIDROIT 2020—C.D. (99) A.8, June 2020, paras 62, 68.

[61] UNCITRAL Secretariat, Note by the Secretariat on 'Adjustments to the draft Legal Guide to Uniform Instruments in the Area of International Commercial Contracts (with a focus on sales), as contained in document A/CN.9/1029', 10 June 2020, UN Doc A/CN.9/1030, para 4, merely adding a recently adopted HCCH Convention in n 37 of the *Guide*.

[62] Representative of UNCITRAL, cited in UNIDROIT Governing Council, Report November 2020 (n 27) para 175. See also Deputy Secretary-General of UNIDROIT, cited ibid para 173; UNIDROIT Secretariat, Item No 9 on the agenda: International Sales Law, UNIDROIT 2020—C.D. (99) B.11, August 2020, para 2.

[63] cf <https://cisgac.com/>.

[64] UNIDROIT Secretariat, Item No 9 (n 62) para 2; Deputy Secretary-General of UNIDROIT, cited in UNIDROIT Governing Council, Report November 2020 (n 27) para 173.

Secretariat of UNIDROIT after the approval given by its Governing Council in May.[65] With the exception of a very minor addition to Chapter III,[66] the amendments all concerned Chapter IV of the *Guide*.[67] Some of them were mere formal corrections, while others were of a more substantial nature.[68] UNCITRAL approved the text with all the twenty proposed adjustments for publication.[69] The Governing Council of UNIDROIT authorized the publication of the revised text of the instrument at its next meeting in September 2020.[70] The Hague Conference did not take a further formal decision, but it has consistently treated the document as approved.[71]

Overall, therefore, the process within all three agencies met their respective requirements for the approval of legislative instruments which do not amount to international treaties.[72] The English-language version of the *Guide* was published in April 2021. In the course of the same year, the text was also made available in the other five official languages of the United Nations, that is, Arabic, Chinese, French, Russian, and Spanish.[73] All versions are freely available online.[74] Since at least 2018, work on the text had been 'commonly referred' to as the 'tripartite project'.[75] From April 2019 onwards, UNIDROIT began to use the designations 'Tripartite Legal Guide' and 'Tripartite Guide' in its official papers,[76] and the term can also be found in the documents of the Hague Conference.[77]

V. Content

In its final and approved version, the *Tripartite Guide* has five chapters, spread across roughly 100 pages.[78] Chapters I and II contain a brief introduction, summarizing the origin and the purposes of the document and introducing the instruments covered (pp 1–8). Chapter III is dedicated to issues of private international law (pp 9–25). It explains how the

---

[65] UNCITRAL Secretariat, Note on 'Adjustments' (n 61) para 24, based on the Communication of UNIDROIT of 11 June 2020, ibid 34, 38 (insertion of a reference to the ICC Force Majeure and Hardship Clauses 2020).

[66] See n 61.

[67] UNCITRAL Secretariat, Note on 'Adjustments' (n 61) paras 5–24.

[68] See text at nn 128–30.

[69] UNCITRAL, Agenda item 3: Approval for publication of a joint UNCITRAL–UNIDROIT–The Hague Conference guide on commercial contract law, 6 July 2020, UN Doc A/CN.9/LIII/CRP.4.

[70] UNIDROIT Governing Council, Report November 2020 (n 27) para 183.

[71] HCCH Permanent Bureau, Overview of Conventions and other instruments drawn up under the auspices of UNCITRAL, UNIDROIT and the HCCH, Info. Doc. No 1 of February 2021, D.11 (p 4) and Info. Doc. No 1 of January 2023, D.13 (p 4). See also HCCH, *Annual Report 2020* (HCCH 2021) 20; HCCH, *Annual Report 2021* (HCCH 2022) 29.

[72] UNCITRAL, *A Guide to UNCITRAL: Basic Facts about the United Nations Commission on International Trade Law* (UNCITRAL 2013) paras 47–49; Arts 11–14 of the UNIDROIT Statute, as amended on 26 March 1993, see also the information under the heading 'Intergovernmental negotiation stage', available at <https://www.unidroit.org/about-unidroit/overview/>; Art 4 of the Statute of the HCCH, as amended on 30 September 2006.

[73] See, eg, Commission des Nations Unies pour le droit commercial international, Conférence de La Haye pour le droit international privé, L'Institut International pour l'unification du droit privé (eds), *Guide juridique de la CNUDCI, la HCCH et Unidroit sur les instruments de droit uniforme relatifs aux contrats du commerce international (notamment de vente)* (UNCITRAL 2021).

[74] For the English version, see <https://uncitral.un.org/sites/uncitral.un.org/files/media-documents/uncitral/en/tripartiteguide.pdf>.

[75] Interim Secretary General of UNIDROIT, quoted in UNIDROIT Governing Council, Report 2018 (n 42) para 158.

[76] UNIDROIT Secretariat, Item No 3 (n 52) 'Action to be taken' and para 11.

[77] See the 'Overviews' of the HCCH Permanent Bureau cited in n 71.

[78] Page references below are to the English language version.

law applicable to international commercial contracts is determined, either by party choice or in the absence of it. While the Hague Principles are given prominent treatment, information is also provided on national regimes of private international law, which are, in turn, sometimes based on international and supranational sets of rules. Chapters IV and V deal with the substantive law of international commercial contracts.

Chapter IV, by far the longest of the chapters, provides relatively detailed coverage of the three most important instruments in the field, that is, the CISG (pp 27–64), the Limitation Convention (pp 64–71), and the PICC (pp 72–88). This is followed by very short surveys of further international instruments (the Uniform Rules on Contract Clauses for an Agreed Sum Due upon Failure of Performance, published by UNCITRAL in 1983, and the OHADA Uniform Act Relating to General Commercial Law) and various model contracts and drafting guides published by non-State actors, such as the International Chamber of Commerce, the International Trade Centre, and the International Bar Association (pp 88–92). Chapter V provides an overview of some recurring legal issues arising in connection with sales contracts. These include the relevant international instruments dealing with types of contract other than sales (agency, barter, and distribution), as well as questions concerning software, data, intellectual property, and the use of electronic means in contracting more generally (pp 93–100). An annex lists the most important materials, reference works, and websites in the field (pp 100–07).

The style of the *Tripartite Guide* resembles that of a basic and extremely concise textbook. The discussion of the various topics is far from exhaustive.[79] It is clearly designed to provide an accessible entry point for potential users with limited experience in international contracting. The text is discursive and accompanied by footnotes. Most of these are simple references to certain uniform law instruments or some of their specific provisions; very few point to further literature;[80] some convey substantive information.[81] Extensive cross-references in the main text and in the footnotes connect the different parts of the *Guide* and contribute to the textbook-like appearance. So do the many subheadings, many of which are framed as questions of the type that non-expert readers might ask ('What are the obligations of the buyer?', 'How would judges and arbitrators apply a clause designating the [PICC] as the applicable law of the contract?', and so on).[82] Importantly, the document does not set forth any rules. It rather provides an overview of the existing provisions of the relevant instruments and explores how they apply. To this extent, it certainly differs from most other publications of the three formulating agencies.

While the focus of the *Tripartite Guide* is on sales, many of the issues covered are equally relevant to other types of contract. The discussion of private international law questions in Chapter III, for example, applies to all international commercial contracts, as does the analysis of the PICC in Chapter IV. Chapter V specifically addresses types of contract other than sales. As a result, the *Tripartite Guide* provides a broad overview of the law of international commercial contracting in general. At the same time, it gives appropriate weight to the most paradigmatic type of contract and the most important conventions on sales by dedicating nearly half the text to a discussion of the CISG and the Limitation Convention.

---

[79] As is acknowledged in *Tripartite Guide* (n 16) paras 12, 18.
[80] For the latter, see ibid para 49 n 33.
[81] ibid nn 19, 38, 39, 43, 52, 72, 75, 80.
[82] ibid paras 236, 343.

CONTENT 293

Yet even these Sections differ from the conventional treatment of the two Conventions to the extent that they consistently highlight the interactions between them, as well as the interfaces with other international texts in the field. Neither Convention is presented exclusively 'on its own terms'. The same holds true for the Section on the PICC. There are, of course, certain passages which exclusively focus on matters relevant to one of the three instruments. These include the accounts of their respective scopes of application and a fully self-contained overview of the content of the PICC.[83] Similarly, the passages dealing with the solutions of the CISG on the determination of the place of business and on the seller's obligation regarding the time of delivery and the conformity of the goods[84] could be straight from an introductory textbook to the Convention.

Most of the discussion, however, is concerned with situating the individual instruments in the broader context of international commercial contract law. Very little attention is paid to how they relate to domestic laws.[85] Rather, it is stressed that, frequently, more than one instrument can apply to the same transaction. An international contract for the sale of goods that is concluded by electronic communications, for example, may engage the CISG, the PICC, the Hague Principles, the Limitation Convention, and the Electronic Communications Convention.[86] The *Guide* also explores potential overlaps between the CISG and other uniform instruments, such as the 1964 Hague Uniform Laws on International Sales of Goods, the UNCITRAL Model Law on International Credit Transfers of 1992, the EU Directive on payment services, the Geneva Conventions for Bills of Exchange and Promissory Notes and for Cheques, and the Uniform Rules on Contract Clauses for an Agreed Sum Due upon Failure of Performance.[87] The relationship between the CISG and international conventions concerning the international carriage of goods is discussed at length,[88] as is its interplay with the International Chamber of Commerce's Incoterms 2020[89] and its potential interactions with the Hague Principles and the PICC.[90]

It is the latter aspect that is dealt with most extensively. The *Guide*'s discussion of the CISG frequently involves comparisons to the treatment of similar topics in the PICC. Sometimes these are confined to stating that specific rules, such as the provisions on the passing of risk, have no equivalent in the PICC.[91] More often, it is pointed out that the PICC contain similar or broadly similar solutions (for example, on force majeure, contractual interpretation, requirements as to form, the seller's right to cure and his obligation to bear the cost of delivery, the relevance of contractual practices and usages, and the requirements for fundamental breach[92]), even if different terminologies are used, as in the case of 'avoidance' and 'termination'.[93]

---

[83] ibid paras 27–33, 106–26, 290–93, 354–57 (scopes of application), paras 358–91 (content of the PICC).

[84] ibid paras 148–50, 192–201.

[85] There are very few references to the interpretation of the CISG by national courts (*Tripartite Guide* (n 16) para 149 n 50, para 150 n 51, para 172 n 53, para 279 n 70) and to domestic legislation (ibid para 147 n 48), most importantly in the area of private international law (ibid para 47 n 31, para 350; see also text following n 78 above).

[86] *Tripartite Guide* (n 16) para 22, with helpful visualization in Table 1; cf ibid para 16: 'emphasis on the complementary nature of these instruments when more than one instrument applies to a transaction.'

[87] ibid paras 242–43, 276, 286.

[88] ibid paras 179–84.

[89] ibid paras 143–47, 176, 180–89, 191, 226.

[90] ibid paras 45–47, 71, 124–25.

[91] ibid para 228.

[92] ibid paras 137 (interpretation), 139 (practices and usages), 155 (form), 190 (cost of delivery), 204 (cure), 264 n 66 (fundamental breach), 277 n 68 (force majeure).

[93] ibid para 264.

Moreover, the *Tripartite Guide* comprehensively highlights issues on which the CISG is silent, while the PICC set forth specific rules, most obviously on validity, hardship, and standard terms.[94] In a similar vein, the passage on the obligation of the buyer to pay the price under the CISG refers to the PICC rules on the risk of adverse currency and monetary control measures; the determination of the price by one party, a third person, or with reference to external factors; the choice of the currency of payment; methods of payment; and the cost of payment.[95] The sub-Section on remedies points out that the rules of the CISG have 'strongly influenced' the respective articles of the PICC, but that the latter 'contain a number of additional provisions covering issues not expressly settled by the CISG'.[96] These include more detailed rules on specific performance, on the interest rate applying to damages, and on specific types of clause (penalty, liquidated damages, limitation, and exclusion clauses).[97] Not least with regard to such clauses, the *Guide* points out that the PICC contain 'a number of provisions that are designed to protect parties with less experience and inferior bargaining power', and that rules 'of this kind are notably absent from the CISG'.[98]

The Section on the Limitation Convention is even more systematic in providing 'a brief comparison' of the substantive rules of the Convention with those on limitation periods in Chapter 10 of the PICC.[99] It also has a specific sub-Section on the interaction of the Convention with other uniform law instruments.[100] A similar sub-Section concludes the Section on the PICC. It includes a comparative overview of the coverage of the PICC on the one hand and the CISG and (to a lesser extent) the Limitation Convention on the other.[101] In a similar vein, the passages on other international instruments show how these are similar to, differ from, or overlap with the corresponding rules in the CISG, the PICC, and, where applicable, the Limitation Convention.[102]

VI. Legal Effect

From what has been said in the previous section of this contribution, it should have become obvious that the *Tripartite Guide* is an important and welcome addition to the legal literature on international commercial contract law. While it cannot rival the existing specialist textbooks and commentaries on the relevant instruments, nor survey the entire ground covered in the much broader overview of Goode, Kronke, and McKendrick's *Transnational Commercial Law*,[103] it provides the most concise, holistic, and up-to-date overview of the transnational law of contract available. What is less clear, though, is whether the text also has any legal relevance.

---

[94] ibid paras 120 n 43 (validity), 157–73 (standard terms; with references to the PICC in paras 157 (n 52), 171, and 172), and 277 (hardship).

[95] ibid paras 237–48; with references to the PICC in paras 237, 238, 240, 241, 245.

[96] ibid para 263.

[97] ibid paras 266, 276, 278, 279.

[98] ibid para 391.

[99] ibid paras 294–312; the quote is in para 289.

[100] ibid paras 315–21.

[101] ibid paras 392–99.

[102] ibid paras 400–05 (Uniform Rules on Contract Clauses for an Agreed Sum), 406–09 (OHADA Uniform Act Relating to General Commercial Law), 410–14 (ICC Model Contracts), 425–30 (Electronic Communications Convention), 437–42 (international conventions on agency).

[103] Goode, Kronke, and McKendrick, *Transnational Commercial Law* (n 5).

At first sight, the *Tripartite Guide* is not more than a purely explanatory document. This is underlined by its very title. In the specific nomenclature of UNCITRAL, the publication of a 'legal guide' is an 'explanatory technique' for achieving legal harmonization.[104] The notion of 'guide' invokes the genres of self-help books, DIY manuals, and travel literature. The analogy of a travel guide is perhaps not entirely inappropriate. Right at its outset, the *Guide* purports simply to give an 'overview of ... the area', 'information', and a 'summary'.[105] It aims to 'provid[e] orientation'[106] in what will be uncharted territory for many of its readers and 'assist ... in navigating' and 'understanding'[107] this complex environment. The exercise is thus, prima facie, descriptive, not normative. The *Tripartite Guide* does not set forth new rules that might be applied to a given commercial transaction. It does not even intend, as is explicitly said early on, 'to favour any particular interpretation, or to offer any new interpretation of uniform texts'.[108] As has been seen above, these statements are in line with what the three formulating agencies emphasized throughout the drafting process, that is, that no new law should be brought into existence.[109]

Yet it would be rash to conclude that the text is devoid of any legal effect. As has been seen above, and as is emphasized in the *Tripartite Guide* itself, the document was jointly authored, examined, amended, voted on, approved, and officially published by the three leading international formulating agencies in the area of international uniform law.[110] One of these is an organ of the United Nations, composed of seventy Member States elected by the General Assembly; the others are independent intergovernmental organizations with sixty-three and ninety Member States, respectively.[111] To the extent that each of these agencies is a 'body having political or administrative power and control in a particular sphere',[112] a more old-fashioned designation would be that they are 'authorities' (such as, for example, the 'High Authority of the European Coal and Steel Community', the predecessor of today's European Commission). As such, their formal communications and publications also have a degree of 'authority', even if they do not amount to a formal act of law-making.

Historically, many legal texts attained 'authoritative' status because of their intrinsic quality and the particular personal or institutional 'authority' of their authors. Examples range from the Accursian gloss to Littleton's *Treatise on Tenures* and Blackstone's *Commentaries on the Laws of England*. The contemporary debate, particularly in the transnational context, centres mostly on the authority of 'soft law' instruments, such as the PICC and comparable European projects.[113] Most importantly, authority must not be confused with bindingness. This is well known from national doctrines of precedent. In civil law systems, for example, judicial decisions of higher courts are not normally binding on the

[104] UNCITRAL, *A Guide to UNCITRAL* (n 72) paras 32, 51–53.
[105] *Tripartite Guide* (n 16) vii (Executive Summary); cf ibid para 16: the 'purpose of the Guide is to provide an introduction to, and a brief summary of, several important legal instruments'.
[106] ibid para 7.
[107] ibid paras 17, 18.
[108] ibid para 7.
[109] See text at nn 31, 39, 42.
[110] See text at nn 53–72; *Tripartite Guide* (n 16) paras 8, 11.
[111] cf the information provided by the agencies at <https://uncitral.un.org/en/about/faq/mandate_composit ion>, <https://www.unidroit.org/about-unidroit/members-states-2/>, and <https://www.hcch.net/en/states/ hcch-members>.
[112] Oxford English Dictionary Online, v° authority, no I.4, <https://www.oed.com>.
[113] See, eg, Nils Jansen, *The Making of Legal Authority: Non-legislative Codifications in Historical and Comparative Perspective* (OUP 2010); Roger Cotterrell and Maksymilian Del Mar (eds), *Authority in Transnational Legal Theory: Theorising across Disciplines* (Edward Elgar 2016).

296   THE 'TRIPARTITE GUIDE'

lower courts, yet they enjoy strong persuasive authority.[114] The same is true for the value of judgments of the House of Lords in English appeals when relied upon in Scottish courts or for decisions of the Judicial Committee of the Privy Council in the courts of England and Wales.[115]

In the complex environment of international commercial contract law, there is a wide variety of potentially authoritative texts. These include both personal and institutional contributions. The former are textbooks and commentaries that are highly regarded because of the reputation of their authors and editors.[116] The latter can be placed on a continuous scale of institutional texts, ranging from clearly authoritative ones, such as the CISG and other binding multilateral treaties, to clearly non-authoritative ones, such as the account of library activities in the Annual Report of UNIDROIT.[117] Non-binding sets of 'Principles', such as the PICC and the Hague Principles, and model contract clauses, such as the ICC Incoterms, might be placed more towards the first end. Opinions by private initiatives, such as the CISG Advisory Council, would be found close to the other end; national court decisions on the interpretation of the CISG would be somewhere in between. All of these texts have some degree of persuasive authority, some stronger, some weaker—although none of them is 'binding' as such.

However, they are legally relevant because, to borrow a phrase from Robert Alexy, they shift the 'burden of argumentation': while it is possible to refute an argument based on persuasive authority in a given legal dispute, it requires particularly strong and, 'weightier' counter-arguments to do so.[118] Now, the *Tripartite Guide*, despite all its efforts to stay neutral and avoid any new interpretations of the law of international commercial contracts, cannot steer clear of making certain assumptions about the current law. UNCITRAL defines a 'legal guide' as 'a text that provides guidance for the drafting of contracts, discussing relevant issues and recommending solutions appropriate to particular circumstances'.[119] The very idea of 'providing guidance' and 'recommending solutions' involves a steer towards a particular result over other possible outcomes. It would, for instance, be hard to argue that contractual freedom is not a guiding principle of the relevant uniform law instruments, seeing the constant reminders in the *Guide* that these sets of rules are supposed to support freedom of contract.[120] While this might be a trivial example, the text makes other assumptions about individual points that are not particularly controversial but at least theoretically open to debate. It affirms, for example, that the choice of the law of a Contracting State does not normally constitute an opt-out from the CISG,[121] and it employs the definition of 'standard terms' in Article 2.1.19(2) of the PICC when discussing the use of standard terms in contracts governed by the CISG.[122]

---

[114] Stefan Vogenauer, 'Precedent, Rule of' in Jürgen Basedow, Klaus Hopt, and Reinhard Zimmermann (eds), *The Oxford Handbook on European Private Law* (OUP 2012) 1304, 1305.

[115] *Willers v Joyce* [2016] UKSC 44, [2018] AC 843.

[116] See, eg, Goode, Kronke, and McKendrick, *Transnational Commercial Law* (n 5); Ingeborg Schwenzer (ed), *Commentary on the UN Convention on the International Sale of Goods (CISG)* (4th edn, OUP 2016).

[117] See, eg, UNIDROIT, *Annual Report—2021* (UNIDROIT 2022) 41–42.

[118] Robert Alexy and Ralf Dreier, 'Precedent in the Federal Republic of Germany', in D Neil MacCormick and Robert S Summers (eds), *Interpreting Precedents: A Comparative Study* (Ashgate 1997) 17, 44.

[119] UNCITRAL, 'Facts about UNCITRAL' (UNCITRAL leaflet 2004, <https://uncitral.un.org/sites/uncitral.un.org/files/media-documents/uncitral/en/uncitral-leaflet-e.pdf>).

[120] cf, among others, *Tripartite Guide* (n 16) paras 6, 25, 40, 68.

[121] ibid para 29 (the Guide is, however, transparent, as to the fact that this view is only based on 'almost unanimous case law and scholarly opinion').

[122] ibid para 171.

Similarly, it is hard to maintain that the passages of the *Guide* on the interplay of the various instruments, on which these instruments themselves are silent, can be dismissed as legally irrelevant. After all, as has been seen above, the *Guide* puts specific emphasis on the 'complementary nature' of the texts[123] and particularly aims 'at clarifying the relationship among' them, and it does so 'with a view to promoting their . . . uniform interpretation and, ultimately, the establishment of a predictable and flexible legal environment for cross-border commercial transactions'.[124]

Perhaps the most pertinent question in this regard is whether the PICC may be used to interpret and supplement the CISG when the rules of the latter are ambiguous or do not provide a solution.[125] The *Guide* acknowledges that this is 'an open issue', but maintains that it is 'the common understanding' that the PICC 'are not, as such, considered to be the general principles of the CISG, but rather as being able to serve to corroborate the existence of a given general principle and, thus, they can be a tool to interpret the CISG (CISG, art. 7, para. 1) or to fill its gaps (CISG, art. 7, para. 2), whenever there is no conflict between the two instruments'.[126] At a later stage, it is said that recourse to the PICC in interpreting the CISG is 'generally accepted' under Article 7(1) of the CISG, and there is a relatively detailed explanation as to how and to what extent they may be used to fill gaps according to Article 7(2) of the Convention.[127] It is noteworthy that these passages received special attention during the drafting process. Their ultimate formulation goes back to the final amendments, mostly based on the 'last minute' intervention of the CISG Advisory Council, and was agreed between the three Secretariats before final approval was given by UNCITRAL in July 2020.[128] In the event, the passages from the previous draft were only slightly rewritten and left the general thrust of the earlier passages in place.[129] In one instance, the change even removed a potential counter-argument against the use of the PICC in filling gaps in the CISG.[130] It would, therefore, be difficult to say that the *Tripartite Guide* does not adopt a position on this contested doctrinal issue. As it reflects the current view of the three formulating agencies (most importantly the position of UNCITRAL, the agency behind the CISG) on the interplay of the CISG and the PICC as mediated by Article 7(2) of the CISG, it provides an authoritative interpretation on this particular question.

Overall, the authoritative approval of the text by the institutions ensures that the document enjoys much stronger authority than other texts in the field. A simple thought experiment may help to make the point. If the five experts involved in the drafting of, but ultimately not responsible for, the final text of the *Guide*[131] had written a textbook with identical content, it would be difficult to argue that their text has particularly authoritative status.

---

[123] ibid para 16 (see n 86).

[124] ibid para 6 (cf ibid para 11: 'to promote uniformity, certainty and clarity in this area of the law').

[125] For an overview of the discussion, see Michaels, 'Preamble I' (n 22) paras 120–36.

[126] *Tripartite Guide* (n 16) para 132.

[127] ibid paras 352, 353. See also ibid para 393.

[128] See text at nn 61–69.

[129] Compare paras 132 and 392 of UNCITRAL Secretariat, Note on the 'Legal Guide' (n 57) with *Tripartite Guide* (n 16) paras 132 (introduced by UNCITRAL Secretariat, Note on 'Adjustments' (n 61) para 7: removal of reference to good faith in Article 7(2) CISG) and 393 (introduced by UNCITRAL Secretariat, Note on 'Adjustments' (n 61) para 22: sentence on the relationship of the CISG and the PICC not affected by changes).

[130] Compare para 352 of UNCITRAL Secretariat, Note on the 'Legal Guide' (n 57) with *Tripartite Guide* (n 16) para 353. For the introduction of the change, see UNCITRAL Secretariat, Note on 'Adjustments' (n 61) para 20.

[131] See text at nn 40, 47; for the division of labour and responsibility, see also *Tripartite Guide* (n 16) para 8: 'It was compiled by the respective secretariats with input from a group of five experts.'

298   THE 'TRIPARTITE GUIDE'

It would, therefore, be fully legitimate if, in a case involving a contract governed by the CISG, a national court or an arbitral tribunal were to refer to the *Guide* as an authority, albeit a non-binding one, for the proposition that whether a term is a standard term or not may be decided on the basis of Article 2.1.19(2) of the PICC, rather than on the basis of other domestic or autonomous interpretations. Likewise, the court or tribunal would be entitled to draw on the *Guide* as an authority for the legitimacy of using the PICC in interpreting and supplementing the CISG. The text is indeed, as was suggested by the HCCH after its adoption, not only 'an overview of the principal legislative texts prepared by each organisation'. It is 'a user-friendly resource for those interested in the adoption, *application, and interpretation* of uniform contract law'.[132]

VII. Conclusion

The *Tripartite Guide* provides a concise and up-to-date overview of the law on international commercial contracting. It has persuasive authority and may be usefully referred to in the adjudication of disputes by either national courts or arbitral tribunals. It does, therefore, have (albeit weak) normative force. Perhaps ironically, this effect was only made possible by the discursive style of the document. In this regard, the contrast to another text authored by the same three agencies is telling. As indicated above, *Comparison and Analysis of Major Features of International Instruments Relating to Secured Transactions*, published in 2012,[133] served as a kind of precedent for the *Tripartite Guide*.[134] It started from the acknowledgement of a similar problem, that is, that it was difficult to determine how the various instruments adopted by the three organizations in the relevant field interrelated and 'fit together'. Moreover, it pursued a similar aim, that is, to assist potential users in 'summarizing the scope and application of those instruments, showing how they worked together and providing a comparative understanding of the coverage and basic themes of each instrument'.[135] Yet the nature of the 2012 text is very different from that of the *Tripartite Guide*. Its fewer than forty pages do not feature a continuous text. They simply set out a number of synoptical tables, or 'charts', which summarize the purpose of each instrument, provide a comparison of their major features, and give an overview of their substantive content, mostly by way of bullet points. There is no discussion of substantive issues. This document, while providing a useful overview, is certainly not 'a text that provides guidance for the drafting of contracts, discussing relevant issues and recommending solutions appropriate to particular circumstances'.[136] In contrast, by engaging with substantive issues the *Tripartite Guide* cannot avoid making certain normative choices.

---

[132] HCCH, 'New Guide for International Commercial Contracts', 20 April 2021, <https://www.hcch.net/en/news-archive/details/?varevent=796> (emphasis added). Almost identical language is used in Permanent Bureau of the Hague Conference on Private International Law, 'News from the Hague Conference on Private International Law (HCCH)' (2022) 26 Uniform Law Review 768, 775. See also *Tripartite Guide* (n 16) para 6, cited at n 124.

[133] HCCH, UNIDROIT, and UNCITRAL, *UNCITRAL, Hague Conference and UNIDROIT Texts on Security Interests: Comparison and Analysis of Major Features of International Instruments Relating to Secured Transactions* (United Nations 2012).

[134] See text at n 37.

[135] HCCH, UNIDROIT, and UNCITRAL, *Texts on Security Interests* (n 133) Preface; see ibid para 3.

[136] UNCITRAL, 'Facts about UNCITRAL' (n 119). It was, therefore, made clear from early on in the preparatory discussions of the *Tripartite Guide* that the latter 'would require more textual description, given the complex interplay between the different instruments in the field': UNIDROIT Governing Council, Report 2017 (n 43) para 111.

It remains to be seen whether the normative potential of the *Guide* will be realized by courts and tribunals. Similarly, only time will tell whether the mere explanatory power of the text is strong enough to achieve the desired result of promoting the CISG, the PICC, and the Hague Principles among its potential users, be they legislators, adjudicators, contracting parties, or their legal counsel. After all, it might be argued that, by adding yet another text to the existing 'plethora of uniform law instruments',[137] the *Guide* is increasing the present confusion, rather than reducing it. Ultimately, much of the success of the document will depend on whether the three formulating agencies live up to their commitment to treat it as a 'living document' that 'will be kept under review by the three secretariats, with a view to its periodic revision'.[138] This would enable future clarification of substantive points that prove to be problematic in the application and the interpretation of the instruments.

Even now it can be predicted, though, that the *Tripartite Guide* will have a lasting impact in three different regards. First, it is the most important and successful cooperation between the three formulating agencies to date. Whatever the historic rivalries between them,[139] it has become obvious that each of them will gain if they combine forces. They have indeed been 'systematically pulling the strings together'.[140] It is noteworthy that in their press releases they referred to themselves as the 'three sister organisations'.[141] Second, it may be expected that the text will function as 'a solid teaching reference', as was envisaged by the formulating agencies early on.[142] It overcomes the thinking in silos that characterizes most of the scholarship in the field of transnational commercial contract law, which, apart from the book by Goode, Kronke, and McKendrick, mostly focuses exclusively on a single instrument. There is at present no better text that explains the overlaps and connections between the relevant instruments—how they 'interact with and complement each other'.[143] Third, and relatedly, the document is pervaded by the underlying idea that the field of transnational commercial transactions is, at least in principle, governed by a coherent body of law, a kind of 'system' that exists despite and beyond the scattered and fragmentary regulatory framework. This might indeed be the most important contribution of the *Tripartite Guide* to the field.

---

[137] *Tripartite Guide* (n 16) para 15.

[138] ibid para 8.

[139] This has been a recurring theme since the establishment of UNCITRAL in 1966, cf Caroline Lucas, 'UNCITRAL's Role in Commercial Law Reform: History and Future Prospects' in Orkun Akseli and John Linarelli (eds), *The Future of Commercial Law: Ways Forward for Change and Reform* (Hart 2020) 11, 16, 17–18, 19, 20, 21, 22, 23, 25, 31–32, 38.

[140] See the text at n 8.

[141] UNIDROIT, 'Legal Guide to Uniform Instruments in the Area of International Commercial Contracts Published', 19 April 2021 <https://www.unidroit.org/legal-guide-to-uniform-instruments-in-the-area-of-international-commercial-contracts-published/>; HCCH, 'New Guide' (n 132).

[142] UNCITRAL Secretariat, Joint proposal (n 34) 4.

[143] *Tripartite Guide* (n 16) para 16.

18

The Sale of Goods Act and the Nature of Sales

HUGH BEALE

I. Introduction

I have been lucky enough to work closely with Ewan McKendrick. Tony Guest invited him to be an editor of *Chitty on Contracts* for the twenty-seventh edition in 1994, taking on the chapters on performance and discharge. Since then he has kindly shouldered responsibility for more chapters—Bailment for the twenty-ninth edition and, since the thirty-second edition, Express Terms and Implied Terms. He has not only brought enormous learning to the book, but has also carried out substantial restructuring of the material to make it more accessible and has been a wonderful source of advice and support to me as general editor.

However, we got to know each other better when we were both heavily involved in the Study Group on a European Civil Code,[1] which often involved meetings of several days, more than once a year. We were both responsible for giving guidance to the teams of mainly young researchers working on Sales, Services Contracts, Long-Term Contracts (Commercial Agency, Franchise and Distribution Contracts), and Mandate Contracts. These were difficult projects whose teams often sought guidance. Ewan's steady hand was perfect for that role, as well as later when he joined the Co-ordinating Committee for the European Civil Code project as a whole. Ewan and I have also taught commercial law seminars together at Oxford.

Ewan's knowledge of contract law and sales law is profound. I have learned an enormous amount from him and the books he has written and edited, and I have enjoyed working with him more than I can say. So I was honoured and delighted to be invited to contribute a chapter to this collection in tribute to him. As Ewan has written extensively on the sale of goods— including three chapters in his edited collection *Sale of Goods*[2] and in Part II of what has now become *Goode and McKendrick on Commercial Law*[3]—and this is one of the topics on which we have worked together, it seems appropriate to write about the sale of goods.

The argument of my chapter is simple: that the Sale of Goods Act 1979 ('the SGA') is no longer fit for the particular purpose for which I believe it is needed most, to govern the kinds of transaction that are most likely to be entered by small businesses. There are two ways in which this is the case. The first is that the Act is too 'mercantilist', by which I mean that it is too much orientated towards purchases for resale as opposed to purchases for use or consumption. The second, which for reasons of space I will discuss only briefly, is that the Act does not cover common types of transaction, in particular the supply of digital

---

[1] See the series Study Group on a European Civil Code, *Principles of European Law*.
[2] Ewan McKendrick (ed), *Sale of Goods* (LLP 2000).
[3] Ewan McKendrick (ed), *Goode and McKendrick on Commercial Law* (6th edn, LexisNexis 2021) (hereafter *Goode and McKendrick*).

Hugh Beale, *The Sale of Goods Act and the Nature of Sales* In: *Shaping the Law of Obligations*. Edited by: Edwin Peel and Rebecca Probert, Oxford University Press. © Hugh Beale 2023. DOI: 10.1093/oso/9780198889762.003.0018

302   THE SALE OF GOODS ACT AND THE NATURE OF SALES

products, the supply of goods other than by way of sale, and the supply of services. The sale of goods and these other kinds of supply should be brought within a single Act, as has been done for consumers.

Any argument for legislation along these lines raises a number of general questions. Why do we need any legislation when most transactions of any significance are governed by detailed sets of terms and conditions, and the parties are businesspeople who will know what they want (or are prepared to pay for), and can bargain for it? Given that nearly all the provisions of any legislation would be only default rules, like the SGA, why does it matter what the rules are? After all, the parties can and will bargain round them. Even with digital products, there is almost certainly some protection at common law: isn't that enough? And the supply of goods of other kinds than sale and the supply of services is already covered by legislation—so why do we need anything more? Let me try to answer some of those questions before going further. The last two questions are not concerned with the sale of goods as such, and I will consider them in the second part of the chapter.

II. General Arguments

A. Detailed Written Contracts

The classic law-and-economics explanation for default rules is that they save the costs of negotiating terms each time.[4] In reality, this argument seems to hold for only the simplest contracts made face to face. The vast majority of other contracts of sale, and especially those made online, are now made subject to a set of terms and conditions. The terms of some very high-value contracts are negotiated in detail. Most, however, are governed by a standard set of terms, most often drafted by or on behalf of the seller. Because the seller can use the same set of terms for multiple contracts, the cost per transaction is low enough to make it worth incurring the expense of having a set of terms and conditions drawn up.

We still need a set of rules to govern sales, however. First, there will always remain some contracts that are not subject to standard terms, whether by design or by accident. Second, even though standard terms are getting longer and longer, it is inevitable that there will be both points that are unclear and points that are not covered. Should a dispute arise and the parties fail to find a compromise, it may then be necessary to fall back on the law in order to interpret the contract or to fill in what is missing. Third, there are some rules that are mandatory, though few if any of them are in the SGA.

B. Business Parties Can Bargain for What They Need

It is true that some businesses can and will ensure that the express terms of any contract they make give them the degree of protection for which they are willing to pay. A large business

---

[4] Classic expositions include Anthony T Kronman and Richard A Posner, *Economics of Contract Law* (Little Brown & Co 1979), 4; Richard A Posner and Andrew M Rosenfield, 'Impossibility and Related Doctrines in Contract Law: an Economic Analysis' (1977) 6 JLS 83, 87–92; Ian Ayres and Robert Gertner, 'Filling Gaps in Incomplete Contracts: an Economic Theory of Default Rules' (1989) 99 Yale LJ 87; Christopher Riley, 'Designing Default Rules in Contract Law' (2000) 20 OJLS 367.

or other organization that is buying, for example, digital products under a site licence may well have the knowledge and bargaining power to ensure that the contract provides adequate warranties and compensation for possible losses, whether that is through the supplier being fully liable, or by having limited liability coupled with adequate insurance on the buyer's side. In contrast, a small business or organization buying a piece of software 'off the shelf' is unlikely to be in a position to achieve such a good outcome, even if the software will be critical to its operations. A small enterprise is much more likely to be dependent on the standard terms used by the supplier, which may or may not provide what is needed by the buyer.

The problems are well known. First, a small business is much less likely to read and understand the supplier's terms, let alone work out their potential impact. If the transaction is not a high-value one, the cost of taking legal advice will probably be considered disproportionate. If most customers concentrate only on the description of the item they wish to buy and the price, and do not read or understand the supplier's terms, the pressure of competition over price is likely to encourage the supplier to reduce its costs by putting more and more risks onto the unwitting customer. The result will be that customers are offered lower prices but harsher terms.[5] So when something goes wrong and the small business has to look at the terms to which it has agreed, it may be taken by surprise. Second, even if it does understand the terms that the supplier is offering, and objects to one or more of them, a small business is unlikely to be a sufficiently important customer—that is, to have the bargaining power—to persuade the supplier to alter its standard terms.[6]

In other words, a small business confronted with standard terms is particularly likely to encounter the problems identified long ago by Lord Reid in the context of exemption clauses: 'In the ordinary way the customer has no time to read them, and if he did read them he would probably not understand them. and if he did understand and object to any of them, he would generally be told he could take it or leave it, and if he then went to another supplier the result would be the same.'[7] Similar problems may well affect even large organizations when they make occasional contracts for goods or digital products that are only incidental to their operations.

It is certainly possible that, to continue my example, the software supplier's standard terms will give what buyers normally want. It has been pointed out that, if even a fairly small margin of customers try to negotiate what they need, the supplier may adjust its terms so as to attract their business. If it uses the same terms for all its customers, the activities of the vocal minority will benefit all the supplier's customers[8] to the extent their needs are similar.[9] But even when there is an active margin of buyers there can be no certainty that the supplier will not try to gain sales among its less discriminating customers by offering cheaper but less generous deals, which the customers may snap up without realizing the risks.

---

[5] See Victor P Goldberg, 'Institutional Change and the Quasi-invisible Hand' (1974) 17 Jo L & Econ 461, 483–86 (hereafter Goldberg, 'Institutional Change').

[6] See Alan Schwartz, 'Seller Unequal Bargaining Power and the Judicial Process' (1974) 49 Indiana LJ 367, 370–71.

[7] *Suisse Atlantique Société d'Armement Maritime SA v NV Rotterdamsche Kolen Centrale* [1967] AC 361, 406.

[8] See Michael Trebilcock, 'Economic Criteria of Unconscionability' in Barry J Reiter and John Swan (eds), *Studies in Contract Law* (Butterworths 1980) 379.

[9] See Goldberg, 'Institutional Change' (n 5) 487; Hugh Beale, 'Unfair Contracts in Britain and Europe' (1989) 42 CLP 197, 212.

THE SALE OF GOODS ACT AND THE NATURE OF SALES

C. The Parties Can Contract Around Default Rules

Does the fact that most of the rules on the sale and supply of goods are only default rules that the parties can contract out of undermine the case for legislation? I have already given one reason why I do not think this is the case: even when the transaction is governed by a fairly complete set of terms and conditions, there are still likely to be uncertainties and gaps, when the default rules can be used as a background for interpretation or to fill gaps.

A second reason is that the terms of many business-to-business contracts, at least in domestic markets, are subject to some form of fairness control, even if the controls apply only to clauses that exclude or restrict liability, or define the user's obligations in a surprising way.[10] Having a set of default rules gives a measure by which a court faced with applying a test of reasonableness or fairness can judge to what extent the claimant's rights will be reduced if the term is enforced. The problem is most clearly illustrated in the consumer context. In the *Aziz* case, the first part of the test of unfairness laid down by Article 3(1) of the Directive on Unfair Terms in Consumer Contracts[11] was interpreted by the CJEU to require consideration of 'what rules of national law would apply in the absence of an agreement by the parties'.[12] Such a test is hard to apply when there is no legislation or case law establishing 'default' obligations for the type of contract in question.

This argument would be of course stronger if controls over the fairness of a wider range of terms applied to small business contracts as well as to consumer contracts, as recommended by the Law Commissions.[13] This is not the place to discuss that issue again; but similar problems can arise under the current law, for example when a court may have to decide what it was reasonable for the claimant to expect in terms of how the supplier would perform.[14]

D. Plain English

Lastly—and since this paper is obviously idealistic, why not cry for the moon?—any new legislation should be drafted in such a way that it is easier for non-lawyers to understand.[15] There is no doubt that legislative drafting has changed dramatically in the past fifty years[16] but the SGA has only seen modest improvements, mainly as the result of the changes made to section 14 by the Sale and Supply of Goods Act 1994.[17] When the Law Commissions

[10] Unfair Contract Terms Act 1977, ss 2, 3, 6, and 7.

[11] Council Directive 93/13/EEC of 5 April 1993 on unfair terms in consumer contracts, OJ L95/93, 29.

[12] *Aziz v Caixa d'Estalvis de Catalunya, Tarragona i Manresa (Catalunyacaixa)* (C-415/11) EU:C:2013:164, para 68.

[13] *Unfair Terms in Contracts* (Law Com No 292; Scot Law Com No 199, 2005) Pt 5 (hereafter Law Commissions, *Unfair Terms*).

[14] Under Unfair Contract Terms Act 1977, s 3(2)(b)(i).

[15] Before the CRA 2015 was passed, it was said that small businesses had especially low understanding of the law: Department for Business Innovation and Skills (2012), *Enhancing Consumer Confidence by Clarifying Consumer Law* [5.71].

[16] See Cabinet Office and Office of Parliamentary Counsel, *When Laws Become Too Complex* (2013) (hereafter *When Laws Become Too Complex*), quoted by Simon Taylor, 'UK Sale of Goods Legislation 1893–2015: Towards Plain(er) Language?' (2018) 74 ASp [Online] 95, available at https://journals.openedition.org/asp/5411?lang=en (accessed 27 November 2022) (hereafter Taylor, 'UK Sale of Goods Legislation').

[17] For a linguistic analysis of the changes to s 14 and the equivalent section in the CRA 2015, see Taylor, 'UK Sale of Goods Legislation' (n 16).

were drafting the terms of reference for the project on unfair terms, I had the temerity to propose that we should be required to draft the legislation in 'Plain English'. I was immediately slapped down by Parliamentary Counsel, who said that they always draft in Plain English, but a compromise was worked out, drawing on the terms of reference for the Tax Law Rewrite[18] that was then being carried out, and the Law Commissions were asked

> to consider the desirability and feasibility of
>
> . . .
>
> (3) Making any replacement legislation clearer and more accessible to the reader, so far as possible without making the law significantly less certain, by using language which is non-technical with simple sentences, by setting out the law in a simple structure following a clear logic and by using a presentation that is easy to follow.[19]

The aim was to have legislation that could be readily understood, not necessarily by consumers, but by consumer advisers who do not have legal training and by businesspeople with some experience of contracting.[20] To indicate what the Law Commissions had in mind, unusually the Law Commissions' Consultation Paper contained a partial draft Bill prepared by Parliamentary Counsel. To Parliamentary Counsels' credit, their efforts were approved by the Plain English campaign.[21] The Law Commissions endeavoured to maintain the same approach in the full draft Bill contained in their final Report, though the final draft did not include the examples that had been contained in the consultative draft. This was largely because of unhappy experience with earlier legislation that used examples, some of which turned out to be wrong. It was argued that readers can look at the Explanatory Notes to the Bill or guides to the legislation.[22] Personally I regretted the decision to drop the examples, because I think lay advisers or businesspeople will often not consult either and should be able to understand the legislation fully without having to do so; but obviously views on this may differ. In any event, the Bill in the Report was never enacted.

When what became the Consumer Rights Act 2015 ('the CRA') was drafted, it was also intended to be in simpler language.[23] There is quite widespread agreement among consumer lawyers that, sadly, this aim was far from being achieved.[24] But there is no reason

---

[18] A statement of the approaches and techniques used in this project can be found in HMRC, *Tax Law Rewrite Report and Plans 2009–10* [2.4] (available at https://webarchive.nationalarchives.gov.uk/ukgwa/20100407044212/http://www.hmrc.gov.uk/rewrite/plans2009-10.htm#1). A general description of the project is available at https://webarchive.nationalarchives.gov.uk/ukgwa/20140206160137/http://www.hmrc.gov.uk/rewrite/index.htm

[19] *Unfair Terms in Contracts* (CP No 166; Scottish Law Commission Discussion Paper No 119, 2002) [1.1].

[20] Law Commissions, *Unfair Terms* (n 13) [2.45]. According to *When Laws Become Too Complex* (n 16) [4.1]: 'In the past, users of legislation tended to be legally qualified; but today's users are a far wider group of people thanks to the web (legislation.gov.uk has over 2 million unique visitors per month)'. The paper contains a useful analysis of the causes of complexity in legislation and suggestions for improvement.

[21] Law Commissions, *Unfair Terms* (n 13) [2.47].

[22] ibid [2.53]. Vijay K Bhatia argues for two versions of legislation, a 'simplified' version for the general public and a more precise one for lawyers, but he still argues for 'easification' of the latter, using the kind of style at which the Law Commissions were aiming: 'Drafting Legislative Provisions: Challenges and Opportunities' [2010] *The Loophole* 5, 10, available at http://calc.ngo/sites/default/files/loophole/dec-2010.pdf (accessed 27 November 2022).

[23] 'There is general agreement across business and consumer groups that the existing UK consumer law is unnecessarily complex. It is fragmented and, in places, unclear, for example where the law has not kept up with technological change or lacks precision or where it is couched in legalistic language': Explanatory Notes, para 5.

[24] See eg Paula Giliker, 'The Consumer Rights Act 2015—A Bastion of European Consumer Rights' (2017) 37 LS 78, 85–86; James Devenney, 'The Legacy of the Cameron–Clegg Coalition Programme of Reform of the Law on the Supply of Goods, Digital Content and Services to Consumers' [2018] JBL 485.

306   THE SALE OF GOODS ACT AND THE NATURE OF SALES

to stop trying to make our legislation clearer, though it would be ironic were legislation on business contracts to end up being easier to understand than the principal statute on consumer contracts.

III. The SGA: Too 'Mercantilist'

Turning now to the classic sale of goods, this is not the place to go through all the many criticisms that have been made of the Act or all the suggestions for its reform.[25] I want to make the simple argument that the SGA is not aimed at the right audience, and then to illustrate some of the changes that would be required to correct its aim.

It follows from the arguments just made that legislation on contracts should focus on the kinds of contract that are most likely to be made by small businesses. I do not think the Act makes sufficient allowance for small business buyers, who may not have the sophistication or the legal advice to enable them to protect themselves adequately. Further, though I do not have empirical evidence for it, I strongly suspect that the vast majority of small business buyers are not buying goods for the purposes of resale but either to use the goods or to consume them. To my mind the Act too often assumes that the buyer is a trader. Let me try to demonstrate both points by considering particular sections of the Act.

A. Section 18 and the Passing of Property

At a guess, small businesses buying parts, materials, or other consumables will usually pay cash on or only shortly before delivery or, if they are dealing with a regular supplier, they will be given credit, with the seller often reserving title until the goods have been paid for (or all monies paid). Small businesses buying equipment for use, in contrast, will often have to order it or, even when the seller has the item in stock, may have to wait for delivery until the seller has made any adjustments required by the buyer, or while the buyer makes adjustments to its premises necessary to install the goods. In these circumstances the seller is very likely to ask for a deposit; and if the seller becomes bankrupt before the goods have been delivered, the buyer may lose it.

Section 18 protects some buyers by providing that, unless otherwise agreed, the property in specific goods will pass at the time the contract is made, even if the goods have not been paid for or delivered (rule 1); but this applies only where the goods were in a deliverable state at the outset or have been put into a deliverable state[26] and the buyer has been informed (rules 1 and 2) and do not have to be weighed or measured, or the like, by the seller in order to ascertain the price, again unless that has been done and the buyer has been informed (rule 3).[27] I suspect that the reason behind the restrictions in rules 2 and 3 is that the

---

[25] See eg Ontario, Ministry of The Attorney-General, *Report on Sale of Goods* (1979); The Law Reform Commission of Western Australia, Project No 89, *The Sale of Goods Act 1895*, Report (1998); Ireland, Sales Law Review Group, Report on the Legislation governing the Sale of Goods and the Supply of Services, Prn A11/ 1576 (TSO 2011); Michael Bridge, 'Do We Need a New Sale of Goods Act?' in John Lowry and Loukas Mistelis, *Commercial Law: Perspectives and Practice* (Butterworths 2006) 15.

[26] It would be very helpful to clarify the requirement of 'deliverable state' along the lines suggested in *Goode and McKendrick* (n 3) [8.87].

[27] *Goode and McKendrick* (n 3) [8.89] may be correct that this rule now has little practical importance.

passing of property also triggers the passing of risk and the action for the price, and that it was thought that the risk should not pass while the seller is still doing things to the goods,[28] while the action for the price cannot be available until the price is known.[29] When the goods have to be obtained or made by the seller, the buyer will not be protected until the goods have been appropriated to the contract, and this is unlikely to occur until they are delivered to the buyer or to a carrier.[30]

The risk posed to the buyer is recognized as a problem for consumers, and the Law Commission has recommended that the rules on passing of property should be relaxed, even to the extent that property should pass in goods that the seller has merely labelled or physically set aside for the buyer, unless it is shown that this was not intended to be permanent.[31]

I strongly suspect that many small businesses are quite unaware of the risk that they are running and, even if they are aware of it, they may find it hard to protect themselves. A company cannot take advantage of section 75 of the Consumer Credit Act 1974 by using a credit card, and the cost and effort of obtaining a 'reverse guarantee' from a bank to ensure they get a refund is likely to be disproportionate to the size of the transaction. The passing of property will not hurt the seller or its creditors, since (unless agreed otherwise) the seller is not obliged to deliver the goods until they have been paid for in full.[32] So why not change the rule for all buyers? The three issues—who is entitled to the goods,[33] who bears the risk of accidental destruction, and when the action for the price is available—should be separated.[34]

---

[28] Admittedly this argument is not made explicitly in the most obvious sources. M Chalmers, *The Sale of Goods Act 1893* (W. Clowes and Sons 1894), 39 (hereafter Chalmers, *Sale of Goods Act*) refers to a number of cases but even the earliest, *Rugg v Minett* (1809) 11 East 210, simply states the rule without attempting to justify it. Chalmers also cites C Blackburn, *The Law of Sale* (1st edn, W Benning, 1845) 152 (hereafter Blackburn, *Law of Sale*), who argues that normally the passing of property benefits the vendor because the risk also passes, but that where the vendor has to put the goods into a deliverable state 'the intention of the parties should be taken to be, that the vendor was to do this before he obtained the benefit of the passing of property'. In *Young v Matthews* (1866-67) LR 2 CP 127 the Court of Common Pleas was prepared to hold that the facts that the purchaser had advanced large sums to the vendor and that the vendor's foreman had said that the vendor 'would hold and deliver' the goods was enough to show that the parties had intended the property to pass even though they were not yet in a deliverable state. Christian Twigg-Flesner and Rick Canavan (eds), *Atiyah and Adams' Sale of Goods* (14th edn, Pearson 2020) 238 (hereafter Twigg-Flesner and Canavan, *Sale of Goods*) point out that the rule does not apply when a buyer who has bought goods knowing of a defect then leaves them with the seller to be repaired.

[29] Thus in *Hanson v Meyer* (1805) 6 East 614, 625 Lord Ellenborough pointed out that the weight of the goods must be ascertained before the price can be known and paid. Chalmers, *Sale of Goods Act* (n 28) 42 says the rule derives from Roman law, under which there could be no sale until the price was fixed. Blackburn, *Law of Sale* (n 28) 153) criticizes this rule, saying it 'seems to be somewhat hastily adopted from the civil law, without adverting to the great distinction made by the civilians between a sale for a certain price in money and an exchange for anything else. The English law makes no such distinction but, as it seems, has adopted the rule of civil law, which seems to have no foundation except in that distinction.'

[30] *Carlos Federspiel & Co SA v Charles Twigg & Co Ltd* [1957] 1 Lloyd's Rep 240. The property in a new vehicle might pass earlier, when it is registered in the buyer's name, though it will not be in a deliverable state until the number plates have been attached, *Kulkarni v Manor Credit (Davenham) Ltd* [2010] EWCA Civ 69; [2010] 2 Lloyd's Rep 431 [25]–[26]; and Rix LJ took the view that property in a new car that the buyer has not seen will generally not pass until delivery, even when the buyer has already paid in full (at [38]–[39]).

[31] Law Commission, *Consumer Sales Contracts: Transfer of Ownership* (Law Com No 398, 2021). See the proposed new s 18B of the SGA 1979, especially ss 18B(3) and (4).

[32] SGA 1979, s 28.

[33] Twigg-Flesner and Canavan, *Sale of Goods* (n 28) 230 makes good arguments for retaining a rule on the passing or property.

[34] *Goode and McKendrick* (n 3) [8.27] remarks that 'The impact of the location of property is all-pervasive'.

B. Section 20 and the Passing of Risk

The rule that, unless otherwise agreed, risk passes with property is probably an even more dangerous trap for the unsophisticated business buyer.[35] Many sales of equipment to small businesses, especially second-hand sales, will be of specific items, and under section 18 rule 1 the property in the equipment may well pass immediately even if the buyer is not going to take delivery immediately. How many small business buyers will know that they need to insure the equipment right away? I suspect they are likely to assume that the goods are only at their risk once they have taken control of them. It is to be hoped that the courts will recognize this and seek to interpret the agreement as being that the risk (or the property) was not intended to pass in accordance with the default rules of the Act.[36] But will non-lawyers know that? And if the Act no longer accords with the law in practice, surely it is time to change the Act.[37]

C. Section 49 and the Action for the Price

Section 49(1) provides that where the property in the goods has passed to the buyer, the seller may maintain an action for the price.[38] This appears to apply though the buyer has not yet taken delivery of the goods and has told the seller that it no longer wants them. In effect, the buyer will have to pay the price and then arrange to dispose of the unwanted goods. That outcome may be acceptable when the buyer is also a trader in the goods and so can be expected to have facilities for resale, but it makes much less sense when the buyer was purchasing them for use or consumption.

It has been held that the buyer may have to pay the price even if the property has not passed at the time of the buyer's repudiation, provided that the seller can and does complete the steps that will result in the property passing without the buyer's cooperation,[39] following the decision of the majority in *White and Carter (Councils) Ltd v McGregor*[40] that the innocent party may ignore a wrongful repudiation and, if it is able to do so without the other party's cooperation, earn the price. Benjamin[41] points out that this may need to be qualified now that the dictum of Lord Reid, that the innocent party must have a 'legitimate interest' in performing rather than accepting the repudiation and claiming damages,[42] appears to have become part of the law;[43] and that the majority approach is inconsistent with the policy of

---

[35] See also Twigg-Flesner and Canavan, *Sale of Goods* (n 28) 265. Consumers are protected by CRA 2015, s 29: the risk will not pass until the goods have been delivered to the consumer or to another person nominated by the consumer, including a carrier, provided the carrier was not chosen from a list provided by the trader. This rule implemented Article 20 of the Consumer Rights Directive (2011/83/EU).

[36] See Diplock LJ in *RV Ward v Bignall* [1967] 1 QB 534, 567 ('in modern times very little is needed to give rise to the inference that the property in specific goods is to pass only on delivery or payment'—though this was not a case on risk); and the decision in *Philip Head & Sons Ltd v Showfronts Ltd* [1970] 1 Lloyd's Rep 140.

[37] See also *Goode and McKendrick* (n 3) [9.02], arguing that risk should pass with control.

[38] Section 49(1) has given rise to other difficulties: see *Goode and McKendrick* (n 3) [15.14].

[39] *Anglo-African Shipping Co of New York Inc v J Mortner Ltd* [1962] 1 Lloyd's Rep 81; appeal dismissed without discussion of this point [1962] 1 Lloyd's Rep 910.

[40] [1962] AC 413.

[41] Michael Bridge (Gen ed), *Benjamin's Sale of Goods* (11th edn, Sweet & Maxwell 2020) [16-031].

[42] *White and Carter (Councils) Ltd v McGregor* [1962] AC 413, 431.

[43] See the discussion by Mindy Chen-Wishart in Hugh Beale (Gen ed), *Chitty on Contracts* (34th edn, Sweet & Maxwell 2021) [30-007] (hereafter *Chitty on Contracts*).

the mitigation rule. I would say that the same should apply when the property has already passed to the buyer at the time of its repudiation. If it is accepted that the Act should focus on sales to small businesses, the default rule should be that the action for the price should be available to the seller only when the property has passed and the goods have been delivered to the buyer.[44] It is true that when the goods have been shipped to a buyer abroad, it may sometimes be more sensible for the buyer to have to dispose of them than for the seller to have to arrange for their storage and subsequent disposal,[45] but in that situation the seller would remain free to make the current rule an express term of the contract.

D. Online Purchases: A Right to Cancel?

What I have just suggested would in effect give the buyer a right to cancel subject to paying the seller for its loss, though only until the moment of delivery. It is probable that in practice more and more purchases by small businesses are made online and the goods are delivered to the buyer's premises by the seller or a third-party carrier. Where the buyer is a consumer, they would have a right to cancel the contract, usually within fourteen days of the goods coming into their physical possession.[46] It may be argued that small businesses also need a right of cancellation, because of the difficulty of assessing the exact nature and the quality of the goods when buying online. It would be very interesting to know if, or to what extent, business buyers ask for, or are granted, a right of cancellation, and if so on what terms.[47]

It might be fair to go further than I have suggested and to allow a business buyer to cancel within a fixed period after delivery and (since few online purchases will be on credit provided by the seller) the price has been paid, but (unlike with consumers) subject to liability for the seller's costs and other loss. How useful that would be in practice is a difficult question. I suspect many sellers would argue that not only have they incurred costs in arranging to receive, store, and re-sell the goods but also that supply exceeds demand, so that even if the goods are ultimately re-sold the seller has lost a sale.[48] Though this would entitle them only to compensation for the profit they would have made, not for the full price of the goods, a small business buyer might quail if confronted with this kind of argument, especially when told that it has the burden of showing that the seller did not lose its profit.[49]

---

[44] In this context 'delivery' should mean not just that the goods have been made available to the buyer for collection but that they have been handed to and received by the buyer (without prejudice, of course, to the buyer's right to reject the goods if they are found not to conform to the contract.) Cf text at n 46.

[45] See Twigg-Flesner and Canavan, *Sale of Goods* (n 28) 403.

[46] See Consumer Contracts (Information, Cancellation and Additional Charges) Regulations 2013, SI 2013/3134) Pt 3.

[47] Online sellers that sell to both consumers and businesses, such as Amazon, do not appear to limit the right of cancellation to people who are not buying in the course of a business. Amazon's conditions of sale do not refer to the fact that the statutory right applies only to consumers: see https://www.amazon.co.uk/gp/help/customer/display.html?nodeId=201909000#GUID-189D34BF-F756-4879-B149-0D73223A3BFD__SECTION_DE2895462 69C476B94AC853787C5CF48.

[48] See *WL Thompson Ltd v Robinson (Gunmakers) Ltd* [1955] Ch 177.

[49] In *Lazenby Garages v Wright* [1976] 1 WLR 459 the Court of Appeal seems to have assumed that the burden of proof was on the buyer but this is contrary to dicta in *Re Vic Mill Ltd* [1913] 1 Ch 465 and *Hill & Sons v Edwin Showell & Sons Ltd* (1918) 87 LJ KB 1106. In *Sony Computer Entertainment UK Ltd v Cinram Logistics UK Ltd* [2008] EWCA Civ 955; [2009] Bus LR 528 [37], [45]–[51] it was said that though a claimant bears the burden of proving its loss, if the seller shows the profit it would have made on the sale to the defendant, the buyer bears the evidential burden of showing that the seller could not have made both the original sale and a second one: 'it is not for the claimant to prove a negative, that he has not recouped the profit by a substitute sale but for the defendant to prove a positive that the profit has been recouped and thus the loss of profit not suffered at all' ([49]).

310 THE SALE OF GOODS ACT AND THE NATURE OF SALES

E. The Buyer's Remedies

Let us suppose now that the seller has failed to deliver the goods, or has delivered goods that do not comply with the express or implied terms of the contract; and, again, that the buyer is a small business purchasing the goods for use or consumption. Should that affect the remedies available to the buyer?

1. Specific performance of the obligation to deliver
In the case in which the seller fails to deliver, logically the first question must be whether the buyer should be able to compel performance. I will not go into the general question of whether specific performance should be more widely available. I do not have the space to discuss the extensive literature on this question from the perspectives of both law-and-economics[50] and comparative law,[51] and in any case I do not see that small businesses need different treatment in this kind of case.

2. A right to repair or replacement?
If the goods delivered to a consumer buyer are not in accordance with the contract, the buyer has the right to demand repair or replacement, enforceable if necessary by an order of specific performance.[52] Should a small business buyer have a similar right? It is probably the case that many contracts for the supply of equipment, or guarantees that accompany them, will provide expressly that the seller or the manufacturer will repair or replace defective goods, or arrange for that to be done; so having a specifically enforceable right to repair or replacement might well meet the buyer's expectations. But I am sceptical of the value of such a right. If the seller is willing to carry out the repair or replacement, a court order is unnecessary; if the seller acts only in response to a court order, it seems unlikely to do a good job. It would be better to get a third person to do it and then claim damages. In many civil law systems, having the goods supplied or work done by a third person at the expense of the debtor is treated as a form of specific performance.[53] Termination of the contract and a claim for damages are functionally almost directly equivalent to this.[54]

3. Termination by the buyer
Michael Bridge has argued that SGA's rules, especially those governing when a buyer may terminate the contract, are more suitable for sales of 'market sensitive' items, such as commodities, than they are for market insensitive items such as heavy machinery.[55] My general argument is not dissimilar, but the focus on small businesses buying goods for use or consumption raises some problematic questions. The topic is tricky because we have to consider a number of rules that are interrelated.

---

[50] See eg Anthony T Kronman, 'Specific Performance' (1978) 45 U Chi L Rev 351; Alan Schwartz, 'The Case for Specific Performance' (1979) 89 Yale LJ 271; Ian R Macneil, 'Efficient Breach of Contract: Circles in the Sky' (1982) 68 Va L Rev 947.

[51] See eg Solène Rowan, *Remedies for Breach of Contract* (OUP 2012).

[52] CRA 2015, ss 23 and 58.

[53] See eg France, Art 1222 Cciv; Germany, §887 ZPO (Zivilprozessordnung).

[54] I have been told that when the European Commission was discussing implementation of the Consumer Sales Directive (1999/44/EC) with officials from London, the Commission indicated that there was no need to change our law to satisfy the Directive.

[55] Michael Bridge, 'A Law for International Sale of Goods' [2007] HKLJ 17, 19 (hereafter Bridge, 'A Law for International Sale of Goods'), arguing that the CISG is more appropriate for the second type of sale.

THE SGA: TOO 'MERCANTILIST'   311

Take first the case of a small business buying a piece of equipment for use in the business. When the equipment is delivered, it is not in conformity with the implied terms under sections 13–15 of the SGA; for example, it does not correspond exactly to the contractual description, or it is not of satisfactory quality. However, the non-conformity is 'minor', in the sense either that it will not prevent the business from using the equipment as intended or that, though it cannot be used in its present state, the defect can easily be put right. Should the buyer have the right to reject the equipment and terminate the contract immediately? Or should it have the right to do so only if the seller fails to put things right within a reasonable time? Or should there be no right of termination for a minor breach?

An initial problem is uncertainty over the current position, in a number of respects.

On the face of it, the goods do not satisfy the implied requirements of the Act. The courts have accepted that small deviations from the contractual description mean that section 13 is not satisfied,[56] while the changes made to section 14(2)[57] after the decision in *The Hansa Nord*[58] mean that goods may not be of satisfactory quality because of cosmetic defects. Any breach of sections 13–15 will normally be a breach of condition, and this may give the buyer the right to reject the goods and terminate the contract. But the position is not completely clear, for a number of reasons.

The first is that matters such as appearance and finish, and freedom from minor defects, are only 'aspects of the quality of the goods' in 'appropriate cases'.[59] The explicit requirements of appearance, finish, and freedom from minor defects seem to have been introduced mainly to protect consumers,[60] and it may be argued that it is not appropriate to take them into account in a business-to-business sale. I suspect the argument would not succeed for a number of reasons: the Law Commission rejected the idea of separate criteria for consumer sales and other sales;[61] if Parliament had intended them not to apply then it would have amended section 14(2) when consumer sales were removed from the scope of the Act; and to say that a minor defect cannot make the quality unsatisfactory would deprive the buyer of any remedy, unless it is protected by an express term of the contract. But it is hard to be sure.

The second reason for uncertainty is that the buyer's right to reject is qualified by section 15A.[62] That was clearly intended to prevent a buyer from abusing the right to reject[63]—for example, using a relatively trivial breach as an excuse for terminating a contract that has become unprofitable.[64] Whether it will be applied to prevent a buyer from rejecting the goods for a minor defect of the kind we are envisaging, when the buyer is not motivated by a fall in the market, is hard to predict. My hunch is that it would not. Section 15A applies only when 'the breach is so slight that it would be unreasonable for [the buyer] to reject' the goods.

---

[56] *Arcos Ltd v EA Ronaasen & Son* [1933] AC 470.

[57] Sale and Supply of Goods Act 1994, s 1.

[58] *Cehave NV v Bremer Handelsgesellschaft mbH (The Hansa Nord)* [1976] QB 44.

[59] SGA 1979, s 14(2B).

[60] Law Commissions, *Sale and Supply of Goods* (Law Com No 160, Scot Law Com No 104, 1987) [3.40] (hereafter Law Commissions, *Sale and Supply of Goods*). The definitions should be generally applicable but are more relevant to consumers. See also Law Commission WP No 85, Scottish Law Commission Consultative Memorandum No 58, *Sale and Supply of Goods* (1983) [1.10].

[61] ibid [3.9–3.10]; and see also Law Commission Working Paper No 85, Scottish Law Commission Consultative Memorandum No 58, *Sale and Supply of Goods* (1983) [3.2].

[62] Introduced by s 4 of the 1994 Act.

[63] Law Commissions, *Sale and Supply of Goods* (n 60) [4.18].

[64] ibid [4.5]. In the light of this, the Law Commission's insistence that the buyer's motive for rejection is irrelevant (ibid [4.19]) seems odd, even though their prime concern was that the strictness of the remedy might lead to the requirements of ss 13–15 being watered down (see ibid [2.26] and [4.1]).

312 THE SALE OF GOODS ACT AND THE NATURE OF SALES

'Slight' might be taken to mean something less than minor;[65] and historically the courts have been very reluctant to limit a party's normal remedies by notions of reasonableness.[66]

A further complication is that it is not clear whether the current law gives the seller a right to cure the problem by either making a second delivery of goods that do conform to the contract or possibly by repairing them, if that can be done in time.[67] We have authority that a party who tenders documents that do not conform to the contract before the time for tender has run out can make a fresh tender of them,[68] but there has been some controversy over whether this applies equally to tendering non-conforming goods or when they have actually been handed over.[69] I am sure that Goode and McKendrick are correct to say that this is possible, at least when it can be done before the contractual date, or within the contractual period, for delivery.[70] In general there is no right to terminate a contract until the other party is in breach, unless the other party's conduct (in our situation, the initial delivery) amounts to a repudiation because it shows that the seller is unwilling or unable to perform the contract save in a way that would ultimately give the buyer the right to terminate it.[71] And I agree also that the seller has the right to cure a breach of contract even after the date or period for performance has passed,[72] if time is not of the essence—neither originally nor having subsequently been 'made of the essence' by the buyer setting a reasonable deadline that has passed[73]—nor has the delay become so serious that it frustrates the purpose of the contract.[74] That is in effect the rule in contracts for services or for the sale of land,[75] and I see no reason why it does not apply generally to delays in the sale of goods.[76] The right to reject is a right to withhold performance—to refuse to accept the goods—until the seller performs properly; it is distinct from termination or, as the SGA puts it, the right to treat the contract as repudiated.

This leads to a last uncertainty in the current law: when is time of the essence? The classic statement is that time for the delivery of goods is of the essence of the contract,[77] and though English law takes a more relaxed view of the time for payment,[78] dates for delivery seem to be regarded as sacrosanct. There is no equivalent of section 15A for late delivery. But the 'time for delivery is of the essence' approach can at most be a presumption and a court will

---

[65] See also Edwin Peel (ed), *Treitel: The Law of Contract* (15th edn, Sweet & Maxwell 2020) [18-060] (hereafter *Treitel*).

[66] See eg *White and Carter (Councils) Ltd v McGregor* [1962] AC 413, 430 (Lord Morton).

[67] *Goode and McKendrick* (n 3) [12.21] regrets that the 1994 Act did not introduce a more extensive right to cure, namely when the seller reasonably believed that the goods would be acceptable to the buyer with or without a monetary allowance, cf UCC §2-508(2). I agree.

[68] *Borrowman, Phillips & Co v Free & Hollis* (1878) 4 QBD 500; *EE & Brian Smith (1928) Ltd v Wheatsheaf Mills Ltd* [1939] 2 KB 302.

[69] See *Goode and McKendrick* (n 3) [12.20].

[70] ibid. See also Twigg-Flesner and Canavan, *Sale of Goods* (n 28) 417.

[71] See Devlin, 'The Treatment of Breach of Contract' (1966) 24 CLJ 192, 194.

[72] See *Goode and McKendrick* (n 3) [12.24].

[73] See *United Scientific Holdings Ltd v Burnley BC* [1978] AC 904, 958; *Bunge Corp v Tradax SA* [1981] 1 WLR 711, 716.

[74] See *Universal Cargo Carriers Corp v Citati (No 1)* [1957] 2 QB 401, 430.

[75] See Hugh Beale, *Remedies for Breach of Contract* (1980) 87–89 (it is now clear that a notice may be served as soon as the date has passed: *Behzadi v Shaftesbury Hotels Ltd* [1992] Ch 1). For discussion of the theoretical basis of this rule, which may appear to change the nature of a term of the contract, see *Chitty on Contracts* (n 43) [27-035] (E McKendrick) and *Treitel* (n 65) [18-127].

[76] It applies explicitly to delay in payment: SGA 1979, s 48(3).

[77] *Hartley v Hymans* [1920] 3 KB 475, 484.

[78] SGA 1979, s 10(1).

not necessarily hold that time is of the essence when a business is buying equipment in order to use it, unless the situation is evidently one of urgency.

Turning back to what remedies our small business needs, rules that make the seller's obligations as to correspondence with description and/or sample and fitness for purpose into 'conditions', so that the buyer has an almost unqualified right to reject the goods for any breach of one of those implied terms, and treat time for delivery as being of the essence seem better suited to purchases of goods for resale—when the buyer may not know on what terms the goods may have been re-sold, or whether what to it seems a minor defect may be of great import to a buyer lower down the chain—than it is when the goods are bought for use. In most cases, it would suffice for our buyer that the goods can be repaired, or replaced if that is necessary, within a reasonable period. In other words, as a default rule I would suggest that time for delivery should not be treated as being of the essence, and the buyer should be entitled to terminate the contract only if the seller does not 'cure' the defect after the buyer has set a reasonable period for this to be done.

Even when the seller has failed to cure the problem, should the buyer have the right to terminate the contract, if despite the non-conformity the goods can in fact be used for the buyer's purpose? Some systems appear to allow this. In German law, for example, it appears that if the goods do not conform to the contract, and the seller has failed to comply with a notice to repair or replace them within a reasonable time (a *Nachfrist*), the buyer may terminate the contract without having to show that the breach was serious,[79] save where it was entirely trivial (*unerheblich*).[80] That might at least give the seller an extra incentive to perform, beyond its potential liability in damages. The argument is parallel to the argument used to justify retaining a consumer's right to reject the goods and terminate the contract immediately, now called 'the short-term right to reject'.[81] It was said that this right is a useful bargaining tool for the consumer to use against a recalcitrant supplier.[82] It can be argued that a small business should have the same kind of leverage. Though it might be useful to investigate the practical experience of small businesses when trying to get suppliers to repair or replace goods, my sense is that small business buyers do not need an immediate right to terminate the contract, but they should be able to do so after they have given a warning to the seller to fix the problem within a reasonable time.

I have so far talked about equipment required for use. Would it be different with goods to be used for consumption? The buyer will be consuming the goods, rather than using them over a period of time, and (especially with 'just in time delivery' becoming more common) may want to use them immediately. In other words, it is more likely that time will be of the essence. However, I don't think a separate rule would be required for this case—or at least no more than a presumption that when a buyer orders consumables, time will be presumed to be of the essence. Under the current law, that would exclude any right to cure after the date or period for delivery has passed.

---

[79] §323 BGB; see Hugh Beale, 'Remedies for Breach of Contract in the Light of the Recent Changes to German Law, English Law and the DCFR' in Uwe Blaurock and Günter Hager (eds), *Obligationenrecht im 21.Jahrhundert* (Nomos 2010) 115, 132–38.

[80] §323 BGB V second sentence.

[81] CRA 2015, s 20.

[82] See Law Commissions, *Consumer Remedies for Faulty Goods* (Law Com No 317, Scot Law Com No 216, 2009) [3.14].

F. Loss of the Right to Reject

Despite the changes that have been made to the sections governing the loss of the buyer's right to reject,[83] there is still some uncertainty over when this occurs, and in particular what amounts to retaining the goods after a reasonable lapse of time.[84] How much improvement is possible I do not know. It might be useful to set minimum periods—for example, that unless the goods are perishable, the period will never be shorter than, say, thirty days. But again, I do not think the needs of small business buyers for use or consumption are different to those of other buyers, except that small businesses might benefit more from legislative clarification of the law.

G. A Long-Term Right to Reject

Consumers now have a right to reject goods that are found to be non-conforming however long they have had them, if the supplier has failed to repair or replace them within a reasonable time of being asked to do so or if the repair or replacement will cause undue inconvenience to the consumer ('the final right to reject').[85] The supplier must then refund the price unless the consumer has had the goods for more than six months or the goods consist of a vehicle, when deductions may be made for the use the consumer has had from the goods.[86] Should small business buyers have a similar right? In 1987 the Law Commissions recommended against a long-term right to reject, mainly because of the difficulties over valuing the buyer's use of the goods.

The remedial structure of the CRA 2015 was dictated by the Consumer Sales Directive and seems to go further than is necessary, for small business buyers if not for consumers. I suspect that in most cases of the sale of equipment to small businesses the buyer will have paid the price within a fairly short period.[87] If the non-conformity—say, lack of durability—emerges only after some months, and the seller fails to replace the goods or make the necessary repairs, termination will no longer have the advantage of being a self-help remedy; the buyer will have to bring a claim against the seller, whether it be for a refund of the price or for damages. In principle a claim for a refund, being liquidated, will be easier to bring, but I doubt that it will be hard for the buyer to prove the basic loss it has suffered. If the goods can be repaired then the claim will be for the cost (and for disruption to the buyer's business, so far as that is not too remote); if they cannot be repaired, the damages will be for the cost of a replacement. I do not see that the long-term right to reject is needed.

H. The Measure of Damages

Michael Bridge has made the point that the rule that normally the buyer's damages are measured by the market price of the goods at the date for delivery is not apt for sales where

---

[83] Sections 34 and 35 were amended by the Sale and Supply of Goods Act 1994, s 2.
[84] See Twigg-Flesner and Canavan, *Sale of Goods* (n 28) 432–35.
[85] CRA 2015, s 24(5).
[86] CRA 2015, ss 24(8), (10).
[87] If the business cannot pay cash, it is more likely to lease the equipment.

the buyer intends to use the goods.[88] It would be better to measure the buyer's damages by the cover price, that is, what the buyer has paid to obtain a substitute, subject to the seller showing that the buyer delayed unreasonably or that the substitute transaction was not reasonable. This is the approach adopted by the Uniform Commercial Code,[89] the UN Convention on Contracts for the International Sale of Goods (1980),[90] and the recent soft law restatements.[91] Although the difference between the two measures is being reduced by the court's willingness to allow the innocent party to consider its position, and thus to measure the damages by a later date,[92] it still seems preferable to allow the buyer to recover the actual cost it incurred in getting what it wanted, provided the buyer did not act unreasonably. The 'abstract' market price measure can be reserved for cases in which the buyer decides not to obtain a substitute.[93]

IV. The Scope of the Legislation

For reasons of space, I will discuss this second issue only briefly, dealing first with digital downloads and services, then with involving the supply of goods other than by way of sale or combined with services.

A. Digital Products

Consumers who have been supplied with digital downloads that are not of the correct description or fit for the purpose, and so on, are now protected by Part 1, Chapter 3 of the Consumer Rights Act 2015.

I believe that at least small businesses should have similar statutory protection. It is true that if a digital product does not work or is not fit for a particular purpose made known to the supplier, there is protection for buyers at common law if not under statute. After the *St Albans* case it now seems to be accepted that if software is supplied on a disk or other tangible medium, the combination of disk and software may count as goods and the transaction may fall within the SGA.[94] If the digital product is not supplied on a disk or the like but is directly up- or downloaded, it seems likely that the supplier can be liable for breach of an implied term at common law, analogous to the implied terms under the SGA.[95] But what

---

[88] Bridge, 'A Law for International Sale of Goods' (n 55) 36, remarks that 'the sale of goods contract is in effect recharacterised by the market damages rule as a market differences contract', but notes (at 37) that though the SGA approach might seem better suited to the commodities markets, the GAFTA conditions also start with the substitute transaction (see now GAFTA 100 cl 24).

[89] UCC §2-712.

[90] CISG Art 75.

[91] Ole Lando and Hugh Beale (eds), *Principles of European Contract Law* (Kluwer 2000) Art 9:506 (Substitute transaction); UNIDROIT, *Principles of International Commercial Contracts* (2016) Art 7.4.5 (Proof of harm in case of substitute transaction).

[92] See generally *Chitty on Contracts* (n 43) [29-105].

[93] UCC §2-713, which applies the date that the buyer learned of the breach, 'uses as a yardstick the market in which the buyer would have obtained cover had he sought that relief' (Comment 1); CISG Art 76, which applies if the buyer has not made a purchase under Art 75; similarly, PECL Art 9:507 (Current Price) and UPICC 7.4.6 (Proof of harm by current price).

[94] *St Albans City & District Council v International Computers Ltd* [1997] FSR 251, 266.

[95] ibid.

the *St Albans* case did not address explicitly was whether the contract was one of sale, so that all the rights in the software were transferred to the Council, or merely a licence to use the software.[96] It has been argued forcefully that the customer does buy a copy of the software that it can use, and that the position is no different to buying a book;[97] and the CJEU in the *Usedsoft* case[98] has held that a person who no longer wants to use software may be able to sell it. In reaction to this decision, however, many software companies now supply software not once-and-for-all but on a subscription basis, so the analogy with sales disappears. As a result, there is considerable doubt what rights the customer will have at common law. For example, it is not wholly clear whether the supplier's obligation will be one of strict liability, by analogy to goods, or only one to use reasonable care and skill.[99]

In any event, common law rules are not readily accessible to anyone except lawyers. Sole traders and small businesses that run into contractual difficulties may often seek advice from organizations that do not employ lawyers, and non-lawyers may not be able to find the relevant common law or may assume that because there is no legislation on the topic, the client has no remedy.

I would like to see legislation which goes further than the CRA currently does, in a number of ways. First, the CRA does not have special rules on the provision of digital services, such as cloud storage;[100] these are left to the chapter of the Act dealing with services. In contrast, the EU's Digital Content Directive[101] (which had to be implemented by Member States only after the UK had left the EU) requires that digital services meet conformity criteria almost identical to those for goods, throughout the period of supply. Second, the Directive tackles a series of issues that can arise with the supply of digital products and services, such as updates that are required to keep the product or service working and secure, and when the supplier may make other changes.[102] We need similar provisions, for both consumers and small businesses.

B. Supply Other Than by Sale

I also think the supply of goods of other kinds than sale and the supply of services should be brought within a single Act, as has been done for consumers. Here we have legislation already. There is already a good deal of statutory protection for the 'business buyer', in the

---

[96] *St Albans v International Computers* [1997] FSR 251, 257, stating that Clause 3 of the contract granted the plaintiffs a licence under the defendant's patents, copyrights, and other intellectual property rights to use the equipment, programs, and any items related to the provision of services, in the form and for the purpose for which they were supplied.

[97] Sarah Green and Djakhongir Saidov, 'Software as Goods' [2007] JBL 161.

[98] *UsedSoft GmbH v Oracle International Corp* (C-128/11) EU:C:2012:407.

[99] See inter alia Robert Bradgate, *Consumer Rights in Digital Products* (BIS 2010), available at https://assets.publishing.service.gov.uk/government/uploads/system/uploads/attachment_data/file/31837/10-1125-consumer-rights-in-digital-products.pdf (accessed 29 November 2022), Pt III.

[100] CRA 2015, s 39(6) applies quality obligations to data which is supplied by the consumer and processed by the trader, but only when the trader has supplied digital content to the consumer first (s 39(3)(b)). Whether this covers digital services seems to depend on whether the consumer has to download an app or other software in order to use the service. A service accessed through the trader's website is not within the section.

[101] Directive (EU) 2019/770 of the European Parliament and of the Council of 20 May 2019 on certain aspects concerning contracts for the supply of digital content and digital services of 22 May 2019, OJ L136.

[102] For a survey of the Directive's provisions on services, see Hugh Beale, 'Digital Content Directive and Rules for Contracts on Continuous Supply' (2021) 12 JIPITEC 96.

Supply of Goods (Implied Terms) Act 1973 and the Supply of Goods and Services Act 1982. So why do we need a new Act which would in effect be merely a consolidation? My answer is again one of accessibility for advisers who do not have legal training, and for businesspeople with some experience in contracting.

This is especially important when the business is contracting not for a simple sale or a simple supply of services but a bundle of obligations, either under a single mixed contract or under a series of linked contracts with the supplier. Many contracts for the supply of goods involve what the industry refers to as 'servitization'. Business Studies literature[103] describes servitization as taking one of three forms.[104] In the first, 'product-orientated services', goods are sold to customers with an accompanying package of services. The services may be provided just at the outset, such as installation and training, or on a continuing basis, such as maintenance. The services may be performed by the goods supplier itself or by a third-party sub-contractor. In the second category, 'use-orientated services', the supplier retains ownership of the goods and maintains them, and so on, while the customer pays to use them. The rental may be for a long period or a short one, and the customer may pay either a flat rent for the period of lease or hire, or according to its use of the goods.[105] In a third form, 'result-orientated services', the customer contracts simply to be provided with an outcome; how the outcome is produced is left to the supplier. The classic example comes from the Netherlands: the Philips company has contracted with an airport to provide light in the airport, of so many lumens for so many hours per day.[106] How it does so, and what equipment to install, is left to Philips.

Advising a business that has problems with a servitization arrangement may thus involve advising on several types of contract, and it would be helpful if the rules were available all in one place, as they are in the CRA. It would be better still if the legislation explained the interrelationship between the parts of mixed contracts and, when the goods and services are supplied under separate contracts, the effect of terminating one of them on the other contracts in the bundle.[107]

---

[103] A useful summary and analysis can be found in Mark Johnson, Jens K Roehrich, Mehmet Chakkol, and Andrew Davies, 'Reconciling and Reconceptualising Servitization Research: Drawing on Modularity, Platforms, Ecosystems, Risk and Governance to Develop Mid-Range Theory' (2021) 41 Int J Operations & Production Management 465 (hereafter Johnson et al, 'Reconciling and Reconceptualising Servitization Research'). For a very readable survey of the ways companies have changed their marketing strategies, including servitization, and a study of the development of car leasing in the Netherlands, see Taneli Vaskelainen, Karla Münzel, Wouter Boon, and Koen Frenken, 'Servitisation on Consumer Markets: Entry and Strategy in Dutch Private Lease Markets' (2021) 24 *Innovation* 231. Those wanting to explore the literature in detail can find a helpful list in María Martín-Peña and Ali Bigdeli, 'Servitization: Academic Research and Business Practice' (2016) 49 Universia Business Rev 18.

[104] See Johnson et al, 'Reconciling and Reconceptualising Servitization Research' (n 103) 6.

[105] This is nothing new. A classic example—Rolls-Royce's 'Power by the Hour' scheme for aeroengines, under which the engines are leased to customers who pay according to the number of hours for which the engine is used—was introduced sixty years ago: https://www.rolls-royce.com/media/press-releases-archive/yr-2012/121 030-the-hour.aspx (accessed 29 November 2022).

[106] Vanessa Mak and Evelyne Terryn, 'Circular Economy and Consumer Protection: The Consumer as a Citizen and the Limits of Empowerment Through Consumer Law' (2020) 43 JCP 227, 239.

[107] See Hugh Beale, 'From Sales to Servitization' in Yeşim M Atamer and Stefan Grundmann (eds), *European Sales Law in the 21st Century* (SECOLA Series, forthcoming).

V. Conclusion

The changes that I have suggested to the Sale of Goods Act 1979 to make it better suited to the needs of small businesses, and the extension of the legislation to cover digital content and services and other forms of supply of goods and services, are probably all wishful thinking. Nonetheless, I hope that Ewan McKendrick will appreciate this short exploration of the possibilities—even though he probably thought of all of them himself long ago.

19

Transnational Commercial Law and Impediments to Its Development

ROY GOODE

I. Introduction

It is a privilege to be invited to contribute to a collection of essays in honour of Professor Ewan McKendrick—a fine scholar; an outstanding law teacher; a superb administrator who for many years, in his capacity as Registrar of the University of Oxford, of which he had been a Pro-Vice-Chancellor, helped steer the university through sometimes difficult times; and a wonderful colleague and friend. Generations of students have benefited from his works on contract law and unjust enrichment, not to mention his contributions to comparative contract law and his co-authorship of *Transnational Commercial Law: Texts, Cases and Materials*.[1] I owe Ewan a particular debt of gratitude for taking on the heavy burden of editorship of *Commercial Law* from the fourth edition onwards[2] and ensuring that its aim of conceptual clarity was maintained despite the plethora of new case law and legislation. His retirement and move, with his wife Rose, to Cheltenham have deprived Oxford of the benefit of his great teaching skills, his down-to-earth approach to management, and his wry sense of humour. But we will not let him escape entirely!

National law governing purely domestic transactions may be ill-suited to cross-border agreements. The parties may, of course, reach agreement on the governing law, failing which the law determined by the forum's conflict of laws rules will apply. But the transaction will remain rooted in national law. Uniform conflict rules will serve to harmonize conflict of laws matters but again it is the given national law that will apply. Hence the drive to develop transnational commercial law to govern cross-border transactions.

Transnational commercial law, a relatively new subject,[3] has been defined as 'that set of private law principles and rules, from whatever source, which governs international commercial transactions and is common to legal systems generally or to a significant number of legal systems'.[4] Thus defined, transnational commercial law is the product of convergence of rules drawn from a variety of sources, both legally binding and facultative.

---

[1] Roy Goode, Herbert Kronke, and Ewan McKendrick, *Transnational Commercial Law, Text, Cases and Materials* (2nd edn, OUP 2015) (hereafter Goode, Kronke, and McKendrick, *Transnational Commercial Law*). A third edition of this work is in progress with new editors, coordinated by Professor Teresa Rodriguez de las Heras Ballel.

[2] Now in its sixth edition: *Goode and McKendrick on Commercial Law* (LexisNexis 2020).

[3] The evolution of the modern concept of transnational commercial law from the 1950s was powered by scholars such as Professors Berthold Goldman of Paris and Clive Schmitthoff of London but took a long time to penetrate the academic world. What is believed to be the first known academic course in the world on transactional commercial was introduced by the writer into the Oxford Law curriculum in the mid-1990s. Now transnational commercial law is taught by law schools in many countries.

[4] Goode, Kronke, and McKendrick, *Transnational Commercial Law* [1.03]. See also Maren Heidemann's excellent work *Transnational Commercial Law* (Red Globe Press 2018).

Roy Goode, *Transnational Commercial Law and Impediments to Its Development* In: *Shaping the Law of Obligations*. Edited by: Edwin Peel and Rebecca Probert, Oxford University Press. © Roy Goode 2023. DOI: 10.1093/oso/9780198889762.003.0019

II. The Approach to Harmonization

Any harmonization project must begin with a survey of existing national laws dealing with the field that is to be harmonized. What, then, should be made of the results of such a survey, which is likely to show widely differing approaches? One way forward is to search for the common core, an approach initiated by the celebrated comparativist Rudolf Schlesinger in his ground-breaking work *Formation of Contracts*[5] and followed by the project *The Common Core of European Private Law*,[6] launched under his auspices in 1993, and at a more specific level *Good Faith in European Private Law*.[7] One aspect of the functional approach to comparative law[8] is to look not at formal doctrinal differences but at solutions to typical problems. The solutions may differ but the problem is common. A comparison of solutions to typical problems was traditionally the province of comparative lawyers, who might use the comparison to determine best solutions, but with the complexities of modern commerce this is less likely than it may once have been. International business organizations nowadays tend to find themselves much more in the driving seat when it comes to identifying problems and their solutions.

The business community looks for three things when examining a proposed rule governing cross-border transactions: clarity, in the sense of giving predictability of outcome of a dispute; reduction of risk (particularly relevant to potential financiers when considering whether to extend credit), as by establishing an international register for the registration of property rights;[9] and efficiency in facilitating the speed of a transaction and reducing transaction costs, as by the use of intermediation for dealings in securities, electronic transfers, and digitalization, or by establishing an international register for the recording of property rights.

III. Sources of Law

A. Legally Binding Rules

Legally binding rules governing relationships in cross-border transactions derive from international instruments, primarily international conventions[10] and protocols thereto,[11]

---

[5] Rudolf B Schlesinger (gen ed), *Formation of Contracts: A Study of the Common Core of Legal Systems* (Stevens & Sons 1968).

[6] On which see <https://common.core.org>.

[7] Reinhard Zimmermann and Simon Whittaker (eds), *Good Faith in European Contract Law* (CUP 2000).

[8] On which see Ralf Michaels, 'The Functional Method of Comparative Law' in Mathias Reiman and Reinhard Zimmermann (eds), *The Oxford Handbook of Comparative Law* (2nd edn, OUP 2019) ch 10. See further the discussion in John Cartwright's chapter in this collection (ch 2).

[9] For example, the registration of a patent under the 1970 Patent Co-operation Treaty (as amended) to secure simultaneous patent protection in a large number of countries or registration of an international interest in mobile equipment in the International Registry established by the 2001 Convention on International Interests in Mobile Equipment (the Cape Town Convention) giving priority over unregistered interests, whether registrable or not.

[10] But some conventions are in substance soft law because they are excludable by contract, as in the case of the UN Convention on Contracts for the International Sale of Goods 1980 (CISG), or are so general in character that they lack true binding force. See generally Alan Boyle, 'Soft Law in International Law-Making' in Malcolm Evans (ed), *International Law* (5th edn, OUP 2018) ch 5; Christine Chinkin, 'The Challenge of Soft Law: Development and Change in International Law' (1989) 38 ICLQ 850.

[11] Such international instruments do, of course, fall within the domain of public international law as treaties, but though the parties are States the primary beneficiaries are the transacting parties, so that the treaty provisions are essentially concerned to confer private rights. Treaties of this kind are rarely mentioned in works on international

and from customary international law[12] and uncodified international trade usage (*lex mercatoria*). They may also result from judicial or legislative parallelism, where national courts or legislatures are influenced by decisions of foreign courts and legislatures or by international restatements of law by leading scholars.[13] This chapter focuses on instruments made by the four main international bodies concerned with the harmonization of commercial law: the International Institute for the Unification of Private Law (UNIDROIT); the United Nations (UN) and its Commission on International Commercial Practice (UNCITRAL); the Hague Conference on Private International Law (HCCH) as regards conflict of laws conventions; and the International Chamber of Commerce (ICC), which prepares and publishes rules for incorporation into contracts. Much of the former unwritten international trade usage has now been codified, thereby losing its character as usage and deriving its force from contract, international conventions, or some other source.[14]

B. Facultative Rules

Facultative rules are of three main kinds: model laws, legislative guides, and contractually adopted or incorporated rules. In contrast to conventions, which become binding by ratification and transplantation into domestic law where not self-executing, model laws come at the harmonization problem from a different direction by offering a set of rules that can be adopted as domestic law in national legal systems. There is no obligation on any State to adopt the rules since these have no effect on the international plane, so that there is no process of ratification. So model laws prepared by UNCITRAL are adopted either by a Diplomatic Conference convened by its General Assembly or, more usually, by the General Assembly itself at one of its annual meetings performing the functions of a Diplomatic Conference, while those prepared by UNIDROIT are adopted by a Joint Session of its General Assembly and the project's committee of governmental experts. Moreover, it is open to states to adopt a model law in a modified form, excluding or varying some of its provisions.

Examples of model laws relating to international commercial contracts are the 1985 UNCITRAL Model Law on International Commercial Arbitration, as amended in 2006, the 2008 UNIDROIT Model Law on Leasing and the 1997 UNCITRAL Model Law on Cross-Border Insolvency. As a form of soft law, model laws do not have either the uniformity or the stability of international conventions because, in an adopting State, they can be changed

---

law generally or treaty law in particular despite the fact that they have distinctive features. See Goode, Kronke, and McKendrick, *Transnational Commercial Law* (n 1) [3.32] *et seq*. It was formerly the practice to have a short convention annexing a uniform law or uniform rules (see, for example, the 1930 Geneva Convention providing Uniform Law for Bills of Exchange and Promissory Notes, Geneva, 7 June 1930). Modern practice is to have the rules as the text of the convention itself.

[12] A treaty may sometimes evidence a rule of customary international law, which will then be applied irrespective of whether the treaty itself has entered into force in the forum State.

[13] See eg the influential UNIDROIT Principles of International Commercial Contracts (hereafter 'UNIDROIT Principles') and the Principles of European Contract Law prepared by the (private) Commission on European Contract Law. Though the latter are regional in form, they have much in common with the UNIDROIT Principles and can be used in international contracts.

[14] See generally Roy Goode, 'Usage and Its Reception in Transnational Commercial Law' (1997) 46 ICLQ 1, reproduced in *The Development of Transnational Commercial Law*, ch 18.

or even abandoned at any time without the formalities required for denunciation of a Convention by a Contracting State. Despite these weaknesses, model laws and other forms of soft law are widely used because of the time and effort required to secure international agreement to a proposed Convention and the difficulty of amending the Convention once adopted, and also because soft laws are designed primarily for domestic transactions, are adaptable, and do not impinge on a State's existing law except so far as that State decides. But where international uniformity is the paramount consideration, the convention will be the instrument of choice.

Model laws are to be distinguished from model rules in that the former are intended for adoption by states while the latter are for adoption by the transacting private parties. Model rules may be either procedural, such as the arbitration rules promulgated by UNCITRAL[15] and the International Chamber of Commerce,[16] which are triggered by a dispute resolution clause in the underlying contract, or substantive, such as the ICC rules governing documentary credits[17] and demand guarantees,[18] which are given effect by incorporation into all relevant contracts.[19]

Finally, there are legislative guides or legal guides covering certain types of transaction issued by bodies such as UNIDROIT and UNCITRAL, which are merely explanatory in character[20] but are nonetheless influential.

IV. Obstacles to Be Overcome

Any examination of the obstacles to the harmonization of commercial law[21] needs to distinguish between issues of process and issues of substance. The former go to the organization of the project; the latter to the scope of a project, differences in national legal philosophies, and the problems of language where there are multilingual texts.

A. Issues of Process

1. *The time factor*
Those experienced in the preparation of uniform law know that they usually have to settle in for the long haul. The process of devising a successful international regime for contracts for

---

[15] See, eg, the UNCITRAL Arbitration Rules as last revised 2021 available at https://uncitral.un.org/en/texts/arbitration/contractualtexts/arbitration, last accessed 3 January 2023.

[16] See, eg, the 2021 ICC Rules of Arbitration, available at https://iccwbo.org/dispute-resolution-services/arbitration/rules-of-arbitration/, last accessed 3 January 2023.

[17] The 2007 Uniform Customs and Practice for Documentary Credits (UCP 600), on which see https://iccwbo.org/media-wall/news-speeches/iccs-new-rules-on-documentary-credits-now-available, last accessed 3 January 2023.

[18] *ICC Uniform Rules for Demand Guarantees: 2010 Revision (URDG 758)* (ICC 2010).

[19] There are also regional rules, the most significant of these being regulations and directives issued by what is now the European Union. These are binding on EU Member States. They are not considered further here.

[20] See, eg, the UNIDROIT *Legislative Guide on Intermediated Securities* (www.unidroit.org/instruments/capital-markets/legislative-guide, last accessed 3 January 2023); the UNCITRAL *Legislative Guide on Secured Transactions* (https://uncitral.un.org/en/texts/securityinterests/legislativeguides/secured_transactions, last accessed 3 January 2023).

[21] See generally José Angelo Estrella Faria, 'Future Directions of Legal Harmonisation and Law Reform: Stormy Seas or Prosperous Voyage?' [2009] Unif L Rev 4.

the international sale of goods proved particularly protracted. The first initiative came from the famous Austrian law professor Ernst Rabel, who in 1928 proposed to the newly established UNIDROIT a project for a uniform sales law. A committee was set up by UNIDROIT in 1931 to carry the project forward. After nine years, during which two successive drafts were produced, work was halted by the outbreak of the Second World War and not resumed until 1950, when UNIDROIT took it up again as a part of a planned coordination of work on contracts for the international sale of goods and agency in international sales. Fourteen more years were to elapse before a Diplomatic Conference convened by UNIDROIT in 1964 adopted the Uniform Law on International Sales and the Uniform Law on Contracts for the International Sale of Goods. Despite the great efforts put into their making they were not a success,[22] though they did provide a foundation for further work by UNCITRAL, which had now taken over the project. In 1980 the UN Convention on Contracts for the Sale of Goods was adopted, more than half a century after Rabel's initial proposal, or forty-six years if one excludes the hiatus created by the Second World War.

Much the same happened with the (UNIDROIT) Convention on Agency in the International Sale of Goods, referred to earlier, which took forty-eight years from start to finish, with thirty-eight Articles.

What is remarkable is the persistence of those involved at different stages of this long-drawn-out project, which was finally brought to a successful conclusion.

Happily, the typical time for bringing projects to a conclusion from start to adoption is now much shorter, though the process is still lengthy and few of the projects are successes in terms of the number of ratifications. The following are figures showing for some other instruments the time elapsed between the formal start of a project (though sometimes preceded by one or more colloquia) and the adoption of the relevant instrument, occasionally with a reduced scope, as in the case of agency:

1. The 1978 Hague Convention on the Law Applicable to Agency, with a total of 28 Articles: twenty-two years.
2-3. The 1988 UNIDROIT leasing and factoring conventions (run together as parallel projects), with twenty-five and twenty-three Articles respectively: fourteen years.
4. The 1997 UNCITRAL Model Law on Cross-Border Insolvency, with a total of thirty-two Articles: 2½ years.
5. The 2001 Cape Town Convention on International Interests in Mobile Equipment and its associated Aircraft Protocol (the only protocol currently in force) with a total of ninety-nine Articles: twelve years.
6. The 2002 Hague Convention on the Law Applicable to Certain Rights in Respect of Intermediated securities, with twenty-four Articles: 2¾ years.[23]
7. The 2009 UNIDROIT Convention on Substantive Rules for Intermediated Securities, with forty-eight Articles: seven years.

---

[22] One factor was the remarkable Article 2 of the Uniform Law, which, against the advice of the Drafting Committee of the Diplomatic Conference and in the teeth of other opposition, purported to exclude the application of rules of private international law altogether, and this despite the fact that only nine years earlier the Hague Convention on the Law Applicable to International Sales of Goods had been adopted. A further weakness was that under Article 3, introduced on the insistence of the United Kingdom, parties to a contract of sale were free to exclude it, expressly or by implication, potentially rendering their state's ratification meaningless.

[23] The text was finalized in February 2003 but the convention is dated 5 July 2006 because of the then practice of the Hague Conference to treat its texts as drafts until the first signature.

324 TRANSNATIONAL COMMERCIAL LAW AND IMPEDIMENTS

Three points may be noted: first, the astonishing achievements of UNCITRAL and the Hague Conference in bringing projects 4 and 6 respectively to fruition in less than three years;[24] second, the remarkably short time taken to bring the Cape Town Convention and Aircraft Protocol to fruition, given their sheer complexity, coupled with the fact that part way through the project ICAO joined UNIDROIT as a co-sponsoring organization, leading to joint meetings and the involvement of two Secretariats. Though the collaboration worked well, it is clear that without the input of the aviation industry and the Aviation Working Group in particular the project would have been much more limited and far less useful.[25] Third, the conclusion of the Hague Convention in a mere 2¾ years was astonishing.[26]

2. *Expediting the process*

What can be done to expedite the process of bringing commercial law harmonization projects to a successful conclusion? The writer's own experience suggests that among possible measures are the following: (a) substantial involvement at the outset of experts in the industry concerned; (b) greater intersessional activity; (c) an energetic, knowledgeable individual, aided by a small group, to drive the project forward; (d) the 'best as the enemy of the good'; and (e) the use of a small group as 'friends of the Chair of the Drafting Committee' to help produce a text to lay before the Drafting Committee.

a) The involvement of industry experts

The traditional process of harmonizing the law governing transactions in a given industry included sending out consultation papers and analysing responses for the benefit of the relevant study group entrusted with the project. But in the past half century it has become increasingly recognized that this procedure is no longer sufficient. Industry experts must be not merely consulted but actively involved in the process as key players, because they are best able to identify the key issues and to determine which of a range of proposed solutions will work and which will not. Lawyers from industry can also play an invaluable rule in proposing or commenting on drafts. So great reliance was placed on industry experts in the preparation of the Hague Convention on Intermediated Securities and the Cape Town Convention on International Interests in Mobile Equipment and its associated protocols.

In the case of the ICC, which is the world's largest business representative organization, with more than 45 million members in more than 100 countries, it is industry itself that takes the lead. The ICC is not a law-making body. Instead, one of its major roles is to harmonize business practice by formulating rules which are given effect by incorporation into all relevant contracts. So in the case of issue of a documentary credit, the relations between the applicant for the credit and the issuer, the issuer and the beneficiary, the issuer and an advising bank, the issuer and a confirming bank, an advising or confirming bank, and the beneficiary and the transferor and transferee of a credit, are all governed by the 2007 Uniform Customs and Practice for Documentary Credits.[27] But though it is industry that plays the dominant role, with successive drafts going out to all ICC members for comment,

---

[24] For the reasons for this as regards the Hague Convention and the unfortunate change of direction which has so far led to the bare minimum of ratifications required to bring it into force, see p.???

[25] See p.**.

[26] For the reasons for this and the unfortunate change of direction which has so far led to its failure see p.**.

[27] UCP 600 (n 17).

academic and practising lawyers also play an important part. The outcome is the product of an immense amount of expertise which has served business well.

b) Greater intersessional activity

For reasons of time and expense, plenary sessions of study groups are usually held not more frequently than annually, and sometimes less often than that. There may be intermediate meetings of sub-committees or working groups to examine particular aspects, but in general each plenary session starts with an examination of the text produced by the previous plenary session a year or more ago. However, some of the procedures adopted in work on the Hague Securities Convention were innovative. At that time the working methods of the Hague Conference and its Permanent Bureau tended to be rather formal, with votes taken on every proposition. But many of the experts involved brought with them the experience of the less formal UNIDROIT working methods which Dr Christophe Bernasconi, then First Secretary and currently Secretary General, was happy to adopt. The Permanent Bureau itself introduced a new technique by which the Drafting Committee was authorized to seek and draft for a consensus on key issues arising from the text resulting from the earlier plenary session, so that at the next meeting of the plenum it was not constrained to take the original text as the starting point, but would work on the revised text produced by the consensus. This saved much time and is a technique that could be usefully used in other harmonizing work. But it was possible only through the existence of an individual driving force, as described in what follows.

Physical meetings among delegates from around the world entail the time and expense of travel and accommodation. But with greater use of online meetings it should be possible to increase the frequency and greatly reduce the time and cost of plenary sessions—albeit provoking unhappiness on the part of those delegates who come for the ride and the shopping and only turn up on the first and last days of the meeting!

c) An individual as the driving force

The organization of a harmonization project is typically the responsibility of a senior member of staff of the sponsoring body. It is his or her responsibility to procure the necessary background information for the project, including the need for the harmonizing measure and the form it might take; to prepare questionnaires as to existing laws and practices and analyse responses; to set up and service the relevant study group or committee; to convene meetings and generally carry the work forward. In all four of the main organizations sponsoring harmonization, this work is carried out both efficiently and diplomatically. But is this enough to promote expeditious conclusion of a project? The problem is that the number of legal staff in sponsoring organizations is usually small and each lawyer is typically engaged in several projects at any given time. Intersessional contact with individual delegates of participating states is thus hard, if not impossible, to achieve. There needs to be an outside expert driver willing to give time to the project. Fortunately, two dynamic lawyers became involved in two different projects: Jeffrey Wool, a US legal expert in aircraft finance, for the UNIDROIT Cape Town project and Richard Potok, a New South Wales lawyer, for the Hague intermediated securities project.

Work on the Cape Town Convention began in 1989. Six years into the project, when progress was slow and the ambit of the work limited, UNIDROIT requested Airbus Industrie and the Boeing Company to produce a second draft of the convention setting out

326 TRANSNATIONAL COMMERCIAL LAW AND IMPEDIMENTS

a representative aviation industry view of the desired content of the convention as regards aircraft. The two aircraft manufacturers then submitted a memorandum in May 1995 on behalf of an Aviation Working Group they had organized, which, with its broad-brush approach, changed everything and led to a major expansion of the project. In due course Wool was appointed as a special guest of the Study Group's sub-committee to bring the views of the AWG to the sub-committee and later became consultant to UNIDROIT on aviation matters. His knowledge and energy, together with forceful advocacy coupled with diplomacy, drove the project forward and secured the active involvement of leaders of the aviation industry, which devoted a huge amount of time and resources to the project, reflecting their understanding of its potential importance to aircraft financing.

The securities project was also fortunate in having a sole individual as the main driving force, aided by a few key experts. The project began with a colloquium in Oxford in 1998 at which a New South Wales lawyer, Richard Potok, acted as rapporteur. He then persuaded the Permanent Bureau of the Hague Conference to adopt and fast-track the project,[28] later becoming legal expert to the Permanent Bureau and, with the assistance of a small group of experts, driving the project forward. Potok made it his business to take up key issues with all the key players from the different jurisdictions and ascertain from extended telephone conference calls where a consensus lay on each issue, the results forming the basis of the next draft.[29] The remarkably short interval between start and finish of the project owed much to this approach.

d) The best as the enemy of the good

Everything was set fair for an early entry into force of the Hague Securities Convention when there was a change of direction which proved unfortunate. Up to that point the project had proceeded on the basis of the place of the relevant intermediary approach (PRIMA), that is to say, the applicable law would be the place of business of the relevant intermediary with which the securities account was maintained. This received widespread support. Then the US delegation correctly pointed out that this could lead to uncertainty in that the different activities involved in the maintenance of an account might be dispersed among activities of the intermediary in different states: the place of opening of the account, the place from which accounts are sent, the place where dividends are received, and so on. This led to a proposal, eventually adopted despite significant opposition, that the relevant law should be that expressly chosen by the parties in the account agreement to govern the issues listed in the convention, provided that the relevant intermediary has an office ('Qualifying Office') in the selected State which provides certain functions relating to securities accounts (the so-called 'reality test' designed to avoid a capricious choice of law).[30] Failing an express choice of law, the Convention provided three alternative fall-back rules to be taken

---

[28] Resulting from the swift and committed reaction of the then Secretary General of the Hague Conference, Hans van Loon, and the Deputy Secretary General, Catherine Kesssedjisan. Dr Bernasconi was put in charge of the project and played a major role in its adoption and in the preparation of the ensuing Explanatory Report.

[29] For the history of the project, an overview of the subject and a description of the law governing intermediated securities in twenty-four jurisdictions see Richard Potok (ed), *Cross Border Collateral: Legal Risk and the Conflict of Laws* (Butterworths LexisNexis 2002). See also Roy Goode, Hideka Kanda, and Karl Kreuzer, assisted by Christophe Bernasconi, *Hague Securities Convention: Explanatory Report* (Martinus Nijhoff Publishers 2005).

[30] Hague Convention of 5 July 2006 on the Law Applicable to Certain Rights in Respect of Securities Held With an Intermediary, art 4. The Convention was actually adopted in December 2002 but as a draft, the practice of the Hague Conference at that time being to treat as a convention as a draft until the first signature.

in sequence.[31] The law thus determined would govern not only the relationship between the account holder and the intermediary but also all connected relationships—for example, that between the intermediary and the account holder's assignee or that between successive and competing assignees.

This was undoubtedly a better solution than the original PRIMA, applying a single law to all relationships. But it was undoubtedly counterintuitive that a contract between A (the intermediary) and B (the account holder) should, for example, be applied to determine priority issue between C (first assignee) and D (second assignee). Further, the solution was strongly opposed by the European Central Bank and a number of other European states, who feared (albeit without grounds) that the choice of law provision might be used to avoid regulatory requirements. So this was a case of the best being the enemy of the good. It would have been better to work out a sequence for applying the different alternatives arising under PRIMA, such as taking first the office of the intermediary where the account was opened and, if that was not a Qualifying Office, then the office from which statements are sent. In the result, a Convention has entered into force that would in its original form have attracted ratifications quickly but has to date secured only the bare minimum of three ratifications.

e) Friends of the Chair of the Drafting Committee

To begin drafting in the Drafting Committee itself is both time-consuming and inefficient. It is important to be able to lay a complete first draft before the Drafting Committee at its first meeting. My own practice as Chairman of a Drafting Committee was to prepare a first draft myself and then discuss it with a small group, 'the friends of the Chairman of the Drafting Committee', including francophones, tasked with examining my draft critically and proposing additions and amendments so as to produce a well worked-out revised text with which the Drafting Committee could begin its work. This process saved a great deal of time and allowed a number of issues to be addressed before the text even reached the Drafting Committee.

B. Issues of Substance

1. *Identifying a subject for a project*

In the case of all the international harmonizing institutions a great deal of preliminary work is undertaken to examine relevant existing national laws, to ensure that there is a need for a harmonizing measure and that it is supported by the relevant industry and is feasible. This raises acute questions of scope. If the project is too broad, it risks failure. Such was the fate of the original convention on agency, first proposed by UNIDROIT in 1935, which covered both the external relations between principal/agent and third parties and the internal relations between principal and agent. The almost unprecedented failure to produce a text at the initial Diplomatic Conference in Bucharest in 1979 led to a decision, on the advice of the renowned English scholar Professor LCB ('Jim') Gower, to confine the project to third-party relationships. This proved successful in leading to the adoption of a shortened text in 1983.[32] Another example of an international Convention so broadly based as

---

[31] ibid art 5.
[32] 1983 Convention on Agency in the International Sale of Goods.

to give rise to complexity is the 2001 UN Convention on the Assignment of Receivables in International Trade, which covers both the international assignment of receivables arising from domestic transactions and the assignment of international receivables arising from cross-border transactions. Requiring five ratifications, the Convention has so far secured only two.[33] The 2016 UNCITRAL Model Law on Secured Transactions has similarly failed to gain traction, having been so far adopted by only four states.[34] This is perhaps because it was again thought too complex, with nine chapters containing 107 Articles, based on highly developed legislation in countries such as the USA which, of course, did not need it.

If, on the other hand, the project is too narrow, its utility is reduced. It is arguable that two other UNIDROIT instruments, the 1988 Convention on International Financial Leasing and its running mate the International Factoring Convention, both of which entered into force, nevertheless did not gain the expected traction because they were too restricted.[35] Both conventions were limited to international transactions. In addition, the Leasing Convention was confined to finance leases, excluding operating leases,[36] while the Factoring Convention was limited to assignments of which notice was given to the debtor when, not so long after, the trend moved sharply towards non-notification invoice discounting where the supplier continues to maintain the ledgers and collect the discounted receivables from the debtors. It is not without significance that UNIDROIT itself has subsequently adopted a Model Law on Leasing covering both finance and operating leases and, on a proposal by the World Bank,[37] is in the process of completing a Model Law on Factoring which embraces both factoring in the traditional sense and invoice discounting.

The problem is that it is sometimes difficult to forecast how large or small a project will turn out to be. For example, the Cape Town Convention and Aircraft Protocol were initially envisaged as relatively small in scale, but with the input of the aviation industry professionals, academic experts, and national and international organizations, more and more issues kept unfolding. What categories of equipment should be covered? Should the proposed convention be a purely conflicts convention or one laying down substantive rules? Should the project be limited to security interests in the strict sense or should a functional approach be adopted so that conditional sale agreements and finance leases would be covered by the same provisions? Alternatively, should the functional approach be rejected while having title reservation and leasing agreements included but governed by distinct rules? Was the nature of the interest to be determined by national or prescribed by the convention itself as an autonomous international interest? Were priority issues to be determined through national registration systems or by the creation of an international registry? Should issues of insolvency—previously regarded, like property issues, as taboo—be included?[38] The end product proved to be one of the largest and most private commercial law harmonization projects ever to be undertaken, from which a number of new techniques emerged. It is fair

---

[33] Liberia and the United States.

[34] Fiji, Kenya, Philippines, and Zimbabwe. The UNCITRAL website gives nine States but four of these precede the model law, though taking a similar approach.

[35] The Leasing Convention has been ratified by eleven States, the Factoring Convention by nine States.

[36] The first meeting of the Restricted Exploratory Working Group did indeed recommend that the scope of the study should not be restricted to financial leasing (see CD. 54—Doc. 4/1, UNIDROIT 1975), but this idea was quickly abandoned.

[37] Which considered that current rules largely focus on international transactions and do not provide sufficient guidance to States to develop functional domestic factoring frameworks.

[38] For a detailed description see Anton Didenko, *The Cape Town Convention: A Documentary History* (Bloomsbury Publishing 2021).

to say that if the scale of the venture had been understood at the outset it is unlikely that it would have been undertaken at all! Fortunately, the progenitors UNIDROIT and, later, ICAO were determined to make a success of the project, and the delegates pressed on resolutely as each new batch of issues unfolded, and against the odds their ambition and utter determination proved justified.

There may be reasons other than scope for the failure of a project. For example, the 1995 UN Convention on Independent Guarantees and Stand-by Letters of Credit has entered force with eight ratifications, only five being required, but without a single ratification from major states in the world's financial markets in the space of its twenty-seven years of existence. There is a story behind this. UNCITRAL and the ICC have a long history of collaboration and UNCITRAL had never intended to prepare a Convention on independent guarantees. Instead, it had urged the ICC to pick up the ball and prepare for independent guarantees the equivalent of the Uniform Customs and Practice for Documentary Credits. Unfortunately, the ICC's response was slow and inadequate. Its eventual answer was the issue of the ICC Uniform Rules for Contract Guarantees,[39] which, unless otherwise agreed by the parties, required the production of a judgment or arbitral award to trigger the right to payment. Though technically documentary in character, this requirement made contract guarantees almost indistinguishable from suretyship guarantees and was not at all what the market wanted. This led to the UN Convention. The ICC began to retrieve its reputation in this field with the publication of the 1992 ICC Uniform Rules for Demand Guarantees,[40] under which the only requirements were a written demand by the beneficiary and a statement that the Principal was in breach and the respect in which it was in breach. This was much more to the liking of the business community but the rules were fairly basic. All this changed with the issue of much more comprehensive rules in 2010,[41] which fully met the needs of the market while at the same time leaving the parties the freedom to vary the rules or exclude particular provisions. In consequence, international business saw no need to rely on the UN Convention, which therefore failed to take off through no fault of its progenitor, UNCITRAL.

A more surprising failure is the well-conceived 2009 UNIDROIT Convention on Substantive Rules for Intermediated Securities,[42] which after thirteen years has not received a single ratification, and this despite the fact that it adopts a neutral approach to the two main alternative holding systems: transparent systems in which participants holding accounts with a securities intermediary continue to have a relationship with the issuer, and non-transparent systems, in which the account holder's relationship is solely with its own intermediary and the account holder has no claims against a higher-tier intermediary or the issuer.

---

[39] ICC Publication No 325.

[40] ICC Publication No 458.

[41] ICC Publication No 758. See Georges Affaki and Roy Goode, *Guide to ICC Uniform Rules for Demand Guarantees* (2nd edn, ICC 2010). A third edition is in progress.

[42] The official shorthand for this is the 'Geneva Securities Convention'. For a comprehensive analysis see Hideki Kanda, Charles Mooney, Luc Thévenoz, and Stéphanie Béraud, assisted by Thomas Keijser, *Official Commentary on the UNIDROIT Convention on Substantive Rules for Intermediated Securities* (OUP 2012).

2. Form of instrument

Assuming agreement on the subject-matter and scope of the instrument, what form should it take: a convention or a model law? This depends in large measure on the degree of the need for uniformity. If a high level of uniformity is required this cannot be left to national legal systems and only a convention will suffice.

a) Successful instruments

There are many examples of successful instruments. The most widely adopted of these is the 1958 UN Convention on the Recognition and Enforcement of Foreign Arbitral Awards, generally known as the New York Convention. This has gained an astonishing 170 ratifications, that is, 88 per cent of the world's countries, making this the most successful private law convention of all time,[43] powered by widespread problems in enforcing in one jurisdiction judgments obtained in another in the absence of a bilateral treaty. Other successful private law conventions include the 1980 UN Convention on Contracts for the International Sale of Goods (CISG), with ninety-five ratifications;[44] the 1995 UNIDROIT Convention on Stolen or Illegally Exported Cultural Objects, with fifty-four ratifications; the 1997 UNCITRAL Model Law on Cross-Border Insolvency, with fifty-three ratifications; the 2001 Cape Town Convention on International Interests in Mobile Equipment and its associated Aircraft Protocol, a product of collaboration between UNIDROIT and ICAO, which a mere two decades are fast catching up on CISG with eighty-six State ratifications of the Convention and eighty-three ratifications of the Protocol, together in each case with what is now the European Union; and the 2005 Hague Convention on Choice of Court Agreements, which, after a slow start, entered into force in 2015 following adoption by the EU and its Member States (except Denmark) and now has thirty-two ratifications. Among successful ICC products are the 2007 Uniform Customs and Practice for Documentary Credits,[45] which are in worldwide use, the 2010 ICC Uniform Rules for Demand Guarantees[46] and INCOTERMS 2020.

3. Differences in legal philosophies

Much of the work of harmonization involves the reconciliation of differing philosophies underlying different legal systems. As a generalization, the common law in general and English law in particular attach great importance to the sanctity of contract and are reluctant to allow judicial intervention to limit or preclude the enforcement of contract terms. London's status as a world financial centre, and the willingness of foreign parties to choose English law as the governing law and English courts as the forum even where neither the transaction nor the parties have any connection with England, depend in no small measure on the fact that under English law parties are held to their agreements and only rarely will

---

[43] The record for ratifications of public law conventions is held by the 1989 UN Convention on the Rights of the Child, ratified by all the countries of the world except the United States.

[44] It is not clear to what extent the number of ratifications reflects the actual application of the Convention, given that the parties to an international sale contract are free to exclude all but one of its provisions, and many do. So the GAFTA 100 contract issued by the Grain and Feed Trade Association provides that ULIS, CISG, the UN Convention on the Limitation Period in the International Sale of Goods, and Incoterms do not apply to the contract. Professor Michael Bridge, a leading authority on international sales, has supported the exclusion of CISG in commodity contracts: 'The CISG and Commodity Sales: A Relationship to Be Revisited' [2021] Sing JLS 271. The UK is one of the major trading nations that has not ratified CISG.

[45] UCP 600 (n 17).

[46] URDG 758 (n 18).

the court intervene to prevent this in commercial transactions.[47] Though the legal traditions of given legal families are far from uniform, it is broadly true that common law countries are relatively creditor-oriented and civil law countries relatively debtor-oriented. It is nevertheless recognized by civil law delegates that conventions dealing with cross-border transactions should give broad scope to freedom of contract, though they will take steps to ensure the inclusion of provisions designed to curb creditor over-reach and delegates from common law jurisdictions accept that this is a legitimate price to pay to secure agreement. In the case of the Cape Town Convention in particular, the problem is mitigated by the inclusion of an extensive system of declarations by which a Contracting State is not bound by a provision running counter to its legal philosophy unless it has opted into it or alternatively is bound by the provision unless it opts out of it.[48]

4. *Predictability versus flexibility*

The business world regularly asserts that it wants predictability in the form of clear rules covering all the main kinds of transaction. But, when faced with rules, it then seeks flexibility either in the formulation of the rules or in their application. In the case of regulations prescribed by a regulatory authority, this typically involves the conferment of discretions on the authority concerned. This in turn leads to requests to the authority to set out guidelines showing when and in what conditions the discretion will usually be exercised, so that over time discretions move towards becoming rules.

In the case of international instruments this problem may be tackled in various ways. The convention in question may allow a Contracting State to make a unilateral reservation, but in modern private law treaty practice reservations are rarely permitted. An alternative is to build into the convention a system of declarations by which a Contracting State (1) may make a declaration disapplying a provision that might run counter to its basic legal philosophy (opt-out provision), or (2) will not be bound by such a provision unless it makes an opt-in declaration. The Cape Town Convention and Protocol have elaborate systems of declarations to this end.[49] A further option is to set out alternative versions of a given Article.

5. *Balancing competing interests*

While industry involvement and support are essential, because only industry experts have the requisite expertise in identifying problems arising from cross-border transactions in their field, they must not be allowed to capture the project. It is important that the interests of other parties, including debtors and guarantors, be safeguarded from unfair treatment. This is where experts from civil law jurisdictions, which as noted earlier tend to be debtor-oriented, have an important, though not exclusive, role to play.

Similar considerations apply to interpretation, discussed below. Understandably enough, industry experts will press vigorously for an interpretation on a given issue that works well for the industry. In most cases this does not raise a problem but there are occasions in which the neutral commentator will have to take a stand and point out that the language of the

---

[47] But see Ewan McKendrick, 'Commercial Contract Law: How Important Is the Quest for Certainty?' [2021] LMCLQ 72.

[48] For a detailed analysis of the declarations system see Roy Goode, *Official Commentary on the Convention on International Interests in Mobile Equipment and Protocol thereto on Matters Specific to Aircraft Equipment* (5th edn, UNIDROIT 2022) (hereafter Goode, *Official Commentary* [2.326] *et seq*, [3.165] *et seq*.

[49] See Goode, *Official Commentary* (n 48) [2.326] *et seq*, [3.165] *et seq* and App XI.

332   TRANSNATIONAL COMMERCIAL LAW AND IMPEDIMENTS

text, even if interpreted in context, simply does not allow the meaning contended for. In the writer's own experience this typically results in vigorous exchanges which are invaluable in sharpening the arguments and the analysis, and which ultimately lead to an agreement which accommodates both viewpoints.

6. *Language issues*

Multiparty instruments involve consideration of parallel language texts. Though English is set to remain the dominant source language (displacing French, which was previously the primary language of diplomacy), it is essential to have at least one other language representative of civil law and other legal systems. That language is French. UNIDROIT has five official languages[50] but two working languages, English and French. The usual practice is to begin with an English text and then produce a French text paragraph by paragraph. This is not a translation but a parallel text, the two texts being equally authentic. ICAO, with which UNIDROIT collaborated in producing the Cape Town Convention and Aircraft Protocol, is a UN specialized agency and as such uses all six of the official languages of the United Nations.[51] This posed a problem for the Cape Town Convention because it is impossible for a drafting committee to work in more than two languages, which in a multilateral instrument will be English and French. So the expedient adopted at the Cape Town Diplomatic Conference was to produce a text in English which, before being released, would be sent to a team of experienced ICAO translators in Montreal to produce parallel texts in the other five official languages of ICAO. These were highly competent and acted with great speed and efficiency, but since they had neither legal qualifications nor prior involvement in the project, the resulting texts unsurprisingly met with criticism by delegates from the countries concerned. Though those were the texts adopted by the Conference, the problem was neatly addressed by a provision of the Final Act of the Conference that the text was subject to verification by the Secretariat of the Conference under the authority of the President of the Conference within a period of ninety days as to the linguistic changes required to make the texts in the six languages consistent with one another. This is a device that could usefully be made standard in relation to all multilateral instruments. Contracting States with other languages will, of course, produce their own texts which are 'official' but not 'authentic'.

Even parallel texts in only two languages, such as English and French, may raise difficulties. For example, French legal delegates will understandably want to ensure that the French text not only parallels the English text but is rendered in elegant French. Where this is not possible, the best solution is to change the English text. A more serious difficulty is that, since legal terms embody the concepts of the legal system in which they are embodied, an accurate parallel rendering may prove impossible. For example, the word 'possession' in English is unavoidably rendered '*possession*' in French, yet these terms are *faux amis*. In French law a person holding goods is a possessor only if holding in the capacity of owner, so that an equipment lessee does not have possession, whereas in English law any person holding for an interest of its own is a possessor even if the interest is only a limited one such as that of a lessee or pledgee. The only way of resolving the problem is to interpret the word in question in the light of the purposes of the instrument.[52]

---

[50] English, French, German, Italian, and Spanish.
[51] Arabic, Chinese, English, French, Russian, and Spanish.
[52] Which in the Cape Town Convention embodies the broader common law concept of possession. See Goode, *Official Commentary* (n 48) [2.30].

According to Article 33(1) of the 1969 Vienna Convention on the Law of Treaties:

> When a treaty has been authenticated in two or more languages, the text is equally authoritative in each language, unless the treaty provides or the parties agree that, in case of divergence, a particular text shall prevail.

This, of course, is necessarily the formal position in treaty law, but it has rightly been described as a fiction.[53] Nowadays the language of the source text is almost invariably English, with a French text as at least one of the parallel texts.

7. Technology

One of the novel features of the Cape Town Convention was its provision for the establishment of an International Registry for the registration of international interests in mobile equipment,[54] accompanied by a rule giving priority over subsequently registered interests and over unregistered interests, whether registrable or not. Competing bids were invited which received the most careful evaluation before the contract was awarded to the Irish company Aviareto, a joint subsidiary of SITA and the Irish government. The technology involved proved much more complex than had been envisaged and it was fortunate that Spain, the third State to ratify the Convention, deferred ratification of the Aircraft Protocol, needed to bring the Convention into force,[55] delaying this for some years, supposedly because of yet another dispute with the UK over Gibraltar. But for this hold-up, the Convention would have entered into force without an operative Registry—a central plank of the Cape Town system—posing an interesting problem for international lawyers.[56] So even obstacles can sometimes turn out to be a blessing!

V. Interpretation

It is customary for harmonizing agencies such as the Hague Conference, UNIDROIT, and UNCITRAL to publish explanatory reports or official commentaries by leading experts in the field in question, giving the history of the project, its underlying principles and policies, and an article-by-article examination of its provisions. These are not binding on national courts but are of high persuasive value and help to ensure consistency of interpretation by

---

[53] Jean-Francois Riffard, 'Is the Duality of Working Languages a Source of Conflict or Mutual Enrichment? The Example of the Cape Town Convention and Its Protocols' (2022) 8 CTCJ 40, 42.

[54] In the words of John G Sprankling, 'The registration system established under the convention is a remarkable achievement—an international mechanism for defining and coordinating security interests among private actors, independent of municipal laws. It is the first global title system for any form of property rights': *The International Law of Property* (OUP 2014) 63.

[55] For a detailed account, see Teresa Rodriguez de las Heras Ballell, 'The Accession by Spain to the Cape Town Convention: A First Assessment' (2014) 19 Unif L Rev 1.

[56] Article 61(1) of the Vienna Convention on the 1969 Law of Treaties provides for suspension of the operation of a treaty while is performance is impossible, and implicitly allows suspension of some of its provisions where performance of those is temporarily impossible but suspension should also extend to other provisions that are inextricably linked to what is impossible—in the case of an inoperable registry, provisions relating not only to registration but to priorities and insolvency.

national courts.[57] They are of two kinds. The first are reports which are intended to be final and definitive and are either presented for approval to a Diplomatic Conference or published subsequently by or under the aegis of the sponsoring organisation. These are very appropriate where the adopted instrument is complete and does not require any additional process but are unsuitable for cases where the instrument in questions provides for further developments which will necessitate an update of the original Official Commentary. The Cape Town Convention and Aircraft Protocol provide a case in point. At the time of adoption of these instruments, no declarations by Contracting States had been made under either of them; the International Registry to record international interests had not been set up, nor had registry regulations been issued; and a range of interpretative issues could be identified only after experience of working with the two instruments had been gained. Indeed, it typically takes many years to gain a full appreciation of the text of an instrument, particularly in the case of complex texts such as the Convention and Aircraft Protocol.[58] Moreover, though these stand up remarkably well to rigorous interpretation, it became apparent over the years that they contained errors, omissions, ambiguities and the like that were not picked up at the outset.[59] Accordingly, the original Official Commentary was necessarily limited in scope and had to be followed by new and expanded editions with each significant new development, particularly the conclusion of an additional Protocol, and the identification of each new issue. Fortunately this was possible, because while each edition is required to be undertaken after consultation with, and in the light of comments from, governments and various other bodies, including observer organizations such as the Aviation Working Group, the final text was the responsibility of the writer alone, subject only to the text receiving formal approval for distribution by the UNIDROIT Governing Council. There was therefore no problem in keeping the text updated. The revised edition is to be published in the autumn of 2023.

Official commentaries and explanatory reports are not, of course, the sole repository of wisdom on matters of interpretation. There are also books and articles by many authors. The difference is that though these may be illuminating, they do not carry the status of officially approved texts. The same, of course, is true of texts of instruments which are not rendered in one of the official languages of a Diplomatic Conference but are translations by national governments.

---

[57] The problem does not, of course, arise in the case of EU regulations and directives, where the final arbiter on issues of interpretation is the European Court of Justice. For ordinary private law conventions, by contrast, there is no appellate court to entertain appeals outside a Contracting State's own appellate system. The national courts of a Contracting State have a duty to interpret a convention in good faith, so that deliberate disregard of its provisions would place the State in question in breach of its international obligations, but apart from this there is no external tribunal competent to rule on the validity of the court's interpretation. This raises a question as to the duty of a court of a Contracting State when asked to enforce a decision of another Contracting State on the Convention pursuant to a bilateral treaty between the two States when that decision is plainly wrong. In the writer's view it is not for the courts of the enforcing State to second-guess the decision of the issuing court even though the enforcing court is itself a Contracting State. This is because the enforcing court is not being asked to interpret the Convention, merely to give effect to the court order.

[58] Official Commentaries have also been published for the Luxembourg (Rail) Protocol.

[59] See Goode, *Official Commentary* (n 48).

VI. Securing Ratifications

It is one thing to have an international instrument adopted but quite another to have it ratified and then implemented in domestic legislation. Governments from all over the world send delegates to participate in preparatory work and diplomatic conferences, which involve hard work and painstaking endeavour; yet when it comes to ratification, a remarkable torpor descends. Two reasons are usually advanced: lack of parliamentary time and lack of industry support. It is true that governments are preoccupied with domestic law and legislative time is precious, but where, as is usual, legislation is needed to make a convention part of domestic law, the process will usually be relatively quick because, except for permitted reservations and declarations, the text of a convention cannot be changed, so the legislature has simply to decide whether to adopt the convention or reject it. Therefore a supposed lack of parliamentary time generally signifies a lack of political will.

Industry support is crucial; hence the importance of involving industry experts, not as mere consultees but as active participants in the preparation of the instrument. Even with industry support, governments can be slow to act in the absence of evidence of the economic benefits of the convention. With this in mind, UNIDROIT took the unusual step of procuring economic impact assessments of the prospective Cape Town Convention and (1) the Aircraft Protocol and (2) the MAC Protocol,[60] all of which concluded that the potential benefits were substantial, running to billions of dollars a year for both developed and developing Contracting States.[61]

Given the limited resources that harmonizing organisations are able to devote to promotion of their products, it is important that industry support does not end with the Diplomatic Conference but extends to post-conference promotion of the text through conferences in different countries and through publications. In the case of the Cape Town Convention, for example, the Aviation Working Group has played a continuing role in vigorously promoting the Convention and the Aircraft Protocol and this has been a significant factor in the success of these two instruments.

VII. Compliance Index

It is one thing for a Contracting State to ratify a convention, another to determine whether the convention has been effectively domesticated in national law and is being correctly applied. The Aviation Working Group introduced a novel concept to test compliance with the Cape Town Convention and Aircraft Protocol. This index, based on information supplied by more than 200 law firms worldwide, assesses for each Contracting State the degree of compliance, on the basis of which it assigns a score to each such State. The relevant activity

---

[60] Formally the Pretoria Protocol, but the abbreviation is convenient as denoting coverage of mining, agricultural and construction equipment. It should be noted that the Convention by itself has no economic benefits because it enters into force as regards a category of objects only where there is a Protocol relating to such category and subject to the terms of that Protocol (art 49).

[61] See, for aircraft objects, Anthony Saunders and Ingo Walter, *Proposed Unidroit Convention on International Interests in Mobile Equipment as Applicable to Aircraft Equipment through the Aircraft Equipment Protocol: Economic Impact Assessment* (A Study Prepared under the Auspices of INSEAD and the New York University Salomon Center 1998), a quantitative study commissioned by the Aircraft Protocol Group. See Jeffrey Wool, 'Economic Analysis and Harmonised Modernisation of Private Law' (2003) ULR 389; Didenko (n 38) 137 *et seq*.

VIII. Envoi

It is fitting to conclude with Ewan McKendrick's comments on the influence of comparative law in discussing the decision of Leggat J in *Yam Seng Pte Ltd v International Trade Corp Ltd*,[62] which reflected a welcome move away from the rigidity of English law in rejecting a general principle of good faith:

> It is important to note that Leggatt J drew on a wide range of legal systems, including civilian, common law, and mixed legal systems. In this respect it is interesting to note that Leggatt J did not commence his analysis with the experience of other common law legal systems. Until relatively recently, that is where one might have expected a judge to look for comparative material. Rather, his starting point was in Europe, specifically the Unfair Terms in Consumer Contracts Regulations 1999, various EU Directives, the Principles of European Contract Law, and the proposed Regulation for a Common European Sales Law. This ordering perhaps illustrates the increasing significance of European law on the development of English private law. The fact that the Unfair Terms in Consumer Contracts Regulations 1999 require the English courts to use and apply the language of good faith may diminish the reluctance of the English judiciary to employ the language of good faith in other contractual contexts. The present case illustrates the important role which comparative law can play in the development of the law within national legal systems. Where a legal system finds itself significantly out of line with the experience of other legal systems, a recognition of the existence of that difference may encourage that legal system to re-examine its own position. This is not to say that legal systems should blindly follow the views of the majority of nation states: there may be good reasons for a particular legal system to adopt its own distinctive legal rule, but that difference should be justified, not simply asserted. But it is necessary to proceed with caution when seeking to draw lessons from comparative law, in particular to ensure that the analogy drawn is an appropriate one and that like cases are being treated alike.[63]

---

[62] [2013] EWHC 111 (QB), [2013] 1 Lloyd's Rep 526.

[63] Ewan McKendrick, 'Good Faith in the Performance of a Contract in English Law' in Larry DiMatteo and Martin Hogg (eds), *Comparative Contract Law: British and American Perspectives* (OUP 2015) 198–99 (footnotes omitted).

PART IV
UNJUST ENRICHMENT

20

Mistakes of Law, Again

HELEN SCOTT

I. Introduction

Peter Birks once remarked that the subject of mistakes of law was 'about as inviting as stale crumbs in a biscuit tin'.[1] That he wrote these words more than twenty years ago suggests that those crumbs are even less appealing now. But recent decisions of the Supreme Court on the subject of limitation[2]—specifically, on the application of section 32(1)(c) of the Limitation Act to cases involving mistaken payments—have refreshed debates apparently long settled. Specifically, renewed focus on the test of reasonable discoverability set out in that section has opened up new perspectives on the role of mistake in the law of unjust enrichment.[3]

The subject strikes me as a particularly appropriate one to address here because it was the subject of Ewan's contribution to a collection of essays, *Lessons of the Swaps Litigation*, that appeared in the wake of *Kleinwort Benson v Lincoln* in 2000.[4] The piece, which argued powerfully that it was unnecessary to rely on the claimant's mistake as the reason for restitution in that case, influenced me profoundly in my subsequent doctoral work, and it is perhaps not surprising that I have reached a rather similar conclusion here. Scholarship aside, for almost twenty years Ewan has been an invaluable colleague and mentor to me and to many others. It is a great pleasure to be able to celebrate his academic career thus far.

II. Mistake as a Cause of Action

It has been settled law since at least *Kelly v Solari*[5] that a payment made under the influence of a mistake is recoverable without reference to the culpability or otherwise of the claimant's error. More recent decisions have established that the claimant's mistake need not be a mistake of fact,[6] nor need it relate to his liability to make the payment.[7] On the other hand, the

---

[1]   Peter Birks, 'Mistakes of Law' (2000) 53 CLP 205, 205 (hereafter Birks, 'Mistakes of Law').

[2]   *Test Claimants in the Franked Investment Income Group Litigation and others v Commissioners for Her Majesty's Revenue and Customs* [2020] UKSC 47; [2020] 3 WLR 1369 (hereafter *Test Claimants*).

[3]   An earlier version of the argument presented in section V is set out in Helen Scott, 'What Mistake Can Do' in Nils Jansen and Sonia Meier (eds), *Iurium itinera: Historical Comparative Law and Comparative Legal History* (Mohr Siebeck 2022) 627, 643–49 (hereafter Scott, 'What Mistake Can Do'). To the extent that the later version avoids the errors of the earlier one, this is due to the very helpful input I received at a meeting of the GSPLT (Global Seminar on Private Law Theory) on 10 December 2021.

[4]   Ewan McKendrick, 'The Reason for Restitution' in Peter Birks and Francis Rose (eds), *Lessons of the Swaps Litigation* (Routledge 2000) 84.

[5]   *Kelly v Solari* (1841) 9 M &W 54 (Exch).

[6]   *Kleinwort Benson Ltd v Lincoln City Council* [1999] 2 AC 349 (HL) (hereafter *Kleinwort Benson*).

[7]   *Barclays Bank Ltd v WJ Simms, Son & Cooke (Southern) Ltd* [1980] QB 677.

Helen Scott, *Mistakes of Law, Again* In: *Shaping the Law of Obligations*. Edited by: Edwin Peel and Rebecca Probert, Oxford University Press. © Helen Scott 2023. DOI: 10.1093/oso/9780198889762.003.0020

340 MISTAKES OF LAW, AGAIN

presence of a valid obligation to make the payment is a reason to deny restitution.[8] Beyond these propositions, unanimity is harder to come by.

According to what is probably the dominant view, mistake provides the reason for restitution in claims such as that at issue in *Kelly v Solari*: it constitutes the 'unjust factor' that is the central element in the claimant's cause of action.[9] Mistake is normatively significant because it shows the vitiation of the claimant's intention in making the payment. On this view, the presence of a valid obligation on the claimant to pay serves as a defence—a new reason, extrinsic to the claim, that explains why it should fail despite the fulfilment of all the elements in the claimant's cause of action—or, more likely, a denial: an argument that defeats one of those elements, namely the requirement that the defendant's enrichment be unjust.[10]

There is, however, is a different way of understanding the role of mistake in a case such as *Kelly v Solari*. According to this alternative thesis, mistake in itself cannot provide a valid reason for restitution: a defect in the knowledge of the claimant cannot justify imposing a restitutionary duty on the defendant.[11] Instead, it is the absence of a valid obligation to pay that provides the reason for restitution. Insofar as it has any role to play, mistake serves, first, as a useful proxy for the absence of any obligation on the claimant to pay—this is of course true only of liability mistakes such as the one at issue in *Kelly v Solari* itself—and, second, to pre-empt the argument that the claimant consented to pay an amount that they did not owe.[12] This argument itself amounts to a defence.[13] A variant of this alternative thesis treats as central not the absence of indebtedness but rather the failure of the payment's purpose. According to this view, in a case such as *Kelly v Solari*, proof of mistake on the part of the claimant serves to demonstrate both the purpose of the payment—that is, the discharge of liability—and the failure of that purpose by virtue of the absence of any such liability.[14] Other sorts of mistakes play a similar dual role: for example, in *Lady Hood of Avalon v Mackinnon*,[15] the claimant's mistake served to demonstrate both her purpose—to equalize her gifts to her daughters—and its failure. In each case, it is the failure of the payment's legitimate[16] purpose that justifies restitution. On neither version of the thesis is mistake an element in the claimant's cause of action.

---

[8] ibid 695.

[9] See eg *Samsoondar v Capital Insurance Co Ltd* [2020] UKPC 33. For a comprehensive account of the nature of mistake qua unjust factor, see Charles Mitchell, Paul Mitchell and Stephen Watterson (eds), *Goff and Jones on Unjust Enrichment* (10th edn, Thomas Reuters 2022) [9-06]–[9.61] (hereafter *Goff and Jones*).

[10] See eg *DD Growth Premium 2X Fund v RMF Market Neutral Strategies (Master) Ltd* [2017] UKPC 36, [62]: 'It is fundamental that a payment cannot amount to enrichment if it was made for full consideration; and that it cannot be unjust to receive or retain it if it was made in satisfaction of a legal right' (Lords Sumption and Briggs). See also Andrew Burrows, *A Restatement of the English Law of Unjust Enrichment* (OUP 2012).

[11] See Robert Stevens, 'The Unjust Enrichment Disaster' (2018) 134 LQR 574, 577–78 and *The Laws of Restitution* (OUP 2023) 78–79 (hereafter Stevens, *The Laws of Restitution*).

[12] Stevens, *The Laws of Restitution* (n 11) 72–78.

[13] Either one that nullifies the defendant's duty to make restitution—a justificatory defence, as per Stevens, *The Laws of Restitution* (n 11) 76—or one that merely creates an immunity from suit: see Scott, 'What Mistake Can Do' (n 3) 636–37.

[14] Scott, 'What Mistake Can Do' (n 3) 638–40.

[15] *Lady Hood of Avalon v Mackinnon* [1909] 1 Ch 476–84 (ChD).

[16] Scott 'What Mistake Can Do' (n 3) 638–40.

III. Mistake as a Factor Delaying Limitation

The role of mistake in the context of limitation is different. According to section 32(1)(c) of the Limitation Act 1980, in the case of claims for relief from the consequences of a mistake, the statutory limitation period does not begin to run until the claimant has discovered their mistake or could with reasonable diligence have discovered it.[17] In other words, only reasonable, non-careless mistakes are sufficient to defer the running of the limitation period. This is different from the treatment of mistakes in *Kelly v Solari*, according to which a mistake need only be genuine in order to found a restitutionary claim. What explains this difference in approach?

Limitation defeats the defendant's liability to pay but leaves the defendant's duty to make restitution intact: rather than justifying their retention of the benefit in question, it merely provides the defendant with immunity from suit. This immunity is founded on considerations of policy and equity: it is both good for society and fair to the defendant that claims should be brought within a reasonable interval after the claimant's cause of action arises or not at all. Proof that the claimant's mistake—the mistake from the consequences of which he is seeking relief—was a reasonable one in the circumstances is in turn sufficient to excuse the claimant from the operation of the defence. Careless claimants do not deserve this assistance.

Section 32(1)(c) has been applied to mistakes of law since the decision in *Kleinwort Benson v Lincoln* in 1998.[18] In that case the House of Lords decided not only that a mistake of law was sufficient to found the restitution of a mistaken payment, but also that section 32(1)(c) should be interpreted to comprise mistakes of law as well as mistakes of fact. But while the House of Lords in *Kleinwort Benson* did consider the question of whether to apply section 32(1)(c) to mistakes of law,[19] the question of how to apply it received little attention: it was simply assumed that the mistake of law at issue in that case became discoverable only when the decision in *Hazell v Hammersmith*[20]—according to which the swaps contracts widely entered into between merchant banks and local authorities during the 1980s were *ultra vires* the powers of the local authorities as set out in the Local Government Act 1972 and were therefore void—was handed down.

Subsequently, in *Deutsche Morgan Grenfell Group v Inland Revenue Commissioners* in 2006,[21] the House of Lords considered that question in more detail. It was decided by a majority of the Court that the mistake of law at issue in that case could be said to be reasonably discoverable for the purposes of the section only at the date on which the decision of the ECJ in *Metallgesellschaft v Inland Revenue Commissioners*[22]—according to which the failure of the Income and Corporation Taxes Act 1988 (ICTA) to afford to UK-based subsidiaries of non-UK-based European parent companies the opportunity to make a group

---

[17] Section 32(1)(c) reads as follows: 'where . . . the action is for relief from the consequences of a mistake; the period of limitation shall not begin to run until the plaintiff has discovered the fraud, concealment or mistake (as the case may be) or could with reasonable diligence have discovered it.'

[18] *Kleinwort Benson* (n 6).

[19] ibid 387–88 (Lord Goff); 416–18 (Lord Hope).

[20] *Hazell v Hammersmith and Fulham London Borough Council and others* [1992] 2 AC 1–47 (HL) (hereafter *Hazell*).

[21] *Deutsche Morgan Grenfell Group plc v Inland Revenue Commissioners* [2006] UKHL 49, [2007] 1 AC 558 (hereafter *Deutsche Morgan Grenfell*).

[22] *Metallgesellschaft Ltd v Inland Revenue Commissioners, Hoechst AG v Inland Revenue Commissioners* (Joined Cases C-397 and 410/98), [2001] ECR I-01727, [2001] Ch 620–669 (ECJ) (hereafter *Metallgesellschaft*).

342 MISTAKES OF LAW, AGAIN

income election and thus delay the payment of advance corporation tax on dividends paid to the parent company was contrary to the right to freedom of establishment then set out in Article 43 of the EC Treaty—was handed down.

It is these questions—the applicability of section 32(1)(c) to mistakes of law and the application of the test of reasonable discoverability—that have now been reopened by the Supreme Court in *Test Claimants in the Franked Investment Income Group Litigation and others v Commissioners for Her Majesty's Revenue and Customs*.[23]

IV. The *Test Claimants* Case

The purpose of the FII group litigation order was to determine a number of questions of law arising out of the tax treatment of UK-based parent companies with non-resident subsidiaries. Like *Deutsche Morgan Grenfell*, it concerned the system of advance corporation tax (ACT) and the taxation of dividend income received from non-resident sources under ICTA and its predecessors. This time, the point at issue was the taxation of dividend income received by UK-based parent companies from non-resident European subsidiaries; again, the test claimants' case was that the differences between their tax treatment and that of wholly UK-based groups of companies breached European law, specifically Article 43 (freedom of establishment) and Article 56 (free movement of capital) of the EC Treaty and their relevant predecessor articles. The claimants sought the repayment of such tax insofar as it was unlawful under EU law, dating back in some cases to the accession of the UK to the EU in January 1973 and the introduction of ACT in April of that year.[24]

Since the payments of tax in issue had been made up to thirty years prior to the issue of the taxpayers' claims, and since a large element of those claims would therefore have been time-barred under section 5 of the Limitation Act, the taxpayers relied heavily on section 32(1)(c). Following a reference from the trial judge, the Court of Justice of the European Union (CJEU) decided that the tax regimes in question were indeed contrary to European Union law.[25] Again, the issues before the Supreme Court in *FII* [2020] were, first, whether section 32(1)(c) applied to mistakes of law as well as mistakes of fact, as had been held in *Kleinwort Benson*; and, second, if it did, whether the majority in *Deutsche Morgan Grenfell* had been right to hold that the claimant's mistake of law had become reasonably discoverable only once the true state of the law had been established by a judicial decision from which there was no right of appeal.

For a minority of the Court (Lord Briggs, Lord Sales, and Lord Carnwath), the House of Lords in *Kleinwort Benson v Lincoln* had been 'plainly wrong'[26] to apply section 32(1)(c) to mistakes of law. For reasons that had to do with the construction of the section, the practical consequences of its application to mistakes of law (specifically, the undermining of legal certainty in relation to settled transactions that this entailed), and the unworkable nature of the test for reasonable discovery proposed by the majority, *Kleinwort Benson* should

---

[23] *Test Claimants* (n 2).

[24] For a summary of the points at issue, see *Test Claimants* (n 2) [3]–[5].

[25] *Test Claimants in the FII Group Litigation v Inland Revenue Commissioners* (Case C-446/04) [2006] ECR I-11753, [2012] 2 AC 436 (ECJ).

[26] *Test Claimants* (n 2) [259].

be overruled on that point and the operation of section 32(1)(c) confined to mistakes of fact only.

For the majority, on the other hand (Lord Reed, Lord Hodge, Lord Lloyd-Jones, and Lord Hamblen), the real mischief was to be found not in the application of section 32(1)(c) to mistakes of law but in the test of reasonable discoverability adopted by the House of Lords in *Deutsche Morgan Grenfell*. To the extent that the House of Lords held there that the claimant's mistake of law had become discoverable only when the CJEU declared (in *Metallgesellschaft*) that the relevant provisions of ICTA were unlawful because they were contrary to European law, *Deutsche Morgan Grenfell* had been wrongly decided and had therefore to be overruled.[27] Not only was a majority of the Supreme Court persuaded that the practical consequences of such a view were unacceptable;[28] the approach to reasonable discoverability adopted by the majority in *Deutsche Morgan Grenfell* (and most clearly articulated by Lord Hoffmann) amounted to a logical paradox.[29] Whereas a cause of action was retrospectively deemed to have accrued at the time at which the payment in question had been made, following the approach to mistakes of law adopted in *Kleinwort Benson*, when it came to limitation a different approach was adopted: for the purposes of section 32(1)(c), the change in the law said to have been brought about by the *Metallgesellschaft* decision was treated as occurring only at the time of that decision, and was therefore discoverable only at that time.[30] In a case in which both the correctness of a particular view of the law and the restitution of a benefit conferred under the influence of that view were decided in a single set of proceedings, this approach produced the absurd result that the mistake that formed the basis of the restitutionary claim was not discoverable until that claim itself had succeeded, and that the applicable limitation period did not begin to run until the proceedings were concluded.[31]

These difficulties could be avoided if the approach to reasonable discoverability taken by Lord Brown in *Deutsche Morgan Grenfell* were adopted.[32] It was undoubtedly possible to investigate how legal thinking on a particular question had developed over time, and to ascertain, by means of evidence, the date by which a reasonably diligent person in the position of the claimant could have known of his previous mistake of law, to the extent of knowing that there was a real possibility that such a mistake had been made and that a worthwhile claim could be brought on that basis.[33] It was at that point that a claim became discoverable for the purposes of section 32(1)(c). This approach cohered with the purpose of the Limitation Act, with the application of section 32(1)(c) to cases of fraud, with the application of other similar statutory tests, and with the case law predating the statutory limitation regime.[34] It was also likely to be reasonably practical and certain in its operation.[35]

---

[27] *Test Claimants* (n 2) [214].

[28] For a compelling account of the negative consequences of the approach to discoverability adopted in *Kleinwort Benson* (n 6) and *Deutsche Morgan Grenfell* (n 21), see Samuel Beswick, 'The Discoverability of Mistakes of Law' (2019) 58 LMCLQ 112, especially the summary at 128, and also 'Discoverability Principles and the Law's Mistakes' (2020) 136 LQR 139.

[29] *Test Claimants* (n 2) [173]–[176].

[30] *Test Claimants* (n 2) [176].

[31] ibid [174], [177].

[32] *Deutsche Morgan Grenfell* (n 21) [165]–[167], and the references to his approach by the majority in *Test Claimants* (n 2) at [180]–[182], [185]–[187], [193], [195], [197] and [209], as well as in the summary at [213].

[33] *Test Claimants* (n 2) [178].

[34] *Test Claimants* (n 2) [179]–[198].

[35] *Test Claimants* (n 2) [209]–[212].

344   MISTAKES OF LAW, AGAIN

The decision in *Test Claimants* has been subject to significant academic criticism since it was handed down. This criticism has largely been confined to the test for reasonable discoverability adopted by the majority. It has been argued that this test is, in fact, uncertain in its application and thus likely to generate unnecessary litigation; it is also said to be insufficient to avert the negative consequences (extremely long limitation periods) created by the application of section 32(1)(c) to mistakes of law in *Kleinwort Benson*.[36] In my view, however, the decision of the majority in *FII* [2020] is significant—and problematic—for more fundamental reasons.

V. Actual Mistakes and Deemed Mistakes

In *Kleinwort Benson*, the majority took the view that the claimant's belief at the time at which the payments were made—that it was liable to make the payments under a valid swap contract with the defendant—constituted a mistake. Critically, the majority's view that the payments had been made under the influence of a mistake also engaged the operation of section 32(1)(c). But because the claimant's mistake was assumed to have become reasonably discoverable only at the time of the *Hazell* decision in 1991,[37] it was unnecessary to determine exactly when their cause of action had arisen. It could have been the case that Kleinwort Benson had—as a matter of historical fact—been mistaken about their liability to pay at the time that the payments were made, in which case their cause of action would have arisen immediately upon payment. Or—less ambitiously—it could have been purely by virtue of the retrospectivity of the decision in *Hazell* that the claimant was mistaken as to whether the money they had paid was due, not by virtue of any variance between their beliefs and the state of the law at the time; in this case, the claimant's cause of action would have arisen only at the date of that decision. Dicta in the speeches of both Lord Goff and Lord Hoffmann in *Kleinwort Benson* support the latter rather than the former view.[38] But in fact the former view is not implausible: the swaps contracts could without great artificiality be said to be void at the time at which the payments were made.[39]

The circumstances at issue in *Deutsche Morgan Grenfell* were different. The relevant provisions in the Income and Corporation Taxes Act did not at the time of the payments permit the claimants to make the group income election that would have allowed them lawfully

---

[36] See eg Adrian Zuckerman, 'Test Claimants 2 in the Supreme Court: Serves Neither Justice Nor the Administration of Justice' (2022) 138 LQR 1; Stevens, *Laws of Restitution* (n 11) 372–74. Stevens in particular argues that since mistake forms no part of the claimant's cause of action (cf the text to n 12 above), the House of Lords was wrong in *Kleinwort Benson* (n 6) to hold that s 32(1)(c) applied to the claim before it.

[37] See eg *Kleinwort Benson* (n 6) 390 (Lord Lloyd).

[38] See in particular Lord Goff in *Kleinwort Benson* (n 6) 378: 'The historical theory of judicial decision, though it may in the past have served its purpose, was indeed a fiction. But it does mean that, when the judges state what the law is, their decisions do, in the sense I have described, have a retrospective effect.' See also his statement that 'it is plain that the money was indeed paid over under a mistake, the mistake being a mistake of law. The payer believed, when he paid the money, that he was bound in law to pay it. He is now told that, *on the law as held to be applicable at the date of the payment*, he was not bound to pay it' (379, my italics). See also Lord Hoffmann in *Kleinwort Benson* ('I therefore do not think that there are any reasons of principle for distinguishing cases in which a subsequent decision changes a settled view of the law, or, for that matter, settles what was previously an unsettled view of the law. The enrichment of the recipient is in each case unjust because he has received money which he would not have received if the payer had known the law to be what *it has since been declared to have been*' (309–401, my italics)) and in *Deutsche Morgan Grenfell* (n 21) [23], speaking of the majority decision in *Kleinwort Benson*.

[39] Thus for Lord Hope, 'If it were necessary to decide this point, I do not think that it would be right to say that the decision in the *Hazell case* "changed" the law'. *Kleinwort Benson* (n 6) 411.

to postpone the payment of ACT. As a matter of historical fact, then, at the time when the payments in question were made, the claimants were not mistaken as to the availability of a group income election under the relevant statutory provision: none was available. Nor could they be said to be mistaken as to their liability to pay ACT: having made no group income election, the ACT was due. This seemed a rather serious obstacle to the restitutionary claim. Indeed, it was the basis of Lord Scott's dissent in *Deutsche Morgan Grenfell*.[40] Nevertheless, according to Lord Hoffmann, 'the mistake was about whether DMG was liable for ACT'.[41] This mistake was 'deemed to have been made because of the retrospective operation of a later decision of the Court of Justice'.[42] In the same way, the claimant's valid obligation to pay at the time at which the payments were made did not pose an obstacle to the restitutionary claim because it was retrospectively effaced by the decision of the Court of Justice in the *Metallgesellschaft* case: 'The effect of the decision in the *Metallgesellschaft/ Hoechst* case ... was that the Inland Revenue had not been entitled to the money'.[43] It necessarily followed from this view of the effect of the decision in *Metallgesellschaft* that the mistake was not reasonably discoverable until after that judgment had been delivered: DMG 'could not have discovered the truth [prior to the *Metallgesellschaft* case] because the truth did not yet exist'.[44]

Although the circumstances at issue in *Test Claimants* were essentially the same as those in *Deutsche Morgan Grenfell*, the majority in the former took a fundamentally different approach. Insofar as it contemplated the possibility that the claimant's mistake could be found to have become reasonably discoverable at some point between the date of payment (T1) and the date of the decision of the CJEU (T2), it necessarily entailed that the claimant's cause of action was complete prior to T2: a mistake could not be reasonably discoverable for the purposes of section 32(1)(c) before it had come into existence. Indeed, the majority were quite clear that the claimant's cause of action accrued at T1:

> Judges cannot avoid having to decide at T2 what the law was at T1, and if their decision does not reflect how the law was understood by the claimant at T1, then it will ordinarily be uncontroversial to say that the claimant was mistaken at T1. The consequence, following the decision on the law of restitution in *Kleinwort Benson*, is that a cause of action accrued at T1 if a payment was made then on the basis of the mistaken understanding, regardless of the date of T2.[45]

In order to sustain this view, it was necessary for the majority in *Test Claimants* to frame the claimant's mistake rather differently to the majority in *Deutsche Morgan Grenfell*. Although the relevant provisions of the Income and Corporation Taxes Act were in fact in force at the time at which the payments were made, they were incompatible with EU law and were therefore unlawful (although not void). To the extent that the claimants believed the relevant provisions to be compatible with EU law, they were mistaken.[46] This mistake—which

---

[40] *Deutsche Morgan Grenfell* (n 21) [88]–[89].
[41] ibid [32].
[42] ibid [31].
[43] ibid [20]
[44] ibid [31].
[45] *Test Claimants* (n 2) [176].
[46] *Test Claimants* (n 2) [178] and [229].

346   MISTAKES OF LAW, AGAIN

had caused the claimants to make the payments in question—was sufficient to found their restitutionary claim.

In analysing the claim in this way, the majority implicitly adopted the orthodox view of mistake as a cause of action set out in section II above. Again, according to this view, mistake is normatively significant because it shows the vitiation of the claimant's intention in making the payment in question. Insofar as it entails a false belief about the present, it must be distinguished from a misprediction, which involves a false belief about the future.[47] But as we have seen, it may be that mistake cannot in itself provide a good reason for restitution. Rather, insofar as it is required that the claimant plead and prove a mistake, it may be that mistake merely serves (at least in cases such as *Kelly v Solari*) as a useful proxy for the absence of any obligation on the claimant to pay and, second, to pre-empt the argument that the claimant consented to pay an amount that they did not owe; a different but closely related view is that mistake serves as a technique for demonstrating both the purpose of the payment—in *Kelly v Solari*, the discharge of liability—and the failure of that purpose. It seems that the majorities in *Kleinwort Benson* and *Deutsche Morgan Grenfell* were prepared to order restitution on grounds of a deemed mistake precisely because they had this alternative conception of the claim in mind, either implicitly or explicitly.[48] On the other hand, to the extent that the majority's view in *Test Claimants* commits English law to the position that the claimants' cause of action accrued at the time of payment, it does not seem possible to accommodate to this alternative thesis the fact that the payments were then due in terms of the relevant legislation, the claimants having made no group income election. Indeed, *Test Claimants* is difficult to reconcile even with the orthodox view that the existence of a valid obligation on the claimant to confer the benefit in question constitutes a denial of the 'unjust' element of the claim.[49]

VI. Mistakes and Errors of Judgement

Furthermore, it is not clear that the majority's approach in *Test Claimants* can without serious strain be applied to the overruling scenario discussed in *Kleinwort Benson*:[50] in this well-known hypothetical case, money paid in accordance with Decision A at T1 is claimed following the overruling of Decision A by Decision B at T2.[51] In resolving to treat this case in the same way as the facts actually before it, the majority were motivated by an understandable desire to avoid the vagueness problem entailed by any attempt to distinguish deemed mistakes from actual ones: distinguishing the facts at issue from those of the hypothetical case would both raise difficult jurisprudential questions and undermine certainty as to the time limit for bringing a claim.[52] But even if the weight of these concerns is conceded, it is difficult to assert—at least without resort to fiction—that—for example—a contract

---

[47] *Dextra Bank v Bank of Jamaica* [2002] 1 All ER Com 193 (PC).

[48] See especially Lord Hope in *Kleinwort Benson* (n 6) 408 and Lord Hoffmann in *Deutsche Morgan Grenfell* (n 21) [20]–[23].

[49] Cf section II.

[50] See, in particular, the speeches of the minority (Lord Browne-Wilkinson and Lord Lloyd) in *Kleinwort Benson* (n 6) 358–59 and 390–94.

[51] It is these facts that the majority appeared to have in mind in setting out the paradox at *Test Claimants* (n 2) [174].

[52] *Test Claimants* (n 2) [175].

declared to be void in Decision B at T2 was as a matter of historical fact void when the claimant performed his obligations under it at T1, Decision A having considered such contracts and declared them to be valid. In the same way, it is difficult to assert that the claimant was as a matter of historical fact mistaken at any point prior to Decision B. Taking up such a position entails denying that judicial decisions have any distinctive effect on the development of the law; it implies that in attesting to the true state of the law, judicial decisions are identical in status to the forcefully expressed views of law professors, or solicitors, or indeed students. Thus it entails confusing two senses of 'law', one normative (law as an ideal system of rules), the other positive (law as those rules that emanate from an authoritative source).[53] Simply put, on this view, it is not clear why *Hazell*, *Metallgesellschaft*, or the decision of the CJEU in *Test Claimants* should have made any difference. This view is not compatible with the modern doctrine of precedent.

In fact, insofar as *Test Claimants* treats the claimants' cause of action as arising at the date of payment (T1), it becomes necessary to confront the full implications of the decision in *Kleinwort Benson v Lincoln*. In that decision, mistake of law was recognized—in general terms—as a sufficient ground of recovery alongside mistake of fact, and the claimant's mistake as to the validity of the swaps contracts treated—in particular—as a sufficient ground for restitution in that case. But mistakes of the sort at issue in *Kleinwort Benson*, *Deutsche Morgan Grenfell*, and *Test Claimants* are different in kind from either mistakes of fact (such as the mistake at issue in *Kelly v Solari*) or from mistakes regarding the existence or contents of an authoritative legal source: for example, where I pay tax in ignorance of a statutory provision that exempts people in my position from doing so.

As we have seen, according to orthodoxy, a mistake is a false belief about the present.[54] Thus mistake entails the possibility of ascertaining the truth; or, put differently, the falsifiability of the claim in question. Beliefs about facts are falsifiable at any time during the course of litigation, whatever a court may subsequently pronounce. In *Kleinwort Benson*, *Deutsche Morgan Grenfell*, and *Test Claimants*, on the other hand, the claimants—or rather their legal advisers—had formed judgements on the basis of a range of legal materials as to the validity of the contract or statute in terms of which the payments were made. These judgements were of course incorrect, and were subsequently found to have been so by the House of Lords and the Supreme Court. But that does not mean that they were falsifiable at the time they were made.[55] In that sense, they were like mispredictions: the crucial difference between mistakes on the one hand and mispredictions and misjudgements on the other consists in the fact that in the latter case there is no impairment of the claimant's decision.[56]

The majority in *Test Claimants* (following Lord Brown in *Deutsche Morgan Grenfell*) criticized the assumption underlying the majority view in *Deutsche Morgan Grenfell* that 'discovery' within the meaning of section 32(1) meant the ascertainment of 'the truth', and that

---

[53] Cf John Finnis, 'The Fairy Tale's Moral' (1999) 115 LQR 170, especially 174: 'Correctly identifying a belief as having been mistaken in law need involve no denial or neglect of any historical fact. The law, in our metaphor, has a double life. One can switch between the descriptive (historical or predictive) and the normative ways of thinking and talking about it, and everyone regularly does.'

[54] Cf Frederick Wilmot-Smith, 'Retrospective Mistakes of Law' in Paul S Davies and Justine Pila (eds), *The Jurisprudence of Lord Hoffmann* (Hart 2015) 289, especially 292–93.

[55] Cf Birks, 'Mistakes of Law' (n 1) 226: 'The rule of recognition in use in our system means that, legislation aside, a belief as to the law can only be falsified by the utterance of a court.'

[56] Cf Birks, 'Mistakes of Law' (n 1) 224.

348 MISTAKES OF LAW, AGAIN

a mistake of law was therefore discoverable only when the point of law in question has been authoritatively decided by a court of final jurisdiction.[57] They pointed out that it is the function of courts to resolve disputes of law and fact, and that until the court has done so, the parties can, at best, have only a reasonable belief that their assertions are correct: 'If a limitation period is to serve its purpose, in fixing a time within which claims must be brought, it can therefore only be concerned with beliefs, and not with the truth established by judicial decisions, whether in the proceedings in question, or in other proceedings.'[58] This is quite right. To the extent that the majority in *Deutsche Morgan Grenfell*, like the majority in *Kleinwort Benson*, treated the claimant's belief in their liability to pay as a mistake in the sense of a belief in a falsifiable claim, they were incorrect. But the majority in *Test Claimants* did not go far enough. To the extent that they took the view that the claimant's belief in the compatibility of ICTA with the relevant European treaty provisions was a mistake—again, a belief as to a falsifiable claim—they too were involved in error. Properly analysed, the facts of *Test Claimants* do not disclose a mistake in the sense required by orthodoxy.[59]

VII. Conclusion

Prior to the decision in *Test Claimants*, it was possible to overlook the difficulties raised by the decisions in *Kleinwort Benson* and *Deutsche Morgan Grenfell*. In particular, if the claimant's mistake became discoverable only with the handing down of the *Hazell* or *Metallgesellschaft* decisions, it was possible to leave open the difficult question of when exactly its cause of action accrued, and of what kind that cause of action was. Those difficulties can no longer be evaded.

First, on facts such as those at issue in *Deutsche Morgan Grenfell* and *Test Claimants*, a cause of action must now be understood to have accrued despite the existence of a valid obligation on the claimant to pay. That is incompatible with any account of the claimant's cause of action that sees absence of basis as the gist of its claim, and indeed with any account that sees the existence of a valid obligation to confer the benefit in question as a denial of the 'unjust' element. Second, even if one accepts the analysis of the cause of action adopted in *Test Claimants*, it seems that the claimant's belief as to the compatibility of ICTA with the relevant European treaty provisions was not after all a mistake in the sense required to justify restitution. It was, rather, a misjudgement: an incorrect view as to the meaning or interpretation of authoritative legal sources.

This means that—whatever view one takes of the cause of action at issue – the decision in *Test Claimants* is problematic. *Deutsche Morgan Grenfell*, too, can no longer be explained if indeed the claimant's cause of action must be understood to have arisen prior to the decision

---

[57] *Test Claimants* (n 2) [180]. Of course, if—as Lord Hoffman claimed in *Deutsche Morgan Grenfell* (n 21) [31]— '[the claimants] could not have discovered the truth because the truth did not yet exist', because their liability to pay had not yet been retrospectively effaced by the decision in *Metallgesellschaft*, then it must be correct to say that they were not in any sense mistaken, nor was their mistaken discoverable, until the handing down of that decision. Cf section V.

[58] *Test Claimants* (n 2) [196].

[59] This argument is distinct from the argument that a 'deemed' mistake is insufficient to ground a claim in unjust enrichment articulated by the minority in *Kleinwort Benson* (n 6) and by Birks in 'Mistakes of Law' (n 1) 223–30. Cf also the remarks of the majority in *Test Claimants* (n 2) at [195]–[196] and [221]: 'a mistake of law is, and always was, a "mistake" in the ordinary sense of the word.' On the view taken here, most mistakes of law are indeed to be treated differently from mistakes of fact, and the distinction does indeed remain of crucial importance.

in *Metallgesellschaft*. As for *Kleinwort Benson*, to the extent that the claimant was not in fact liable to pay at the time at which the payments were made, that decision remains defensible, even if the *Test Claimants* approach to the coming into existence of the claimant's cause of action is adopted. That is because *Kleinwort Benson* is susceptible to alternative analysis, in terms of the absence of a legal ground for the payment. Rather than providing the reason for restitution, the claimant's mistake can be understood as pre-emptively refuting a defence of consent (ie that the claimant knew that the money was not due and paid regardless) or serving to establish that the claimant's purpose in making the payment was the discharge of liability. Whereas Kleinwort Benson's misjudgement regarding the applicable law is insufficient to found a cause of action, it may still be enough to establish the absence of donative intent.

There remains some difficulty: given the analysis offered here, can the claim in *Kleinwort Benson* coherently be described as one for 'relief from the consequences of mistake' for the purposes of section 32(1)(c)? Some have doubted it.[60] But it is at least plausible to argue that the role assigned to mistake in the alternative analysis set out above could be described in those terms. Nor is there any conceptual obstacle to treating such a mistake as a factor capable of excusing the claimant from the operation of the limitation defence.

---

[60] Cf the treatment of this issue in *Deutsche Morgan Grenfell* (n 21) and *Test Claimants in the FII Group Litigation v HMRC* [2012] UKSC 19; [2012] 2 AC 337, discussed in *Goff and Jones* (n 9) 33-48–33-49. Also Stevens *Laws of Restitution* (n 11) 372–74, discussed in n 36.

21

The External Shield of a Contract—Torts, Equity, and Restitution

NILI COHEN*

I. Introduction

This chapter is a broad overview of an issue that lies at the intersection of contracts, torts, equity, and restitution, and is a heartfelt tribute to Ewan McKendrick for his extraordinary scholarship, leadership, and friendship. It focuses on the transformation of legal rights following social and technological changes; in particular, the transformation of the right to personal services from property to status, ending up finally as the weakest type of contract from the point of view of legal enforceability. The paradox is that the contract for personal services, originally rooted in property concepts, served as a vehicle for the fortification of other types of contractual rights. When the personal services contract accomplished its role in turning other contractual rights into a kind of property, the personal services contract itself became in a sense the most fragile of contracts.

The chapter is divided into four main sections. Section II briefly addresses the process whereby contract gradually assumed proprietary traits. Section III refers to the historical roots of tort liability for inducing breach of contract, namely torts that allowed master and husband to sue third parties who induced their servant or wife to leave them. These torts were in the background of *Lumley v Gye*,[1] which established tort liability for inducing breach of contract. I shall point to the criticism this tort has faced, and also to a parallel doctrine in equity which protected specifically enforceable contracts against interference by third parties.

Section IV of the chapter considers the scope of liability in restitution for inducing breach of contract. Even before *Lumley v Gye*, a rule parallel to the one in tort allowed a former master to claim benefits obtained by a second master who unlawfully induced the former master's servant to work for him. This rule however did not develop into a general principle allowing a claim for benefits emanating from inducing breach of contract.

Section V, the final section, examines the radical changes that the old torts of inducement have undergone. They themselves were abolished altogether, and the territories covered by them—namely, family law and employment law—became subject to different disciplines, allowing freedom to the once fettered wives and employees. Following the historical and sociological development of third-party liability for breach of contract, it transpires that the special relations which once gave birth to the tort of inducing breach of contract, nowadays

---

* I am grateful to my friends and colleagues Professor Guy Mundlak and Professor Hila Shamir for their excellent remarks and to my research assistant Omer Rosenwaks for her excellent assistance.

[1] *Lumley v Gye* (1853) 2 El & Bl 216 (QB) (hereafter *Lumley v Gye*).

Nili Cohen, *The External Shield of a Contract—Torts, Equity, and Restitution* In: *Shaping the Law of Obligations*. Edited by: Edwin Peel and Rebecca Probert, Oxford University Press. © Nili Cohen 2023. DOI: 10.1093/oso/9780198889762.003.0021

352 THE EXTERNAL SHIELD OF A CONTRACT

form a major exception to the general rule of tort liability and to a large extent permit third parties to interfere with employment and marital contracts.

II. From Contract to Property

The year 2023 marks the 170th anniversary of *Lumley v Gye*, a landmark decision in English private law and a meeting point of contract, torts, and property. The decision established the tort of inducing breach of contract, thereby protecting contractual rights from external interference and adding a building block to the proprietary nature of contract. It reflected the importance of the contractual interest, the seeds of which were sown at the beginning of the nineteenth century following the industrial revolution and the emergence of the idealistic belief in human rights and in the individual's ability to forge his own destiny.

Nowadays talking about the importance of contractual rights is a cliché. In a market economy based on credit and the accelerated exchange of goods and services, contract constitutes a major component of wealth. It is no wonder that an owner of property may sometimes choose to convert property rights into contract rights, for example, by depositing banknotes or currency in a bank account. The depositor prefers her contractual right against the bank to the ownership of the currency. Being a lender in this case is preferable to being an owner.

The exterior protection of contract reflects the transformation that contract has undergone during the nineteenth and twentieth centuries.[2] The privity of contract concept reflected the original view of contract as a personal relation both in its inner circle and in its impact on third parties. The creditor had control over the debtor, even over his body. A debtor who did not repay his debt became the creditor's chattel, who could do with him as he wished: 'the borrower is servant to the lender'.[3] In the period of the Twelve Tables in Rome (fifth century BCE), and even in the Middle Ages, when a debtor did not repay his debt he could be subjected to physical torments, including the amputation of limbs.[4] The contract in *The Merchant of Venice*,[5] which provided that if Antonio did not repay Shylock within three months, Shylock would be entitled to a pound of Antonio's flesh, is therefore by no means a figment of the imagination, but a somewhat exaggerated reflection of a practice that existed in the past.

The gradual weakening of the perception of every contract as personal in modern law has an effect both on internal relations, as well as on the contract's impact on third parties.[6] Thus, the death of one of the parties does not terminate the contract (if it is not of an inherent personal character). This enables the transfer of contractual right *mortis causa*. The possibility of assigning contractual rights *inter vivos* enabled strangers to replace the

---

[2] John Danforth, 'Tortious Interference with Contract—A Reassertion of Society's Interest in Commercial Stability and Contractual Integrity' (1981) 81 Colum L Rev 149, 150.

[3] Proverbs 22:7.

[4] Raymond Westbrook, 'Slave and Master in Ancient Near Eastern Law' (1994) 70 Chi Kent L Rev 1631; Donald E Phillipson, 'Development of the Roman Law of Debt Security' (1968) 20 Stan L Rev 1230.

[5] William Shakespeare, *The Merchant of Venice* (first published 1596).

[6] Charles R Noyes, *The Institution of Property* (Longmans, Green, 1936) 326–30.

original parties to the contract and third parties can, in some circumstances, benefit from a contract to which they were not parties.[7]

The deviations from the privity doctrine and the weakening of the personal character of the contract were both prerequisites and justification for its greater external protection. The creditor's weaker control over the debtor requires machinery to deter the debtor and strangers from interfering with the creditor's right. The justification stems from the existence of an analytical rationale which expands the territory of contract liability. The shattering of the concept of privity led to the application of contract territory to strangers. That being so, imposing liability on strangers to respect the contractual right seems to be a natural outcome of the whole process.[8] The law which transformed contractual rights has endowed it with some of the natural attributes of property,[9] namely, assignability and opposability against third parties.[10] This has been effectively accomplished by the tort of inducing breach of contract.[11]

III. Tort Liability

A. Historical Origin of Tort Liability—Inducing Servant, Inducing Wife

The tort of inducing breach of contract was created in *Lumley v Gye*, where Johanna Wagner, a famous opera singer, was under a contract to perform exclusively for Benjamin Lumley, an opera-house owner, for a period of three months. Knowing of this contract, Frederick Gye, the owner of another opera-house, induced Johanna Wagner to break her contract with Lumley and to perform for Gye for a higher wage. Gye was held liable in tort for the damage inflicted upon Lumley as a result of the breach.[12]

[7] In English law only at a relatively late stage: Contract (Rights of Third Parties) Act 1999, but under Continental systems and US law much earlier: see Edwin Peel (ed), *Treitel: The Law of Contract* (15th edn, Sweet & Maxwell 2020) [14-099-14-136] (hereafter *Treitel*).

[8] On the relations between the tort of inducing breach of contract and the doctrine of privity, see Wei Jian Chan, 'Contractual Privity and Inducing Breach of Contract' [2014] Oxford Univ Undergraduate LJ 24. On whether the tort forms an accessory liability to the contractual liability, see Roderick Bagshaw, 'Lord Hoffmann and the Economic Torts' in PS Davies and J Pila (eds) *The Jurisprudence of Lord Hoffmann* (Hart Publishing 2015) 59(hereafter Bagshaw, 'Lord Hoffmann and the Economic Torts'). On the relations between assignability of contract and the tort of inducing breach, see Fred S McChesney, 'Tortious Interference with Contract versus "Efficient" Breach: Theory and Empirical Evidence' (1999) 28 JLS 131, 143–59 (hereafter McChesney, 'Tortious Interference with Contract versus "Efficient" Breach').

[9] On 'property-transfer' theories of contract, see Peter Benson, 'Contract as a Transfer of Ownership' (2006) 48 Wm & Mary L Rev 1673; Andrew S Gold, 'A Property Theory of Contract' (2009) 103 Nw UL Rev 1; Ralph Cunnington, 'Contract Rights as Property Rights' in Andrew Robertson (ed), *The Law of Obligations: Connections and Boundaries* (Routledge 2004). For scepticism about property-transfer theories of contract, see JW Harris, *Property and Justice* (OUP 1996) 19–20; Stephen A Smith, *Contract Theory* (OUP 2004) 97–103.

[10] Richard Epstein, 'Intentional Harms' (1975) 4 JLS 391; Hirsch Lauterpacht, 'Contracts to Break a Contract' (1936) 52 LQR 494, 509; Francis B Sayre, 'Inducing Breach of Contract' (1923) 36 Harv L Rev 663, 675–76; Joseph Gabriel Starke, 'Unlawful Interference with Contractual Relations' (1956) 7 Res Iudicata 136, 148; John T Nockleby, 'Tortious Interference with Contractual Relations in the Nineteenth Century—The Transformation of Property, Contract and Tort' (1980) 39 Harv L Rev 1510, 1529–37 (hereafter Nockleby, 'Tortious Interference'). On the circularity of the property argument: Sarah Swan, 'A New Tortious Interference With Contractual Relations: Gender and Erotic Triangles in Lumley v Gye' (2012) 35 Harv JL & Gender 167, 191–93 (hereafter Swan, 'A New Tortious Interference').

[11] Richard Epstein, 'Inducement of Breach of Contract as a Problem of Ostensible Ownership' (1987) 16 JLS 1; Benjamin L Fine, 'Analysis of the Formation of Property Rights Underlying Tortious Interference with Contracts and other Economic Relations' (1983) 50 U Chi L Rev 1116.

[12] For a historical account, see Stephen Waddams, 'Johanna Wagner and the Rival Opera Houses' (1998) 117 LQR 431.

354 THE EXTERNAL SHIELD OF A CONTRACT

The contract with Johanna Wagner was for personal services. Such a contract at the time was similar to a contract between master and servant which had unique traits. It initially granted the master a proprietary right (later converted to status) in the servant and in his services, as attested by the actions available to the master against third parties. One action arose where a servant suffered a personal injury as a result of a tort committed by a third party. In such a case the master could sue the tortfeasor for the loss of services of his servant—*per quod servitium amisit*. A second action originated in the Statute of Labourers,[13] which regulated the work force following the chaos caused by the 'Black Death'. The ordinance led to involuntary servitude at wages which pre-dated the plague, and criminalized not only a servant who unlawfully left his master, but also any third party who knowingly enticed away another's servants.[14] It applied also to a third party who continued to employ the servant after learning that he had left his previous master.[15]

Similar actions were at the disposal of a husband and father. The first was a claim against a third party who wrongfully injured the wife and children causing loss of their services to the husband and father—*per quod consortium amisit, per quod servitium amisit*. The second action was available to the husband against a third party for knowingly enticing the wife to leave the husband,[16] or for continuing his relations with her after learning that she had left her husband.[17]

In *Lumley v Gye* the relevant action was enticement. This action could not directly apply to the case as the contract therein was not between a master and servant. But the court expanded the action of enticement, or inducement, and applied it to a mere contract for personal services.

The actions of inducement, *per quod servitium* or *consortium amisit*, were based upon the idea of wrongful appropriation of an asset belonging to another, namely the property right of the master in his servant's, or the husband in his wife's and children's, services.[18] Such proprietary relations did not exist in the contractual context dealt with in *Lumley v Gye*.[19] The challenge faced by the court in *Lumley v Gye* was lessened by the analogy to master–servant relations and to the gendered character of the case.[20] The fact that the owners of the opera-houses were men and the opera singer a woman facilitated the analogy to the patriarchic concepts that stood behind the actions of inducement and *per quod servitium*

---

[13] Statute of Labourers 1351.

[14] Gareth H Jones, 'Per Quod Servitium Amisit' (1958) 74 LQR 39; Swan, 'A New Tortious Interference' (n 10).

[15] For liability imposed for continuous employment: *Blake v Lanyon* (1795) 6 TR 221 (hereafter *Blake*); *De Francesco v Barnum* (1890) 45 Ch D 430 (hereafter *De Francesco*). In *Jones Brothers (Hunstanton) Ltd v Stevens* [1955] 1 QB 275 (hereafter *Jones Brothers*) it was held that a continuous employment would impose liability only if the first employer showed that the employee would have returned to him but for the interference. However, following the abolition of these actions (n 25) the continuous employment after the employee has left by his own will is not likely to subject the second employer to tort liability. See text to nn 55–56.

[16] Originally the enticement action was available only to husbands: *Winsmore v Greenbank* (1745) Willes 577. Later, it was hesitantly granted to a wife for the enticement of her husband: *Gray v Gee* [1923] 39 TLR 42.

[17] *Winsmore v Greenbank* (1745) Willes 577. This latter type of action was not granted to the wife: *Winchester v Fleming* [1958] 1 QB 259 (appeal allowed on other grounds: [1958] 3 All ER 51).

[18] On the relations between the actions, see P Brett, 'Consortium and Servitium' (1957) 29 ALJ 321.

[19] Nowadays a contract for personal services is regarded as a relatively weak contract as it is usually not subject to the remedy of specific performance (even in legal systems where this is the primary remedy): see n 31 and accompanying text.

[20] Lea VanderVelde, 'Binding Men's Consciences and Women's Fidelity' (1992) 101 Yale LJ 775; Swan, 'A New Tortious Interference' (n 10).

amisit which were available in those times to masters (men) and husbands.[21] This might well explain the willingness of the court to grant in the purely contractual sphere an injunction prohibiting Johanna Wagner from performing for Gye.[22] The court emphasized that though this injunction might indirectly prompt Wagner to sing for Lumley, it was not a direct court order to perform for him. The decision has been criticized for the reason that the injunction might put great economic pressure on the services-provider and force her to perform the original contract. Current ideas of competition, fair trade, and personal autonomy allow greater freedom to the worker or services-provider even when they break the contract, but an injunction in the *Lumley*-type scenario is still available.[23]

Eventually, the court extended the action of inducement and the concept behind the claim to a situation where the original rationale for the old actions did not exist. It did so by extending the master-husband actions against third parties to other factual situations. In doing so, the court built a new proprietary theory that underlies the current concept of contract according to which the creditor has a property interest in the contract.[24] The creation of the tort of inducing breach of contract was the swan song of the old torts available to the husband and the master. The tort of interference with contractual relations extended the inducement action to a great variety of contract relations, while the old torts themselves gradually faded and finally were abolished by legislation.[25] Nowadays, husbands are no longer protected against third parties inducing their wives,[26] but employers who have lost their employees' services following an unlawful inducement by others can still avail themselves of the tort of inducing breach of contract.

B. Inducing Breach, Privity, and Efficient Breach

The tort of inducing breach of contract has faced challenges since its inception. A major challenge related to the personal character of the contract, which arguably precludes a third party from being liable under it.[27] Yet a third party interfering with a contract need not be a party to the contract, just as a third party inducing a public servant to breach her duty is not required to have a governmental position or capacity.[28] Other objections concerned its

---

[21] See the references in *Lumley v Gye* (n 1) to these actions by Erle J (755) and Wightman J (757); Coleridge J, who was in the minority, remarked that the analogy was unjustified because a woman did not have a legal personality separate to her husband (761).

[22] *Lumley v Wagner* [1852] EWHC (Ch) J96 (hereafter *Lumley v Wagner*). This might still be the current position with regard to a party with special skills: see *Warner Brothers Pictures Inc v Nelson* [1937] 1 KB 209 (an actor); *Evening Standard Co Ltd v Henderson* [1987] ICR 588 (a reporter). Other authorities are more reluctant to issue an injunction if it is likely to impose undue pressure on the services-provider to perform: see *Warren v Mendy* [1989] 1 WLR 853 (an athlete); *Treitel* (n 7) [21-065]. See also n 70 and accompanying text.

[23] The prevailing view is that an injunction would be granted if it leaves the employee or services-provider with reasonable possibilities of earning a leaving: *Treitel* (n 7) [21-065] (and *cf* n 70). See also *American Broadcasting Co v Wolf* [1980] 430 NYS 2d 275, 283–84 (App Div).

[24] For a historical analysis, see Nockleby, 'Tortious Interference' (n 10).

[25] The inducement actions within the family were abolished by the Law Reform (Miscellaneous Provisions) Act 1970, s 5. The loss of services actions and the inducement of a servant were abolished by the Administration of Justice Act 1982, s 2(a). For a view supporting a revival of these torts in American law to defend family values, see William R Corbett, 'A Somewhat Modest Proposal to Prevent Adultery and Save Families: Two Old Torts Looking for a New Career' (2001) 33 Ariz St LJ 985.

[26] See text to nn 86–89.

[27] Dan B Dobbs, 'Tortious Interference with Contractual Relations' (1980) 34 Arkans LR 335, 350–58.

[28] Bagshaw, 'Lord Hoffmann and the Economic Torts' (n 8) 19.

356 THE EXTERNAL SHIELD OF A CONTRACT

vagueness and its intrusion into individual liberties.[29] The tort is considered as imposing constraints on abandoning undesirable or inefficient contracts. This is linked to the performance interest of the creditor,[30] and the concept of efficient breach.

Under the common law, the injured party does not have a right to specific performance. Where the contract is for personal services, specific performance is not granted even in systems where it is the main remedy.[31] Yet this did not hinder the court in *Lumley v Gye* from establishing the tort of inducement in a case where the contract under consideration was a personal one, though as noted earlier the court was inspired by the property and gendered traits of the master–servant relations, and also by the special skills of the singer.

The efficient breach theory came to life many years after *Lumley v Gye*. According to the Holmesian dictum, a contractual party has an option either to perform or to breach and pay damages. Under this view the creditor is not entitled to the performance of the contract, if the breaching party has apparently a 'right' to break the contract subject to paying damages.[32] If so, the argument goes, there is no real justification for granting the creditor a cause of action against a third party who induced the debtor to take advantage of her right not to perform, in particular where the latter contract is more efficient than the former. The creditor should thus be satisfied with the claim for damages against the debtor under the contract.[33]

But is there really an inherent right, or option, to break a contract where no order for performance is awarded? Is there a real clash between the doctrine of efficient breach and the tort of inducing breach? Some suggest that broadening the scope of specific performance, and positing it as a major remedy, would eliminate the concept of efficient breach and also reduce the gap between the contract and tort doctrines.[34] But this does not resolve the very essence of the problem of efficient breach and its moral and efficiency justifications.[35]

As to the moral aspect: a contract creates a moral and legal obligation to perform irrespective of whether performance is efficient. An efficient breach is still a breach and therefore a wrong; the law should not encourage wrongful behaviour. A contract does not grant the breaching party a right to purchase the duty to perform by paying damages. The creditor has a substantive right to the other party's performance, even if the remedy for breach is deficient.[36] Indeed, the remedies' territory might affect the substantive right. Inefficient

---

[29] Gary D Wexler, 'Intentional Interference with Contract: Market Efficiency and Individual Liberty Considerations' (1994) 27 Connecticut L Rev 279 (hereafter Wexler, 'Intentional Interference with Contract'); David Howarth, 'Against Lumley v Gye' (2005) 68 MLR 195 (hereafter Howarth, 'Against Lumley v Gye').

[30] On the different contractual interests with an emphasis on the performance interest, see Daniel Friedmann, 'The Performance Interest in Contract Damages' (1995) 111 LQR 628.

[31] As in the Israeli system: Israeli Contracts (Remedies for Breach) Law, 1971 s 2(2) states that 'The injured party is entitled to enforcement of the contract, except if any of the following applies: (2) enforcement of the contract consists in compelling the doing or acceptance of personal work or a personal service'.

[32] Oliver W Holmes, Jr, 'The Path of the Law' (1897) 10 Harv L Rev 457; Oliver W Holmes, Jr, *The Common Law* (Little, Brown 1881) 300–01; Richard A Posner, *Economic Analysis of Law* (3rd edn, Aspen 1986) 106–07. For its evolution see Daniel Friedmann, 'The Efficient Breach Fallacy' (1989) 18 JLS 1, 2–4 (hereafter Friedmann, 'The Efficient Breach Fallacy').

[33] Harvey S Perlman, 'Interference with Contract and other Economic Expectancies—A Clash of Contract and Tort Doctrine' (1982) 49 U Chic L Rev 61; Wexler, 'Intentional Interference with Contract' (n 29).

[34] Deepa Varadarajan, 'Tortious Interference and the Law of Contract: The Case for Specific Performance Revisited' (2001) 111 Yale LJ 735.

[35] Friedmann, 'The Efficient Breach Fallacy' (n 32); Douglas Laycock, *The Death of the Irreparable Injury Rule* (OUP 1991) ch 11; Frank Menetrez, 'Comment, Consequentialism, Promissory Obligation, and the Theory of Efficient Breach' (2000) 47 U Cal LA L Rev 859; Richard O'Dair, 'Restitutionary Damages for Breach of Contract and the Theory of Efficient Breach' (1993) 46 CLP 113; Seana Valentine Shiffrin, 'The Divergence of Contract and Promise' (2007) 120 Harv L Rev 708, 723–32.

[36] Gareth Jones, 'The Recovery of Benefits Gained from a Breach of Contract' (1993) 9 LQR 443, 453–54.

contracts should not be enforced,[37] but in principle this cannot erase the very existence of the right. If the creditor's right is incontestable, the duty to perform the contract imposes on third parties a duty to abstain from knowingly interfering with the contract. If they do interfere with no justification,[38] they are accomplices to a wrong, not in the contract sphere—they are not parties to the contract—but in the tort sphere, as infringing a legally protected right.

The efficient breach theory is not convincing from the internal economic-efficiency perspective either.[39] Under the theory, if the breach is economically efficient, then interference by a third party that brings about an efficient allocation of resources is permissible and should not be regarded as tortious.[40] Yet economic justification ignores[41] costs and litigation costs against the party in breach and the third party involved in the breach. And in general terms the contractual system is not focused only on monetary values. It is based on trust. One of its main goals is furthering cooperation. This would be severely damaged in a regime that encourages breach and disregards the involvement of third parties knowingly interfering with the contract.[42]

It is even arguable that the need for external protection of the contract is greater where specific performance is unavailable. The contract for services which originally led to the creation of the tort of inducing breach of contract was a personal contract. The non-availability of specific performance reflects justifiable considerations of rejecting personal servitude and honouring to some extent changes in personal preferences. Such a contract requires striking a delicate balance between personal autonomy of the promisor and reliance by the promisee. Yet in such a contract, and in effect in all relational contracts—employment, long-term business—building trust and maintaining it is a major factor.[43] The very existence of the tort implements this goal.

C. Reception

The American case of *Texaco Inc v Pennzoil Co*[44] provides a definitive affirmation of the tort of causing breach of contract. In this case there was an agreement between Pennzoil

---

[37] See *Co-operative Insurance Society v Argyll Stores* [1998] AC 1 (HL). See Daniel Friedmann, 'Economic Aspects of Damages and Specific Performance Compared' in Djakhongir Saidov and Ralph Cunnington (eds), *Contract Damages: Domestic And International Perspectives* (Hart Publishing 2008) 128–32. On the relation between rights and remedies, see Daniel Friedmann, 'Rights and Remedies' in Nili Cohen and Ewan McKendrick (eds), *Comparative Remedies for Breach of Contract* (Hart Publishing 2005) 3; Stephen A Smith, 'Remedies for Breach of Contract, One Principle or Two' in Gregory Klass, George Letsas, and Prince Saprai (eds), *The Philosophical Foundations of Contract Law* 341 (OUP 2014) (hereafter Klass et al, *Philosophical Foundations*).

[38] Would a third party be justified if she induced the party to break the inefficient contract? If it is conceived as an advice bona fide it might constitute a justification and remove tort liability. On justification see text to nn 46–47.

[39] Friedmann, 'The Efficient Breach Fallacy' (n 32). Only a very few cases can give basis to an argument of efficient breach: Robert E Scott, 'Contract Law and the Shading Problem' (2015) 99 Marq L Rev 1, 10–11.

[40] The theory assumes that the interference requires fewer transactions to bring about an efficient allocation: McChesney, 'Tortious Interference with Contract Versus "Efficient" Breach' (n 8) 148–56.

[41] Daphna Lewinsohn-Zamir, 'The Questionable Efficiency of the Efficient-Breach Doctrine' (2012) 168 JITE 5.

[42] For a survey and attenuated efficient breach theory based on useful design, see Gregory Klass, 'Efficient Breach' in Klass et al, *Philosophical Foundations* (n 37).

[43] See Lillian R BeVier, 'Reconsidering Inducement' (1990) 76 Va L Rev 877. For strong support of the application of the tort in the ambit of relational contracts, particularly in the music industry, see David F Partlett, 'From Victorian Opera to Rock and Rap: Inducement to Breach of Contract in the Music Industry' (1992) 66 Tul L Rev 771 (hereafter Partlett, 'From Victorian Opera to Rock and Rap').

[44] [1986] 784 F2d 1133, 1157 [2d Cir 1986], rev'd, 107 S Ct 1519 [1987].

358 THE EXTERNAL SHIELD OF A CONTRACT

and Getty under which Pennzoil agreed to purchase billions of dollars' worth of Getty oil stock. Aware of that agreement, Texaco offered Getty a higher price, and a contract was signed between them. The court held that Texaco knowingly interfered with the agreement between Pennzoil and Getty and held Texaco liable towards Pennzoil for an unprecedented amount of damages.[45] This case dramatically exposes the proprietary feature of the contractual right. The centre of gravity of wealth has been constantly moving from static wealth, such as land and other tangibles, to dynamic wealth, such as contracts, securities, intellectual property, and even economic expectancies.

The tort of inducing breach of contract has gained its proper basis but its limits are somewhat vague. Contracts are pluralistic and their inner strength varies accordingly. A contract to convey property is different from one to convey fungibles or one for personal services. Employment is different from a contract to supply services; some contracts are non-assignable by nature, some can be terminated easily. The tort is based on a breach of a valid contract. The nature and contents of the contract have an impact on its validity and ongoing effect. In addition, an existing contract can be challenged by a competing interest which might be regarded as preferable. The competing interest constitutes a justification for the interference that absolves the interfering party from tortious liability. The various justifying causes will not be enumerated here.[46] The decision in *Edwin Hill & Partners v First National Finance Corp*[47] will serve as an example. The defendant bankers had lent money to a developer. The loan was secured by a first legal charge over the latter's property. When the developer required further financing, the defendant agreed but only on the condition that the developer dismiss the plaintiff architects to appoint a more prestigious firm. The developer reluctantly acceded to this request. The architects sued for inducing breach of contract, and it was held that the defendant's conduct was justified. As legal chargee, the defendant could have recalled the loan and enforced the security, which would also have resulted in the termination of the plaintiffs' contract. In procuring the breach of the plaintiffs' contract, the defendant was protecting its equal or superior right as legal chargee.

Tort protection of contracts and other economic interests is not limited to the *Lumley* mode of interference, and questions as to its scope still arise. This is demonstrated by the House of Lords' landmark decision in *OBG Ltd v Allan*,[48] the definitive modern case on economic torts. The defendants were receivers purportedly appointed under a floating charge which was admitted to have been invalid. Acting in good faith, they took control of the claimant company's assets and undertakings. The claimant argued that this constituted *inter alia* unlawful interference with its contractual rights and that the defendants were liable in tort for the value of the assets and undertakings, including the value of the contractual claims, as of the date of their appointment. Lord Hoffmann held that the invalidly appointed receivers were not liable for wrongful interference with contractual relations.

---

[45] On 17 November 1985, a Texas jury awarded Pennzoil $10.53 billion in compensatory and punitive damages. Judgment was entered in the amount of $11.12 billion, which included costs and pre-judgment interest. The punitive portions of the damages were lowered, on appeal, from $3 billion to $1 billion. See Timothy S Feltham, 'Tortious Interference with Contractual Relations: The Texaco Inc v Pennzoil Co Litigation' (1988) 33 NY L Sch L Rev 111.

[46] Andrew Burrows, *The Law of Restitution* (3rd edn, OUP 2011) 523–614; The American Law Institute, *A Concise Restatement of Torts* (2nd edn, Ellen M Bublick and Kenneth S Abraham eds, American Law Institute Publishers 2010) 338–61. For the justification in the context of marriage and employment, see text to nn 78–90.

[47] [1989] 1 WLR 225.

[48] [2007] UKHL 21, [2008] 1 AC 1.

Such a receiver acting in good faith did not employ any unlawful means and did not intend to cause any loss.

OBG v Allan distinguished between two types of economic torts, the first following *Lumley*, namely knowingly inducing breach of contract,[49] and the second causing injury by unlawful means.[50] The latter, a vehicle for regulating commercial competition, is not limited to contract and may apply to other economic advantages such as expectancies. The following analysis will mainly relate to the tort of inducing breach.

D. Parallel Equity Doctrines and the Function of Specific Performance

The relationship between specific performance, trust, and inducing breach is reflected in the protection given to a contract to convey specific property. This is the type of contract where specific performance is available as a matter of course. Furthermore, enforceable contracts relating to specific, unique property have always been regarded as constituting constructive trust, thus creating equitable interests.[51] Under equity doctrines an equitable right is valid against a third person who acquires the property unless she is a purchaser for value in good faith. A third party who acquired a property knowing about a prior contract relating to the property can be ordered to hand it over to the prior purchaser. In different territory, in the equity sphere, long before *Lumley v Gye*, liability was imposed upon a third party who knowingly thwarted a prior enforceable contractual right. Assuming attributes of property—an equitable right—such a contract gained protection against third parties, not available to a mere contractual right. The protection of equitable interests via the law of torts is quite complicated and its subtle distinctions will not be dealt with here.[52] For our purposes it suffices to note that there is a partial overlapping liability in tort and in equity, yet the equitable protection is wider: it applies to a bona fide recipient who gave no value, and also to a purchaser who acted in good faith when the transaction was made but gave value only after learning about the previous transaction.[53]

As noted earlier, a parallel rule which imposed liability for knowledge acquired after entering into a conflicting transaction was relevant in the old days of master–servant relations.[54] The continuous employment of a servant, after learning that he abandoned his former master, imposed liability on the second master.[55] This was in line with the equitable protection given to a contract for the sale of property: both such contracts assumed proprietary features. Nowadays the situation with regard to contracts of employment differs. The fact that the first contract is unenforceable and that the second employer did not induce

---

[49] Mere inconsistent dealing does not suffice. The tort requires direct inducement or persuasion: see *Kawasaki Kisen Kaisha Ltd v James Kemball Limited* [2021] EWCA Civ 33, [2021] 3 All ER 978. See also n 53.

[50] For analysis: Bagshaw, 'Lord Hoffmann and the Economic Torts' (n 8).

[51] Jill Martin, *Hanbury & Martin Modern Equity* (19th edn, Sweet & Maxwell 2012) [12-035].

[52] See *Treitel* (n 7) [14-149]–[14-154]; Nili Cohen, 'Interference with Contractual Relations and Equitable Doctrines' (1982) 45 MLR 241.

[53] See the proposal to abolish the equitable action for dishonest assistance, and to assimilate common law and equitable liability for third party interferences under the 'general principle' *of Lumley v Gye*: Leonard Hoffmann, 'The Redundancy of Knowing Assistance' in Peter Birks (ed), *The Frontiers of Liability*, vol 1 (OUP 1994). But in the commercial sphere a mere inconsistent dealing does not suffice. The tort requires a direct inducement or persuasion (see n 49).

[54] Text to nn 15 and 17.

[55] See *De Francesco* (n 15) and *Blake* (n 15).

360 THE EXTERNAL SHIELD OF A CONTRACT

its breach relieves the latter from liability in torts.[56] Absent a right of enforcement, the employee is regarded as having solely caused the damage resulting from the breach. In other words, there is no causal connection between the breach and the involvement of the second employer.

The modern concept of labour relations is devoid of the proprietary features which once gave birth to the continuing requirement of innocence by the second master. With the withering of the roots, there is no valid reason for maintaining the dry branch. Therefore the tort is not committed now if the knowledge of the second employer is acquired after entering into the conflicting transaction.

IV. Restitution Liability

A. Historical Origin of Restitution Liability—Inducing Servant

Historically, the recovery of benefits derived from a wrong is rooted in the doctrine of waiver of tort under which the injured party could waive the tort and claim the gain that the tortfeasor obtained by committing the wrong. The waiver doctrine was confined to a number of specific torts and it was not clear whether it applied to the tort of inducing breach of contract.

Case law in this context antedated *Lumley v Gye* and was initially applied in the cases of usurpation of an office[57] and conversion.[58] Their reasoning was subsequently applied in the context of master and servant relations. These relations, which were crucial in establishing the tort of inducing breach, had a similar impact in the sphere of restitution. Several decades before *Lumley v Gye*, two cases applied the waiver of tort doctrine to the following scenario: a master brought an action against a rival who induced a servant to leave the plaintiff and work for him. The claim was for the value of the services of the servant. In the first case, *Lightly v Clouston*,[59] Lord Mansfield, drawing an analogy to the tort of conversion, upheld the claim with no reservations; in the second, *Foster v Stewart*,[60] the same principle was applied with some reservations by Lord Ellenborough who remarked that the preferable legal rule would justify only an action in tort.

Later on, following *Lumley v Gye*, as we have seen, the increasing importance of contract led to a general tort liability for knowingly interfering with a contract unconnected with the master–servant relation. However, the restitutionary claim faced great challenges and to the best of my knowledge no decision in English law has recognized a general rule of restitutionary liability for interference with contractual relations.

Although the master–servant inducement claim can be regarded as the ancestor of the tort of inducing breach of contract, it was not clear whether the waiver of tort claim of restitution for inducing a servant can be similarly extended to other instances of inducing breach of contract. It may well be that the need to grant restitutionary protection against a third party was less acute due to the existing tort protection. Hence, after establishing

---

[56] *Jones Brothers* (n 15).
[57] *Arris v Stukely* (1677) 2 Mod 260, *Howard v Wood* (1679) 2 Lev 245.
[58] *Lamine v Dorrell* (1705) 2 Ld Raym 1216.
[59] (1808) 1 Taunt 112.
[60] (1814) 3 M & S 192.

general tort protection to the contract, no similar energy was recruited in endowing the contractual right with a restitutionary claim against the party causing its breach.

B. Doubts and Reception

Since the first half of the twentieth century the controversy in this area has boiled down to the questions whether there is a *numerus clausus* of torts which can be waived, and whether the tort of inducing breach of contract is included in the list.[61] Nowadays scholarship tends in principle to allow a restitutionary claim for inducing breach.[62] There are also a number of American cases supporting this position to which I shall shortly refer.[63]

Eventually this approach was adopted in the *Restatement Restitution Third*, which recognizes a broad application of restitution for the tort of interference with contract.[64] Section 44(1) states that a person who obtains a benefit by conscious interference with a claimant's legally protected interests (or in consequence of such interference by another) is liable in restitution as necessary to prevent unjust enrichment, unless competing legal objectives make such liability inappropriate. Section 44(2) goes on to explain that interference with legally protected interests includes conduct that is tortious, or that violates another's legal duty or prohibition (other than a duty imposed by contract)[65] if the conduct constitutes an actionable wrong to the claimant. And comment b to section 44 clarifies that it applies generally to interference with contract or with prospective economic advantage, to the extent that such interference is tortious under the applicable law. The issue turns then into the question of application and delineating the proper boundaries.

We have seen that the tort of inducing breach of contract is subject to exceptions according to the kind of competing interests and the manner of interference. The same applies to liability in restitution which depends on the nature of the contractual interest, the kind of interference, and the mode by which the interferer benefitted from the interference.

In general, a contract that has clear proprietary features fortifies the right of restitution against a third party benefiting from the breach. A conspicuous example is a contract to sell a specific property. If a third party knowingly induced the seller to breach her contract with the first purchaser, and that third party acquires the property and sells it profitably, the

---

[61] For not including the tort, see PH Winfield, *The Law of Quasi Contract* (Sweet & Maxwell 1952) 98, 100; for a doubtful though favourable approach, see Robert Goff and Gareth Jones, *The Law of Restitution* (7th edn, Sweet & Maxwell 2007) [36-005] (hereafter Goff and Jones, *The Law of Restitution*). This is the last edition edited by Professor Jones in which the topic is included, and states that a claimant may obtain restitution following a tortious act, possibly including the tort of inducing a breach of contract. For conflicting authorities in American law, see *Developers Three v Nationwide Ins* [1990] 582 NE 2d 1130, 1135 (not allowing a restitution claim for inducing breach); *TruGreen Companies v Mower Brothers* [2008] 199 P3d 929 (allowing such a claim).

[62] See Richard RW Brooks, 'The Efficient Performance Hypothesis' (2006) 116 Yale LJ 568, 572–73; John P Dawson, 'Restitution or Damages?' (1959) 20 Oh St LJ 175, 186–87; Melvin A Eisenberg, 'The Disgorgement Interest in Contract Law' (2006) 105 Mich L Rev 559, 578–81; Daniel Friedmann, 'Restitution of Benefits Obtained through the Appropriation of Property or the Commission of a Wrong' (1980) 80 Colum L Rev 504, 513–27 (hereafter Friedmann, 'Restitution').

[63] Text to nn 67 and 68.

[64] Nicholas McBride, 'Restitution for Wrongs' in Charles Mitchell and William Swadling (eds), *The Restatement Third: Restitution and Unjust Enrichment—Critical and Comparative Essays* (Hart Publishing 2013).

[65] Section 39 of Restatement (Third) of the Law of Restitution refers to breach of contract, and grants a right of restitution for gain resulting out of opportunistic breach. On restitution against the party in breach: Friedmann, 'Restitution' (n 62) 513–26; *Treitel* (n 7) [20-009]–[20-013].

362 THE EXTERNAL SHIELD OF A CONTRACT

first purchaser would be entitled to the gain.[66] This stems from the equitable right that the first purchaser acquires when her contract is concluded. The benefit is conceived as derived from the property and the proprietary interest that the first purchaser has in the property.

Does the non-availability of equitable remedies, namely specific performance and injunction, affect the first buyer's right against the third party? Specific performance against the seller might be impossible, for example, because the latter transferred the property to a third party who, knowing about the first transaction, sold it to his buyer for value in good faith. In this case, the first buyer has lost the property due to priority rules. She did not voluntarily give up her right in the asset. Therefore, she is entitled to the profits that the third party gained from the sale of the property. The result would be different where the first buyer, following a breach by the seller, rescinded the contract and claimed damages. Assuming she did so before the seller entered into a second sale, she is deemed to have given up her right to performance in specie. This means that she was no longer committed to carrying out the transaction, thereby giving up her right to the contract's performance and accordingly to the proceeds of the second sale promised to the seller by the second buyer.

The link between enforcement against the party in breach and the availability of restitution against the interferer is demonstrated also in the context of contractual prohibition. A notable example is the American case of *National Merchandising Corp v Leyden*[67] which dealt with a non-compete provision. Company A recruited advertisements and printed them on the cover of a phone directory which was distributed among the phone subscribers. Several of its employees resigned and went to work for a competitor in violation of a non-competition agreement. Company A sued its employees and the competing company, and an order was issued with the consent of all parties, forbidding the employees to engage in telephone directory covers intended for publication. C, one of the managers of company A, then retired and founded another company, which intended to engage in the same business as company A. C persuaded B, who was subject to the said order, to manage his business. In the claim against C for inducing breach of contract, A requested an order preventing C from employing workers who were subject to the restraining order. A also claimed the profit that C had gained from the sale of advertisements during the period in which B ran his business. The court awarded both remedies. The strength of the injured party's right, which is reflected in its enforcement both against the party in breach and the intervener, has an impact on the victim's right to restitution. Profits generated as a result of the violation of the contractual right (which was fortified by an injunctive relief) belong to its owner, to the same extent that profits wrongfully extracted from another's property belong to the owner of the property.

A relevant consideration affecting the right to restitution relates to the manner in which the intervention was made. The American case of *Federal Sugar Refining Co v US Sugar Equalization Board* can serve as an example.[68] A seller, A, undertook to sell sugar to a buyer,

---

[66] This applies naturally against the seller as well: if she breaks the contract and sells the property profitably to a third person, the injured purchaser is entitled to the proceeds of the sale even if they exceed her loss: *Lake v Bayliss* [1974] 1 WLR 1073. See also Nicholas W Sage, 'Disgorgement: From Property to Contract' (2016) 66 Toronto LJ 244. The Supreme Court of Israel ruled in the case of FH 20/82 *Adras v Harlo and Jones* 37(4) PD 225 that a breaching seller of fungible goods was under a duty to restore the profits—which exceeded the buyer's damage—to the buyer. The case is discussed in Daniel Friedmann, 'Restitution of Profits Gained by Party in Breach of Contract' (1988) 104 LQR 383.

[67] [1976] 348 NE 2d 771 (hereafter *National Merchandising Corp*).

[68] [1920] 268 F 575. This is the leading case on the subject referred to with approval by Goff and Jones, *The Law of Restitution* (n 61) [36-007].

B. The contract required a licence. C, a government official, informed B that the licence would not be granted unless B signed a contract to purchase sugar from a government company of which C was a director. This message was false. B consequently wrongfully terminated his contract with A and entered into a contract with the government company for the purchase of the sugar. The contract yielded a benefit to C exceeding the sum that A would have gained from the transaction with B. A's claim to recover the profit C made from the transaction was successful. This judgment given in 1920 was a landmark decision recognizing a claim for unjust enrichment resulting from a tortious breach of contract. The misrepresentation, which was also an abuse of C's position as a public official, led to the obvious conclusion of allowing A's claim.

C. A Contract for Personal Services

Restitution claims against a third party who has induced a breach of contract become particularly problematic in the case of a contract for personal services. The non-enforceability of this contract apparently cuts off the relationship between the injured party and the subject of the contract. Furthermore, unlike a contract for the transfer of property, in a contract for personal services, the services provided to the third party are not necessarily the same as those that would have been provided to the injured party, had the contract with her been fulfilled.

Also, in a contract to transfer property there is a strong link between the right to restitution and the injured party's right to specific performance or an injunction (on the contractual level).[69] In a services contract, by its very nature, the injured party is not entitled to specific performance. However, its non-availability does not always preclude restitution. The nature of the services and their importance to the injured party are decisive factors in deciding whether that party is entitled to any profits derived by the interference. Furthermore, granting an injunction against the party in breach (and sometimes also against the interferer) indicates an intention to block the enrichment of the interferer. If profits were gained before the injunction, they should inure to the injured party. The prospects of an order are greatly improved when the employee has special skills. Her services can be regarded as a 'unique asset' that cannot be replaced.[70] The right to restitution therefore lies in the special relationship between the injured party and the 'subject' of the contract. Thus, suppose that a singer contracts with an opera manager to perform thirty performances for a year and refrain from performing during that year in any other setting. A competing promoter convinces her to break the contract, and within that year she performs forty shows for him. As the subject matter of the contract is the special skills of the singer, restitution is warranted.

---

[69] This point is not necessarily decisive and there are cases where restitution is granted though these remedies are unavailable: text preceding n 67.

[70] See Partlett, 'From Victorian Opera to Rock and Rap' (n 43), remarking that injunctive relief and the tort build trust in the music industry and in the whole plethora of relational contracts. See also Geoffrey Christopher Rapp, 'Affirmative Injunctions in Athletic Employment Contracts: Rethinking the Place of the Lumley Rule in American Sports Law' (2006) 16 Marq Sport L Rev 261, arguing that, in the common case of a professional player who simply holds out for midterm contract renegotiation, an injunction will not suffice: the threat of not being able to play for any other team has no particular salience. Therefore, an affirmative injunction should be granted, and that requires a change in the law that till now has followed *Lumley v Wagner* (n 22).

The question thus relates to the measure of recovery: the profits arising from the first thirty performances or 75 per cent of the profits, or perhaps the full profits?[71]

The question of restitution could have arisen in *Hivac Ltd v Park Royal Scientific Instruments*,[72] where the plaintiff's employees used their free hours in order to work for a competitor. The court granted an injunction preventing the competitor from hiring them. The plaintiff did not claim restitution from the competitor, but such a claim should have been available for two reasons: first, there was no issue of coercing labour relations, since the employees were ready and willing to continue to work for their original employer; second, the injunction against the competitor indicates that he was not entitled to benefit from the work of the employees.

Restitution may be appropriate also in the context of breach of a non-competition covenant. When such a covenant is enforced by an injunction against the party in breach and against the inducer of the breach, the profit that the inducer gained as a result of his wrong ought to belong to the injured party, as was actually decided in the *Leyden* case.[73]

V. Conclusion—Master–Servant and Marriage Relations—A Dialectical Process of Rule and Exception

The process which the tort of inducing breach of contract and the restitution remedy for inducing breach of contract have undergone began with the status relations of master–servant and husband–wife, where the master and husband had a property interest in the servant and wife. As has been observed:

> The law of husband and wife and the law of parent and child were . . . proximate to . . . the law of master and servant. This pattern corresponded with a social order in which cohabitation, legitimate sexual relations, reproduction, and productive labor were assumed to belong in one place: the *household*. . . . The wife, the child, and the servant were not just subordinate; they were similarly subordinate.[74]

Both relations gave birth to the old torts of enticement against competitors who induced the servant or the wife to leave the master or husband. The tort of enticing a servant gave also a rise to a claim against the competitor for disgorgement.

The flourishing of the tort of interference with contractual relations marked the demise of the ancient torts of enticement, which reflected an anachronistic social and legal order, and eventually were abolished by the legislator.[75] The new order marked

> the separation of the law of familial intimacy from the law of productive labor. It coincided with the emancipation of the servant from indenture and slavery and with the emergence

---

[71] A similar question can be raised regarding the first thirty performances which might result from the special skills of the second manager. For a general discussion: Daniel Friedmann, 'Restitution for Wrongs: The Measure of Recovery' (2001) 79 Tex L Rev 1879.

[72] [1946] Ch 169.

[73] *National Merchandising Corp* (n 67).

[74] Janet Halley, 'What Is Family Law? A Genealogy Part 1' (2011) 23 Yale JL & Human 1, 2 (hereafter Halley, 'What Is Family Law?').

[75] See n 25.

of the laborer and employee selling his work for a wage. Socially, it coincided with the emergence of a market for labor, an ideology of *laissez faire* for the market.[76]

The master–servant relation on which the enticement tort was grounded has undergone dramatic upheavals. The application of the tort to labour relations resulted in an overzealous defence of the employer's right. This protection was no longer desirable. The special proprietary nature of the master–servant relationship, manifested in the master's control over his servant, no longer exists. The participants changed both contents and titles—the master is now employer; the servant an employee. A contractual relationship of a unique nature was created,[77] governed extensively by legislation.[78]

At the individual level many contracts of employment, in particular long-term contracts, are terminable at will.[79] Covenants which limit competition are occasionally void as a restraint of trade.[80] Consequently, interference in such contracts is not always actionable, either because of the absence of a breach or the lack of a binding contract.

Furthermore, since the nineteenth century trade unions have restructured labour relations from the individual to the collective level. Hence collective relations reside side by side with the individual. The social and legal map has dramatically changed. Initially the activity of unions was considered illegal. Their interference with both the employment contract and other contracts of the employer was actionable in tort.[81] The over-protective attitude towards employers by the courts led the legislator to intervene.[82] Legislation nowadays partly governs the field of collective labour disputes, granting immunity for interference in contracts of employment and other contracts made in contemplation or furtherance of a trade dispute.[83] Yet there is still strong opposition to the very existence of the tort based on its problematic application to industrial relations.[84] This might be resolved by formulating a proper immunity or enlarging its current scope. It cannot justify a call for abolishing the tort altogether.[85]

The contract of employment served in the past as the leverage which enabled the master to impose tort liability on a third-party interferer and recover profits from a third party who caused the breach. Nowadays we have a general rule imposing tort liability on parties that interfere with a contract and allowing a disgorgement claim in some instances against them, though the employment contract is often excluded from the general rule.

A similar process has occurred with regard to marriage relations.[86] The institution of family and marriage has undergone dramatic changes, at least in the Western world. A wife is not the property of her husband, nor are his children. The

---

[76] Halley, 'What Is Family Law?' (n 74) 2–3.
[77] For a general survey: Hugh Collins, *Employment Law* (2nd edn, OUP 2010). Labour law deals with the contract, industrial law, and social law.
[78] Employment Relations Act 1999; Equality Act 2010 s 57.
[79] Jay M Feinman, 'The Development of the Employment at Will Rule' (1976) 20 Am JL Hist 118; Rachel Arnow-Richman, 'Modifying at-Will Employment Contracts' (2016) 57 BCL Rev 427.
[80] *Treitel* (n 7) [11-112] ff.
[81] ibid [11-142]; Christian Witting, *Street on Torts* (14th edn, OUP 2015) 406.
[82] Already in the Trade Union Act 1871, and later in the Trade Disputes Act 1906, which enshrined into law the rights of unions to strike.
[83] Currently Trade Union Reform and Employment Rights Act 1993.
[84] Swan, 'A New Tortious Interference' (n 10) 196–200; Howarth, 'Against Lumley v Gye' (n 29).
[85] As was suggested by Howarth, 'Against Lumley v Gye' (n 29).
[86] As is thoroughly described by Halley, 'What Is Family Law?' (n 74), and part 2, 23 Yale JL & Human 189.

366 THE EXTERNAL SHIELD OF A CONTRACT

patriarchal–proprietary–discriminatory arrangement which governed family relations has totally changed. Marriage is founded nowadays on equality, on both partners' autonomy. In most countries, a process of secularization regulating marriage has taken place. From a closed relationship marriage has turned into a relationship enabling a mutual right to withdraw without a cause.[87]

This transformation has had a deep impact on tort liability. In most jurisdictions, the tort of inducing breach of contract does not apply to marriage,[88] or to a contract to marry. Liability is excluded either as an initial exception or as a justification to the tort, and occasionally due to the absence of a binding contract.[89]

This reversal with regard to tort liability of third parties interfering with employment and marriage relations actually demonstrates the vicissitudes these relations have gone through, and also rather a conceptual continuity. Based on property concepts in *Lumley v Gye*, they paved the road to the general tort of inducing breach of contract. Property features are now attached to other contracts which are protected against third-party inducement. Eventually, the domestic relations governed by husbands and masters changed not only the nomenclature but also the substance. In liberal democracies proprietary control over servants and wives vanished; employment and marriage now offer more balance and freedom to once subordinate parties. This freedom in the internal relations has an impact on a third party's liability. Third parties who knowingly interfere with employment and contracts of marriage or those relating to them are to a large extent exempt from liability.[90]

In an interesting dialectical process regarding a rule and its exception, the master–servant and marriage relations have maintained their special character. In the past, these relations were unique in imposing liability on third parties who interfered with them. Nowadays there is a general tort liability protecting any contract from external interference, yet the relations of employment and marriage are still regarded as unique and constitute a significant exception to the tort they forged in *Lumley v Gye*.

---

[87] See Divorce, Dissolution and Separation Act 2020.

[88] Under Jewish law marriage, though religiously officiated, is considered a contract. Under Israeli law it is excluded from the application of the tort: s 62(b) The Civil Wrongs Ordinance, enacted during the British Mandate in 1944 and later on ratified in the Hebrew version in 1968 by the Israeli Parliament.

[89] This is the case under English law: a promise of marriage is not binding as a contract: Law Reform (Miscellaneous Provisions) Act 1970, s 2. Before the passing of the 1970 Act, some dicta indicated that inducing a breach of a promise of marriage would not be actionable: *National Phonograph Co Ltd v Edison Bell Co* [1908] Ch 335, 350.

[90] The affinity between the exceptions is reflected in Israeli law. The Civil Wrongs Ordinance states in s 62(b): 'For the purpose of this section, the relationship created by marriage shall not be considered a contract, and a strike and a shutdown shall not be considered a breach of contract.'

22

Unjustified Enrichment in China: An Uncertain Path

QIAO LIU*

I. Introduction

This chapter is devoted to Professor Ewan McKendrick, whose works have greatly influenced my learning of the English law of contract and unjust enrichment.

The new Chinese Civil Code ('CCC')[1] seems to give one the impression that a brand new, and relatively complete, law of unjustified[2] enrichment has just emerged in China. The new scheme, occupying the entirety of Chapter 29 'Unjustified Enrichment' (Book III 'Contract' Part 3 'Quasi-Contract') and consisting of four articles (Articles 985–988), certainly represents one of the most significant changes introduced with the enactment of the Code.[3] Yet, to say that those provisions are new to the Chinese legal system is misleading, for it overlooks a vast body of foundational jurisprudence developed over the years by the Chinese judiciary. One striking feature attending to the development of the Chinese law of unjustified enrichment, which continues to this day, has indeed been the tension between a short supply of legislative rules and a huge demand, demonstrated in the judicial practice,[4] for more rules and clearer guidance. Naturally, the Supreme People's Court ('SPC'), the top judiciary in China, has stepped in from time to time with an attempt to provide such rules and guidance. It would be missing a vital (albeit not necessarily the easiest or most orderly) part of the law should any study of the subject leave the relevant judicial practice unexplored.

The purpose of this chapter is to delineate some of the bright lines emerging from a vast body of Chinese cases, with a particular focus on an issue going into the foundation of this area of law: *what constitutes the reason for the restitution of an enrichment*? In the Chinese context, the contest is between an open-ended, discretionary approach focusing on the impropriety, unconscionability, unfairness, or unreasonableness of the enrichment (the 'unjust' approach) and a more controlled and refined approach requiring a search for a 'legal

---

* I am grateful for insightful comments on an earlier draft of this article by Professor Hugh Beale. I am also grateful for valuable feedback received from participants of the School of Law, City University of Hong Kong Research Seminar Series on 3 February 2023.

[1] The Civil Code of the People's Republic of China (中华人民共和国民法典) (adopted at the 3rd meeting of the 13th National People's Congress on 28 May 2020, effective from 1 January 2021).

[2] For reasons why the German terminology of 'unjustified' enrichment should be preferred, in the Chinese context, to the English 'unjust' enrichment, see section IV.

[3] The pre-Code law, at the level of the National People's Congress (or its Standing Committee, hereafter 'NPC' and 'NPCSC')—China's top legislature, takes the form of a simple rule which still finds its way into the Code through Article 122 (Bk I 'General Rules' Ch 5 'Civil Rights').

[4] Court decisions on the subject are, to say the least, voluminous. A search of 'unjustified enrichment' as the cause of action in the official case publication website 'China Judgements Online' returns more than 478,000 cases: <http://wenshu.court.gov.cn> (last accessed 2 February 2023).

Qiao Liu, *Unjustified Enrichment in China: An Uncertain Path* In: *Shaping the Law of Obligations*. Edited by: Edwin Peel and Rebecca Probert, Oxford University Press. © Qiao Liu 2023. DOI: 10.1093/oso/9780198889762.003.0022

basis' (the 'unjustified' approach).[5] Which of these two approaches, the 'unjust' approach or the 'unjustified' approach, have found favour with Chinese courts? It is impossible to depict something close to a full picture here, especially when such a picture will necessarily call for an assessment of a gigantic number of decisions delivered by lower courts. Thus, the study to be presented in what follows is confined to a few dozen representative cases, either because the cases were assigned high importance by the SPC, were themselves decided by the SPC, or otherwise involved points of legal significance. In discussing these cases within the conceptual framework laid down by the CCC, I will strive to, where appropriate, draw upon comparative law materials (particularly those concerning English and German law) for comparison and inspiration.

II. An Overview

For readers not familiar with the evolution of the Chinese law on the subject, it is necessary to take a quick look at how the law got to where it is today. The present unjustified enrichment scheme under the Code is a continuance (as well as expansion) of the relevant provisions of earlier national laws, which were enacted as discrete 'parts' to be assembled into the Code.[6] Its prototype can be traced back to Article 92 of the 1986 General Principles of Civil Law ('GPCL'), a mini civil code promulgated at the early stage of the reform and opening up era, which stated that 'where *improper benefit* is obtained without *lawful grounds*, resulting in loss to another party, the improper benefit obtained must be returned to the person who suffered the loss'.[7]

Remarkably, the above general provision for unjustified enrichment under the GPCL was intended as a new conceptualization of unjustified enrichment as one of the four causes giving rise to a right *in personam* or an obligation (the other three being contract, tort, and *negotiorum gestio*), rather than a special form of tortious liability as it had been previously conceived of.[8] Article 92 was thus placed under the chapter entitled 'Civil Rights' and made reference to 'loss' instead of 'harm/injury'. The above four causes of obligations were

---

[5] Therefore, the debate to be discussed here is different from the debate in England as to whether the traditional 'unjust factors' approach, captured by the term 'unjust enrichment', should yield to a modified version of the 'absence of basis' approach. The modified 'absence of basis' approach was advocated in Peter Birks, *Unjustified Enrichment* (2nd edn, OUP 2005) 109 (hereafter Birks, *Unjustified Enrichment*). For counter-arguments in support of the 'unjust factors' approach, see Andrew Burrows, *The Law of Restitution* (3rd edn, OUP 2011) 97 et seq (hereafter Burrows, *The Law of Restitution*). For a criticism of the 'unjust factors' approach from a civilian perspective, see Reinhard Zimmermann, 'Unjustified Enrichment: The Modern Civilian Approach' (1995) 15 OJLS 403, 416 (hereafter Zimmermann, 'Unjustified Enrichment').

[6] For the parts-assembling approach and the systematic issues that this has created, see Qiao Liu, 'The Chinese Civil Code: The Problem of Systematisation' in Michele Graziadei and Lihong Zhang (eds), *The Making of the Civil Codes* (Springer 2022) 104.

[7] General Principles of Civil Law of the People's Republic of China (中华人民共和国民法通则) (adopted at the fourth session of the sixth NPC, amended on 27 August 2009) art 92 (my emphasis). A translation is provided by Whitmore Gray and Henry Ruiheng Zheng, 'General Principles of Civil Law of the People's Republic of China' (1986) 34 Am J Com L 715, 734 (hereafter Gray and Zheng, 'General Principles of Civil Law of the PRC'). 'Improper benefit' is a literal translation of '不当利益', and 'lawful grounds' a literal translation of '合法根据'.

[8] Guangyu Fu (傅广宇), 'The Chinese Civil Code and Unjustified Enrichment: Retrospect and Prospect' (中国民法典与不当得利：回顾与前瞻) [2019] Issue 1 ECUPL Journal, 116, 120 (hereafter Fu, 'Retrospect and Prospect'). While the law of unjustified enrichment can be said to be 'the mirror image of the law of delict', it is concerned with the defendant's gains, not the claimant's losses: Zimmermann, 'Unjustified Enrichment' (n 5) 403–04, 413–14.

subsequently reaffirmed and solidified in the 2017 General Rules of Civil Law ('GRCL'),[9] a 'Law' adopted by the National People's Congress ('NPC') to be integrated in 2020 into the CCC as its general part. Thus, Article 122 in CCC Book I (General Provisions), identical to the same numbered article in the GRCL, provides that 'a person who sustains a loss as a result of another person obtaining *improper benefit* without *a legal basis* is entitled to claim a restitution by that other person of the *improper benefit*'.[10]

Subject to one major proviso, Article 122 reads very much alike the general provision for an action for unjustified enrichment in German law.[11] If Article 122 of the CCC is compared to Article 92 of the GPCL, the most significant change is no doubt the substitution of a 'legal basis', which is said to refer simply to a 'provision of law or agreement of the parties', for a 'lawful ground', which misleadingly connotes an emphasis on the lawfulness or legality of the enrichment.[12] However, it should be noted that Article 122 continues with the use of 'improper benefit' which first appeared under Article 92. Although it is said that 'improper benefit' 'presumably covers what might be called "unjust" enrichment in some legal systems',[13] such an expression raises questions about whether concepts of propriety, fairness, or reasonableness might be seen as controlling factors in this area of law. Therefore, while the legislature has moved in favour of a more disciplined approach based on the absence of a 'legal basis', it has left loose ends that need to be sorted out when Article 122 is applied.

Having a single provision for unjustified enrichment in the form of CCC Article 122 and its predecessors has long been criticized as overly brusque and rough, and hence inadequate.[14] The response by the CCC was to introduce a Chapter 29 ('Unjustified Enrichment') within Book III (Contract) Part 3 ('Quasi-Contract'). The NPC's decision to adopt the bizarre term 'quasi-contract' is surprising, but should be regarded as no more than a convenient or symbolic move. It appears that in doing so the NPC purported to borrow from certain foreign legal systems, including Anglo-American legal systems, under which it was said equivalents to unjustified enrichment and *negotiorum gestio* tended to be treated together as 'quasi-contract' given the lack of a 'general part' of the law of obligations.[15] In reality, the NPC opted for stability by continuing with a time-honoured law-making practice which involved stuffing into the law of contract rules concerning non-contractual, non-tortious obligations. The term 'quasi-contract', although founded upon a misconceived and obsolete understanding of Anglo-American law, is hence decorative and inconsequential.[16]

---

[9] General Rules of Civil Law of the People's Republic of China (中华人民共和国民法总则) (adopted at the 5th meeting of the 12th NPC on 15 March 2017).

[10] CCC, art 122 (emphasis added). A 'legal basis' is a literal translation of '法律根据'.

[11] German Bürgerliches Gesetzbuch (BGB) §812(1). The proviso concerns the dichotomy between enrichment 'by performance' and enrichment 'other than by performance': see n 19.

[12] Hong Shi (石宏) (ed), *The General Rules of Civil Law of the People's Republic of China: Interpretation of Provisions, Legislative Reasons and Related Rules* (中华人民共和国民法总则：条文说明、立法理由及相关规定) (Beijing University Press 2017) 286 (hereafter Shi, *General Rules*).

[13] Gray and Zheng, 'General Principles of Civil Law of the PRC' (n 7) fn 30.

[14] Substantial expansion of the law had been attempted before the CCC in two major scholarly drafts of the Civil Code: Huixing Liang (梁慧星) (ed), *The Draft Civil Code of the People's Republic of China: English Translation* (Martinus Nijhoff 2010), latest Chinese original version [中国民法典草案建议稿] (2nd edn, Law Press 2011); Liming Wang (王利明), *A Propositional Version with Legislative Reasons for Civil Code Draft of China* (original translation, 中国民法典学者建议稿及立法理由) (Law Press 2005).

[15] Wei Huang (黄薇) (gen ed), *Interpretations on the Civil Code of the People's Republic of China* (中华人民共和国民法典释义) (Law Press 2020) vol II, 1776 (hereafter Huang, *Interpretations*). The authors are from the Civil Law Office of the NPCSC Legal Work Commission, the institution responsible for drafting and revising the text of the CCC. The views expressed in the book are generally regarded as representing the lawmakers' position.

[16] See also Zhicheng Wu and William Swadling, 'Unjustified Enrichment in the Chinese Civil Code: Questions from the Common Law' (2021) 29 Asia Pac L Rev 402, 405–06. Incidentally, one major early Chinese work on

370 UNJUSTIFIED ENRICHMENT IN CHINA

Most relevantly, unjustified enrichment in China has never been associated with something like a general 'implied contract' theory,[17] which finds no place in the contemporary Chinese jurisprudence.

Chapter 29 of the CCC starts with Article 985, whose first paragraph essentially repeats Article 122 by stating that 'a person who suffers a loss may claim a restitution by the enrichee of the obtained benefit'. The second paragraph of Article 985 goes on to set out three defences against a claim for unjustified enrichment: (1) where a performance is rendered for the purpose of fulfilling a moral duty; (2) where an obligation is discharged before its due date; or (3) where an obligation is discharged by a party knowing that the obligation does not exist. Notably, all three defences in paragraph 2 are confined to cases involving enrichment 'by performance', defined as a juristic act with an intention to increase another person's wealth for a certain purpose,[18] such as a delivery of goods under a contract of sale or a bequeathal of a gift. However, the main provision in Article 985 paragraph 1 (or Article 122 for that matter) does not explicitly adopt the distinctive German dichotomy between enrichment 'by performance' and enrichment 'other than by performance'.[19] Although there are signs that the German model of bifurcating unjustified enrichment into two categories may eventually gain currency in China,[20] uncertainty as to the two categories' demarcation and the differences in their applicable rules lingers on.

In a provision of a judicial interpretation issued by the SPC on Article 92 of the GPCL, the scope of restitution based on unjustified enrichment was confined to 'the original property plus any accrued interest', leaving any other enrichment to be confiscated by the State.[21] The 'confiscation' option has since faded away.[22] However, it remains the law that a claim

---

unjustified enrichment used the term 'quasi-contract' in its title: Daming Shen (沈达明), *The Law of Quasi-Contract and Restitution* (准合同法与返还法) (University of International Business and Economics Press 1999).

[17] The theory, as endorsed in *Sinclair v Brougham* [1914] AC 398 (HL), has been firmly abandoned in modern authorities such as *Lipkin Gorman v Karpnale Ltd* [1991] 2 AC 548 (HL); *Westdeutsche Landesbank Girozentrale v Islington London Borough Council* [1996] 2 WLR 802 (HL).

[18] Huang, *Interpretations* (n 15) 1790. Also, Reinhard Zimmermann and Jacques du Plessis, 'Basic Features of the German Law of Unjustified Enrichment' (1994) 2 RLR 14, 25–26 (hereafter Zimmermann and du Plessis, 'Basic Features').

[19] BGB §812(1). Further, Gerhard Dannemann, *The German Law of Unjustified Enrichment and Restitution: A Comparative Introduction* (OUP 2009) 21–25 (hereafter Dannemann, *The German Law of Unjustified Enrichment and Restitution*; Zimmermann and du Plessis, 'Basic Features' (n 18) 25; Zimmermann, 'Unjustified Enrichment' (n 5) 405–07.

[20] The dichotomy has been approved by the SPC in *Liu Zhongyou v Nanchang City Municipal Construction Co Ltd and Jiangxi Province Fuzhen Road & Bridge Construction Co Ltd* (刘忠友与南昌市市政建设有限公司、江西省福振路桥建筑工程有限公司建设工程合同纠纷申诉、申请民事判决书), SPC, 27 Dec 2017, (2017) Zui Gao Fa Min Zai No 287 Civil Judgment (hereafter *Liu Zhongyou v Nanchang Construction Co Ltd*); *Shenzhen Hongye Investment Holdings Group Co Ltd v Wang Xiaoling et al* (深圳鸿烨投资控股集团有限公司等诉王晓玲等建筑工程合同纠纷再审案), SPC, 21 July 2017, (2016) Zui Gao Fa Min Zai No 153 Civil Judgment (hereafter *Shenzhen Hongye v Wang*). The dichotomy is also supported by both lawmakers and a majority of scholars: Huang, *Interpretations* (n 15) 1790 et seq; Fu, 'Retrospect and Prospect' (n 8) 122.

[21] Opinion (for Trial Use) of the Supreme People's Court on Questions Concerning the Implementation of the *General Principles of Civil Law of the People's Republic of China* (关于贯彻执行＜中华人民共和国民法通则＞若干问题的意见(试行), adopted at the SPC Judicial Committee on 26 January 1988, issued and effective as of 2 April 1988); Fa (Ban) Fa [1988] No 6, art 131. A translation is provided by Whitmore Gray and Henry Ruiheng Zheng, 'Opinion (for Trial Use) of the Supreme People's Court on Questions Concerning the Implementation of the *General Principles of Civil Law of the People's Republic of China*' (1989) 52 LCP 59, 78.

[22] It might be queried whether the 'confiscation' option might be retained for illegal enrichment, but such a solution does not seem to be countenanced by Chinese courts, see for example *Wang Liangqun v Shenzhen Fuyuan School et al* (王良群诉深圳市富源学校、吕继刚、王彦荣不当得利案), Shenzhen Baoan District Court, 20 March 2009, (2009) Shen Bao Fa Min Yi Chu Zi No 420 Civil Judgment (bribes paid for school admission held recoverable as unjustified enrichment).

for unjustified enrichment entails first and foremost the restitution of either the ownership or possession of the original property plus interest.[23] Interest is calculated by a simple rate adopted by the central bank. When it is impossible or unnecessary to make restitution in species, the value of the original property or its substitute must be paid.[24] Chinese law is thus aligned with German law not only in designating restitution as the only legal response to unjustified enrichment, but also in viewing restitution as always personal (including an obligation to give up a specific property) and never proprietary.[25]

Against the background of the above general rules about the scope of recovery in a claim of unjustified enrichment, the rest of Chapter 29 (Articles 986–988) of the CCC make some significant additions to the remedial aspect of unjustified enrichment. Similar to the German law,[26] CCC Articles 986 and 987 regard what is equivalent to the English concept of 'disenrichment' not as a defence, but as going into the measurement of the restitutionary liability. A bona fide enrichee, one who has no actual or presumed knowledge of the absence of a legal basis, is not liable to make restitution of benefits that no longer exist,[27] while a mala fide enrichee, one with such knowledge, is liable not only to return all the benefits obtained, but also to compensate further losses sustained by the claimant.[28] In addition, CCC Article 988 provides that 'where the enrichee has transferred gratuitously the obtained benefits to a third party, the person suffering a loss may claim that the third party assume an obligation of restitution to a corresponding extent'. This claim appears to be more readily available than its German counterpart under section 822 of the German Bürgerliches Gesetzbuch (BGB), in that it may lie wherever, and only to the extent that, the claimant fails to (either because it is not entitled or chooses not to) recover unjustified enrichment in full from the initial enrichee under Articles 986 or 987, irrespective of whether the initial enrichee is bona fide or mala fide.[29]

Over the years, a number of scholarly works have been produced in China introducing the law of unjustified enrichment in Germany, Taiwan, and other jurisdictions to a Chinese audience.[30] In fact, the above sketch of the unjustified enrichment regime under the CCC

---

[23] Huang, *Interpretations* (n 15) 1796–97.

[24] Huang, *Interpretations* (n 15); *Shanghai Xinhong Freight Service Co Ltd v Liu Yang* (上海鑫鸿货运服务有限公司与刘洋不当得利纠纷案), Zhengzhou IPC, 19 Mar 2011, (2011) Zheng Min Er Zhong Zi No 236 Civil Judgment.

[25] Dannemann, *The German Law of Unjustified Enrichment and Restitution* (n 19) 7, Ch 6 sec 1.

[26] BGB §818(3). See further Dannemann, *The German Law of Unjustified Enrichment and Restitution* (n 19) 139–41.

[27] *Liu Zhongyou v Nanchang Construction Co Ltd* (n 20).

[28] The legal basis of such compensation is presently unclear, but presumably associated with Chinese courts' broad discretion to apportion losses or distribute gains based on the general principle of 'good faith', which entails consideration of either party's 'fault': The Minutes of the National Courts' Civil and Commercial Adjudicative Work Conference (全国法院民商事审判工作会议纪要) (hereafter 'SPC Minutes'), Fa [2019] No 254 (adopted at the 319th meeting of the Civil and Administrative Specialized Committee of the Judicial Committee of the Supreme People's Court on 11 September 2019) art 32(2) (restitution aims 'to achieve a reasonable distribution between the parties and to prevent a party in bad faith from benefiting from the non-existence or invalidation of the contract').

[29] Huang, *Interpretations* (n 15) 1802. Cf Dannemann, *The German Law of Unjustified Enrichment and Restitution* (n 19) 145. Of course, a third party who has paid a reasonable price for the enrichment is not liable: *Guangdong Zhenrong Energy Co Ltd v Zhangjiakou Qintong Industrial Co Ltd* (广东振戎能源有限公司、张家口市秦同实业有限责任公司买卖合同纠纷再审民事判决书), SPC, 19 Dec 2017, (2017) Zui Gao Fa Min Zai No 114 Civil Judgment.

[30] Some notable earlier works include Hailin Zou (邹海林), *Unjustified Enrichment in Chinese Civil Law* (我国民法上的不当得利), (1996) 5 Civil and Commercial L Rev 1 (民商法论丛); Jianyuan Cui (崔建远), 'A Study on Unjustified Enrichment' (不当得利研究) (1987) Issue 4 The Chinese Journal of Law (法学研究) 58; Zejian Wang (王泽鉴), *Theories of the Law of Obligations: Unjustified Enrichment* (债法原理·不当得利) (CUPL Press 2002).

has shown a remarkable resemblance to some provisions of the BGB. Borrowed legislative texts, however, do no more than transplant a tree and do not guarantee its thriving in a non-native soil. It is hence critical to study the process of the judicial internalization of the legal texts, structures, and concepts originating from overseas. More recently in China, there have been calls for a renewed interest in domestic judicial practice.[31] The present chapter is an attempt to shed some light on the judicial path(s) taken by, mostly, the SPC. It is commonplace that China has no system of precedent resembling the one in common law jurisdictions like England. The SPC is, however, given the power to—and regularly does—'make law' by issuing legally binding 'judicial interpretations'[32] and 'guiding cases'.[33] We have seen one provision from a 'judicial interpretation' above, but there is no 'guiding case' directly relating to unjustified enrichment.[34] My ensuing analysis is primarily based on 'gazette cases', namely cases published in the official Gazette of the SPC, which are, although not strictly binding, widely regarded as wielding a general de facto influence over Chinese judges.[35] I will start with the general structure of a claim for unjustified enrichment in China, before turning to an issue which goes into the foundation of this area of law, namely whether China has a law of 'unjust' or 'unjustified' enrichment.

III. The Four-Point Test

It is generally accepted by Chinese courts that unjustified enrichment as formulated under Article 92 of the GPCL and its successors enshrines a four-point test.[36] Accordingly, to make out a claim for unjustified enrichment, Chinese law requires that: (1) the defendant is enriched; (2) the claimant suffers a loss; (3) there is a 'causal link' between the enrichment and the loss; and (4) the enrichment is received/retained without a legal basis.

---

[31] See eg Mingyi Ye (叶名怡), 'The Hilbert's Problems in the Law of Unjustified Enrichment' (不当得利法的希尔伯特问题) (2022) 34 Peking University LJ 944, 965–66.

[32] A Judicial Interpretation (usually with 'Interpretation', 'Opinion' or 'Reply' in its title) issued by the SPC is a legal instrument setting out relatively detailed rules concerning the interpretation and application of a 'law' enacted by the top legislature (the National People's Congress or its Standing Committee). A judicial interpretation is binding on all people's courts in China. See generally Nanping Liu, *Judicial Interpretations in China: Opinions of the Supreme People's Court* (Sweet & Maxwell Asia 1997).

[33] 'Guiding Cases' are case summaries edited and issued by the SPC. One specific part of a 'guiding case', 'essential reasons', is binding on all courts. See generally Qiao Liu, 'Chinese "Case Law": Illusions and Complexities' (2019) 14 ASJCL S97 (hereafter Liu, 'Chinese "Case Law"').

[34] To date only 211 'guiding cases' (including two abolished cases) have been issued. One of the abolished 'guiding cases', Guiding Case No 20 (*Shenzhen Siruiman Fine Chemicals Co Ltd v Shenzhen Kengzi Water Supply Co Ltd and Shenzhen Kangtailan Water Treatment Equipment Co Ltd* (深圳市斯瑞曼精细化工有限公司诉深圳市坑梓自来水有限公司、深圳市康泰蓝水处理设备有限公司侵害发明专利权纠纷案), SPC Gazette, 2014, Issue 5, was abolished by the SPC for mistaking a restitutionary claim based on a civil wrong for a restitutionary claim based on unjustified enrichment: The Implementation Work Leading Group Office of the SPC's Working Progress Report on the Comprehensive Tidy-up of Judicial Interpretations to Ensure Implementation of the Civil Code (最高人民法院民法典贯彻实施工作领导小组办公室关于为确保民法典实施进行司法解释全面清理的工作情况报告) (adopted by the 1826th meeting of the SPC Judicial Committee on 28 Dec 2020), section 2(5).

[35] Liu, 'Chinese "Case Law"' (n 33) 104–08.

[36] Eg *Liu Zhongyou v Nanchang Construction Co Ltd* (n 20); *Jiangsu Bright Trading Co Ltd v Zhang Yuehong* (江苏百锐特贸易有限公司诉张月红不当得利纠纷案), Dongtai People's Court, 14 Nov 2016, SPC Gazette, Issue 5, 2018, 38–40 (hereafter *Jiangsu Bright*). For the structurally similar English test, see Charles Mitchell, Paul Mitchell, and Stephen Watterson (eds), *Goff & Jones: The Law of Unjust Enrichment* (9th edn, Sweet & Maxwell 2016) [1-09] et seq (hereafter Mitchell et al, *Goff & Jones*; Burrows, *The Law of Restitution* (n 5) 27.

THE FOUR-POINT TEST   373

In the following passages, I will discuss some issues of significance with respect to points 1–3, then moving on to give a separate treatment to an issue of continuing controversy with respect to point 4 in the next section.

First, 'enrichment' is generally understood to comprise any form of benefit or swelling of one's wealth, taking a wide range of forms such as acquisition of a proprietary right, possession or registration (of a property), discharge of an obligation, (receipt of) labour/service, and use of a thing.[37] Such various forms of 'enrichment' have been recognized by Chinese courts, such as in two SPC Gazette cases where it was held that unauthorized possession of another's property constituted an 'enrichment' to the possessor.[38] However, while some courts seem to be of the view that an improvement on another's property constitutes an 'enrichment' only where it conforms to that person's 'subjective will' and is 'freely accepted' by that person,[39] it remains to be seen to what extent Chinese courts are inclined to endorse what is equivalent to the common law test of 'subjective devaluation'.[40]

Second, the claimant must have suffered a 'loss', which is required for establishing a claim for unjustified enrichment. We are not here concerned with the use of 'loss' as a limiting factor in determining the scope of recovery.[41] Instead, the question is whether 'loss' in Chinese law entails something more than the common law notion of 'at the expense of'.[42] Some courts have unwarily made a false association between 'loss' and the law of damages by speaking of, for example, unjustified enrichment as a means to make good 'unexpected losses' and restore the claimant's lawful interests to status quo.[43] Even the SPC No 1 Civil Tribunal has once asserted that where a lessee sub-lets the property without the lessor's permission, the lessor is not entitled to recover the difference between their agreed rent and the higher sub-letting rent since the lessor, having received the agreed rent from the lessee, does not suffer a 'loss'.[44] However, the better view is that such positive or negative losses are not required; rendering a performance or a mere infringement of one's lawful interests,

---

[37] Huang, *Interpretations* (n 15) 1790.

[38] *Xu Jinliang v Wang Zhonghai* (徐进良诉王忠海不当得利案), Antu County People's Court of Jilin Province, SPC Gazette, 1996, issue 2; *Korean Samyung Co v Panjin Qingdao Clothing Co Ltd* (韩国三荣公司诉盘锦庆道服装有限公司), Dalian Maritime Court, 6 May 1996, SPC Gazette, Issue 4, 1997.

[39] See eg the first-instance decision by Fengzhen People's Court ((2017) Nei 0981 Min Chu No 758 Civil Judgment) in *Ulanqab Branch, CNPC (China National Petroleum Co) v Fengzhen City Yifeng Petrochemical Co Ltd et al* (中国石油天然气股份有限公司内蒙古乌兰察布销售分公司与丰镇市益丰石化有限公司、杨淑芬等不当得利纠纷二审民事判决书), affirmed on other ground by Ulanqab IPC, 24 May 2018, (2018) Nei 09 Min Zhong No 302 Civil Judgment. Also, Daxi Wu (武大喜) and Songbao Wang (王宋宝) (Fengzhen People's Court), 'Acquisition of Affixed Property According to Contract Is No Unjustified Enrichment' (依合同取得他人添附财产不构成不当得利), (2019) People's Judicature (人民司法), issue 11, 11–13.

[40] Mitchell et al, *Goff & Jones* (n 36) [4-43] et seq, [4-54]; Peter Birks, *An Introduction to the Law of Restitution* (rev edn, OUP 1989) 109–10; Burrows, *The Law of Restitution* (n 5) ch 3.

[41] As suggested by some Chinese lawmakers, recovery seems to be limited to either the claimant's loss or the defendant's enrichment, whichever is lower in value: Huang, *Interpretations* (n 15) 1798.

[42] For the meaning of the phrase under English law, see Mitchell et al, *Goff & Jones* (n 36) pt 4; Burrows, *The Law of Restitution* (n 5) ch 4. For the German law, see Dannemann, *The German Law of Unjustified Enrichment and Restitution* (n 19) 30–33.

[43] *Shi Jianwei v Xu Xiuying* (施建伟诉徐秀英不当得利纠纷案), Shanghai No 2 IPC, (2009) Hu Er Zhong Min Yi (Min) Zhong Zi No 1221 Civil Judgment.

[44] SPC No 1 Civil Tribunal, Understanding and Applying the SPC Judicial Interpretation on the Adjudication of Cases Involving Urban House Leasing Contract Disputes (最高人民法院关于审理城镇房屋租赁合同纠纷案件司法解释的理解和适用) (2nd edn, People's Court Press 2016) 220–21. Now, Interpretation of the Supreme People's Court on Several Issues concerning the Application of Law in the Adjudication of Cases Involving Urban House Leasing Contract Disputes (最高人民法院关于审理城镇房屋租赁合同纠纷案件具体应用法律若干问题的解释) (adopted at the 1469th meeting of the Judicial Committee of the SPC on 22 June 22, 2009, last amended on 23 December 2020), SPC, 29 Dec 2020, Fa Shi [2020] No 17, art 10.

such as by placing an advertisement board on the roof of one's house without permission (irrespective of whether the roof is damaged or might be put to a commercial use by the owner), is itself a 'loss' for the purpose of establishing a claim for unjustified enrichment.[45] This view is also supported by a number of SPC decisions, which do not appear to regard the 'loss' element as bearing a different meaning from 'at the expense of'. Hence, an assignee of a debt suffers no 'loss' from the debtor's payment to the assignor, which does not discharge the debtor's obligation to the assignee, in the sense that the payment is not made 'at the assignee's expense'.[46] Where a cement manufacturer who is ordered to cease production for twenty days in order to dismantle a dust precipitator which infringes the claimant's intellectual property right manages to dismantle the precipitator without ceasing production, the claimant suffers no 'loss' in the sense that the continuance of production is not 'at his expense'.[47] The point is not that the claimant has not suffered any damage or injury, but that it is not a party entitled to claim a restitution of the enrichment identified.

Third, there must be a 'causal link' between the claimant's loss and the defendant's enrichment. The term 'causal link' is, of course, misleading, since it is usually not the defendant's 'enrichment', but some other causative event, that has led to the claimant's 'loss'. One key issue that appears to have been resolved by Chinese courts relates to whether both 'loss' and 'enrichment' must result from one single causative event.[48] The SPC has answered this question in the negative in two of its decisions.[49] This can be illustrated by *Liu Zhongyou v Nanchang Construction Co Ltd*.[50] The claimant (Liu) was deceived by a fraudster into paying RMB 20 million yuan to a highway company (HC) as a deposit for a construction project. Subsequently, HC paid 6 of the 20 million to the defendant, Nanchang Construction Company (NCC), who then paid the 6 million to the fraudster, as a deposit for another construction project. When it transpired that both construction projects were fabricated, the claimant brought an action against the defendant (NCC) claiming for the restitution of the 6 million. The SPC held that there was a 'causal link' between the claimant's loss and the defendant's enrichment, even though they arose respectively from two separate transactions. In the words of the SPC, what the law requires is a 'substantive link' between the two, which should be established 'according to fairness and common understanding of the society'. On this point, the SPC did not adopt the reasoning of the first instance court (Nanchang Intermediate People's Court, or Nanchang IPC) that the claim was precluded by privity of contract. Instead, it agreed with the appellate court (Jiangxi High People's Court, or Jiangxi HPC) that neither the lack of a contractual relationship between the parties nor the absence of fault on the part of the defendant barred the claim. Hence, the SPC favoured

---

[45] Huang, *Interpretations* (n 15) 1791, 1794.

[46] *Qingdao Honghai Investment Co Ltd v Weifang Branch, Agriculture Bank of China* (青岛泓海投资有限公司与中国农业银行潍坊市分行不当得利纠纷申请案), SPC, 15 Nov 2013, (2013) Min Shen Zi No 1631 Civil Ruling; *Meiyan v Shiyan People's Road Branch, Industrial and Commercial Bank of China* (梅艳、中国工商银行股份有限公司十堰人民路支行不当得利纠纷再审审查与审判监督民事裁定书), SPC, 29 Nov 2017, (2016) Zui Gao Fa Min Shen No 2681 Civil Ruling.

[47] *Zhang Peiyao, Hui Deyue and Jiangsu Funing County Dust-Cleaning Equipment Factory v Suzhou City Nanxin Cement Co Ltd* (张培尧、惠德跃、江苏省阜宁县除尘设备厂诉苏州南新水泥有限公司侵犯商业秘密、财产损害赔偿纠纷上诉案), SPC, 6 Nov 2000, (2000) Zhi Zhong Zi No 3 Civil Judgment.

[48] Such a requirement for the 'directness' of enrichment was once insisted upon under the German law: Zimmermann and du Plessis, 'Basic Features' (n 18) 31; Dannemann, *The German Law of Unjustified Enrichment and Restitution* (n 19) 22–23.

[49] *Liu Zhongyou v Nanchang Construction Co Ltd* (n 20); *Shenzhen Hongye v Wang* (n 20).

[50] *Liu Zhongyou v Nanchang Construction Co Ltd* (n 20).

a rather liberal interpretation of the 'causal link' element and rejected the claim only because the defendant, as a bona fide recipient,[51] had parted with the money by paying all the 6 million to the fraudster. Nevertheless, the SPC did not in that case offer much in the way of definition or explanation what amounts to a 'substantive' or sufficient link and this point awaits further clarification. As Chinese lawmakers cautioned, an 'indirect causal link' might be a helpful solution 'in individual cases' but requires 'further research'.[52]

Finally, the claimant in an action for unjustified enrichment has the burden of showing 'enrichment', 'loss', and a 'causal link'. This may not always be an easy task to fulfil. In two SPC Gazette cases, it has been held that a bank's internal accounting rules or transaction records were insufficient to show an 'enrichment', that is, overpayment to a customer either in cash or by crediting his/her account with an incorrect figure.[53] However, once the claimant makes out the above three elements, the SPC appears to favour the position that, at least in some cases, it is primarily for the defendant to disprove the fourth element, which is a 'negative fact', by adducing 'direct evidence' of the presence of a legal basis.[54] This is still a matter of some controversy and here is not the place to visit it in detail. Next, I will focus my inquiry on a related issue as to the meaning and scope of the fourth element, the 'absence of a legal basis'.

IV. Unjust or Unjustified Enrichment?

Thus far we have been using the term 'unjustified enrichment' to refer to this area of law in China. The more faithful literal translation of the Chinese phrase '不当' is, however, 'improper' or 'unjust'. As noted above, the legislature has abandoned 'lawful ground' in favour of 'legal basis' in drafting first the 2017 GRCL and then the 2020 CCC.[55] In this respect, the general provision for unjustified enrichment under CCC Articles 122 and 985 is in line with the German model set out in BGB §812(1). Does this mean that Chinese law has decisively adopted the German 'absence of basis' approach, as reflected by the name 'unjustified enrichment'?[56] Therefore, these two apparently contradictory terms, 'improper benefit' and 'legal basis', are both in use under the 2017 GRCL and then the 2020 CCC. This legislative ambivalence naturally leads one to look to the Chinese judicial practice for an answer to the following question: is the reason for the restitution of an enrichment the unjustness or unjustifiability of that enrichment?

---

[51] No evidence was found showing that the defendant had been aware of the fraud at the relevant time, therefore it was concluded that the defendant had been 'subjectively bona fide'.

[52] Huang, *Interpretations* (n 15) 1792.

[53] *Shilin County Branch, China Construction Bank v Yang Fubin* (中国建设银行石林县支行诉杨富斌不当得利纠纷案), Kunming IPC, 8 Nov 2002, SPC Gazette, Issue 6, 2003; *Xin Lianhua v Xingang Commercial Bank* (信连华诉新港商业银行存单纠纷案), Tianjin No 2 IPC, 23 Feb 2004, SPC Gazette, Issue 5, 2005.

[54] See eg *Shanghai Quncan Construction Materials Business Department v TBEA Co Ltd* (上海群灿建材经营部与特变电工股份有限公司二审民事判决书), SPC, 16 Dec 2016, (2016) Zui Gao Fa Min Zhong No 223 Civil Judgment; *Zheng Xiang v Hong Yeshan* (郑祥、洪叶珊不当得利纠纷再审民事判决书), SPC, 28 Dec 2017, (2016) Zui Gao Fa Min Zai No 39 Civil Judgment; *Lu Qiujie v Sun Jian* (路秋洁与孙剑不当得利纠纷再审案), SPC, 21 Nov 2013, (2013) Min Shen Zi No 1639 Civil Ruling.

[55] Text to and following n 10 above.

[56] Dannemann, *The German Law of Unjustified Enrichment and Restitution* (n 19) 37.

376   UNJUSTIFIED ENRICHMENT IN CHINA

The answer can be gleaned from a series of SPC Gazette cases. In the first case, *Wang Chunlin v Yinchuan*,[57] an employer paid its employees' salaries in the form of term deposit certificates as a substitute for cash. Each certificate had a face value of RMB 100 yuan and would, when redeemed, win a prize of (in most cases) small value. Subsequently, the defendant employee won the top prize of RMB 10,000 yuan with one of the certificates he received. The employer sought to recover as unjustified enrichment the net benefits obtained by the defendant, namely RMB 9,900 yuan, alleging that the winning certificate had been given away under 'fundamental misapprehension' (the Chinese version of mistake). The Ningxia HPC, following a SPC Reply[58] and reversing the lower courts' decision, dismissed the claim on the ground that the employer had not been mistaken and that there was a valid and effective agreement between the parties which constituted the 'legal basis' for the employee's enrichment. As stated by the SPC, the reason why there was no mistake was that the employer, 'knowing full well that every certificate would win a prize, should be taken to have transferred the right to the prize when giving it away without making provision for such a right'.[59] This is not, of course, based on a finding of the employer's subjective status of mind; rather, a critical finding seems to be that the employer, through its manager, had carelessly failed to discover that the winning certificate had been announced before delivery to the employee.

If the decision in the first case is uncontroversial, we quickly encounter uncertainty in our second and third cases, where opposite outcomes were arrived at on similar facts. In the second case, *Yu Shanlan v ICBC*,[60] the claimant customer had his IC card replaced by the defendant issuing bank and paid the fees (RMB 100 yuan) charged by the defendant. The customer brought an action to recover the difference (RMB 69.2 yuan) between the fees paid and the cost incurred by the defendant in making the new card (RMB 30.8 yuan) on the ground of a departmental regulation[61] limiting card replacement fees to the cost of making the card. At first instance it was held by the Beijing Xuanwu District People's Court that the fees had been charged by the defendant under a lawful and valid contract and hence did not constitute unjustified enrichment. On appeal, Beijing No 1 IPC overturned the first instance decision by holding that the defendant ought to have adjusted the fees according to the regulation and that since the defendant 'could not present a lawful ground' for the fees charged over and above the cost of making the card, the claim for unjustified enrichment should be allowed. The main difficulty with the appellate decision is that under Chinese law a contract is generally not invalidated by reason of a contravention of a departmental regulation.[62] Unfortunately, the appellate decision failed to explain why the defendant should be

---

[57]   *Wang Chunlin v Yinchuan Aluminum Materials Factory* (王春林与银川铝型材厂有奖储蓄存单纠纷再审案), Ningxia HPC, 27 March 1995, SPC Gazette, Issue 4, 1995 (hereafter *Wang Chunlin*).

[58]   A reply may be issued when a lower court requests instruction from the SPC. It is a form of judicial interpretation and hence a binding instrument. See The Reply of the Supreme People's Court concerning the Term Deposit Certificate Dispute between Wang Chunlin and Yinchuan Aluminum Materials Factory (最高人民法院关于王春林与银川铝型材厂有奖储蓄存单纠纷一案的复函), SPC, 1 January 1995 (hereafter SPC Reply on *Wang Chunlin*).

[59]   SPC Reply on *Wang Chunlin* (n 58).

[60]   *Yu Shanlan v Xuanwu Branch and Beijing Branch, Industrial and Commercial Bank of China* (喻山澜与工行宣武分行、工行北京分行不当得利纠纷案), Beijing No 1 IPC, 1 January 2005, SPC Gazette, Issue 6, 2005 (hereafter *Yu Shanlan*).

[61]   A departmental regulation is a regulation, order, direction, etc issued by a department of the State Council. The departmental regulation in the case was issued by the National Development and Reform Commission.

[62]   For the latest enunciation of the rule, see SPC Minutes (n 28), arts 30–31 (a contravention of a departmental regulation, as opposed to 'validity provisions' in a 'law' passed by the NPC or NPCSC or an 'administrative

precluded from relying upon the contract as the 'legal basis' for charging the fees. Nor did it address the part (if any) played by the defendant's 'fault' in not updating its fee schedule according to the departmental regulation before the conclusion of the contract. Another intriguing aspect of the decision, adverted to at the end of the final section of this chapter, concerns the appellate court's unequivocal confirmation that the burden was on the defendant to prove the presence of the 'legal basis'.

The decision in *Yu Shanlan* can be contrasted to the third case, *Jiangnan Credit Union v Luo Yuanling*,[63] where the claimant credit union entered into an eight-year term deposit contract featuring a preferential rate of 17.1 per cent per annum with the defendant customer. After having paid all of the interest (as well as the principal), the credit union sought to claim back any interest paid in excess of that calculated by reference to a normal rate of 2.88 per cent per annum by arguing that such was the effect dictated by a departmental regulation issued by the People's Bank which had taken effect when the contract was concluded. The Meizhou IPC allowed the defendant's appeal from the lower court's decision, in which it was erroneously held that the departure from the departmental regulation invalidated the term deposit contract. Accordingly, and contrary to the *Yu Shanlan* case, the contract between the parties stood as a 'legal basis' foreclosing the credit union's claim for unjustified enrichment.[64]

Are these two decisions reconcilable, if we accept that the outcomes in both cases are correct? In both cases, the contract between the bank/credit union and the customer was in contravention of a regulation which did not result in the invalidation of the contract. Further, there was a patent disparity between the bargaining positions of the two parties in both cases and the stronger party (the bank/credit union) was more or less 'at fault', in not complying with the regulation or disclosing it to the customer. The only material difference between the two cases seems to stem from the fact that in one case the benefit accrues to the stronger party and in the other case to the weaker party. In the *Yu Shanlan* case, the extra fees were repayable given the unilateral, non-negotiable nature of the fees charged and the bank's responsibility to make sure that all fees were lawful. In the *Jiangnan* case, the excess interest was not recoverable since the customer's reasonable expectation arising from the contract deserved protection against a careless, undisciplined financial institution. Thus interpreted, the courts might have tacitly allowed an element of (un)fairness, (un)conscientiousness, or (un)lawfulness to enter into their reasoning in determining a 'legal basis' in an unjustified enrichment claim.

The subtlety of Chinese courts' approach to 'legal basis' can be further seen from the remaining two SPC Gazette cases. In *Jiangsu Bright Trading Co Ltd v Zhang Yuehong*,[65] the defendant's father, who was a worker employed by the claimant, suffered an industrial

---

regulation' passed by the State Council, does not generally invalidate a contract unless it also constitutes a breach of public order and good morale).

[63] *Jiangnan Branch, Rural Credit Cooperatives Union of Meijiang District, Meizhou City v Luo Yuanling* (梅州市梅江区农村信用合作联社江南信用社诉罗苑玲储蓄合同纠纷案), Meizhou IPC, 15 Dec 2009, SPC Gazette, 2011, Issue 1 (hereafter *Jiangnan*).

[64] Similarly, where a borrower voluntarily pays interests not required by the loan contract, it may not recover the interests since their 'legal basis' lies in a contract implied from the borrower's conduct of payment and the lender's conduct of (free) acceptance: SPC No 1 Civil Tribunal (ed), *Guidance and Reference for Civil Adjudication* (民事审判指导与参考) (People's Court Press 2015) vol 1, 283–84.

[65] *Jiangsu Bright* (n 36).

injury and was awarded compensation amounting to RMB 368,333 yuan calculated on the basis of a twenty-year term in which the father required care. Subsequently, the parties concluded a settlement agreement reducing the total sum to RMB 300,000 yuan, which the claimant duly paid to the defendant. Unfortunately, the father died merely two and a half years after the agreement. The claimant then sought to recover the compensation paid for the 'unspent' 17.5 years. This claim was rightfully rejected and it was held that the settlement agreement constituted a 'lawful ground' for the payment.[66] In its reasoning, however, the court placed much reliance on the fact that the sum of compensation resulted from a fair and reasonable 'comprehensive determination within the legally permissible discretion' of likely future losses. This seemingly opens the door for the argument that some parts of the payment might be recoverable should they be based on a prior unfair or unreasonable determination.

Likewise, in *Sun Wei v Baichuan Co*,[67] the claimant, Sun Wei, was a warehouse keeper employed by the defendant company and he and two other employees were found to have embezzled the defendant's goods. The claimant agreed to, and did, pay more than RMB 40,000 yuan to the defendant in exchange for the defendant's promise not to inform the prosecutors of his offence. When criminally convicted, the claimant brought a civil action against the defendant to recover RMB 30,000 yuan as unjustified enrichment, alleging that the criminal verdict fixed the proceeds obtained by the claimant through reselling the goods at RMB 10,000 yuan. This claim was rejected on the ground that the figure fixed by the criminal verdict did not constitute complete or conclusive evidence of the value of the embezzled goods. There is some uncertainty as to whether the agreement between the parties, which purported to settle away a criminal liability by preventing a prosecution, was valid and effective as a matter of civil law in the Chinese context.[68] Even if it was, no reliance was placed by the court on it as a 'legal basis' for the payment. Instead, the decision suggests that should the claimant be shown to have over-compensated the defendant, the excess would likely be recoverable.

Several points may be noted with respect to the above Gazette cases. First, all these cases were decided in accordance with Article 92 of the GPCL, which still used the obsolete term of 'lawful ground'. However, in none of the cases did the decision turn upon the distinction between 'lawful ground' and 'legal basis'. *Yu Shanlan* is the only case that could be interpreted as suggesting that unlawfulness in the form of a contravention of the regulation, albeit not invalidating the contract, was of itself sufficient to justify the restitution of the enrichment. This interpretation is, however, unlikely to be sustainable, not only because there is some self-contradictoriness in it, but also because it clearly goes against the recognition in most other cases of a valid and binding contract as a 'lawful ground'.[69] Therefore, even before the more accurate expression of 'legal basis' found its way into the GRCL and then

---

[66] Similarly, *Li Xinfu v Chengdu Public Transport Group Co Ltd* (李新付诉成都市公共交通集团公司城市公交运输合同案), Chengdu IPC, 25 July 2005, [2005] Cheng Min Zhong Zi No 1561 Civil Judgment (a claim for proportionate restitution of fares paid for a monthly bus ticket which entitled the passenger to 100 trips when only 67 trips were taken was rejected on the ground that there was a valid and binding contract).

[67] *Sun Wei v Nantong Baichuan Flour Co Ltd* (孙卫与南通百川面粉有限公司不当得利纠纷案), Hai'an County People's Court, 15 July 2014, SPC Gazette, Issue 7, 2015 (No 225).

[68] An affirmative answer was given in, eg, Ling Zhang (张凌) and Chanyuan Li (李婵媛), 'Criminal Settlement Agreement from the Perspective of A Public Law View of Contract' (公法契约观视野下的刑事和解协议) (2008) 26(6) Tribune of Political Science and Law (政法论坛) 32, 39–40.

[69] Especially *Jiangsu Bright* (n 36), but also including *Wang Chunlin* (n 57) and *Jiangnan* (n 63).

the CCC, the German 'absence of basis' approach had been followed by Chinese courts, including the SPC.

Second, the Gazette cases discussed above reveal that Chinese courts have not saddled themselves with a narrow understanding that confines a reason for the restitution of an enrichment to a 'provision of law or agreement of the parties',[70] but have allowed some additional factors to enter the equation. For example, a party's 'fault' has lurked behind the decision in the first three cases: the claimant's 'fault' might militate against restitution (*Wang Chunlin* and *Jiangnan*), whereas the defendant's 'fault' might militate in favour of it (*Yu Shanlan*). In the other two cases, there were hints that substantive 'unfairness' between the parties might be a potential reason for restitution. Of course, accepting that the contract in both *Jiangsu Bright* and *Sun Wei* was lawful and valid, it is questionable whether such 'unfairness' should be relevant at all. This can be seen from a robust statement by a Chinese court in another case that it was 'the lessee's business judgement and responsibility' to have agreed upon a contractual rate much higher than the market rate, which consequently precluded any recovery of the difference on the ground of unjustified enrichment.[71] Nevertheless, it has been the practice of Chinese courts that such factors as 'fault' and 'fairness' might be taken into account in the search for a reason for restitution and it is doubtful that this practice will be departed from in the era of the CCC given the general nature of the term 'legal basis'. Two further reasons also lend support to this proposition. One is that since, as is openly acknowledged in *Yu Shanlan*, the onus of proof lies with the defendant, Chinese courts are likely to be attracted to the view that where the defendant seeks to establish any reason beyond 'provision of law or agreement of the parties', this should be given appropriate consideration. The other reason relates to the fact that all the SPC Gazette cases discussed above are cases involving enrichment 'by performance'. Since cases involving enrichment 'other than by performance' are, due to their variety and complexity, less amenable to a simple fixed formula, Chinese courts might regard it fitting to apply in those cases an approach more accommodating of such considerations as 'fault' or 'fairness'.[72]

Third, the above approach adopted by Chinese courts must incorporate proper controls and checks which qualify the range of relevant considerations and the weight given to them. In this respect, there is much to be learned from the common law. In the above Gazette cases, neither 'fault' nor 'fairness' was openly discussed, let alone properly defined. There is thus a real danger that, if more clarity is not given to the judicial reasoning and an unfettered pathway is created for the reversal of 'improper' or 'unjust' benefits, the search for a reason for restitution might slip into the abyss of palm tree justice. In view of this, it seems advisable for Chinese jurists to pay heed to the Canadian 'absence of juristic reason' approach, which allows the law to develop and refine specific reasons for restitution under a civilian conceptual structure. According to the Canadian approach, once the claimant shows the absence of any of the 'established categories' of juristic reason, which are largely aligned with the reference in China to 'provision of law or agreement of the parties', restitution is prima facie to be ordered unless the defendant successfully establishes a countervailing

---

[70] Shi, *General Rules* (n 12) 286.

[71] *Dai Mingan v Yang Tao* (代明安与杨㳋房屋租赁合同纠纷二审民事判决书), Xiaogan IPC, 25 March 2015, (2015) E Xiao Gan Zhong Min Er Zhong Zi No 63 Civil Judgment.

[72] Such has been suggested to be the case in the Roman law tradition since enrichment 'other than by performance' has historically been developed from claims based on '*actio de in rem verso*' rather than *condictio* type of claims: Francesco Giglio, 'A Systematic Approach to "Unjust" and "Unjustified" Enrichment' (2003) 23 OJLS 455.

reason for retaining the enrichment, which reason comprises particularly public policy and the parties' reasonable expectation.[73] The reason for dividing the approach into two separate steps was said to lie in the need to restrict the claimant's exposure to a duty of 'proof of a negative'.[74] That Chinese courts have consistently determined the issue in one single step may be explained by the recognition in cases like *Yu Shanlan* that, at least in some cases, the defendant bears the burden to prove the presence of a 'legal basis' for retaining the enrichment. As suggested above, the decision in *Yu Shanlan* effectively allowed factors beyond 'provision of law or agreement of the parties', such as 'fault' and 'unconscionability', to be taken into account even where there was a valid and enforceable contract between the parties. This illustrates the path that Chinese courts are most likely to follow in the future but it is a path whose trajectory and shape are still subject to further adjustments. There seem to be two respects in which the case law in common law jurisdictions might offer valuable lessons to the future development of Chinese law. The first respect concerns the way in which (such as in Canada) specific 'juristic reasons' outside 'established categories' might be developed and defined under the umbrella of 'public policy' and 'reasonable expectation of the parties'. Case law (such as in England) relating to 'unjust factors', as far as they are relevant to the devising of a Chinese solution, might also help. For example, the English concept of 'unconscientious receipt'[75] might inform how some forms of 'fault' on the defendant's side are to take shape in China. Conversely, some other 'unjust factors' might be of more limited value. An example is a mere mistake which, under Chinese law, cannot of itself justify the restitution of the enrichment and is considered of little relevance if it does not invalidate a contract or a statutory obligation.[76] The second respect concerns the relationship between 'established categories' and additional considerations. For example, in the Chinese context, an issue requiring resolution is the extent to which an additional consideration might trump an existing 'established' legal basis. In *Yu Shanlan*, 'fault' or 'unconscionability' on the part of the bank was allowed to trump an existing contract. However, arguments based on substantive unfairness have been dismissed in the face of a voluntarily concluded contract (such as in the overpriced lease case). Even though it is recognized that Chinese law will probably draw a markedly different line than common law jurisdictions, the common law may provide a guidepost as to where the line is drawn in the Chinese context.

---

[73] Such 'established categories' are composed of a contract, disposition of law or donative intent, or 'other common law, equitable or statutory obligations': *Garland v Consumers' Gas Co* [2004] 1 SCR 629, (2004) 237 DLR (4th) 385 (SCC) [44] (Iacobucci J). In the Chinese context, there is no equitable jurisdiction and a donation is characterized as a contract: CCC, Book III 'Contract' Part 2 Ch 11 'Gift Contract'. For more details about the Canadian approach, see Mitchell McInnes, 'Juristic Reasons and Unjust Factors in the Supreme Court of Canada' (2004) 120 LQR 554; Mitchell McInnes, 'Making Sense of Juristic Reasons: Unjust Enrichment After *Garland v. Consumers' Gas*' (2004) 42 Alta L Rev 399; Mitchell McInnes, 'The Reason to Reverse: Unjust Factors and Juristic Reasons' (2012) 92 BUL Rev 1049.

[74] *Garland v Consumers' Gas Co* (n 73) [44].

[75] Peter Birks and Robert Chambers (eds), *The Restitution Research Resource* (2nd edn, Mansfield Press Oxford 1997) 2–3; Birks, *Unjustified Enrichment* (n 5) 42.

[76] *Wang Chunlin* (n 57). This might also be the reason why the claimant did not allege mistake in *Yu Shanlan* (n 60), *Jiangnan* (n 63), or *Jiangsu Bright* (n 36). Contra, *Deutsche Morgan Grenfell Group plc v Inland Revenue Commissioners* [2006] UKHL 49, [2007] 1 AC 558, 572.

V. Concluding Remarks

In a new chapter entitled 'unjustified enrichment' within the Chinese Civil Code, the top legislature in China has imparted a German-type framework for this area of law. While this framework has a long line of judicial decisions as part of its foundation and opens up a new direction or space for future development, there is no denial that the principal task of carving out a coherent system of operable rules lies with the Chinese judiciary particularly the SPC. It is inevitable that the SPC, when embarking on what is a 'test and error' approach, has made wrong turns (such as by taking a damages-based view of 'loss') and undertook new paths still covered in mist (such as by adopting an 'indirect causal link').

The greatest uncertainty attending to this area of the law is whether, and if so to what extent, Chinese courts might, tacitly or otherwise, resort to such general concepts as 'unjustness', 'impropriety', 'fault', and 'unfairness' in determining the presence or absence of a 'legal basis'. In some cases, such as *Yu Shanlan* and *Jiangnan*, the seemingly inconsistent decisions could be reconciled by a sensible desire to protect the weaker party, who was a consumer dealing with a financial institution. The difficulty with the courts' reasoning process is that it left too much in the dark, with the true reasons not being spelt out, subjected to open debate, or formalized into the legal construct. Chinese law seems to be at a crossroads in shaping the foundation and future of the law of unjustified enrichment. The leading cases surveyed in this chapter demonstrate that the SPC might not easily yield to a rigid interpretation of a 'legal basis' favoured by some lawmakers and scholars, but might in all probability continue with a path which entails opaque edges, shifting ground, and discretionary turns. The key to the usefulness of such a path is that it must be clear for followers to see and that uncertainty is minimized. It is in this aspect that the SPC, and Chinese courts in general, would benefit from learning from practical solutions developed in the common law cases, through detailed and specifically targeted (as opposed to framework-level and general) comparative studies.

23

Implied Terms and Restitution

EDWIN PEEL

I. Introduction

As one of the editors of this collection, I have already had the welcome opportunity to pay tribute to Ewan McKendrick in the Preface. To what is said there, I will add one further expression of thanks. I returned to Oxford in 1992 to read for the BCL, unsure as to whether I wanted to pursue a career as an academic or a practitioner, both of which were in a fledgling state (I did at least know that I wanted to be a lawyer). Ultimately, I did both, but I began as an academic and that is where my greater interest lies. I may not have realized it at the time, but that path was sealed by the influence of three teachers, whom I now have the good fortune to regard as colleagues (or former colleagues): Adrian Briggs, Andrew Burrows, and Ewan McKendrick. I hope they will take it as the compliment which is intended when I say that it is to their brand[1] of 'practical legal scholarship' that I have always aspired. In Ewan's case, this has been most evident to me in his writing. I cannot recall ever needing to read anything he has written more than once in order to have a very clear sense of what was being said, and why it mattered, without recourse to theatrical overstatement. My regret is that we have not often shared a platform, whether when teaching or in conference, but when we have, the same calm, reflective, and assured manner seen in his writing has always been to the fore. If I have learned well, my hope is that this short chapter might demonstrate some of the qualities which I so admire in Ewan McKendrick. It takes as its starting point an observation in one of his earliest published papers: 'where a contract has been concluded, there is no case for permitting a person to proceed with a restitutionary claim.'[2]

This chapter is included in the section of this collection entitled 'Unjust Enrichment'. One potential difficulty with writing any paper on unjust enrichment, or restitution, is that it can easily be sidetracked into a broader debate about 'restitution theory'. That is something which is consciously resisted at the outset, by explaining the relatively narrow scope of this chapter. It addresses the circumstances in which a claim for restitution may be made for a benefit conferred, whether the payment of money or the provision of services, under a valid and subsisting contract. It is not concerned with the effect which an underlying contract may have on such a claim if the contract is not valid and subsisting, for example because it has been terminated for breach or discharged by frustration, or because it is an anticipated contract which never materialized or it is a contract which is void and of no legal effect. It is also concerned only with the circumstances where the ground for a claim in restitution

---

[1] There are various 'brands': see Andrew Burrows, 'Professor Sir Guenter Treitel (1928–2019)' in James Goudkamp and Donal Nolan (eds), *Scholars of Contract Law* (Hart Publishing 2022).

[2] Ewan McKendrick, 'The Battle of the Forms and the Law of Restitution' (1988) 8 OJLS 197, 202. See also Jack Beatson, 'Restitution and Contract: Non-Cumul?' (2000) 1 Theoretical Inquiries in Law 83.

Edwin Peel, *Implied Terms and Restitution* In: *Shaping the Law of Obligations.* Edited by: Edwin Peel and Rebecca Probert, Oxford University Press. © Edwin Peel 2023. DOI: 10.1093/oso/9780198889762.003.0023

is 'failure of basis',[3] and not where a contract, or supposed contract, is part of the context in which a claim in restitution may arise on other grounds, such as 'mistake'.[4]

So far as 'failure of basis' is concerned, this paper adopts the view of Carr LJ in *Dargamo Holdings Ltd v Avonwick Holdings Ltd*,[5] derived from *Goff & Jones on Unjust Enrichment*,[6] that the 'core concept' is that 'a benefit has been conferred on a joint understanding that the recipient's right to retain it is conditional. If the condition is not fulfilled, the recipient must return the benefit.'[7] In the cases which are the subject of this chapter, the 'joint understanding' of the parties is to be found in the contract under which the relevant benefit has been bestowed by one upon the other. The central thesis is that Lord Leggatt was right when he said, in the recent decision in *Barton v Morris*, in the context of a claim in restitution for failure of basis, and in words which echo the observation of Ewan McKendrick above: 'there is no room for an unjust enrichment claim where there is a subsisting contract between the parties.'[8]

It is submitted that both are right because the work that would need to be done by any claim in restitution has already been done by the terms of the contract, including any implied terms. The principal focus is on implied terms,[9] since it is obvious that any express term which entitled, or disentitled, a party to the repayment of sums already paid, or payment for services rendered, would prevail.[10] Put at its simplest, if one party has made a payment under a valid and subsisting contract which they claim is not due, and there is no express term indicating that it was not due, or entitling them to repayment, they need to establish an implied term to that effect. Similarly, if one party provides their services under the contract, and no payment is due under the express terms, they need to establish an implied term that payment was due. If they succeed in establishing the necessary implied term, they recover under the implied term, that is, under the contract. If they do not, there is no alternative claim in restitution.[11] There will have been no failure of basis. A contract which is enforced in accordance with its terms, after also taking account of any implied terms, has not 'failed'; quite the contrary, the basis (the 'joint understanding') upon which the parties proceeded will have been fulfilled. If correct, this calls into question the decisions in two of the leading cases, in part[12] or in full.[13]

---

[3] 'Failure of basis' is used throughout this chapter, but some of the citations from the decided cases use the term 'failure of consideration'. For the reasons to prefer 'failure of basis', see *Barnes v Eastenders Cash & Carry Plc* [2014] UKSC 26, [2015] AC 1 [104]–[106] (Lord Toulson) (hereafter *Barnes v Eastenders*); cf Peter Birks, 'Failure of Consideration and Its Place on the Map' (2002) 2 OUCLJ 1, 3 ('It would permanently avert a recurrent misunderstanding if "failure of basis" could once and for all displace "failure of consideration"') (hereafter Birks, 'Failure of Consideration').

[4] See eg *Kelly v Solari* (1841) 9 M & W 54.

[5] [2021] EWCA Civ 1149; [2021] 2 CLC 583 (hereafter *Dargamo*)

[6] See now Charles Mitchell, Paul Mitchell, and Stephen Watterson (eds), *Goff & Jones on Unjust Enrichment* (10th edn, Sweet & Maxwell 2022) para 12-01 (hereafter Goff & Jones); an earlier edition is cited by Carr LJ in *Dargamo*.

[7] *Dargamo* (n 5) [79].

[8] [2023] UKSC 3; [2023] AC 684 [188] (hereafter *Barton v Morris*).

[9] The submission, more broadly, that 'the contractual allocation of risk must be respected' is hardly a novel one: Goff & Jones (n 6) para 3-21.

[10] See eg *Dargamo* (n 5).

[11] Insofar as this is just a question of 'construction', this too is not an entirely new idea. See Andrew Tettenborn, 'Subsisting Contracts and Failure of Consideration—A Little Scepticism' 10 RLR 1, 3 (no claim in restitution where 'on their proper interpretation, the terms of a contract between the parties are inconsistent with the existence of a claim to restitution for failure of consideration'); cf Robert Stevens, 'Is There a Law of Unjust Enrichment' in Simone Degeling and James Edelman (eds), *Unjust Enrichment in Commercial Law* (Thomson Reuters 2008).

[12] See the discussion of *Barnes v Eastenders* (n 3) in section IV.

[13] See the discussion of *Roxborough v Rothmans of Pall Mall Australia Ltd* [2001] HCA 68; 208 CLR 516 (hereafter *Roxborough v Rothmans*) in section IV.

II. Four Cases

This chapter is constructed primarily around four cases: *Roxborough v Rothmans of Pall Mall Australia Ltd*;[14] *Barnes v Eastenders Cash & Carry Plc*;[15] *Bank of New York Mellon (International) Ltd v Cine-UK Ltd, London Trocadero (2015) LLP v Picturehouse Cinemas Ltd*;[16] and *Barton v Morris*.[17] The potential overlapping of claims based on an implied term and in restitution is perhaps most apparent from the decisions in *BNY v Cine-UK* and *Barton v Morris*, but to begin with a chronological approach is adopted.

A. *Roxborough v Rothmans*

In *Roxborough v Rothmans*, retailers of cigarettes purchased them from licensed wholesalers for a price which included a licence fee payable by the wholesalers to the state authorities. The licence fee was subsequently held to be an invalid tax. The retailers sought recovery of the licence fee element of the price which had been paid to the wholesalers, but not remitted to the state, following the tax ruling. A majority of the High Court of Australia held in favour of the retailers; Kirby J dissented. Gleeson CJ and Gaudron and Hayne JJ held that, while a claim based on an implied term for repayment failed, a claim in restitution was available:

> Although an attempt was made by the appellants to invoke an implied agreement under which they could claim repayment of any unpaid tax, it was artificial and unconvincing. The parties made no agreement, express or implied, about what was to happen if the tax was held to be invalid. If there is here a right to enforce repayment upon the basis of a failure of consideration, it is because, in the circumstances, the law imposes upon the respondent [the wholesalers] an obligation to make just restitution for a benefit derived at the expense of the appellants [the retailers].[18]

Similarly, Gummow J held that an implied term for repayment was not 'necessary',[19] but a claim in restitution was justified on the basis that it was 'unconscionable for Rothmans to enjoy the payments in respect of the licence fee, in circumstances in which it was not specifically intended or specially provided that Rothmans should so enjoy them'.[20]

A potential obstacle to the claim in restitution was the requirement of a 'total' failure of consideration, but this was overcome by the fact that the licence fee was dealt with in the invoices paid by the retailers on a quite separate basis and easily identified as a 'severable part of the consideration'.[21] A further obstacle was the fact that the burden of the licence fee

---

[14] ibid.
[15] *Barnes v Eastenders* (n 3).
[16] [2022] EWCA Civ 1021, [2023] L&TR 2 (heard as a conjoined appeal) (hereafter *BNY v Cine-UK*).
[17] *Barton v Morris* (n 8).
[18] *Roxborough v Rothmans* (n 13) [20].
[19] ibid [60].
[20] ibid [104].
[21] ibid [20]; cf [109] (Gummow J: 'can be broken up').

386 IMPLIED TERMS AND RESTITUTION

actually fell on the customers to whom the retailers had sold the cigarettes, but according to Gleeson CJ and Gaudron and Hayne JJ the 'critical question' was which of the wholesalers or the retailers had the 'superior claim'. The answer was the retailers because they had paid 'for a consideration which has failed, and the respondent [the wholesalers] has no title to retain the moneys'.[22]

In his dissenting judgment, Kirby J rejected both the implied term case *and* the claim in restitution. A notable feature of his approach to the former is that he took into account the fact that the licence fee payment had been passed on to the retailers' customers, whereas the majority addressed this issue only as an aspect of the claim in restitution. According to Kirby J, this feature meant that it was not the case that, had they been asked by the 'officious bystander',[23] both the retailers and the wholesalers would have said 'of course' the licence fee element of the price should be repaid. At its highest, the answer from a reasonable person in the position of the wholesalers was more likely to be it would 'all depend', including whether the retailers intended to reimburse their customers or simply to obtain a windfall.[24] He concluded this part of his judgment in the following terms:

> By the application of current doctrine governing the implication of contractual terms and, indeed, of any reformulation of that doctrine of which I am aware, no legal basis is established in law to imply the two terms[25] propounded by the retailers. Those terms are neither reasonable nor equitable. Still less are they essential to give business efficacy to the retailer's contracts with the wholesaler.[26]

The alternative claim in restitution also foundered on the terms of the contract. In the absence of any implied term, the express terms required the retailers to pay the price of the cigarettes in full; that was their '*legal* obligation' and it was only upon fulfilment of that obligation that property in the cigarettes passed to the retailers.[27] A claim in restitution on the ground of failure of basis could only succeed if the wholesalers were bound by an unperformed promise to pay the licence fee element as licence fees[28] and that was one of the implied terms which had already been rejected.[29]

B. *Barnes v Eastenders*

In *Barnes v Eastenders* the Crown Prosecution Service (CPS) sought and obtained management receivership orders over two defendants and associated companies. The

---

[22] ibid [27].

[23] See *Shirlaw v Southern Foundries (1926) Ltd* [1939] 2 KB 206, 207 (CA) (MacKinnon LJ).

[24] *Roxborough v Rothmans* (n 13) [163]. Callinan J allowed the claim in restitution, but unlike the rest of the majority thought that it 'might be appropriate to imply a term' for repayment (ibid [204]). However, he too acknowledged that the prospect of a windfall for the retailers was problematic in this regard (ibid: 'I need not express any concluded opinion on this question').

[25] Either a term providing for repayment, or a term that the wholesaler would pay the licence fee element as a licence fee: ibid [156].

[26] *Roxborough v Rothmans* (n 13) [164].

[27] ibid [165] (emphasis in the original).

[28] ibid [168].

[29] See n 25.

orders provided that the expenses and remuneration of the receiver would be paid out of the receivership property and in accordance with a letter of agreement sent by the CPS to the receiver. The letter of agreement stated that the receiver would have a lien over the defendants' assets and that the CPS did not undertake to indemnify him if those assets were insufficient to cover the expenses and remuneration. The orders were subsequently quashed, by which time the receiver had incurred expenses and an entitlement to remuneration. The House of Lords held that the receiver had no recourse to the assets of the associated companies,[30] but since, as a result, he would not be able to recover his expenses and remuneration, he was entitled to recover them from the CPS in restitution.

In Lord Toulson's speech, there is some limited discussion about the possible 'construction' of the letter of agreement, in the following terms:

> There is an argument that the statement 'you will have a lien over the defendants' assets for payment of your fees' should be interpreted as a promise that the receiver would have a legally enforceable lien over the receivership property, whatever its value might be, but to resort to that solution would involve a strained and artificial construction of the letter. The alternative is that the CPS made no such promise to the receiver, but that this was their mutual expectation and was the premise on which the receiver agreed to act. If the latter is the preferable analysis, does the receiver have a remedy against the CPS under the law of restitution or unjust enrichment?[31]

The existence of a 'mutual expectation' which is not reflected in the express terms of the contract might be viewed as fertile territory for an implied term,[32] but it led Lord Toulson to formulate the question above about the law of restitution, to which the answer was yes. The basis which had failed was the anticipated lien over the companies' assets. This was viewed as the failure of 'a non-promissory condition as to the future', on a par with the subsequent invalidity of the licence fee in *Roxborough v Rothmans*.[33] It was also described as 'fundamental to the basis' on which the receiver had agreed to act, so as to distinguish it from a mere 'failure of an expectation' which may motivate a party to enter into a contract, which would not be sufficient. As Lord Toulson concluded:

> in the present case the expectation that the receiver would have a legal right to recover his remuneration and expenses was not just a motivating factor. Nobody envisaged that the receiver should provide his services in managing the companies as a volunteer; those services were to be in return for his right to recover his remuneration and expenses from the assets of the companies, such as they might be.[34]

---

[30] This was on the basis that the companies had not been defendants nor had there been any reasonable cause, at the time when the orders had been made, for regarding their assets as those of the defendants.

[31] *Barnes v Eastenders* (n 3) [99].

[32] *Equitable Life Assurance Society v Hyman* [2002] 1 AC 408 (HL) 459 (Lord Steyn: 'The implication is essential to give effect to the reasonable expectations of the parties') (hereafter *Equitable Life v Hyman*).

[33] *Barnes v Eastenders* (n 3) [109]–[114].

[34] ibid [115].

The only other feature of this decision to note for later reference is the disposal. This was dealt with by reinstating the order of Underhill J.[35] The relevant elements of that order were that the CPS was to pay the receiver's remuneration and disbursements, subject to an assessment by the taxing authority of the Crown Court under the Criminal Procedure Rules and was also to pay the legal costs incurred by the receiver in the exercise of his functions as receiver.

C. BNY v Cine-UK

In *BNY v Cine-UK* the tenant of cinema premises resisted the payment of rent for periods when operation of the cinemas was unlawful as a consequence of the regulations imposed to deal with the Covid-19 pandemic. This rested on one of two grounds: either an implied term that there was no obligation to pay rent during the periods in question, or that any rent payable would be recoverable for a failure of basis, the basis for payment being the use of the premises as a cinema. It may be noted that Flaux C said of the two grounds that 'the substance of the argument is the same'.[36] It may also be noted that a curious feature of the failure of basis claim in one of the cases before the Court of Appeal[37] is that it did not lead to a claim in restitution as such. The rent in question had not been paid. The pragmatic answer of the trial judge was to suggest that it could be pleaded by way of counterclaim and set-off to the landlord's claim for the rent,[38] but he, like the Court of Appeal, held that the failure of basis claim failed in any event.

The implied term ground was approached as a term implied in fact. It failed to meet the requirement either of 'obviousness' or of 'business efficacy',[39] primarily on the basis that it was an argument for an extension to the express cesser of rent provision in the leases. The inclusion of that express term clearly indicated that the parties had turned their minds to the circumstances in which rent was not payable if the premises could not be used by the tenant; and such circumstances did not extend to those which had arisen to deal with the pandemic. This was a 'deliberate allocation of risk' with which there was no basis to interfere.[40]

The alternative claim in restitution was rejected on the basis of what Carr LJ has referred to, in the *Dargamo* case, as the 'Obligation Rule'. In its simplest form this is the rule that 'an unjust factor will not override a valid and subsisting legal obligation of the claimant to confer the benefit on the defendant'[41] or, put in even simpler form, 'the claim in unjust

---

[35] Though for different reasons. Underhill J held that the receiver's right to recover from the CPS could be derived from the Proceeds of Crime Act 2002: 4 April 2012, Case No: U20110135/1/2011. The House of Lords disagreed, but allowed the claim under the law of restitution.

[36] *BNY v Cine-UK* (n 16) [4] cf. *Barton v Morris* in the Court of Appeal: [2019] EWCA Civ 1999, [2020] 2 All ER (Comm) 652 [76] ('two sides of the same coin').

[37] *London Trocadero (2015) LLP v Picturehouse Cinemas Ltd.*

[38] *BNY v Cine-UK* (n 16) [39].

[39] The law in this regard was derived from *Marks and Spencer Plc v BNP Paribas Securities Services Trust Co (Jersey) Ltd* [2015] UKSC 72, [2016] AC 742 (hereafter *Marks & Spencer*) and *Yoo Design Services Limited v Iliv Realty Pte Limited* [2021] EWCA Civ 560.

[40] *BNY v Cine-UK* (n 16) [141]. Though not cited by Flaux C, there is an obvious echo here of a similar observation made by Lord Neuberger in *Marks & Spencer* (n 39) [40].

[41] *Dargamo* (n 5) [70].

enrichment is not allowed to contradict the terms in the contract'.[42] The failure of basis claim in *BNY v Cine-UK* plainly fell foul of this rule. If the express cesser of rent provision did not apply and there was no basis for extending it by implication, the rent was payable; there was nothing unjust in its retention by the landlord. As Flaux C observed: 'The leases contain a carefully worked out contractual regime for the allocation of risk and the proposed "failure of basis" would subvert that regime and contradict the terms of the contracts in a way which . . . the law does not permit.'[43] The decision in *Roxborough v Rothmans* was distinguished on the basis that that was 'a case where the claim in unjust enrichment was consistent with the terms of the contract'.[44] The decisions in both *Roxborough* and *Barnes v Eastenders* are distinguished on the basis that 'there was some wider arrangement which gave rise to an extraneous or extra-contractual understanding the operation of which did not subvert the contract'.[45]

D. *Barton v Morris*

In *Barton v Morris* the claimant lost £1.2m in two failed attempts to buy a property from the defendant.[46] The parties then entered into an oral agreement under which the claimant was entitled to a commission of £1.2m if he introduced a buyer for the property who would purchase it for £6.5m. The property was sold to a buyer introduced by the claimant, but only for £6m. The contract was silent as to what, if anything, was to happen in those circumstances.

A majority of the Supreme Court held that nothing was to happen. There was no implied term that a reasonable commission should be paid for the introduction, which the trial judge assessed at £435k. They held that the contract between the parties was one in which the claimant was entitled to the inflated fee 'if and only if' the target price of £6.5m was achieved, and the claimant had taken the risk that, if it was not achieved, he would not be paid at all. The finding that the claimant had taken this risk also ruled out any claim in restitution for the reasonable value of his services, which was also assessed at £435k. There was no 'failure of basis' where the contract had operated as the parties intended.

The minority (Lord Leggatt and Lord Burrows) held in favour of the claimant on the basis of an implied term for payment of a reasonable commission. All members of the Court agreed that there was no room for a term implied in fact,[47] save to the extent that the defendant would not, in bad faith, deliberately engineer a sale at less than £6.5m so as to avoid the commission.[48] The minority found in the claimant's favour on the basis of a term implied

---

[42] ibid [75]. The claim in *Dargamo* plainly contradicted an express term of the contract. The term in question stated that the price had been paid for x, but the claimant argued that there was a non-contractual understanding that the price had in fact been paid for x and y.

[43] *BNY v Cine-UK* (n 16) [147].

[44] ibid [148].

[45] ibid [150].

[46] Things were a little more complicated than the reference to just the two parties may imply (including a corporate vehicle which was in insolvency), but such complication is not material to the issues which the Supreme Court had to address and which are the concern of this chapter.

[47] The majority held that such a term would contradict the express terms: (n 8) [25]. Lord Burrows ruled it out without offering any reasons: ibid [205]. It is more accurate to say of Lord Leggatt simply that he focused only on a term implied in law.

[48] This was not such a case. The expected sale price of £6.5m was not achieved because the value of the property was affected by the plans for HS2.

390 IMPLIED TERMS AND RESTITUTION

term in law, that is, a term which is a 'standardized', or 'default', feature of certain types of contract. The relevant type of contract here was a 'services' contract, or an 'agency' contract, and the standardized term was the payment of a reasonable fee for the service, or the introduction. This might have been based on section 15(1) of the Supply of Goods and Services Act 1982, which states that 'where, under a relevant contract for the supply of a service, the consideration for the service is not determined by the contract . . . there is an implied term that the party contracting with the supplier will pay a reasonable charge'. The majority ruled out the application of this section on the basis that there was no contract for the supply of a service (the agreement was a unilateral contract under which the claimant had no obligation to find a buyer) and 'the consideration for the service' *had* been determined by the contract. The minority acknowledged the first difficulty, but held that, if section 15(1) itself did not apply, it nonetheless reflected the common law position, as illustrated by a number of cases involving estate agents.[49] The majority distinguished those cases on the basis that the clamant was not acting as an estate agent, or any sort of agent as such. His contract with the defendant was very much a 'one-off' in which he took the risk of only getting paid if there was a sale at £6.5m.[50]

The principal difference between the majority and the minority was their approach to what Lord Leggatt referred to as the 'burden of expression'.[51] With a term implied in fact, the burden is on the party arguing for the implied term. With a term implied in law, because it is a standardized or default rule, the burden is on the party seeking to exclude the term in question. As it was put by Lord Burrows, did the parties agree 'if and only if' in the 'weak sense' that the claimant would only be paid £1.2m if the sale was at £6.5m, or did they agree 'if and only if' in the 'strong sense' that the claimant would only be paid at all (but at an inflated level) if the sale was at £6.5m. The majority held the latter. The minority held the former.

When it came to the alternative claim in restitution, the majority adopted the same approach as the Court of Appeal in *BNY v Cine-UK*; that is, the failure of any implied term ruled out any failure of basis: with no implied term in *BNY v Cine-UK*, the payment of rent was due, the landlord was not unjustly enriched by its receipt, and it could not be recovered; with no implied term in *Barton v Morris*, no payment was due for the claimant's introduction of the purchaser, the defendant was not therefore unjustly enriched,[52] and the claimant was not entitled to a sum representing the value of the work he had done. As Lady Rose put it:

> The 'silence' of the contract as to what obligations arise on the happening of the particular event means that no obligations arise as Lord Hoffmann made clear in [*Attorney General of*

---

[49] See, in particular, *Firth v Hylane Ltd* [1959] EWCA Civ J0211-3 (vLex); [1959] EGD 212 which bore some resemblance to the facts of *Barton v Morris* and was heavily relied upon by the claimant.

[50] The closer analogy was said to be with *Cutter v Powell* (1795) 6 Term Rep 320; 101 ER 573 (KB) (shipowner agreed to pay mariner a lump sum of 30 guineas 'provided he proceeds, continues and does his duty as second mate in the said ship from hence to the port of Liverpool'. No payment due when the mariner died shortly before the voyage was completed).

[51] *Barton v Morris* (n 8) [135].

[52] Lady Rose acknowledged ([97]) that the defendant benefited from the introduction, but he could hardly have rejected it (cf a buyer of non-conforming goods who must pay their value to the seller if he decides nonetheless to accept) and such non-denial would not have assisted the claimant since he would then have been entitled to no commission as there would have been no sale at all.

Belize v Belize Telecom Ltd[53]]. This excludes not only an implied contractual term but [also] (sic) a claim in unjust enrichment.[54]

In the minority, Lord Leggatt agreed with this analysis. Had he rejected the implied term, he would also have rejected the claim in restitution. It is in this context that he agreed with the submission that 'there is no room for an unjust enrichment claim where there is a subsisting contract between the parties'.[55] He elaborated as follows:

> In relation to the subject matter of the contract, the law of contract determines, and governs the consequences of, not only the existence but also the absence of an obligation on one contracting party to confer a benefit on the other. To redistribute the allocation of benefits and losses provided for by the law of contract by applying another set of legal principles would undercut this regime.[56]

By contrast, Lord Burrows *appears*[57] to take a different view. If there had been no implied term for reasonable remuneration, the claimant would have been entitled to the same sum in restitution. The failure of basis was simply the fact that the sale proceeded at a price below £6.5m and the prima facie right to restitution to which this gave rise was not excluded by the terms of the contract because it was not an 'if but only if' contract in the strong sense, as explained above. As he put it: 'in the absence of any implied term the contract simply did not provide for what was to happen where the contract price was less than £6.5m: the contract (even if regarded as subsisting) has 'run out' and there is no good reason to stop unjust enrichment stepping in.'[58]

E. Summary

The outcome of the four cases considered in this part may be summarized as follows. In two of them (*BNY v Cine-UK* and *Barton v Morris*, excluding for the moment the speech of Lord Burrows) the claims made failed both in contract (on the basis of an implied term) and in restitution. However, in the other two (*Roxborough v Rothmans* and *Barnes v Eastenders*) the claims made in contract failed (or at least were regarded as 'artificial and unconvincing',[59] or 'strained and artificial'[60]) but the claim in restitution succeeded. The main question to which this gives rise is whether the outcomes in the latter two cases are an infringement of

---

[53] [2009] UKPC 10, [2009] 1 WLR 1988 [17].
[54] *Barton v Morris* (n 8) [96].
[55] ibid [189].
[56] ibid [191], drawing on the similar observations of Lord Goff in *Pan Ocean Shipping Co Ltd v Creditcorp Ltd (The Trident Beauty)* [1994] 1 WLR 161 (HL) 164 ('the law of restitution has no part to play in the matter; the existence of the agreed regime renders the imposition by the law of a remedy in restitution both unnecessary and inappropriate').
[57] The hesitant way this is expressed stems from the fact that Lord Burrows may have been saying that the claim for reasonable remuneration could be explained either on the basis of an implied term, or by way of restitution, but it seems that he would have allowed the latter even if there was no implied term: see further at n 72.
[58] *Barton v Morris* (n 8) [239].
[59] See text at n 18.
[60] See text at n 31.

392 IMPLIED TERMS AND RESTITUTION

the 'Obligation Rule', or an undercutting of the law of contract and, therefore, incorrectly decided.

III. Gaps, Implied Terms, and Fundamental Bases

In cases where a claim in restitution has been made notwithstanding a valid and subsisting contract between the parties, it has sometimes been described as remedying a 'gap' in the contract. Thus, in *Roxborough v Rothmans* Gummow J described the claim in restitution by the retailers as 'illustrative of the gap-filling . . . role of restitutionary remedies'.[61] In *BNY v Cine-UK* Flaux C concluded that there was no 'gap' in the lease which required to be filled by the law of unjust enrichment.[62] But where there is a 'gap' in a valid and subsisting contract, the first option for filling it is to ask if a term should be implied. As Lord Steyn has pointed out, terms implied in law operate as 'general default rules'[63] while terms implied in fact operate as 'ad hoc gap fillers'.[64] This description is referred to by Lord Leggatt in *Barton v Morris* in which, throughout his speech, he refers to the default rule that a reasonable sum should be paid for services rendered under a contract which is silent as to remuneration as filling the 'gap'.[65] This no doubt explains why he concluded that either the gap was filled by the implied term for reasonable payment (as he held) or, if it was not, there was no gap which required to be filled and therefore no basis for a claim in restitution.

Why then was there a 'gap' in the contracts in *Roxborough v Rothmans*, *Barnes v Eastenders* and *Barton v Morris* (at least according to Lord Burrows) which, if it could not be filled by an implied term, could be filled by a claim in restitution? One possible answer is to say that the two claims, implied term and restitution, address different sorts of 'gaps'. For example, in *Barton v Morris* Lord Burrows thought it was more a case that, if the contract did not provide for what was to happen if the sale price was less than £6.5m, the contract had 'run out', rather than that it was silent or there was any gap to be filled.[66] In *Barnes v Eastenders* Lord Toulson referred to the quashing of the receivership order and the loss of the receiver's lien as the failure of 'a non-promissory condition as to the future', which was 'fundamental to the basis' on which the receiver had agreed to act. And in *Roxborough v Rothmans* Gleeson CJ and Gaudron and Hayne JJ referred to the licence fee element as having been 'externally imposed' and 'not agreed by negotiation',[67] so that to permit its recovery 'would not result in confusion between enforcing a contract and claiming a right by reason of events which have occurred in relation to a contract'.[68] The common theme in all of these observations appears to be that the events which led to the claim in restitution were not the subject of any contractual allocation of risk at all.

---

[61] *Roxborough v Rothmans* (n 13) [75].

[62] *BNY v Cine-UK* (n 16) [147]; cf. *Dargamo* (n 5) [75]–[76].

[63] *Equitable Life v Hyman* (n 32) 458, citing *Scally v Southern Health and Social Services Board* [1992] 1 AC 294 (HL).

[64] ibid 459.

[65] *Barton v Morris* (n 8) [143], [160], [211]–[212].

[66] This comment of Lord Burrows is made by way of disagreement with the view expressed that if the contract was silent that meant the loss should lie where it fell: see William Day and Graham Virgo, 'Risks on the Contract/ Unjust Enrichment Borderline' (2020) 136 LQR 349 (commenting on the decision of the Court of Appeal).

[67] Cf. Birks, 'Failure of Consideration' (n 3) 5 ('neither the payment of the tax nor the amount of that payment were viewed as negotiable').

[68] *Roxborough v Rothmans* (n 13) [21] (emphasis added).

There is no doubt that a claim in restitution may arise by reason of events which have occurred merely 'in relation to a contract', that is, where the contract between the parties is, in effect, incidental. In *Barton v Morris*, Lord Leggatt gives as an example 'where a party performs or claims to have performed services additional to or different from those covered by the contract'.[69] There may be, in such a case, a claim in restitution, and it may be a claim for 'failure of basis', but it would not contradict the terms of the contract because the 'basis' is not regulated by the contract. Of course, even in such a case, there would, as Lord Leggatt observes, be a question first about the 'scope of the applicable contractual regime',[70] in order to establish if the services are 'additional' or 'different', but if they are then the contract would, in the words of Lord Burrows, have 'run out'. Lord Leggatt concluded that *Barton v Morris* was not such a case, and it is submitted that he was correct to do so, but what of cases such as *Roxborough v Rothmans* and *Barnes v Eastenders*, and Lord Burrows' apparently contrary view in *Barton v Morris*?

If we start with *Roxborough v Rothmans*, it cannot be enough simply to say that the licence fee element of the price was 'externally imposed' and 'not agreed by negotiation'. Its imposition and the assumption that it was, and would remain, payable was part of the context in which the parties negotiated the price so as to include the licence fee. What falsified the assumption that it was payable was its subsequent invalidation, but most implied terms arise to deal with events, or a state of affairs, which the parties did not expressly contemplate at the time of the contract. In *BNY v Cine-UK* the parties plainly did not expressly contemplate the outbreak of an external event like the Covid-19 pandemic and the measures taken to deal with it; and in *Barton v Morris* the parties did not expressly contemplate that the plans for the HS2 rail line would reduce the market value of the property below £6.5m. When they occurred, it was simply an exercise in assessing how the risk of such events was allocated by the contract. Similarly, to say in *Barnes v Eastenders* that the quashing of the receivership order was the failure of 'a non-promissory condition as to the future' is, at one level, only to conclude that there was no express promise about what should happen if it was not sustained.

Lord Burrows' view in *Barton v Morris* is perhaps most difficult.[71] As noted above, for him the failure of basis was simply the fact that the sale proceeded at a price below £6.5m and the right to restitution to which this gave rise was not excluded by the terms of the contract because it was not an 'if but only if' contract in the strong sense. But there seems, with respect, to be an element of circularity about this. The fact that the contract was not an 'if and only if' contract in the strong sense leads to the conclusion that there was an implied term for reasonable payment, in which case there would be no inconsistency in allowing the claim in restitution, but the latter is simply not necessary. This is a further reason why it may be that Lord Burrows was pointing out only that the claim for reasonable remuneration could be explained either on the basis of an implied term, or by way of restitution, but he prefaces his conclusions on the claim in restitution on more than one occasion with the assumption that there was no implied term.[72]

---

[69] *Barton v Morris* (n 8) [193].
[70] ibid.
[71] Not least because I find myself in disagreement with my mentor and colleague: see text at n 1.
[72] *Barton v Morris* (n 8) [227], [236].

IV. Consequences

It does not necessarily follow from the submissions made in this chapter that any of the decisions reached in the four cases under most direct consideration are incorrect. The principal submission made is that the alternative claim in restitution must not contradict the terms of the valid and subsisting contract. It seems clear that the decisions in *BNY v Cine-UK* and *Barton v Morris* are consistent with this submission, but the decisions in *Roxborough v Rothmans* and *Barnes v Eastenders* are not necessarily inconsistent. The basis for this observation lies in the less than entirely dismissive way in which the implied term claim was rejected. While Gleeson CJ and Gaudron and Hayne JJ did state that the parties made no agreement, express or implied, about what was to happen if the tax was held to be invalid, this is prefaced by the observation that any implied agreement was 'artificial and unconvincing'.[73] Similarly, in *Barnes v Eastenders* an implied term solution was said by Lord Toulson to involve 'a strained and artificial construction of the letter'.[74] That does not necessarily rule it out. It has already been noted that the 'mutual expectation' of the parties in *Barnes v Eastenders* that the receiver would have a lien over the associated companies' assets could provide the foundation for an implied term, particularly as it was a mutual expectation about something which was described as 'fundamental' to the basis of the contract.

A parallel may be drawn in this regard with debate about the juristic basis of discharge for frustration. One explanation is that if the parties 'must have made their bargain on the footing that a particular thing or state of things would continue to exist . . . a term to that effect will be implied'.[75] This has fallen out of favour on the basis that it is 'not realistic',[76] but it is not an implausible alternative explanation once it is realized that any question of the intention of the parties is determined objectively.[77] Similarly, that *Roxborough v Rothmans* might be explained on the basis of an implied term that the licence fee element of the price was to be repaid if no such fee was payable,[78] or that *Barnes v Eastenders* might be explained on the basis of an implied term that payment was to be made by the CPS if there was no recourse to the defendants' assets, is not ruled out, even it has an element of artificiality about it.[79] There is, in a very obvious sense, an element of artifice about any implied term based on an objective assessment of the parties' intentions.

It is important to stress that any such ex post facto rationalization of the decisions in *Roxborough v Rothmans* or *Barnes v Eastenders* can only be justified if, in fact, the alternative implied term analysis can be sustained, even if perceived as artificial; that is, the claim in restitution which succeeded must not have resulted in a dilution of the requirements for an implied term. For example, the 'stringent test'[80] for a term implied in fact must have been

---

[73] See text to n 18.

[74] See text to n 31.

[75] *Tamplin SS Co Ltd v Anglo-Mexican Petroleum Co* [1916] 2 AC 397 (HL) 404 (Lord Loreburn).

[76] *The Great Peace* [2002] EWCA Civ 1407, [2003] QB 679 (CA) [73] (Lord Phillips MR).

[77] Edwin Peel (ed), *Treitel on The Law of Contract* (15th edn, Sweet & Maxwell 2020) para 19-124 (hereafter Peel, *Treitel*). What the alternative juristic basis may be, and whether it has any practical significance, is far from clear: ibid paras 19-123-19-130.

[78] To the extent that a term implied in fact is an exercise in giving effect to the intention of the parties, note the dictum of Gummow J set out above (text to n 20) about what was, or was not, 'specifically intended' by the parties.

[79] To be clear, this is not an attempt to resurrect the theory of implied or 'quasi' contract. It is a submission solely about the content of the contract which the parties did enter into in the context of establishing a 'failure of basis'.

[80] *Equitable Life v Hyman* (n 32) 459 (Lord Steyn); *Marks & Spencer* (n 39) [23] (Lord Neuberger); cf *Philips Electronique Grand Public SA v BSkyB Ltd* [1995] EMLR 472 (CA) 480 (Lord Bingham MR: an 'ambitious undertaking'). Given the central thesis of this chapter, it is perhaps worth noting that, in *Marks & Spencer*, an implied

met, but that may have been on the mind of Lord Toulson in *Barnes v Eastenders* when he stressed that the mutual expectation of a lien over the defendant's assets must have been 'fundamental' to the basis of the contract 'because it should not be thought that mere failure of an expectation which motivated a party to enter into a contract may give rise to a restitutionary claim'.[81] Such an expectation would be equally insufficient to meet the stringent test for implication of a term.

But while some form of ex post facto rationalization of the two decisions may be possible, it is nonetheless submitted that there is reason to doubt the outcome in *Barnes v Eastenders* in part, and in *Roxborough v Rothmans* in full. The hesitation about *Barnes v Eastenders* stems from the disposal. As noted above, the CPS was ordered to pay the receiver's remuneration and disbursements, subject to an assessment by the taxing authority of the Crown Court under the Criminal Procedure Rules, and was also to pay the legal costs incurred by the receiver in the exercise of his functions as receiver.[82] If the claim which succeeded was the claim in restitution, the CPS should have been ordered to pay a reasonable sum based on the objective market value of the services rendered and not the contract 'price', though the latter may be taken into account as evidence of the objective market value.[83] As acknowledged in *Barton v Morris*, the quantum meruit in contract and the quantum meruit in unjust enrichment may be the same where, for example, the contract is silent as to the remuneration payable.[84] But the contract in *Barnes v Eastenders* appears not to have been silent as to the remuneration payable,[85] and the order of Underhill J which the Supreme Court reinstated seems more consistent with the enforcement of the payment agreed[86] than with the assessment of a restitutionary quantum meruit.[87] More fundamentally, the contract between the CPS and the receiver imposed a 'cap' on recovery by the receivers, in the form of the assets covered by the receivership order. It may be that this cap was never likely to be exceeded,[88] leaving aside the difficulty of putting a figure on it once the receivership order had been quashed, but it surely had to apply or the claim in restitution would have contradicted one of the express terms of the contract.

The greater hesitation about the decision in *Roxborough v Rothmans* is based simply on the fact that the reasoning of Kirby J is more persuasive than the reasoning of the majority.

---

term that the landlord should refund two months' worth of rent when the tenant had paid for three months in advance, but would only get one month of occupation because of a lawful break of the lease, was rejected and no alternative claim in restitution was even pursued when the failure of basis was arguably stronger than in *BNY v Cine-UK*. The tenant in the latter was at least entitled to exclusive occupation of the premises, even if they could not put them to their intended use.

[81] *Barnes v Eastenders* (n 3) [115].

[82] See text following n 35.

[83] Peel, *Treitel* (n 77), para 22-028; cf. *Benedetti v Sawiris* [2013] UKSC 50, [2013] 3 WLR 351 [9]; *Energy Venture Partners Ltd v Malabu Oil & Gas Ltd* [2013] EWHC 2118 (Comm) [283] ('the exercise of ascertaining what objectively [the parties] would have contemplated was a reasonable amount is a very different exercise from that which is required of the court in the context of a restitutionary quantum meruit claim') (Gloster LJ).

[84] See *Barton v Morris* (n 8) [227].

[85] The receiver's remuneration, costs, and expenses were to be paid in accordance with a Framework Agreement between the CPS and a panel of approved receivers: *Barnes v Eastenders* (n 3) [17], [19].

[86] The sums involved are addressed at ibid [29]. There is no suggestion that the figures are anything other than the sums charged under the contract with the CPS.

[87] All of which perhaps assists the suggested ex post facto rationalization of the decision previously referred to.

[88] In the Court of Appeal, it is noted that the receiver took possession of £774,556 in cash but asserted a lien over it in the sum of £474,779: [2012] EWCA Crim 2436, [2013] 1 WLR 1494 [7]. The figures referred to in the Supreme Court appear a little larger, but less than the cash taken into possession: *Barnes v Eastenders* (n 3) [29].

In particular, the fact that Kirby J took into account the passing on of the licence fee to the retailers' customers as part of the question of whether the case turned on any implied term. It is respectfully submitted that the majority erred when considering this only in the context of the claim in restitution This resulted in the conclusion that, *as between* the wholesalers and the retailers, the requirements for a claim in restitution were established and the passing on of the licence fee to the retailers' customers was, in effect, *res inter alios acta*. As Kirby J points out, the passing on of the licence fee and the very unlikely prospect of it being claimed by, or reimbursed to, the retailers' customers, was an important part of the context in which any implied term fell to be assessed. His conclusion that there was no basis for such an implied term (rather than its rejection as artificial and unconvincing) and his further conclusion that there was, as a result, no failure of basis when the licence fee was paid under the terms and conditions of the contract is to be preferred.[89]

V. Conclusion

This chapter started with the observation of Ewan McKendrick that 'where a contract has been concluded, there is no case for permitting a person to proceed with a restitutionary claim'. Taken entirely out of context, that is, of course, too dogmatic. As Jack Beatson has explained, 'it should, in principle, be possible to bring a restitution claim where it would not reallocate risks . . . as an alternative to an action for breach of contract',[90] but, as he went on to acknowledge, such circumstances will be very rare[91] and 'restitution will almost never be appropriate before a valid contract has been discharged'.[92] We have seen that one possible example is where a party performs services which are additional to or different from those covered by the contract.[93] Where the benefit conferred falls within the 'scope of the applicable contractual regime' (ie where the contract has not 'run out'), one starts with the claim for breach of contract and, if there is no breach (because there is no applicable express or implied term), there is no failure of basis to support an alternative claim in restitution.

---

[89] Goff & Jones (n 6) para 3-27 ('the fact remains that, by requiring its repayment in the absence of any contractual term, the court reallocated the risk to the wholesaler'); cf. Jack Beatson and Graham Virgo, 'Contract, Unjust Enrichment and Unconscionability' (2002) 118 LQR 352, 355–56.

[90] Jack Beatson, 'The Temptation of Elegance: Concurrence of Restitutionary and Contractual Claims' in William Swadling and Gareth Jones (eds), *The Search for Principle: Essays in Honour of Lord Goff of Chievely* (OUP 1999) 142, 153 (hereafter Beatson, 'The Temptation of Elegance').

[91] Cf Birks, 'Failure of Consideration' (n 3) 4.

[92] Beatson, 'The Temptation of Elegance' (n 90) 169.

[93] See text to n 69.

List of Publications

EWAN MCKENDRICK

Books

Sole-authored

Contract Law (1st to 14th edn, Palgrave/Macmillan 1990–2021; 15th edn, Bloomsbury 2023)
Contract Law, Text, Cases and Materials (1st to 9th edn, Oxford University Press 2003–2020)
The Creation of a European Law of Contracts (Kluwer 2004)
Goode and McKendrick on Commercial Law (6th edn, LexisNexis 2020)

Co-authored

Andrew Burrows and E McKendrick, *Cases and Materials on the Law of Restitution* (Oxford University Press 1997)
Andrew Burrows, E McKendrick, and James Edelman, *Cases and Materials on the Law of Restitution* (2nd edn, Oxford University Press 2007)
Roy Goode, Herbert Kronke, and E McKendrick, *Transnational Commercial Law, Text, Cases and Materials* (1st to 2nd edn, Oxford University Press 2007 and 2015)
Roy Goode, Herbert Kronke, E McKendrick, and Jeffrey Wool, *Transnational Commercial Law: Primary Materials* (Oxford University Press 2007)
E McKendrick and Qiao Liu, *Contract Law (Australian edition)* (1st edn, Palgrave/Macmillan 2016)
Norman Palmer and Ewan McKendrick, *Product Liability in the Construction Industry* (LLP 1993)

Edited Books

Nili Cohen and E McKendrick (eds), *Comparative Remedies for Breach of Contract* (Hart Publishing 2005)
Roy Goode, Herbert Kronke, E McKendrick, and Jeffrey Wool (eds), *Transnational Commercial Law: International Instruments and Commentary* (1st to 2nd edn, Oxford University Press 2004 and 2012)
E McKendrick (ed), *Commercial Aspects of Trusts and Fiduciary Obligations* (Oxford University Press 1992)
E McKendrick (ed), *Force Majeure and Frustration of Contract* (2nd edn, LLP 1995)
E McKendrick (ed), *Sale of Goods* (LLP 2000)
E McKendrick (ed), *Goode on Commercial Law* (4th edn, LexisNexis/Penguin 2009)
E McKendrick (ed), *Goode on Commercial Law* (5th edn, LexisNexis and Penguin 2016)
Norman Palmer and E McKendrick (eds), *Interests in Goods* (LLP 1998)

Journal Articles

Sole-authored

'The Battle of the Forms and the Law of Restitution' (1988) 8 Oxford Journal of Legal Studies 197
'Breach of Contract and the Meaning of Loss' (1999) 52 Current Legal Problems 37
'Commercial Contract Law: How Important Is the Quest for Certainty?' [2021] Lloyd's Maritime and Commercial Law Quarterly 72
'The Common Law at Work: The Saga of *Alfred McAlpine Construction Ltd v Panatown Ltd*' (2003) 3 Oxford University Commonwealth Law Journal 145

'Contracts, The Common Law and the Impact of Europe' [2001] Europa e diritto privato 769

'Doctrine and Discretion in the Law of Contract Revisited' (2019) 7 Chinese Journal of Comparative Law 1

'Economic Duress: A Reply' [1985] Scots Law Times 277

'Interpretation of Contracts and the Admissibility of Pre-Contractual Negotiations' (2005) 17 Singapore Academy of Law Journal 248

'Liquidated Damages, Delay and the Termination of Contracts' [2019] Journal of Business Law 577

'*Pirelli* Re-examined' (1991) 11 Legal Studies 326

'Promises to Perform–How Valuable?' (1992) 5 Journal of Contract Law 6

'The Rights of Trade Union Members—Part I of the Employment Act 1988' (1988) 17 Industrial Law Journal 141

'Specific Implement and Specific Performance—A Comparison' [1986] Scots Law Times 249

'Trade Unions and Non-Striking Members' (1986) 6 Legal Studies 35

'Traditional Concepts and Contemporary Values' [2002] European Review of Private Law 95

'Vicarious Liability and Independent Contractors—A Re-examination' (1990) 53 Modern Law Review 770

Co-authored

E McKendrick, JM Luycks, and AMM Hendrikx, 'A NCC Case on Contract Interpretation from an English and Dutch Law Perspective' (2021) 29 European Review of Private Law 71

E McKendrick and Iain Maxwell, 'Specific Performance in International Arbitration' (2013) 1 Chinese Journal of Comparative Law 195

E McKendrick and Matthew Parker, 'Drafting Force Majeure Clauses: Some Practical Considerations' (2000) 11 International Company and Commercial Law Review 132

Lord Wedderburn of Charlton, E McKendrick, and Alison Real, 'Il Diritto del Lavoro in Gran Bretagna 1980–1983' (1985) 28 Giornale di Diritto del Lavoro e di Relazioni Industriali 833

Chapters

Sole-authored

'Arbitrations, Multiple References and Apparent Bias: A Case Study of *Halliburton Co v Chubb Bermuda Insurance Ltd* (2018)' in Axel Calissendorff and Patrik Scholdstrom (eds), *Stockholm Arbitration Yearbook 2019* (Kluwer Law International 2019)

'Breach of Contract, Restitution for Wrongs and Punishment' in Andrew Burrows and Edwin Peel (eds), *Commercial Remedies: Current Issues and Problems* (Oxford University Press 2003)

'The Consequences of Frustration—The Law Reform (Frustrated Contracts) Act 1943' in E McKendrick (ed), *Force Majeure and Frustration of Contract* (LLP 1995)

'Contract Law and Codification: A View from England' in Manuel Carlos Lopes Porto and Jorge Sinde Monteiro (eds), *A Civil Code for Europe* (Coimbra Editora 2002)

'Commerce' in William Swadling (ed), *The Quistclose Trust: Critical Essays* (Hart Publishing 2004)

'Coming to Terms with Good Faith' in Dennis Faber, Ben Schuijling, and Niels Vermunt (eds), *Trust and Good Faith across Borders: Liber Amicorum Prof Dr SCJJ Kortmann* (Wolters Kluwer 2017)

'Contract: In General' in Andrew Burrows (ed), *Principles of the English Law of Obligations* (Oxford University Press 2015)

'The Contracting Society: A Misplaced Faith' in Paul Beaumont (ed), *Christian Perspectives on the Limits of the Law* (Paternoster Press 2002)

'Economic Frustration Revisited' in Andrew RC Simpson, Scott Crichton Styles, Euan West, and Adelyn LM Wilson (eds), *Continuity, Change and Pragmatism in the Law: Essays in Memory of Professor Angelo Fort* (Aberdeen University Press 2016)

'English Contract Law: A Rich Past, An Uncertain Future?' in Michael Freeman (ed), *Law and Opinion at the End of the Twentieth Century* (Oxford University Press 1997)

'Express Terms, Implied Terms, Performance, Discharge by Agreement, Discharge by Frustration, Discharge by Breach, Other Modes of Discharge, Bailment' in Hugh Beale (ed), *Chitty on Contracts Vols I and II* (Sweet & Maxwell 2015)

LIST OF PUBLICATIONS   399

'Express Terms, Implied Terms, Performance, Discharge by Agreement, Discharge by Frustration, Discharge by Breach, Other Modes of Discharge and Bailment' in Hugh Beale (ed), *Chitty on Contracts Volumes 1 and 2* (Sweet & Maxwell 2018)

'Force Majeure and Frustration—Their Relationship and a Comparative Assessment' in E McKendrick (ed), *Force Majeure and Frustration of Contract* (LLP 1995)

'Force Majeure Clauses: The Gap between Doctrine and Practice' in Andrew Burrows and Edwin Peel (eds), *Contract Terms* (Oxford University Press 2007)

'Frustration: Automatic Discharge of Both Parties?' in Andrew Dyson, James Goudkamp, and Frederick Wilmot Smith (eds), *Defences in Contract* (Bloomsbury 2017)

'Frustration, Restitution and Loss Apportionment' in Andrew Burrows (ed), *Essays on the Law of Restitution* (Oxford University Press 1991)

'The Further Travails of Duress' in Andrew Burrows and Lord Rodger of Earlsferry (eds), *Mapping the Law: Essays in Memory of Peter Birks* (Oxford University Press 2006)

'Good Faith: A Matter of Principle?' in Angelo DM Forte (ed), *Good Faith in Contract and Property Law* (Hart Publishing 1999)

'Good Faith in the Performance of a Contract in English Law' in Larry DiMatteo and Martin Hogg (eds), *Comparative Contract Law: British and American Perspectives* (Oxford University Press 2016)

'Interpretation' in William Day and Sarah Worthington (eds), *Challenging Private Law: Lord Sumption on the Supreme Court* (Hart 2020)

'The Interpretation of Contracts: Lord Hoffmann's Re-Statement' in Sarah Worthington (ed), *Commercial Law and Commercial Practice* (Hart Publishing 2003)

'Hardship Clauses and Damages' in Stefan Vogenauer (ed), *Commentary on the Unidroit Principles of International Commercial Contracts (PICC)* (Oxford University Press 2015)

'Harmonisation of European Contract Law: The State We Are In' in Stefan Vogenauer and Stephen Weatherill (eds), *The Harmonisation of European Contract Law: Implications for European Private Laws, Business and Legal Practice* (Hart Publishing 2006)

'Innominate Terms Revisited' in Louise Gullifer and Stefan Vogenauer (eds), *English and European Perspectives on Contract and Commercial Law: Essays in Honour of Hugh Beale* (Hart Publishing 2014)

'Judicial Control of Contractual Discretion' in Mark Freedland and Jean-Bernard Auby (eds), *The Public Law/Private Law Divide: Une Entente Assez Cordiale?* (Hart Publishing 2006)

'La Buona Fede Tra Common Law E Diritto Europeo' in Carlo Castronovo and Salvatore Mazzamuto (eds), *Manuale di Diritto Privato Europeo* (Giuffre Editore 2007)

'Liquidated Damages and Related Clauses in Claims Involving Chattels' in Norman Palmer and E McKendrick (eds), *Interests in Goods* (LLP 1998)

'Local Authorities and Swaps: Undermining the Market?' in Ross Cranston (ed), *Making Commercial Law: Essays in Honour of Roy Goode* (Oxford University Press 1997)

'The Meaning of "Good Faith"' in Mads Andenas, Silvia Diaz Alabart, Sir Basil Markesinis, Hans Micklitz, and Nello Pasquini (eds), *Liber Amicorum Guido Alpa: Private Law Beyond the National Systems* (British Institute of International and Comparative Law 2007)

'Mistake of Law—Time for a Change?' in William Swadling (ed), *The Limits of Restitutionary Claims: A Comparative Analysis* (British Institute of International and Comparative Law 1997)

'Negligence and Human Rights: Re-Considering *Osman*' in Daniel Friedmann and Daphne Barak-Erez (eds), *Human Rights in Private Law* (Hart Publishing 2001)

'The Passing of Property in Part of a Bulk' in Norman Palmer and E McKendrick (eds), *Interests in Goods* (LLP 1998)

'Performance, Discharge by Agreement, Discharge by Frustration, Discharge by Breach, Other Modes of Discharge' in AG Guest (ed), *Chitty on Contracts Vol I* (Sweet & Maxwell 1994)

'Performance, Discharge by Agreement, Discharge by Frustration, Discharge by Breach, Other Modes of Discharge, Bailment' in Hugh Beale (ed), *Chitty on Contracts Vols I and II* (Sweet & Maxwell 1999)

'Performance, Discharge by Agreement, Discharge by Frustration, Discharge by Breach, Other Modes of Discharge, Bailment' in Hugh Beale (ed), *Chitty on Contracts Vols I and II* (Sweet & Maxwell 2004)

'Performance, Discharge by Agreement, Discharge by Frustration, Discharge by Breach, Other Modes of Discharge, Bailment' in Hugh Beale (ed), *Chitty on Contracts Vols I and II* (Sweet & Maxwell 2008)

E McKendrick, 'Performance, Discharge by Agreement, Discharge by Frustration, Discharge by Breach, Other Modes of Discharge, Bailment' in Hugh Beale (ed), *Chitty on Contracts Vols I and II* (Sweet & Maxwell 2012)

'The Reason for Restitution' in Peter Birks and Francis Rose (eds), *Lessons of the Swaps Litigation* (Mansfield Press 2000)

'The Regulation of Long-Term Contracts in English Law' in Jack Beatson and Daniel Friedmann (eds), *Good Faith and Fault in English Contract Law* (Oxford University Press 1995)

'Restitution and the Misuse of Chattels—The Need for a Principled Approach' in Norman Palmer and Ewan McKendrick (eds), *Interests in Goods* (LLP 1998)

'Sale of Goods' in Andrew Burrows (ed), *Principles of English Commercial Law* (Oxford University Press 2015)

'Taxonomy: Does It Matter?' in David Johnston and Reinhard Zimmermann (eds), *Unjustified Enrichment: Key Issues in Comparative Perspective* (Cambridge University Press 2002)

'Total Failure of Consideration and Counter-Restitution: Two Issues or One?' in PBH Birks (ed), *Laundering and Tracing* (Oxford University Press 1995)

'Two "Truly Fundamental Issues in the Law of Contract": An Analysis of *MWB Business Exchange Centres Ltd v Rock Advertising Ltd*' in Daniel Clarry (ed), *The UK Supreme Court Yearbook, Volume 9: 2017–2018 Legal Year* (Appellate Press 2019)

'The Undue Influence of English Law?' in Hector L MacQueen (ed), *Scots Law into the 21st Century: Essays in Honour of WA Wilson* (W Green/Sweet & Maxwell 1996)

'Work Done in Anticipation of a Contract which Fails to Materialise' in William Cornish, Richard Nolan, Janet O'Sullivan, and GJ Virgo (eds), *Restitution Past, Present and Future: Essays in Honour of Gareth Jones* (Hart Publishing 1998)

Co-authored

E McKendrick and Rachel Kapila, 'Contract Law Harmonisation' in Adam Brzozowski, Wojciech Kocot, and Katarzyna Michalowska (eds), *Towards Europeanization of Private Law: Essays in Honour of Professor Jerzy Rajski* (C H Beck 2007)

E McKendrick and Qiao Liu, 'Good Faith in Contract Performance in the Chinese and Common Laws' in Larry DiMatteo and Lei Chen (eds), *Chinese Contract Law: Civil and Common Law Perspectives* (Cambridge University Press 2018)

E McKendrick, Qiao Liu, and Xiang Ren, 'Remedies in International Instruments' in Roger Halson and David Campbell (eds), *Research Handbook on Remedies in Private Law* (Edward Elgar 2019)

E McKendrick and Iain Maxwell, 'Specific Performance in International Arbitration' in Qiao Liu and Wenhua Shan (eds), *China and International Commercial Dispute Resolution* (Brill Nijhoff 2016)

E McKendrick and Hannes Unberath, 'Supervening Events' in Gerhard Dannemann and Stefan Vogenauer (eds), *The Common European Sales Law in Context: Interactions with English and German Law* (Oxford University Press 2013)

E McKendrick and Stefan Vogenauer, 'Supervening Events in Contract Law: Two Cases on the Interaction of National Contract Laws, International Uniform Law and "Soft Law" Instruments' in Christoph Benicke und Stefan Huber (ed), *National, International, Transnational: Harmonischer Dreiklang im Recht Festschrift fur Herbert Kronke zum 70 Geburtstag* (Verlag Ernst und Werner Gieseking Bielefeld 2020)

E McKendrick and Katherine Worthington, 'Damages for Non-Pecuniary Loss' in Nili Cohen and Ewan McKendrick (eds), *Comparative Remedies for Breach of Contract* (Hart Publishing 2005)

Case Notes

Sole-authored

'Auctioneers, "Sleepers" and Actions in Negligence' (1992) 1 International Journal of Cultural Property 207

'Brexit, Uncertainty and the Doctrine of Frustration' (2019) 34 Journal of International Banking Law and Regulation 199

'Economic Duress—A Reasonable Alternative?' [1985] Scottish Law Gazette 54

'Economic Duress and Industrial Action' (1990) 20 Industrial Law Journal 195

'Equal Pay, Material Difference and Market Forces' [1985] Scots Law Times 13

'Incontrovertible Benefit—A Postscript' [1989] Lloyd's Maritime and Commercial Law Quarterly 401

'Invitations to Tender and the Creation of Contracts' [1991] Lloyd's Maritime and Commercial Law Quarterly 31

'The Legal Effect of an Anti-Oral Variation Clause' (2017) 32 Journal of International Banking Law and Regulation 439

'Negotiations "Subject to Contract"' (1995) 3 Restitution Law Review 100

'No Place for *O'Brien* in Scots Law' (1996) 4 Restitution Law Review 100

'Public Nuisance and the Environment' (1993) 1 Journal of Tort Law 14

'Restitution, Misdirected Funds and Change of Position' (1992) 55 Modern Law Review 377

'Restitution of Tax Unlawfully Demanded' (1991) 107 Law Quarterly Review 526

'Restitution of Unlawfully Demanded Tax' [1993] Lloyd's Maritime and Commercial Law Quarterly 88

'Self-Induced Frustration and Force Majeure Clauses' [1989] Lloyd's Maritime and Commercial Law Quarterly 3

'Self-Induced Frustration and the Construction of Force Majeure Clauses' [1990] Lloyd's Maritime and Commercial Law Quarterly 153

'Tracing Misdirected Funds' [1991] Lloyd's Maritime and Commercial Law Quarterly 378

'Vicarious Liability and Industrial Action' (1989) 19 Industrial Law Journal 161

'Who Is an Employee? A Contextual Approach?' (1996) 25 Industrial Law Journal 136

Co-authored

E McKendrick and James Edelman, 'Employee's Liability for Statements' (2002) 118 Law Quarterly Review 4

E McKendrick and Lee Gleeson, 'The Rotting Away of Caveat Emptor?' [1987] The Conveyancer and Property Lawyer 121

E McKendrick and Martin Graham, 'The Sky's the Limit: Contractual Damages for Non-Pecuniary Loss' [2002] Lloyd's Maritime and Commercial Law Quarterly 161

Reviews

E McKendrick and Richard Brent, 'Banking Review: An Interim Report' (1999) 14 Journal of International Banking Law 313

Index

For the benefit of digital users, indexed terms that span two pages (e.g., 52–53) may, on occasion, appear on only one of those pages.

Tables are indicated by *t* following the page number

absence of basis approach 348, 367–68, 375, 378–79
absence of juristic reason approach 379–80
abuse of right (*abus de droit*) 29
accession, doctrine of 228–29, 241, 242n.98
accessory before the fact 213
accessory liability theory 253, 353n.8
Ackner, Lord 33–34, 42, 43
action for the price 306–7, 308–9
agencies
    formulating 283n.1, 284–85, 287–89, 290, 295, 299
    harmonizing 284–85, 333
Arden, Lady 40n.6, 63, 64–65, 71–72, 200
assumption of liability approach 49n.30
Atkin, Lord 32n.43, 81–82
attribution of acts 212, 213, 216, 217, 224–25
    performed by an agent 218–19, 222
    performed by a delegate 219–22
    see also direct liability
Australian contract law
    attribution of acts 218–19, 221
    breach of contract 193–94
    breach requirement 197–98, 207*t*
    Federal Court of Australia 217, 222–23
    High Court of Australia 166, 193–94, 197, 204, 216, 217, 230–31
    reliance damages 53
    sue, right to 279–80, 281
    transportation for life 80
    unconscionability 83
    unconscionable bargains 5–6
    vicarious liability 215
Australian Law Reform Commission 212
aviation industry 119–20, 324, 325–26, 328–29
Aviation Working Group 333–34, 335

bad bargains 39–40, 41–56, 51n.34, 98, 135
    failure to prove 53
    mitigated losses and 46–49
    overall expectations and 46–49
    pre-contractual expenditure 41–44
bad faith 6–7, 16, 20, 75, 78–79, 371n.28, 389–90
    demand
        criticisms 84–88
    Lord Burrows' test 84–91, 102n.64
        application 89
        bargaining power, inequality of 84–85

        monopolies, common law regulation of 85
        scope 89
        waiver versus new contract 87–88
        uncertainty and 86–87
bargaining
    see also bad bargains
    business parties can bargain for what they need 302–3
    power, inequality of 84–85
Black, Lady 63, 64–65
Blackburn, Lord 115–16, 122, 221
blackmail 3–4, 82
bona fide purchasers 357n.38, 359, 371, 374–75
    doctrine of 30–31
    Roman law concept 27–28
    Said v Butt case 253
Brandon, Lord 229–30
breach, doctrine of 96
breach of contract
    alternatives to 396
    Cavendish Square Holdings v Makdessi 193–94, 196, 197–98, 199–200, 201, 204–5
    contractual interpretation 166
    damages 171–72, 173, 174, 175–76, 177, 181, 182, 184, 185n.76, 190–91
    frustration and 115
    Law Reform (Frustrated Contracts) Act 127–28, 136
    lawful act duress 83, 86, 88
    love and trust, contracts of 96, 98
    meaning 143
    PIAC conduct 4–5
    reliance damages 39–58
    remedies for 35
    Sale of Goods Act 312
    tort of inducing 351–52, 353, 355–56, 357–58, 359, 360–61, 362–63, 364, 366
    vicarious liability 224–25
    wrongs 245–47, 248–50, 251, 252, 253, 254, 255–56, 257n.86, 259–60
breach requirement 196, 197–204, 206
    B, In re 199–200
    Brown's Bay Resort Ltd v Pozzoni 198
    Hayfin Opal Luxco 3 SARL v Windermere VII CMBS Plc 198
    Heritage Travel and Tourism v Windhorst 199
    international overview 207*t*

404 INDEX

breach requirement (*cont.*)
  Law Ting Pong Secondary School v Chen Wai Wah 199
  Richards v IP Solutions Ltd 199
  Signia Wealth v Vector Trustees 199
Bridge, Lord 229–30, 236–37
Briggs, Lord 71–72, 73, 166n.61, 342–43
Brown, Lord 343, 347–48
Buckmaster, Lord 96
Burrows, Lord 4, 5, 16, 36, 75, 79, 82, 83, 85–86, 87, 88–89, 90, 284, 368n.5, 383, 389–90, 391, 392–93
  test of bad faith demand 77
buyers' remedies 310–13
  right to repair or replacement 310
  specific performance of the obligation to deliver 310
  termination by the buyer 310–13
business efficacy test 117–18, 121, 386, 388

Canadian contract law
  absence of juristic reason approach 379–80
  bad bargain 42
  common law system 32n.44
  legislative reform 138–39
  liquidated damages clauses 206
  situational disadvantage 83
  Supreme Court of Canada 61n.5
cancellation rights 115, 120n.73, 205–6, 309
Carnwath, Lord 342–43
cause of action 88, 206, 229–30, 245, 259–60, 273–74, 275–76, 356
  mistake and 339–40, 344, 345–46, 347, 348–49
Cavendish Square Holdings v Makdessi case
  127 Hobson Street Ltd v Honey Bees Preschool Ltd 203
  Ahuja Investments v Victorygame Ltd 205
  applying the test for a penalty 200–1
  B, In re 199–200
  Blu-Sky Solutions v Be Caring Ltd 205–6
  breach requirement 197–204
  Brown's Bay Resort Ltd v Pozzoni 198
  Cargill International Trading Pte Ltd v Uttam Galva Steels Ltd 205
  Cavendish case 195–96
  critical reception 193–208
  Eco World—Ballymore Embassy Gardens Co Ltd v Dobler UK 203
  Gray v Braid Group (Holdings) Ltd 202
  Hayfin Opal Luxco 3 SARL v Windermere VII CMBS Plc 198
  Heritage Travel and Tourism v Windhorst 199
  Indigo Park Services v Watson 202
  international overview 207t
  Law Ting Pong Secondary School v Chen Wai Wah 199, 203–4
  legitimate interest requirement 200–4
  Luxury Italian KBB Co Ltd v Boutros 203
  Makdessi appeal 202
  penalty rule, 'engaging' 197–200

  Permavent v Makin 203, 205
  proportionality requirement 204–6
  Richards v IP Solutions Ltd 199
  Signia Wealth v Vector Trustees 199, 202–3
  Slowikowska v Rogers 205
  Wilaci Pty Ltd v Torchlight Fund No 1 202
charge 271–72
Chinese law of unjust enrichment 367–81
  context 367–68
  four-point test 372–75
  overview 368–72
  unjust vs. unjustified enrichment 375–80
circumvention
  ground of invalidity, as a 7–8
  Lindsay's Executor v Outlook Finance Ltd case 6–7
  Scots law 11–15
CISG *see* United Nations Convention on Contracts for the International Sale of Goods (CISG)
Clarke, Lord 61, 164
Cohen, N. 289
comity 123
commercial reality test 242
Commission on European Contract Law 24n.6, 321n.13
common law
  illegality 67–70
  Law Reform (Frustrated Contracts) Act 130–31
  monopolies, regulation of 85
complex structure theory 236
compliance index 335–36
confidence
  breach of 189–90
  duties of 180n.46, 189–91
  equitable and contractual obligations of 187–90
  trust and 80, 214
confidentiality 275, 281
  agreements 172, 173, 189, 190–91
  confidential information 172n.7, 179–80, 187–89
conflict of laws 123–24, 319, 320–21
consent
  doctrine/principle of 153
  pure consent, principles of 154
contempt of court 252n.52, 258
  Marex tort 260
contextualism 160
contra proferentum principle 112–13, 114
contract law 283–99
  content 291–94
  context 285–86
  damages 180–83
  institutional approval 290–91
  legal effect 294–98
  preparatory work 286–89
  publication 290–91
  transnational *see* transnational contract law
contractual interpretation 141–52
  'all agreements are like this' 145–47
  antinomies 153–69
  appointing 145–47

boundaries of 164–68
context 141–42, 153–64
delegating 145–47
frustrations of unforeseen circumstances 148–51
'I agree the terms, whatever they are' 145
interpreters 147
Lord Leggatt's rational choice theory 147–48
objective principle is not itself a problem, but nor is it an answer 142–43
outsourcing 145–47
shortcuts 145–47
'you don't have to think it to mean it' 143–44
contractual performance 55, 111, 114, 119–20, 124, 137
impossibility of 115–17
contractual purpose 90, 91, 119
impossibility of 117–19
copyright 184, 185, 316n.96
corporate veil 17–18, 20
see also piercing the veil
COVID-19 pandemic 114, 119–20, 148n.27, 388, 393
cure, right to 293, 312, 313

damages 171–91
see also property damage; reliance damages
cases where there is no use of C's property 183–85
concept of damage 230
confidence, equitable and contractual obligations of 187–90
context 171
contract cases 180–83
controversial cases 187–90
injunctions 185–87
Lord Cairns' Act (LCA) damages 185–87
measure of 314–15
older authorities 176–85
One Step argument 172–76
tort cases 176–80
deceit 7–8, 10–11, 12–13, 75, 91, 127, 143–44, 211, 214
deception 7, 144n.11
defences 260n.104, 370
see also illegality defence
Marex tort 254–55
deemed mistakes see mistake
Denning, Lord 18, 33nn.47–48, 42, 96–97, 106, 178–79, 181, 218–19, 220–22, 256n.75
digital products 315–16
Diplock, Lord 308n.36
direct liability 213–25
see also vicarious liability
attribution of acts performed by an agent 218–19
attribution of acts performed by a delegate 219–22
systems of action 222–25
broad application 212–13
categorisations 211–12
context 211

disclosure, duty of 31–32, 33–35, 82, 256
non-disclosure agreements 188
unauthorized disclosure 189, 190
diseases, concept of notifiable 149n.28
disenrichment 371
Dunedin, Lord 121–22, 195–96, 200
Dunlop test 207–8
duress, doctrine of see economic duress; Times Travel v PIAC case

economic duress 3–5, 11–12, 16–17, 33–34, 36, 37, 75, 82, 83, 87, 88, 91
economic loss 172, 175, 176–77, 178, 179, 181, 186
see also pure economic loss
efficient breach doctrine 355–57
Ellenborough, Lord 307n.29, 360
English contract law 87
good faith 23–37
lawful act duress 75
property damage 235–39
English language
see also language issues
plain English 304–6
envoi 336
equitable assignment 269–71
general 269
no notice to the obligor 275–80
notice to the obligor 270–71
equity
concepts of 167
doctrines 359–60
errors of judgement 346–48
see also mistake
European Civil Code 3, 24n.6, 301
European Commission 295, 310n.54
European Union (EU) 285–86, 322n.19, 330, 342
exception
rule and exception, dialectical process of 364–66
expense, 'at the expense of' 197–98

facility and circumvention, doctrine of 3–4, 14, 15, 20–21
ground of invalidity, as a 7–8
Scots law 11–15
factoring 266–67
fairness 3–4, 27n.18, 28, 29–30, 32, 36, 86, 97n.31, 154, 186, 304, 374–75, 377, 379
see also unfairness
family law 93–94, 97, 99, 101, 106, 108–9, 351–52
see also marriage
fault 94–95, 116–17, 125, 138, 374–75
no-fault divorce 97, 98
financing models 266–68
factoring 266–67
invoice discounting 249
security interests 267–68
force and fear doctrine 3–4, 11–15
force majeure 111, 119, 120n.73, 120n.76, 121–22, 149–50, 293
frustration 112–14

406 INDEX

four-point test 372–75
fraud 7–8, 12n.47, 18, 31, 56, 75, 89, 91, 341n.17,
  343, 374–75
  Civil Fraud 245, 254–55, 259–60
  concept of 7
  doctrine of 20–21
  employees 202
  judgments 252
  mortgage 62–63, 64
  on a power, doctrine of 166–67
fraudulent misrepresentation 6–7, 11, 125, 126
freedom of contract 33–34, 84, 197–98, 206–8,
  296, 330–31
freedom of establishment 341–42
freezing orders 245–46, 248, 250, 257
  Marex tort 258
French contract law 25, 27n.19
  civil code 28
  civil law system 33n.48, 34n.53
  good faith 34n.53
  language issues 332, 333
  reforms in 2016 29
French, P. 223
frustration 111–24
  see also implied terms
  context 111–12
  doctrine of 111, 112, 121, 123–24
  force majeure 112–14
  implied terms 115–21
  public policy 121–24

Gama, L. 289
General Principles of Civil Law (GPCL) 368
German contract law 122, 367–68
  see also Weiterfresserschäden, German doctrine of
  absence of basis approach 378–79
  Bürgerliches Gesetzbuch (BGB) 371, 375
  court system 230, 235n.41
  doctrine 231
  good faith 27n.18, 28, 30, 34n.53
  restitution 370–71
  sale of goods 313
  unjustified enrichment 367n.2, 369, 370, 371,
    373n.42, 374n.48
Gleeson, L. 221, 385–86, 392, 394
Goff, Lord 136–37, 168, 344, 361n.61, 384, 391n.56
good faith 6–7, 11, 15, 19–20, 23, 75–76, 78, 79, 87,
    88, 89, 90, 164n.47, 297n.129, 320, 334n.57,
    358–59, 362
  comparative law 24–30
  English contract law 23–37
  future prospects 36–37
  general principles of 336, 371n.28
  historical developments 30–36
  language of 336
Goode, R. 265, 272n.42, 284, 294, 299, 301, 306nn.26–
    27, 307n.34, 312, 331n.48, 332n.52

Hague Principles 285, 287–88, 291–92, 293, 296, 299
Hale, Lady 61, 100–1

Halsbury, Lord 13–14, 277–78
Hamblen, Lord 64–65, 67, 73, 343
harmonization, legal 24, 284–85, 295, 320–21, 322,
    324, 325, 328–29, 330–31
Hodge, Lord 5–6, 16, 17, 33n.49, 61, 63, 64–65, 75,
    79, 80, 82–85, 86, 87, 90, 155, 160, 161, 201,
    204, 343
Hoffman, Lord 35, 49n.30, 141, 147, 151, 155–56,
    163–64, 219, 222, 343, 344–45, 348n.57, 358–
    59, 390–91
Hope, Lord 344n.39, 346n.48
Hutchinson, Lord 96
hypothetical bargain 172–73

illegality defence 59–74
  common law illegality 67–70
  context 59
  court taking the point on its own initiative 71–72
  Patel v Mirza 59–62
    background 60
    decision 60–62
  restraint of trade 72–74
  standard of review, by an appellate court 70–71
  statutory illegality 67–70
  subsequent decisions 62–66
    Grondonav Stoffel & Co 62–64
    *Henderson v Dorset Healthcare Foundation
      Trust* 64–66
illegality doctrine 62
implied contract 65n.18, 369–70, 390–91
  theory of 394n.79
implied terms 115–21
  contractual performance, impossibility of 115–17
  contractual purpose, impossibility of 117–19
  doctrine of 151
  limits 121
  restitution and 383–96
    Barnes v Eastenders 386–88
    Barton v Morris 389–91
    BNY v Cine-UK 388–89
    consequences 394–96
    context 383–84
    fundamental bases 392–93
    gaps 392–93
    implied terms 392–93
    Roxborough v Rothmans 385–86
  underlying state of affairs, change to 119–20
impropriety 27–28, 381
industry experts 324–25
inequality of (bargaining) power 5–6, 33–34, 84–85, 101
intellectual property (IP) 172, 175, 178, 188, 190–91,
    292, 316n.96
intention
  concept of 106
  to create legal relations, doctrine of 93, 105–
    6, 108–9
intergovernmental organizations 295
International Bar Association (IBA) 289, 292
International Chamber of Commerce (ICC) 114, 292,
    293, 296, 320–21, 322, 324–25, 329, 330

INDEX 407

international organizations 286–87, 328–29
International Registry for the registration
       of international contracts in mobile
       equipment 320, 328–29, 333–34
International Trade Centre (ITC) 292
interpretation *see* contractual interpretation
interpreters 147
intersessional activity 325
invalidity
   circumvention as a ground of 7–8
   facility as a ground of 7–8
   Lindsay's Executor v Outlook Finance Ltd case 6–7
invoice discounting 249

Jauncey, Lord 236–37, 240–41
judicial decision 295–96, 342, 346–47, 381
   historical theory of 344n.38
juristic personality 18

Keith, Lord 236–37, 240–41
Kerr, Lord 61
Kitchin, Lord 64–65
Kronke, H. 284, 299, 320–21n.11
Kyllachy, Lord 8

labour relations 360, 364, 365
laissez faire principles 206–7, 364–65
language issues 332–33
   see also linguistic communication
   English and French legal texts 332, 333
   official UN languages 291, 332
Law Commission in England and Wales 24n.7, 60, 61,
      207n.113, 304–5, 307, 311, 314
Law Reform (Frustrated Contracts) Act 1943 125–39
   common law 130–31
   non-money benefits 134–37
   payments 132–34
   restitution, reasons for 126–29
   when the act applies 137–38
lawful act doctrine 85
lawful act duress 75–91
   see also Times Travel v PIAC case
   context 75–76
   resurrection of 90–91
leases 116, 299, 328–29, 388–89
legal basis 138, 368–69, 371, 372, 375–80, 381, 386
legal guide, definition of 296
legal philosophies 330–31
legitimate interest requirement 200–4
   127 Hobson Street Ltd v Honey Bees Preschool
      Ltd 203
   applying the test for a penalty 200–1
   Eco World—Ballymore Embassy Gardens Co Ltd v
      Dobler UK 203
   Gray v Braid Group (Holdings) Ltd 202
   Indigo Park Services v Watson 202
   Law Ting Pong Secondary School v Chen Wai Wah
      (2021) 203–4
   Luxury Italian KBB Co Ltd v Boutros 203
   Makdessi appeal 202

Permavent v Makin 203
Signia Wealth v Vector Trustees 202–3
Wilaci Pty Ltd v Torchlight Fund No 1 202
Leggatt, Lord 26–27, 34–35, 70, 82, 87, 142n.5,
      145n.14, 336, 384, 389–90, 391, 392, 393
   rational choice theory 147–48
lesion (loss) 6–7, 10–11
liability *see* direct liability; product liability; restitution
      liability; tort liability; vicarious liability
licence fees 172–73, 175, 183–84, 186, 189–90, 385–
      86, 387, 392, 393, 394, 395–96
licences 103
Lindley, Lord 177, 255–56
Lindsay's Executor v Outlook Finance Ltd case 6–10
   action 6–7
   circumvention 6–7
   decision 10–11
   facility 6–7
   facts 8–10
   ground of invalidity 6–7
linguistic communication 144
   pragmatic theory 144n.12
   relevance theory 147–48
Liu, Q. 368n.6
Lloyd-Jones, Lord 63, 64–65, 260, 342–43
loan agreements 6, 10
locus poenitentiae doctrine 60–61
Lord Cairns' Act (LCA) 171n.3, 172, 185–87
love
   see also marriage; trust
   contracts and relationships of 93–109
   termination of contract 94–98
Lyndhurst, Lord 96

Mance, Lord 18, 157, 160, 193, 197, 201–2, 204,
      206n.107, 207, 258
Mansfield, Lord 31–32, 214, 360
merchantilism 306–15
   see also Sale of Goods Act
Marex tort
   added value 257–58
   contempt of court 260
   defences 254–55
   development of 245–48
   discreteness of 259–60
   entry of a judgment 249–51
   freezing orders 258
   mere omissions 253
   need for an actual breach 253
   orders 252
   procedure 256
   relationship with other torts 257–58
   remedies 256
   remoteness 255–56
   Said v Butt, rule in 253–54
   scope of 248–54
   status of judgment 252
   type of judgment 252
   underlying obligation, nature of 249
   wider issues 258–60

408 INDEX

marriage
  see also pre-nuptial agreements
  breach of contract 358
  concept of 94–98
  contract, as a 93–94
  contracting for obligations outside legal 103–8
  contracting out of obligations of 99–103
  inducing wife 353–55
  relations 364–66
  validity of 108
master-servant relations 364–66
  inducing servant 353–55
  restitution liability 360–61
  tort liability 353–55
Material Adverse Effect 114
McCluskey, Lord 13
McDonald, Lord 12–13
McKendrick, E.
  academic career 3, 75, 93, 111, 319, 351
  accessory liability 253
  duress 6, 20–21
  employees 211
  English contract law, impact on 367
  frustration 111, 126
  good faith 23, 34, 336
  Goode and McKendrick on Commercial Law 301,
    306nn.26–27, 307n.34, 308n.37, 308n.38, 312
  impact on non-specialists 194
  international trade contracts 120n.76
  legislation 138–39
  linguistic meaning 160–61
  loss apportionment 126
  pragmatic approach 141
  pre-contractual negotiations 147n.19
  rational choice theory 148
  responsibility for wrongdoing 225–26
  restitution 126, 383, 396
  sale of goods 301, 318
  secondary liability 253
  tort law, contribution to 227
  Transnational Commercial Law, effect of 294, 299,
    320–21n.11
  transnational contract law 283–85
  undue influence 6
  unjust enrichment 367, 384
  victims' consent 16
mere omissions 253
mistake 339–49
  see also unjust enrichment
  actual mistakes 344–46
  cause of action, as a 339–40
  context 339
  deemed mistakes 344–46
  errors of judgement 346–48
  factor delaying limitation, as a 341–42
  Test Claimants case 342–44
mitigated losses 46–49
monopolies
  common law regulation of 85

power of 86
  rights 183–84
morality
  concepts of 167
  public 122–23
  sexual 73
Morris, Lord 144n.11
multi-factorial test 112–13, 117n.44, 124
mutuality of contract principle 11n.45

National People's Congress (NPC) 367nn.1–2, 368–
  69, 372n.32
natural justice 88
negligence 56, 62–63, 64, 70, 113, 178, 215, 218, 219–
  20, 221–22, 227, 230, 232, 238, 255
Neuberger, Lord 18, 61, 150n.40, 193–94, 195–96,
  197–98, 200n.60, 201, 204, 388n.40
Nicholls, Lord 157, 216, 236
non-money benefits 134–37
novation 265–66, 266n.4, 268–69

object of the bargain test 233n.33, 241–42
objective interpretation of contracts, principle
  of 153, 165
objective principle 142–43, 147–48
obligors
  see also sue, right to
  action against 272–80
  charge 280
  financing models 266–68
  legal techniques 268–72
  no notice to the obligor 275–80
  notice to the obligor 270–71, 275
  novation 268–69
  receivables, financing of 265–81
  statutory assignment 268–69
occupation, concept of 158
Oliver, Lord 229–30, 234n.37, 236–37
online purchases 309
operate markets, right to 183–84
Organization for the Harmonization of Commercial
  Law in Africa (OHADA) 285–86, 292
Organization of American States (OAS) 286n.22
outsourcing 145–47, 288–89

pandemics 114
  see also COVID-19 pandemic
parallel equity doctrines 359–60
parallelism, legislative 320–21
Parker, M. 275
Patel v Mirza 59–62
  background 60
  decision 60–62
payment, right to 131, 329
penalties doctrine 194n.12, 197
  applying the test for a penalty 200–1
  definition of penalty 196
  'engaging' the penalty rule 197–200
Perales Viscasillas, P. 289

performance, right to 251, 362
personal property 227
  accession doctrine 241
  contract for 363–64
personal responsibility, principle of 145, 220
Phillips, Lord 100, 101
PICC *see* UNIDROIT Principles of International
    Commercial Contracts (PICC)
piercing the veil 17, 18, 20
  see also corporate veil
  definition of 17, 18
place of the relevant intermediary approach
    (PRIMA) 326–27
policy-based approach 60, 61, 63, 65, 66, 216
possession, concept of 332n.52
poverty 5–6
pre-contractual negotiations 3–4, 147n.19, 249–50
  entry into the contract 49–51
  mis-characterisation of pre-contractual
    expenditure 44–45
  spending 41–44
pre-existing freedom test 73
pre-nuptial agreements 99–103
  see also marriage
precedent, doctrine of 346–47
price or hire, of, principle 177–78
primary liability *see* direct liability
Principles of European Contract Law (PECL) 321n.13
private international law 123–24, 285–86, 289, 290,
    291–92, 293n.85, 323n.22
  Hague Conference 284–85, 320–21
private ownership 177
privity doctrine 352, 353, 355–57, 374–75
product liability 227
promise 49–51
promissory estoppel 206
property
  see also intellectual property (IP); personal
    property; property damage
  contracts and 352–53
  passing of 306–7
  rights 103, 183–84, 230, 231, 232–35, 241–42, 320,
    333n.54, 352, 354–55, 373–74
property damage
  American jurisprudence 239–40
  analysis 240–42
  component added after transfer of property to
    claimant 232–33
  component added before transfer of property to
    claimant 233–34
  context 227–29
  core questions 235–42
  damage to the property itself 229–31
  English case law 235–39
  final product, flawed nature of 234–35
  pure economic loss and 227–43
  timing issues 232–35
proportionality 56n.50, 61–62, 63, 64, 65, 69, 71, 196,
    201, 204–6

Ahuja Investments v Victorygame Ltd 205
Blu-Sky Solutions v Be Caring Ltd 205–6
*Cargill International Trading Pte Ltd v Uttam Galva
    Steels Ltd* 205
Permavent v Makin 205
Slowikowska v Rogers 205
propriety 27–28, 367–68, 369, 381
public policy 62, 68, 72–73, 88, 99, 103, 111, 121–
    24, 379–80
pure economic loss 227–43

quasi contract, theory of 394n.79

Radcliffe, Lord 36, 61n.5, 150–51, 152
range-of-factors approach 60
rational choice theory 100, 147–48
real entity theory 223
realism 162
reality test 241–42
reasonable discoverability test 339, 342–44
reasonableness 27n.18, 29–30, 44n.17, 73–74, 148,
    201, 304, 311–12, 367–68, 369
reception 357–59
Reed, Lord 63, 64–65, 172, 174, 176, 184–
    85, 186n.82, 187–88, 343
reflective loss, doctrine of 246
Reid, Lord 303, 308–9
reject goods, right to 309n.44, 311–13
  long-term right to reject 314
  loss of the right to reject 314
reliance damages 39–58
  Australia 53
  bad bargains 41–56
    failure to prove 53
  context 39–40
  counter-examples to current orthodoxy 54–56
  fuller and perdue soft-shoe shuffle 51–52
  mis-characterisation of pre-contractual expenditure
    as reliance 44–45
  mitigated losses 46–49
  overall expectations 46–49
  post-contractual reliance on the promise 49–51
  pre-contractual reliance in entering into the
    contract 49–51
  pre-contractual spending 41–44
  propositions 40–41
  rebuttal presumption that reliance expenditure
    would be recouped 44–45
  responsibility, assumptions of 49–51
remedies 310–13
  right to repair or replacement 310
  specific performance of the obligation to
    deliver 310
  termination by the buyer 310–13
remoteness test 49n.30
  Marex tort 255–56
remuneration and expenses, right to recovery of 387
repair or replacement, right to 310, 313, 314
reprehensible means, requirement of 82–83

410 INDEX

responsibility
  assumptions of 49–51
  principles of 212
restitution
  implied terms and 383–96
    Barnes v Eastenders 386–88
    Barton v Morris 389–91
    BNY v Cine-UK 388–89
    consequences 394–96
    context 383–84
    fundamental bases 392–93
    gaps 392–93
    implied terms 392–93
    Roxborough v Rothmans 385–86
  Law Reform (Frustrated Contracts) Act 1943 126–29
  reasons for 126–29
restitution liability 360–64
  doubts 361–63
  historical origin 360–61
  inducing servant 360–61
  personal services, contract for 363–64
  reception 361–63
restitution theory 383–84
  right to restitution 362–64, 391, 393
restoration principle 177
restraint of trade doctrine 72–74, 172, 173, 188, 190–91
risk, passing of , 293, 306–7, 308
Rose, Lady 390–91
royalties 178, 179, 184, 189–90, 203
rules *see* sources of law
Rylands v Fletcher
  the rule in, 255n.71, 259n.97

Sale of Goods Act
  action for the price (s49) 308–9
  business parties can bargain for what they
    need 302–3
  buyer's remedies 310–13
  cancellation rights 309
  context 301–2
  damages, measure of 314–15
  detailed written contracts 302
  digital products 315–16
  general arguments 302–15
  long-term right to reject 314
  loss of the right to reject 314
  merchantilism 306–15
  online purchases 309
  parties can contract around default rules 304
  plain English 304–6
  property, passing of (s18) 306–7
  right to repair or replacement 310
  risk, passing of (s20) 308
  sales, nature of 301–17
  scope of legislation 315–17
  specific performance of the obligation to deliver 310
  supply other than by sale 316–17
  termination by the buyer 310–13
Sales, Lord 147, 246n.13, 259–60, 342–43

Scarman, Lord 81–82
Schrödinger' cat 75
  see also lawful act duress
Scott, Lord 86, 344–45
Scott, R. E. 340n.13, 357n.39
secondary liability *see* vicarious liability
security interests 266n.5, 267–68, 280, 287–88, 328–
  29, 333
servants *see* master-servant relations
Shaw, Lord 177, 178n.35
shortcuts 145–47
Simon of Glaisdale, Lord 153
'soft-shoe shuffle' 51–52
Sono, H. 289
sources of law 320–22
  facultative rules 321–22
  legally binding rules 320–21
specific performance 35, 115, 185, 294, 354n.19, 357,
  362, 363–64
  function of 359–60
  of the obligation to deliver 310
  right to 356
  right to repair or replacement 310
Sperber, D. 144n.12
standard of review, by an appellate court 70–71
standard terms 294, 302–3
  definition of 296
statutory assignment 266, 268–69, 270–71, 272
subjective devaluation test 181, 373
sue, right to
  assignees 273–74
  assignor's right to sue 274–80
    no notice to the obligor 275–80
    notice to the obligor 275
  representative capacity 280–81
Suez crisis 120
Sumption, Lord 18, 162, 173n.17, 188n.95, 197–98,
  221–22, 260

taxation 141, 342
technology 333
termination of contract 94
  love and trust 94–98
'test and error' approach 381
textualism 160
Times Travel v PIAC case 4–6, 76–89
  see also bad faith
  background to case 4–5
  bad faith demand, Burrows' test of 84–89
  bargaining power, inequality of 5–6, 84–85
  Court of Appeal finds no duress 78–79
  discussion 16–21
  duress to the person or illegality 81
  facts 76–77
  High Court finds lawful act duress 77–78
  lawful act duress, categories of 79–77
  monopolies, common law regulation of 85
  nature of demand 81–82
  reprehensible means, requirement of 82–83

Supreme Court decision 79–89
  uncertainty 86–87
  unconscionability 83–84
  undue influence 80–81
  waiver versus new contract 87–88
tort law 247, 251, 261
  damages cases 176–80
tort liability 353–60
  efficient breach 355–57
  historical origin 353–55
  inducing breach 355–57
  inducing servant 353–55
  inducing wife 353–55
  parallel equity doctrines 359–60
  privity 355–57
  reception 357–59
  specific performance, function of 359–60
Toulson, Lord 61–60, 64, 65, 67, 196, 392, 394–95
trade unions 3n.3, 15, 76, 365
'trading society' test 73
transnational commercial law 284–85, 294, 319
transnational contract law 283–85, 319–36
  'best as the enemy of the good' 326–27
  competing interests, balance of 331–32
  compliance index 335–36
  concept of 319n.3
  context 319
  definition of 319
  differences in legal philosophies 330–31
  envoi 336
  expediting the process 324–27
  flexibility 331
  form of instrument 330
  Friends of the Chair of the Drafting
    Committee 327
  harmonization, approach to 320
  identifying a subject for a project 327–29
  individual as the driving force 325–26
  industry experts, involvement of 324–25
  intersessional activity 325
  issues of process 322–27
  issues of substance 327–33
  interpretation 333–34
  language issues 332–33
  obstacles 322–33
  predictability 331
  ratifications, securing 335
  successful instruments 330
  technology 333
  time factor 322–24
treaties, international 94–95, 287–88, 291, 296, 320–
  21n.11, 333
Tripartite Guide 285, 291–92, 293nn.85–86, 294–95,
  296, 297, 298, 299
trust, contracts and relationships of 93–109
  see also love; marriage

uncertainty 86–87
unconscientious receipt 379–80

unconscionability 5, 7–8, 20–21, 81, 85, 206, 207,
  367–68, 379–80
  Times Travel v PIAC case 83–84
unconscionable bargains, doctrine of 5–6, 16, 17, 19,
  20–21, 83, 90
undue influence 11–15
  banks 15, 71
  doctrine of 3–4, 14, 20–21, 91
  duress, unity of relationship with 6, 20–21
  inequality and 85
  intimidation and 11–12
  lawful act duress 79–80, 81
  nuptial agreements 101
  pressure arising from 3–4
  Scottish reception of 7, 11–12, 14
  sibling relationships 13
  third parties 16–17
  Times Travel v PIAC case 16, 80–81
  unconscionable contract 5, 17, 19, 82, 90
unfair advantage 5, 7
unfair bargaining 20
unfairness 3–4, 20–21, 32, 101–2, 304, 367–68, 379–
  80, 381
  see also fairness
  procedural vs. substantive 3–4
unforeseen circumstances 146, 148
  frustrations of 148–51
UNIDROIT Principles of International Commercial
  Contracts (PICC) 285–86, 287, 289, 290–91,
  296, 320–21, 322–24, 325–26, 327–29, 330,
  332, 333–34, 335
United Kingdom (UK)
  damage to other property 227–28
  non-delegable duties 221–22
  parties to a contract of sale 323n.22
  vicarious liability 217
United Nations (UN) 320–21
  conventions 286–87
  official languages 291, 332
  organs of 295
United Nations Commission on International Trade
  Law (UNCITRAL) 284–88, 289, 290–91, 292,
  293, 295, 296, 297, 320–23, 324, 327–28, 329,
  330, 333–34
United Nations Convention on Contracts for the
  International Sale of Goods (CISG) 285–88,
  290–91, 292, 293–94, 296–98, 299, 310n.55,
  314–15, 320n.10, 330
United Nations Convention on the Rights of the Child
  (UNCRC) 330n.43
United States (US)
  American jurisprudence 239–40
  common law system 32n.44
  damage to other property 227–28
  fair dealing 90n.103
  good faith 33–34
  penalty jurisdiction 201
  UN Convention on the Rights of the Child, failure
  to ratify 330n.43

412 INDEX

unjust contract, theory of 394
unjust enrichment 59, 65n.18
  see also mistake
  Barton v Morris 391
  China 367–81
    context 367–68
    four-point test 372–75
    overview 368–72
  claims 190–91, 390–91
  concepts 384
  contract terms 388–89
  contractual interpretation 168
  damages 180, 181–83
  definitions 368n.5
  'gaps' in leases 392
  Law Reform (Frustrated Contracts) Act 135–36
  McKendrick, influence of 319
  mistake, role of the law of 339
  One Step argument 173–74, 175–76, 184
  'by performance', definition of 370
  remuneration payable 395
  restitution and 60–61, 66, 126, 178–79, 361, 362–
    63, 383–84, 387
  unjustified enrichment versus 375–80
  use value remedy 182–83, 187
unjust factors approach 340, 368n.5, 379–80, 388–89
unjustness 375
unlawful conduct 3–4, 83, 90
Upjohn, Lord 166, 188n.95
'use value' approach 18, 172–73, 175, 178, 179, 180,
    181, 182–83, 185, 187
user principle 183–84

vicarious conduct 217
vicarious liability 213–17
  see also direct liability
  broad application 212–13
  categorisations 211–12
  context 211, 225–26
Vogenauer, S. 289

waiver of tort doctrine 360–61
  new contract versus 87–88
Walker of Gestingthorpe, Lord 18
Weiterfresserschäden, German doctrine of 230–31
Wilberforce, Lord 18, 112, 166, 215
wills 7, 12–13, 219
Wilson, D. 144n.12
Wilson, Lord 61, 73
withhold performance, right to 312
Wolffe, Lady 7, 8, 9–11
Wool, J. 325, 335n.61
Woolf, Lord 200, 204n.91
Woolman, Lord 3
World Bank 328
World War I 6n.18, 113, 119, 121–22
World War II 138–39, 322–23
Wrenbury, Lord 224
Wright, Lord 106n.90, 118n.52, 164–65, 205n.96
Wright, M. 99
written contracts 35n.62, 145–47, 302
wrong, procurement of 245–61
  see also Marex tort
wrongdoing 18, 35, 66n.19, 69, 81, 179, 185, 186, 212–
    13, 217, 225–26, 245